CCH®
WHAT EVERY SUPERVISOR MUST KNOW ABOUT OSHA —
CONSTRUCTION

Joe Teeples

Wolters Kluwer
Law & Business

Vice President, Business Compliance Unit: Paul Gibson, J.D.
Executive Editor: Jeff Reinholtz, J.D.
Managing Editor: Joy Waltemath, J.D.
Coordinating Editor: Debra Levin, J.D.
Contributing Editor: Kari Smith
Production Coordinators: Theresa J. Jensen, Jennifer Wintczak
Cover Design: Craig Arritola
Interior Design: Jason Wommack
Layout: Craig Arritola

This publication is designed to provide accurate and authoritative information in regard to the subject matter covered. It is sold with the understanding that the publisher is not engaged in rendering legal, accounting, or other professional service. If legal advice or other expert assistance is required, the services of a competent professional person should be sought.

ISBN 978-0-8080-1628-1
©2007 **CCH**. All Rights Reserved.
4025 W. Peterson Ave.
Chicago, IL 60646-6085
1 800 248 3248
www.safety.cch.com

TABLE OF CONTENTS

AUTHOR BIOGRAPHY

Author Joe Teeples has over 25 years in the field of occupational safety. He has served as the safety manager of a federal installation where he was instrumental in reducing lost time injuries by 66 percent. Teeples also served the government in the role of director of one of OSHA's Training Institute education centers. In his role as a "train the trainer" in OSHA's Outreach program for various educational centers, he has prepared written training materials, slides, movies, online courses and books for other trainers to use. His company has taught safety around the world in locations such as Saudi Arabia, Trinidad, Guam, Saipan and the Virgin Islands. In the United States, he has trained students on federal requirements from the East Coast to the West Coast, from Alaska to Hawaii.

Teeples holds an M.B.A. from the University of Wisconsin and is a certified member of the World Safety Organization that serves a consultative role to the United Nations. He is also a member of the American Society of Safety Engineers. As a measure of his dedication to safety, Teeples maintains a web site at www.wisafety.com with many useful items for safety professionals to download and use at no charge.

CONSTRUCTION PRE-TEST
(See appendix for answers)

1. **The controlling employer can be cited whether or not his or her own employees are exposed to a hazard.**
    a. True
    b. False

2. **What is a key element of a comprehensive safety and health program?**
    a. Identification and control of hazards
    b. Tool box meetings
    c. Exchange of Hazard Communication Programs
    d. OSHA poster on site
    e. None of the above

3. **On a multi-employer worksite, penalties for employers with no exposed employees will be calculated using the exposed employees of all employers as the number of employees for probability assessment.**
    a. True
    b. False

4. **The four hazards that are relevant to a focused inspection include falls, electrocutions, struck-by, and caught in between.**
    a. True
    b. False

5. **Employers are required to have a program in which frequent and regular safety and health inspections are made by a competent person.**
    a. True
    b. False

6. **Employers are not responsible for instructing each employee in the recognition and avoidance of unsafe conditions, but they have to instruct employees on the regulations that are applicable to their own work environment.**
    a. True
    b. False

7. **Each employee who is constructing a leading edge 5 ft. or more above lower levels shall be protected from falling by the use of guardrail systems, safety net systems or personal fall arrest systems.**
    a. True
    b. False

8. **On residential construction, when the employer can demonstrate that it is infeasible or creates a greater hazard to use the conventional fall protections, including guard rails, safety nets, and personal fall arrest systems, the employer shall develop and implement a:**
    a. System of interventions designed to protect employees at the moment they appear to be falling
    b. Fall protection plan that meets the requirements of 1926.502(k)
    c. Blue prints, detailing scaffold availability throughout each construction phase
    d. None of the above

9. A stairway or ladder shall be provided at all personnel points of access where there is a break in elevation of 12 in. or more and no ramp, runway, sloped embankment or personnel hoist is provided.
   a. True
   b. False

10. Fixed ladders shall be provided with cages, wells, ladder safety devices or self-retracting lifelines where the length of climb is less than 24 ft., but the top of the ladder is at a distance greater than 24 ft. above lower levels.
    a. True
    b. False

11. No scaffold shall be erected, moved, dismantled, or altered except under the supervision of competent persons.
    a. True
    b. False

12. When freestanding mobile scaffold towers are used, the height shall not exceed ____ times the minimum base dimension.
    a. Five
    b. Six
    c. Eight
    d. Four

13. In steel erection operations, when bolts or drift pins are being knocked out, means shall be provided to keep them from falling.
    a. True
    b. False

14. In steel erection operations, when rivet heads are knocked off or backed out, means shall be provided to keep them from_____.
    a. Bouncing
    b. Falling
    c. Curling
    d. Sticking
    e. None of the above

15. The employer shall be responsible for the development of a fire protection program to be followed throughout all phases of construction and demolition work, and it shall provide for the firefighting equipment as specified in Subpart F. As fire hazards occur, there shall be no delay in providing the necessary equipment.
    a. True
    b. False

16. Not more than _____ gallons of flammable or _____ gallons of combustible liquids shall be store in any one storage cabinet. Not more than three such cabinets may be located in a single storage area. Quantities in excess of this shall be stored in an inside storage room.
    a. 50 and 100
    b. 40 and 150
    c. 60 and 120
    d. None of the above

17. Portable heaters, including salamanders, shall be equipped with an approved automatic device to shut off the flow of gas to the main burner and pilot, if used, in the event of flame failure. Such heaters, having inputs of more than 50,000 BTUs per hour shall be equipped with either a pilot, which must be lighted and proved before the burner can be turned on, or an electrical ignition system.
   a. True
   b. False

18. All construction equipment cab glass shall be ____ glass, or equivalent, that introduces no visible distortion affecting the safe operation of any machine covered by Subpart O.
   a. Clear
   b. Stained
   c. Safety
   d. Rust-resistant
   e. None of the above

19. Employers can use any motor vehicle equipment having an obstructed view to the rear whether or not it is equipped with a reverse signal alarm that is audible above the surrounding noise level.
   a. True
   b. False

20. No grounded conductor shall be attached to any terminal or lead so as to reverse designated polarity.
   a. True
   b. False

21. A written description of the employer's assured equipment grounding conductor program, including the specific procedures adopted by the employer, shall be available at the ____ for inspection and copying by the Assistant Secretary and any affected employee.
   a. Home office
   b. Employee's house
   c. Job site
   d. General contractor's headquarters
   e. None of the above

22. All hand and power tools and similar equipment, whether furnished by the employer or the employee, shall be maintained in a safe condition.
   a. True
   b. False

23. All hand-held powered platen sanders, grinders with wheels 2 in. in diameter or less, routers, planers, laminate trimmers, nibblers, shears, scroll saws and jigsaws with blade shanks measuring ¼ in. or less may be equipped with only a positive ____ control.
   a. Toggle switch
   b. Trigger finger
   c. Quick release
   d. On/Off
   e. All of the above

24. "Limited access zone" means an area along a masonry wall that is under construction and is clearly demarcated to limit access by employees.
    a. True
    b. False

25. No construction loads shall be placed on a concrete structure or portion of a concrete structure unless the employer determines, based on information received from a person who is competent in structural design, that the structure or portion of the structure is capable of supporting the loads.
    a. True
    b. False

COURSE OBJECTIVES
For Construction Safety Supervisor

- Be able to explain the Occupational Safety and Health Act, 29 CFR 1926 and relevant interpretations and applications
- Explain the history of, and the reason for, federal safety and health regulations
- Identify common causes of accidents and fatalities in hazardous areas of construction
- Identify abatement strategies for hazards found in the construction industry
- Understand basic instructional methods and techniques and the use of visual aids, student workshops and supplementary course material
- Be able to present 10 and 30 hour training programs using the OSHA construction regulations and guidelines

Note: This 2005 version of the construction manual type course material has been revised based upon comments from instructors and students in the field. The original material that was provided by the OSHA Training Institute in Arlington Heights was found to be of such high quality that only minor changes were required. Wherever possible the original intent, text and artwork of the 1995 manual was retained in order to allow current instructors to remain familiar with the manual by maintaining the "feel" that they have been used to as well as to keep the material in the public domain.

It was felt that the material needed to be updated (the last update was in 1995) in order to:
- Create a flow of educational topics that tended to enhance the educational process as opposed to skipping from one section to another in the book. For example, following a discussion of Industrial Hygiene where the student learns about PEL's and TWA's, the discussion leads to asbestos, lead and hearing conservation programs to reinforce the use of those IH terms.
- Update the manual to reflect changes that have been made in Federal regulations since 1995.
- Reduce the number of pages and bulk of the overall book in order to make it more useable and less expensive to print, publish, distribute and ship.
- Include page numbers for each tab for easy reference by instructors and students alike in the classroom.
- Additional information that has been included:
  - A chapter on confined space entry as it pertains to construction
  - A chapter on Safety Committees
  - The OSHA Field Inspection Reference Manual

What Every Supervisor Must Know About OSHA Construction

Suggested Matrix

TIME	MONDAY	TUESDAY	WEDNESDAY	THURSDAY
8:00 8:50	Opening Remarks Bio Sheets Objectives	Subpart J Welding	Subpart N Cranes	Subpart I Tools
9:00 9:50	Intro To OSHA, Inspections, Penalties Standards	Subpart K Electrical	Subpart H Rigging	Training Techniques
10:00 10:50	Focused Inspections Multi-employer Sites	Subpart K Electrical	Subpart Q Concrete	OSHA Outreach Program
11:00 11:45	Subpart D & Z Health Hazards In Construction	Subpart X Stairs And Ladders	Subpart F Fie Protection And Prevention	Review For Exam
11:45 12:45	Lunch	Lunch	Lunch	Lunch
12:45 1:35	Subpart D Hazard Communication	Subpart M Fall Protection	Subparts G & W Vehicles And Equipment	Exam
1:45 2:35	Subpart E Personal Potective Equipment	Subpart M Fall Protection	Subpart O Forklift Operator Training	Exam And Course Evaluations
2:45 3:35	Subpart E Resiratory Protection	Subpart L Scaffolds	Subpart P Excavations	Q & A OSHA Rep.
3:45 4:30	1910 Subpart J Confined Space Entry Ansi Z117	Subpart R Steel Erection	Record Keeping 29 Cfr 1904	Certificate Awards Course Closes

INTRODUCTION TO OSHA

The American worker represents a valuable national resource, with more than 90 million Americans spending their days on the job. Yet, until 1970, no uniform and comprehensive provisions existed for their protection against workplace safety and health hazards.

In 1970, the Congress considered these annual figures:

- Job-related accidents accounted for more than 14,000 worker deaths;
- Nearly 2½ million workers were disabled;
- Ten times as many person-days were lost from job-related disabilities as from strikes; and
- Estimated new cases of occupational diseases totaled 300,000.

In terms of lost production and wages, medical expenses and disability compensation, the burden on the nation's commerce was staggering. Human cost was beyond calculation. Therefore, the Occupational Safety and Health Act of 1970 (the Act) was passed by a bipartisan Congress "to assure so far as possible every working man and woman in the Nation safe and healthful working conditions and to preserve our human resources."

OSHA's Purpose

Under the Act, the Occupational Safety and Health Administration (OSHA) was created within the Department of Labor to:

- Encourage employers and employees to reduce workplace hazards and to implement new or improve existing safety and health programs;
- Provide for research in occupational safety and health to develop innovative ways of dealing with occupational safety and health problems;
- Establish "separate but dependent responsibilities and rights" for employers and employees for the achievement of better safety and health conditions;
- Maintain a reporting and recordkeeping system to monitor job-related injuries and illnesses;
- Establish training programs to increase the number and competence of occupational safety and health personnel;
- Develop mandatory job safety and health standards and enforce them effectively; and
- Provide for the development, analysis, evaluation, and approval of state occupational safety and health programs.

While OSHA continually reviews and redefines specific standards and practices, its basic purposes remain constant: OSHA strives to implement its mandate fully and firmly with fairness to all concerned. In all its procedures, from standards development through implementation and enforcement, OSHA guarantees employers and employees the right to be fully informed, to participate actively and to appeal actions.

The Act's Coverage

Coverage of the Act extends to all employers and their employees in the 50 states, the District of Columbia, Puerto Rico, and all other territories under federal government jurisdiction. Coverage is provided either directly by federal OSHA or through an OSHA-approved state program.

As defined by the Act, an employer is any "person engaged in a business affecting commerce that has employees, but does not include the United States or any State or political subdivision of a State." Therefore, the Act applies to employers and employees in such varied fields as manufacturing, construction, long shoring, agriculture, law and medicine, charity and disaster relief, organized labor, and private education. Such coverage includes religious groups to the extent that they employ workers for secular purposes.

The following are not covered under the Act:

- Self-employed persons;
- Farms at which only immediate members of the farm employer's family are employed; and
- Working conditions regulated by other federal agencies under other federal statutes.

Even when another federal agency is authorized to regulate safety and health working conditions in a particular industry, if it does not do so in specific areas, OSHA standards then apply.

Provisions for Federal Employees

Under the Act, federal agency heads are responsible for providing safe and healthful working conditions for their employees. The Act requires agencies to adhere to standards that are consistent with those OSHA issues for private sector employers. OSHA conducts federal workplace inspections in response to employees' reports of hazards and as part of a special program that identifies federal workplaces with higher than average rates of injuries and illnesses.

Federal agency heads are required to operate comprehensive occupational safety and health programs that include:

- Recording and analyzing injury/illness data;
- Providing training to all personnel; and
- Conducting self-inspections to ensure compliance with OSHA standards.

OSHA conducts comprehensive evaluations of these programs to assess their effectiveness.

OSHA's federal sector authority is different from that in the private sector in several ways. The most significant difference is that OSHA cannot propose monetary penalties against another federal agency for failure to comply with OSHA standards. Instead, compliance issues unresolved at the local level are raised to higher organizational levels until resolved. Another significant difference is that OSHA does not have authority to protect federal employee "whistleblowers." However, the Whistleblower Protection Act of 1989 affords present and former federal employees (other than those in the U.S. Postal Service and certain intelligence agencies) an opportunity to file their reports of alleged violations.

Provisions for State and Local Governments

OSHA provisions do not apply to state and local governments in their role as employers. The Act does provide that any state desiring to gain OSHA approval for its private sector occupational safety and health program must provide a program that covers its state and local government workers and that is at least as effective as its program for private employees. State plans may also cover only public sector employees.

Standards

OSHA is responsible for promulgating legally enforceable standards. OSHA standards may require conditions, or the adoption or use of one or more practices, means, methods, or processes reasonably necessary and appropriate to protect workers on the job. It is the responsibility of employers to become familiar with standards applicable to their establishments and to ensure that employees have and use personal protective equipment when required for safety. Employees must comply with all rules and regulations that are applicable to their own actions and conduct. Where OSHA has not promulgated specific standards, employers are responsible for following the Act's general duty clause.

General Duty Clause

The Act's General Duty Clause requires that employers provide a safe and healthy environment for their workers:

Each employer shall furnish to each of his employees employment and a place of employment which are free from recognized hazards that are causing or are likely to cause death or serious physical harm to his or her employees.

There are four elements that must be present to prove a violation of this clause.
1. There must be a hazard to which employees are exposed.
2. The hazard must be recognized.
3. The hazard was causing or was likely to cause death or serious physical harm.
4. The hazard may be corrected by a feasible useful method.

Some examples of citations from the General Duty Clause include:
- Employee riding backhoe/front end loader bucket;
- Open side of a self-propelled scissor lift;
- Failure to use the installed safety belt on a forklift;
- Using a forklift as a work platform;
- Wearing tennis shoes on a construction site;
- No reflective vests during asphalt operations; and
- Backhoe within 10 ft. of power lines.

States with OSHA-approved occupational safety and health programs must set standards that are at least as effective as the federal standards. Many state plan states adopt standards identical to the federal. OSHA standards fall into four major categories:
1. General Industry;
2. Maritime;
3. Construction; and
4. Agriculture.

The Federal Register is one of the best sources of information on standards, since all OSHA standards are published there when adopted, as are all amendments, corrections, insertions or deletions. The *Federal Register* is available in many public libraries. Annual subscriptions are available from the U.S. Government Printing Office.

OSHA can begin standards-setting procedures on its own initiative, or in response to petitions from other parties, including the Secretary of Health and Human Services (HHS), the National Institute for Occupational Safety and Health (NIOSH), state and local governments, any nationally recognized standards-producing organization, employers or labor representatives, or any other interested person.

Advisory Committees

If OSHA determines that a specific standard is needed, any of several advisory committees may be called upon to develop specific recommendations. There are two standing committees and ad hoc committees may be appointed to examine special areas of concern to OSHA. All advisory committees, standing or ad hoc, must have members representing management, labor and state agencies, as well as one or more designees of the Secretary of HHS. The occupational safety and health professions and the general public also may be represented. The two standing advisory committees are the:
1. National Advisory Committee on Occupational Safety and Health (NACOSH), which advises, consults with, and makes recommendations to the Secretary of HHS and to the Secretary of Labor on matters regarding administration of the Act; and
2. Advisory Committee on Construction Safety and Health, which advises the Secretary of Labor on formulation of construction safety and health standards and other regulations.

NIOSH Recommendations

Recommendations for standards also may come from NIOSH, established by the Act as an agency of the Department of HHS. NIOSH conducts research on various safety and health problems, provides technical assistance to OSHA, and recommends standards for OSHA's adoption. NIOSH may make workplace investigations, gather testimony from employers and employees, and require that employers provide information to them. NIOSH also may require employers to provide medical examinations and tests to determine the incidence of occupational illness among employees.

Standards Adoption

Once OSHA has developed plans to propose, amend or revoke a standard, it publishes these intentions in the *Federal Register* as a "Notice of Proposed Rulemaking," or often as an earlier "Advance Notice of Proposed Rulemaking." An "Advance Notice" or a "Request for Information" is used, when necessary, to solicit information that can be used in drafting a proposal. The Notice of Proposed Rulemaking will include the terms of the new proposed rule and provide a specific time (at least 30 days from the date of publication, but usually 60 days or more) for the public to respond. Interested parties who submit written arguments and pertinent evidence may request a public hearing on the proposal when none has been announced in the notice. When such a hearing is requested, OSHA will schedule one, and will publish, in advance, the time and place for it in the *Federal Register*. After the close of the comment period and public hearing, OSHA must publish the full, final text of any standard amended or adopted and the date it becomes effective in the *Federal Register*. OSHA also will publish an explanation of the standard and the reasons for implementing it. Likewise, OSHA also may publish a determination that no standard or amendment needs to be issued.

Emergency Temporary Standards

Under certain limited conditions, OSHA is authorized to set emergency temporary standards that take effect immediately. First, OSHA must determine that workers are in grave danger due to exposure to substances or agents that have been determined to be toxic or physically harmful or due to new hazards and that an emergency standard is needed to protect them. Then, OSHA publishes the emergency temporary standard in the *Federal Register*, where it also serves as a proposed permanent standard. It is then subject to the usual procedure for adopting a permanent standard; however, in this case, a final ruling must be made within six months of its publication. It also should be noted that the validity of an emergency temporary standard may be challenged in a U.S. Court of Appeals.

Appealing a Standard

No decision on a permanent standard is ever reached without due consideration of the arguments and data received from the public in written submissions and at hearings. Any person who may be adversely affected by a final or emergency standard, however, may file a petition (within 60 days of the rule's promulgation) for judicial review of the standard with the U.S. Court of Appeals for the circuit in which the objector lives or has his or her principal place of business. Filing an appeals petition, however, will not delay the enforcement of a standard, unless the Court of Appeals specifically orders it.

Variances

Employers may ask OSHA for a variance from a standard or regulation if they cannot fully comply by the effective date due to shortages of materials, equipment, or professional or technical personnel, or can prove their facilities or methods of operation provide employee protection that is "at least as effective." Employers located in states with their own occupational safety and health programs should apply to the state for a variance. If, however, an employer operates facilities in states under both federal OSHA jurisdiction and state-plan states, the employer may apply directly to federal OSHA for a single variance applicable to all the establishments in question. OSHA will work with state-plan states to determine if a variance can be granted that will satisfy both the state and federal OSHA requirements. Variances are not retroactive. An employer who has been cited for a standards violation may not seek relief from that citation by applying for a variance. The fact that a citation is outstanding, however, does not prevent an employer from filing a variance application.

Temporary Variance

A temporary variance may be granted to an employer who cannot comply with a standard or regulation by its effective date due to unavailability of professional or technical personnel, materials or equipment, or because the necessary construction or alteration of facilities cannot be completed in time. Employers must demonstrate to OSHA that they are taking all available steps to safeguard employees in the meantime, and that the employer has put in force an effective program for coming into compliance with the standard or regulation as quickly as possible. A temporary variance may be granted for the period needed to achieve compliance or for one year, whichever is shorter. A temporary variance is renewable twice, each time for six months. An application for a temporary variance must identify the standard or portion of the standard from which the variance is requested and the reasons why the employer cannot comply with the standard. The employer must document those measures already taken and to be taken (including dates) to comply with the standard.

The employer must certify that workers have been informed of the variance application, that a copy has been given to the employees' authorized representative, and that a summary of the application has been posted wherever notices are normally posted. Employees also must be informed that they have the right to request a hearing on the application. The temporary variance will not be granted to an employer who simply cannot afford to pay for the necessary alterations, equipment, or personnel.

Permanent Variance

A permanent variance (alternative to a particular requirement or standard) may be granted to employers who prove their conditions, practices, means, methods operations, or processes provide a safe and healthful workplace as effectively as would compliance with the standard.

OSHA weighs the employer's evidence and arranges a variance inspection and hearing where appropriate. If OSHA finds the request valid, it prescribes a permanent variance detailing the employer's specific exceptions and responsibilities under the ruling. When applying for a permanent variance, the employer must inform employees of the application and of their right to request a hearing. Anytime after six months from the issuance of a permanent variance, the employer or employees may petition OSHA to modify or revoke it.

Interim Order

Employers may apply to OSHA for an interim order to continue to operate under existing conditions until a variance decision is made. Application for an interim order may be made either at the same time as, or after, application for a variance. Reasons why the order should be granted may be included in the interim order application. If OSHA denies the request, the employer is notified of the reason for denial. If the interim order is granted, the employer and other concerned parties are informed of the order and the terms of the order are published in the *Federal Register*. The employer must inform employees of the order by giving a copy to the authorized employee representative and by posting a copy wherever notices are normally posted.

Experimental Variance

If an employer is participating in an experiment to demonstrate or validate new job safety and health techniques and that experiment has been approved by either the Secretary of Labor or the Secretary of HHS, a variance may be granted to permit the experiment.

In addition to temporary, permanent, and experimental variances, the Secretary of Labor also may find certain variances justified when the national defense is impaired.

Public Petitions

OSHA continually reviews its standards to keep pace with developing and changing industrial technology. Therefore, employers and employees should be aware that, just as they may petition OSHA for the development of standards, they also may petition OSHA for the modification or revocation of standards.

Recordkeeping and Reporting

Before the Act became effective, no centralized, systematic method existed for monitoring occupational safety and health problems.

Statistics on job injuries and illnesses were collected by some states and by some private organizations; national figures were based on not-altogether-reliable projections. With OSHA came the first basis for consistent, nationwide procedures — a vital requirement for gauging problems and solving them.

Employers of 11 or more employees must maintain records of occupational injuries and illnesses as they occur. The purpose of keeping records is to permit survey material to be compiled, to help define high-hazard industries, and to inform employees of the status of their employer's record. Employers in state-plan states are required to keep the same records as employers in other states.

OSHA recordkeeping is not required for certain retail trades and some service industries. Exempt employers, like nonexempt employers, must comply with OSHA standards, display the OSHA poster and report to OSHA within eight hours of the occurrence of any accident that results in one or more fatalities or the hospitalization of three or more employees. If an on-the-job accident occurs that results in the death of an employee or in the hospitalization of three or more employees, all employers, regardless of the number of employees, must report the accident, in detail, to the nearest OSHA office within eight hours. In states with approved plans, employers report such accidents to the state agency responsible for safety and health programs.

Injury and Illness Records

Recordkeeping forms are maintained on a calendar-year basis. They are not sent to OSHA or any other agency. They must be maintained for five years at the place of business and must be available for inspection by representatives of OSHA, HHS or the designated state agency. Many specific OSHA standards have additional recordkeeping and reporting requirements. (See Chapter 21, Recordkeeping.)

Keeping Employees Informed

Employers are responsible for keeping employees informed about OSHA and the various safety and health matters with which they are involved. Federal OSHA and states with their own occupational safety and health programs require that each employer post certain materials at a prominent location in the workplace, including:

- The Job Safety and Health Protection workplace poster (OSHA 2203 or state equivalent) informing employees of their rights and responsibilities under the Act. Any official edition of the poster is acceptable. In addition displaying the workplace poster, the employer must make available to employees, upon request, copies of the Act and copies of relevant OSHA rules and regulations;
- Summaries of petitions for variances from standards or recordkeeping procedures;
- Copies of all OSHA citations for violations of standards. These copies must remain posted at or near the locations of the alleged violations for three days or until the violations are corrected, whichever is longer; and
- The Log and Summary of Occupational Injuries and Illnesses (OSHA No. 300). The log must be maintained and a summary (OSHA No. 300A) must be signed by an officer of the company and posted no later than February 1. It must remain posted until May 1.

All employees have the right to examine any records kept by their employers regarding their exposure to hazardous materials or the results of medical surveillance. Occasionally, OSHA standards or NIOSH research activities will require an employer to measure and record employee exposure to potentially harmful substances. Employees have the right (in person or through their authorized representative) to be present during the measuring as well as to examine records of the results.

Under these substance-specific requirements, each employee or former employee has the right to see his or her examination records, and must be told by the employer if his or her exposure has exceeded the levels set by the standards. The employee must also be told what corrective measures are being taken.

In addition to having access to records, employees in manufacturing facilities must be provided with information about all of the hazardous chemicals in their work areas. Employers must provide this information by labeling containers, posting material safety data sheets, and conducting training programs.

Inspections

To enforce its standards, OSHA representatives are authorized under the Act to conduct workplace inspections. Every establishment covered by the Act is subject to inspection by OSHA compliance safety and health officers, who are hired for their knowledge and experience in the occupational safety and health field. Compliance officers are vigorously trained in OSHA standards and in recognition of safety and health hazards. Similarly, states with their own occupational safety and health programs also conduct inspections using qualified compliance safety and health officers.

Under the Act, "upon presenting appropriate credentials to the owner, operator or agent in charge," an OSHA compliance officer is authorized to:

> Enter without delay and at reasonable times any factory, plant, establishment, construction site or other areas, workplace, or environment where work is performed by an employee of an employer....
>
> Inspect and investigate during regular working hours, and at other reasonable times, and within reasonable limits and in a reasonable manner, any such place of employment and all pertinent conditions, structures, machines, apparatus, devices, equipment and materials therein, and to question privately any such employer, owner, operator, agent or employee.

Inspections are conducted without advance notice. There are, however, special circumstances under which OSHA may indeed give notice to the employer, but even then, such a notice will be given less than 24 hours in advance. These special circumstances include:

- Imminent-danger situations that require correction as soon as possible;
- Inspections that must take place after regular business hours or that require special preparation;
- Cases where notice is required to ensure that the employer and employee representative or other personnel will be present; and
- Situations in which the OSHA area director has determined that advance notice would produce a more thorough or effective inspection.

Employers receiving advance notice of an inspection must inform their employees' representative or arrange for OSHA to do so. If an employer refuses to admit an OSHA compliance officer or if an employer attempts to interfere with the inspection, the Act permits appropriate legal action to be taken.

Based on a 1978 Supreme Court ruling (Marshall v. Barlows, Inc.), OSHA may not conduct warrantless inspections without an employer's consent. It may however inspect after acquiring a judicially authorized search warrant based upon administrative probable cause or evidence of a violation.

Inspection Priorities

Obviously, not all 6 million workplaces covered by the Act can be inspected immediately. The worst situations need attention first. Therefore, OSHA has established a system of inspection priorities.

Imminent Danger

Imminent-danger situations are given top priority. An imminent danger is any condition where there is reasonable certainty that a danger exists that can be expected to cause death or serious physical harm immediately or before the danger can be eliminated through normal enforcement procedures.

Serious physical harm is any type of harm that could cause permanent or prolonged damage to the body or while not damaging the body on a prolonged basis, could cause such temporary disability as to require in-patient hospital treatment. OSHA considers "permanent or prolonged damage" to have occurred when, for example, a part of the body is crushed or severed; an arm, leg or finger is amputated, or sight in one or both eyes is lost. This kind of damage also includes that which renders a part of the body either functionally useless or substantially reduced in efficiency on or off the job. For example, the damage could be bones in a limb shattered so severely that mobility or dexterity will be permanently reduced.

Temporary disability requiring in-patient hospital treatment includes injuries, such as simple fractures, concussions, burns, or wounds involving substantial loss of blood and requiring extensive suturing or other healing aids. Injuries or illnesses that are difficult to observe are classified as serious if they inhibit a person in performing normal functions, cause reduction in physical or mental efficiency, or shorten life.

Health hazards may constitute imminent-danger situations when they present a serious and immediate threat to life or health. For a health hazard to be considered an imminent danger, there must be a reasonable expectation that toxic substances, such as dangerous fumes, dusts or gases, are present and that exposure to them will cause immediate and irreversible harm to such a degree as to shorten life or cause a reduction in physical or mental efficiency, even though the resulting harm is not immediately apparent.

Employees should inform the supervisor or employer immediately if they detect or even suspect an imminent-danger situation in the workplace. If the employer takes no action to eliminate the danger, an employee or an authorized employee representative may notify the nearest OSHA office and request an inspection. The request should identify the workplace location, detail the hazard or condition, and include the employee's name, address and telephone number. Although the employer has the right to see a copy of the complaint if an inspection results, the name of the employee will be withheld if the employee so requests.

After a case of imminent danger is reported, the OSHA area director will review the information and immediately determine whether there is a reasonable basis for the allegation. If it is decided the case has merit, the area director will assign a compliance officer to conduct an immediate inspection of the workplace.

Upon inspection, if an imminent danger situation is found, the compliance officer will ask the employer to voluntarily abate the hazard and to remove endangered employees from exposure. Should the employer fail to do so, OSHA, through the regional solicitor, may apply to the nearest federal district court for appropriate legal action to correct the situation. Judicial action can produce a temporary restraining order (immediate shutdown) of the operation or section of the workplace where the imminent danger exists. Before the OSHA

inspector leaves the workplace, he or she will advise all affected employees of the hazard and post an imminent-danger notice. Should OSHA "arbitrarily or capriciously" decline to bring court action, the affected employees may sue the Secretary of Labor to compel the Secretary to do so.

Walking off the job because of potentially unsafe workplace conditions is not ordinarily an employee right. To do so may result in disciplinary action by the employer. However, an employee does have the right to refuse (in good faith) to be exposed to an imminent danger. OSHA rules protect employees from discrimination if:

- Where possible, he or she asked the employer to eliminate the danger and the employer failed to do so;
- The danger was so imminent that there was not sufficient time to have the danger eliminated through normal enforcement procedures;
- The danger facing the employee was so grave that "a reasonable person" in the same situation would have concluded there was a real danger of death or serious physical harm; or
- The employee had no reasonable alternative to refusing to work under such conditions (e.g., asking for reassignment to another area).

Catastrophes and Fatal Accidents
Second priority is given to investigation of fatalities and catastrophes that resulted in hospitalization of three or more employees. The employer must report such situations to OSHA within eight hours of their occurrence. Investigations are made to determine whether OSHA standards were violated and to avoid the recurrence of similar accidents.

Employee Complaints
Third priority is given to employee complaints of an alleged violation of standards or of unsafe or unhealthful working conditions. Also included in this category are serious referrals of unsafe or unhealthful working conditions from other sources, such as local or state agencies or departments.

The Act gives each employee the right to request an OSHA inspection when the employee feels he or she is in imminent danger from a hazard or when he or she feels there is a violation of an OSHA standard that threatens physical harm. OSHA will maintain confidentiality if requested, will inform the employee of any action it takes regarding the complaint and, if requested, will hold an informal review of any decision not to inspect. Just as in situations of imminent danger, the employee's name will be withheld from the employer, if the employee so requests.

Programmed High-Hazard Inspections

Next in priority are programmed, or planned, inspections aimed at specific high-hazard industries, occupations, or health substances. Industries are selected for inspection on the basis of factors such as death, injury and illness incidence rates and employee exposure to toxic substances. Special emphasis may be regional or national in scope, depending on the distribution of the workplaces involved. States with their own occupational safety and health programs may use somewhat different systems to identify high-hazard industries for inspection.

Follow-up Inspections

A follow-up inspection determines whether previously cited violations have been corrected. If an employer has failed to abate a violation, the compliance officer will inform the employer that it is subject to alleged "Notification of Failure to Abate" violations and may face additional proposed daily penalties while such failure or violations continue.

Inspection Process

Prior to inspection, the compliance officer will become familiar with as many relevant facts as possible about the workplace, taking into account such things as the history of the establishment, the nature of the business, and the particular standards likely to apply. Preparing for the inspection also involves selecting appropriate equipment for detecting and measuring such things as fumes, gases, toxic substances, noise and other potential hazards.

Inspector's Credentials

An inspection begins when the OSHA compliance officer arrives at the establishment. He or she will display official credentials and ask to meet an appropriate employer representative.

Employers should always insist upon seeing the compliance officer's credentials. An OSHA compliance officer carries U.S. Department of Labor credentials bearing his or her photograph and a serial number that can be verified by phoning the nearest OSHA office. Anyone who tries to collect a penalty at the time of inspection or promotes the sale of a product or service at any time is not an OSHA compliance officer. Posing as a compliance officer is a violation of law; suspected impostors should be promptly reported to local law enforcement agencies.

Opening Conference

In the opening conference, the compliance officer (CSHO) will explain why the establishment was selected for inspection. The CSHO also will ascertain whether an OSHA-funded consultation program is in progress or whether the facility is pursuing or has received an inspection exemption; if programmed, the inspection will usually be terminated. If the inspection is not terminated the employer will then be asked to select an employer representative to accompany the CSHO during the inspection.

The CSHO will explain the purpose of the visit, the scope of the inspection and the standards that apply. The employer will be given a copy of any employee complaint that may be involved.

An authorized employee representative also will be given the opportunity to attend the opening conference and to accompany the compliance officer during inspection. If a recognized bargaining representative represents the employees, the union ordinarily will designate the employee representative to accompany the compliance officer. Similarly, if there is a plant safety committee, the employee members of the committee will designate the employee representative (in the absence of a recognized bargaining representative) to accompany the compliance officer. Where neither employee group exists, the employees themselves may select an employee representative or the compliance officer will determine if any employee suitably represents the interest of other employees. Under no circumstances may the employer select the employee representative for the walk-around.

The Act does not require that there be an employee representative for each inspection.

Where there is no authorized employee representative, however, the compliance officer must consult with a reasonable number of employees concerning safety and health matters in the workplace; such consultations may be held privately.

Inspection Tour

After the opening conference, the compliance officer and accompanying representatives will proceed through the establishment, inspecting work areas for compliance with OSHA standards. The compliance officer will determine the route and duration of the inspection. When speaking with employees, the compliance officer will make every effort to minimize any work interruptions. The compliance officer will observe conditions, consult with employees, take instrument readings, examine records and, for record purposes, may take photos and/or videos.

Trade secrets observed by the compliance officer will be kept confidential. An inspector who releases confidential information without authorization is subject to a $1,000 fine, one year in jail, or both. The employer may require that the employee representative have a security clearance for any area in question.

Employees will be consulted during the inspection tour. The compliance officer may stop and question workers in private about safety and health conditions and practices in their workplaces. Each employee is protected under the Act from discrimination for exercising their safety and health rights.

Posting and recordkeeping also will be checked. The compliance officer will inspect records of deaths, injuries and illnesses that the employer is required to keep. He or she will check to see that a copy of the totals from the last page of OSHA No. 300 has been posted and that the OSHA workplace poster (OSHA 2203) is prominently displayed. Where records of employee exposure to toxic substances and harmful physical agents are required, they also will be examined.

The CSHO also will explain the requirements of the Hazard Communication Standard, which requires employers to establish a written, comprehensive hazard communication program that includes provisions for container labeling, material safety data sheets and an employee-training program. The program must provide a list of the hazardous chemicals in each work area and the means the employer will use to inform employees of the hazards of non-routine tasks.

During the course of the inspection, the CSHO will point out to the employer any unsafe or unhealthful working conditions he or she observes. At the same time, the CSHO will discuss possible corrective action if the employer so desires. Some apparent violations detected by the compliance officer can be corrected immediately. However, even if immediately corrected the apparent violations may still serve as the basis for a citation and/or notice of proposed penalty.

Closing Conference

After the inspection tour, a closing conference will be held between the compliance officer and the employer or the employer representative. It is a time for free discussion of problems and needs—a time for frank questions and answers.

The compliance officer will discuss with the employer all unsafe or unhealthful conditions observed on the inspection and indicate all apparent violations for which a citation may be issued or recommended. The employer also will be told of its appeal rights. The compliance officer will not indicate any proposed penalties. Only the OSHA area director has that authority, and only after having received a full report.

During the closing conference, the employer may wish to produce records to show its compliance efforts and to provide information that can help OSHA determine how much time may be needed to abate an alleged violation. When appropriate, more than one closing conference may be held. This is usually necessary when health hazards are being evaluated or when laboratory reports are required.

A closing discussion will then be held with the employees, or their representative if requested, to discuss matters of direct interest to employees. The employees' representative may be present at the closing conference.

The CSHO will explain that OSHA area offices are full-service resource centers that provide a number of services, including guest speakers, handout materials that can be distributed to interested persons, and training and technical materials on safety and health matters.

Citations and Penalties

The OSHA area director issues citations. After the compliance officer reports his or her findings, the area director will determine what citations, if any, will be issued and what penalties, if any, will be proposed.

Citations inform the employer and employees of the regulations and standard alleged to have been violated and of the proposed length of time set for the abatement. The employer will receive citations and notices of proposed penalties by certified mail. The employer must post a copy of each citation or notice near the place the violation occurred for three days or until the violation is abated, whichever is longer.

There are several types of violations that may be cited and penalties that may be proposed. Citation and penalty procedures may differ somewhat in states that administer their own occupational safety and health programs.

Other Than Serious Violation. A violation that has a dire relationship to job safety and health, but probably would not cause death or serious physical harm. A proposed penalty of up to $7,000 for each violation is discretionary.

A penalty for an other-than-serious violation may be adjusted downward by as much as 95 percent, depending on the employer's good faith (demonstrated efforts to comply with the Act), history of previous violations and business size. When the adjusted penalty amounts to less than $100, no penalty is proposed.

Serious Violation. A violation where there is substantial probability that death or serious physical harm could result and that the employer knew, or should have known, of the hazard.

A mandatory penalty of up to $7,000 for each violation is proposed. A penalty for a serious violation may be adjusted downward, based on the employer's good faith, history of previous violations, the gravity of the alleged violation, and size of business.

Willful Violation. A violation that the employer knowingly commits or commits with plain indifference to the law. The employer either knows that what it is doing constitutes a violation, or is aware that a hazardous condition existed and made no reasonable effort to eliminate it.

Penalties of up to $70,000 may be proposed for each willful violation, with a minimum penalty of $5,000 for each violation. A proposed penalty for a willful violation may be adjusted downward, depending on the size of the business and its history of previous violations. Usually, no credit is given for good faith.

If an employer is convicted of a willful violation of a standard that has resulted in the death of an employee, the offense is punishable by a court-imposed fine, imprisonment for up to six months, or both. A fine of up to $250,000 for an individual or $500,000 for a corporation may be imposed for a criminal conviction.

Repeated Violation. A violation of any standard, regulation, rule or order where, upon reinspection, a substantially similar violation has occurred can bring a fine of up to $70,000 for each such violation. To be the basis of a repeated citation, the original citation must be final; a citation under contest may not serve as the basis for a subsequent repeated citation.

Failure to Abate Prior Violation. Failure to abate a prior violation may bring a civil penalty of up to $7,000 for each day the violation continues beyond the prescribed abatement date.

De Minimis Violation. De minimis violations are violations of standards that have no direct or immediate relationship to safety or health. When de minimis conditions are found during an inspection, they are documented in the same way as any other violation, but are not included on the citation.

Additional violations for which citations and proposed penalties may be issued upon conviction include:

- Falsifying records, reports, or applications, which can bring a fine of $10,000, up to six months in jail, or both;
- Failing to comply with posting requirements, which can bring a civil penalty of up to $7,000;
- Assaulting a compliance officer or otherwise resisting, opposing, intimidating or interfering with a compliance officer while he or she is engaged in the performance of his or her duties, which is a criminal offense, subject to a fine of not more than $5,000 and imprisonment for not more than three years.

Table 1-1.

OSHA PENALTIES	
Willful	
– Maximum	$70,000
– Minimum	$5,000
Repeated – Maximum	$70,000
Serious, Other-than-Serious, Other Specific Violations	
– Maximum	$7,000
Failure to Abate for each calendar day beyond abatement date	
– Maximum	$7,000
OSHA Notice	$1,000
Posting of OSHA Record Keeping Summary	$1,000
Posting of Citation	$3,000
Maintaining OSHA 300, OSHA Record Keeping	$1,000
Reporting Fatality/Catastrophe	$5,000
Access to Records under 1904	$1,000
Notification Requirements under 1903.6 (Advance Notice)	$2,000

Appeals Process

Appeals by Employees

If an inspection was initiated due to an employee complaint, the employee or authorized employee representative may request an informal review of any decision not to issue a citation.

Employees may not contest citations, amendments to citations, penalties or lack of penalties. They may contest the time in the citation for abatement of a hazardous condition. They also may contest an employer's Petition for Modification of Abatement (PMA), which requests an extension of the abatement period. Employees must contest the PMA within 10 working days of its posting or within 10 working days after an authorized employee representative has received a copy. Within 15 working days of the employer's receipt of the citation, the employee may submit a written objection to OSHA. The OSHA area director will forward the objection to the Occupational Safety and Health Review Commission, which operates independently of OSHA.

Employees may request an informal conference with OSHA to discuss any issues raised by an inspection, citation, and notice of proposed penalty or employer's notice of intention to contest.

Appeals by Employers

When issued a citation or notice of a proposed penalty, an employer may request an informal meeting with OSHA's area director to discuss the case. Employee representatives may be invited to attend the meeting. The area director is authorized to enter into settlement agreements that revise citations and penalties to avoid prolonged legal disputes.

Petition for Modification of Abatement

Upon receiving a citation, the employer must correct the cited hazard by the prescribed date unless it contests the citation or abatement date. Factors beyond the employer's reasonable control may prevent the completion of corrections by that date.

The written petition should specify all steps taken to achieve compliance, the additional time needed to achieve complete compliance, the reasons such additional time is needed, all temporary steps being taken to safeguard employees against the cited hazard during the intervening period, that a copy of the PMA was posted in a conspicuous place at or near each place where a violation occurred and that the employee representative (if there is one) received a copy of the petition.

Notice of Contest

If the employer decides to contest either the citation, the time set for abatement or the proposed penalty, it has 15 working days from the time the citation and proposed penalty are received in which to notify the OSHA area director of its disagreement in writing. An orally expressed disagreement will not suffice.

There is no specific format for the Notice of Contest; however, it must clearly identify the employer's basis for contesting the citation, notice of proposed penalty, abatement period or notification of failure to correct violations.

A copy of the Notice of Contest must be given to the employees' authorized representative. If a recognized bargaining agent does not represent any affected employees, a copy of the notice must be posted in a prominent location in the workplace or personally served upon each unrepresented employee.

Review Procedure

If the written Notice of Contest has been filed within the required 15 working days, the OSHA Area Director will forward the case to the Occupational Safety and Health Review Commission. The commission is an independent agency not associated with OSHA or the Department of Labor. The commission will assign the case to an administrative law judge, who may disallow the contest if it is found to be legally invalid or may schedule a hearing in a public place near the employer's workplace or, if it is found to be legally invalid, disallow the contest. The employer and the employees have the right to participate in the hearing; the commission does not require that attorneys represent them. Once the administrative law judge has ruled, any party to the case may request a further review by the OSHRC. Any of the three OSHRC commissioners also may, at his or her own motion, bring a case before the commission for review. OSHRC rulings may be appealed to the appropriate U.S. Court of Appeals.

Appeals in State-Plan States

States with their own occupational safety and health programs have a state system for review and appeal of citations, penalties and abatement periods. The procedures are generally similar to federal OSHA's, but a state review board or equivalent authority hears cases.

OSHA-Approved State Programs

The Act encourages states to develop and operate, under OSHA guidance, state job safety and health plans.

Once a state plan is approved, OSHA funds up to 50 percent of the program's operating costs. State plans are required to provide standards and enforcement programs, as well as voluntary compliance activities that are at least as effective as the federal program. State plans developed for the private sector also must, to the extent permitted by state law, provide coverage for state and local gov-

ernment employees. OSHA rules also permit states to develop plans limited in coverage for state and local government, or public schools, employees only; in such cases, private sector employment remains under federal jurisdiction. Employers and employees should find out if their state operates an OSHA-approved state program and, if so, become familiar with it (See Exhibit 1-2.).

Exhibit 1-2. State-plan states.

The following states and territories have OSHA-approved state plans:

Alaska	New Mexico
Arizona	New York*
California	North Carolina
Connecticut*	Oregon
Hawaii	Puerto Rico
Indiana	South Carolina
Iowa	Tennessee
Kentucky	Utah
Maryland	Vermont
Michigan	Virgin Islands*
Minnesota	Virginia
Nevada	Washington
New Jersey*	Wyoming

*Plans only cover public-sector employees.

To gain OSHA approval as a developmental plan, a state must have adequate legislative authority and must demonstrate that within three years it will provide:

- Standards-setting, enforcement, and appeals procedures;
- Public employee protection;
- A sufficient number of competent enforcement personnel; and
- Training, education and technical assistance programs.

If, at any time during this period or later, it appears that the state is capable of enforcing standards in accordance with the above requirements, OSHA may enter into an "operational status agreement" with the state. OSHA generally limits its enforcement activity to areas not covered by the state in the agreement and suspends all concurrent federal enforcement.

Scheduled accident and complaint inspections generally become the primary responsibility of the state. OSHA closely monitors state programs.

When all developmental steps concerning resources, procedures, and other requirements have been completed and approved, OSHA then certifies that a state has the legal, administrative, and enforcement means necessary to operate effectively. This action renders no judgment on how well or poorly a state is actually operating its program, but merely attests to the structural completeness of its program. After this certification, there is a period of at least one year to determine if a state is effectively providing safety and health protection.

State safety and health standards under approved plans must keep pace with federal standards, and state plans must guarantee employer and employee rights as does OSHA. If it is found that the state is operating at least as effectively as federal OSHA and other requirements, including compliance staffing levels, final approval of the plan may be granted and federal authority will cease in those areas over which the state has jurisdiction.

Anyone finding inadequacies or other problems in the administration of a state's program may file a complaint about state program administration (CASPA) with the appropriate regional administrator for OSHA. The complainant's name will be kept confidential. OSHA investigates all such complaints and, where complaints are found to be valid, requires appropriate corrective action on the part of the state.

Services Available

Consultation Assistance

Consultation assistance is available to employers who want help in establishing and maintaining a safe and healthful workplace. Largely funded by OSHA, this service is provided at no cost to the employer. No penalties will be proposed or citations issued for hazards identified by the consultant. Consultation is provided to the employer with the assurance that his or her name and firm and any information about the workplace will not be routinely reported to the OSHA inspection staff.

Primarily developed for smaller employers with more hazardous operations, the consultation service is delivered by state government agencies or universities employing professional safety consultants and health consultants. When delivered at the worksite, consultation assistance includes an opening conference with the employer to explain the ground rules

for consultation, a walk through the workplace to identify any specific hazards and to examine those aspects of the employer's safety and health program that relate to the scope of the visit, and a closing conference followed by a written report to the employer of the consultant's finding and recommendations.

This process begins with the employer's request for consultation and the commitment to correct any serious job safety and health hazards identified by the consultant. Possible violations of OSHA standards will not be reported to OSHA enforcement staff unless the employer fails or refuses to eliminate or control worker exposure to any identified serious hazard or imminent danger situation. In such unusual circumstances, OSHA may investigate and begin enforcement action.

Employers who receive a comprehensive consultation visit, correct all identified hazards, and demonstrate that an effective safety and health program is in operation may be exempted from OSHA programmed enforcement inspections (not complaint or accident investigations) for a period of one year. Comprehensive consultation assistance includes an appraisal of all mechanical, physical, work practice, and environmental hazards of the workplace and all aspects of the employer's present job safety and health program.

Additional information concerning consultation assistance, including a directory of OSHA-funded consultation projects, can be obtained by requesting OSHA Publication No. 3047, Consultation Services for the Employer.

Voluntary Protection Programs

The voluntary protection programs (VPPs) represent one part of OSHA's effort to extend worker protection beyond the minimum required by OSHA standards. These programs as well as expanded onsite consultation services and full-service area offices are cooperative approaches that when coupled with an effective enforcement program, expand worker protection to help meet the goals of the Occupational Safety and Health Act of 1970.

The three VPPs-Star, Merit, and Demonstration-are designed to:

■ Recognize outstanding achievement of those who have successfully incorporated comprehensive safety and health programs into their total management systems;

- Motivate others to achieve excellent safety and health results in the same outstanding way; and
- Establish a relationship between employers, employees, and OSHA that is based on co-operation rather than coercion.

Star Program. This program is the most demanding and the most prestigious. It is open to employers in any industry who have successfully managed a comprehensive safety and health program to reduce injury rates below the national average for that industry. Specific requirements for the program include:

- Management commitment and employee participation;
- A high quality worksite analysis program;
- Hazard prevention and control programs; and
- Comprehensive safety and health training for all employees.

These requirements must all be in place and operating effectively.

Merit Program. Primarily a stepping stone to the Star Program, the Merit Program is appropriate for an employer with a basic safety and health program built around the Star requirement who is committed to improving the company's program. Usually the employer can show it has the resources to improve its program within a specified period of time and may work with OSHA to meet Star qualifications.

Demonstration Program. This program is for companies that provide Star-quality worker protection in industries where certain Star requirements may not be appropriate or effective. It allows OSHA both the opportunity to recognize outstanding safety and health programs that would otherwise be unreached by the VPP and to determine whether general Star requirements should be changed to include these companies as Star participants.

OSHA will review an employer's VPP application and conduct an onsite review to verify that the safety and health program described is in operation at the site. Evaluations are conducted on a regular basis—annually for Merit and Demonstration Programs and triennially for the Star Program. All participants must send their injury information annually to their

OSHA regional office. Sites participating in the VPPs are not scheduled for programmed inspections; however, any employee complaints, serious accidents or significant chemical releases that may occur are handled according to routine enforcement procedures.

An employer may make application for any VPP at the nearest OSHA regional office. Once OSHA is satisfied that, on paper, the employer qualifies for the program, an on-site review will be scheduled. The review team will present its findings in a written report for the company's review prior to submission to the Assistant Secretary of Labor, who heads OSHA. If approved, the employer will receive a letter from the Assistant Secretary informing the site of its participation in the VPP. A certificate of approval and flag are presented at a ceremony held at or near the approved worksite. Star sites receiving reapproval after each triennial evaluation receive plaques at similar ceremonies.

These VPPs are available in states under federal OSHA jurisdiction. Some state-plan states have similar programs. Interested companies in these states should contact the appropriate state designee for more information.

Training and Education

OSHA's area offices are full-service centers offering a variety of informational services, including publications, audio-visual aids on workplace hazards, technical advice, and speakers.

The OSHA Training Institute in Arlington Heights, Ill., provides basic and advanced training and education in safety and health for federal and state compliance officers; state consultants; other federal agency personnel; and private sector employers, employees and their representatives. Institute courses cover areas such as electrical hazards, machine guarding, ventilation and ergonomics. The Institute facility includes classrooms, laboratories, a library, and an audiovisual unit. The laboratories contain various demonstrations and equipment, such as power presses, woodworking and welding shops, a complete industrial ventilation unit and a sound demonstration laboratory.

OSHA also grants funds on an annual basis to nonprofit organizations to conduct workplace training and education in subjects where OSHA identifies areas of unmet needs for safety and health education. Current grant subjects include agricultural health and safety and hazard communication programs for small businesses that do not have safety and health staff to assist them.

Organizations awarded grants use funds to develop training and educational programs, reach out to workers and employers for whom their program is appropriate, and provide these programs to workers and employers. Grants are awarded annually, with a one-year renewal possible. Grant recipients are expected to contribute 20 percent of the total grant cost.

All OSHA publications can be downloaded at no costs from the agency web site at www.osha.gov. In addition, most are available in hard-copy form, some at no cost, from OSHA and others for sale from the U.S. Government Printing Office. For a list of available publications, visit www.osha.gov or call 1-800-321-OSHA.

Occupational Safety and Health Administration Regional Offices

Region I
(CT, MA, ME, NH, RI, VT)
JFK Federal Building
Room E340
Boston, MA 02203
Telephone: (617) 565-9860

Region VI
(AR, LA, NM, OK, TX)
525 Griffin Street
Room 602
Dallas, TX 75202
Telephone (214) 767-4731

Region II
(NJ, NY, PR,VI)
201 Varick Street
Room 670
New York, NY 10014
Telephone: (212) 337-2378

Region VII
(IA, KS, MO, NE)
City Center Square
1100 Main Street, Suite 800
Kansas City, MO 64105
Telephone: (816) 426-5861

Region III
(DC, DE, MD, PA, VA, WV)
The Curtis Center, Suite 740 West
170 S. Independence Mall West
Philadelphia, PA 19106-3309
Telephone: (215) 861-4900

Region VIII
(CO, MT, ND, SD, UT, WY)
1999 Broadway, Suite 1690
P.O> Box 46550
Denver, CO 80201-6550
Telephone: (303) 844-1600

Region IV
(AL, FL, GA, KY, MS, NC, SC, TN)
61 Forsyth Street, SW
Atlanta, GA 30303
Telephone: (404) 562-2300

Region IX
(American Samoa, AZ, CA, Guam, HI, NV)
71 Stevenson Street, Room 420
San Francisco, CA 94105
Telephone: (415) 975-4310

Region V
(IL, IN, MI, MN, OH, WI)
230 South Dearborn Street
Room 3244
Chicago, IL 60604
Telephone: (312) 353-2220

Region X
(AK, ID, OR, WA)
1111 Third Avenue
Suite 715
Seattle, WA 98101-3212
Telephone: (206) 553-5930

Employer Responsibilities and Rights

Employers have certain responsibilities and rights under the Occupational Safety and Health Act of 1970. Employer responsibilities and rights in states with their own occupational safety and health programs are generally the same as in federal OSHA states. Employers must cooperate with the OSHA compliance officer by furnishing names of authorized employee representatives who may be asked to accompany the compliance officer during an inspection. If none, the compliance officer will consult with a reasonable number of employees concerning safety and health in the workplace.

Employees must comply with all applicable OSHA standards. In addition, Employers should:

- Read the OSHA poster at the job site
- Follow all employer safety and health rules and regulations and wear or use prescribed protective equipment while engaged in work.
- Report hazardous conditions to the supervisor
- Cooperate with the OSHA compliance officer conducting an inspection if he or she inquires about safety and health conditions in the workplace.
- Meet the general duty responsibility to provide a workplace free from recognized hazards that are causing or are likely to cause death or serious physical harm to employees and comply with standards, rules and regulations issued under the Act.
- Be familiar with mandatory OSHA standards and make copies available to employees for review upon request.
- Inform all employees about OSHA.
- Examine workplace conditions to make sure they conform to applicable standards.
- Minimize or reduce hazards.
- Make sure employees have and use safe tools and equipment (including appropriate personal protective equipment) and that such equipment is properly maintained.
- Use color codes, posters, labels or signs when needed to warn employees of potential hazards.
- Establish or update operating procedures and communicate them so that employees follow safety and health requirements.

- Provide training required by OSHA standards (e.g., hazard communication, lead).
- Report to the nearest OSHA office within eight hours any fatal accident or one that results in the hospitalization of three or more employees.
- Keep OSHA-required records of work-related injuries and illnesses and post a copy of the OSHA 300A from February through April each year. (This applies to employers with 11 or more employees.)
- Post, at a prominent location within the workplace, the OSHA poster (OSHA 2203) informing employees of their rights and responsibilities.
- Provide employees, former employees and their representatives' access to the Log and Summary of Occupational Injuries and Illnesses (OSHA 300) at a reasonable time and in a reasonable manner.
- Provide access to employee medical records and exposure records to employees or their authorized representatives.
- Not discriminate against employees who properly exercise their rights under the Act.
- Post OSHA citations at or near the worksites involved. Each citation, or copy thereof, must remain posted until the violation has been abated or for three working days, whichever is longer.
- Abate cited violations within the prescribed period.

Employers have the right to:

- Seek advice and off-site consultation as needed by writing, calling or visiting the nearest OSHA office. (OSHA will not inspect merely because an employer requests assistance.)
- Be active in industry association job safety and health programs.
- Request and receive proper government-issued identification from OSHA compliance officers prior to inspections.
- Be advised of the reason for the inspection.
- Have an opening conference with the compliance officer.
- Accompany the compliance officer during the inspection.
- Have a closing conference at the end of the inspection.
- File a written Notice of Contest with the OSHA area director within 15 working days

of the receipt of a notice of citation or a proposed penalty.

- Apply to OSHA for a temporary variance from a standard if unable to comply because of the unavailability of materials, equipment or personnel to make necessary changes within the required time.
- Apply to OSHA for a permanent variance from a standard if able to furnish proof its facilities or method of operation provide employee protection at least as effective as that required by the standard.
- Take an active role in developing safety and health standards through participation in OSHA Standard Advisory Committees, nationally recognized standards-setting organizations, and evidence and views presented in writing or at hearings.
- Be assured of the confidentiality of any trade secrets observed by an OSHA compliance officer during an inspection.
- Submit a written request to NIOSH for information on whether any substance in its workplace has potentially toxic effects in the concentrations being used.

Employee Responsibilities and Rights

Although OSHA does not cite employees for violations of their responsibilities, each employee "shall comply with all occupational safety and health standards and all rules, regulations, and orders Issued under the Act" that are applicable. Employee responsibilities and rights in states with their own occupational safety and health programs are generally the same as for workers in federal OSHA states.

Employees must comply with all applicable OSHA standards. In addition, employers should:

- Read the OSHA poster at the job site.
- Follow all employer safety and health rules and regulations and wear or use prescribed protective equipment while engaged in work.
- Report hazardous conditions to the supervisor.
- Cooperate with the OSHA compliance officer conducting an inspection if he or she inquires about safety and health conditions in the workplace.

While the part of the law covering employee responsibilities is not considered the "general duty clauses," it is an important part of the act. It means employees must follow the rules established by the employer. Employees must obey all safety rules and regulations and cannot pick and choose which ones to abide by.

11(c) Rights: Protection for Using Rights

Employees have a right to seek safety and health on the job without fear of punishment as described in Section 11(c) of the Act. The law says employers shall not punish or discriminate against workers for exercising rights such as:

- Complaining to an employer, union, OSHA or any other government agency about job safety and health hazards;
- Filing safety or health grievances;
- Participating on a workplace safety and health committee or in union activities concerning job safety and health; and
- Participating in OSHA inspections, conferences, hearings, or other OSHA-related activities.

If an employee is exercising these or other OSHA rights, the employer is not allowed to discriminate against that worker in any way, such as through firing, demotion, taking away seniority or other earned benefits, transferring the worker to an undesirable job or shift, or threatening or harassing the worker.

If the employer has knowingly allowed the employee to do something in the past (e.g., leaving work early), he or she may be violating the law by punishing the worker for doing the same thing following a protest of hazardous conditions. If the employer knows that a number of workers are doing the same thing wrong, it cannot legally single out for punishment the worker who has taken part in safety and health activities.

Workers believing they have been punished for exercising safety and health rights must contact the nearest OSHA office within 30 days of the time they learn of the alleged discrimination. A union representative can file a 11(c) complaint for a worker. The worker does not have to complete any forms. An OSHA staff member will complete the forms, asking what happened and who was involved.

Following an 11(c) complaint, OSHA will investigate. If an employee has been illegally punished for exercising safety and health rights, OSHA will ask the employer to restore that worker's job earnings and benefits. If necessary, and if it can prove discrimination, OSHA will take the employer to court. In such cases, the worker does not pay any legal fees. If a state agency has an OSHA-approved state program, employees may file their complaint with either federal OSHA or a state agency under its laws.

Other Rights

Employees have the right to:
- Review copies of appropriate OSHA standards, rules, regulations and requirements that the employer should have available at the workplace.
- Request information from the employer on safety and health hazards in the area, precautions that may be taken and procedures to be followed if an employee is involved in an accident or is exposed to toxic substances.
- Receive adequate training and information on workplace safety and health hazards.
- Request the OSHA area director to investigate if you believe hazardous conditions or violations of standards exist in your workplace.
- Have your name withheld from your employer, upon request to OSHA, if you file a written and signed complaint.
- Be advised of OSHA actions regarding your complaint and have an informal review, if requested, of any decision not to inspect or to issue a citation.
- Have your authorized employee representative accompany the OSHA compliance officer during the inspection tour.
- Respond to questions from the OSHA compliance officer, particularly if there is no authorized employee representative accompanying the compliance officer.
- Observe any monitoring or measuring of hazardous materials and have the right to see these records and your medical records, as specified under the Act.
- Have your authorized representative, or yourself, review the Log and Summary of Occupational Injuries (OSHA 300) at a reasonable time and in a reasonable manner.
- Request a closing discussion with the compliance officer following an inspection.

- Submit a written request to NIOSH for information on whether any substance in your workplace has potentially toxic effects in the concentration being used and have your name withheld from your employer if you so request.
- Object to the abatement period set in the citation issued to your employer by writing to the OSHA area director within 15 working days of the issuance of the citation.
- Participate in hearings conducted by the Occupational Safety and Health Review Commission.
- Be notified by your employer if it applies for a variance from an OSHA standard and testify at a variance hearing and appeal the final decision.
- Submit information or comment to OSHA on the issuance, modification or revocation of OSHA standards and request a public hearing.

Section 405: Surface Transportation Assistance Act Protection for Truck Industry Workers

Section 405 of the Surface Transportation Assistance Act (STAA) provides protection from reprisal by employers for truckers and certain other employees in the trucking industry involved in activities related to interstate commercial motor vehicle safety and health. Secretary of Labor's Order No. 9-83 (48 FR 35736, August 5, 1983) delegated to the Assistant Secretary of OSHA the authority to investigate and to issue findings and preliminary orders under Section 405.

Employees who believe they have been discriminated against for exercising their rights under Section 405 can file a complaint with OSHA within 180 days of the incident. The Secretary will then investigate the complaint and, within 60 days after it was filed, issue findings as to whether there is a reason to believe Section 405 has been violated.

If the Secretary finds that a complaint has merit, he/she also will issue an order requiring, where appropriate, abatement of the violation, reinstatement with back pay and related compensation, payment of compensatory damages, and the payment of the employee's expenses in bringing the complaint. Either the employee or employer may object to the findings. If no objection is filed within 30 days, the finding and order are final. If a timely filed objection is made, however, the objecting party is entitled to a hearing on the objection before an Administrative Law Judge of the Department of Labor.

Within 120 days of the hearing, the Secretary will issue a final order. A party aggrieved by the final order may seek judicial review in a court of appeals within 60 days of the final order. The following activities of truckers and certain employees involved in inter-state commercial motor vehicle operation are protected under Section 405:

Filing of safety or health complaints with OSHA or another regulatory agency relating to a violation of a commercial motor vehicle safety rule, regulation, standard, or order.

Instituting or causing to be instituted any proceedings relating to a violation of a commercial motor vehicle safety rule, regulation, standard or order.

Testifying in any such proceedings relating to the above items.

Refusing to operate a vehicle when such operation constitutes a violation of any Federal rules, regulations, standards or orders applicable to commercial motor vehicle safety or health; or because of the employee's reasonable apprehension of serious injury to himself or the public due to the unsafe condition of the equipment.

Complaints under Section 405 are filed in the same manner as complaints under 11(c). The filing period for Section 405 is 180 days from the alleged discrimination, rather than 30 days as under Section 11(c).

OSHA Standards Simplified

Initially, the OSHA standards were taken from three sources:
- Consensus standards;
- Proprietary standards; and
- Federal laws in effect when the Occupational Safety and Health Act became law.

Consensus standards are developed by industry-wide, standard-developing organizations and are discussed and substantially agreed upon through consensus by industry. OSHA has incorporated the standards of the two primary standards groups, the American National Standards Institute (ANSI) and the National Fire Protection Association (NFPA), into its set of standards.

For example, ANSI Standard B56.1-1969, Standard for Powered Industrial Trucks, covers the safety requirements relating to the elements of design, operation and maintenance of powered industrial trucks.

Another consensus standard source is the NFPA standards. NFPA No. 301969, Flammable and Combustible Liquids Code was the source standard for Part 1910, Section 106. It covers the storage and use of flammable and combustible liquids with flash points below 200°F.

Professional experts within specific industries, professional societies, and associations prepare proprietary standards. The proprietary standards are determined by a straight membership vote, not by consensus. An example of these would be the "Compressed Gas Association, Pamphlet P-1, Safe Handling of Compressed Gases." This proprietary standard covers requirements for safe handling, storage and use of compressed gas cylinders.

Some federal laws in effect before the OSH Act are enforced by OSHA, including the Federal Supply Contracts Act (Walsh-Healey); Federal Service Contracts Act (McNamara-O'Hara); Contract Work Hours and Safety Standards Act (Construction Safety Act); and the National Foundation on the Arts and Humanities Act.

Horizontal and Vertical Standards

Standards are sometimes referred to as being either "horizontal" or "vertical" in their application. Most standards are horizontal or "general," which means they apply to any employer in any industry. Standards relating to fire protection, working surfaces and first aid are examples of horizontal standards.

Some standards, however, are relevant only to a particular industry, and are called vertical, or "particular" standards. Examples are standards applying to the long shoring industry or the construction industry, and to the special industries covered in Subpart R.

OSHA is responsible for promulgating legally enforceable standards. OSHA standards may require conditions or the adoption or use of one or more practices, means, methods or processes reasonably necessary and appropriate to protect workers on the job. It is the responsibility of employers to become familiar with standards applicable to their establishments and to ensure that employees have and use personal protective equipment when required for safety.

Employees must comply with all rules and regulations that are applicable to their own actions and conduct. Where OSHA has not promulgated specific standards, employers are responsible for following the Act's general duty clause.

The general duty clause of the Act states that each employer "shall furnish ... a place of employment which is free from recognized hazards that are causing or are likely to cause death or serious physical harm to his employees."

States with OSHA-approved occupational safety and health programs must set standards that are at least as effective as the federal standards. Many state plan states adopt standards identical to their federal counterparts. OSHA standards fall into four categories: General industry, maritime, construction and agriculture.

Code of Federal Regulations

One of the most common complaints from people who must comply with the Part 1910 standards is "How do you wade through hundreds of pages of standards and make sense out of them?" From time to time you may have experienced this frustration and been tempted to toss the standards in the "round file."

The Code of Federal Regulations is a codification of the general and permanent rules published in the *Federal Register* by the executive departments and agencies of the federal government. The code is divided into 50 titles that represent broad areas subject to federal regulation. Each title is divided into chapters that usually bear the name of the issuing agency. Each chapter is further subdivided into parts covering specific regulatory areas. Based on this breakdown, the Occupational Safety and Health Administration is designated Title 29 – Labor, Chapter XVII.

Each volume of the code is revised at least once each calendar year and issued on a quarterly basis approximately as follows:
- Title 1 – Title 16 as of January 1
- Title 17 – Title 27 as of April 1
- Title 28 – Title 41 as of July 1
- Title 42 – Title 50 as of October I

The Code of Federal Regulations is kept up to date by individual issues of the *Federal Register*. These two publications (the CFR and the *Federal Register*) must be used together to determine the latest version of any given rule.

To determine whether there have been any amendments since the revision date of the Code volume in which the user is interested, the following two lists must be consulted: the "Cumulative List of CFR Sections Affected" issued monthly and the "Cumulative List of Parts Affected" which appears daily in the Federal Register. These two lists will refer you to the Federal Register page where you may find the latest amendment of any given rule. The pages in the Federal Register are numbered sequentially from January 1 to January 1 of the next year. Federal Register is one of the best sources of information on standards, since all OSHA standards are published there when adopted, as are all amendments, corrections, insertions or deletions.

Parts, Subparts, and Sections

The regulations are broken down into Parts. Part 1926, for example, is "Occupational Safety and Health Standards for Construction." Under each part, such as Part 1926, major blocks of information are broken down into Subparts.

Major Subparts in the 1926 standards include:
- Subpart A – General
- Subpart B – General Interpretations
- Subpart C – General Safety and Health Provisions
- Subpart D – Occupational Health and Environmental Control
- Subpart E – Personal Protective and Life Saving Equipment
- Subpart F – Fire Protection and Prevention
- Subpart G – Signs, Signals and Barricades
- Subpart H – Materials Handling, Storage, Use and Disposal
- Subpart I – Tools -Hand and Power
- Subpart J – Welding and Cutting

- Subpart K ~ Electrical
- Subpart L ~ Scaffolds
- Subpart M ~ Fall Protection
- Subpart N ~ Cranes, Derricks, Hoists, Elevators and Conveyors
- Subpart O ~ Motor Vehicles, Mechanized Equipment, Marine
- Subpart P ~ Excavations
- Subpart Q ~ Concrete and Masonry Construction
- Subpart R ~ Steel Erection
- Subpart S ~ Underground Construction, Caissons, Cofferdams and Compressed air
- Subpart U ~ Blasting and the Use of Explosives
- Subpart V ~ Power Transmission and Distribution
- Subpart W ~ Rollover Protective Structures, Overhead Protection
- Subpart X ~ Stairways and Ladders
- Subpart Y ~ Commercial Diving Operations
- Subpart Z ~ Toxic and Hazardous Substances

Subparts are then broken down into sections. For example, Subpart M ~ Fall Protection is divided into the following sections:
- 1926.500 ~ Scope, application and definitions
- 1926.501 ~ Duty to have fall protection
- 1926.502 ~ Fall protection systems criteria and practices
- 1926.503 ~ Training requirements
- Appendix A ~ Determining roof widths (non-mandatory)
- Appendix B ~ Guardrail systems (non-mandatory)
- Appendix C ~ Personal fall arrest systems (non-mandatory)
- Appendix D ~ Positioning device systems (non-mandatory)
- Appendix E ~ Sample fall protection plan (non-mandatory)

It should be noted that appendices can be mandatory or non-mandatory. Mandatory appendices carry the same weight and regulatory controls as the rest of the regulation and must be followed. Non-mandatory appendices, such as those in Subpart M, provide information to employers to help them comply with the regulation, but cannot be cited alone. In this case, OSHA has developed appendices to help employers determine the width of roofs, establish a guardrail or personal arrest system, and develop that meets the code as well as providing a sample fall protection plan. Prudent employers follow the guidance in the non-mandatory as well as the mandatory appendices.

Paragraph Numbering System

The OSHA standards are easier to deal with once you become familiar with the paragraph numbering system in the Federal Register. For example, Part 1926, Section 501 will appear as:

29 CFR 1926.501

The first number, 29, stands for the Title, which in this case relates to Labor. Next, CFR, stands for Code of Federal Regulations. Next, 1926, is the part number. After 1926 is a period, followed by an Arabic number. This is the section number; in this case, the number is 501. If you followed this system to its place in the standards, you would find information on the duty to have fall protection.

After the section level, there will be more numbers and letters within parentheses. These represent subsections. The following example refers to a specific subsection within the standard:

29 CFR 1926.501(b)(2)(i)

Like parts and sections, subsections appear in a specific order as well. As noted in the example above, the first level consists of lowercase letters. If the section has three major paragraphs of information in it, they will be numbered 501(a), 501(b) and 501(c). The letter b in the example above refers to the second paragraph or subsection in section 501.

The next level of numbering involves Arabic numbers. If there are three paragraphs of information between subsections (a) and (b), they will be numbered (a)(1), (a)(2) and (a)(3). The number 2 appears in the example, representing the second paragraph, or subsection, in subsection (b).

The next level uses the lowercase Roman numeral. If there are three paragraphs of information between subsections (a)(1) and (a)(2), they will be numbered (a)(1)(i), (a)(1)(ii) and (a)(1)(iii). The lowercase Roman numeral i appears in the example, representing the first paragraph or subsection in subsection (b)(2). If you followed this system to its place in the standards, you would find information on fall protection for employees constructing leading edges.

Color Coding

To further simplify the reading of standards, it is suggested that you color code your standards book. For example, go through the book and find all the section numbers and highlight them in pink. Also highlight every section head full column width in pink. Then go through the book and highlight the subsections (i.e., lowercase letter, Arabic number, lowercase Roman numeral in parentheses) in yellow:

			PINK	YELLOW
Title	Code of Fed. Reg.	Part	Section	Subsections
29	CFR	1926	.501	(b)(2)(i)

Also note there is a subject index in the back of the standards book; this index can be very helpful when trying to locate specific standards based on a key word. If you try to locate information within the standards by using the Table of Contents, remember that the particular section number contained on each page is printed in the upper corner of that page.

Construction vs. General Industry

Because OSHA is responsible for ensuring the safety and health of workers in a variety of industries, it has developed regulations for each industry, such as maritime, construction and general industry (manufacturing). Often these regulations may seem to overlap and the worker must understand what regulation applies to his or her work. OSHA considers the work being performed as the key element to this "entry argument" into the regulations. So even though a worker has a job title of construction operator, he or she may fall under the general industry rules depending on the job that is being performed.

For example, OSHA defines "construction work" as "work for construction, alteration, and/or repair, including painting and decorating."

The general industry standard 1910.23(c)(1) for fall protection starts at 4 ft. and requires a guardrail:

Every open-sided floor or platform 4 feet or more above adjacent floor or ground level shall be guarded by a standard railing (or the equivalent as specified in paragraph (e)(3) of this section) on all open sides except where there is entrance to a ramp, stairway, or fixed ladder. The railing shall be provided with a toeboard wherever, beneath the open sides, workers can pass.

The construction standard 1926.501(b)(15) for fall protection starts at 6 ft. and allows for such protective devices as guardrails and personal fall arrest systems:

Each employee on a walking/working surface (horizontal and vertical surface) with an unprotected side or edge which is 6 feet (1.8 m) or more above a lower level shall be protected from falling by the use of guardrail systems, safety net systems, or personal fall arrest systems.

To continue the example, a company has one maintenance worker who fixes heating and ventilation systems and a building with a roof that is 5 ft. tall. On Monday the worker goes to the rooftop to replace a bad motor. That work would be considered an alteration of the system, so it would fall under the construction standard. Under that standard, the work surface must be at least 6 ft. before fall protection is needed. Two weeks later, the same worker returns to the same heating unit to change filters. However, he is not altering, constructing, painting or decorating, he is simply performing routine maintenance. In this instance, the general industry standard applies, which holds that fall protection must be provided for work surfaces more than 4 ft. above ground level. Same person, same roof, same heating system. Different regulation.

Most Frequently Cited Construction Standards
Listed below are the standards cited by OSHA during the period October 2004 through September 2005.

Standard	Cited	Insp	Penalty ($)	Description
Total	41811	13878	33719436	
19260451	8050	3134	7226613	Scaffolding
19260501	5455	4867	6864349	Fall Protection Scope/Applications/Definitions
19261053	2032	1543	921544	Ladders
19260651	1712	986	2010299	Excavations, General Requirements
19260503	1518	1458	806797	Fall Protection Training Requirements
19260020	1492	1292	827176	Construction, General Safety and Health Provisions
19260100	1469	1453	774133	Head Protection
19101200	1428	725	143876	Hazard Communication
19260453	1316	1159	1208323	Manually Propelled Mobile Ladder Stands and Scaffolds
19260404	1284	1058	632878	Electrical, Wiring Design and Protection
19260652	1203	1082	2966595	Excavations, Requirements for Protective Systems
19260405	1131	848	336951	Elec. Wiring Methods, Components and Equip,Gen'l Use
19260021	920	893	695233	Construction, Safety Training and Education
19260502	919	630	797209	Fall Protection Systems Criteria and Practices
19261052	760	586	365588	Stairways
19260403	636	548	320297	Electrical, General Requirements
19100134	486	251	114754	Respiratory Protection
19260062	367	68	412118	Lead
19260095	365	359	288539	Criteria for Personal Protective Equipment
19261060	352	342	88614	Stairways and Ladders, Training Requirements
19261101	331	87	164506	Asbestos
19260416	325	306	312255	Electrical, Safety-Related Work Practices,Gen Rqts
19260025	304	303	160164	Construction, Housekeeping
19260350	301	204	119293	Gas Welding and Cutting
5A0001	279	258	360015	General Duty Clause
19260602	270	227	197234	Material Handling Equipment
19260701	252	249	157234	Concrete/Masonry, General Requirements
19100178	242	198	104664	Powered Industrial Trucks
19260150	235	216	59807	Fire Protection
19261051	232	231	104430	Stairways and Ladders,General Requirements
19260550	215	136	384132	Cranes and Derricks
19260304	179	120	78749	Woodworking Tools
19260251	158	113	65215	Rigging Equipment for Material Handling
19260300	152	147	93880	Hand and Power Tools, General Requirements
19260152	148	103	35303	Flammable and Combustible Liquids
19260200	145	129	116978	Accident Prevention Signs and Tags
19260028	122	121	60222	Construction, Personal Protective Equipment
19260050	115	102	32840	Medical Services and First Aid
19260153	100	71	114561	Liquefied Petroleum Gas

Introduction to OSHA Quiz

(See appendix for answers.)

1. OSHA was formed in 1970 in order to:
a. Provide income to the federal government
b. Establish and enforce occupational health and safety rules and to preserve human resources
c. Establish an agency that would work with the EPA to enforce pollution
d. Provide for worker safety by reducing the need for unions

2. On a construction site, the OSHA inspector conducting a Focused Inspection will look mainly at hazards caused by falls, struck by, struck against and:
a. Drowning
b. Chemical exposure
c. Electrical exposure
d. Safety program violations

3. On a large construction site the general contractor and subcontractors can be viewed as one organization under the multi-employer rule. OSHA may not issue citations to companies that:
a. Create the hazard
b. Control the hazard
c. Are responsible for correcting the hazard
d. Observe the hazard indirectly

4. The General Duty Clause states that each employer shall furnish to each employee a place of employment that:
a. Is free from recognized hazards
b. Complies with OSHA regulations
c. Recognizes organized bargaining units
d. Provides minimum safety and health provisions

5. States that develop their own safety and health rules must ensure that those rules are:
a. Identical to the federal rules
b. Providing safety to workers that equal or exceed federal standards
c. In the best interest of the state
d. Available to all workers in the state

6. OSHA has the authority to conduct inspections. Employers may:
a. Require the inspector to wait until the safety director arrives
b. Reschedule the inspection for a more appropriate time
c. Be informed of the name of the employee who filed an anonymous complaint
d. Request a search warrant

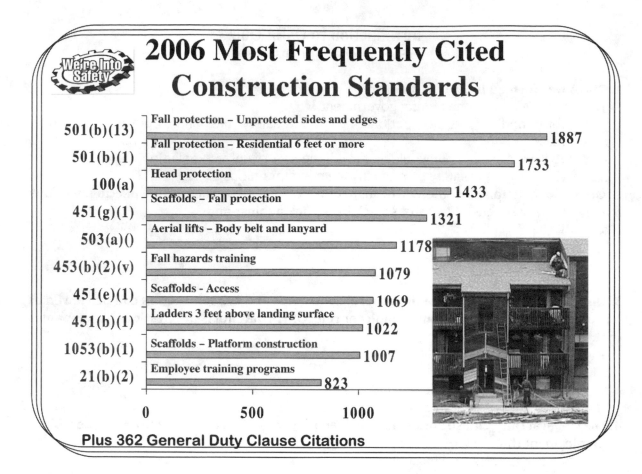

2006 Most Frequently Cited Construction Standards

Standard	Description	Citations
501(b)(13)	Fall protection – Unprotected sides and edges	1887
501(b)(1)	Fall protection – Residential 6 feet or more	1733
100(a)	Head protection	1433
451(g)(1)	Scaffolds – Fall protection	1321
503(a)()	Aerial lifts – Body belt and lanyard	1178
453(b)(2)(v)	Fall hazards training	1079
451(e)(1)	Scaffolds – Access	1069
451(b)(1)	Ladders 3 feet above landing surface	1022
1053(b)(1)	Scaffolds – Platform construction	1007
21(b)(2)	Employee training programs	823

Plus 362 General Duty Clause Citations

SAFETY PROGRAMS AND COMMITTEES

Companies recognize the need for a safety and health program. A program addresses work-related hazards including potential hazards that can result from changes in work conditions or practices whether or not they are regulated by government standards. A good safety and health program makes a big impact on loss prevention, worker productivity and the bottom line of a company.

Major Elements of a Safety Program

There are common elements in any safety program. Those companies with an effective safety and health program are rewarded with fewer and less severe accidents. Employee morale and productivity also is increased, and there is a significant reduction in workers' compensation costs and other costs associated with on-the-job injuries. The key components of any safety and health program consist of:

- Hazard analysis—Assessment of the hazard;
- Hazard prevention—Steps taken to keep workers safe;
- Polices and procedures—Rules that can be used by workers and subcontractors;
- Employee training—Type and frequency of training for all construction workers;
- Follow-up inspections—Audits or walk around inspections of the job site; and
- Enforcement—What specific steps are taken when a worker violates a safety rule.

A safety and health program describes the policies, procedures and practices that an organization uses to provide effective safety protection on the job. These guidelines are normally performance oriented. A large number of worksites lack the professional resources to develop this type of program on their own. Most small and medium-sized business do not have a full time safety staff to create such guidelines and this task often falls to a worker who picks up the additional job as a "collateral duty." In these cases it is even more important to have a written document to guide the safety program. This document should reflect the commitment by management, methods to involve the workforce, analysis of the workplace to identify hazardous situations and procedures used to control identified hazards. Safety training and enforcement of the rules are also key elements of an effective safety program.

The safety program should spell out the authority, responsibility and accountability of all parties concerned. These roles and responsibilities also should be documented in writing to prevent confusion and uncertainty. Understanding the practices can be too easily confused considering personnel turnover, cultural differences, and other factors that influence the work performance on any job. Written guidance is needed to cover basic polices, practices, procedures, emergency plans, posted signs, performance objectives and disciplinary actions.

An effective program includes provisions for the systematic identification and control of hazards in the workplace. The system must go beyond mere regulatory compliance to address all hazards.

Safety programs can be described as a system. Individual parts of the system work together to achieve a common goal. Companies often develop a baseline comprehensive worksite audit and then perform surveys on a routine basis to update that audit. Safety teams or committees work with those audits to correct unsafe conditions. Management and employees must work together to make the system work and they should review the safety program annually to make sure it still fits the needs of the organization.

Management Commitment and Employee Involvement

Safety is a team effort where management is convinced that on-the-job safety is just as important as productivity and cost control. Managers demonstrate their safety leadership by communicating freely with their staff on safety matters. The legal responsibility for safety and health lies with the employer. The employer establishes the program and is responsible for decision making in the facility.

A clearly stated safety policy involves top management and is understood by all workers on a site. An example of demonstrated commitment on the part of management can be found in a company letter from the senior manager explaining that safety is of the utmost importance and is a requirement for the job. The person in charge of a facility often signs a policy statement on safety and health protection.

The role of management in the safety system is to create the needed resources so that responsible workers have the authority and ability to react to safety needs. Management must also hold supervisors accountable for enforcing the safety standards.

Individual workers have a right to a safe and healthy workplace. In successful safety programs, individuals feel that they are involved in the overall safety culture, accept responsibility for their workplace and realize that they have an active role in the safety of others. Safety programs should have committees that meet periodically. Hazard analysis teams or other worker-led groups should assist in inspections or the revision of safety rules as well as accident investigations. This will encourage employees to report workplace conditions that appear to be hazardous.

When workers are involved in decisions that affect safety, the results are better management decisions, more effective safety protection and increased employee support for the safety program. A work site that solicits safety suggestions is a better place to work. This type of solicitation should be systematic and workers should feel that they are protected from reprisal for reporting an unsafe condition, and they should be provided with the appropriate response to their suggestion in a timely fashion. Workers will support a company where they know that management wants to be made aware of safety issues and will take action to correct them.

A key part of any program is affixing responsibility at the correct level. Both management and workers share responsibility for safety. Management establishes and enforces the rules and provides financial support for safety training and equipment. When the disciplinary procedures are fairly enforced and clearly understood, and management is held accountable for enforcing those standards, there is little opportunity to push workers into taking short cuts. Management must be held accountable for enforcing safety rules.

Workers are required to follow the rules. They must understand that there is no tolerance for unsafe behavior. Discipline is an indispensable piece of the whole approach to safety and health protection. Safe work procedures must be enforced and must cover all personnel, from site manager to hourly employee. Accountability can be demonstrated by a written human resource policy that provides for corrective actions to be taken when a safety rule is ignored. This may involve a verbal reprimand, a written reprimand, suspension without pay or even termination. A clearly communicated system of progressive discipline lets all workers and supervisors know what is expected of them as well as the consequences for failing to meet those expectations. By using readily available counseling forms from the human resources department to accomplish counseling for safety misconduct, the supervisors reinforce the company's commitment to safety.

Work Site Analysis

Companies should examine the work site to identify existing hazards or conditions that could create hazards. Dangerous operations should be analyzed in such a way that hazards can be anticipated. This involves time and resources that must be approved by management. Safety committees, hazard evaluation teams, insurance carriers or outside consultants can assist in a workplace analysis. The people performing the inspections should be familiar with the safety program and applicable regulations for the work site.

The analysis can take the form of a comprehensive walk-through audit to establish a baseline for future safety audits. Some companies conduct a Job Hazard Analysis that involves reviewing each step of a job in a systematic way to determine the safest method to perform that task. Safety inspections should be performed on a periodic basis. A weekly inspection is recommended, although some companies perform a walk around inspection every other week. Checklists can be developed that identify regulations that apply to the operation or safety challenges that have developed in the past. A review of accident records or injury reports often provides an insight into hazardous operations. The safety team should review new facilities and processes, materials, and equipment that may be brought into the facilities. The team should also look into accidents and even "near-miss" incidents to find ways to prevent future accidents from occurring.

Workers who report safety problems should be able to notify management or committees about unsafe conditions without fear of reprisal. They should receive feedback in a timely manner and should be encouraged to use the system.

Hazard Prevention and Control

Armed with a list of hazardous operations, the employees can begin a systematic analysis of how to control the hazards. Effective design or engineering controls often eliminate the hazard at the source. In OSHA's hierarchy the first method of hazard management is to establish an engineering control. If that is not feasible, some form of administrative control, personal protective equipment, or another form of work safety practice may be used. Such things as installing a guardrail or electrical insulation often are cost-effective ways of eliminating the hazard. This change must be done in a timely manner to minimize the exposure of workers to the danger.

If the hazard cannot be eliminated, workers may have to use some form of hazard control, such as using a spotter or wearing personal protective equipment to continue to work in a safe manner. Sometimes the hazard is the result of poor maintenance or use or abuse of the facility and normal maintenance procedures correct the problem. In other cases, an emergency event such as the release of chlorine gas or reaction to a fire highlight the need for special training for the workers.

The best preventive measure for controlling unsafe conditions is to create an engineered solution, such as a guardrail or a physical system to protect the worker. Sometimes a feasible physical solution cannot be found. In these cases a procedure for safe work can be established. These procedures may not be as effective at ensuring a safe workplace by building engineered controls, but with the right type of training, positive reinforcement and correction of unsafe worker performance, the workplace can be made significantly safer. Firms should consider the use of a clearly communicated disciplinary system to enforce worker safety performance. In the event that the unsafe act cannot be engineered to a safe degree, or procedures do not provide sufficient safety, the firm may rely on personal protective equipment that can protect the workers. If none of these protective systems are deemed sufficient, the firm may rely on administrative controls to maintain safety. For example, the facility may rotate workers through the hazardous area in order to minimize the amount of time that the employees are exposed to a hazard.

The hazard prevention and control methodology can be illustrated with an example.

Imagine there is a wastewater treatment facility that has a lot of toxic gases being vented into an area. The first thing to do is try an engineering control, such as installing a ventilation system that continuously vents the air to the outside. If that is not feasible, the second best system is to develop procedures for safe work by requiring workers to manually vent the area prior to entering the work area by opening the doors and putting fans in the windows. If that procedure is not feasible, the company may elect to use personal protective equipment and require the workers to wear respirators when they are in that area. Finally, if none of those solutions are feasible, the firm may rotate workers through that area so that no single worker is exposed to toxic gases for more than 30 minutes at a time, based on the maximum amount of exposure listed for short-term exposures on the material safety data sheet.

Safety and Health Training

Training is a key element in any business. In order to maximize the human element, workers must be trained in new and productive techniques. Maintaining a safety system is no different than maintaining a production system. Some training is required by federal or state regulations, while other safety training topics enhance the overall safety and even the productivity of the job.

The safety program should identify the types of training required, the personnel who need the training and the frequency of that training. A test should be given to ensure that workers understand the training material. This test can be a written quiz or a hands-on demonstration. It is important to provide sufficient training for safety so that responding to emergencies becomes second nature to the workers.

Workers must understand the hazards to which they may be exposed and the training must ensure that they understand how to prevent themselves from getting injured as a result of those hazards.

Training can easily be broken into two areas: initial training and refresher training. When new employees are brought into the job site, they must be taught about the hazards of their new position. If a new machine or process is brought into place, the workers must receive initial training so that they can perform their required tasks safely.

Once they have been on the job for a while, refresher training helps to improve their performance and update the worker regarding any changes in policy or procedures.

Workers need to understand the hazards associated with their jobs, how to identify hazards and how to use the safety equipment that is provided to them. This training should be incorporated into their other training. Contractors and short-term workers must receive orientation training to prepare them to work in the area safely in an environment that may be new to them or hazards that they normally do not encounter. All workers must be trained on how to report incidents and accidents that may require posting in the OSHA 300 log.

Supervisors must understand company polices and procedures, hazard detection and control, how to conduct accident investigations, how to handle emergencies and how to reinforce training. Management training should be different than training that is provided to new hires, contract workers and other employees. It is important to stress to management that their role is to guide the safety program and provide support so that the workers can accomplish the job in a safe and efficient manner.

EMPLOYEE SAFETY AND HEALTH RECORD

Name: Permanent___
Job Title: Temporary___
Department: Date Hired:

List Hazards Associated with Present Duties:

_____
_____

Occupational Health Medical Examination Required:

Asbestos: Hearing:
Lead: Other (specify):

_____
_____

MANDATORY TRAINING TOPICS (To be briefed to all personnel, initial when conducted)

_____Location of required and appropriate safety bulletin boards, OSHA Poster
_____OSHA and Company Safety Rules that apply to the job and work place
_____Hazards of the work area to include physical, physiological and chemical.
_____Reason for specific medical evaluation
_____Hazards of the assigned job or tasks and safety procedures to be followed
_____Personal Protective Equipment (PPE), required, how, when and where to use it
_____Emergency procedures for evacuation, fire reporting, emergency equipment
_____Location of alarms and extinguishers
_____ Emergency Telephone Numbers
_____Location of medical facilities or first aid kits
_____Need to report of unsafe/unhealthful equipment, conditions or procedures
_____How to report unsafe/unhealthful equipment, conditions or procedures
_____Requirements for documentation and notification of on-the-job injury or illness
_____Hazard Communications Program
_____Company Safety Program

INITIAL INDIVIDUAL TRAINING TOPICS (As needed, initial when conducted)

_____Respirator Protection Program   _____ Lockout/Tagout
_____Permit Required Confined Space Program   _____Back Injury Prevention
_____Hearing Conservation   _____Bloodborne Pathogens
_____Jewelry Safety   _____PPE Use and Care
_____Fall Protection   _____Others (List and initial)

_____   _____

PERSONAL PROTECTION ISSUED (initial when issued)

___Head Protection   ___Eye Protection   ___Face Protection
___Arm/Hand Protection   ___Foot Protection   ___Hearing Protection
___Respiratory Protection   ___Other (specify)   ___Other (specify)

PERSONAL PROTECTION PROVIDED IN THE WORK AREA

___Head Protection   ___Eye Protection   ___Face Protection
___Arm/Hand Protection   ___Foot Protection   ___Hearing Protection
___Respiratory Protection   ___Other (specify)   ___Other (specify)

RECORD OF CONTINUOUS JOB SAFETY TRAINING

DATE	TOPIC	SUPERVISOR SIGN	EMPLOYEE SIGN

RECORD OF JOB SAFETY NON-COMPLIANCE

Verbal Warning _____   Date: _____   Supervisor: _____
Written Warning _____   Date: _____   Supervisor: _____
Referred to Human Resources: Date: _____   Supervisor: _____

Elements of a Written Safety Program

These safety programs can be published as a written document and stored in a three-ring binder for easy updating. There are some topics that are common in any safety and health program. The basic plan sets the safety policy of the company and establishes responsibility, accountability and disciplinary procedures. Some topics included in the basic plan are:

- Safety policy
- Management responsibilities
- Supervisor responsibilities
- Employee responsibilities
- Safety committee or safety team (employee participation)
- Safety meetings
- Hazard recognition
- Incident investigation
- Elimination of workplace hazards
- Basic safety rules
- Job related safety rules
- Disciplinary policy
- Emergency planning
- Reporting accidents and incidents (OSHA 300 log)
- Training
  - Initial (new employee or new process)
  - Refresher
  - Specialized
  - Supervisory

Appendices can then be added to the basic program to provide specific guidance on site-specific hazards that workers will encounter. This approach allows a company or a facility to personalize the plan to handle situations that may be unique to that area. Some examples of appendices that may be added to the safety program are:

- Personal protective equipment hazard analysis and program
- Respirator program
- Lockout/tagout (control of hazardous energy)
- Permit-required confined space entry
- Electrical safety
- First-aid plan
- Hazard communication program
- Hearing conservation program
- Welding hot work program
- Bloodborne pathogen plan
- Violence in the workplace plan
- Emergency action plan
- Hazardous waste operations plan

Safety Committees

The principal function of the safety committee is to consult and provide policy advice on and monitor the performance of the safety and health program. Committees should be established at company facilities or groupings of facilities consistent with the mission, size and organization of the company and its collective bargaining configuration. The company shall form committees at the lowest practicable local level. The principal function of these committees is to monitor and assist in the execution of the company's safety and health policies and program at its work sites.

- Committees shall have equal representation of management and non-management employees, who shall be members of record.
- Management members of both national-level and establishment-level committees shall be appointed in writing by the person empowered to make such appointments.
- Non-management members of establishment-level committees shall represent all employees of the establishment and shall be determined according to the following rules:
- Where employees are represented under collective bargaining arrangements, members shall be appointed from among those recommended by the exclusive bargaining representative;
- Where employees are not represented under collective bargaining arrangements, members shall be determined through procedures devised by the company that provide for effective representation of all employees; and
- Where some employees are covered under collective bargaining arrangements and others are not, members shall be representative of both groups.

Non-management members of national level committees shall be determined according to the following rules:

- Where employees are represented by organizations having exclusive recognition on a company basis or by organizations having national consultation rights, some members shall be determined in accordance with the terms of collective bargaining agreements and some members shall be selected from those organizations having consultation rights, and
- Where employees are not represented by the above types of organizations, members shall be determined through procedures devised by the agency that provide for effective representation of all employees.
- Committee members should serve overlapping terms. Such terms should be of at least two years duration, except when the committee is initially organized.
- The committee chairperson shall be nominated from among the committee's members and shall be elected by the committee members. Management and non-management members should alternate in this position. Maximum service time as chairperson should be two consecutive years.

- Committees ought to establish a regular schedule of meetings and special meetings shall be held as necessary; establishment level committees should meet at least quarterly and national committees should meet at least annually.

Adequate advance notice of committee meetings should be furnished to employees and each meeting should be conducted pursuant to a prepared agenda. Written minutes of each committee meeting shall be maintained and distributed to each committee member, and upon request, shall be made available to employees and to the Secretary.

- The employer must provide all committee members with appropriate training
- The safety and health committee is an integral part of the safety and health program, and helps ensure effective implementation of the program at the establishment level.
- Monitor and assist the safety and health program at establishments under its jurisdiction and make recommendations to the official in charge on the operation of the program;
- Monitor findings and reports of workplace inspections to confirm that appropriate corrective measures are implemented

YOUR SAFETY COMMITTEE

Name of the Committee (be creative)

_____

Committee Motto:. _____

Elected Leader: _____

Recorder . _____

Member Name: _____.

Member Name: _____.

Member Name: _____.

Member Name: _____.

Member Name: _____.

Member Name: _____.

Member Name: _____.

Member Name: _____.

Member Name: _____.

Member Name: _____.

State Programs

States often develop regulations that provide safety for their workers that are as effective or even more so than the federal regulations. Two such states are Washington and California. California enacted Senate Bill 198, a worker safety bill that applies to all employers in the state of California. Washington State requires that all companies have an "Accident Prevention Program." Both states require that the program be written and meet certain criteria.

California Requirements

The State of California passed S.B. 198 requiring that all California employers have a safety program. California compares workers' compensation data to target employers for safety inspections. S.B. 198 requires employers to:

- Designate a responsible person;
- Periodically conduct inspections and accident investigations, as necessary;
- Identify workplace hazards;
- Correct safety deficiencies or hazards;
- Train employees;
- Establish a system for employee communication; and
- Establish a disciplinary system.

Washington State Requirements

The State of Washington requires companies to develop an accident prevention plan (APP) in writing. This plan must be tailored to the workplace. The written plan must contain an orientation and a description of the company safety program. The plan should detail the requirement for a safety committee as well as how to report injuries and unsafe conditions.

Washington's plan requires specific training for employees, such as the initial on-the-job orientation; use and care of personal protective equipment; emergency actions to be taken to evacuate the workplace; and how to identify, store and use hazardous gases, chemicals and materials. Other training topics should include materials-handling equipment, machine tool operations, toxic materials and the operation of utility systems. The plan should require employers to enforce training programs and

procedures to ensure that the work is performed in a safe manner. Washington companies must establish, supervise and enforce accident prevention programs in a manner that is effective.

A large part of the APP is the establishment of a safety committee and the use of safety meetings. Companies with more than 11 employees at the same location in the same shift are required to have a safety committee. The committee should have an equal number of employee-elected and employer-selected members. It also is important to include union members in the selection of the committee if a union is present. The committee should serve for a maximum of one year. The group must elect a chairperson of the committee and decide how often, when, and where to meet. The committee meetings should not last longer than one hour.

Firms with less than 10 employees may elect to have safety meetings instead of a safety committee. These safety meetings must be held monthly and there must be at least one representative of management at the meetings. The purpose of these meetings should be to review safety inspections, evaluate accident investigations and the overall performance of the APP. A record of the meeting must be made and include the names of the attendees and the subjects discussed.

The safety committee shall:

- Document the attendance at the meeting;
- Record subjects discussed;
- Review safety inspection reports;
- Evaluate accident investigations;
- Evaluate the workplace APP; and
- Maintain meeting records for one year.

The State of Washington allows companies to establish additional programs, plans and other rules that go beyond the APP described in order to develop a total safety and health plan.

Example Plan

The federal program as well as the two state programs provide an insight into how organizations are expected to respond with safety programs. By combining the intent of those programs into one document, a sample safety program that companies can use to meet the requirements of the overall safety program can be created. Companies can use this form by filling in the blank spaces with the pertinent information. Once it is completed it is important to review the plan with the management and staff to ensure that the plan is workable for the facility as well as understood by all.

The safety plan provided here is a sample that can be used to develop a facility safety program. The base document describes roles and responsibilities and sets forth guidelines for the effective operation of a safety system. The guidelines may be modified to include more specific details as necessary.

With the overall plan in place, the facility should add appendices as needed to establish site-specific safety operations for detailed tasks. These appendices can be added or deleted as the facility establishes or discontinues procedures.

Sample Safety and Health Policy

It is the policy of _____ to provide a safe and healthy workplace for all of our employees. We feel that all accidents are preventable and that safety is a team effort involving the workforce, supervisors and management.

This company has established a safety and health program that is designed to involve all workers in the identification and reduction of hazards on each of our work sites. This program is designed to protect our most valuable resource, our workers, as well as meet federal and state regulations.

Safety is a key element in all workers' jobs. Unsafe behavior will not be tolerated and supervisors are required to enforce safety rules the same as they would enforce quality and timeliness issues with the employees. Active participation and adherence to our Safety Program is a condition of employment. No worker is allowed to work on a job that he or she knows is not safe. That includes our contractors and subcontractors.

Our goal is to eliminate accidents and injuries. There is no excuse or reason to take a shortcut or cut corners when they could result in an unsafe condition or action.

We're all in this together. If we work together, we will all go home safe and sound.

_____
Senior person

Responsibilities

Safety is a team effort and all employees and subcontractors of _____ are responsible for ensuring that the work area is safe. Different levels of management hold levels of responsibility. The person identified to maintain this program is _____, who is the head of _____ _____ and can be reached at telephone extension _____. Management is responsible to ensure that a safety committee is formed, staffed and resourced to allow it to complete its task of assisting the safety program. Managers will ensure that workers have sufficient time, resources and support from their supervisors to carry out the program. Managers will include an evaluation of safety performance in the annual review of workers' performance. Managers are responsible to ensure that all incidents (accidents and close calls) are investigated within five days and that corrective action is taken to prevent hazardous conditions from recurring. Managers will ensure that the OSHA 300 form is maintained in an up-to-date, accurate manner with all recordable incidents being posted within seven calendar days of their occurrence. Managers are expected to report unsafe practices and to take action to correct unsafe behavior when they see it. Managers of this facility are required to set a good example by following established safety rules, attending required safety training and encouraging all workers to do the same. Managers must enforce the disciplinary rules established in this safety program by ensuring that supervisors counsel workers as necessary.

Supervisors are responsible for the workers entrusted to their care. They must ensure that workers receive initial safety training prior to being allowed to work. Such training should be documented and evaluated to ensure that the worker understands what is expected of him or her. Supervisors are responsible for ensuring workers have the correct personal protective equipment and that the equipment is maintained correctly and used in the correct manner.

Supervisors are required to conduct a daily walk-around safety check of the work area and to direct the correction of any safety deficiencies found. In the event that the safety deficiency is caused by worker misconduct or non-compliance with established safety rules, the supervisor is required to counsel the individual and record that counseling on the employee's work record as outlined in the section on discipline.

Supervisors are not allowed to remove or defeat any safety device or to encourage workers by word or example to take short cuts that could result in an unsafe condition or act. Supervisors are required to support the safety committee by allowing workers the time needed to participate in safety activities.

Employees are required to comply with the safety rules established by the facility, federal or state law, safety training and any actions directed by their supervisors with regard to safety. When employees identify unsafe conditions, they are to report those to their supervisors or the safety committee promptly. All injuries or accidents are to be reported immediately to supervisors. All personal protective equipment should be maintained in good working condition and used correctly. Workers may not remove or defeat any safety device nor encourage coworkers by word or deed to take short cuts that may lead to an unsafe condition or act.

The Safety Committee has been formed to help employees and management work together to resolve safety problems and develop solutions identified to ensure that the safety program works smoothly. The safety committee consists of an equal number from management and employees. The union is invited to sit on the safety committee. The leader of the safety committee reports directly to _____ who has responsibility for the safety program. The leader is elected from the group. Members of the safety committee serve for one year and the group meets once a quarter on company time. The committee will review the OSHA 300 log and any accident reports or audits that have occurred during that time. The Safety Committee will conduct a monthly safety audit of the facility and the results of the audit will be posted on the company safety bulletin board.

The safety committee meets for one hour on the first Tuesday of the month in the employee lunchroom. The minutes of each meeting will be posted on the company's safety bulletin board and kept on file for two years.

Safety meetings for all employees will be held monthly by the supervisor. All employees are required to attend these meetings to enhance safety-related communication in the facility.

Employees are required to report any injury or work-related illness to their immediate supervisor regardless of how serious. Minor injuries such as cuts and scrapes can be entered on the minor injury log that is posted at _____.

The site supervisor will:

Investigate a serious injury or illness using procedures in the "Incident Investigation" section below. Complete an "Incident Investigation Report" form. Give the "Employee's Report" and the "Incident Investigation Report" to _____, who is responsible for this form.

Determine from the Employee's Report, Incident Investigation Report, and any loss and injury claim form associated with the incident, whether it must be recorded on the OSHA Injury and Illness Log and Summary according to the instructions for that form.

- Enter a recordable incident within six days after the company becomes aware of it.
- If the injury is not recorded on the OSHA log, add it to a separate incident report log, which is used to record non-OSHA recordable injuries and near misses.
- Each month before the scheduled safety committee meeting, make any new injury reports and investigations available to the safety committee for review, along with an updated OSHA and incident report log.

The safety committee will review the log for trends and may decide to conduct a separate investigation of any incident.

The management will post a signed copy of the OSHA log summary for the previous year on the safety bulletin board each February 1 until April 30. The log will be kept on file for at least five years. Any employee can view an OSHA log upon request at any time during the year.

Incident Investigation

If an employee dies while working or is not expected to survive, or when employees are admitted to a hospital as a result of a work-related incident the management will contact the OSHA representative (federal or state) within eight hours after becoming aware of the incident. The scene of the incident should not be disturbed except to aid in rescue or make the scene safe.

Whenever there is an incident that results in death or serious injuries that have immediate symptoms, a preliminary investigation should be conducted by the immediate supervisor of the injured person(s), a person designated by management, an employee representative of the safety committee, and any other persons whose expertise would help the investigation.

The investigation team should take written statements from witnesses and photograph the incident scene and equipment involved. The team also should document as soon as possible after the incident, the condition of the equipment and any anything else in the work area that may be relevant. The team should make a written report of its findings. The report also should include a sequence of events leading up to the incident, conclusions about the incident and any recommendations to prevent a similar incident in the future. The safety committee should review the report at its next regularly scheduled meeting.

When a supervisor becomes aware of an employee injury where the injury was not serious enough to warrant a team investigation as described above, the supervisor should write an Incident Report to accompany the "Employee's Injury/Illness Report Form" and forward them to _____, who maintains the OSHA 300 log.

Whenever there is an incident that did not but could have resulted in serious injury to an employee (a near-miss), the incident should be investigated by the supervisor or a team depending on the seriousness of the injury that would have occurred. The "Incident Investigation Report" form should be used to investigate the near miss. The form should be clearly marked to indicate that it was a near miss and that no actual injury occurred. The report should be forwarded to the bookkeeper to record on the incident log.

Safety Inspection Procedures

This company is committed to aggressively identifying hazardous conditions and practices that are likely to result in injury or illness to employees. We will take prompt action to eliminate any hazards we find. In addition to reviewing injury records and investigating incidents for their causes, management and the safety committee will regularly check the workplace for hazards as described below:

Annual Site Survey—An inspection team made up of members of the safety committee will do a wall-to-wall, walk-through inspection of the entire worksite. They will write down any safety hazards or potential hazards they find. The results of this inspection will be used to eliminate or control obvious hazards, target specific work areas for more intensive investigation, assist in revising the checklists used during regular monthly safety inspections and as part of the annual review of the effectiveness of our accident prevention program.

Weekly Safety Inspection—Each week, safety representatives will inspect their areas for hazards using the standard safety inspection checklist. They will talk to employees about their safety concerns. Committee members will report any hazards or concerns to the whole committee for consideration. The results of the area inspection and any action taken will be posted in the affected area. Occasionally, committee representatives may agree to inspect each other's area rather than their own.

Job Hazard Analysis—As a part of our ongoing safety program, we will use a "Job Hazard Analysis" form to look at each type of job task our employees perform. The supervisor of that job task or a member of the safety committee will conduct this analysis. We will change how the job is performed as needed to eliminate or control any hazards. We will also determine whether the employee needs to use personal protective equipment (PPE)

while performing the job. Employees will be trained in the revised operation and to use any required PPE. The results will be reported to the safety committee. Each job task will be analyzed at least once every two years, whenever there is a change in how the task is performed or if a serious injury occurs while the task is being performed.

Hazard Prevention and Control

This company is committed to eliminating or controlling workplace hazards that could cause injury or illness to our employees. We will meet the requirements of federal and state safety standards where there are specific rules about a hazard or potential hazard in our workplace. Whenever possible we will design our facilities and equipment to eliminate employee exposure to hazards. Where these engineering controls are not possible, work rules that effectively prevent employee exposure to the hazard will be established. When the above methods of control are not possible or are not fully effective, we will require employees to use personal protective equipment (PPE) such as safety glasses, hearing protection, and foot and hand protection.

Basic Safety Rules

The following basic safety rules have been established to help make our company a safe and efficient place to work. These rules are in addition to safety rules that must be followed when doing particular jobs or operating certain equipment. Those rules are listed elsewhere in this program. Failure to comply with these rules will result in disciplinary action.

- Never do anything that is unsafe in order to get the job done. If a job is unsafe, report it to your supervisor or safety committee representative. We will find a safer way to do that job.
- Do not remove or disable any safety device! Keep guards in place at all times on operating machinery.
- Never operate a piece of equipment unless you have been trained on it and are authorized to use it.
- Use your personal protective equipment whenever it is required.

- Obey all safety-warning signs.
- Working under the influence of alcohol or illegal drugs or using them at work is prohibited and will not be tolerated.
- Do not bring firearms or explosives onto company property.
- Smoking is only permitted in designated areas.
- Horseplay, running and fighting are prohibited
- Clean up spills immediately. Replace all tools and supplies after use. Do not allow scraps to accumulate where they will become a hazard. Good housekeeping helps prevent injuries.

Disciplinary Policy

This facility has established a disciplinary policy to provide appropriate consequences for failure to follow safety rules. This policy is designed not so much to punish as to bring unacceptable behavior to the employee's attention in a way that the employee will be motivated to make corrections. The following consequences apply to the violation of the same rule or the same unacceptable behavior:

- First instance—Verbal warning, notation in employee file, and instruction on proper actions.
- Second instance—One-day suspension, written reprimand, and instruction on proper actions.
- Third instance—One-week suspension, written reprimand, and instruction on proper actions.
- Fourth instance—Termination of employment.

An employee may be subject to immediate termination when a safety violation places the employee or his or her coworkers at risk of permanent disability or death.

If an Injury Occurs

A first-aid kit is maintained at _____ _____. Each company vehicle is equipped with a first-aid kit located in the glove box or under the driver's seat. Members of the safety committee check these kits monthly. An inventory of each kit is taped to the inside cover of the box. If you are injured, promptly report it to any supervisor.

All supervisors are required to have first-aid cards. Other employees may have been certified. A list of current first-aid and CPR-certified supervisors and employees is posted on the company safety bulletin board along with the expiration dates of their cards.

In case of serious injury, do not move the injured person unless absolutely necessary. Only provide assistance to the level of your training. Call for help. If there is no response, call 911.

Safety Training

Training is an essential part of our plan to provide a safe workplace at this facility. To ensure that all employees are trained *before* they start a task that requires training, we have a training coordinator whose name is posted on the company safety bulletin board. Our safety-training supervisor is

_____.

That person is responsible for verifying that each employee has received an initial orientation by his or her supervisor has received any training needed to do the job safely and that the employee file includes documentation of the training. The coordinator will make sure that an outline and materials list is available for each training course we provide:

Course	Who must attend
Basic Orientation	All employees (given by the employee's supervisor)
Chemical Hazards (General)	All employees
Chemical Hazards (Specific)	An employee who uses or is exposed to a particular chemical
Fire extinguisher Safety	All employees
Respirator Training	Employees who use respirators
Forklift Training	Employees who operate forklifts
Electrical Safety	Employees who work with electricity
Power Tool Safety	Employees who use power tools

Safety and Health Program

According to the OSHA Instruction STD 3-1, dated June 22, 1987, OSHA will look for the following elements in a safety program.

Management Commitment and Leadership

- Policy statement: goals established, issued, and communicated to employees.
- Program revised annually.
- Participation in safety meetings, inspections; agenda items in meetings.
- Commitment of resources is adequate.
- Safety rules and procedures incorporated into site operations.
- Management observes safety rules.

Assignment of Responsibility

- Safety designee on site, knowledgeable, and accountable.
- Supervisors (including foremen) safety and health responsibilities understood.
- Employees adhere to safety rules.

Identification and Control of Hazards

- Periodic site safety inspection program involves supervisors.
- Preventive controls in place (PPE, maintenance, engineering controls).

- Action taken to address hazards.
- Safety Committee, where appropriate.
- Technical references available.
- Enforcement procedures by management.

Training and Education

- Supervisors receive basic training.
- Specialized training taken when needed.
- Employee training program exists, is ongoing, and is effective.

Recordkeeping and Hazard Analysis

- Records maintained of employee illnesses/injuries and posted.
- Supervisors perform accident investigations, determine causes, and propose corrective action.
- Injuries, "near misses", and illnesses are evaluated for trends, similar causes; corrective action is initiated.

First Aid and Medical Assistance

- First-aid supplies and medical service available.
- Employees informed of medical records.
- Emergency procedures and training, where necessary.

How This Safety Program Meets Federal and State Requirements

	Federal Guidelines	California	Washington
Written Plan	X	X	X
Policy Statement by Management	X		
Responsible Person		X	
Accountability	X	X	
Employee Involvement	X	X	X
Hazard Identification	X	X	
Hazard Control	X	X	
Training	X	X	X
Safety Committee	X	X	
Safety Rule Enforcement		X	X
Disciplinary Guides		X	X

Sample Safety and Health Program

This GENERIC Written Safety and Health Program has been developed in order to help employers understand how to develop the required Written Safety and Health Program. This employer understands that this plan will be only partially completed by filling in the blanks.

The final determination of compliance with OSHA regulations including compliance with the written Safety and Health Program requirement under 1926.21 is made by evaluation of all factors pertaining to potential hazards at a particular worksite with respect to employee safety and health. Employers who are contemplating the use of this guide should be aware that it is not to be considered a substitute for any provisions of the Occupational Safety and Health Act or for any standards issued by OSHA. The standards themselves are the legal requirements to which and employer will by held.

This is a generic safety and health program. It is designed to be used as a guideline for developing a company safety and health program. Since each company is different, this program must be tailored to meet specific needs, by adding or deleting parts of this guide. Determine based on the hazards or potential hazards of your job site.

POLICY STATEMENT

It is *COMPANY NAME* belief that our people are our most important asset and that the preservation of employee Safety and Health must remain a constant consideration in every phase of our business. It is our intent to provide a work environment as free of hazards as possible.

All employees are responsible for working safely and productively, always remaining aware of hazards in their jobs and following recognized safe work practices, including the use of Personal Protective Equipment (PPE).

It is also *COMPANY NAME* belief that any safety and health program must have total employee involvement. Therefore this program has management's highest priority, support, and participation.

PRODUCTION IS NOT SO URGENT THAT WE CANNOT TAKE TIME TO DO OUR WORK SAFELY.

Signed by
Presiden

GOALS

Safety begins at the top and goes downward throughout the company. Our goal is to have an injury free work place. This can be achieved by delegating responsibility and accountability to all involved in this company's operation.

Responsibility: Having to answer for activities and results.

Accountability: The active measurement by management to ensure compliance or management doing something to ensure action.

In other words, to reach our goal of a safe work place everyone needs to take responsibility. Then everyone will be held accountable.
- Benefits of achieving our goals are:
- The minimizing of all injury accidents
- The loss to property and equipment
- No fatalities
- No permanent disabilities
- Having the best Safety and Health conditions possible in the work place.
- ENTER YOUR COMPANY'S OWN GOALS HERE

OBJECTIVES and SAFETY MEETINGS

The Safety and Health program shall be reviewed annually, and be revised, updated or changed at that time if needed. All employees of *COMPANY NAME* shall attend and participate in the (Daily/Weekly/Biweekly/Monthly) safety meetings.

A minimum of min./hrs. shall be given each (Day/Week/Month) to the safety meeting. This shall be conducted by *SAFETY PERSON*. Problems that have arisen or that are anticipated shall be discussed along with any other safety and health topics. To keep the meeting a valuable educational experience the following is suggested:
- Keep the meeting moving.
- Start and stop on time.
- Use illustrated material and demonstrations to make the point.
- Each topic should be discussed thoroughly.
- Review accidents, injuries.
- Evaluate close calls or near misses for trends; similar causes, and initiate corrective actions.
- ENTER YOUR COMPANY'S OBJECTIVES HERE

MANAGEMENT COMMITMENT

The management of *COMPANY NAME* is committed to the company's safety policy, and to provide direction and motivation by:

- The appointment of *SAFETY COORDINATOR NAME* as our Safety Coordinator.
- Establishing our annual Company safety goals and objectives.
- Having a written safety and health program and being totally committed to it. Take part in employees' safety training. Establish and enforce disciplinary procedures for employees.
- Support for the safety and health program with people, authority and training.
- Establish accountability and responsibilities for management and employees to follow.
- ENTER YOUR MANAGEMENT'S COMMITMENT HERE

ASSIGNMENT OF RESPONSIBILITY

Safety Officer

COMPANY NAME has designated *PERSONS NAME* as our safety and health officer. The location of his/her office is * *.

It shall be the duty of the safety officer to assist the Supervisor/Foreman and all other levels of Management in the initiation, education, and execution of an effective safety program generally and more specifically the following:

- Introduce the safety program to new employees.
- Follow up on recommendations, suggestions, etc., made at the Daily/ Weekly/ Biweekly/ Monthly safety meetings. All topics of safety concerns shall be documented accordingly.
- Be thoroughly familiar with the company safety program and assist the personal in the execution of standard policies.
- Conduct safety inspection on a periodical basis.
- Address all hazards or potential hazards as needed.
- The preparation of monthly accident reports and investigations.
- Maintain adequate stock of first aid supplies and other safety equipment to ensure their immediate availability, and make sure there is adequate number of qualified first aid certified people on the job.
- Be thoroughly familiar with the OSHA, local and state safety codes and regulations.

NOTE: Employers should incorporate current copies of such codes and regulations in to your safety and health program as resource material.

EMPLOYEES

It is the duty of each and every employee to know the safety rules, and conduct his/her work in compliance. Disregard of the safety and health rules shall be grounds for disciplinary action up to and including termination. It is the duty of each employee to make full use of the safeguards provided for their protection. Every employee will receive an orientation when hired and receive a Company Safety and Health Program. This is a partial list of these rules:

- Read, understand and follow safety and health rules and procedures.
- Employees working in areas where there is a possible danger of injury preventable with Personal Protection Equipment (PPE) will wear PPE at all times.
- Suitable work clothes will be worn; see your supervisor
- Employees observed working in a manner which might cause injury to either themselves or other workers shall be warned of the danger and will immediately correct their method of operation.
- Employees shall report all injuries, no matter how slight to their supervisor/ foreman immediately, and seek treatment promptly.
- Employees shall be aware of the location of first aid, fire fighting equipment, and other safety devices.
- Attend any and all required safety and health meetings.
- Until they are properly trained, employees are not to perform potentially hazardous tasks, or to use any hazardous material. Employees are to follow all procedures when performing those tasks.

ADDITIONAL

ADDITIONAL

IF EVER IN DOUBT ABOUT SOMETHING, STOP AND ASK SOMEONE

SUPERVISOR/FOREMAN

Supervisor/Foreman will establish an operating atmosphere that insures that safety and health is managed in the same manner and with the same emphasis as production, cost, and quality control.

- Define the responsibilities for safety and health of all subordinates and hold each person accountable for their results through the formal appraisal system and where necessary, disciplinary procedures.
- Regularly emphasizing that accident and health hazard exposure prevention are not only moral responsibilities, but also a condition of employment. Accidents create unnecessary loss both personal and financial.
- Identifying operational oversights that could contribute to accidents which often result in injuries and property damage. Example :(*lockout/tagout*).
- Participate in safety and health related activities, including routinely attending safety meetings, reviews of the facility, correcting employee behavior that can result in accidents and injuries, and quality control problems.
- Spend some time with each person hired explaining the safety policies and the hazards of his/her particular work. See that this initial orientation of "new hires" is carried out by *SAFETY OFFICER'S NAME*
- Make sure that if a "Competent Person" is required, that one is on hand to oversee, and instruct employees when necessary.
- Never short-cut safety for expediency, nor allow workers to do so.
- Enforce safety rules consistently, and follow company's discipline/enforcement procedures.
- Conduct daily, job site walkarounds and correct noted safety violations.

DISCIPLINE/ENFORCEMENT

Two types or degrees of violation are:

A. Serious Violation - Violation of any company rule or regulation without premeditation. For a serious violation, *SAFETY OFFICER'S NAME* can use his/her judgment to determine the degree of discipline regarding the number of days off without pay or * *.

B. Willful Violation - Violation of any company rule or regulation with premeditation or forethought. For a willful violation, the discipline indicated below is the minimum that can be given. However, the degree of discipline may be extended or increased to termination of employment for willful violations. This decision is to be made by *PERSONS NAME*.

ENTER YOUR COMPANY'S DISCIPLINE POLICY HERE

CONTROL OF HAZARDS

Where feasible, workplace hazards are prevented by effective design of the job site or job. Where it is not feasible to eliminate such hazards, they must be controlled to prevent unsafe and unhealthy exposure. Once a potential hazard is recognized, the elimination or control must be done in a timely manner. These procedures should include measures such as the following:

- Using engineering techniques where feasible and appropriate.
- Maintaining the facility and all equipment to prevent equipment breakdowns.
- Using administrative controls, such as reducing the duration of exposure.
- Supervisors/Foreman shall maintain a periodic site inspection program.
- Establishing a medical program that includes first aid on site, as well as nearby physician and emergency medical card to reduce the risk of any injury or illness that occurs.
- Address any and all safety hazards to employees whenever one is observed.

SAFETY COMMITTEE

The Committee shall consist of representatives from management and employees with *SAFETY COORDINATOR NAME* as the chairman. The committee is a forum, created for the purpose of fostering safety and health through communication.

The responsibilities of Safety Committee Members include:

- Discuss safety policies and procedures with management and make recommendations for improvements.

- Serve as liaison between workers and management in safety matters.
- Provide technical reference materials.
- Review accident investigation reports on all accidents and "near miss".
- Identify unsafe conditions and practices and make recommendations for remedies.

TRAINING AND EDUCATION

Training is an essential component of an effective safety and health program. It addresses the responsibilities of both management and employees at the site. Training is often most effective when incorporated into other education on performance requirements and job practices.

Training programs should be provided as follows:

- Initially when the plan is developed
- For all new employees
- When new equipment, materials, or processes are introduced
- When procedures have been updated or revised
- When experiences/operations show that employee performance must be improved
- At least annually

Besides the standard training, employees should also be trained in the recognition of hazards. Be able to look at something or someone and know that there is a problem; a list may include:

- Falls from- Floors, Roofs and roof openings, Ladders (Straight and Step), Scaffolds, Wall openings, Tripping, Trenches, Steel Erection, Stairs, Chairs
- Electrical- Appliances, Damaged cords, Outlets, Overloads, Overhead High Voltage, Extension cords, Portable Tools(broken casing or damaged wiring), Grounding, Metal Box's, Switches, Ground fault circuit interrupters(GFCI)
- Housekeeping- Exits, Walkways, Floors, Trash, Storage of Materials (Hazardous and Non-Hazardous), Protruding Nails etc.
- Fire- Oily-Dirty Rags, Combustibles, Fuel Gas Cylinders, Exits (blocked)
- Trips/Slips- Stairs, Un-even flooring, Electrical cords, icy walkways
- Health- Silicosis, Asbestos, Loss of hearing, Eye injury due to flying objects

Employees trained in the recognition of hazards are less likely to be injured on the job. Overall production will increase, workers' compensation insurance will decrease and management/employee relations will be substantially improved.

EMPLOYER ENTER YOUR TRAINING POLICY AND PROCEDURES HERE

Training is not just for the worker, but for everyone.

RECORDKEEPING AND HAZARD ANALYSIS

If an injury or accident should ever occur, you are to report it to your supervisor/foreman as soon as possible.

A log and summary report shall be maintained for every recordable injury and illness. The entry should be done as soon as practicable, but no later than 6 working days after receiving information that a recordable injury or illness has occurred. The OSHA log No. 300 or equivalent shall be used for the recording.

A recordable injury or illness would be a fatality, loss work days, transfer to another job or termination of employment, an incident requiring medical treatment (other than first aid) or involve loss of consciousness or restriction of work or motion.

First Aid is any one-time treatment, and any follow-up visit for the purpose of observation, of minor scratches, cuts, burns, splinters, and so forth which do not ordinarily require medical care.

An annual summary of recordable injuries and illnesses shall be posted and contain the following information: Calendar year, company name-establishment name, establishment address, certification signature, title, and date. OSHA 300 should be evaluated by the employer to determine trends or patterns in injuries in order to address hazards to which employees are exposed to.

The summary covering the previous calendar year shall be posted no later than February 1, and remain in place until May 1. If no injury or illness occurred in the year zeros must be entered on the total line, and be posted. This form must be signed by an officer of the company.

ACCIDENT INVESTIGATION
Supervisors/Foreman
- Provide first aid, call for emergency medical care if required
- If further medical treatment is required, arrange to have an employee accompany the injured employee to the medical facility. Encourage return to work with the physician if possible.
- Secure area, equipment and personnel from injury and further damage.
- Investigate the incident (injury)--gather facts, employee and witness statements; take pictures and physical measurements of incident site and equipment involved. Complete an incident investigation report form within 24 hours whenever possible.
- If the injury warrants time away from work, insure that the absence is authorized by a physician and that you maintain contact with your employee while he/she remains off work.
- Insure that corrective action to prevent a recurrence is taken.
- Discuss incident, where appropriate, in safety and other employee meetings with the intent to prevent a recurrence. Discuss with other supervisors and other management.
- Monitor status of employee(s) off work, maintain contact with employee and encourage return to work even if restrictions are required by the physician.
- When injured employee(s) return to work they should not be allowed to return to work without "return to work" release forms from the physician. Review the release carefully and insure that the employee follows the restrictions indicated by the physician.

FIRST AID
COMPANY NAME has designated *PERSON OR PERSON'S NAME* as having adequate training to render first aid in the event of a medical emergency.

First aid kits are located at the following locations:
- Job Shack at entrance to construction site
- Each company owned truck behind the driver seat
- Every even numbered floor on multi-story buildings
- Every employee shall be trained in emergency procedures:
- Evacuation plan
- Alarm systems
- Shutdown procedures for equipment
- Types of potential emergencies

ENTER ANY SPECIAL PROCEDURES YOUR COMPANY HAS HERE
Employer should review their typical job site and address any and all of their hazards or potential hazards by adding to this section.

SAFETY RULES AND PROCEDURES
- No employee is expected to undertake a job until that person has received adequate training.
- All employees shall be trained on every potential hazard that they could be exposed to and how to protect themselves.
- No employee is required to work under conditions which are unsanitary, dangerous or hazardous to their health.
- Only qualified trained personnel are permitted to operate machinery or equipment.
- All injuries must be reported to your supervision/foreman. Manufacturer's specifications /limitations /instructions shall be followed.
- Particular attention should be given to new employees and to employees moving to new jobs or doing non-routine tasks. All OSHA posters shall be posted.
- Emergency numbers shall be posted and reviewed with employees
- Each employee in an excavation/trench shall be protected from cave-ins by an adequate protective system. (See your own detailed section on excavations).
- Employees working in areas where there is a possible danger of head injury, exces-

sive noise exposure, or potential eye and face injury shall be protected by Personal Protection Equipment (PPE).

- All hand and power tools and similar equipment, whether furnished by the employer or the employee, shall be maintained in a safe condition.
- All materials stored in tiers shall be stacked, racked, blocked, interlocked, or otherwise secured to prevent sliding, falling or collapse.
- The employer shall ensure that electrical equipment is free from recognized hazards that are likely to cause death or serious physical harm to employees.
- All scaffolding shall be erected in accordance with the CFR 1926.451 subpart L. Standard guardrails for fall protection and ladders for safe access shall be used. (See your own detailed section on scaffolding).
- All places of employment shall be kept clean, the floor of every workroom shall be maintained, so far as practicable, in a dry condition; standing water shall be removed. Where wet processes are used, drainage shall be maintained and false floors, platforms, mats or other dry standing places or appropriate waterproof footgear shall be provided.
- To facilitate cleaning, every floor, working place, and passageway shall be kept free from protruding nails, splinters, loose boards, and holes and openings.
- All floor openings, open sided floor and wall openings shall be guarded by a standard railings and toeboards or cover (see your own detailed section on fall hazards).
- The employer shall comply with the manufacturer's specifications and limitations applicable to the operation of any and all cranes and derricks.
- All equipment left unattended at night, adjacent to a highway in normal use, or adjacent to construction areas where work is in progress, shall have appropriate lights or reflectors, or barricades equipped with appropriate lights or reflectors, to identify the location of the equipment.
- No construction loads shall be placed on a concrete structure or portion of a concrete structure unless the employer determines, based on information received from a person who is qualified in structural design, that the structure or portion of the structure is capable of supporting the loads.
- A stairway or ladder shall be provided at all personnel points of access where there is a break in elevation of 19 inches or more, and no ramp, runway, sloped embankment, or personnel hoist is provided (see your own detailed section on ladders).

Emergency Response to Hazardous Substance

The employer shall determine beforehand whether they will be involved in a hazardous substance cleanup; if so, the employer shall develop and implement a written safety and health program for their employees involved in hazardous waste operations. The program shall be designed to identify, evaluate, and control safety and health hazards, and provide for emergency response for hazardous waste operations. The plan shall incorporate the following:

- An organizational structure
- A comprehensive work plan
- Site-specific safety and health plan
- Safety and health training program
- Employer's standard operating procedures for safety and health
- Any necessary interface between general program and site-specific activities.

INITIAL TRAINING

General site worker (such as equipment operators, general laborers and supervisory personnel) engaged in hazardous substance removal or other activities which expose or potentially expose workers to hazardous substances and health hazards shall receive a minimum of 40 hours of instruction off the site, and a minimum of three days actual field experience under the direct supervision of a trained, experienced supervisor.

COMPANY NAME WILL FOLLOW THE RULES AND REGULATIONS FROM THE 29 CFR 1910.120 PERTAINING TO HAZARDOUS WASTE OPERATIONS AND EMERGENCY RESPONSE.

Employer shall also read and follow the standard in 1910.1200

NOTE: Employers should incorporate current copies of such codes and regulations in to your safety and health program as resource material.

EMPLOYEE EMERGENCY ACTION PLAN

The emergency action plan will be in writing and will cover those designated actions employers and employees must take to ensure employee safety from fire and other emergencies. The following elements, at a minimum, shall be included in the plan:

(1) Emergency escape procedures and emergency escape route assignments.
(2) Procedures to be followed by employees who remain to operate critical plant operations before they evacuate.
(3) Procedures to account for all employees after emergency evacuation has been completed.
(4) Rescue and medical duties for those employees who are to perform them.
(5) Means of reporting fires and other emergencies.
(6) Names or regular job titles of persons or departments who can be contacted for further information or explanation of duties under the plan.

ALARMS SYSTEMS

COMPANY NAME will establish an employee alarm system which complies with 29 CFR 1926.159.

* If the employee alarm system is used for alerting fire brigade members, or for other purposes, a distinctive signal for each purpose will be used.

EVACUATION

* *COMPANY NAME* will establish in the emergency action plan the types of evacuation to be used in emergency circumstances.

TRAINING

Before implementing the emergency action plan, *COMPANY NAME* will designate and train a sufficient number of persons to assist in the safe and orderly emergency evacuation of employees.

COMPANY NAME will review the plan with each employee covered by the plan at the following times.

(1) Initially when the plan is developed.
(2) Whenever the employee's responsibilities or designated actions under the plan change.
(3) Whenever the plan is changed.

COMPANY NAME will review with each employee upon initial assignment those parts of the plan which the employee must know to protect the employee in the event of an emergency. The plan shall be kept at the workplace and made available for employee review. For those employers with 10 or fewer employees the plan may be communicated orally to employees and the employer need not maintain a written plan.

ENTER ANY SPECIAL PROCEDURES YOUR COMPANY HAS HERE

Checklist to Assess Your Safety Program

- ❑ Title, signature and phone number of Responsible Person
- ❑ Policy statement of company safety and health
- ❑ Administrative responsibilities for implementing the plan
- ❑ Identification and accountability of worksite personnel responsible for accident prevention
- ❑ Means for controlling work activities of subcontractors and suppliers
- ❑ Responsibilities of subcontractors and vendors
- ❑ Plans for safety indoctrination of new employees
- ❑ Plans for continued safety training
- ❑ Provisions for safety inspections
- ❑ Responsibilities for investigation and reporting accidents/exposure
- ❑ Responsibilities for maintaining accident data, reports and logs
- ❑ Emergency response plan for disasters
- ❑ Public safety requirements (e.g., fencing/signs)
- ❑ Plans for monthly safety meetings and weekly employee safety meetings.
- ❑ Meetings shall be documented, including the date, attendance, subjects, and the names of the individuals who conducted the meeting.
- ❑ Documents shall be available for inspection on the job site.

Appendices and Local Requirements as Needed for the Job

- ❑ First-aid procedures—local emergency phone numbers posted
- ❑ Personal protective equipment—warning signs posted
- ❑ Hazard communications—list of chemicals on the job site/container labels
- ❑ Confined space entry—identification, entry procedures, rescue procedures
- ❑ Hearing conservation
- ❑ Respirator program
- ❑ Hot work program (welding)
- ❑ Bloodborne pathogens
- ❑ Violence in the workplace
- ❑ Emergency action plan
- ❑ Hazardous waste operations
- ❑ Fire prevention/protection
- ❑ Electrical safety
- ❑ Machinery and mechanized equipment
- ❑ Hand and power tools
- ❑ Fall protection
- ❑ Working over water or liquids

Injured Workers May Sue Government

A construction worker injured on an Army installation after a contracting officer failed to enforce contractual safety standards may sue the government under the Federal Tort Claims Act (FTCA), a federal district court ruled June 4, 1999. In *Pelham v. U.S.* (No. 84-1395), the U.S. District Court for the District of New Jersey affirmed its earlier ruling that while a contracting officer's implementation of a safety inspection program is discretionary, once the officer suspects safety deficiency, he or she must act upon it.

The accident occurred when a forklift was used to lift a garbage dumpster in which Jerry Pelham was standing in order to attach cables to a 20-ft. roof-support suspension beam. When the forklift lurched, Pelham lost his balance and caught his hand between the forklift mast chain and pulley, amputating parts of three fingers and severely cutting a fourth.

Shortly before Pelham was injured, the contracting officer observed a worker in a metal container being hoisted by a forklift. The contracting officer testified that he "raised the issue" with the job superintendent, who told him that it was standard practice.

Under the terms of the contract, the contractor was required to take safety measures prescribed by the government's contracting officer. The contracting officer was required to notify the contractor of any non-compliance with safety provisions and had authority to issue a stop-work order if the contractor failed to comply promptly.

Discretionary Function Exception

Lawsuits against the United States for injuries caused by government employees in situations where a private person, would be liable are authorized by the FTCA. Under an exception to the act, the government is not liable for claims based on a discretionary function, whether or not the discretion involved is abused.

The court distinguished the Pelham case from two other Third Circuit decisions that applied the discretionary function exemption to the government's alleged failure to inspect a radioactive extraction facility and remove asbestos. Negligence in the development of safety provisions or a spot check program is not the kind of conduct at issue here the court stated, where the issue is "ministerial implementation of safety regulations" rather than "the discretionary authority to develop such provisions."

The contracting officer accepted the contractor's response rather than assume his ministerial responsibility under the contract to enforce compliance. The court found that under the contract "there is nothing discretionary about this responsibility." Once the contracting officer suspected a safety violation, his duty to check safety requirements was ministerial and not discretionary under the FTCA, the court ruled. Decisions made at the operational level, as distinguished from the planning level, are not protected by the exception, the court found.

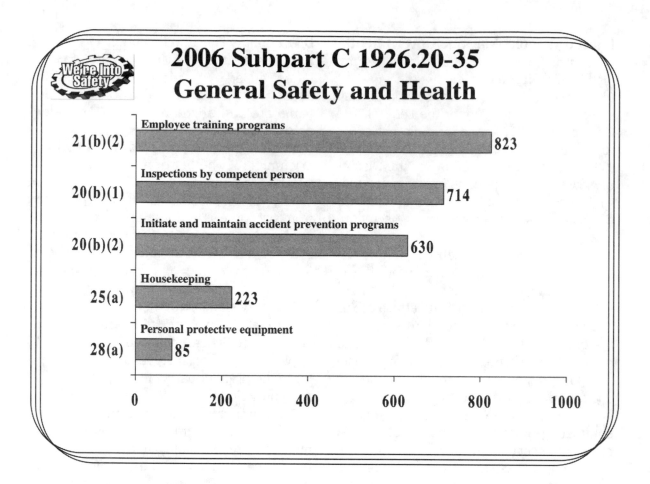

FOCUSED INSPECTIONS

The Focused Inspections Initiative that became effective October 1, 1994 is a significant departure from how OSHA has previously conducted construction inspections. This initiative recognizes the efforts of responsible contractors who have implemented effective safety and health programs/plans. It also encourages other contractors to adopt similar programs. The number of inspections is no longer driving the construction inspection program.

The Focused Inspections Initiative enables OSHA to focus on the leading hazards that cause 90 percent of the injuries and deaths:
- Falls (e.g., floors, platforms, roofs);
- Struck by (e.g., falling objects, vehicles);
- Caught in or between (e.g., cave-ins, unguarded machinery, equipment); and
- Electrical (e.g., overhead power lines, power tools and cords, outlets, temporary wiring).

Under the Focused Inspection Initiative, CSHOs shall determine whether or not there is project coordination by the general contractor, prime contractor, or other such entity and conduct a brief review of the project's safety and health program/plan to determine whether the project qualifies for a focused inspection.

To qualify for a focused inspection, the following conditions must be met:
- The project safety and health program/plan meets the requirements of 29 CFR 1926, Subpart C, General Safety and Health Provisions; and
- There is a designated competent person responsible for and capable of implementing the program/plan.

If the project meets the above criteria, an abbreviated walk-around inspection will be conducted focusing on:
- Verification of the safety and health program/plan's effectiveness through interviews and observation;
- The four leading hazards; and
- Other serious hazards observed by the CSHO.

The CSHO conducting a focused inspection is not required to inspect the entire project. Only a representative portion of the project need be inspected.

The CSHO will make the determination as to whether a project's safety and health program/plan is effective. If the conditions observed on the project indicate otherwise, the CSHO will immediately terminate the focused inspection and conduct a comprehensive inspection. The discovery of serious violations during a focused inspection need not automatically convert the focused inspection into a comprehensive inspection. These decisions will be based on the professional judgment of the CSHO.

The Focused Inspection Initiative should be publicized to the maximum extent possible so as to encourage contractors to establish effective safety and health programs/plans and concentrate on the four leading hazards before the inspection. Contractors that qualify for a focused inspection may be eligible to receive a full "good-faith" adjustment of 25 percent on any penalty issued.

Guidelines

- The Focused Inspections Initiative policy applies only to construction safety inspections. Construction health inspections will continue to be conducted in accordance with current agency procedures.
- A project determined not to be eligible for a focused inspection shall be given a comprehensive inspection with the necessary time and resources to identify and document violations.
- To ensure that all employers provide adequate protection for their employees, the general contractor, prime contractor or other such entity shall conduct a comprehensive inspection when there is no coordination.
- A request for a warrant will not affect the determination as to whether a project will receive a focused inspection.

- On job sites where unprogrammed inspections (for complaints, fatalities, etc.) are being conducted, the determination as to whether to conduct a focused inspection shall be made only after the complaint or fatality has first been addressed.
- All contractors and employee representatives shall, at some time during the inspection, be informed as to why a focused or a comprehensive inspection is being conducted. This may be accomplished either by personal contact or posting the "Handout for Contractors and Employees" (Field Inspection Reference Manual, Chapter 11, Section A.3).

A brief justification will be included in each case file as to why a focused inspection was or was not conducted. The optional "Construction Focused Inspection Guideline" may be used for this purpose.

Although the walk-around inspection shall focus on the four leading hazards, citations shall be issued for any serious violations found during a focused inspection and for any other-than-serious violations that are not immediately abated. Other-than-serious violations that are immediately abated shall not normally be cited or documented.

For focused inspections, an OSHA-1 will be completed in accordance with the multi-employer policy as stated in the Field Inspection Reference Manual for the:

- General contractor;
- Prime contractor;
- Other such entity; and
- Each employer that is issued a citation.

CONSTRUCTION FOCUSED INSPECTION GUIDELINE

This guideline is to assist the professional judgment of the compliance officer to determine if there is an effective project plan, to qualify for a Focused Inspection.

	YES/NO
PROJECT SAFETY AND HEALTH COORDINATION. Are there procedures in place by the general contractor, prime contractor, or other such entity to ensure that all employers provide adequate protection for their employees ?	
Is there a DESIGNATED COMPETENT PERSON responsible for the implementation and monitoring of the project safety and health plan who is capable of identifying existing and predictable hazards and has authority to take prompt corrective measures?	
PROJECT SAFETY AND HEALTH PROGRAM/PLAN* that complies with 1926 Subpart C and addresses, based upon the size and complexity of the project, the following:	

_____ Project Safety Analysis at initiation and at critical stages that describes the sequence, procedures, and responsible individuals for safe construction.

_____ Identification of work/activities requiring planning, design, inspection or supervision by an engineer, competent person or other professional.

_____ Evaluation/monitoring of subcontractors to determine conformance with the Project Plan. (The Project Plan may include, or be utilized by subcontractors.)

_____ Supervisor and employee training according to the Project Plan including recognition, reporting and avoidance of hazards, and applicable standards.

_____ Procedures for controlling hazardous operations such as: cranes, scaffolding, trenches, confined spaces, hot work, explosives, hazardous materials, leading edges, etc.

_____ Documentation of: training, permits, hazard reports, inspections, uncorrected hazards, incidents and near misses.

_____ Employee involvement in hazard: analysis, prevention, avoidance, correction and reporting.

_____ Project emergency response plan.

* For examples, see owner and contractor association model programs, ANSI A10.33, A10.38, etc.

The walkaround and interviews confirmed that the plan has been implemented, including:

_____ The four leading hazards are addressed: falls, struck by, caught in\between, electrical.

_____ Hazards are identified and corrected with preventative measures instituted in a timely manner.

_____ Employees and supervisors are knowledgeable of the project safety and health plan, avoidance of hazards, applicable standards, and their rights and responsibilities.

THE PROJECT QUALIFIED FOR A FOCUSED INSPECTION.

OSHA Instruction CPL 1-0.124
December 10, 1999
Multi-employer Citation Policy

Multi-Employer Worksites

On multi-employer worksites (in all industry sectors), more than one employer may be citable for a hazardous condition that violates an OSHA standard. A two-step process must be followed in determining whether more than one employer is to be cited.

Step One. The first step is to determine whether the employer is a creating, exposing, correcting, or controlling employer. The definitions in paragraphs (B) – (E) below explain and give examples of each. Remember that an employer may have multiple roles (see paragraph H). Once you determine the role of the employer, go to Step Two to determine if a citation is appropriate (NOTE: only exposing employers can be cited for General Duty Clause violations).

Step Two. If the employer falls into one of these categories, it has obligations with respect to OSHA requirements. Step Two is to determine if the employer's actions were sufficient to meet those obligations. The extent of the actions required of employers varies based on which category applies. Note that the extent of the measures that a controlling employer must take to satisfy its duty to exercise reasonable care to prevent and detect violations is less than what is required of an employer with respect to protecting its own employees.

The Creating Employer
Step 1: Definition: The employer that caused a hazardous condition that violates an OSHA standard.

Step 2: Actions Taken: Employers must not create violative conditions. An employer that does so is citable even if the only employees exposed are those of other employers at the site.

Example 1: Employer Host operates a factory. It contracts with Company S to service machinery. Host fails to cover drums of a chemical despite S's repeated requests that it do so. This results in airborne levels of the chemical that exceed the Permissible Exposure Limit.

Analysis: Step 1: Host is a creating employer because it caused employees of S to be exposed to the air contaminant above the PEL. **Step 2:** Host failed to implement measures to prevent the accumulation of the air contaminant. It could have met its OSHA obligation by implementing the simple engineering control of covering the drums. Having failed to implement a feasible engineering control to meet the PEL, Host is citable for the hazard.

Example 2: Employer M hoists materials onto Floor 8, damaging perimeter guardrails. Neither its own employees nor employees of other employers are exposed to the hazard. It takes effective steps to keep all employees, including those of other employers, away from the unprotected edge and informs the controlling employer of the problem. Employer M lacks authority to fix the guardrails itself.

Analysis: Step 1: Employer M is a creating employer because it caused a hazardous condition by damaging the guardrails. **Step 2:** While it lacked the authority to fix the guardrails, it took immediate and effective steps to keep all employees away from the hazard and notified the controlling employer of the hazard. Employer M is not citable since it took effective measures to prevent employee exposure to the fall hazard.

The Exposing Employer
Step 1: Definition: An employer whose own employees are exposed to the hazard.

Step 2: Actions Taken: If the exposing employer created the violation, it is citable for the violation as a creating employer. If another employer created the violation, the exposing employer is citable if it (1) knew of the hazardous condition or failed to exercise reasonable diligence to discover the condition, and (2) failed to take steps consistent with its authority to protect is employees. If the exposing employer has authority to correct the hazard, it must do so. If the exposing employer lacks the authority to correct the hazard, it is citable if it fails to do each of the following: (1) ask the creating and/or controlling employer to correct the hazard; (2) inform its employees of the hazard; and (3) take reasonable alternative protective measures.

In extreme circumstances (e.g., imminent danger situations), the exposing employer is citable for failing to remove its employees from the job to avoid the hazard.

Example 3: Employer Sub S is responsible for inspecting and cleaning a work area in Plant P around a large, permanent hole at the end of each day. An OSHA standard requires guardrails. There are no guardrails around the hole and Sub S employees do not use personal fall protection, although it would be feasible to do so. Sub S has no authority to install guardrails. However, it did ask Employer P, which operates the plant, to install them. P refused to install guardrails.

Analysis: Step 1: Sub S is an exposing employer because its employees are exposed to the fall hazard. **Step 2:** While Sub S has no authority to install guardrails, it is required to comply with OSHA requirements to the extent feasible. It must take steps to protect its employees and ask the employer that controls the hazard — Employer P — to correct it. Although Sub S asked for guardrails, since the hazard was not corrected, Sub S was responsible for taking reasonable alternative protective steps, such as providing personal fall protection. Because that was not done, Sub S is citable for the violation.

Example 4: Unprotected rebar on either side of an access ramp presents an impalement hazard. Sub E, an electrical subcontractor, does not have the authority to cover the rebar. However, several times Sub E asked the general contractor, Employer GC, to cover the rebar. In the meantime, Sub E instructed its employees to use a different access route that avoided most of the uncovered rebar and required them to keep as far from the rebar as possible.

Analysis: Step 1: Since Sub E employees were still exposed to some unprotected rebar, Sub E is an exposing employer. **Step 2:** Sub E made a good faith effort to get the general contractor to correct the hazard and took feasible measures within its control to protect its employees. Sub E is not citable for the rebar hazard.

The Correcting Employer

Step 1: Definition: An employer who is engaged in a common undertaking, on the same worksite, as the exposing employer and is responsible for correcting a hazard. This usually occurs where an employer is given the responsibility of installing and/or maintaining particular safety/health equipment or devices.

Step 2: Actions Taken: The correcting employer must exercise reasonable care in preventing and discovering violations and meet its obligations of correcting the hazard.

Example 5: Employer C, a carpentry contractor, is hired to erect and maintain guardrails throughout a large, 15-story project. Work is proceeding on all floors. C inspects all floors in the morning and again in the afternoon each day. It also inspects areas where material is delivered to the perimeter once the material vendor is finished delivering material to that area. Other subcontractors are required to report damaged/missing guardrails to the general contractor, who forwards those reports to C. C repairs damaged guardrails immediately after finding them and immediately after they are reported. On this project few instances of damaged guardrails have occurred other than where material has been delivered. Shortly after the afternoon inspection of Floor 6, workers moving equipment accidentally damage a guardrail in one area. No one tells C of the damage and C has not seen it. An OSHA inspection occurs at the beginning of the next day, prior to the morning inspection of Floor 6. None of C's own employees are exposed to the hazard, but other employees are exposed.

Analysis: Step 1: C is a correcting employer since it is responsible for erecting and maintaining fall protection equipment. **Step 2:** The steps C implemented to discover and correct

damaged guardrails were reasonable in light of the amount of activity and size of the project. It exercised reasonable care in preventing and discovering violations; it is not citable for the damaged guardrail since it could not reasonably have known of the violation.

The Controlling Employer

Step 1: Definition: An employer who has general supervisory authority over the worksite, including the power to correct safety and health violations itself or require others to correct them. Control can be established by contract or, in the absence of explicit contractual provisions, by the exercise of control in practice. Descriptions and examples of different kinds of controlling employers are given below.

Step 2: Actions Taken: A controlling employer must exercise reasonable care to prevent and detect violations on the site. The extent of the measures that a controlling employer must implement to satisfy this duty of reasonable care is less than what is required of an employer with respect to protecting its own employees. This means that the controlling employer is not normally required to inspect for hazards as frequently or to have the same level of knowledge of the applicable standards or of trade expertise as the employer it has hired.

Factors Relating to Reasonable Care Standard. Factors that affect how frequently and closely a controlling employer must inspect to meet its standard of reasonable care include:

- The scale of the project;
- The nature and pace of the work, including the frequency with which the number or types of hazards change as the work progresses;
- How much the controlling employer knows both about the safety history and safety practices of the employer it controls and about that employer's level of expertise.
- More frequent inspections are normally needed if the controlling employer knows that the other employer has a history of non-compliance. Greater inspection frequency may also be needed, especially at the beginning of the project, if the controlling employer had never before worked with this other employer and does not know its compliance history.

- Less frequent inspections may be appropriate where the controlling employer sees strong indications that the other employer has implemented effective safety and health efforts. The most important indicator of an effective safety and health effort by the other employer is a consistently high level of compliance. Other indicators include the use of an effective, graduated system of enforcement for non-compliance with safety and health requirements coupled with regular jobsite safety meetings and safety training.

Evaluating Reasonable Care. In evaluating whether a controlling employer has exercised reasonable care in preventing and discovering violations, consider questions such as whether the controlling employer:

- Conducted periodic inspections of appropriate frequency;
- Implemented an effective system for promptly correcting hazards;
- Enforces the other employer's compliance with safety and health requirements with an effective, graduated system of enforcement and follow-up inspections.

Types of Controlling Employers

Control Established by Contract. In this case, the Employer Has a Specific Contract Right to Control Safety: To be a controlling employer, the employer must itself be able to prevent or correct a violation or to require another employer to prevent or correct the violation. One source of this ability is explicit contract authority. This can take the form of a specific contract right to require another employer to adhere to safety and health requirements and to correct violations the controlling employer discovers.

Example 6: Employer GH contracts with Employer S to do sandblasting at GH's plant. Some of the work is regularly scheduled maintenance and so is general industry work; other parts of the project involve new work and are considered construction. Respiratory protection is required. Further, the contract explicitly requires S to comply with safety and health requirements. Under the contract GH has the right to take various actions against S for failing to meet contract requirements,

including the right to have non-compliance corrected by using other workers and back-charging for that work. S is one of two employers under contract with GH at the work site, where a total of five employees work. All work is done within an existing building. The number and types of hazards involved in S's work do not significantly change as the work progresses. Further, GH has worked with S over the course of several years. S provides periodic and other safety and health training and uses a graduated system of enforcement of safety and health rules. S has consistently had a high level of compliance at its previous jobs and at this site. GH monitors S by a combination of weekly inspections, telephone discussions and a weekly review of S's own inspection reports. GH has a system of graduated enforcement that it has applied to S for the few safety and health violations that had been committed by S in the past few years. Further, due to respirator equipment problems S violates respiratory protection requirements two days before GH's next scheduled inspection of S. The next day there is an OSHA inspection. There is no notation of the equipment problems in S's inspection reports to GH and S made no mention of it in its telephone discussions.

Analysis: Step 1: GH is a controlling employer because it has general supervisory authority over the worksite, including contractual authority to correct safety and health violations. **Step 2:** GH has taken reasonable steps to try to make sure that S meets safety and health requirements. Its inspection frequency is appropriate in light of the low number of workers at the site, lack of significant changes in the nature of the work and types of hazards involved, GH's knowledge of S's history of compliance and its effective safety and health efforts on this job. GH has exercised reasonable care and is not citable for this condition.

Example 7: Employer GC contracts with Employer P to do painting work. GC has the same contract authority over P as Employer GH had in Example 6. GC has never before worked with P. GC conducts inspections that are sufficiently frequent in light of the factors listed above in (G)(3). Further, during a number of its inspections, GC finds that P has violated fall protection requirements. It points the violations out to P during each inspection but takes no further actions.

Analysis: Step 1: GC is a controlling employer since it has general supervisory authority over the site, including a contractual right of control over P. **Step 2:** GC took adequate steps to meet its obligation to discover violations. However, it failed to take reasonable steps to require P to correct hazards since it lacked a graduated system of enforcement. A citation to GC for the fall protection violations is appropriate.

Example 8: Employer GC contracts with Sub E, an electrical subcontractor. GC has full contract authority over Sub E, as in Example 6. Sub E installs an electric panel box exposed to the weather and implements an assured equipment grounding conductor program, as required under the contract. It fails to connect a grounding wire inside the box to one of the outlets. This incomplete ground is not apparent from a visual inspection. Further, GC inspects the site with a frequency appropriate for the site in light of the factors discussed above in (G)(3). It saw the panel box but did not test the outlets to determine if they were all grounded because Sub E represents that it is doing all of the required tests on all receptacles. GC knows that Sub E has implemented an effective safety and health program. From previous experience it also knows Sub E is familiar with the applicable safety requirements and is technically competent. GC had asked Sub E if the electrical equipment is OK for use and was assured that it is.

Analysis: Step 1: GC is a controlling employer since it has general supervisory authority over the site, including a contractual right of control over Sub E. **Step 2:** GC exercised reasonable care. It had determined that Sub E had technical expertise, safety knowledge and had implemented safe work practices. It conducted inspections with appropriate frequency. It also made some basic inquiries into the safety of the electrical equipment. Under these circumstances GC was not obligated to test the outlets itself to determine if they were all grounded. It is not citable for the grounding violation.

Control Established by a Combination of Other Contract Rights: Where there is no explicit contract provision granting the right to control safety, or where the contract says the employer does *not* have such a right, an employer may still be a controlling employer. The ability of an employer to control safety in this circumstance can result from a combination of contractual rights that, together, give it broad responsibility at the site involving almost all aspects of the job. Its responsibility is broad enough so that its contractual authority necessarily involves safety. The authority to resolve disputes between subcontractors, set schedules and determine construction sequencing is particularly significant because they are likely to affect safety. (NOTE: citations should only be issued in this type of case after consulting with the Regional Solicitor's office).

Example 9: Construction manager M is contractually obligated to: set schedules and construction sequencing, require subcontractors to meet contract specifications, negotiate with trades, resolve disputes between subcontractors, direct work and make purchasing decisions, which affect safety. However, the contract states that M does not have a right to require compliance with safety and health requirements. Further, Subcontractor S asks M to alter the schedule so that S would not have to start work until Subcontractor G has completed installing guardrails. M is contractually responsible for deciding whether to approve S's request.

Analysis: Step 1: Even though its contract states that M does not have authority over safety, the combination of rights actually given in the contract provides broad responsibility over the site and results in the ability of M to direct actions that necessarily affect safety. For example, M's contractual obligation to determine whether to approve S's request to alter the schedule has direct safety implications. M's decision relates directly to whether S's employees will be protected from a fall hazard. M is a controlling employer. **Step 2:** In this example, if M refused to alter the schedule, it would be citable for the fall hazard violation.

Example 10: Employer ML's contractual authority is limited to reporting on subcontractors' contract compliance to owner/developer O and making contract payments. Although it reports on the extent to which the subcontractors are complying with safety and health infractions to O, ML does not exercise any control over safety at the site.

Analysis: Step 1: ML is not a controlling employer because these contractual rights are insufficient to confer control over the subcontractors and ML did not exercise control over safety. Reporting safety and health infractions to another entity does not, by itself (or in combination with these very limited contract rights), constitute an exercise of control over safety. **Step 2:** Since it is not a controlling employer it had no duty under the OSH Act to exercise reasonable care with respect to enforcing the subcontractors' compliance with safety; there is therefore no need to go to Step 2.

Architects and Engineers: Architects, engineers, and other entities are controlling employers only if the breadth of their involvement in a construction project is sufficient to bring them within the parameters discussed above.

Example 11: Architect A contracts with owner O to prepare contract drawings and specifications, inspect the work, report to O on contract compliance, and to certify completion of work. A has no authority or means to enforce compliance, no authority to approve/reject work and does not exercise any other authority at the site, although it does call the general contractor's attention to observed hazards noted during its inspections.

Analysis: Step 1: A's responsibilities are very limited in light of the numerous other administrative responsibilities necessary to complete the project. It is little more than a supplier of architectural services and conduit of information to O. Its responsibilities are insufficient to confer control over the subcontractors and it did not exercise control over safety. The responsibilities it does have are insufficient to make it a controlling employer. Merely pointing out safety violations did not make it a controlling employer. NOTE: In a circumstance such as this it is likely that broad control over the project rests with another entity. **Step 2:** Since A is not a controlling employer it had no duty

under the OSH Act to exercise reasonable care with respect to enforcing the subcontractors' compliance with safety; there is therefore no need to go to Step 2.

Example 12: Engineering firm E has the same contract authority and functions as in Example 9.

Analysis: Step 1: Under the facts in Example 9, E would be considered a controlling employer. **Step 2:** The same type of analysis described in Example 9 for Step 2 would apply here to determine if E should be cited.

Control Without Explicit Contractual Authority. Even where an employer has no explicit contract rights with respect to safety, an employer can still be a controlling employer if, in actual practice, it exercises broad control over subcontractors at the site (see Example 9). NOTE: Citations should only be issued in this type of case after consulting with the Regional Solicitor's office.

Example 13: Construction manager MM does not have explicit contractual authority to require subcontractors to comply with safety requirements, nor does it explicitly have broad contractual authority at the site. However, it exercises control over most aspects of the subcontractors' work anyway, including aspects that relate to safety.

Analysis: Step 1: MM would be considered a controlling employer since it exercises control over most aspects of the subcontractor's work, including safety aspects. **Step 2:** The same type of analysis on reasonable care described in the examples in (G)(5)(a) would apply to determine if a citation should be issued to this type of controlling employer.

Multiple Roles

A creating, correcting or controlling employer will often also be an exposing employer. Consider whether the employer is an exposing employer before evaluating its status with respect to these other roles.

Exposing, creating and controlling employers can also be correcting employers if they are authorized to correct the hazard.

Liability of Controlling/General Contractor/Construction Managers and Owners on Multi-Employer Work Sites

The commission has established a presumption that an employer with supervisory authority over other employers can be held liable for safety violations of those employers that it could reasonably prevent or abate by reason of its authority. This liability exists even though the supervisory employer's employees are not exposed and that it did not create the hazard itself. The commission announced this policy with regard to general contractors (GCs) but has applied it to construction managers and owners as well based upon their supervisory authority.

In order to hold a General Contractor or other supervisory employer liable for a subcontractor's violations, we therefore must demonstrate that the General Contractor had the authority to ensure compliance with the safety standards. The best evidence of this would be a specific provision in a contract between the General Contractor and the subcontractor. A contract between the owner and the General Contractor giving it the authority and responsibility to ensure compliance would be excellent evidence. If there were no contract provision that specifies the General Contractor's authority, then we would need some proof of that authority from actual practice. Proof of prior instances in which the General Contractor obtained compliance from a subcontractor would be helpful. If a General Contractor had the practice of reviewing work, inspecting the site or resolving the complaints by contractors against other contractors, it would also tend to prove supervisory authority.

The commission has held that a mere title is not alone proof of supervisory authority. Therefore we must prove that the General Contractor has the actual power to compel and not merely to report violations or recommend compliance with the safety standards. Moreover, a purported General Contractor can rebut the presumption that it possessed sufficient authority over another contractor.

Obviously the best case to present to a judge is one in which a specific contract provision gives the obligation and the authority to a General Contractor to assure compliance with the safety standards. The minimum would be convincing evidence that the General Contractor actually exercised this authority over subcontractors.

What is the most difficult factor to predict is what an Administrative Law Judge will find to be a violation that a General Contractor could reasonably prevent or abate. It seems clear that a General Contractor's responsibility would not be as extensive as the subcontractor's because of the subcontractor's expertise in its own area. The minimum responsibility of a General Contractor would probably be responding to subcontractor complaints regarding other subcontractors' violations, conducting visual inspections and having familiarity with all of the applicable safety standards. Each case will have to be evaluated to determine the extent of supervisory authority, the obviousness of the violation and the reasonableness of the General Contractor's conduct or response to the violation.

Occupational Safety and Health Review Commission — 1975

Commission-Grossman Steel and Aluminum Corporation

The commission reevaluated its policy regarding GCs at multi-employer work sites. The Commission reviewed the Second Circuit's opinion In Brennan v. OSAHRC and Underhill Constr. Corp., (2nd Cir. 1975) and the Seventh Circuit's opinion in the case of Anning-Johnson Company v. OSAHRC, 516 F2d 1081 (7th Cir. 1975). The facts in Grossman involved a subcontractor whose employees were exposed to open sides of a building under construction. The GC in this case was actually responsible for the erection of guardrails where needed. Presumably this was a contractual matter although the opinion does not clarify this issue. The Commission reasoned in dicta that a GC on a multi-employer worksite normally has the responsibility to ensure that other contractors fulfill their obligations with respect to employee safety and those that affect the entire site. The Commission stated:

The general contractor is well situated to obtain abatement of hazards, either through its own resources or through its supervisory role with respect to other contractors. It is therefore reasonable to expect the General Contractor to assure compliance with the standards insofar as all employees on site are affected, thus we will hold the general contractor responsible for violations it could reasonably been expected to prevent or abate by reason of its supervisory capacity.

In the case of Anning-Johnson Co., 4 OSHC 1193 (OSHRC 1976), the Commission also noted in dicta that a typical GC in a multi-employer project possesses sufficient control over the entire worksite to give rise to a duty under Section 5 (a)(2) of the Act either to comply fully with the standard or to take the necessary steps to assure compliance.

The Commission has reaffirmed its general rule regarding GC liability in a number of subsequent cases. In Gil Haugan d/b/a Haugan Constr. Co., 7 OSHC 2004 (OSHRC 1979) the Commission dealt with the GC's liability for violations by the scaffolding subcontractor at a multi-employer worksite. There were no guardrails on or access ladder to the scaffold at the time of the inspection. The GC stated that it did not control the subcontractor's employees but that it exercised a limited right to direct those employees. The contract was not introduced into evidence. The Commission however concluded that the GC was responsible for safety on the site and compliance with OSHA regulations because, as the GC, it retained sufficient control over the site. The violations were found to be readily apparent to a casual inspection and that a GC should have known of them and taken steps to correct them (or, through the exercise of reasonable diligence, could have or should have known of their existence).

The Commission reiterated its policy that on multi-employer construction sites, the GC could reasonably be expected to prevent or detect and abate by reason of its supervisory authority over the entire work site. The Commission stated that this policy is predicated on the presumption that, by virtue of its supervisory capacity, the GC has sufficient control over the

subcontractors to require them to comply with OSHA standards and to abate violations. The Commission did however note that the GC can rebut this presumption and that the burden of proof on this issue is on the GC.

The decision in the case of National Industrial Constructors, Inc., 10 OSHC 1081 (OSHRC 1981) held the GC liable for a violation that a subcontractor created. The violation involved a fall hazard because of a ladder that was placed too close to a wall. The Commission did not elaborate on where the GC derived its authority (contract or practice) but was satisfied on the basis of the GC's status as such. Similarly unilluminating opinions by the Commission can be found in Sierra Constr. Corp., 6 OSHC 1278 (OSHRC 1978) and Gelco Builders, Inc., 6 OSHC 1104 (OSHRC 1977).

An administrative law judge in Rogers Constr., Inc., 10 OSHC 2186 (1982), dealt with the failure of a subcontractor's employees to give proper hand signals to a crane operator. The ALJ stated that the GC had an obligation to ensure that all persons giving hand signals were trained in proper procedures, either by posting instructions or by requiring a demonstration of proficiency. Thus, the ALJ went beyond requiring a casual inspection of conditions on the work site to requiring the GC to become more involved with the subcontractor's employees.

The Eighth Circuit in Marshall v. Knutson Constr. Co. & OSAHRC, 6 OSHC 1077 (8th Cir. 1977) reviewed the Commission's multi-employer worksite doctrine. The case involved a GC who was cited for failure to equip the scaffold with guardrails and toe boards. Four employees of a subcontractor were injured in the collapse of the scaffolding. The GC employed a safety administrator who inspected the scaffolding in question on two different occasions at a distance of 20 feet. The Commission held that the GC violated its duty with respect to guardrails and toe boards because under the circumstances it could reasonably have known the scaffold lacked both items. However, the Commission concluded that the general contractor had not violated its duty with regard to the lack of adequate support for the scaffolding because the GC could not reasonably have known that the scaffold was incapable of meeting the minimal weight requirement. The OSHA inspector found a 1-inch preexisting crack in the underside of the scaffolding after the collapse. The Eighth Circuit upheld both findings of the Commission and also the reasonableness of the multi-employer worksite doctrine as a whole.

The Court interpreted the Commission's policy (that GCs under 654 (a)(2) are responsible where they could reasonably have been expected to prevent or abate by reason of their supervisory capacity) to require the consideration of three factors: (1) degree of supervisory authority, (2) nature of the safety standard violated, and (3) nature and extent of precautionary measures taken by the GC. The GC's duty depends on what measures are commensurate with its degree of supervisory control.

An ALJ in Bethlehem Steel Corp., 9 OSHC 2025 (1981), found the owner of a worksite liable for safety violations of other employers' truck drivers. The owner was in complete control of the worksite and could easily have provided head or foot protection to the drivers or could have kept them from the hazardous area. Therefore, the owner's supervisory authority was sufficient and the hazard easily could have been abated.

Red Lobster Inns of America, Inc., 8 OSHC 1762 (OSHRC 1980) dealt with a construction site in which the owner of the site contracted directly with the subcontractors. A job site superintendent was responsible for coordinating the subcontractors and for ensuring the work was performed to specifications.

The superintendent was an employee of the owner. The citation at issue involved a nonconforming electric generator. Because of the superintendent's authority over the subcontractor responsible for the violation, the owner was liable for the violation. The Commission focused on the superintendent's authority to review and approve work, to settle disputes between contractors and the fact that he was the sole party in charge.

An engineering firm was held to be responsible for the violations by other contractors. An ALJ in the case of Kaiser Engineers. Inc., 1978 OSHC 22,599 (1978) determined that the use of a safety supervisor by the engineering firm did not render it liable even though the

supervisor monitored the worksite for violations. The supervisor could only report to the management group of contractors and did not have the authority to order abatement.

In Cauldwel-Winaate Com., 6 OSHC 1619 (OSHRC 1978) the Commission found that the difference in the title of the respondent construction manager, rather than GC, was not important. Even though there were several prime contractors including a GC, the respondent had the authority to coordinate the contractors, to review work performed and to effect abatement of hazards. The architect/construction manager in Bertrand Goldbera Assocs., 4 OSHC 1587 (OSHRC 1976) was also found to possess authority similar to a general contractor and therefore liable for other contractors' violations.

Review Commission Final Orders

Classic Homes, Div. of Elite Inc. v. Secretary of Labor (1/17/95). Serious citation item alleging violation of 1926.451(u)(3), which requires catch platforms to be installed below working area of roofs more than 16 feet above ground is affirmed with $1,000 penalty assessed; employer was engaged in construction of home, and subcontractor was performing roofing work.

Parties agreed that employees of subcontractor were not protected from falling when working on roof 17 feet high, and that catch platforms were not installed. The project manager for the employer testified that he was responsible for about 20 homes, that he inspected various job sites assigned to him, and that he had authority to correct hazards and ensure abatement of violations. If there were two or more safety violations, subcontractors were subject to termination.

Employer disclaimed responsibility for safety infractions on grounds that the subcontractor's workers were not employees of employer, that the subcontractor was the controlling employer and the subcontractor created the violations.

However, the Occupational Safety and Health Review Commission has rejected the notion that liability under the Occupational Safety and Health Act should be solely based on employment relationship. General contractors normally have the responsibility and means to ensure that other contractors fulfill their obligations with respect to employee safety.

General Contractors' Duty

The Commission holds general contractors responsible for violations they could have reasonably been expected to prevent or abate. This duty is not limited to the protection of their own employees, but extends to the protection of all employees at the work site.

Accordingly, violation is affirmed; Secretary of Labor proposed penalty of $2,500,

however, based on fact that employer had program of checking subcontractors for adherence to safety regulations, that employer had safety superintendents to check on work habits of subcontractors, and that none of its employees were exposed to dangers involved, penalty is assessed at $1,000. Serious citation item alleged violation of 1926.500(c)(1), which requires guarding wall openings from which there is drop of more than 4 feet, and where bottom of openings is less than 3 feet above the working surface, is affirmed, with $600 penalty assessed. Parties agreed employee of subcontractor was exposed to unguarded wall openings from which there was drop of more than 4 feet, and bottom of opening was less than 3 feet above the working surfaces.

Noble Steel Inc. v. Secretary of Labor (1/ 17/95). Employer's argument that videotape of work site taken by Occupational Safety and Health Administration Compliance officer should not be admitted into evidence because employer did not give permission is rejected; employer quoted extensively from OSHA's Field Operations Manual and argued that compliance officer failed to follow FOM in conducting opening conference; however, Occupational Safety and Health Review Commission precedent has established that FOM is internal manual that provides OSHA officials with guidance and does not have force or effect of law; therefore, compliance officer's conformance with FOM has no bearing on admissibility of videotape.

Evidence established that employer's representative gave permission to compliance officer to videotape; testimony of compliance

officer and employee conflicted as to events that occurred; however, employee wavered in his testimony and videotape supported compliance officer's version of events; even if employee had not given permission, evidence showed that general contractor did give its permission to compliance officer to inspect facility; while employer would still with regard to enclosed spaces at work site, such as trailer or tool shed, evidence established that chlorine basin in which employer was working was open area; fact that basin was below ground level did not make it enclosed space used for preserving privacy.

Serious citation item alleging violation of 1926.701 (b) for failure to guard protruding reinforcing steel, is affirmed, with $1,125 penalty assessed; Secretary of Labor established that there were exposed pieces of 7/8-inch rebar on floor of basin, that employees entered and exited basin by climbing rebar on one of basin's walls, and that violative condition was in plain view.

Creation of Hazard

Employer's defense that it should not be held liable because it did not create hazard is rejected; even if employer's workers did not create hazard, their exposure to violative condition required employer to take appropriate action to protect its employees; evidence showed that general contractor provided strips of plywood to cover rebar, but that plywood was too small to cover entire area and was constantly knocked off by employees who passed by; employer stated that its contract with general contractor required general contractor to provide mushroom caps; however, general contractor's failure to provide caps does not excuse employer's action; asking twice for caps from general contractor and then taking no further action is insufficient; employer should have purchased caps itself.

Employer's impossibility defense is also rejected; employer's defense rested solely on use of plywood strip to guard rebar; employer did not use alternative protective measures and failed to provide there was no feasible alternative measure; employer conceded that mushroom caps would have abated violation.

Serious citation item alleging violation of

1926.1051(a), for failure to provide stairway or ladder at point of elevation where there was a break in elevation of 19 inches or more, is affirmed, with $1,125 penalty assessed; employees entered and exited basin by climbing rebar held in place with wire ties; compliance officer explained that rebar was not attached to wire ties, meaning they could roll around on wire ties, creating unsteady footing; compliance officer stated that ladder could have been used and that there was ladder at work site.

Employer's defenses of infeasibility and impossibility are rejected; employer argued that if it had used ladder, it could not have placed it at angle in compliance with OSHA ladder standards; however, except for testimony of its witness, the employer did not present any evidence to support its allegation the ladder could not have been used properly; employer's greater hazard defense is also rejected; employer did not seek variance from cited standard; although employer argued that it would have been inappropriate to apply for a variance because the use of a rebar wall as a ladder is common in industry, the employer failed to explain why this should make application inappropriate.

Penalties assessed are based on compliance officer's number of employees and severe gravity of both violations; no evidence was provided regarding employer's prior history with OSHA or its good faith (No. 93-3066).

Secretary of Labor v. Shelly & Sands, Inc.

Inadequate Safety Program— Site-Specific Program Not Needed

It is the Secretary of Labor's position that the employer should have had a site-specific accident program to comply with 29 CFR 1926.20(b)(1) is rejected. Given that the hazards faced by workers paving country road were similar to hazards faced by workers at employer's other work sites and that deceased employee had experience and had received training regarding hazard that resulted in her death. Accordingly, serious citation is vacated.

Digest of Judge's Report

A compliance officer with the Occupational Safety and Health Administration following the October 1991 fatality of an employee inspected Shelly & Sands, Inc.

Shelly was cited for an alleged serious violation of 29 CFR 1926.20(b)(1), for failure to initiate and maintain an accident prevention program as necessary to comply with Part 1926. The facts of the accident are undisputed (direct cause). Shelly was repaving a country road near Senecaville, Ohio.

While operating a finish roller, the deceased, contrary to accepted safe practices, drove her roller into a deep area of asphalt that had not yet sufficiently cooled even though the area had been identified as a deep area by other crew members. As the roller skidded over the edge of the berm, the deceased either jumped or was thrown into the adjacent ditch. She died of injuries received due to the roller landing on her.

The compliance officer testified that he issued the citation based upon the belief that Shelly should have had a site-specific safety program, where it would address the hazards that they (workers) would encounter at that particular job site. The compliance officer testified that there should have been an inspection of the area before the employees were allowed to conduct the work that they were to do to make a determination as to what hazards existed at that specific job site.

The specific hazards, according to the compliance officer, were the fact that the edge of the road or the berm was adjacent to a ditch, and there were possibilities of the equipment going over the edge of the ditch causing an accident, which it did.

Several witnesses established that the deceased, a full-time employee of Shelly since 1989, completed her union apprenticeship over a period of four years ending in 1985. Her apprenticeship included safety training that encompassed roller operations.

When she was first assigned to one of Shelly's crews, she received finish roller operating training under an operator with 25 years of experience, and she was specifically trained in the conditions of working alongside berms. She was familiar with the procedures to be used when rolling such deep spots, having encountered them numerous times previously. There is some indication in the record that at times she operated the roller in a standing position that other operators felt was less safe than operating in a seated position.

The Secretary argued that Shelly violated the standard because "[r]ules were not developed or enforced for the safe operation of the tandem rollers." Noting that the deceased failed to wait for the first run of asphalt to cool completely before starting her, the secretary noted that "[n]o specific rules were established on this procedure."

Shelly responded that its only obligation under the cited standard is to demonstrate how it will comply with Part 1926 and reasoned that since Part 1926 does not deal with roller operations and no violation of any other specific standard in Part 1926 had been alleged or even suggested, it cannot be found in violation of 29 CFR 1926 20(b)(1).

Shelly further argued that its safety program is not inadequate and claimed that an adequate program need not cover every potential hazard in writing. The employer accurately pointed out that the compliance officer was mistaken in his belief as to the extent to the deceased's training and job experience. Shelly also noted that included in its regular safety activities are weekly tool box meetings, annual safety meetings for foremen, and the presentation of safety awards to employees and foremen.

The evidence shows that the hazards encountered at the work site were virtually the same as on numerous other country roads that Shelly crews and the deceased had previously worked. There is unrefuted evidence that the deceased had received training in these particular hazards. It is reasonable for an employer to rely on the training an employee received as part of an extensive apprenticeship program and under the supervision of highly experienced personnel.

The Secretary's perceived inadequacies in Shelly's program do not withstand scrutiny. The use of written materials prepared by someone other than the particular employer, in this case the safety committee of the Ohio Contractors Association, does not, by itself, mean that the materials are inadequate. Given the fact that the hazards encountered were not unique to the particular work site, that the foreman had reviewed the site to check for possible hazards prior to the work commencing and the deceased had received training, Shelly did not violate the cited standard.

Multi-Employer Work Sites—Practical Exercise

On multi-employer work sites, citations shall normally be issued to the employer whose employees are exposed to hazards. This would be the exposing employer. In addition,, employers may be cited whether or not their own employees are exposed if any of the following conditions apply:

- The employer actually creates the hazard (creating employer).
- The employer is responsible by contract or through actual practice for safety and health conditions on the worksite, such as having authority for ensuring that the hazardous conditions are corrected (controlling employer).
- The employer has the responsibility for correcting the hazard (correcting employer).

The employer may use the following legitimate defense to the citation by ensuring that all of the following are true:

- Did not create the hazard;
- Did not have responsibility or authority to have the hazard corrected;
- Did not have the ability to correct or remove the hazard;
- Can demonstrate that it specifically notified the controlling/correcting employer of the hazard;
- Instructed workers to avoid hazard;
- Established an alternative means of protection; and
- Removed workers from the hazardous site.

Multi-Employer Work Sites— Practical Exercise

Exercise 1

Idaho Potato Flake Company hired Hightone Paints, a painting contractor, to do some repair and painting. During the repair work, Hightone removed a railing near a walkway and posted a sign warning customers of the hazard. Some of Hightones employees almost fell 20 ft., but caught themselves.

Who should be cited for the missing rail and why?

Exercise 2

California Widgets contracted with McKay Plumbing to repair sewer pipes on its property. The contract stated that McKay Plumbing was responsible for all safety and health conditions related to the sewer job. McKay Plumbing dug a trench and did not provide protection against cave-ins for three of their employees who were working in the 6-ft. deep trench.

Which company(ies) should receive citations and why?

Exercise 3

Washington Maintenance has five employees who clean Teeples Clinic on a daily basis. These employees come in contact with contaminated sharps and other regulated waste. No exposure control plans, nor related precautions, are in effect. Washington Maintenance sent a letter to Teeples Clinic expressing concern about employee protection, but received no response. Furthermore, Teeples Clinic is under contract to Medicinal Medical Inc., (a group of physicians) to run day-to-day operations. Medicinal Medical is responsible for the clinic's safety and health program and all related decisions. Teeples Clinic and Medicinal Medical Inc. both have employees at the site who are potentially exposed to potentially infectious materials.

Which company(ies) should receive citations and why?

Exercise 4

Chicago Construction, Inc., is the general contractor at a construction site. It has contracted with Detroit Surveying and Red Hot Construction for work on the site. During an inspection, a compliance officer finds that Red Hot Construction created a floor-opening hazard, but none of its employees were exposed. Detroit Surveying has notified both Chicago Construction and Red Hot Construction of the hazard and has told their employees to avoid that area until further notice. Detroit Surveying is unable to repair the opening.

Which company(ies) should receive citations and why?

Exercise 5

Cornhusker, Inc., hired Dingy Tank Company to clean two of its storage tanks. In the contract, Cornhusker, Inc., maintains responsibility for the safety and health conditions at the workplace. During the cleaning operations, three Dingy Tank Company employees are in the tank. Cornhusker has no confined space program.

Which company(ies) should receive citations and why?

HEALTH HAZARDS IN CONSTRUCTION

Some significant events in occupational safety in the United States include:

In 1812, the Embargo of the War of 1812 spurred the development of the New England textile industry and the founding of factory mutual companies. These early insurance companies inspected properties for hazards and suggested loss control and prevention methods in order to secure low rates for their policyholders.

In 1864 the Pennsylvania Mine Safety Act (PMSA) was passed into law.

In 1864 North America's first accident insurance policy was issued.

In 1867 the state of Massachusetts instituted the first government-sponsored factory inspection program.

In 1877 the state of Massachusetts passed a law requiring guarding for dangerous machinery, and took authority for enforcement of factory inspection programs.

In 1878 the first recorded call by a labor organization for a federal occupational safety and health law is heard.

In 1896 an association to prevent fires and write codes and standards, the National Fire Protection Association (NFPA), was founded.

In 1902 the state of Maryland passed the first workers' compensation law.

In 1904 the first attempt by a state government to force employers to compensate their employees for on-the-job injuries was overturned when the U.S. Supreme Court declared Maryland's workers' compensation law to be unconstitutional.

In 1911 a professional, technical organization responsible for developing safety codes for boilers and elevators, the American Society of Mechanical Engineers (ASME), was founded.

From 1911 to 1915 30 states passed workers' compensation laws.

In 1911 the American Society of Safety Engineers (ASSE) was founded. The ASSE was dedicated to the development of accident prevention techniques and the advancement of safety engineering as a profession.

In 1912 a group of engineers representing insurance companies, industry and government met in Milwaukee to exchange data on accident prevention. The organization formed at this meeting was to become the National Safety Council (NSC). (Today, the NSC carries on major safety campaigns for the general public, as well as assists industry in the development of safety promotion programs.)

In 1916 the U.S. Supreme Court upheld the constitutionality of state workers' compensation laws.

In 1918 the American Standards Association was founded. Responsible for the development of many voluntary safety standards, some of which are referenced into laws it is now called the American National Standards Institute (ANSI).

In **1936** Frances Perkins, Secretary of Labor, called for a federal occupational safety and health law. This action came a full 58 years after organized labor's first recorded request for a law of this nature.

In **1936** the Walsh-Healey (Public Contracts) Act passed. This law required that all federal contracts be fulfilled in a healthful and safe working environment.

In **1948** all 48 states had workers' compensation laws.

In **1952** Coal Mine Safety Act (CMSA) was passed into law.

In **1960** specific safety standards were promulgated for the Walsh-Healey Act.

In **1966** the Metal and Nonmetallic Mines Safety Act (MNMSA) was passed.

In **1966** the U.S. Department of Transportation (DOT) and its sections, the National Highway Traffic Safety Administration (NHTSA) and the National Transportation Safety Board (NTSB), were established.

In **1968** President Lyndon Johnson called for a federal occupational safety and health law.

In **1969** the Construction Safety Act (CSA) was passed.

In **1969** the Board of Certified Safety Professionals (BCSP) was established. This organization certifies practitioners in the safety profession.

In **1970** President Richard Nixon signed into law the Occupational Safety and Health Act thus creating the Occupational Safety and Health Administration (OSHA) and the National Institute for Occupational Safety and Health (NIOSH).

Industrial Hygiene

Industrial hygiene has been defined as

> that science and art devoted to the anticipation, recognition, evaluation, and control of those environmental factors or stresses arising in or from the workplace, which may cause sickness, impaired health and well-being, or significant discomfort among workers or among the citizens of the community.

Industrial hygienists use environmental monitoring and analytical methods to detect the extent of worker exposure and employ engineering, work practice controls and other methods to control potential health hazards.

There has been an awareness of industrial hygiene since antiquity. The environment and its relation to worker health was recognized as early as the fourth century B.C. when Hippocrates noted lead toxicity in the mining industry. In the first century A.D., Pliny the Elder, a Roman scholar, perceived health risks to those working with zinc and sulfur. He devised a face mask made from an animal bladder to protect workers from exposure to dust and lead fumes. In the second century A.D., the Greek physician Galen accurately described the pathology of lead poisoning and also recognized the hazardous exposures of copper miners to acid mists.

In the Middle Ages, guilds worked at assisting sick workers and their families.

In 1556, the German scholar Agricola advanced the science of industrial hygiene even further when in his book *De Re Metallica*, he described the diseases of miners and prescribed preventive measures. The book included suggestions for mine ventilation and worker protection, discussed mining accidents and described diseases associated with mining occupations such as silicosis.

Industrial hygiene gained further respectability in 1700 when in Italy, Bernardo Ramazzini, known as the "father of industrial medicine," published the first comprehensive book on industrial medicine, *De Morbis Artificum Diatriba* (*The Diseases of Workmen*). The book contained accurate descriptions of the occupational diseases of most of the workers of his time. Ramazzini greatly affected the future of industrial hygiene because he asserted that occupational diseases should be studied in the work environment rather than in hospital wards.

Industrial hygiene received another major boost in 1743 when Ulrich Ellenborg published a pamphlet on occupational diseases and injuries among gold miners. Ellenborg also wrote about the toxicity of carbon monoxide, mercury, lead, and nitric acid.

In England in the 18th century, Percival Pott, as a result of his findings on the insidious effects of soot on chimney sweepers, was a major force in getting the British Parliament to pass the *Chimney-Sweepers Act of* 1788. The passage of the English Factory Acts beginning in 1833 marked the first effective legislative acts in the field of industrial safety. The acts, however, were intended to provide compensation for accidents rather than to control their causes. Later, several other European nations developed workers' compensation acts, which stimulated the adoption of increased factory safety precautions and the establishment of medical services within industrial plants.

In the early 20th century in the United States, Dr. Alice Hamilton led efforts to improve industrial hygiene. She observed industrial conditions first hand and startled mine owners, factory managers and state officials with evidence that there was a correlation between worker illness and exposure to toxins. She also presented definitive proposals for eliminating unhealthful working conditions.

At about the same time, U.S. federal and state agencies began investigating health conditions in industry. In 1908 public awareness of occupationally related diseases stimulated the passage of compensation acts for certain civil employees. States passed the first workers' compensation laws in 1911. In 1913 the New York Department of Labor and the Ohio Department of Health established the first state industrial hygiene programs. All states enacted such legislation by 1948. In most states, there is some compensation coverage for workers who contract occupational diseases.

The U.S. Congress has passed three landmark pieces of legislation related to safeguarding workers' health:

- The Metal and Nonmetallic Mines Safety Act of 1966;
- The Federal Coal Mine Safety and Health Act of 1969; and
- The Occupational Safety and Health Act of 1970.

Today nearly every employer is required to implement the elements of an industrial hygiene and safety, occupational health, or hazard communication program and to be responsive to the Occupational Safety and Health Administration (OSHA) and its regulations.

OSHA and Industrial Hygiene

Under the OSH Act, OSHA develops and sets mandatory occupational safety and health requirements applicable to the more than 6 million workplaces in the United States. OSHA relies on, among many others, industrial hygien-

ists to evaluate jobs for potential health hazards. Developing and setting mandatory occupational safety and health standards involves determining the extent of employee exposure to hazards and deciding what is needed to control these hazards to protect workers. Industrial hygienists are trained to anticipate, recognize, evaluate and recommend controls for environmental and physical hazards that can affect the health and well-being of workers.

More than 40 percent of the OSHA compliance officers who inspect U.S. workplaces are industrial hygienists. Industrial hygienists also play a major role in developing and issuing OSHA standards to protect workers from health hazards associated with toxic chemicals, biological hazards and harmful physical agents. They also provide technical assistance and support to the agency's national and regional offices. OSHA also employs industrial hygienists who assist in setting up field enforcement procedures and issue technical interpretations of OSHA regulations and standards.

Industrial hygienists analyze, identify and measure workplace hazards or stresses that can cause sickness, impaired health or significant discomfort in workers through chemical, physical, ergonomic or biological exposures. The two main roles of the OSHA industrial hygienist are to spot those conditions and help eliminate or control them through appropriate measures.

Worksite Analysis

A worksite analysis is an essential first step that helps an industrial hygienist determine the jobs and workstations where problems could arise. During the worksite analysis, the industrial hygienist measures and identifies exposures, problem tasks and risks. The most effective worksite analyses include all jobs, operations and work activities. The industrial hygienist inspects, researches or analyzes how the particular chemicals or physical hazards at that worksite affect worker health. If a situation hazardous to health is discovered, the industrial hygienist recommends the appropriate corrective actions.

Recognizing and Controlling Hazards

Industrial hygienists recognize that engineering, work practice and administrative controls are the primary means of reducing employee exposure to occupational hazards. Engineering controls minimize employee exposure by either reducing or removing the hazard at the source or isolating the worker from the hazard. Engineering controls include eliminating toxic chemicals and substituting nontoxic chemicals, enclosing work processes or confining work operations, and installing general and local ventilation systems.

Work practice controls alter the manner in which a task is performed. Some fundamental and easily implemented work practice controls include:

- changing existing work practices to follow proper procedures that minimize exposures when operating production and control equipment;
- inspecting and maintaining process and control equipment on a regular basis;
- implementing good housekeeping procedures;
- providing good supervision; and
- mandating that eating, drinking, smoking, chewing tobacco or gum and applying cosmetics in regulated areas is prohibited.

Administrative controls include controlling employees' exposure by scheduling production and tasks, or both, in ways that minimize exposure levels. For example, the employer might schedule operations with the highest exposure potential during periods when the fewest employees are present.

When effective work practices or engineering controls are not feasible or while such controls are being instituted, appropriate personal protective equipment must be used. Examples of personal protective equipment are gloves, safety goggles, helmets, safety shoes, protective clothing and respirators. To be effective, personal protective equipment must be:

- individually selected;
- properly fitted and periodically refitted;
- conscientiously and properly worn;
- regularly maintained; and
- replaced, as necessary.

Examples of Job Hazards

To be effective in recognizing and evaluating on-the-job hazards and recommending controls, industrial hygienists must be familiar with the hazards' characteristics. Potential hazards can include air contaminants and chemical, biological, physical and ergonomic hazards.

Air Contaminants

Air contaminants are commonly classified as either particulate or gas and vapor contaminants. The most common particulate contaminants include dusts, fumes, mists, aerosols and fibers. Dusts are solid particles generated by handling, crushing, grinding, colliding, exploding and heating organic or inorganic materials such as rock, ore, metal, coal, wood and grain. Any process that produces dust fine enough to remain in the air long enough to be inhaled or ingested should be regarded as hazardous until proven otherwise.

Fumes are formed when material from a volatilized solid condenses in cool air. In most cases, the solid particles resulting from the condensation react with air to form an oxide.

The term mist is applied to liquid suspended in the atmosphere. Mists are generated by liquids condensing from a vapor back to a liquid or by a liquid being dispersed by splashing or atomizing. Aerosols are also a form of a mist characterized by highly respirable, minute liquid particles.

Fibers are solid particles whose length is several times greater than their diameter, such as asbestos.

Gases are formless fluids that expand to occupy the space or enclosure in which they are confined. They are atomic, diatomic or molecular in nature as opposed to droplets or particles that are made up of millions of atoms or molecules.

Through evaporation, liquids change into vapors and mix with the surrounding atmosphere. Vapors are the volatile form of substances that are normally in a solid or liquid state at room temperature and pressure. Vapors are gases in that true vapors are atomic or molecular in nature.

Chemical Hazards

Harmful chemical compounds in the form of solids, liquids, gases, mists, dusts, fumes and vapors exert toxic effects by inhalation (breathing), absorption (through direct contact with the skin) or ingestion (eating or drinking). Airborne chemical hazards exist as concentrations of mists, vapors, gases, fumes or solids. Some are toxic through inhalation and some of them irritate the skin on contact; some can be toxic by absorption through the skin or through ingestion; and some are corrosive to living tissue.

The degree of worker risk from exposure to any given substance depends on the nature and potency of the toxic effects and the magnitude and duration of exposure.

Information on the risk to workers from chemical hazards can be obtained from the material safety data sheet (MSDS) that OSHA's *Hazard Communication Standard* requires be supplied by the manufacturer or importer to the purchaser of all hazardous materials (29 CFR 1910.1200). The MSDS is a summary of the important health, safety, and toxicological information on the chemical or the mixture's ingredients. Other provisions of the *Hazard Communication Standard* require that all containers of hazardous substances in the workplace have appropriate warning and identification labels.

Biological Hazards

These include bacteria, viruses, fungi and other living organisms that can cause acute and chronic infections by entering the body either directly or through breaks in the skin. Occupations that deal with plants, animals or their products, or with food and food processing may expose workers to biological hazards. Laboratory and medical personnel also can be exposed to biological hazards. Any occupations that result in contact with bodily fluids pose a risk to workers from biological hazards.

In occupations where animals are involved, biological hazards are dealt with by preventing and controlling diseases in the animal population as well as properly caring for and handling infected animals. Also, effective personal hygiene, particularly proper attention to minor cuts and scratches, especially on the hands and forearms, helps keep worker risks to a minimum.

In occupations where there is potential exposure to biological hazards, workers should practice proper personal hygiene, particularly hand washing. Hospitals should provide proper ventilation, proper personal protective equipment such as gloves and respirators, adequate infectious waste disposal systems, and appropriate controls, including isolation in instances of particularly contagious diseases such as tuberculosis.

Physical Hazards

These include excessive levels of ionizing and nonionizing electromagnetic radiation, noise, vibration, illumination and temperature.

In occupations where there is exposure to ionizing radiation, time, distance and shielding are important tools in ensuring worker safety. Danger from radiation increases with the amount of time one is exposed to it; hence, the shorter the time of exposure, the smaller the radiation danger.

Distance also is a valuable tool in controlling exposure to both ionizing and nonionizing radiation. Radiation levels from some sources can be estimated by comparing the squares of the distances between the worker and the source. For example, at a reference point of 10 ft. from a source, the radiation is 1/100 of the intensity at 1 ft. from the source.

Shielding also is a way to protect against radiation. The greater the protective mass between a radioactive source and the worker, the lower the radiation exposure.

Similarly, shielding workers from nonionizing radiation can also be an effective control method. For example, workers exposed to radiant heat can be protected by installing reflective shields and providing them with protective clothing. In some instances, however, limiting exposure to or increasing distance from certain forms of nonionizing radiation, such as lasers, is not effective. For example, an exposure to laser radiation that is faster than the blinking of an eye can be hazardous and would require workers to be miles from the laser source before being adequately protected.

Noise, another significant physical hazard, can be controlled by various measures. Noise can be reduced by:

- Installing equipment and systems that have been engineered, designed, and built to operate quietly;
- Enclosing or shielding noisy equipment;
- Making certain that equipment is in good repair and properly maintained with all worn or unbalanced parts replaced;
- Mounting noisy equipment on special mounts to reduce vibration; and
- Installing silencers, mufflers or baffles.

Substituting quiet work methods for noisy ones is another significant way to reduce noise (e.g., welding parts rather than riveting them). Also, treating floors, ceilings and walls with acoustical material can reduce reflected or reverberant noise. In addition, erecting sound barriers at adjacent workstations around noisy operations will reduce those workers' exposure to noise.

It is also possible to reduce noise exposure by:

- Increasing the distance between the source and the receiver;
- Isolating workers in acoustical booths;
- Limiting workers' exposure time to noise; and
- Providing hearing protection.

OSHA also requires that workers in noisy surroundings be periodically tested as a precaution against hearing loss.

Ergonomic Hazards

The science of ergonomics is the study and evaluation of a range of tasks including, but not limited to, lifting, holding, pushing, walking and reaching. Many ergonomic problems result from technological changes, such as increased assembly line speeds, added specialized tasks and increased repetition. However, some problems arise from poorly designed job tasks. Any of those conditions can cause ergonomic hazards such as excessive vibration and noise, eye strain, repetitive motion and heavy lifting problems. Improperly designed tools or work areas also can be ergonomic hazards. Repetitive motions or repeated shocks over prolonged periods of time as in jobs involving sorting, assembling and data entry can often cause irritation and inflammation of the tendon sheath of the hands and arms, a condition known as carpal tunnel syndrome.

Ergonomic hazards are avoided primarily by the effective design of a job or job site and by better designed tools or equipment that meet workers' needs in terms of physical environment and job tasks. Through thorough worksite analyses, employers can set up procedures to correct or control ergonomic hazards by:

- Using the appropriate engineering controls (e.g., designing or redesigning workstations, lighting, tools, equipment);
- Teaching correct work practices (e.g., proper lifting methods);

- Employing proper administrative controls (e.g., shifting workers among several different tasks, reducing production demand and increasing rest breaks); and
- Providing and mandating personal protective equipment, if necessary.

Evaluating working conditions from an ergonomics standpoint involves looking at the total physiological and psychological demands of the job on the worker. Overall, the benefits of a well-designed, ergonomic work environment can include increased efficiency, fewer accidents, lower operating costs and more effective use of personnel.

Routes of Entry

For a harmful agent to exert its toxic effect, it must come into contact with a body cell and must enter the body through inhalation, skin absorption or ingestion. Chemical compounds in the form of liquids, gases, mists, dusts, fumes and vapors can cause problems by inhalation, absorption or ingestion.

Inhalation

Inhalation involves those airborne contaminants that can be inhaled directly into the lungs and can be physically classified as gases, vapors and particulate matter that includes dusts, fumes, smokes and mists.

Inhalation, as a route of entry, is particularly important because of the rapidity with which a toxic material can be absorbed in the lungs, pass into the bloodstream and reach the brain. Inhalation is the major route of entry for hazardous chemicals in the work environment.

Absorption

Penetration through the skin can occur quite rapidly if the skin is cut or abraded. Intact skin, however, offers a reasonably good barrier to chemicals. Unfortunately, there are many compounds that can be absorbed through intact skin.

Some substances are absorbed via hair follicle openings and others dissolve in the fats and oils of the skin, such as organic lead compounds, many nitro compounds and organic phosphate pesticides. Compounds that are good solvents for fats (e.g., toluene, xylene) also can cause problems by being absorbed through the skin.

Many organic compounds, such as cyanides and most aromatic anilines, amides and phenols, can produce systemic poisoning by direct contact with the skin. Absorption of toxic chemicals through the skin and eyes is the second most important route of entry.

Ingestion

In the workplace, people can unknowingly eat or drink harmful chemicals if they store drinking containers in the workplace or do not wash before eating. Toxic compounds are capable of being absorbed from the gastrointestinal tract into the blood stream. Lead oxide can cause serious problems if people working with this material are allowed to eat or smoke in work areas. In this situation, careful and thorough washing is required both before eating and at the end of every shift.

Inhaled toxic dusts can also be ingested in amounts that may cause trouble. If the toxic dust swallowed with food or saliva is not soluble in digestive fluids, it is eliminated directly through the intestinal tract. Toxic materials that are readily soluble in digestive fluids can be absorbed into the blood from the digestive system.

In addition to studying all routes of entry when evaluating the work environment (e.g., snack foods or lunches in the work area, solvents being used to clean work clothing and hands), specific types of air contaminants must be identified.

Types of Air Contaminants

There are precise meanings of certain words commonly used in industrial hygiene. These must be used correctly in order to:

- Understand the requirements of OSHA's regulations;
- Effectively communicate with other workers in the field of industrial hygiene; and
- Intelligently prepare purchase orders to procure health services and personal protective equipment.

For example, a fume respirator is worthless as protection against gases or vapors. Too frequently, terms (e.g., gases, vapors, fumes, mists) are used interchangeably. Each term has a definite meaning and describes a certain state of matter. Air contaminants are commonly classified as either particulate contaminants or gas and vapor contaminants.

Particulate Contaminants

The most common particulate contaminants include dusts, fumes, mists and fibers.

Dusts

Dusts are solid particles generated by handling crushing grinding, rapid impact, detonation and decrepitation (breaking apart by heating) of organic or inorganic materials, such as rock, ore, metal, coal, wood and grain.

Dust is a term used in industry to describe airborne solid particles that range in size from 0.1 to 25 micrometers. One micrometer is a unit of length equal to one millionth of a meter. A micrometer is also referred to as a "micron" and is equal to 1/25,400 of an inch. Dust can enter the air from various sources, such as the handling of dusty materials, or during such processes such as grinding, crushing, blasting and shaking.

Most industrial dusts consist of particles that vary widely in size, with the small particles greatly outnumbering the large ones. Consequently (with few exceptions), when dust is noticeable in the air near a dusty operation, more invisible dust particles than visible ones are probably present. A process that produces dust fine enough to remain in the air long enough to be inhaled should be regarded as hazardous until proven otherwise.

An airborne dust of a potentially toxic material will not cause pulmonary illness if its particle size is too large to gain access to the lungs. Particles 10 ppm in diameter and larger are known as nonrespirable These particles will be deposited in the respiratory system long before they reach the alveolar sacs — the most important area in the lungs.

Particles less than 10 ppm in diameter are known as respirable. Because the particles are likely to reach the alveoli in great quantities, they are potentially more harmful than larger particles.

By using a size-selective device (e.g., a cyclone) ahead of a filter at a specific airflow-sampling rate, it is possible to collect respirable-sized particles on the filter. This allows one to determine the dust concentration of respirable particles.

Fumes

Fumes are formed when the material from a volatilized solid condenses in cool air. The solid particles that are formed make up a fume that is extremely fine — usually less than 1.0 micron in diameter. In most cases, the hot vapor reacts with the air to form an oxide. Gases and vapors are not fumes, although the terms are often mistakenly used interchangeably.

Welding, metalizing and other operations involving vapors from molten metals may produce fumes; these may be harmful under certain conditions. Arc welding volatilizes metal vapor that condenses as the metal or its oxide in the air around the arc. In addition, the rod coating is partially volatilized. Because these fumes are extremely small, they are readily inhaled.

Other toxic fumes, such as those formed when welding structures that have been painted with lead-based paints or when welding galvanized metal, can produce severe symptoms of toxicity rather rapidly in the absence of good ventilation or proper respiratory protection.

Mists

Mists are suspended liquid droplets generated by condensation of liquids from the vapor back to the liquid state or by breaking up a liquid into a dispersed state, such as by splashing or atomizing. The term mist is applied to a finely divided liquid suspended in the atmosphere. Examples include oil mist produced during cutting and grinding operations, acid mists from electroplating acid or alkali mists from pickling operations, and spray mist from spray-finishing operations.

Fibers

Fibers are solid particles that have a slender, elongated structure with length several times as great as their diameter. Examples include asbestos, fibrous talc, and fiberglass. Airborne fibers may be found in construction activities, mining, friction product manufacturing and fabrication, and demolition operations.

Gas and Vapor Contaminants

Gases

Gases are formless fluids that expand to occupy the space or enclosure in which they are confined. Gases are a state of matter in which the molecules are unrestricted by cohesive forces. Examples are arc-welding gases, internal combustion engine exhaust gases and air.

Vapors

Vapors are the volatile form of substances that are normally in the solid or liquid state at room temperature and pressure. Evaporation is the process by which a liquid is changed into the vapor state and mixed with the surrounding atmosphere. Some of the most common exposures to vapors in industry occur from organic solvents. Solvents with low boiling points readily form vapors at room temperature. Solvent vapors enter the body mainly by inhalation, although some skin absorption can occur.

Units of Concentration

In addition to the definitions concerning states of matter that find daily usage in the vocabulary of the industrial hygienist, other terms used to describe degree of exposure include the following:

ppm. Parts per million. Parts of contaminated air on a volumetric basis. It is used for expressing the concentration of a gas or vapor.

mg/m3. Milligrams of a substance per cubic meter of air. The term is most commonly used for expressing concentrations of dusts, metal fumes or other particles in the air.

mppcf. Millions of particles of a particulate per cubic foot of air.

f/cc. The number of fibers per cubic centimeter of air. This term is used for expressing the concentration of airborne asbestos fibers.

The concentration of a gas or vapor in air is usually expressed in parts per million (ppm), but may be converted to mg/m3 at a temperature of 25°Celsius and a pressure of 760 mm Hg:

$$mg/m3 = ppm \times (Molecular\ Weight/24.45)$$

Example: A 50-ppm concentration of carbon monoxide (molecular weight = 28) is equivalent to a concentration of 57.26 mg/m3 at 25°Celsius and 760 mm Hg. Note also that:

Concentration (ppm) = Concentration (%) x 10,000

Example: A concentration of a gas or vapor equal to 0.01% is equivalent to a concentration of 100 ppm.

The health and safety professional recognizes that air contaminants exist as a gas, dust, fumes, mist or vapor in the workroom air. In evaluating the degree of exposure, the measured concentration of the air is compared to limits or exposure guidelines.

Threshold Limit Values

Threshold limit values (TLVs) have been established for airborne concentrations of many chemical compounds. It is important to understand something about TLVs and the terminology in which their concentrations are expressed.

The American Conference of Governmental Industrial Hygienists (ACGIH) publishes annually the list of "Threshold Limit Values and Biological Exposure Indices." The ACGIH is not an official government agency. Membership is limited to professional personnel in government agencies or educational institutions engaged in occupational safety and health programs.

The data for establishing TLVs comes from animal studies, human studies and industrial experience. The limit may be selected for several reasons; it may be based on the fact that a substance is very irritating to the majority of people exposed, or, other substances may be asphyxiants. Other reasons for establishing a TLV include the fact that certain chemical compounds are anesthetic, or fibrogenic, or can cause allergic reactions or malignancies. Some additional TLVs have been established because exposure above a certain airborne concentration is a nuisance.

The basic idea of TLVs is fairly simple. They refer to airborne concentrations of substances and represent conditions under which it is believed that nearly all workers may be repeatedly exposed, day after day, without adverse effect.

Because individual susceptibility varies widely, an occasional exposure of an individual at (or even below) the threshold limit may not prevent discomfort, aggravation of a preexisting condition or occupational illness. In addition to the TLVs set for chemical compounds, there are limits for physical agents, such as noise, microwaves, and heat stress.

Several important points should be noted concerning TLVs. First, "TLV" is a copyrighted trademark of the ACGIH. It should not be used to refer to the values published in OSHA or other standards. OSHA's limits are known as permissible exposure limits and will be discussed later. The ACGIH TLVs are not mandatory federal or state employee exposure standards. These limits are not fine lines between safe and dangerous concentrations nor are they a relative index of toxicity. Three categories of TLVs are specified.

Time-weighted average (TLV-TWA) is the time-weighted average concentration for a normal eight-hour workday or 40-hour workweek to which nearly all workers may be repeatedly exposed, day after day, without adverse effect. Time-weighted averages permit excursions above the limit, provided they are compensated by equivalent excursions below the limit during the workday.

Short-term exposure limit (TLV-STEL) is the maximal concentration to which workers can be exposed continuously for a short period of time without suffering from any of the following:

- Irritation;
- Chronic or irreversible tissue change; or
- Narcosis of sufficient degree to increase accident proneness, impair self-rescue or materially reduce work efficiency.

The STEL is a 15-minute TWA exposure that should not be exceeded at any time during a workday, even if the eight-hour time weighted average is within the TLV-TWA. Exposures above the TLV-TWA up to the STEL should not be longer than 15 minutes and should not occur more than four times per day. There should be at least 60 minutes between successive exposures in this range.

The STEL is not a separate independent exposure limit; rather it supplements the time-weighted average limit where there are recognized acute effects from a substance whose toxic effects are primarily of a chronic nature. STELs are recommended only where toxic effects have been reported from high short-term exposures in humans or animals.

Ceiling (TLV-C) is the concentration that should not be exceeded even instantaneously. Although the time-weighted average concentration provides the most satisfactory, practical way of monitoring airborne agents for compliance with the limits, there are certain substances for which it is inappropriate. In the latter group are substances that are predominantly fast acting and whose threshold limit is more appropriately based on this particular response. A ceiling limit that should not be exceeded best controls substances with this type of response.

For some substances (e.g., irritant gases), only one category, the TLV-C, may be relevant. For other substances, either two or three categories may be relevant, depending upon their physiologic action. It is important to observe that if any one of these three TLVs is exceeded, a potential hazard from that substance is presumed to exist.

Skin Notation

Nearly one-fourth of the substances in the TLV list are followed by the designation "Skin." This refers to the potential significant contribution to the overall exposure by the cutaneous route, including mucous membranes and the eyes, usually by direct contact with the substance. This designation is intended to suggest appropriate measures for the prevention of cutaneous absorption.

Federal Occupational Safety and Health Standards

The first compilation of health and safety standards promulgated by the Department of Labor's OSHA in 1970 was derived from the then-existing federal standards and national consensus standards. Thus, many of the 1968 TLVs established by the ACGIH became federal standards or permissible exposure limits (PEL).

Also, certain workplace quality standards known as maximal acceptable concentrations of the American National Standards Institute (ANSI) were incorporated as federal health standards in 29 CFR 1910.1000 as national consensus standards. These PEL values for general industry were subsequently updated in 1989. Unlike the TLVs, OSHA's PELs are enforceable by law. Employers must keep employee exposure levels below the PELs of regulated substances. As with TLVs, there are three types of PELs.

Time-Weighted Average

In adopting the TLVs of the ACGIH, OSHA also adopted the concept of the time-weighted average concentration for a workday. The eight-hour time-weighted average (TWA) is the average concentration of a chemical in air over an eight-hour exposure period. In general:

$$TWA = \frac{C_aT_a + C_bT_b + C_cT_c \ldots C_rT_r}{8}$$

Where:
- T_a is the time of the first exposure period.
- C_a is the concentration of contaminant in period "a."
- T_b is another time period during the shift.
- C_b is the concentration during period "b."
- C_r is the concentration during the "no" time period.
- T_r is the "nth" time period.

To illustrate the formula prescribed above, assume that a substance has an eight-hour TWA PEL of 100 ppm. Assume that an employee is subject to the following exposure:
- Two hours exposure at 150 ppm;
- Two hours exposure at 75 ppm; and
- Four hours exposure at 50 ppm.

Substituting this information in the formula, we have:

$$TWA = \frac{(150)(2) + (75)(2) + (50)(4)}{8} = 81.25 \text{ ppm}$$

Since 81.25 ppm is less than 100 ppm, the eight-hour TWA limit, the exposure is acceptable.

Amendments to OSHA's Air Contaminant Standard

On January 19, 1989, OSHA amended its Air Contaminant standard, 1910.1000 (54 Fed. Reg. 2332). New limits were established for many substances and many new PELs were set for substances previously not regulated by OSHA.

The Eleventh Circuit Court of Appeals issued a decision vacating the "Final Rules" of the Air Contaminants Standard (29 CFR 1910.1000) on July 7, 1992. The court's decision struck down the entire standard. However, PELs specified in 29 CFR 1910.1001 through the end of Subpart Z of Part 1910 are unaffected by the court's decision.

Effective March 22, 1993, OSHA is enforcing only the following Permissible Exposure Limits (PELs) in 29 CFR 1910.1000:

- Those limits specified in the "Transitional Limits" column of Table Z-1-A;
- All limits in Table Z-2; and
- All limits in Table Z-3.

PELs specified in 29 CFR 1910.1001 through the end of Subpart Z of Part 1910 are unaffected by the Court's decision.

Asbestos and Lead Awareness

OSHA regulations apply for industrial applications and construction uses of asbestos and lead. OSHA enforces safety rules through their regional offices. OSHA can issue citations to federal agencies, but cannot issue fines.

Asbestos is a naturally occurring mineral that is used in vehicle brakes and building materials. It is highly resistant to heat and corrosion and has been used extensively in the past.

Inhaling asbestos fibers can cause serious lung disease that may not appear for years. Asbestos can cause a buildup of scar-like tissue in the lungs, resulting in a loss of lung functions and often disability and death.

Simply being exposed to asbestos does not mean a person will become ill or die. In an eight-hour work shift, employees can be exposed to 0.1 fiber per cubic centimeter of air. This small amount of asbestos is normally filtered by the body's system of defense, such as mucous membranes and nose hairs.

Lead Exposure

Like Asbestos, lead is very resistant to corrosion and has a low melting temperature. For these reasons it is used extensively in manufacturing, construction work, welding, cutting, brazing and some painting. Lead also can be found in radiator repair shops, motor gaskets and firing ranges.

Once lead gets into the blood, it settles in the blood and soft tissues, such as the kidney, bone marrow, liver and brain. It also settles in the bones and teeth of workers. Overexposure to lead is a leading cause of workplace illnesses. Lead has a permissive exposure level based on an eight-hour day of less than 50 micrograms per cubic meter of air.

Worker Protection

Both asbestos and lead must enter the body to cause damage. The primary route of entry is inhalation. In some small cases, they may enter via ingestion when a worker eats or smokes in an area where airborne lead or asbestos is found.

The best way to protect workers is to keep the material from getting into the air, typically by using a wet method or process. If the asbestos or lead is wet, it cannot float in the air and thus cannot enter workers' lungs. For example, if materials contain lead or asbestos, the worker may wet the material using a spray bottle or mister to reduce or eliminate the possibility of inhalation.

Employees should never use compressed air to clean asbestos or lead particles because the resulting blast of air throws the contaminant into the air where it will float for a long time, often until someone inhales it.

Personal protective equipment, gloves and respirators with a HEPA filter provide protection as well. If there is a possibility of eye irritation, employees must wear the goggles and face shields (See Exhibit 4.1).

Exhibit 4-1.
Respirators and goggles can provide protection from asbestos.

After working with asbestos or lead, the employee should immediately wash his or her hands when finished with the procedure. Naturally, smoking should not be allowed in any area where these contaminants are used.

Medical Considerations

Before any work with asbestos begins, the facility should be monitored to determine if the level of asbestos exceeds the permissible exposure limit of 0.1 fibers per cubic centimeter. If a process has changed and more asbestos is possibly being released into the air through a particular process, contact the safety office to arrange for another evaluation.

If the company's work requires that workers be exposed beyond the PEL, they should alert their personal physicians so that the physicians can monitor them for possible asbestos-related problems.

If exposed to lead or asbestos on a routine basis beyond the PEL, workers also should contact the local safety office and enroll in a medical surveillance program.

Significant Changes in the Asbestos Standard for Construction

This handout is designed to acquaint interested persons with significant changes to OSHA's new Asbestos Standard for Construction, 29 CFR 1926.1101. It is not intended to be a comprehensive review of the entire standard. Persons who wish to learn more about the specific provisions of the standard should consult the preamble and regulatory text of the standard as published in the *Federal Register*.

The issues that are discussed here are the permissible exposure limit (PEL); duties of building/facility owners; duties and training of the competent person; aspects of exposure monitoring; and control measures, especially for the four classes of asbestos work defined by the standard. Basic definitions that are important to understanding these issues are presented.

Definitions

Asbestos-Containing Material (ACM)—means any material containing more than one percent asbestos.

Presumed Asbestos-Containing Material (PACM)—means thermal system insulation and surfacing material found in buildings constructed no later than 1980. The designation of a material as "PACM" may be rebutted following procedures specified in the standard.

Surfacing ACM—means material that is sprayed, troweled-on or otherwise applied to surfaces (such as acoustical plaster on ceilings and fireproofing materials on structural members, or other materials on surfaces for acoustical, fireproofing, and other purposes) and that contains more than 1% asbestos.

Thermal System Insulation (TSI) ACM—means ACM applied to pipes, fittings, boilers, breeching, tanks, ducts or other structural components to prevent heat loss or gain and that contains more than 1% asbestos.

Class I Asbestos Work—means activities involving the removal of TSI and surfacing ACM and PACM.

Class II Asbestos Work—means activities involving the removal of ACM which is not thermal system insulation or surfacing material. This includes, but is not limited to, the removal of asbestos-containing wallboard, floor tile and sheeting, roofing and siding shingles, and construction mastics.

Class III Asbestos Work—means repair and maintenance operations, where "ACM," including TSI and surfacing ACM and PACM, may be disturbed.

Class IV Asbestos Work—means maintenance and custodial construction activities during which employees contact but do not disturb ACM or PACM and activities to clean up dust, waste and debris resulting from Class I, II and III activities.

Notes: 1. The removal of intact cements, coatings, mastics, and flashings during roofing work is not covered by the class system.

2. The installation of asbestos-containing products is covered by the standard but does not fall into any of the four classes.

Building/Facility Owner—means the legal entity, including a lessee, which exercises control over management and recordkeeping functions relating to a building and/or facility in which activities covered by this standard take place.

Permissible Exposure Limit (PEL)

The time-weighted average (TWA) permissible exposure limit has been reduced to 0.1 fibers per cubic centimeter. The Excursion Limit remains at 1.0 fibers per cubic centimeter averaged over 30 minutes. Both of these values are considered PELs.

There is no established action level in the new standard because the sampling and analytical method is not reliable below the time-weighted average limit of 0.1 fibers per cubic centimeter.

Requirements for Building/Facility Owners

Most asbestos-related construction activities involve previously installed building materials. Building owners often are the only and/or best sources of information concerning them. Therefore they are assigned specific information conveying and retention duties under the new asbestos standard. Where a building/facility owner also is an employer with employees who may be exposed to asbestos-containing materials, the duties of employers also apply.

The following materials must be treated as asbestos-containing, unless specified procedures are followed to determine otherwise:

- TSI and surfacing materials in buildings or substrates constructed no later than 1980;
- Asphalt and vinyl flooring material installed not later than 1980; and
- Any other materials that the building owner has actual knowledge that it is, or should have known it to be, asbestos-containing.

Notification Requirements

Before work is begun, building/facility owners must identify the presence, location, and quantity of ACM/PACM and notify the following persons:

- Prospective employers applying for or bidding for work whose employees reasonably can be expected to work in or adjacent to areas containing such material;
- Employees of the owner who will work in or adjacent to areas containing such material;
- On multi-employer worksites, all employers of employees who will be performing work within or adjacent to areas containing such materials; and

- Tenants who will occupy areas containing such materials.

Notification may be in writing or by personal communication to the affected person(s) or their authorized representatives.

Note: When materials labeled as containing asbestos according to the requirements of this standard are installed on non-residential roofs, the contractor must notify the building owner of the presence and location of such asbestos-containing materials. This facilitates the owner's future notification requirements.

Signs and Labels

Building/facility owners must post signs at the entrance to mechanical rooms/areas in which employees reasonably can be expected to enter and which contain TSI and surfacing ACM/PACM. The signs must identify the material which is present, its location, and appropriate work practices that will ensure ACM/PACM will not be disturbed.

Previously installed PACM/ACM that is identified by a building owner or employer must be labeled in areas where the label will clearly be noticed. Posting of signs may be used as an alternative to labels.

The wording for labels is:

**DANGER
CONTAINS ASBESTOS FIBERS
AVOID CREATING DUST
CANCER AND LUNG DISEASE HAZARD**

Labels must also contain a warning statement against breathing asbestos fibers.

Records Retention

Where a building/facility owner has communicated and/or received notification concerning the identification, location, and quantity of ACM/PACM, written records of such notifications and their content must be maintained by the building owner for the duration of ownership and transferred to successive owners.

Where a building/facility owner has relied on data to demonstrate that PACM is not asbestos-containing, such data must be maintained for as long as they are relied upon to rebut the presumption.

Competent Person

The new standard requires that a competent person be designated for all worksites covered by the standard. The competent person must have the qualifications and authority required by 29 CFR 1926.20 through 1926.32, the basic construction requirements.

The standard specifies additional duties and training for the competent person on asbestos worksites.

The competent person must make frequent and regular inspections of the job site, materials, and equipment. On jobsites where Class I or II work is being performed, the competent person must perform or supervise the following duties:

- Set-up the regulated area, enclosure, or other containment
- Ensure (by on-site inspection) the integrity of the enclosure or containment
- Set up procedures to control entry to and exit from the enclosure and/or area
- Supervise all employee exposure monitoring
- Ensure that employees working within the enclosure and/or using glove bags wear protective clothing and respirators
- Ensure through on-site supervision, that employees set up and remove engineering controls, use work practices and personal protective equipment in compliance with all requirements
- Ensure that employees use the hygiene facilities and observe the decontamination procedures
- Ensure through on-site inspection that engineering controls are functioning properly and employers are using proper work practices
- Ensure that notification requirements are met
- For Class I jobs, on-site inspections must be made at least once during each work shift, and at any time at employee request.
- For Class II and III jobs, on-site inspections must be made frequently enough to assess whether conditions have changed, as well as at any reasonable time at employee request.

Training

For Class I and II asbestos work, training of the competent person must include all aspects of asbestos removal and handling, including:

- Abatement, installation, removal, and handling;

- Contents of the standard;
- Identification of asbestos;
- Removal procedures, where appropriate; and
- Other practices for reducing the hazard.

This training will be obtained in a comprehensive course for supervisors that meets the criteria of EPA's Model Accreditation Plan (40 CFR Part 763), or a course equivalent in stringency, content, and length.

For Class III and IV, training of the competent person must include aspects of asbestos handling appropriate to the work, including:

- Procedures for setting up glove bags and mini-enclosures;
- Use of wet methods;
- Contents of the standard; and
- Identification of asbestos.

Training must include successful completion of a course meeting EPA requirements for training local education agency maintenance and custodial staff [40 CFR 763.92(a)(2)], or its equivalent in stringency, content, and length.

Training required for Class I and II competent persons also satisfies the requirements for Class III and IV.

Exposure Monitoring

Initial Exposure Assessment

A competent person must make an "initial exposure assessment" before or at the initiation of all covered operations to determine expected exposures. An initial exposure assessment is not the same as initial exposure monitoring. Initial employee exposure monitoring cannot adequately predict all future exposures on construction jobs. First-day exposures may reflect set-up activities and thus be lower than later exposures. In addition, results of monitoring are not instantaneously available. Therefore, the initial exposure assessment will identify jobs likely to exceed the PEL in time for employers to install and implement the extra controls required to reduce exposures.

The bases for the initial exposure assessment are:

1) Employee exposure monitoring, if feasible, and

2) All observations, information, or calculations that indicate employee exposure to asbestos; this includes any previous monitoring conducted in the workplace, or of the operations of the employer that indicate the levels of airborne asbestos likely to be encountered on the job.

For Class I jobs, exposures are to be assumed to exceed the PELs until and unless the employer is able to make a "negative exposure assessment."

If a "negative exposure assessment" has been made, the "initial exposure assessment" is not required.

Negative Initial Exposure Assessment

A "negative initial exposure assessment" is a demonstration by the employer that employee exposure during an operation is expected to be consistently below the PELs.

The determination of a "negative exposure assessment" is job-specific. It can apply only to jobs performed by trained employees.

An employer may demonstrate that exposure will be below the PELs by data conforming to the following criteria:

1) Objective data – demonstrating that the product or material containing asbestos minerals or the activity involving such product or material cannot release airborne fibers in concentrations in excess of the PELs (TWA or Excursion Limit) under those work conditions having the greatest potential for releasing asbestos (the worst case), or

2) Prior exposure monitoring results – for both PELs; within the previous 12 months; using the sampling and analytical methods of the asbestos standard in effect; work operations closely resemble current or projected operations in terms of processes, types of material, control methods, work practices, environmental conditions, and employee training; results indicate that employee exposures will not exceed PELs, or

3) Results of initial exposure monitoring of the current job – cover operations that are most likely during the performance of the entire asbestos job to result in exposures over the PELs.

Periodic Monitoring

Daily monitoring is required for Class I and II operations unless the employer has made a negative exposure assessment for the entire operation.

For Class I work, daily monitoring may be dispensed with only if all employees are equipped with supplied-air respirators operated in the pressure demand mode (or other positive pressure mode respirator) and only control methods listed in the standard are used.

For Class II work, daily monitoring may be dispensed with if all employees are equipped with supplied-air respirators operated in the positive-pressure mode.

All work operations, other than Class I and II work, where exposures are expected to exceed a PEL, must be monitored at intervals sufficient to document the validity of the exposure prediction.

Methods of Compliance

Some methods of compliance specified in the new standard apply to all covered asbestos jobs. Others are Class-specific.

Requirements Applying to All Jobs

Controls and practices that must always be used, regardless of the level of exposure, are:
- Vacuum cleaners with HEPA filters to collect asbestos-containing debris and dust,
- Wet methods or wetting agents during handling, mixing, removal, cutting, application, and clean-up (unless infeasible or creates a greater hazard) - see paragraph (g)(8)(ii) for roofing exceptions; and
- Prompt clean-up and disposal of wastes and debris contaminated with asbestos in leak-tight containers.

Controls and work practices that may never be used, regardless of the level of exposure, are:
- High-speed abrasive disc saws that are not equipped with point of cut ventilator or enclosures with HEPA filtered exhaust air;
- Compressed air to remove asbestos-containing materials, unless used in conjunction with an enclosed ventilation system to capture the dust cloud;
- Dry sweeping, shoveling or other dry clean-up of dust and debris containing ACM and PACM;

- Employee rotation to reduce employee exposure.

  For all work covered by the standard, one or more of the following controls must be used, as necessary, to achieve compliance with the PELs:

- Local exhaust ventilation equipped with HEPA filter dust collection systems;
- Enclosure or isolation of processes producing asbestos dust;
- Ventilation of the regulated area to move contaminated air away from the employee's breathing zone to a filtration or collection device equipped with a HEPA filter; or
- Other work practices and engineering controls that the Assistant Secretary for OSHA can show to be feasible.

  Note: Where the above controls are not sufficient to achieve compliance with the PELs, they must still be used and then supplemented with respiratory protection.

Requirements Applying to Specific Classes of Asbestos Work

Requirements for controls and work practices that apply to a specific Class or type of asbestos work are found in the sections of the Standard as indicated in the following table:

Class or Type of Asbestos Work	Paragraph of the Standard
Class I Requirements	(g)(4), (g)(5), (g)(6)
Class II Requirements	(g)(7), (g)(8)
Class III Requirements	(g)(9)
Class IV Requirements	(g)(10)
Installing, removing, repairing, or maintaining intact pipeline asphaltic wrap	(g)(11)
Installing, removing, repairing, or maintaining intact roof cements, mastics, coatings, or flashings which contain asbestos fibers encapsulated or coated by bituminous or resinous compounds	(g)(11)

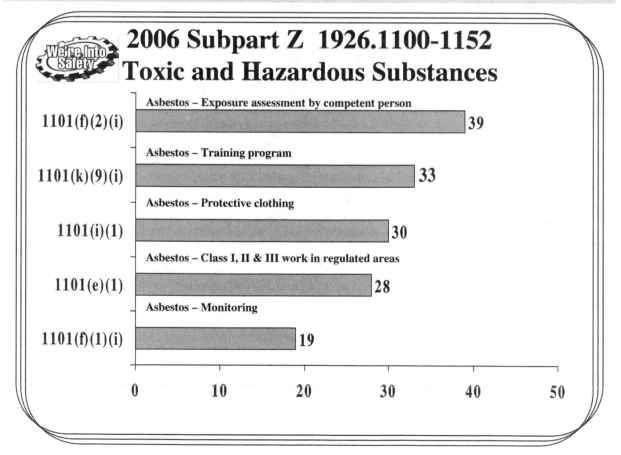

2006 Subpart Z 1926.1100-1152
Toxic and Hazardous Substances

Paragraph	Description	Value
1101(f)(2)(i)	Asbestos – Exposure assessment by competent person	39
1101(k)(9)(i)	Asbestos – Training program	33
1101(i)(1)	Asbestos – Protective clothing	30
1101(e)(1)	Asbestos – Class I, II & III work in regulated areas	28
1101(f)(1)(i)	Asbestos – Monitoring	19

Lead in Construction: Task-Specific Engineering Control Options

The focus of this handout is on types of engineering controls that may be effective for specific construction activities or tasks. The section for lead\task is divided into "Task Description" and "Engineering Controls" segments. The "Task Description" segment briefly describes the activity and the sources of the lead exposure. Highest documented time-weighted average exposures for each specified task are indicated here. Also noted in this segment is whether OSHA requires that interim respiratory protection be used during the initial exposure assessment.

The "Engineering Controls" segment lists methods that have been shown by experience to reduce airborne exposure to lead and, consequently, the level of lead in the body. The use of feasible engineering controls, along with work practice and administrative controls, is required by OSHA's Interim Final Rule on Lead Exposure in Construction, 29 CFR 1926.62, to reduce lead exposures to or below the permissible exposure limit (PEL) of 50 micrograms per cubic meter of air. Persons wishing to review the definitions of engineering, work practice, and administrative controls should consult Appendix A of this handout.

No *specific* engineering controls are mandated. Employers are free to select any feasible engineering controls that effectively reduce exposure.

Not all of the listed controls will be effective for any given set of construction conditions. In particular, outdoor activities may be more difficult to control through engineering methods than those activities carried out indoors or in partially finished structures.

If feasible engineering, work practice and administrative controls have been instituted and found to be insufficient to reduce exposure to or below the PEL they must continue to be used and supplemented by respirators. Required respiratory protection for different levels of exposure is described in Table I of the standard. For a number of activities, OSHA has determined that interim respiratory protection is required even during the initial exposure assessment because of the severity of the anticipated exposure. In most cases, the anticipated exposure is not the highest documented exposure. It is the average exposure level that, statistically, would only be exceeded five percent of the time the activity was monitored.

Employers should note that, where interim respiratory protection is required, the standard also requires that employees be provided with personal protective clothing and equipment, change areas, hand washing facilities, blood sampling, and training.

In all cases, employers are free to use additional controls to further reduce lead exposures below the level required by the standard.

Abrasive Blasting

Abrasive blast cleaning is a process through which paint, rust, and mill scale are removed from a structure, usually prior to repainting. The blasting process usually uses compressed air to propel the blasting medium to the surface being cleaned.

The blasting medium will either be manufactured (e.g., steel shot or steel grit), a natural mineral (e.g., silica sand, garret, etc.) or slag (a product of coal boiling operations, mineral smelter operations, etc.), or an agricultural by-product (e.g., walnut shells). Health hazards produced in these operations come primarily from airborne lead dust and particulate that may be inhaled or ingested. Additional health problems may be created by the medium used (e.g., airborne crystalline silica). Current research has found concentrations as high as 58,700 micrograms per cubic meter in these operations. Potential environmental contamination of air, soil and water at the job site must be evaluated and controlled.

Interim *Respiratory Protection Required*: Yes; any type of respirator in Table I that provides adequate protection for an airborne concentration of lead greater than 2,500 *micrograms per cubic meter*.

Engineering Controls
Less Dusty Abrasive
Examples are coal slag, steel shot, and steel grit.

Containments or Enclosures (partial or full)
Partial containment total enclosure of a section of a structure (usually more convenient due to size of most structures and much easier to ventilate). Full containment: total enclosure of all of a structure (usually difficult to accomplish due to size of most structures and wind loads created by "sail-effects" of containment materials).

Ventilation
1. Containment structures using ventilation should be designed to allow sufficient air movement for lead dust/abrasive removal.
2. Filtration system must be adequate to remove lead dust/abrasive from exhausted air.
3. Containment structure must be properly sealed and maintained to ensure proper removal of airborne dusts/abrasive.

Recyclable Abrasive Systems
This system, like conventional blasting, uses compressed air to propel the abrasive medium to the surface being cleaned. The difference, however, is that the spent abrasive and waste are collected and separated and the abrasive reused.
1. Less waste from abrasive materials is produced than when blasting with expendable abrasive.
2. Containment area must be deigned to ensure effective removal of waste and abrasive.
3. Recycling equipment must be monitored to ensure waste is removed from abrasive and not reblown into the containment area.
4. Airborne silica hazard is eliminated.

Vacuum Blasting Systems
This system uses a specially designed blasting nozzle that applies abrasive medium like conventional blasting but simultaneously vacuums the spent abrasive and waste. The abrasive is later separated from the waste and reused.
1. Airborne lead exposures are significantly reduced.
2. More time consuming than conventional blasting.

Wet Abrasive Blast Cleaning
This system uses compressed air to propel the abrasive medium to- the surface being cleaned; however, water is injected into the abrasive stream either before or after the abrasive exits the nozzle.
1. Airborne lead exposures are eliminated.
2. Waste produced can create containment and removal difficulties.

High Pressure Water Jetting with Abrasive Injection
This system uses an expendable abrasive medium that is metered into a pressurized water jet (up to 20,000 psi) for surface preparation.
1. Airborne lead exposures are eliminated.
2. Waste produced can create containment and removal difficulties.

Ultra-High Pressure Water Jetting
This system uses pressurized water (above 20,000 psi up to 40,000 psi or greater) to prepare surface. No abrasive medium is used.
1. Airborne lead exposures are eliminated.
2. Waste produced can create containment and removal difficulties.

Ultra-High Pressure Water Jetting with Abrasive Injection
This system uses an expendable abrasive medium that is metered into a pressurized water jet (above 20,000 psi up to 40,.000 psi or greater) for surface preparation.
1. Airborne lead exposure are eliminated.
2. Waste produced can create containment and removal difficulties.

Other Paint or Isolation Removal Alternative Methods
1. Chemical Stripping
2. Encapsulation
3. Power tool cleaning

Welding and Cutting
Welding and cutting are processes by which metal pieces are joined together or severed apart, usually performed with an oxy-acetylene torch or an arc welding rod holder. This operation is typically seen in new construction, maintenance or demolition of steel structures. Health hazards created by

this process are from lead-based paint on the structure becoming superheated and released into the air in the form of a fume. Current research has found concentrations as high as 28,000 micrograms per cubic meter in these operations.

Interim Respiratory Protection Required:
Yes; any type of respirator in Table I that provides adequate protection for an airborne concentration of lead greater than 2,500 micrograms per cubic meter.

Engineering Controls
Portable Local Exhaust Ventilation (LEV)
Method of removing from work area lead fume and gases.
1. Must be equipped with HEPA or equivalent filter.
2. Use is limited by location of welding operation.

Removal of Lead-Based Paint Area
This method involves the stripping back of at least 4 inches of paint from area of heat application. Abrasive blasting or other methods can be used.

Hydraulic Shears for Cutting Steel Coated with Lead-Based Paint
Method of mechanically cutting metal.
1. Lead fume hazard is eliminated.
2. Use is limited by access of shears to cutting area.

Working Upwind of Welding/Cutting Areas
Containment or Enclosure:
1. Use limited by work location.
2. Must be used in conjunction with exhaust ventilation system.
3. Must be properly sealed to ensure effective operation of exhaust ventilation system.

Partitions
1. Help confine lead fume to local area.
2. Must be used in conjunction with LEV.

Lead Burning

Lead burning is a process by which lead or alloyed lead is melted with a torch or otherwise fused to another lead object. This operation is typically seen in maintenance operations of electrostatic precipitators or the installation of lead shot, bricks, or sheets in the walls and/or floors of health care X-ray units and/or industrial sites. Lead health hazards in this operation are from lead that is superheated and released into the air in the form of a fume. Additional exposures occur from airborne lead dust released during handling of materials. Current research has documented exposures as high as 2,557 micrograms per cubic meter.

Interim Respiratory Protection Required:
Yes; any type of respirator in Table I that provides adequate protection for an airborne concentration of lead greater than 500 micrograms per cubic meter.

Engineering Controls
Portable Local Exhaust Ventilation (LEV)
Method of vacuuming from work area lead fume and other gases.
LEV must be equipped with HEP A or equivalent filter. Use is limited by location of burning operation

Containment or Enclosure
1. Use limited by work location.
2. Must be used in conjunction with exhaust ventilation system.
3. Must be properly sealed to ensure effective operation of exhaust ventilation system.

Use of Power Tools for Cleaning and Rivet Busting

The use of power tools for cleaning involves tools such as needle guns, grinders, brushes, and sanders to remove dirt, scale, or lead-based paints from coated surfaces. This activity is seen in various construction activities including lead abatement. Health hazards in this operation come from lead dust and paint chips created during tool use. Current research has indicated exposure levels as high as 20,600 micrograms per cubic meter.

Rivet busting involves the use of pneumatic tools to remove rivets from steel structures where lead-containing paints are present. Rivet busting can also involve the use of torches as well as mechanical means for rivet extraction.

Health hazards in this operation come from lead dust and paint chips. Where torches are used, lead fumes will be present as well.

If you are doing residential lead abatement, there may be specific requirements for engineering controls, work practice controls and PPE. These requirements are beyond the scope of this [manual] and it is recommended that you contact the appropriate State agency for additional information.

Interim Respiratory Protection Required:
Yes; for power tool cleaning with dust collection systems, any type of respirator in Table L. For power tool cleaning without dust collection systems, any type of respirator in Table I that provides adequate protection from airborne concentrations of lead greater than 500 micrograms per cubic meter.

For rivet busting, any type of respirator in Table I that provides adequate protection for an airborne concentration of lead greater than 500 micrograms per cubic meter.

Engineering Controls
**Use of Shrouded Tool
with Exhaust Ventilation**
Must be equipped with HEPA or equivalent filter and appropriate collection system.

Painting with Lead-Based Paint
Painting with lead-based paint involves the application of lead-containing paints, typically primers, through spray equipment or by hand. These paints are still used in interior and exterior spray operations. The health hazard in this operation is from airborne lead created through the overspray and rebound of paint spray off the structure being painted. Current research has indicated exposure levels as high as 460 micrograms per cubic meter. Interim Respiratory Protection is required for any type of respirator listed in OSHA's Table L.

Engineering Controls
**Non-Lead Containing Paints and Primers
Hand Applying Lead-Based Paint
Portable Local Exhaust Ventilation (LEV)**
Method of removal of paint overspray and solvents from work area.

1. HEPA or equivalent filtration must be used.
2. Use is limited by location of painting operation.

Containments or Enclosures
1. Use limited by work location.
2. Must be used in conjunction with exhaust ventilation system.
3. Must be properly sealed to ensure effective operation of exhaust ventilation system.

Hand Scraping and Sanding of Lead-Based Paint

Hand scraping and sanding of lead-based paints involves the use of hand-held scraping or sanding tools to remove paint from coated surfaces. These operations are usually seen in lead abatement projects. The health hazards in this activity are from dust and paint chips produced in the scraping or sanding process. Current research has indicated exposure levels as high as 167 micrograms per cubic meter. If you are doing residential lead abatement, there may be specific requirements for engineering controls, work practice controls and PPE in your State. Interim Respiratory Protection is required for any type of respirator listed in OSHA's Table L.

Engineering Controls
No specific controls are suggested.

Heat Gun Removal of Lead-Based Paint
In this activity the worker uses a heat gun, a tool similar in design to a hand held hair dryer, to produce a stream of hot air. This is used to partially melt the lead contaminated paint that is then scraped off. This activity is typically seen in lead-abatement projects. The health hazards encountered are from lead fumes released into the air during the heating process and lead particulate created during the scraping process. Current research has indicated exposure levels as high as 916 micrograms per cubic meter.

If you are doing residential lead abatement, there may be specific requirements for engineering controls, work practice controls and PPE in your State. Interim Respiratory Protection is required for any type of respirator listed in OSHA's Table L.

Engineering Controls
Monitor Temperature Level of Heat Gun to Reduce Burning of Lead-Based Paint

Manual Demolition and/or Removal of Plaster or Gypsum Walls or Building Components

This activity usually involves the demolition or removal of plaster or gypsum walls or building components by striking them with a sledge hammer or similar tool. Demolition and/or removal is seen in lead abatement projects and other construction activities. The health hazards encountered are from dust and paint chips generated in the break-up and removal process. Current research has indicated exposure to levels as high as 168 micrograms per cubic meter.

If you are doing residential lead abatement, there may be specific requirements for engineering controls, work practice controls and PPE in your State. Interim Respiratory Protection is required for any type of respirator listed in OSHA's Table L.

Engineering Controls
Partitions or Other Temporary Barriers
This allows for partial containment of dust.

Use of Lead Pots
If activity involves the use of a lead pot to melt lead for use in the joining or sealing of cast iron pipes. Additional exposures can occur during repair and maintenance operations in which pipe joints are heated to melt the lead caulking and then pulled apart. This activity is usually seen in plumbing trades. The health hazards in this operation are from lead fume and particulate becoming airborne. Time-weighted average exposure levels are expected to be low.

Interim Respiratory Protection Required:
No, unless the employer has any reason to believe that an employee may be exposed to lead above the PEL.

Engineering Controls
Portable Local Exhaust Ventilation (LEV)) for Use of Lead Pot
Method of removing from localized area lead fume and other gases. Must be equipped with HEPA or equivalent filter.

Lead Pot with Thermostatic Control to Reduce Fume Production

Cutting Above and Below Leaded Joints of Cast Iron Pipes
This is done during repair operations to reduce lead fume production.

Soldering and Brazing
These activities use a heat source (propane, gas or oxy-acetylene flame) and a filler metal (tin/lead composition, rosin core, brazing rods) for the joining of metal pieces or parts. This activity is usually seen in the plumbing trades. The health hazard in these operations is from lead fumes in the air.

Interim Respiratory Protection Required:
No; unless the employer has any reason to believe that an employee may be exposed to lead above the PEL.

Engineering Controls
Portable Local exhaust Ventilation (LEV)
Method of removing from localized area lead fume and other gases.
1. Must be equipped with HEPA or equivalent filter.
2. Necessary only for frequent soldering and brazing in confined spaces.

Use of Lead-Containing Mortar in Chemical (Acid) Storage and Processing Tanks

This activity involves the construction or repointing of high-pressure acid tanks with a specialized lead-containing mortar (grout). These tanks are used in the mining industry (especially during gold refining), older paper, (in tanks called "accumulations") and possibly in other industries. The tanks are constructed with either a specialized tile or lead brick lining, which periodically requires repointing, repairing, or relining. Specialty contractors usually do construction of this nature. The health hazards are from lead dust and particulate. Exposure levels are assumed to be similar to those for lead burning.

Interim Respiratory Protection Required:
Yes; any type of respirator in Table I that provides adequate protection for an airborne con-

centration of lead greater than 500 micrograms per cubic meter.

Engineering Controls
Portable Local Exhaust Ventilation (LEV)
Method of removing from localized area lead fume and particulate must be equipped with a HEPA or equivalent filter

Full Enclosure of Work Area Maintained Under Negative Pressure

Removal and Repair of Stained Glass Windows

These tasks involve several distinct activities:
- Removal of the glass from the building structure;
- Tracing the locations of the pieces of glass;
- Disassembly of the lead strips (cane) and removal of the lead putty which seals it;
- Cleaning of the individual pieces of glass; and
- Reassembly and soldering of lead strips (cane).

Only the first activity, removal, takes place at the construction site. The latter steps usually occur at the workshop. Glaziers usually do these operations during restoration or repair jobs. The health hazards are from lead dust released into air during glass removal. Current research has indicated exposure levels as high as 79 micrograms per cubic meter.

Interim Respiratory Protection Required:
No; unless the employer has any reason to believe that an employee may be exposed to lead above the PEL.

Engineering Controls
Portable Local Exhaust Ventilation (LEV)
Method of removing from localized area lead particulate.
1. Must be equipped with HEPA or equivalent filter.
2. Use limited by location of repair operation.

Enclosure Movement and Associated Miscellaneous Activities

The workers involved with these tasks support in various ways the jobs that produce the primary lead exposures. The tasks include:
- Setting up, tearing down and moving of containment structures/materials;
- Support activities for burning, cutting and welding operations;
- Support activities for abrasive blasting;
- Support activities for power tool cleaning;
- Support activities for lead-based painting operations; and
- Support activities for demolition operations.

The lead exposures encountered from these operations are from fumes, dusts and other particulates. Current research has indicated exposure levels as high as 2,100 micrograms per cubic meter for abrasive blasting enclosure movement. In general, the level of protection offered these support workers would probably need to be equivalent to the protection used by those individuals either directly or indirectly involved in the job being done.

Interim Respiratory Protection Required: See below.
For Cleanup Activities Where Dry Expendable Abrasives are Used: Any type of respirator in Table I that provides adequate protection for an airborne concentration of lead greater than 0.500 micrograms per cubic meter.

For Abrasive Blasting Enclosure Movement and Removal: Any type of respirator in Table I that provides adequate protection for an airborne concentration of lead greater than 500 micrograms per cubic meter.

For Other Activities: None, unless the employer has any reason to believe that an employee may be exposed to lead above the PEL.

Engineering Controls
The engineering controls used will vary depending upon the support activities being done. Refer to the activity being supported to determine engineering control options.

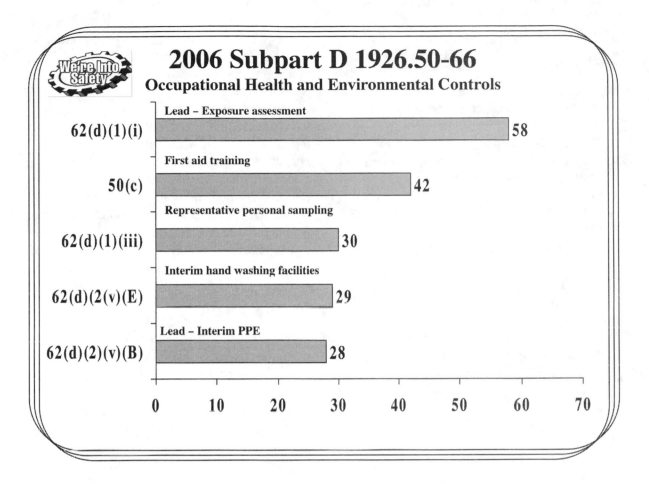

2006 Subpart D 1926.50-66
Occupational Health and Environmental Controls

We're Into Safety

Standard	Description	Value
62(d)(1)(i)	Lead – Exposure assessment	58
50(c)	First aid training	42
62(d)(1)(iii)	Representative personal sampling	30
62(d)(2(v)(E)	Interim hand washing facilities	29
62(d)(2)(v)(B)	Lead – Interim PPE	28

(axis: 0 10 20 30 40 50 60 70)

Bloodborne Pathogens

Bloodborne pathogens are pathogenic micro-organisms that are present in human blood and can infect and cause disease in humans. These pathogens include, but are not limited to, Hepatitis B Virus (HBV), which causes Hepatitis B, a serious liver disease and Human Immune Deficiency Virus (HIV), which causes Acquired Immunodeficiency Syndrome (AIDS).

OSHA has determined that certain employees (particularly healthcare employees) face a significant health risk as a result of occupational exposure to blood and other potentially infectious materials (OPIM) because they may contain bloodborne pathogens.

To minimize or eliminate the risk of occupational exposure to bloodborne pathogens, OSHA issued the Occupational Exposure to Bloodborne Pathogens Standard (29 CFR 1910.1030). This standard prescribes actions that employers must take to reduce the risk of exposure to bloodborne pathogens in the workplace. These actions include the use of:

- Engineering and work practice controls;
- Personal protective equipment;
- Training;
- Medical surveillance;
- Hepatitis B vaccinations; and
- Signs and labels.

Scope and Application

The standard applies to all employees with occupational exposure to blood and OPIM. Occupational exposure means "a reasonably anticipated skin, eye, mucous membrane or parenteral contact with blood or OPIM that may result from the performance of the employees duties." Blood is defined as "human blood, human blood components, and products made from human blood."

OPIM includes the following human body fluids:

- Semen;
- Vaginal secretions;
- Cerebrospinal fluid;
- Synovial fluid;
- Pleural fluid;
- Perinicardial fluid;
- Peritoneal fluid;
- Amniotic fluid;

- Saliva in dental procedures;
- Any body fluid visibly contaminated with blood; and
- All body fluids in situations where it is difficult or impossible to differentiate between body fluids.
  OPIM also includes:
- Unfixed tissue or organs from a human;
- FHV-containing cells or tissue cultures;
- Organ cultures and HIV- or HBV-containing culture medium or other solutions; and
- Blood, organs or other tissue from experimental animals infected with HIV or HBV.

The Bloodborne Pathogens Standard covers many types of employees including those in healthcare, non-healthcare, and permanent and temporary worksites. Examples of employees in healthcare facilities include physicians and surgeons, nurses, dentists and dental workers, and laboratory personnel. Non-healthcare facilities employees include those who service and repair medical and dental equipment, infectious waste disposal employees and employees in law enforcement and correctional institutions.

Exposure Control Plan

The Exposure Control Plan (ECP) is the key provision of the standard. It requires the employer to identify employees who will receive training, protective equipment, vaccination and other provisions of the standard.

The ECP requires employers to identify, in writing, tasks and procedures as well as job classifications where occupational exposure to blood occurs without regard to personal protective equipment. The plan must also set forth the schedule for implementing other provisions of the standard and specify the procedure for evaluating circumstances surrounding exposure incidents. It must be accessible to employees and available to OSHA and National Institute for Occupational Safety and Health (NIOSH) representatives. Employers must review and update the plan annually or more often if changes in exposure occur.

Methods of Compliance

The standard describes various methods of compliance that the employer must take to protect their employees from exposure to bloodborne pathogens. These methods include universal precautions, engineering and work practice controls, personal protective equipment and housekeeping.

Universal precautions is an approach to infection control in which all human blood and certain body fluids are treated as if known to be infectious for HIV, HBV, and other bloodborne pathogens. Universal precautions are OSHA's required method of control to protect employees from exposure to all human blood and OPIM.

Engineering controls are controls that isolate or remove the bloodborne pathogens hazard from the workplace. Examples of engineering controls include puncture-resistant sharps containers; mechanical needle recapping devices; and biosafety cabinets. To ensure effectiveness, engineering controls must be examined and maintained or replaced on a regularly scheduled basis.

Work practice controls reduce the likelihood of exposure by altering the manner in which a task is performed. Some examples of work practice requirements in the standard include not bending or breaking contaminated sharps and hand washing when gloves are removed and as soon as possible after contact with body fluids.

Personal protective equipment must be used if occupational exposure remains after instituting engineering and work practice controls or if these controls are not feasible. Personal protective equipment is specialized clothing or equipment that is worn by an employee for protection against a hazard. Employers must provide, at no cost, and require employees to use appropriate personal protective equipment such as gloves, gowns, masks, mouthpieces, and resuscitation devices. The employer must clean, repair and replace these safety items when necessary.

In addition to other compliance methods, the standard requires that the employer maintain the work site in a clean and sanitary condition. Employees must follow certain procedures for cleaning and decontaminating the environment, equipment and work surfaces and for handling contaminated laundry and regulated waste.

Contaminated work surfaces must be decontaminated with a disinfectant upon completion of procedures or when contaminated by splashes, spills or contact with blood or OPIM. The employer must develop a written schedule for cleaning and decontaminating the work site based on the location within the facility, type of surface to be cleaned, amount of soil and the task being performed. Reusable trash containers must also be cleaned on a regular basis and after contamination.

Contaminated laundry is any laundry that may contain blood or OPIM or may contain sharps. The standard requires that contaminated laundry be handled as little as possible with a minimum of agitation. It must be bagged or containerized at the location where it was used and not be sorted or rinsed where it was used. Contaminated laundry must also be placed and transported in bags or containers and properly labeled. When a facility uses universal precautions in handling soiled laundry, alternative labeling or color-coding is sufficient if it permits all employees to recognize the containers as requiring compliance with universal precautions.

Regulated waste is defined in the standard as:
- Liquid or semi-liquid blood or OPIM;
- Contaminated items that would release blood or OPIM in a liquid or semi-liquid state if compressed;
- Items that are caked with dried blood or OPIM and are capable of releasing these materials during handling;
- Contaminated sharps; and
- Pathological and microbiological waste containing blood or OPIM.

Regulated waste must be placed in closeable, leak-proof containers designed to contain all contents during handling, storing, transporting, or shipping and labeled appropriately.

Hepatitis B Vaccination and Post-Exposure Evaluation and Follow-up

The employer is required to make available the Hepatitis B vaccine and vaccination series to all employees who may be exposed in the workplace and post-exposure evaluation and follow-up to all employees who have had an exposure incident. All medical evaluations and procedures must be provided:

- At no cost to the employee;
- At a reasonable time and place;
- Under the supervision of a licensed physician or health care professional; and
- According to current recommendations of the U.S. Public Health Service.

The Hepatitis B vaccine and vaccination series must be offered within 10 working days of initial assignment to employees who have occupational exposure to blood or OPIM. Exceptions to this requirement are:
- When employees have previously completed the Hepatitis B vaccination series;
- Immunity is confirmed through anti-body testing; or
- The vaccine is contraindicated for medical reasons.

Employees must sign a declination form if they choose not to be the vaccinated; however, they may request and obtain the vaccination at a later date at no cost.

A confidential medical evaluation and follow-up must be made available to an employee involved in an exposure incident. An exposure incident is a specific eye, mouth, other mucous membrane, nonintact skin or parenteral contact with blood or OPIM that results from the performance of an employee's duties.

The evaluation and follow-up procedures must include
- Documenting the circumstances of exposure;
- Identifying and testing the source individual, if feasible;
- Testing the exposed employee's blood if he or she consents; and
- Conducting post-exposure prophylaxis, counseling and evaluation of reported illnesses.

Following the post-exposure evaluation, the healthcare professional must provide a written opinion to the employer. This opinion is limited to a statement that the employee has been informed of the need, if any, for further evaluation or treatment. All other findings are confidential. The employer must provide a copy of the written opinion to the employee within 15 days of the evaluation.

Communication of Hazards to Employees

The hazards of bloodborne pathogens must be communicated to employees through signs, labels and training. The standard requires that warning labels be attached to containers of regulated waste, refrigerators or freezers containing blood or OPIM, and other containers used to store, transport, or ship blood or OPIM.

The warning label must include the universal biohazard symbol followed by the term "BIOHAZARD" in a fluorescent orange or orange-red color with lettering or symbols in a contrasting color.

The labels are not required when:

- Red bags or red containers are used for regulated waste;
- Regulated waste has been decontaminated;
- Individual containers of blood or OPIM are placed in a labeled container during storage, transport, shipment or disposal; and
- Containers of blood or blood products are labeled as to their content and have been released for transfusion or other clinical use.

Contaminated equipment must also be marked with a label that states which portion of the equipment remains contaminated.

The biohazard label must also be posted at the entrance to HIV and HBV research laboratories and production facilities work areas. The employer must ensure that all employees with occupational exposure participate in an effective training program. Training must be provided within 90 days after the effective date of the standard and annually thereafter.

An individual who is knowledgeable in the subject matter must provide training at no cost to employees during a time that is regularly accessible to employees. The training program must include an:

- Accessible copy of the regulatory text and explanation of its contents;
- Explanation of the modes of transmitting and epidemiology of HBV and HIV;
- Explanation of the written exposure control plan and how to obtain a copy;

- Explanation of use and limitations of engineering controls, work practices and personal protective equipment.

The training materials must be appropriate in content, language and vocabulary to the educational, literacy, and language background of the employees.

Recordkeeping

Employers must establish and maintain accurate records for each employee with occupational exposure. The standard requires employers to maintain two types of employee-related records: medical and training. The medical records must include:

- Employee's name and social security number,
- Employee's Hepatitis B vaccination status;
- Post-exposure evaluation and follow-up procedures results, as necessary;
- The healthcare professional's written opinion, as necessary; and
- Other specific information that has been provided to the healthcare professional.

The medical record must be kept confidential and retained for the duration of employment plus 30 years in accordance with OSHA's Access to Employee Exposure and Medical Records Standard. These records must be made available upon request to employees, anyone with the written consent of the employee and OSHA and NIOSH representatives.

Training records must include:

- Training dates;
- Contents or summary of the training session;
- Names and qualifications of the trainers; and
- Names of job titles of trainees.

All training records must be kept for three years from the date of the training. If the employer ceases to do business, medical and training records must be transferred to the successor employer. If there is no successor employer, the employer must notify the Director of NIOSH for instructions regarding the disposal of records. This must be done at least three months prior to the disposing of the records.

Work Activities Involving Potential Exposure to Bloodborne Pathogens

Below are listed the tasks and procedures in our facility where human blood and other potentially infectious materials are handled that may result in exposure to bloodborne pathogens:

Procedure/Task	Job Classification	Location/Department

Vaccination Declination Form

DATE:_____

Employee Name: _____

Employee ID #: _____

I understand that due to my occupational exposure to blood or other potential infectious materials I may be at risk of acquiring Hepatitis B virus (HBV) infection. I have been given the opportunity to be vaccinated with Hepatitis B vaccine at no charge to myself.

However, I decline the Hepatitis B vaccination at this time. I understand that by declining this vaccine, I continue to be at risk of acquiring Hepatitis B, a serious disease. If, in the future, I continue to have occupational exposure to blood or other potentially infectious materials and I want to be vaccinated with Hepatitis B vaccine, I can receive the vaccination series at no charge to me.

_____   _____

Employee Signature   Date

_____   _____

Facility Representative Signature   Date

Hearing Conservation

OSHA has recognized the hazards caused by noise on construction projects for many years. OSHA's noise standard for construction stems from the occupational noise standard originally published in 1969 by the Bureau of Labor Standards under the authority of the Construction Safety Act (40 USC 333).

Another section of the construction standard (29 CFR 1926.101) contains a provision requiring employers to provide hearing protection devices when needed. Both sections 1926.52 and 1926.101 apply to employers engaged in construction and renovation work when high noise levels are present.

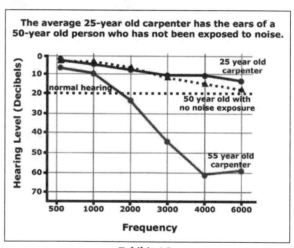

Exhibit 4-2.
Hearing loss due to long-term exposure.

Occupational Noise Exposure Standards in Construction

Paragraph (a) of section 1926.52 requires protection against the effects of noise exposure when eight-hour time-weighted average sound levels exceed a permissible exposure limit (PEL) of 90 decibels (dBA) measured on the A scale of a sound level meter set at slow response. The exposure level is raised 5 dB for every halving of exposure duration as shown in Table D-2 of the standard (See Exhibit 4-3.).

Exhibit 4-3. Table D-2. Construction permissible noise exposure.

Duration per day in hours	Sound level dBA slow response
8	90
6	92
4	95
3	97
2	100
1½	102
½	110
¼ or less	115

Paragraph 29 CFR 1926.52(b) states that when employees are subjected to noise doses exceeding those shown in Table D-2, feasible administrative or engineering controls must be used to lower employee noise exposure. If such controls fail to reduce sound to the levels shown in the table, personal protective equipment must be provided and used to reduce noise exposure to within acceptable levels.

Paragraph (c) defines continuous noise as noise levels where the maxima occur at intervals of 1 second or less, and paragraph (d)(1) requires that a "continuing, effective hearing conservation program" be administered whenever levels exceed those in Table D-2. However, no details are given about the components of such a program. Paragraph (d)(2) gives instruction on how to calculate an employee's noise exposure when the employee is exposed to two or more periods of noise at different levels, and paragraph (e) states that exposure to impulsive or impact noise should not exceed a peak sound pressure level of 140 dB.

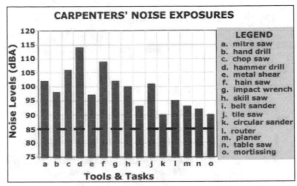

Exhibit 4-4.
Noise levels of carpenters' tools.

Hearing Protection—1926.101

- Wherever it is not feasible to reduce the noise levels or duration of exposures to those specified in Table D-2, Permissible Noise Exposures, in §1926.52, ear protective devices shall be provided and used.
- Ear protective devices inserted in the ear shall be fitted or determined individually by competent persons.
- Plain cotton is not an acceptable protective device.

Occupational Noise Exposure—1926.52

Protection against the effects of noise exposure shall be provided when the sound levels exceed those shown in Table D-2 of this section when measured on the A-scale of a standard sound level meter at slow response.

When employees are subjected to sound levels exceeding those listed in Table D-2 of this section, feasible administrative or engineering controls shall be utilized. If such controls fail to reduce sound levels within the levels of the table, personal protective equipment as required in subpart E, shall be provided and used to reduce sound levels within the levels of the table.

If the variations in noise level involve maxima at intervals of 1 second or less, it is to be considered continuous.

- In all cases where the sound levels exceed the values shown herein, a continuing, effective hearing conservation program shall be administered.
- When the daily noise exposure is composed of two or more periods of noise exposure of different levels, their combined effect should be considered, rather than the individual effect of each. Exposure to different

levels for various periods of time shall be computed according to the formula set forth in paragraph (d)(2)(ii) of this section.

$$F_e = (T1 \div L1) + (T2 \div L2) + \cdots + (Tn/Ln)$$

Where:

F_e = The equivalent noise exposure factor.

T = The period of noise exposure at any essentially constant level.

L = The duration of the permissible noise exposure at the constant level (from Table D-2).

If the value of F_e exceeds unity (1) the exposure exceeds permissible levels.

(iii) A sample computation showing an application of the formula in paragraph (d)(2)(ii) of this section is as follows. An employee is exposed at these levels for these periods:

110 db A ¼ hour.

100 db A ½ hour.

90 db A 1½ hours.

$F_e = (\frac{1}{4} \div \frac{1}{2}) + (\frac{1}{2} \div 2) + (1\frac{1}{2} \div 8)$

$F_e = 0.500 + 0.25 + 0.188$

$F_e = 0.938$

Since the value of F_e does not exceed unity, the exposure is within permissible limits.

Exposure to impulsive or impact noise should not exceed 140 dB peak sound pressure level.

Occupational Noise Exposure Standard as It Applies to General Industry

Workers in general industry are covered by the Agency's Occupational Noise Standard (29 CFR 1910.95), which sets maximum noise exposure levels and certain other requirements that are similar to those found in 29 CFR 1926.52 and 1926.101. However, the general industry noise standard provides more protection for general industry workers than the construction standards provide for construction workers, due to the provisions of OSHA's 1983 Hearing Conservation Amendment (HCA). The HCA requires employers to implement a hearing conservation program if employee noise exposures exceed a time-weighted average level of 85 dBA over an eight-hour workday, using an exchange rate of 5 dB for each doubling or halving of exposure time.

The HCA program (29 CFR 1910.95(c) through (o)) includes, among other things:

- Baseline and annual audiometric testing;
- The monitoring of noise exposure levels;
- Requirements to provide effective hearing protection devices;
- Training and education; and
- The maintenance of employee exposure and hearing loss records.

HAZARD COMMUNICATION

About 32 million workers are potentially exposed to one or more chemical hazards. There are an estimated 575,000 existing chemical products, and hundreds of new ones being introduced annually. This poses a serious problem for exposed workers and their employers. Chemical exposure may cause or contribute to many serious health effects such as rashes, burns, heart ailments, kidney and lung damage, sterility, and cancer. Some chemicals may also be safety hazards and have the potential to cause fires and explosions and other serious accidents.

The Occupational Safety and Health Administration (OSHA) has issued a rule called "Hazard Communication." The goals of the standard are first, to educate employers and employees about work hazards and how to protect themselves and second, to reduce the incidence of chemical source illness and injuries. This program ensures that all employers receive the information they need to inform and train their employees properly and to design and implement employee protection programs. It also provides necessary hazard information to employees so they can participate in and support the protective measures in place at their workplaces. OSHA has developed a variety of materials and publications to help employers and employees develop and implement effective hazard communication programs.

Chemical manufacturers and importers must convey the hazard information they learn from their evaluations to downstream employer-customers by means of labels on containers and material safety data sheets (MSDSs). All covered employers must have a hazard communication program to convey this information to their employees through labels on containers, MSDSs and training. The rule incorporates a "downstream flow of information," which means that producers of chemicals have the primary responsibility for generating and disseminating information, while purchasers of chemicals must obtain the information and transmit it to their employees who work with and use the chemicals. In general, the downstream flow of information works as follows:

- **Chemical manufacturers/importers**
  - Determine the hazards of each product.
- **Chemical manufacturers/importers/distributors**
  - Communicate the hazard information to customers through labels and MSDSs.
- **Employers**
  - Identify and list hazardous chemicals in their workplaces;
  - Obtain MSDSs and labels for each hazardous chemical;
  - Develop and implement a written hazard communication program, including labels, MSDSs, and employee training based on the list of chemicals, MSDSs and label information; and
  - Communicate hazard information to their employees through labels, MSDSs and formal training programs.

Hazard Evaluation

The quality of the hazard communication program depends on the adequacy and accuracy of the hazard assessment. Chemical manufacturers and importers are required to review available scientific evidence concerning the hazards of chemicals they produce or import and to report the information they find to their employees and to employers who distribute or use their products. Downstream employers can rely on the evaluations performed by the chemical manufacturers or importers to establish the hazards of the chemicals they use.

The chemical manufacturers, importers, and any employers who choose to evaluate hazards are responsible for the quality of the hazard determinations they perform. Each chemical must be evaluated for its potential to cause adverse health effects and its potential to pose physical hazards such as flammability. (Definitions of covered hazards are included in the standard.) Chemicals that are listed in one of the following sources are to be considered hazardous in all cases:

- 29 CFR 1910, Subpart Z, Toxic and Hazardous Substances, Occupational Safety and Health Administration; and
- Threshold Limit Values for Chemical Substances and Physical Agents in the Work Environment, American Conference of Governmental Industrial Hygienists (ACGIH).

In addition, chemicals that have been evaluated and found to be a suspected or confirmed carcinogen in the following sources must be reported as such:

- National Toxicology Program (NTP) Annual Report on Carcinogens; and
- International Agency for Research on Cancer (IARC) Monographs.

Chemicals that are regulated by OSHA as a carcinogen also must be reported as a carcinogen.

Written Hazard Communication Program

Employers must develop, implement, and maintain at the workplace a written, comprehensive hazard communication program that includes provisions for container labeling, the collection and availability of material safety data sheets, and an employee-training program. It also must contain a list of the haz-ardous chemicals in each work area, the means the employer will use to inform employees of the hazards of non-routine tasks (e.g., the cleaning of reactor vessels) and the hazards associated with chemicals in unlabeled pipes. If the workplace has multiple employers on site (e.g., a construction site), the standard requires each employer to ensure that information regarding hazards and protective measures be made available to all other employers at the location, where appropriate.

The written program does not have to be lengthy or complicated, and some employers may be able to rely on existing hazard communication programs to comply with the above requirements. The written program must be available to employees, their designated representatives, the Assistant Secretary of Labor for Occupational Safety and Health, and the Director of the National Institute for Occupational Safety and Health (NIOSH).

Labels and Others Forms of Warning

Chemical manufacturers, importers, and distributors must be sure that containers of hazardous chemicals leaving the workplace are labeled, tagged, or marked with the identity of the chemicals, appropriate hazard warnings, and the name and address of the manufacturer or other responsible party.

Each container in the workplace must be labeled, tagged, or marked with the identity of hazardous chemicals that it contains. This marking must show hazard warnings appropriate for employee protection. The hazard warning can be any type of message, words, pictures, or symbols that convey the hazards of the chemicals in the container. Labels must be legible and be in English (plus other languages, if desired). Labels must be prominently displayed.

There are, however, certain exemptions to the requirement for in-plant individual container labels:

- Employers can post signs or placards that convey the hazard information if there are a number of stationary containers within a work area that have similar contents and hazards.
- Employers can substitute various types of standard operating procedures, process sheets, batch tickets, blend tickets, and

similar written materials for container labels on stationary process equipment if they contain the same information and are readily available to employees in the work area.

- Employers are not required to label portable containers into which hazardous chemicals are transferred from labeled containers and that are intended only for the immediate use of the employee who makes the transfer.
- Employers are not required to label pipes or piping systems.

Material Safety Data Sheets

Chemical manufacturers and importers must develop an MSDS for each hazardous chemical they produce or import and must automatically provide the MSDS at the time of the initial shipment of a hazardous chemical to a downstream distributor or user. Distributors must also ensure that downstream employers are provided an MSDS.

Each MSDS must be written in English and include:

- The specific chemical identities of the hazardous chemicals involved and their common names;
- The physical and chemical characteristics of the hazardous chemicals;
- Known acute and chronic health effects and related health information;
- Exposure limits;
- Whether the chemicals are considered to be carcinogenic by NTP, IARC, or OSHA;
- Precautionary measures;
- Emergency and first-aid procedures; and
- The identification of the organization responsible for preparing the sheet.

Copies of the MSDS for hazardous chemicals in a given work site are to be readily accessible to employees in that area. As a source of detailed information on hazards, they must be located close to workers and readily available to them during each work shift.

List of Hazardous Chemicals

Employers must prepare a list of all hazardous chemicals in the workplace. When the list is complete, it should be checked against all of the MSDSs the employer has been sent. If there are hazardous chemicals used for which no MSDS

has been received, the employer must write to the supplier, manufacturer, or importer to obtain an MSDS. If employers do not receive an MSDS within a reasonable period of time, they should contact the nearest OSHA office.

Employee Information and Training

Employers must establish a training and information program for employees exposed to hazardous chemicals in their work areas at the time of their initial assignment and whenever a new hazard is introduced into their work areas. At a minimum, the discussion topics must include:

- The existence and requirements of the hazard communication standard;
- The components of the hazard communication program;
- Operations in work areas where hazardous chemicals are present; and
- Where the employer will keep the written hazard evaluation procedures, communications program, lists of hazardous chemicals, and the required MSDSs.

The employee training plan must consist of the following elements:

- How the hazard communication program is implemented in that workplace, how to read and interpret information on labels and MSDSs, and how employees can obtain and use the available hazard information.
- The hazards of the chemicals in the work area (some hazards may be discussed by individual chemical or by hazard categories such as flammability);
- Measures employees can take to protect themselves from the hazards;
- Specific procedures put into effect by the employer to provide protection, such as engineering controls, work practices, and the use of personal protective equipment (PPE); and
- Methods and observations, such as visual appearance or smell, workers can use to detect the presence of a hazardous chemical to which they may be exposed.

Trade Secrets

A trade secret is something that gives an employer an opportunity to obtain an advantage over competitors who do not know about the trade secret or who do not use it. For example, a trade secret may be a confidential device, pattern, information, or chemical make-up. The standard strikes a balance between the need to protect exposed employees and the employer's need to maintain the confidentiality of a bona fide trade secret. This is achieved by providing for limited disclosure to health professionals who are furnishing medical or other occupational health services to exposed employees or to employees and their designated representatives, under specified conditions of need and confidentiality.

Medical Emergency

The chemical manufacturer, importer, or employer must immediately disclose the specific chemical identity of a hazardous chemical to a treating physician or nurse when the information is needed for proper emergency or first-aid treatment. As soon as circumstances permit, the chemical manufacturer, importer, or employer may obtain a written statement of need and a confidentiality agreement. The treating physician or nurse has the ultimate responsibility for determining that a medical emergency exists. At the time of the emergency, the professional judgment of the physician or nurse regarding the situation must form the basis for triggering the immediate disclosure requirement. Because the chemical manufacturer, importer, or employer can demand a written statement of need and a confidentiality agreement to be completed after the emergency is abated, further disclosure of the trade secret can be effectively controlled.

Non-Emergency Situations

In non-emergency situations, chemical manufacturers, importers, or employers must disclose the withheld specific chemical identity to health professionals providing medical or other occupational health services to exposed employees, and to employees and their designated representatives only if certain conditions are met. In this context, "health professionals" include physicians, occupational health nurses, industrial hygienists, toxicologists, and epidemiologists. The request for information must be in writing and must describe with reasonable detail the medical or occupational health

need for the information. The request will be considered if the information will be used for one or more of the following activities:

- To assess the hazards of the chemicals to which employees will be exposed;
- To conduct sampling of the workplace atmosphere to determine exposure levels;
- To conduct medical surveillance of exposed employees;
- To provide medical treatment to exposed employees;
- To select or assess personal protective equipment for exposed employees;
- To design or assess protective measures for exposed employees; or
- To conduct studies to determine the health effects of exposure.

The health professional, employee, or employee's designated representative also must specify why alternative information is insufficient. The request for information must explain in detail why disclosure of the specific chemical identity is essential and include the procedures to be used to protect the confidentiality of the information. It must include an agreement not to use the information for any purpose other than the health need stated or to release it under any circumstances, except to OSHA.

Guidelines for Compliance

The Hazard Communication Standard (HCS) is based on a simple concept—that employees have both a need and a right to know the identities of the chemicals they are exposed to when working and the hazards the chemicals present. They also need to know what protective measures are available to prevent adverse effects from occurring. Accordingly, the HCS is designed to provide employees with this information.

Knowledge acquired under the HCS will help employers provide safer workplaces for their employees. When employers have information about the chemicals being used, they can take steps to reduce exposures, substitute less hazardous materials, and establish proper work practices. These efforts will help prevent the occurrence of work-related illnesses and injuries caused by chemicals.

The HCS addresses the issues of evaluating and communicating hazards to workers. The evaluation of chemical hazards involves a number of technical concepts, and is a process that requires the professional judgment of experienced experts. That is why the HCS is designed so that employers who simply use chemicals, rather than produce or import them, are not required to evaluate the hazards of those chemicals. Hazard determination is the responsibility of the producers and importers of the materials, who are then required to provide the hazard information to the employers that purchase their products.

Employers that do not produce or import chemicals need only focus on those parts of the rule that deal with establishing a workplace program and communicating information to their workers. This manual provides a general guide for such employers to help them determine what is required under the rule. It does not supplant or serve as a substitute for the regulatory provisions, but rather provides a simplified outline of the steps an average employer would follow to meet those requirements.

Become Familiar with the Rule

The standard is long and some parts of it are technical, but the basic concepts are simple. In fact, the requirements reflect what many employers have been doing for years. You may find that you are already largely in compliance with many of the provisions, and will simply have to modify your existing programs somewhat. If you are operating in an OSHA-approved state plan state, you must comply with the state's requirements, which may be different than those of the federal rule. Many of the state plan states had hazard communication or "right-to-know" laws prior to the promulgation of the federal rule. Employers in state plan states should contact their state OSHA offices for more information regarding applicable requirements.

The rule requires information to be prepared and transmitted regarding all hazardous chemicals and covers both physical hazards (e.g., flammability) and health hazards (e.g., irritation, lung damage, cancer). Most chemicals used in the workplace have some hazard potential and thus are covered by the rule.

One difference between this rule and many others adopted by OSHA is that this rule is performance oriented. That means that you have the flexibility to adapt the rule to the needs of your workplace, rather than having to follow specific, rigid requirements. It also means that you have to exercise more judgment to implement an appropriate and effective program.

The standard's design is simple. Chemical manufacturers and importers must evaluate the hazards of the chemicals they produce or import. Using that information, they must then prepare labels for containers and more detailed technical bulletins called material safety data sheets (MSDS).

Chemical manufacturers, importers, and distributors of hazardous chemicals are all required to provide the appropriate labels and MSDSs to the employers to whom they ship the chemicals. The information is to be provided automatically. Every container of hazardous chemicals you receive must be labeled, tagged, or marked with the required information. Your suppliers also must send you a properly completed MSDS at the time of the first shipment of the chemical and with the next shipment if the MSDS has been updated with significant, new information about the hazards. Workers can rely on the information received from your suppliers because they have no independent duty to analyze the chemical or evaluate the hazards of it.

Employers that use hazardous chemicals must have a program to ensure the information is provided to exposed employees. "Use" means to package, handle, react, or transfer. This is an intentionally broad scope and includes any situation where a chemical is present in such a way that employees may be exposed under normal conditions of use or in a foreseeable emergency.

Identify Responsible Staff

Hazard communication will be a continuing program for every company. Compliance with the rule is not a one-shot deal. To have a successful program, it will be necessary to assign responsibility for both the initial and ongoing activities that have to be undertaken to comply with the rule. In some cases, these activities may already be part of current job assignments. For example, site supervisors are frequently responsible for on-the-job training sessions. Early identification of the responsible employees and involvement of them in the development of your plan of action will result in a more effective program design. Evaluation of the effectiveness of your program will also be affected by the involvement of affected employees.

Identify Hazardous Chemicals in the Workplace

The standard requires a list of hazardous chemicals in the workplace as part of the written hazard communication program. The list will eventually serve as an inventory of everything for which an MSDS must be maintained. At this point, however, preparing the list will help you complete the rest of the program since it will give you some idea of the scope of the program required for compliance in your company.

The best way to prepare a comprehensive list is to survey the workplace. Purchasing records may also help. In fact, you should establish procedures to ensure that in the future, the purchasing process includes a check for an MSDS, which must be received before a material can be used in the workplace. The broadest possible perspective should be taken when conducting the survey. Sometimes people think of chemicals as being only liquids in containers. The HCS covers chemicals in all physical forms—liquids, solids, gases, vapors, fumes, and mists—whether they are contained or not. The hazardous nature of the chemical and the potential for exposure are the factors that determine whether a chemical is covered. If it is not hazardous, it is not covered. For example, if there is no potential for exposure (e.g., the chemical is inextricably bound and cannot be released), the rule does not cover the chemical.

Identify chemicals in containers, including pipes, but also think about chemicals generated in the work operations. For example, welding fumes, dusts, and exhaust fumes are all sources of chemical exposures. Read labels provided by the suppliers for hazard information. Make a list of all chemicals in the workplace that are potentially hazardous. For your own information and planning, you may also want to note on the list the locations of the products within the workplace and an indication of the hazards as found on the label.

After compiling the complete list of chemicals, you should review paragraph (b) to determine if any of the items can be eliminated from the list because they are exempted materials. For example, food, drugs, and cosmetics brought into the workplace for employee consumption are exempt; rubbing alcohol in the first-aid kit also is exempt.

Once you have compiled as complete a list as possible of the potentially hazardous chemicals in the workplace, the next step is to determine if you have received MSDSs for all of them. Check your files against the inventory you have just compiled. If any are missing, contact your supplier and request one. It is a good idea to document these requests, either by copy of a letter or a note regarding telephone conversations. If you have MSDSs for chemicals that are not in your list, figure out why. Maybe you do not use the chemical anymore. Or maybe you missed it in your survey. Some suppliers do provide MSDSs for products that are not hazardous. In these instances, you do not have to maintain the MSDS.

You should not allow employees to use any chemicals for which you have not received an MSDS. The MSDS provides information you need to ensure proper protective measures are implemented prior to exposure.

Preparing and Implementing a Hazard Communication Program

All workplaces where employees are exposed to hazardous chemicals must have a written plan that describes how the standard will be implemented in that facility. Preparation of a plan is not just a paper exercise: All of the elements must be implemented in the workplace in order to be in compliance with the rule. See paragraph (e) of the standard for the specific requirements regarding written hazard communication programs. The only work operations that do not have to comply with the written plan requirements are laboratories and work operations where employees only handle chemicals in sealed containers. The plan does not have to be lengthy or complicated. It is intended to be a blueprint for the implementation of your program—an assurance that all aspects of the requirements have been addressed.

Many trade associations and other professional groups have provided sample programs and other assistance materials to affected employers. These have been very helpful to many employers since they tend to be tailored to the particular industry involved. Although such general guidance may be helpful, you must remember that the written program has to reflect what you are doing in your workplace. Therefore, if you use a generic program it must be adapted to address the facility it covers. For example, the written plan must list the chemicals present at the site, indicate who is to be responsible for the various aspects of the program in your facility, and indicate where written material will be made available to employees. If OSHA inspects your workplace for compliance with the HCS, the OSHA compliance officer will ask to see your written plan at the outset of the inspection.

The written program must describe how the requirements for labels and other forms of warnings, MSDSs, and employee information and training, are going to be met in your facility. The following discussion provides the type of information compliance officers will be looking for to decide whether these elements of the hazard communication program have been properly addressed.

Labels and Other Forms of Warning

In-plant containers of hazardous chemicals must be labeled, tagged, or marked with the identity of the material and appropriate hazard warnings. Chemical manufacturers, importers, and distributors are required to ensure that every container of hazardous chemicals they ship is appropriately labeled with such information and with the name and address of the producer or other responsible party. Employers purchasing chemicals can rely on the labels provided by their suppliers. If the employer subsequently transfers the material from a labeled container to another container, the employer will have to label that container unless it is subject to the portable container exemption.

The primary information to be obtained from an OSHA-required label is an identity for the material and appropriate hazard warnings. The identity is any term that appears on the label, the MSDS, and the list of chemicals and thus links these three sources of information. The identity used by the supplier may be a common or trade name ("Black Magic Formula"), or a chemical name (1,1,l-trichloro-ethane). The hazard warning is a brief statement of the hazardous effects of the chemical ("flammable," "causes lung damage"). Labels frequently contain other information, such as precautionary measures ("do not use near open flame"), but this information is provided voluntarily and is not required by the rule. Labels must be legible, and prominently displayed. There are no specific requirements for size, color, or any specific text.

With these requirements in mind, the compliance officer will be looking for the following types of information to ensure that labeling will be properly implemented in your facility:

- Designation of person(s) responsible for ensuring labeling of in-plant containers;
- Designation of person(s) responsible for ensuring labeling of any shipped containers;
- Description of labeling system(s) used;
- Description of written alternatives to labeling of in-plant containers (if used); and
- Procedures to review and update label information when necessary.

Employers that are purchasing and using hazardous chemicals—rather than producing or distributing them—will primarily be concerned with ensuring that every purchased container is labeled. If materials are transferred into other containers, the employer must ensure that these are labeled as well, unless they fall under the portable container exemption (paragraph (f)(7)). In terms of labeling systems, you can simply choose to use the labels provided by your suppliers on the containers. These will generally be verbal text labels and do not usually include numerical rating systems or symbols that require special training. The most important thing to remember is that this is an ongoing duty: All in-plant containers of hazardous chemicals must always be labeled. Therefore, it is important to designate someone to be responsible for ensuring that the labels are maintained as required on the containers in your facility and that newly purchased materials are checked for labels prior to use.

Material Safety Data Sheets

Chemical manufacturers and importers are required to obtain or develop a material safety data sheet for each hazardous chemical they produce or import. Distributors are responsible for ensuring that their customers are provided a copy of these MSDSs. Employers must have an MSDS for each hazardous chemical they use. Employers may rely on the information received from their suppliers. The specific requirements for MSDSs are in paragraph (g) of the standard.

There is no specified format for the MSDS under the rule, although there are specific information requirements. OSHA has developed a non-mandatory format, OSHA Form 174, which may be used by chemical manufacturers and importers to comply with the rule. The MSDS must be written in English. You are entitled to receive from your supplier a data sheet that includes all of the information required under the rule. If you do not receive one automatically, you should request one. If you receive one that is obviously inadequate, with, for example, blank spaces that are not completed, you should request an appropriately completed one. If your request for a data sheet or for a corrected data sheet does not produce the information needed, you should contact your local OSHA area office for assistance in obtaining the MSDS.

The role of MSDSs under the rule is to provide detailed information on each hazardous chemical, including its potential hazardous effects, its physical and chemical characteristics, and recommendations for appropriate protective measures. This information should be useful to you as the employer responsible for designing protective programs as well as to the workers. If you are not familiar with MSDSs and chemical terminology, you may need to learn to use them yourself. A glossary of MSDS terms may be helpful in this regard. Generally speaking, most employers using hazardous chemicals will primarily be concerned with MSDS information regarding hazardous effects

and recommended protective measures. Focus on the sections of the MSDS that are applicable to your situation.

MSDSs must be readily accessible to employees when they are in their work areas during their work shift. This may be accomplished in several ways. You must decide what is appropriate for your particular workplace. Some employers keep the MSDSs in a binder in a central location (e.g., in the pick-up truck on a construction site). Others, particularly in workplaces with large numbers of chemicals, computerize the information and provide access through terminals. As long as employees can get the information when they need it, any approach may be used. The employees must have access to the MSDSs themselves—simply having a system where the information can be read to employees over the phone is only permitted under the mobile worksite provision, paragraph (g)(9), when employees must travel between workplaces during the shift. In this situation, employees have access to the MSDSs at the primary worksite so the telephone system is simply an emergency arrangement.

To ensure you have a current MSDS for each chemical in the plant as required, and that employee access is provided, the compliance officers will be looking for the following types of information in your written program:

- Designation of person(s) responsible for obtaining and maintaining the MSDSs;
- How such sheets are to be maintained in the workplace (e.g., in notebooks in the work area(s) or in a computer with terminal access) and how employees can obtain access to them when they are in their work area during the work shift;
- Procedures to follow when the MSDS is not received at the time of the first shipment; and
- Description of alternatives to actual data sheets in the workplace, if used.

For employers using hazardous chemicals, the most important aspect of the written program in terms of MSDSs is to ensure that someone is responsible for obtaining and maintaining the MSDSs for every hazardous chemical in the workplace. The list of hazardous chemicals required to be maintained as part of the written program will serve as an inventory. As new chemicals are purchased, the list should be updated. Many companies have found it convenient to include on their purchase orders the name and address of the person designated in their company to receive MSDSs.

Employee Information and Training

Each employee who may be exposed to hazardous chemicals when working must be provided information and be trained prior to his or her initial assignment to work with a hazardous chemical and whenever the hazard changes. "Exposure" or "exposed" under the rule means "an employee is subjected to a hazardous chemical in the course of employment through any route of entry (inhalation, ingestion, skin contact or absorption, etc.) and includes potential (e.g., accidental or possible) exposure." See paragraph (h) of the standard for specific requirements. Information and training may be conducted for each chemical or for categories of hazards. If there are only a few chemicals in the workplace, you may want to discuss each one individually. Where there are large numbers of chemicals or the chemicals change frequently, you may want to train generally based on the hazard categories (e.g., flammable liquids, corrosive materials, carcinogens). Employees will have access to the substance-specific information on the labels and MSDSs.

Information and training are a critical part of the hazard communication program. Information regarding hazards and protective measures is provided to workers through written labels and MSDSs. However, through effective information and training, workers will learn to read and understand such information, determine how it can be obtained and used in their own workplaces, and understand the risks of exposure to the chemicals in their workplace as well as ways to protect themselves. Properly conducted training programs will ensure employee comprehension and understanding. It is not sufficient to simply read material to the workers or hand it to them. You want to create a climate where workers feel free to ask questions. This will help you to ensure the information is understood. You must always remember that the underlying purpose of the HCS is to reduce the incidence of illnesses and injuries caused by chemical exposure. This will be accomplished by modifying behavior through the provision of hazard information and information about protective measures. If your program works, you and your workers will better understand the chemical hazards within the workplace. The procedures you establish regarding, for example, purchasing, storage, and handling of these chemicals will improve and thereby reduce the risks posed to employees exposed to the chemical hazards involved. Furthermore, your workers' comprehension will also be increased and proper work practices will be followed in your workplace.

In reviewing your written program with regard to information and training, the following items need to be considered:

- Designation of person(s) responsible for conducting training;
- Format of the program to be used (e.g., audiovisuals, classroom instruction);
- Elements of the training program; and
- Procedures to train employees at the time of their initial assignment to work with a hazardous chemical and when a new hazard is introduced into the workplace.

The written program should provide enough details about the employer's plans in this area to assess whether a good-faith effort is being made to train employees. In general, the most important aspects of training under the HCS are to ensure that employees are aware that they are being exposed to hazardous chemicals, that they know how to read and use labels and MSDSs, and that as a consequence of learning this information, they are following the appropriate protective measures established by the employer.

The rule does not require employers to maintain records of employee training, but many employers choose to do so. This helps monitor the program to ensure that all employees are appropriately trained. If you already have a training program, you may simply have to supplement it with whatever additional information is required under the HCS. For example, construction employers that are already in compliance with the construction standard (29 CFR 1926.21) will have little extra training to do.

An employer can provide employees information and training through whatever means found appropriate and protective. Although there would always have to be some training onsite (e.g., informing employees of the location and availability of the written program and MSDSs), employee training may be satisfied in part by general training about the requirements of the HCS and about chemical hazards on the job which is provided by, for example, trade associations, unions, colleges, and professional schools. In addition, previous training, education and experience of a worker may relieve the employer of some of the burdens of informing and training that worker. Regardless of the method relied upon, however, the employer is ultimately responsible for ensuring that employees are adequately trained. If the compliance officer finds that the training is deficient, the employer will be cited for the deficiency regardless of who actually provided the training on behalf of the employer.

Other Requirements

In addition to these specific items, compliance officers will also be asking the following questions in assessing the adequacy of the program:

- Does a list of the hazardous chemicals exist in each work area or at a central location?
- Are methods the employer will use to inform employees of the hazards of non-routine tasks outlined?
- Are employees informed of the hazards associated with chemicals contained in unlabeled pipes in their work areas?
- On multi-employer work sites, has the employer provided other employers with information about labeling systems and precautionary measures where the other employers have employees exposed to the initial employer's chemicals?
- Is the written program made available to employees and their designated representatives?

If the program adequately addresses the means of communicating information to employees in your workplace, and provides answers to the basic questions outlined above, it will be found to be in compliance with the rule. The following checklist will help to ensure you are in compliance with the rule:

- Get a copy of the rule.
- Read and understood the requirements.
- Assign responsibility for tasks to be accomplished.
- Prepare an inventory of chemicals and keep it current.
- Ensure all containers of hazardous chemicals are labeled.
- Obtain MSDS for each chemical.
- Prepare written program.
- Make MSDSs available to workers.
- Conduct training of workers who work with hazardous chemicals.
- Establish procedures to maintain current program such as an annual review.
- Establish procedures to evaluate effectiveness.

The Hazard Communication Program

Most employees work with some type of chemicals at one time or another. The federal government has established a Hazard Communication Program (often called the Right To Know Program). This program informs the worker about the chemicals that he or she may encounter so they can work safely.

There are several important parts of the program that need to be addressed:

1. A hazard evaluation must be conducted initially to determine what types of chemicals are present or are subject to be present.
2. A program must be established, in writing, that addresses who is responsible for doing what with regard to hazardous materials. For example, who is responsible for getting the MSDSs for all of the chemicals the company already has? Some points that you may want to ensure are in your plan are:
   a. Employees are required to read container labels and MSDSs.

b. Always add acids to water, not the other way around. (If you add water to acid, you risk splashing and boiling).

c. Employees must use personal protective equipment (PPE) when working with chemicals. PPE such as splash goggles, aprons, gloves, or boots should be specified.

d. Employees must know the location of eye wash stations and how to use them.

3. Labels and other forms of warnings are needed to let present and future workers know about the risks in the area.

4. MSDSs must be available for all hazardous substances.

5. Employees must be trained about their rights and responsibilities regarding hazardous materials.

Hazard Evaluation

Determine who is the best qualified to conduct the initial evaluation for hazards in the area. Review this evaluation as your organization grows and changes. If you move to another building or purchase a new piece of equipment, your evaluation and risk assessment will probably change. Part of this evaluation will be to develop a list of all of the hazardous materials that you have in your area. If you find stuff that you have not used for years, now is a good time to get rid of it! The chemicals that you retain should be listed on paper so that you can insure that you have the MSDS for each item.

The Plan Itself

The plan must be in writing. And it must be updated periodically. In order to be effective it must specify who is required to do specific things. MSDSs will come with all new chemicals, but you should specify who is responsible for contacting the manufacturer or other agency when you cannot locate an MSDS. You may want to attach the list of hazardous materials that you found in your assessment as an appendix to this plan. Another appendix may discuss the responsibilities that outside contractors must comply with in order to meet the goals of the plan. For example, outside contrac-

tors should provide a copy of any MSDSs for chemicals that they are exposing your workers to. Additionally, contractors must be provided with MSDSs for any chemical to which they may be exposed.

Material Safety Data Sheets

There should be an MSDS for every hazardous material that you have. These should be stored in a location where the employees can retrieve them. Some organizations keep them in a computer. In the event of an emergency, can the worker get to the data? The information should be readily accessible, 24 hours a day to the workers who are exposed to the danger. Often, a three-ring notebook containing the sheets will be maintained on site. All employees must be able to use the sheets. If your organization has employees who do not speak English, you have an extra challenge to insure that MSDSs are available and that the worker understands the training provided and labels that come with the product.

Employee Training

Do not forget to train your temporary help. Often these are the people who will spill something without proper equipment and then will not know what to do. All employees should be trained initially and some form of refresher training should be done annually. Then, when an accident does occur, they can respond with the proper personal protective equipment and know how to use it. Employees should realize that when they transfer chemicals to portable containers, the same rules for labeling and MSDSs apply. Different employees remember different types of training. So managers must determine which method is the best one to use to train their workers.

Often, the worker has been trained, but when asked about the hazards, they don't remember. This could be a result of the stress of "being on the spot" or it could be an indicator that the training program needs to be reviewed and possibly "beefed up." Workers should be comfortable and confident when discussing something as important as this.

Hazardous Chemicals Commonly Found on Construction Projects

This list was prepared by the Associated General Contractors of California as an example of the type of hazardous chemicals to which construction workers are exposed. The list is not complete, especially considering new chemicals are used daily. This list serves only as an example.

Acetone	Cutting oil	Cobalt	Hydrochloric acid
Acetylene gas	De-emulsifier for oil	Concrete curing compounds	Inks
Adhesives	Diesel gas or oil		
Aggregate	Drywall	Creosol	Iron
Aluminum etching agent	Enamel	Kerosene	Photogravure ink (copy machine ink)
Ammonia	Etching agents		
Antifreeze	Ethyl alcohol	Lead	Pipe (fiberglass, copper, PVC)
Arsenic compounds	Explosives	Lime (calcium oxide)	Pipe threading oil
Asbestos	Fiberglass, mineral wool	Lubricating oils	Plastics
Asphalt (petroleum)	Foam insulation and fire proofing	Lye	Polishes
		Magnesium	Propanal
Bentonite clay	Form oils	Masonry material	Putty
Benzene (and derivatives)	Freon products	Metal conduit	PVC pipe cement
Bleaching agents	Galvanized junction boxes/outlets	Methanol	Resins, epoxy/synthetics
		Mortar	Roofing felts (asbestos/tarred, etc)
Carbon black	Gasoline (petrol, ethyl)		
Caulking, sealant agents	Glues	Motor oil additives	Shellac
Cement	Graphites	Muriatic acid	Thinner/ solvents
Chromium	Greases	Naphtha (coal tar)	Tin
Cleaners	Grouts	Nitroglycerine	Transite
Cleaning agents	Gypsum (calcium sulfate)	Oxygen	Varnishes
		Ozone	Waxes
Coal tar pitch	Helium (in cylinders)	Paint remover	Wood alcohol
Coatings	Hydraulic brake fluid	Particle board	Wood preservative

Sample MSDS

OATEY ALL PURPOSE CEMENT 4 & 8 oz   Latest Revision Date   06/21/93

SECTION 1	IDENTITY OF MATERIAL
TRADE NAME	CEMENT 001 ~ OATEY ALL PURPOSE CEMENT
PRODUCT NUMBERS	30818 4 oz., 30821 8 oz.
FORMULA	PVC Resin in Solvent Solution
CHEMICAL FAMILY	PVC Organisol
SYNONYMS	PVC Plastic Pipe Cement

SECTION 2 — HAZARDOUS INGREDIENTS			
INGREDIENTS	%	CAS NUMBER	C 313
CPVC Resin (non-hazardous)	12-17%	686-48-B2-8	No
Tetrahydrofuran	40-55%	109-99-9	No
Acetone	<0.25%	67-W-1	Yes
Methyl Ethyl Ketone	25-35%	7S-93-3	Yes
Cyclohexanone	11-16%	108-94-1	No
Fumed Silica (non-hazardous)	1-2%	7631-86-9	No

SECTION 3 — KNOWN HAZARDS UNDER 29 CFR 1910.1200

HAZARDS	YES	NO	HAZARDS	YES	NO
Combustible liquid	X		Skin hazard		X
Flammable liquid	X		Eye hazard		X
Pyrophoric material		X	Toxic agent		X
Explosive material		X	Highly toxic agent		X
Unstable material		X	Sensitizer		X
Water reactive material		X	Kidney toxin	X	
Oxidizer		X	Reproductive toxin		X
Organic peroxide		X	Blood toxin		X
Corrosive material		X	Nervous system toxin		X
Compressed gas		X	Lung toxin		X
Irritant	X		Liver toxin		X

SECTION 4 — REGULATIONS

	TLV (TEA)	PEL (Transitional Limit) STEL	Hazard Action Level
Tetrahydrofuran	200ppm,590mg/cm	200ppm,590mg/cm	250ppm,35mg/cm
Acetone	750ppm,1800mg/cm	1000ppm,2400mg/cm	1000ppm,2400mg/cm
Cyclohexanone	25ppm,100mg/cm (skin)	50ppm,200mg/cm	N/A
Methyl ethyl ketone	200ppm,5909mg/cm	200ppm,5990mg/cm	300ppm,885mg/cm

HAZARD COMMUNICATION

SECTION 5 — REGULATED IDENTIFICATION

DOT PROPER SHIPPING NAME	CEMENT
DOT HAZARD CLASS	Flammable Liquid
SHIPPING ID NUMBER	NA 1133 (Gallons Only)
EPA HAZARDOUS WASTE ID NUMBER	D-001
EPA HAZARD WASTE CLASS	Ignitable Waste/Toxic Waste

SECTION 6 — EFFECTS OF EXPOSURE

ENTRY ROUTE	INHALE–YES	INGES–YES	SKIN–YES	EYE–YES

INHALATION	May cause irritation of mucous membranes, nose and throat, headache, dizziness, nausea, numbness of the extremities and narcosis in high concentrations. Has caused CNS depression and liver damage in animals, high concentrations have caused retardation of fetal development in rats.
SKIN	Chronic contact may lead to irritation and dermatitis. Chronic exposure to vapors of high concentration may cause dermatitis. May be absorbed through the skin.
EYE	Vapors or direct contact may cause irritation.
INGESTION	May be aspirated into the lungs/cause effects described under inhalation.
TARGET ORGANS	Eye, Skin, Kidney, Lung, Liver, Central Nervous System

SECTION 7 — EMERGENCY AND FIRST-AID PROCEDURES—303/623-5716

SKIN	If irritation arises, wash thoroughly with soap and water. Seek medical attention if irritation persists.
EYES	If fumes cause irritation, move to fresh air and irrigate eyes with water for 15 minutes. If irritation persists, seek medical attention. If eye is struck with wire, seek medical attention.
INHALATION	Move to fresh air. If breathing is difficult, give oxygen. If not breathing, give artificial respiration. Keep victim quiet and warm. Call a poison control center or physician immediately.
INGESTION	Drink water and call a poison control center or physician immediately. Avoid alcoholic beverages. Never give anything by mouth to an unconscious person.

SECTION 8 — PHYSICAL AND CHEMICAL PROPERTIES

NFPA HAZARD SIGNAL	HEALTH STABILITY FLAMMABILITY
BOILING POINT	15° F/66° C
MELTING POINT	N/A
VAPOR PRESSURE	145 nmHg 2 20° psi
VAPOR DENSITY (AIR = 1)	2.5
VOLATILE COMPONENTS	84-88X
SOLUBILITY IN WATER	Negligible
PH	N/A
SPECIFIC GRAVITY	0.90 +/- 0.02
EVAPORATION RATE	(8UAC = 1) = 5.5 - 8.0
APPEARANCE	Milky liquid
COLOR	Ether-like
WILL DISSOLVE IN	Tetrahydrofuran
MATERIAL IS	Liquid

SECTION 9   FIRE AND EXPLOSION HAZARD DATA

FLAMMABILITY	LEL =1.8 X Volume LIEL= 11.8 X Volt
FLASHPOINT AND METHOD USED	0-5°F/ PMCC
STABILITY	Stable
CONDITIONS TO AVOID:	Heat, sparks and open flame
HAZARDOUS DECOMPOSITION POTENTIAL:	Carbon monoxide/ carbon dioxide/hydrogen chloride/smoke.
HAZARDOU S POLYMERIZATION	Will Not Occur.
CONDITIONS TO AVOID:	None
INCOMPATIBILITY/MATERIAL TO AVOID	Acids, oxidizing materials, alkalis, chlorinated inorganics (potassium, calcium and sodium hypochlorite), copper or copper alloys.
SPECIAL FIRE FIGHTING PROCEDURE	FOR SMALL FIRES: Use dry chemical, CO_2, water or foam extinguisher.
	FOR LARGE FIRES: Evacuate area and call fire department Immediately.

SECTION 10   SPILL AND DISPOSAL INFORMATION

SPILL OR LEAK PROCEDURES	Ventilate area. Stop leak if it can be done without risk. Take up with sand, earth, or other non-combustible absorbing material.
WASTE DISPOSAL	Dispose of according to local, state, and federal regulations.

SECTION 11   SAFE USAGE DATA

PROTECTIVE EQUIPMENT TYPES

EYES:	Safety glasses with side shields.
RESPIRATORY:	NIOSH-approved canister respirator in absence of adequate ventilation.
GLOVES:	Rubber gloves
OTHER:	Eyewash and safety shower should be available.

VENTILATION...

GENERAL MECHANICAL:	Exhaust ventilation capable of maintaining emissions at the point of use below PEL.
LOCAL EXHAUST:	Open doors and windows. If used in enclosed area, use exhaust fans.

PRECAUTIONS

HANDLING and STORAGE:	Keep away from heat, sparks, and flames. Store in cool, dry place.
OTHER:	Containers, even empties, still retain residue and vapors.

SECTION 12   MANUFACTURER, OR SUPPLIER DATA

FIRM NAME AND MAILING ADDRESS	OATEY COMPANY, P.O. BOX 35906, 4700 West 160th Street, Cleveland, Ohio 44135
OATEY PHONE NUMBER	(216) 267-7100
EMERGENCY PHONE NUMBER	For emergency first aid (303) 623-5716 (COLLECT)

SECTION 13   DISCLAIMER

The information herein has been compiled from sources believed to be reliable, up-to-date, and is accurate to the best of our knowledge. However, Oatey cannot give any guarantees regarding information from other sources and expressly does not make warranties nor assumes any liability for its use.

Sample Letter Requesting an MSDS

Blitz Manufacturing Company
1923 Oak Grove Lane
Springfield, Massachusetts 02110

Dear Sir:

The Occupational Safety and Health Administration (OSHA) Hazard Communication Standard (29 CFR 1910.1200) requires employers be provided Material Safety Data Sheets (MSDSs) for hazardous substances used in their facility, and to make these MSDSs available to employees potentially exposed to these hazardous substances.

We, therefore, request a copy of the MSDS for your product listed as Stock Number _____. We did not receive an MSDS with the initial shipment of the Blitz Solvent 90 we received from you on October 1st. We also request any additional information, supplemental MSDSs, or any other relevant data that your company or supplier has concerning the safety and health aspects of this product.

Please consider this letter as a standing request to your company for any information concerning the safety and health aspects of using this product that may become known in the future.

The MSDS and any other relevant information should be sent to us within 10, 20, 30 days (select appropriate time). Delays in receiving the MSDS information may prevent use of your product. Please send the requested information to Mr. Robert Smith, Safety and Health Manager, XYZ Company, Boston, Massachusetts 02109.

Please be advised that if we do not receive the MSDS on the above chemical by (date), we may have to notify OSHA of our inability to obtain this information. It is our intent to comply with all provisions of the Hazard Communication Standard (1910.1200) and the MSDSs are integral to this effort.

Your cooperation is greatly appreciated. Thank you for your timely response to this request. If you have any questions concerning this matter, please contact Mr. Smith at (555) 123-4567.

Sincerely,
George Rogers, President
XYZ Company

Material Safety Data Sheet Checklist

Ensure that each MSDS contains the following information:

1. Product or chemical identity used on the label.
2. Manufacturer's name and address.
3. Chemical and common names of each hazardous ingredient.
4. Name, address, and phone number for hazard and emergency information.
5. Preparation or revision date.
6. The hazardous chemical's physical and chemical characteristics, such as vapor pressure and flashpoint, physical hazards the chemical presents, including the potential for fire, explosion, and reactivity.
7. Known health hazards.
8. OSHA permissible exposure limit (PEL), ACGIH threshold limit value (TLV) or other exposure limits.
9. Emergency and first-aid procedures.
10. Whether OSHA, NTP or IARC lists the ingredient as a carcinogen.
11. Precautions for safe handling and use.
12. Control measures such as engineering controls, work practices, hygienic practices, or personal protective equipment required.
13. Primary routes of entry.
14. Procedures for spills, leaks, and clean-up.

Hazard Evaluation Procedures

1. The hazard evaluation procedures required by the standard are performance oriented. Basically, OSHA's concern is that the information on labels and data sheets, and in the training program, is adequate and accurate. Although specific procedures to follow and number of sources to be consulted cannot be established, general guidance can be provided. The hazard evaluation process can be characterized as a "tiered" approach—the extent to which a chemical must be evaluated depends to a large degree upon the common knowledge regarding the chemical, whether its health effects are under review, and how prevalent it is in the workplace. The first step for evaluating chemicals is to determine whether the chemical is part of the "floor" of chemicals to be considered hazardous in all situations.

   a. The floor of chemicals consists of three sources. They are as follows:

      (1) Any substance for which OSHA has a permissible exposure limit (PEL) in 1910.1000 or a comprehensive substance-specific standard in Subpart Z. This includes any compound of such substances where OSHA would sample to determine compliance with the PEL.

      (2) Any substance for which the American Conference of Governmental Industrial Hygienists (ACGIH) has a Threshold Limit Value (TLV) in the latest edition of their annual list is to be included in the Hazard Communication Program. Any mixture or combination of these substances would also be included.

      (3) Any substance that the National Toxicology Program (NTP) or the International Agency for Research on Cancer (IARC) has found to be a suspected or confirmed carcinogen or that OSHA regulates as a carcinogen is to be included in the Hazard Communication Program.

   b. Sources to generally establish hazards of the chemicals that are part of the floor of hazardous chemicals covered by the standard:

      1) The OSHA Chemical Information Manual, OSHA Instruction CPL 2-2.43, October 20, 1987.

HAZARD COMMUNICATION

2) NIOSH/OSHA Occupational Health Guidelines.
3) Documentation for the Threshold Limit Values.
4) NTP Summary of the Annual Report on Carcinogens.
5) IARC Monographs.

In addition, the CSHO should check the NIOSH Registry of Toxic Effects of Chemical Substances (RTECS) to see if any hazards are indicated which do not appear in these sources. If there are, further study should be done to evaluate the hazards. RTECS should never be considered a definitive source for establishing a hazard since it consists of data that has not been evaluated. It is, however, a useful screening resource.

2. The second step is to consult other generally available sources to see what has been published regarding the chemical. Patty's *Industrial Hygiene and Toxicology* would be one such source. OCIS contains a number of other chemical information sources. Material safety data sheets available through information services would also be useful.

3. The third step, for those chemicals where information is not readily available or where such available information is not complete, is to perform searches of bibliographic databases. In general, the National Library of Medicine (NLM) services should be used. These include the Toxicology Data Bank (TDB), TOXLINE, and MEDLARS. The information generated by these databases should be evaluated using the criteria in Appendix B of the HCS; i.e., to qualify as an acceptable study, it must be conducted according to scientific principles (e.g., in animal studies, number of subjects is adequate to do statistical analyses of the results; control group is used, and the study must show statistically significant results indicating an adverse health effect). This evaluation obviously requires a subjective, professional assessment. Any questions should be referred to the Directorate of Compliance Programs, Office of Health Compliance Assistance (through the Regional Office) for assistance. In general, uncorroborated cases reports and in vitro studies, such as Ames tests, are useful pieces of information, but not definitive findings of hazards. Animal studies involving species other than those indicated in the acute hazard definitions must be evaluated as well. The acute hazard definitions are not included in the standard to "categorize" chemicals but rather to establish that chemicals meeting those definitions fall under the coverage of the standard.

4. In some cases, the only information available on a substance may be employer-generated data. If the employer indicates that such information is the basis for the hazard evaluation, the CSHO shall ask to see it to complete the OSHA evaluation.

5. In cases where the employer denies the CSHO access to its own hazard data and no published data on the chemical can be found to review the sufficiency of the hazard determination, the Regional Office shall be contacted for assistance in obtaining an administrative subpoena. The Directorate of Compliance Programs shall be contacted if assistance is required in order to obtain unpublished chemical hazard information available from other federal agencies such as the Environmental Protection Agency.

6. If an employer has found any chemical to be non-hazardous, and the CSHO has reason to believe it is hazardous, further investigation is required. The definitions of hazard in the standard are very broad and it is not expected that many chemicals can be considered non-hazardous under this approach. Those most likely to be exempted would be chemicals that pose no physical hazards and have lethal dose findings above the limits found in the acute hazard definitions.

7. In some cases, the employer may not have addressed in the Hazard Communication Program a specific chemical that the CSHO knows to be present through knowledge of the process, sampling, or other investigation of the workplace. This situation also should be further investigated. If the CSHO has information to indicate that there is a hazard, the employer must be able to defend its finding of no hazard.

Guide for Reviewing MSDS Completeness

1. Do chemical manufacturers and importers have an MSDS for each hazardous chemical produced or imported into the United States?
2. Do employers have an MSDS for each hazardous chemical used?
3. Is each MSDS written in English, at least?
4. Does each MSDS contain at least the:
   (a) Identity used on the label?
   (b) Chemical and common name(s) for single-substance hazardous chemicals?
   (c) For mixtures tested as a whole:
      (1) Chemical and common name(s) of the ingredients that contribute to the known hazards?
      (2) Common name(s) of the mixture itself?
   (d) For mixtures not tested as a whole:
      (1) Chemical and common name(s) of all ingredients that are health hazards (1 percent concentration or greater), including carcinogens (0.1 percent concentration or greater)?
      (2) Chemical and common name(s) of all ingredients that are health hazards and present a risk to employees, even though they are present in the mixture in concentrations of less than 1 percent or 0.1 percent for carcinogens?
   (e) Chemical and common name (s) of all ingredients that have been determined to present a physical hazard when present in the mixture?
   (f) Physical and chemical characteristics of the hazardous chemical (e.g., vapor pressure, flashpoint)?
   (g) Physical hazards of the hazardous chemical, including the potential for fire, explosion, and reactivity?
   (h) Health hazards of the hazardous chemical (including signs and symptoms and medical conditions aggravated)?
   (i) Primary routes of entry? OSHA permissible exposure limit (PEL)? The American Conference of Governmental Industrial Hygienists (ACGIH) Threshold limit value (TLV)? Other exposure limit(s) (including ceiling and other short-term limits)?
   (k) Information on carcinogen listings (reference OSHA-regulated carcinogens, those indicated in the National Toxicology Program (NTP) Annual Report on Carcinogens and those listed by the International Agency for Research on Carcinogens (IARC))?

   NOTE: Negative conclusions regarding carcinogenicity or the fact that there is no information do not have to be reported unless there is a specific space or blank for carcinogenicity on the form.

   (1) Generally applicable procedures and precautions for the safe handling and use of the chemical (hygienic practices, maintenance, and spill procedures)?
   (m) Generally applicable control measures (e.g., engineering controls, work practices, personal protective equipment)?
   (n) Pertinent emergency and first-aid procedures?
   (o) Date the MSDS was prepared or the date of the last change to it?
   (p) Name, address and telephone number of the responsible party?
   (q) Are all sections of the MSDS completed?

Hazard Communication Quiz
(See appendix for answers.)

1. The Hazard Communication Act is also known as the:
   a. Chemical Identification Act of 1984
   b. MSDS Law
   c. Chemical Protective Act
   d. Right to Know Law

2. PEL stands for:
   a. Permissible exposure level
   b. Priority evacuation ladder
   c. Permissive exposure limit
   d. Post-mortem exposure level

3. The hazard communication standard requires that construction firms have a written, site-specific program, located at each site, that:
   a. Lists chemicals on site and how they are labeled
   b. Lists chemicals on site and what they look like
   c. List chemicals on site and where they are stored
   d. List chemicals on site and how to safely dispose of them

4. Material safety data sheets must be:
   a. Available to the supervisor on shift
   b. Stored in a central location at the company headquarters
   c. Available to all workers
   d. Available to workers who are exposed to the chemical

5. Two common types of labels are the HMIS label and the:
   a. NFPA label
   b. ANSI label
   c. CGA label
   d. PEL label

6. Regarding chemicals, workers must be trained to:
   a. Identify the chemicals they are using
   b. Protect themselves from the chemicals they are using
   c. Know what chemicals to which they are occupationally exposed
   d. All of the above

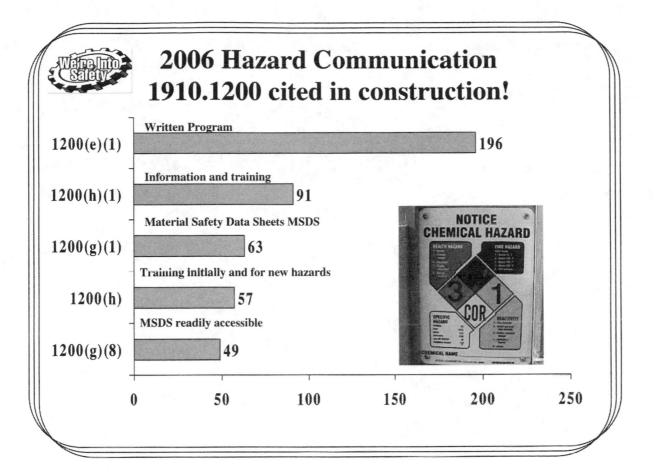

PERSONAL PROTECTIVE EQUIPMENT AND CLOTHING

OSHA requires the use of personal protective equipment (PPE) to reduce employee exposures to hazards when engineering and/or administrative controls are not feasible or effective in reducing these exposures to acceptable levels. Employers are required to determine all exposures to hazards in their workplace and determine whether PPE should be used to protect their workers.

If PPE is to be used to reduce the exposure of employees to hazards, a PPE program should be initialized and maintained. This program should contain identify and evaluate hazards in the workplace and state whether use of PPE is an appropriate control measure; if PPE is to be used, the program should state how it will be selected, maintained, and its use evaluated; how employees will be trained in the use of PPE; and the vigilance of the program to determine its effectiveness in preventing employee injury or illness.

Criteria for Personal Protective Equipment—1926.95

Protective equipment, including personal protective equipment for eyes, face, head, and extremities; protective clothing; respiratory devices; and protective shields and barriers, shall be provided, used, and maintained in a sanitary and reliable condition wherever it is necessary by reason of hazards of processes or environment, chemical hazards, radiological hazards, or mechanical irritants encountered in a manner capable of causing injury or impairment in the function of any part of the body through absorption, inhalation, or physical contact.

Employee-Owned Equipment

When employees provide their own protective equipment, the employer shall be responsible for ensuring its adequacy, including the proper maintenance and sanitation of such equipment.

Design

All personal protective equipment shall be of safe design and construction for the work to be performed.

PPE must be used as the manufacturer intends. Hard hats have a band that is designed to disperse the shock of impact to the head. Wearing a baseball cap beneath the hard hat defeats that protection and can result in injury as well as an OSHA citation.

Head Protection—1926.100

The prevention of head injuries is an important factor in every safety program. A survey by the Bureau of Labor Statistics (BLS) of accidents and injuries noted that most workers who suffered impact injuries to the head were not wearing head protection. The majority of workers were injured while performing their normal jobs at their regular worksites.

The survey showed that in most instances where head injuries occurred, employers had not required their employees to wear head protection. Of those workers wearing hard hats, all but 5 percent indicated that they were required by their employers to wear them. It was found that the vast majority of those who wore hard hats all or most of the time at work believed that hard hats were practical for their jobs. According to the report, in almost half of the accidents involving head injuries, employees knew of no actions taken by employers to prevent such injuries from recurring.

The BLS survey noted that more than one-half of the workers were struck on the head while they were looking down and almost three-tenths were looking straight ahead. While a third of the unprotected workers were injured when bumping into stationary objects, such actions injured only one-eighth of hard-hat wearers. The elimination or control of a hazard leading to an accident should, of course, be given first consideration, but many accidents causing head injuries are of a type difficult to anticipate and control. Where these conditions exist, head protection must be provided to eliminate injury.

Head protection, in the form of protective hats, must do two things:
- Resist penetration; and
- Absorb the shock of a blow.

Protective hats also are used to protect against electrical shock. This is accomplished by making the shell of the hat of a material hard enough to resist the blow and by using a shock-absorbing lining composed of head band and crown straps to keep the shell away from the wearer's skull.

The standards recognized by OSHA for protective hats are contained in American National Standards Institute Z89.1-1969, Safety Requirements for Industrial Head Protection, and ANSI Z89.2-1971, Safety Requirements for Industrial Protective Helmets for Electrical Workers. These requirements should be consulted for details. Later editions of these standards are available and acceptable for use.

Selection

Each type and class of head protection is intended to provide protection against specific hazardous conditions. An understanding of these conditions will help to select the right hat for the particular situation. Protective hats are made in the following types and classes:
- Type 1: Helmets with full brim, not less than 1¼ in. wide; and
- Type 2: Brimless helmets with a peak extending forward from the crown.

For industrial purposes, three classes are recognized:
- Class A: General service, limited voltage protection;
- Class B: Utility service, high-voltage helmets; and
- Class C: Special service, no voltage protection.

For firefighters, head protection must consist of a protective head device with ear flaps and a chin strap that meet the performance, construction, and testing requirements stated in 29 CFR 1910.156(e)(5).

Hats and caps under Class A are intended for protection against impact hazards. They are used in mining, construction, shipbuilding, tunneling, lumbering, and manufacturing.

Class B utility service hats and caps protect the wearer's head from impact and penetration by falling or flying objects and from high-voltage shock and burn. Electrical workers use them extensively.

The safety hat or cap in Class C is designed specifically for lightweight comfort and impact protection. This class is usually manufactured from aluminum and offers no dielectric protection. Class C helmets are used in certain construction and manufacturing occupations, oil fields, refineries, and chemical plants where there is no danger from electrical hazards or corrosion. They also are used on occasions where there is a possibility of bumping the head against a fixed object.

Materials used in helmets should be water-resistant and slow burning. Each helmet consists essentially of a shell and suspension. Ventilation is provided by a space between the headband and the shell. Each helmet should be accompanied by instructions explaining the proper method of adjusting and replacing the suspension and headband. The wearer should be able to identify the type of helmet by looking inside the shell for the manufacturer.

Fit

Headbands are adjustable in 1/8-size increments. When the headband is adjusted to the right size, it provides sufficient clearance between the shell and the headband. The removable or replaceable type sweatband should cover at least the forehead portion of the headband. The shell should be of one-piece seamless construction and designed to resist the impact of a blow from falling material. The internal cradle of the headband and sweatband forms the suspension. Any part that comes into contact with the wearer's head must not be irritating to normal skin.

Inspection and Maintenance

Manufacturers should be consulted with regard to paint or cleaning materials for their helmets because some paints and thinners may damage the shell and reduce protection by physically weakening it or negating electrical resistance.

A common method of cleaning shells is dipping them in hot water (approximately 140°F) containing a good detergent for at least one minute. Shells should then be scrubbed and rinsed in clear hot water. After rinsing, the shell should be inspected for any signs of damage.

All components, shells, suspensions, headbands, sweatbands, and any accessories should be visually inspected daily for signs of dents, cracks, penetration, or any other damage that might reduce the degree of safety originally provided.

Users are cautioned that if unusual conditions occur (e.g., higher or lower extreme temperatures than described in the standards) or if there are signs of abuse or mutilation of the helmet or any component, the margin of safety may be reduced. If damage is suspected, helmets should be replaced. Helmets should not be stored or carried on the rear-window shelf of an automobile because sunlight and extreme heat may adversely affect the degree of protection they provide.

Hearing Protection—1926.101

Wherever it is not feasible to reduce the noise levels or duration of exposures to those specified in Table D-2 in 1926.52, ear protective devices shall be provided and used (See Exhibit 6-1.). Hearing protective devices inserted in the ear shall be individually fitted or determined by competent persons.

Exhibit 6-1. Table D-2.
Permissible Noise Exposures.
Duration per day, hours dBA slow response

8	90
6	92
4	95
3	97
2	100
1½	102
1	105
½	110
¼ or less	115

Exposure to high noise levels can cause hearing loss or impairment, and physical and psychological stress. There is no cure for noise-induced hearing loss, so the prevention of excessive noise exposure is the only way to avoid hearing damage. Specifically designed protection is required, depending on the type of noise encountered.

A professional should individually fit preformed or molded earplugs. Waxed cotton, foam, or fiberglass wool earplugs are self-forming. When properly inserted, they work as well as most molded earplugs. Some earplugs are disposable, to be used one time and then thrown away. Non-disposable earplugs should be cleaned after each use for proper protection. Plain cotton is ineffective as protection against hazardous noise and should not be used.

Earmuffs need to make a perfect seal around the ear to be effective. Glasses, long sideburns, long hair, and facial movements, such as chewing, can reduce protection. Special equipment is available for use with glasses or beards.

Torso Protection

Many hazards can threaten the torso: heat, splashes from hot metals and liquids, impacts, cuts, acids, and radiation. A variety of protective clothing is available to protect the torso, including vests, jackets, aprons, coveralls, and full body suits.

Wool and specially treated cotton are two natural fibers that are fire resistant and comfortable since they adapt well to changing workplace temperatures. Duck, a closely woven cotton fabric, is good for light-duty protective clothing. It can protect against cuts and bruises on jobs where employees handle heavy, sharp, or rough material. Heat-resistant material, such as leather, is often used in protective clothing to guard against dry heat and flame. Rubber and rubberized fabrics, neoprene, and plastics give protection against some acids and chemicals. It is important to refer to the manufacturers' selection guides for the effectiveness of specific materials against specific chemicals.

Disposable suits of paper-like material are particularly important for protection from dusty materials or materials that can splash. If the substance is extremely toxic, a completely enclosed suit may be necessary. The clothing should be inspected to ensure proper fit and function for continued protection.

Arm and Hand Protection

Examples of injuries to arms and hands are burns, cuts, electrical shock, amputation, and absorption of chemicals. There is a wide assortment of gloves, hand pads, sleeves, and wristlets for protection against various hazardous situations.

The protective device should be selected to fit the job. For example, some gloves are designed to protect against specific chemical hazards. Employees may need to use gloves made of materials such as wire mesh, leather, or canvas that have been tested and provide insulation from burns and cuts. The employee should become acquainted with the limitations of the protective equipment used.

Certain occupations require special protection. For example, electricians need special protection from shocks and burns while plumbers may need protection from acids and corrosives. Rubber is considered the best material for insulating gloves and sleeves from electrical hazards. Rubber protective equipment for electrical workers must conform to the requirements established by ANSI in Exhibit 6-2.

Exhibit 6-2.
ANSI rubber protective equipment requirements.

Item	ANSI Standard
Rubber insulating gloves	J6.6-1967
Rubber insulating blankets	J6.4-1970
Rubber insulating hoods	J6.2-1950 (R 1962)
Rubber insulating line hose	J6.1-1950 (R 1962)
Rubber insulating sleeves	J6.5-1962
Rubber matting for use around electrical apparatus	J6.7-1935 (R 1962)

Occupational Foot Protection—1926.96

According to the BLS survey previously mentioned, most of the workers in selected occupations who suffered foot injuries were not wearing protective footwear. Furthermore, most of their employers did not require them to wear safety shoes. Objects falling fewer than 4 ft. and the median caused the typical foot injury. Weight was about 65 lbs. Most workers were injured while performing their normal job activities at their worksites.

Safety-toe footwear for employees must meet the requirements and specifications in ANSI Z41.1-1967, the American National Standard for Men's Safety-Toe Footwear.

To protect their feet and legs from falling or rolling objects, sharp objects, molten metal, hot surfaces, and wet slippery surfaces, workers should use appropriate foot guards, safety shoes, or boots and leggings. Leggings protect the lower leg and feet from molten metal or welding sparks. Safety snaps permit their rapid removal.

Aluminum alloy, fiberglass, or galvanized steel foot guards can be worn over usual work shoes, although they may present the possibility of catching on something and causing workers to trip. Heat-resistant soled shoes protect against hot surfaces like those found in the roofing, paving, and hot metal industries.

Safety shoes should be sturdy and have an impact-resistant toe. In some shoes, metal insoles protect against puncture wounds. Additional protection, such as metatarsal guards, may be found in some types of footwear. Safety shoes come in a variety of styles and materials, such as leather and rubber boots and oxfords. Safety footwear is classified according to its ability to meet minimum requirements for both compression and impact tests. These requirements and testing procedures may be found in ANSI Z41-1967.

Eye and Face Protection—1926.102

Employees shall be provided with eye and face protection equipment when machines or operations present potential eye or face injury from physical, chemical, or radiation agents. Eye and face protection equipment required by this section shall meet the requirements specified in American National Standards Institute, ANSI Z87.1-1968, Practice for Occupational and Educational Eye and Face Protection.

Goggles or spectacles of one of the following types shall protect employees who need to use corrective lenses:

- Spectacles whose protective lenses provide optical correction;
- Goggles that can be worn over corrective spectacles without disturbing them; or
- Goggles that incorporate corrective lenses mounted behind the protective lenses.

Face and eye protection equipment shall be kept clean and in good repair. The use of this type equipment with structural or optical defects shall be prohibited. Protectors shall meet the following minimum requirements:

- Provide adequate protection against the particular hazards for which they are designed;
- Be reasonably comfortable when worn under the designated conditions;
- Fit snugly and not unduly interfere with the movements of the wearer;
- Be durable;
- Be capable of being disinfected; and
- Be easily cleanable.

A survey by the Bureau of Labor Statistics of accidents and injuries found that about 60 percent of workers who suffered eye injuries were not wearing eye protective equipment. When asked why they were not wearing face protection at the time of the accident, workers indicated that face protection was not normally used or worn in their job, or it was not required for the type of work performed at the time of the accident.

OSHA requires eye and face protective equipment where there is a reasonable probability of preventing injury when such equipment is used. Employers must provide a type of protector suitable for the work to be performed and require employees to use the protectors. These stipulations also apply to supervisors and management personnel and applies to visitors who are in hazardous areas. Every protector shall be distinctly marked to identify its manufacturer. When the manufacturer indicates limitations or precautions, they shall be transmitted to the user and care taken to see that such limitations and precautions are strictly observed.

Selection

Each eye, face, or face-and-eye protector is designed for a particular hazard. When selecting a protector, consideration should be given to the kind and degree of hazard. Where a choice of protectors is given, and the degree of protection required is not an important issue, worker comfort may be a deciding factor. The BLS survey showed that few workers ever complained about poor vision or discomfort with personal eye protection equipment.

The survey noted that common injuries were lacerations, fractures, broken teeth, and contusions. These injuries were often caused by flying or falling blunt metal objects.

Over the years, many types and styles of eye and face-and-eye protective equipment have been developed to meet the demands for protection against a variety of hazards. When the manufacturer indicates limitations or precautions, they should be transmitted to the user and strictly observed.

Goggles come in a number of different styles: eyecups, flexible or cushioned goggles, plastic eye shield goggles, and foundry men's goggles. Goggles are manufactured in several styles for specific uses such as protecting against dusts and splashes and in chippers, welders, and cutter's models.

Safety spectacles require special frames. Combinations of normal street wear frames with safety lenses are not in compliance. Persons using corrective spectacles and those who are required by OSHA to wear eye protection must wear face shields, goggles, or spectacles of one of the following types:

- Spectacles with protective lenses providing optical correction;
- Goggles worn over corrective spectacles without disturbing the adjustment of the spectacles; or
- Goggles that incorporate corrective lenses mounted behind the protective lenses.

Many hard hats and nonrigid helmets also are designed with face and eye protective equipment. Design, construction, tests, and use of eye and face protection must be in accordance with ANSI Z87.1-1968.

Fit

Someone skilled in the procedure should ensure the proper fit goggles and safety spectacles. Only qualified optical personnel should fit prescription safety spectacles.

Inspection and Maintenance

It is essential that the lenses of eye protectors be kept clean. Continuous vision through dirty lenses can cause eye strain—a common workers use not to wear eye protectors. Daily inspection and cleaning of the eye protector with soap and hot water or with a cleaning solution and tissue is recommended. Pitted lenses, like dirty lenses, can be a source of reduced vision. They should be replaced. Deep scratches or excessively pitted lenses are apt to break more readily.

Slack, worn-out, sweat-soaked, or twisted headbands do not hold eye protectors in proper position. Visual inspection can determine when the headband elasticity is reduced to a point beyond proper function.

Goggles should be kept in a case when not in use. Spectacles, in particular, should be given the same care as one's own glasses because the frame, nose pads, and temples can be damaged by rough usage.

Personal protective equipment that has been previously used should be disinfected before being issued to another employee. Even when each employee is assigned protective equipment for extended periods, it is recommended that such equipment be cleaned and disinfected regularly.

Several methods for disinfecting equipment for eye protection are acceptable. The most effective method is to disassemble the goggles or spectacles and thoroughly clean all parts with soap and warm water. Carefully rinse all traces of soap and replace defective parts with new ones. Swab thoroughly or completely and immerse all parts for 10 minutes in a solution of germicidal deodorant fungicide. Remove all parts from the solution and suspend them in a clean place for air-drying at room temperature or with heated air. Do not rinse after removing parts from the solution because this will remove the germicidal residue that retains its effectiveness after drying.

The dry parts or items should be placed in a clean, dust-proof container, such as a box, bag, or plastic envelope, to protect them until reissue.

Protection Against Radiant Energy

Table E-2 in 1926.102(b)(1) shall be used as a guide for the selection of the proper shade numbers of filter lenses or plates used in welding. Shades more dense than those listed may be used to suit the individual's needs. Employees whose occupation or assignment requires exposure to laser beams shall be furnished suitable laser safety goggles that will protect for the specific wavelength of the laser and be of optical density (OD) adequate for the energy involved. Table E-3 in 1926.102(b)(2) lists the maximum power or energy density for which adequate protection is afforded by glasses of optical densities from 5 through 8.

All protective goggles shall have an identifying label with the following data:
- The laser wavelengths for which they are intended to be used;
- The optical density of those wavelengths; and
- The visible light transmission.

Respiratory Protection—1926.103

On October 5, 1998, OSHA's revised Respiratory Protection Standard took effect. It replaces the standards adopted in 1971 (29 CFR 1910.134 and 29 CFR 1926.103) and applies to general industry, construction, shipyard, longshoring, and marine terminal workplaces. The respiratory protection standard is discussed in more detail at the end of this chapter.

Safety Belts, Lifelines, and Lanyards— 1926.104

Lifelines, safety belts, and lanyards shall be used only for employee safeguarding. Any lifeline, safety belt, or lanyard actually subjected to in-service loading, as distinguished from static load testing, shall be immediately removed from service and shall not be used again for employee safeguarding. Lifelines shall be secured above the point of operation to an anchorage or structural member capable of supporting a minimum dead weight of 5,400 lbs. Lifelines used on rock-scaling operations or in areas where the lifeline may be subjected to cutting or abrasion shall be a minimum of 7/8-inch wire core manila rope. For all other lifeline applications, a minimum of ¾-in. manila or equivalent, with a minimum breaking strength of 5,400 lbs., shall be used. Safety belt lanyards shall be a minimum of ½-in. nylon, or equivalent, with a maximum length to provide for a fall of no greater than 6 ft. The rope shall have a nominal breaking strength of 5,400 lbs.

All safety belt and lanyard hardware shall be drop forged or pressed steel, cadmium plated in accordance with Type 1, Class B plating specified in federal specification QQ-P-416. The surface shall be smooth and free of sharp edges.

All safety belt and lanyard hardware, except rivets, shall be capable of withstanding a tensile loading of 4,000 lbs. without cracking, breaking, or taking a permanent deformation.

Safety Nets—1926.105

Safety nets shall be provided when workplaces are more than 25 ft. above the ground or water surface, or other surfaces where the uses of ladders, scaffolds, catch platforms, temporary floors, safety lines, or safety belts is impractical. Where safety net protection is required by this section, operations shall not be undertaken until the net is in place and has been tested. Nets shall extend 8 ft. beyond the edge of the work surface where employees are exposed and shall be installed as close under the work surface as practical, but in no case more than 25 ft. below such work surface. Nets shall be hung with suf-ficient clearance to prevent user's contact with the surfaces or structures below. Such clearances shall be determined by impact load testing. It is intended that only one level of nets be required for bridge construction. The mesh size of nets shall not exceed 6 in. × 6 in. All new nets shall meet accepted performance standards of 17,500 ft.-lbs. minimum impact resistance as determined and certified by the manufacturers and shall bear a label of proof test. Edge ropes shall provide a minimum breaking strength of 5,000 lbs. Forged steel safety hooks or shackles shall be used to fasten the net to its supports. Connections between net panels shall develop the full strength of the net.

Working Over or Near Water—1926.106

Employees working over or near water, where the danger of drowning exists, shall be provided with U.S. Coast Guard-approved life jacket or buoyant work vests. Prior to and after each use, the buoyant work vests or life preservers shall be inspected for defects that could alter their strength or buoyancy. Defective units shall not be used. Ring buoys with at least 90 ft. of line shall be provided and readily available for emergency rescue operations. Distance between ring buoys shall not exceed 200 ft. At least one life-saving skiff shall be immediately available at locations where employees are working over or adjacent to water. Night workers and flagmen who might be struck by moving vehicles need suits or vests designed to reflect light.

Enforcing the rules on personal protective equipment is important. The negotiated agreement between a federal institution and the American Federation of Government Employees (affiliated with the AFL-CIO) includes the following:

Health and safety plays an important part in the condition of employment. Union contracts call for the employer to provide a safe and sanitary workplace for all employees.

Regarding Personal Protective Equipment

The Employer will furnish protective clothing and equipment when employees are assigned to work areas that have been des-

Personal Protective Equipment and Clothing

ignated as requiring use of specific types of personal protective equipment.

Within available resources, the furnished safety items shall be replaced in accordance with established standards, upon becoming unsafe, unsanitary or ineffective.

Employees who have been issued protective clothing and/or equipment, and who are required to wear protective clothing and/or equipment, and who report to work without said clothing and/or equipment, will not be permitted to work, and will be placed on AWOL until such time as they are wearing said clothing and/or equipment.

(Section 2, Part 29 Health and Safety of the Negotiated Contract)

Personal protective equipment should not be used as a substitute for engineering, work practice, and/or administrative controls. Personal protective equipment should be used in conjunction with these controls to provide for employee safety and health in the workplace. Personal protective equipment includes all clothing and other work accessories designed to create a barrier against workplace hazards. The basic element of any management program for personal protective equipment should be an in-depth evaluation of the equipment needed to protect against the hazards at the workplace. Management dedicated to the safety and health of employees should use that evaluation to set a standard operating procedure for personnel, then train employees on the protective limitations of personal protective equipment and on its proper use and maintenance.

Using personal protective equipment requires hazard awareness and training on the part of the user. Employees must be aware that the equipment does not eliminate the hazard. If the equipment fails, exposure will occur. To reduce the possibility of failure, equipment must be properly fitted and maintained in a clean and serviceable condition.

Selection of the proper personal protective equipment for a job is important. Employers and employees must understand the equipment's purpose and its limitations. The equipment must not be altered or removed even though an employee may find it uncomfortable. Sometimes equipment may be uncomfortable simply because it does not fit properly.

Personal Protective Equipment for Women

The following is an excerpt from "Women in the Construction Workplace: Providing Equitable Safety and Health Protection," written by the Health and Safety of Women in Construction (HASWIC), a workgroup established by the DOL's Advisory Committee on Construction Safety and Health (ACCSH), and submitted to OSHA in June 1999. The full ACCSH adopted the report on March 13, 19997.

Sources for this report include two research studies conducted by the National Institute on Occupational Safety and Health and one conducted by Chicago Women in Trades (CWIT). More than 450 women were interviewed via phone, mail, in-person one-on-one interviews, and focus groups.

Many women in nontraditional jobs, such as the construction trades, complain of ill-fitting personal protective clothing (PPC) and equipment (PPE). Clothing or equipment that is not sized, or does not fit, properly can compromise personal safety. It also may not function effectively in the manner for which it was designed. Poor fit compromises the protection offered by the garment or equipment. The lack of appropriate PPC and PPE can cause serious safety and health risks for women, and men of smaller sizes, who rely on protective clothing and equipment to help them keep safe. Having inadequate or ill-fitting clothing, boots, gloves, or safety equipment presents a safety hazard for any worker.

Studies by NIOSH and the U.S. Department of the Army found that most tools, equipment, and clothing are not designed for a women's physique. When asked if they could easily find protective clothing to fit, 46% of women in the second NIOSH [survey] said "no" with respect to work shoes and 41% with respect to finding work gloves. One survey of manufacturers of protective equipment, taken at a National Safety Council Annual meeting, found that only 14 percent offered ear, head, and face protection in women's sizes. The highest percentages, 59 percent, were manufacturers who offered foot protection in women's sizes.

Ill-fitting personal protective equipment may be due to unavailability (i.e., manufacturers don't make or distributors don't stock), limited availability, or lack of knowledge among employers and workers about where equipment designed for a woman's body structure can be obtained. Personal protective equipment intended for use by women workers should be based upon female anthropometric (body measurement) data.

Work gloves must fit properly. Overly large gloves impair the transfer of sensory information from the hand, resulting in excessive force being applied. Tight gloves can restrict blood flow. Hand tools should be designed so that the stress concentrations can be spread evenly throughout the hand.

A recent NIOSH review found that few tools, equipment, or clothing are designed for a woman's physique. A recent study commissioned for the U.S. Army had similar findings.

Women in the first NIOSH study were particularly outspoken about this concern. One of the participants said:

When I went through the welding apprenticeship, they issued us welding boots, size 9½, I had to wear two pairs of socks to wear them.

They gave me a welding leather jacket that was a foot longer than my hand. I had to roll it up. And they said that they couldn't order anything smaller. They gave me gloves so humongous I couldn't even pick anything up.

Another woman's story reflects the frustration felt by these women: "I went to get up in a full suit the other day, and you couldn't see me! I mean, I don't want these. Just give me my coat, and I'll put on a couple pairs of coveralls. Sizes ... we need our sizes ... women's sizes."

Beyond frustration is fear and the real danger of poor fitting and ineffective clothes and personal protective equipment:

You can be hurt ... if you happen to have a pair of gloves on and they're too big, and say you're doing some work, that glove could get wrapped up in a fan belt or ... anything ... with moving parts ... you can get hurt if your clothing is not fitted right.

They need to get in touch with apprenticeship programs, with contractors, and push if they have women's work boots and women's gloves for non-traditional trades. The information is not getting out there.

April 17, 1997
MEMORANDUM FOR: REGIONAL ADMINISTRATORS AND STATE DESIGNEES
FROM: FRANK STRASHEIM
Acting Deputy Assistant Secretary
SUBJECT: Citations for the wearing of short pants by employees engaged in hot tar and asphalt construction work

In response to concerns raised by the Senate Appropriations Committee, OSHA has reviewed its enforcement policy regarding the standard on personal protective equipment (PPE) in the construction industry and the hazards arising from employees wearing short pants during hot tar and asphalt construction activities. The committee has expressed concern that the agency may apply the standard without taking into account the risk that may be imposed by literal compliance with the standard. The standard that has sometimes been cited for violations relating to the use of PPE, including protective clothing, is 29 CFR 1926.28(a). Federal citation policy issued some time ago, however, is that the use of appropriate PPE be governed by 29 CFR 1926.95(a) rather than 1926.28(a).

As you know, 1926.95(a) requires protective equipment to be worn "whenever it is necessary by reason of hazards." Thus, where employees are exposed to the hazard of hot tar or asphalt getting on their skin and burning them while doing work on a road surface, it is appropriate that proper skin covering be worn to provide protection. While the standard does not specify any particular kind of protection, such as long pants, employers do have the responsibility to decide which workers are exposed to the hazard and thus require protective clothing and which methods should be used to comply with the standard.

Other factors may exist, however, which would pose a greater safety or health hazard than that of being burned by hot tar or asphalt. In such cases a citation of the PPE standard for lack of skin protection may not be appropriate. Naturally, workers at the site who are not exposed to the hazard of hot tar or asphalt coming into contact with their skin would not be required by the regulation to wear any kind of PPE intended to provide protection against that danger.

To ensure consistency in the future application of 1926.95(a), compliance officers shall be instructed to carefully balance the need for personal protective clothing, such as long pants, during hot tar and asphalt operations against the need for clothing that is appropriate for severe environmental conditions such as extremely warm weather.

State Plans: Regional Administrators should discuss this policy with their State Designees and ask that they adopt an equivalent policy.

Respiratory Protection—1926.103

In 1998 OSHA established criteria for respiratory protection for construction workers. Those criteria are outlined in 1910.134 and are set forth here. The construction and general industry requirements are identical.

OSHA standards require employers to establish and maintain a respiratory protective program whenever respirators are necessary to protect the health of employees.

Respiratory protective devices fall into three classes:
- Air purifying;
- Atmosphere or air supplying; and
- Combination air-purifying and air-supplying.

Class 1: Air-Purifying Devices

The air-purifying device cleanses the contaminated atmosphere. Chemicals can be used to remove specific gases and vapors and mechanical filters can remove particulate matter. This type of respirator is limited in its use to those environments where the air contaminant level is within the specified concentration limitation of the device. These devices do not protect against oxygen deficiency.

"Oxygen deficiency" occurs in an atmosphere with an oxygen content below 19.5 percent by volume.

Types of air-purifying devices include:
- Mechanical-filter cartridge;
- Chemical-cartridge;
- Combination mechanical-filter/chemical-cartridge;
- Gas masks; and
- Powered air-purifying respirators.

Mechanical-filter respirators offer respiratory protection against airborne particulate matter, including dusts, mists, metal fumes and smoke, but do not provide protection against gases or vapors.

Chemical-cartridge respirators afford protection against low concentrations of certain gases and vapors by using various chemical filters to purify the inhaled air. They differ from mechanical-filter respirators in that they use cartridges containing chemicals to remove harmful gases and vapors.

Combination mechanical-filter/chemical-cartridge respirators use dust, mist or fume filters with a chemical cartridge for dual or multiple exposures.

Gas masks provide respiratory protection against certain gases, vapors and particulate matter. Gas masks are designed solely to remove specific contaminants from the air; therefore, it is essential that their use be restricted to atmospheres that contain sufficient oxygen to support life. Gas masks may be used for *escape only* from atmospheres that are immediately dangerous to life or health, and never for entry into such environments.

Immediately dangerous to life or health (IDLH) means an atmospheric concentration of any toxic, corrosive or asphyxiant substance that poses an immediate threat to life or would cause irreversible or delayed adverse health effects or would interfere with an individual's ability to escape from a dangerous atmosphere.

Canisters for gas masks are color-coded according to the contaminant against which they provide protection. This information is included in the standard.

Powered air-purifying respirators protect against particulates, gases and vapors, or both. The air-purifying element may be a filter, chemical cartridge, combination filter and chemical cartridge, or canister. The powered air-purifying respirator uses a power source (usually a battery pack) to operate a blower that passes air across the air-cleaning element to supply purified air to the respirator. The great advantage of the powered air-purifying respirator is that it usually supplies air at positive pressure (relative to atmospheric) so that any leakage is outward from the face piece. However, it is possible at high work rates to create a negative pressure in the face piece, thereby increasing face-piece leakage.

Class 2: Atmosphere- or Air-Supplying Devices

Atmosphere- or air-supplying devices are the class of respirators that provide a respirable atmosphere to the wearer, independent of the ambient air. Atmosphere-supplying respirators fall into three groups: supplied-air respirators, self-contained breathing apparatus (SCBA), and combination-SCBA and supplied-air respirators.

Supplied-air respirators deliver breathing air through a supply hose connected to the wearer's face piece or enclosure. The air delivered must be free of contaminants and must be from a source located in clean air. The OSHA requirements for compressed air used for breathing, including monitoring for carbon monoxide, are listed in 1910.134(d). Supplied-air respirators should only be used in non-IDLH atmospheres.

There are three types of supplied-air respirators, which are classified by type. Type A supplied-air respirators are also known as hose masks with blower. A motor-driven or hand-operated blower through a strong, large diameter hose supplies air. Type B supplied-air respirators are hose masks as in Type A,

but without a blower. The wearer draws air through the hose by breathing. Type C supplied-air respirators are commonly referred to as airline respirators. An airline respirator must be supplied with respirable air conforming to Grade D Compressed Gas Association's Standard CGA G-7.1-73, Commodity Specification for Air, 1973. This standard requires air to have the oxygen content normally present in the atmosphere, no more than 5 mg/NV of condensed hydrocarbon contamination, no more than 20-ppm carbon monoxide, no pronounced odor and a maximum of 1,000 ppm of carbon dioxide.

There are three basic classes of airline respirators.

Continuous flow. A continuous-flow unit has a regulated amount of air fed to the face piece and is normally used where there is an ample air supply such as that provided by an air compressor.

Demand flow. These airline respirators deliver airflow only during inhalation. Such respirators are normally used when the air supply is restricted to high-pressure compressed air cylinders. A suitable pressure regulator is required to make sure that the air is reduced to the proper pressure for breathing.

Pressure-demand flow. For those conditions where the possible inward leakage (caused by the negative pressure during inhalation that is always present in demand systems) is unacceptable and there cannot be the relatively high air consumption of the continuous-flow units, a pressure-demand airline respirator may be the best choice. It provides a positive pressure during both inhalation and exhalation.

Types A, B, and C that are approved for abrasive blasting are designated AE, BE and CE, respectively. These respirators are equipped with additional devices designed to protect the wearer's head and neck against impact and abrasion from rebounding abrasive material and with shielding to protect the windows of face pieces, hoods and helmets.

Self-contained breathing apparatus (SCBA) provide complete respiratory protection against toxic gases and oxygen deficiency. The wearer is independent of the surrounding atmosphere because he or she is breathing with a system that is portable and admits no outside air. The oxygen or air supply of the apparatus itself takes care of respiratory requirements.

There are two basic types of self-contained breathing apparatus: closed circuit and open-circuit. In a closed-circuit apparatus, the exhalation is rebreathed by the wearer after the carbon dioxide has been effectively removed and a suitable oxygen concentration restored from sources composed of compressed oxygen, chemical oxygen or liquid oxygen. In an open-circuit apparatus, exhalation is vented to the atmosphere and is not rebreathed. There are two types of open-circuit SCBAs: demand and pressure-demand.

Combination SCBA and supplied-air respirators are airline respirators with auxiliary self-contained air supplies. An auxiliary SCBA is an independent air supply that allows a person to evacuate an area or enter such an area for a very short period of time where a connection to an outside air supply can be made. These devices are approved for use in IDLH atmospheres. The auxiliary air supply can be switched to in the event the primary air supply fails to operate. This allows the wearer to escape from the IDLH atmosphere. Combination airline respirators with auxiliary SCBA are designed to operate in three modes: continuous-flow, demand flow, and pressure-demand flow.

Class 3: Combination Air-Purifying and Atmosphere-Supplying Devices

Lately, another type of respirator is gaining in popularity. It is a device that is a combination of an airline respirator with an auxiliary air-purifying attachment, which provides protection in the event the air supply fails. These respirators are available in either continuous-flow or pressure-demand flow and are most often used with a high-efficiency filter as the air purifying element. Use in the filtering mode is allowed for escape only. Because of the positive pressure and escape provisions, these respirators have been recommended for asbestos work.

Exhibit 6-3. Classifications of respiratory protective devices.

I. Air-Purifying Devices
  A. Mechanical-filter cartridge
  B. Chemical-cartridge
  C. Combination mechanical-filter/chemical cartridge
  D. Gas masks
  E. Powered air purifying
II. Atmosphere- or Air-Supplying Devices
  A. Supplied-air
    1. Types A and AE
    2. Types B and BE
    3. Types C and CE (airline)
      a. Continuous-flow
      b. Demand-flow
      c. Pressure-demand flow
  B. Self-contained breathing apparatus (SCBA)
    1. Closed-circuit
    2. Open-circuit
    a. Demand
    b. Pressure-demand
  C. Combination SCBA and supplied-air
    1. Continuous-flow
    2. Demand-flow
    3. Pressure-demand flow
III. Combination Air-Purifying and Atmosphere Supplying Devices
  A. Continuous-flow
  B. Pressure-demand flow

Written Operating Procedures
OSHA standards state that the employer is responsible not only for providing appropriate respirators, but also for developing written standard operating procedures for their selection, use and care.

Program Selection
Respirators shall be selected on the basis of hazards to which the worker is exposed. A qualified individual supervising the respiratory protective program usually specifies the respirator type in the work procedures. The individual issuing them shall be adequately instructed to ensure that the correct respirator is issued.

In selecting the correct respirator for a given circumstance, many factors must be taken into consideration (e.g., the nature of the hazard, location of the hazardous area, employee's health, work activity, and respirator characteristics, capabilities and limitations).

In order to make subsequent decisions, the nature of the hazard must be identified to ensure that an overexposure does not occur. One important factor to consider is oxygen deficiency. NIOSH/MSHA approval for supplied-air and air-purifying respirators is valid only for atmospheres containing greater than 19.5 percent oxygen. If oxygen deficiency is not an issue, then the contaminant(s) and their concentrations must be determined.

Training and Fitting

The user must be instructed and trained in the selection, use and maintenance of respirators. Every respirator user shall receive fitting instructions, including demonstrations and practice in how the respirator should be worn, how to adjust it, and how to determine if it fits properly.

Cleaning and Disinfecting

Respirators must be regularly cleaned and disinfected. Those issued for the exclusive use of one worker should be cleaned after each day's use or more often if necessary.

Storage

OSHA standards require that respirators be stored in a "convenient, clean, and sanitary location." The purpose of good respirator storage is to ensure that the respirator will function properly when used. Care must be taken to ensure that respirators are stored in such a manner as to protect against dust, harmful chemicals sunlight, excessive heat or cold and moisture.

Inspection and Maintenance

Respirators used routinely shall be inspected during cleaning. Worn or deteriorated parts shall be replaced. Respirators for emergency use, such as self-contained devices, shall be thoroughly inspected at least once a month and after each use.

Work Area Surveillance

The OSHA standard requires that "appropriate surveillance of work area conditions and degree of employee exposure or stress be maintained." This should include identification of the contaminant, nature of the hazard and concentration at the breathing zone.

Inspection and Evaluation of the Program

The standard requires regular inspection and evaluation to determine the continued effectiveness of the respirator program. Many factors affect the employee's acceptance of respirators, including comfort, ability to breathe without objectionable effort, adequate visibility under all conditions, provisions for wearing prescription glasses (if necessary), ability to communicate, ability to perform all tasks without undue interference and confidence in the face piece fit. Failure to consider these factors is likely to reduce cooperation of the users in promoting a satisfactory program.

Medical Examinations

Persons should not be assigned to tasks requiring the use of respirators unless it has been determined that they are physically able to perform the work and use the equipment. A physician shall determine the health and physical conditions that are pertinent for an employee's ability to work while wearing a respirator. The user's medical status should be reviewed periodically.

Approved Respirators

The standard states that "approved or accepted respirators shall be used when they are available." A respirator is approved as the whole unit with specific components. OSHA recognizes a respirator as approved if NIOSH and the Mine Safety and Health Administration (MSHA) have jointly approved it.

Respirator Selection

In emergencies, or when controls required by Subpart D, *Occupational Health and Environmental Controls*, either fail or are inadequate to prevent harmful exposure to employees, appropriate respiratory protective devices shall be provided by the employer and shall be used.

The U.S. Bureau of Mines shall approve respiratory protective devices or respirators shall be acceptable to the U.S. Department of

Labor for the specific contaminant to which the employee is "exposed.

The chemical and physical properties of the contaminant, as well as the toxicity and concentration of the hazardous material, shall be considered in selecting the proper respirators. The nature and extent of the hazard, work requirements, and conditions, as well as the limitations and characteristics of the available respirators, shall also be factors considered in making the proper selection. Table E-4 in 1926.103(b)(3) lists the types of respirators required for protection in dangerous atmospheres.

Issuance, Use and Care of Respirators

Employees required to use respiratory protective equipment approved for use in atmospheres immediately dangerous to life shall be thoroughly trained in its use. Employees required to use other types of respiratory protective equipment shall be instructed in the use and limitations of such equipment.

Respiratory protective equipment shall be inspected regularly and maintained in good condition. Gas mask canisters and chemical cartridges shall be replaced as necessary so as to provide complete protection. Mechanical filters shall be cleaned or replaced as necessary so as to avoid undue resistance to breathing.

Respiratory protective equipment that has been previously used shall be cleaned and disinfected before it is issued by the employer to another employee. Emergency rescue equipment shall be cleaned and disinfected immediately after each use.

Use of Respirators

Standard operating procedures shall be developed for respirator use. These should include all information and guidance necessary for their proper selection, use, and care. Possible emergency and routine uses of respirators should be anticipated and planned for.

The correct respirator shall be specified for each job. A qualified individual supervising the respiratory protective program usually specifies the respirator type to be used in the work procedures. The individual issuing them shall be adequately instructed to ensure that the correct respirator is issued.

Written procedures shall be prepared that cover safe use of respirators in dangerous atmospheres that might be encountered in normal operations or in emergencies. Personnel shall be familiar with these procedures and the available respirators.

In areas where the wearer, if the respirator were to fail, could be overcome by a toxic or oxygen-deficient atmosphere, at least one additional person shall be present. Communications (visual voice, or signal line) shall be maintained between both or all individuals present. Planning shall be such that one individual will be unaffected by any likely incident and have the proper rescue equipment to be able to assist the other(s) in case of emergency.

When self-contained breathing apparatus are used in atmospheres immediately dangerous to life or health (IDLH); stand-by persons must be present with suitable rescue equipment. Persons using approved air line respirators in IDLH atmospheres shall be equipped with safety harnesses and safety lines for lifting or removing persons from hazardous atmospheres or other and equivalent provisions for the rescue of persons from hazardous atmospheres shall be used. A stand-by person(s) with suitable SCBA shall be at the nearest fresh air base for emergency rescue.

Respiratory protection is no better than the respirator in use, even though it is worn conscientiously. To ensure respirators are properly selected, used, cleaned, and maintained, a qualified individual shall conduct frequent random inspections. For safe use of any respirator, it is essential that the user be properly instructed in its selection, use, and maintenance. Both supervisors and workers shall be so instructed by competent persons. Training shall provide workers with an opportunity to handle the respirator, have it fitted properly, test its face-piece-to-face seal, wear it in normal air for a long familiarity period, and, finally, wear it in a test atmosphere.

Every respirator wearer shall receive fitting instructions including demonstrations and practice in how the respirator should be worn, how to adjust it, and how to determine if it fits properly. Respirators shall not be worn when conditions prevent a good face seal. Such conditions may be a growth of beard, sideburns, a skull cap that projects under the face piece, or temple pieces on glasses. The absence of one or both dentures can seriously affect the fit of a face piece. The worker's diligence in observing these factors shall be evaluated by periodic checking. To ensure proper protection, wearers shall check the face piece fit each time they put on the respirator. This may be done by following the manufacturer's face piece fitting instructions.

Providing respiratory protection for individuals wearing corrective glasses is a serious problem. A proper seal cannot be established if the temple bars of the eyeglasses extend through the sealing edge of the full-face piece. As a temporary measure, glasses with short temple bars or without temple bars may be taped to the wearer's head. The wearing of contact lenses in contaminated atmospheres with a respirator shall not be allowed. Systems have been developed for mounting corrective lenses inside full-face pieces. When a worker must wear corrective lenses as part of the face piece, the face piece and lenses shall be fitted by qualified individuals to provide good vision, comfort, and a gas-tight seal.

If corrective spectacles or goggles are required, they shall be worn so as not to affect the fit of the face piece. Proper selection of equipment will minimize or avoid this problem.

Maintenance and Care of Respirators

A program for maintenance and care of respirators shall be adjusted to the type of plant, working conditions, and hazards involved, and shall include the following basic services:

- Inspection for defects (including a leak check);
- Cleaning;
- Repair; and
- Storage.

Equipment shall be properly maintained to retain its original effectiveness. All respirators shall be routinely inspected before and after each use. A respirator that is not routinely used but is kept ready for emergency use shall be inspected after each use and at least monthly to ensure that it is in satisfactory working condition. In addition, a record shall be kept of inspection dates and findings for respirators maintained for emergency use.

SCBAs shall be inspected monthly to determine, at a minimum, that air and oxygen cylinders are fully charged according to the manufacturer's instructions, and the regulator and warning devices function properly.

Respirator inspection shall include a check of the tightness of connections and the condition of the face piece, headbands, valves, connecting tube, and canisters. Rubber or elastomer parts shall be inspected for pliability and signs of deterioration. Stretching and manipulating rubber or elastomer parts with a massaging action will keep them pliable and flexible and prevent them from taking a set during storage.

Routinely used respirators shall be collected, cleaned, and disinfected as frequently as necessary to ensure that proper protection is provided for the wearer. Respirators maintained for emergency use shall be cleaned and disinfected after each use.

Only experienced persons shall perform repairs or make replacements with parts designed for the respirator. No attempt shall be made to replace components or to make adjustments or repairs beyond the manufacturer's recommendations. Reducing or admission valves or regulators shall be returned to the manufacturer or to a trained technician for adjustment or repair.

After being inspected, cleaned, and repaired, if necessary, respirators shall be stored to protect against dust, sunlight, heat, extreme cold, excessive moisture, and damaging chemicals. Respirators placed at stations and work areas for emergency use should be quickly accessible at all times and should be stored in compartments built for the purpose. The compartments should be clearly marked. Routinely used respirators, such as dust respirators, may be placed in plastic bags. Respirators should not be stored in such places as lockers or toolboxes unless they are in carrying cases or cartons.

Respirators should be packed or stored so that the face piece and exhalation valve will rest in a normal position and function will not be impaired by the elastomer sitting in an abnormal position. Instructions for proper storage of emergency respirators, such as gas masks and SCBA, are found in the "Use and care" instructions, which are usually mounted inside the carrying case lid.

Permissible Practice

In the control of those occupational diseases caused by breathing air contaminated with harmful dusts, fogs, fumes, mists, gases, smokes, sprays, or vapors, the primary objective shall be to prevent atmospheric contamination. This shall be accomplished as far as feasible by accepted engineering control measures (for example, enclosure or confinement of the operation, general and local ventilation, and substitution of less toxic materials). When effective engineering controls are not feasible, or while they are being instituted, appropriate respirators shall be used pursuant to the following requirements:

- The employer shall provide respirators when such equipment is necessary to protect the health of the employee.
- The employer shall provide the respirators that are applicable and suitable for the purpose intended.
- The employer is responsible for the establishment and maintenance of a respiratory protective program that shall include the requirements outlined in the following section.
- The employee shall use the provided respiratory protection in accordance with instructions and training received.

Requirements for a Minimal Acceptable Program

- Written standard operating procedures governing the selection and use of respirators shall be established.
- Respirators shall be selected on the basis of hazards to which the worker is exposed.
- The user shall be instructed and trained in the proper use of respirators and their limitations.
- Respirators shall be regularly cleaned and disinfected. Those used by more than one worker shall be thoroughly cleaned and disinfected after each use.
- Respirators shall be stored in a convenient, clean, and sanitary location.
- Respirators used routinely shall be inspected during cleaning. Worn or deteriorated parts shall be replaced. Respirators for emergency use such as self-contained devices shall be thoroughly inspected at least once a month and after each use.
- Appropriate surveillance of work area conditions and degree of employee exposure or stress shall be maintained.
- There shall be regular inspection and evaluation to determine the continued effectiveness of the program.
- Persons should not be assigned to tasks requiring use of respirators unless it has been determined that they are physically able to perform the work and use the equipment. The local physician shall determine what health and physical conditions are pertinent. The respirator user's medical status should be reviewed periodically (e.g., annually).
- Respirators shall be selected from among those jointly approved by the Mine Safety and Health Administration and the National Institute for Occupational Safety and Health under the provisions of 30 CFR Part 11.

Air Quality

Compressed air, compressed oxygen, liquid air, and liquid oxygen used for respiration shall be of high purity. Oxygen shall meet the requirements of the U.S. Pharmacopoeia for medical or breathing oxygen. Breathing air shall meet at least the requirements of the specification for Grade D breathing air as described in Compressed Gas Association-Commodity Specification G-7.1-1966. Compressed oxygen shall not be used in supplied-air respirators or in open circuit self-contained breathing apparatus that have previously used compressed air. Oxygen must never be used with airline respirators.

Breathing air may be supplied to respirators from cylinders or air compressors. Cylinders shall be tested and maintained as prescribed in the Specifications for Packagings by the Department of Transportation (49 CFR Part 178, Subpart C).

The compressor for supplying air shall be equipped with necessary safety and stand-by devices. A breathing air-type compressor shall be used. Compressors shall be constructed and situated so as to avoid entry of contaminated air into the system and suitable in-line air purifying sorbent beds and filters installed to further ensure breathing air quality. A receiver of sufficient capacity to enable the respirator wearer to escape from a contaminated atmosphere in event of compressor failure and alarms to indicate compressor failure and overheating shall be installed in the system. If an oil-lubricated compressor is used, it shall have a high-temperature or carbon monoxide alarm, or both. If only a high-temperature alarm is used, the air from the compressor shall be frequently tested for carbon monoxide to ensure that it meets the specifications for Grade D breathing air described earlier in this section.

Airline couplings shall be incompatible with outlets for other gas systems to prevent inadvertent servicing of airline respirators with nonrespirable gases or oxygen.

Identification of Gas Mask Canisters

The primary means of identifying a gas mask canister shall be by means of properly worded labels; the secondary means shall be by a color code. All who issue or use gas masks falling within the scope of this section shall see that all gas mask canisters purchased or used by them are properly labeled and colored in accordance with these requirements before they are placed in service and that the labels and colors are properly maintained at all times thereafter until the canisters have completely served their purpose.

On each canister shall appear in bold letters the following:

Canister for_____

(name of atmospheric contaminant) or

_____

Type N Gas Mask Canister _____

In addition, essentially the following wording shall appear beneath the appropriate phrase on the canister label: "For respiratory protection in atmospheres containing not more than ___ percent by volume of (name of atmospheric contaminant)."

Canisters having a special high-efficiency filter for protection against radionuclides and other highly toxic particulates shall be labeled with a statement of the type and degree of protection afforded by the filter. The label shall be affixed to the neck end of, or to the gray stripe that is around and near the top of, the canister. The degree of protection shall be marked as the percent of penetration of the canister by a 0.3- micron-diameter dioctyl phthalate (DOP) smoke at a flow rate of 85 liters per minute.

Each canister shall have a label warning that gas masks should be used only in atmospheres containing sufficient oxygen to support life (at least 16 percent by volume), since gas mask canisters are only designed to neutralize or remove contaminants from the air.

Each gas mask canister shall be painted a distinctive color or combination of colors indicated in Table E-5 in 1926.103(i)(6). All colors used shall be such that they are clearly identifiable by the user and clearly distinguishable from one another. The color coating used shall offer a high degree of resistance to chipping, scaling, peeling, blistering, fading, and the effects of the ordinary atmospheres to which they may be exposed "under normal conditions of storage and use. Appropriately colored pressure sensitive tape may be used for the stripes.

Can I wear a beard with a respirator?

Letter to Mr. William P. Richardson Facial hair in the face sealing area is unacceptable. OSHA policy limits the presence of facial hair when certain types of respirators are worn. This is because of studies which show that a satisfactory fit cannot be obtained by persons with beards.

Mr. William P. Richardson   Dec 24, 1985
3812 Kansas Street
Bellingham, Washington 98226

Dear Mr. Richardson:

This is in response to your November 10 Freedom of Information Act (FOIA) request, addressed to Acting Assistant Secretary Patrick R. Tyson, for information relating to health protection policies which affect bearded employees.

The Occupational Safety and Health Administration (OSHA) considered the protection of all employees in developing its air contaminant standards, and requires that employers ensure that workers are not overexposed to these harmful substances. Workers with beards were not studied separately. When administrative or engineering controls have not kept workplace exposure within permissible limits, then appropriate respirators must be worn by exposed employees.

We can provide information concerning OSHA policy relating to its standard (29 CFR 1910.134) on respirator use, as it affects employees who wear beards. The standard does limit beards or other facial hair when certain types of respirators are utilized. This policy is directed at ensuring that those respirators fit the face properly, and protect against air contaminants. Studies have shown that bearded persons cannot achieve a satisfactory seal of the respirator facepiece, and therefore, it is necessary that the face is clean-shaven. We have enclosed several studies which support this.

As you may know, the FOIA does not require an agency to create a record which is not in existence at the time of the request.

Again, since OSHA did not study bearded workers separately in development of its air contaminant standards, we do not have material in our files concerning their incidence of lung disease, nor do we possess material in our files relating to your other inquiries.

We believe that the information provided sufficiently satisfies your request.

Sincerely,
Bruce Hillenbrand, Director Federal-State Operations

Letter to Honorable J. Bennett Johnston United State Senate

Prohibition of beards for respirators. A response to a letter protesting a company respirator program prohibiting beards. Beards are prohibited for respirators which require a face seal. Respirators that do not require a face seal are unaffected by beards.

The Honorable J. Bennett Johnston   November 18, 1987
United States Senate
Washington, D.C. 20510

Dear Senator Johnston:

This is in response to your correspondence of July 27, on behalf of your constituent, Mr. Tom Laiche of Baton Rouge, Louisiana, who is employed at Exxon's Baton Rouge refinery. Please accept my apology for the delay in responding to your letter.

Mr. Laiche wrote you protesting a company respirator program policy which would mean that none of the men at the plant could wear a beard. He believes that the Occupational Safety and Health Administration (OSHA) required the company to adopt this policy which in his opinion is a violation of the personal freedom of the plant employees.

Provision 29 CFR 1910.134(e)(5)(i) in the standard for respiratory protection states that, "Respirators shall not be worn when conditions prevent a good face seal." This prohibition applies to any personal respiratory protection device of a design relying on the principle of forming a face seal to perform at maximum effectiveness.

Hair growing on the face at points where the seal with respirator is to occur is a condition preventing a good face seal. Therefore, employers may not use a respiratory protection device of the type described above for protecting employees having hair growth where the face seal must form.

There are respirators of designs that are not based on the principle of forming a face seal for assuring protection and hence are unaffected by beards. Perhaps the possibility of using this type of respirator for protecting employees with beards can be explored with the company.

I appreciate the opportunity to comment on this matter. If I may be of further service, please contact me.

Sincerely,
John A. Pendergrass, Assistant Secretary

Common Citations in the Personal Protective Equipment Area

No head protection. This is a common citation where the controlling employer does not mandate the use of hard hats on a construction site. Employers have a difficult time anticipating when an exposure will occur, and this decision not to require head protection in a hazardous situation has resulted in many citations. As one worker explained to an inspector, "Heck, you only need the hard hat when something hits you in the head."

No eye and face protection. Many injuries result from flying particles as a result of grinding welds, cutting concrete products, and cutting rebar and wire mesh. Most citations for welding eye protection occur, not for the welder, but for the welder's helper.

No respiratory protection. Respiratory protection should be worn when exposures cannot be controlled and the potential to exceed the permissible exposure limit (PEL) exists. Once the employee has become overexposed and a citation is issued, the inspector will look for other examples of a poor safety program.

No safety nets. Even though it is not worn, the safety net is covered in the personal protective equipment section because it protects employees. Section 105(a) is the generic standard that is used when fall exposures occur above 25 ft. and there is no specific standard applicable.

No life vests. On bridge jobs where there is a danger of free falling into a body of water, life vests are required. Wearing vests do not alleviate the responsibility for fall protection above 25 ft.

Employers must provide training for their workers and verify in writing that each of the affected employees has received and understood the training through written certification.

Training must include:

- When PPE is necessary;
- What type of PPE is necessary;
- How to properly put on, take off, adjust and wear PPE;
- The limitations of the PPE; and
- The proper care, maintenance, useful life and disposal of the PPE.

Personal Protective Equipment Quiz
(See appendix for answers.)

1. On a construction site, who is responsible to ensure that workers have the PPE?
a. The employee
b. The labor service company
c. The employer
d. OSHA

2. For head protection, workers should wear a hard hat that complies with:
a. ANSI Standard Z64.1
b. ANSI Standard Z89.1
c. NFPA 101
d. NFPA 93

3. Safety shoes must meet the requirements of:
a. LeHigh Safety Shoe specification
b. ANSI Standard Z89.1
c. ANSI Standard Z41.1
d. ANSI Standard Z87.1

4. Eye protection must have the name of the manufacturer and the ANSI Standard stamped on them. In order to be effective, they must:
a. Have side shields
b. Be tinted to preclude sun glare
c. Not disturb other types of PPE, such as hard hats or respirators
d. Be provided by the employee

5. When working over water if there is a danger of falling in, workers must:
a. Be provided with a U.S. Coast Guard-approved life jacket
b. Have a certified swimmer available to fish them out
c. Be trained in basic life-saving techniques
d. Understand the danger of hypothermia

6. Hard hats must be worn:
a. With the bill facing front at all times
b. Over the top of any other type of hat, such as baseball caps
c. At all times
d. When there is a danger of objects striking the head

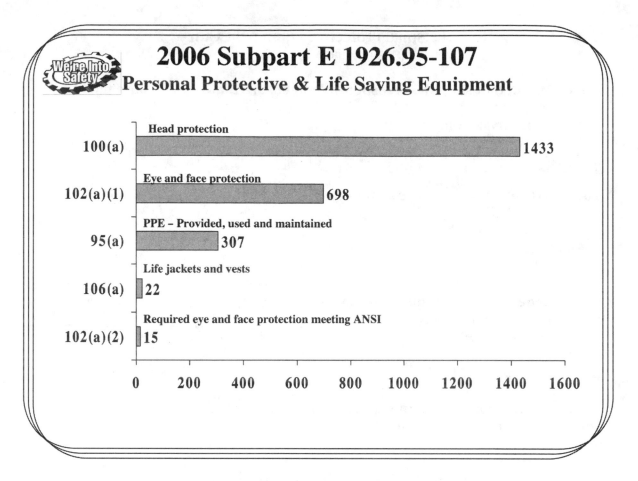

2006 Subpart E 1926.95-107
Personal Protective & Life Saving Equipment

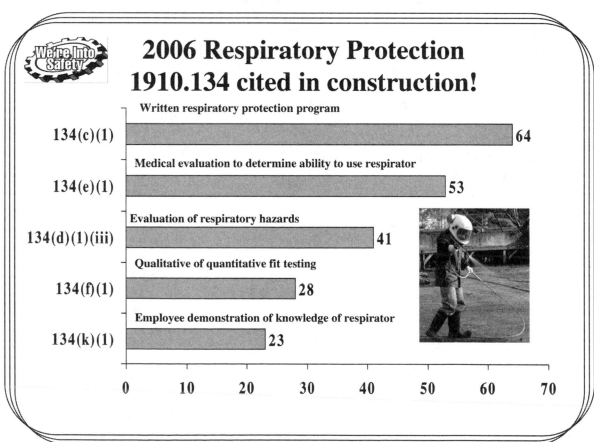

2006 Respiratory Protection
1910.134 cited in construction!

PERMIT-REQUIRED CONFINED SPACES

OSHA's Construction Safety and Health Regulations, Part 1926, do not contain a specific permit-required confined space regulation. Subpart C, 1926.21, Safety Training and Education, states:

> All employees required to enter into confined or enclosed spaces shall be instructed as to the nature of the hazards involved, the necessary precautions to be taken, and in the use of protective and emergency equipment required. The employer shall comply with any specific regulations that apply to work in dangerous or potentially dangerous areas.

This section also defines a confined or enclosed space as:

> [A]ny space having a limited means of egress, which is subject to the accumulation of toxic or flammable contaminants or has an oxygen deficient atmosphere. Confined or enclosed spaces include, but are not limited to, storage tanks, process vessels, bins, boilers, ventilation or exhaust ducts, sewers, underground utility vaults, tunnels, pipelines, and open top spaces more than 4 feet in depth such as pits, tubs, vaults, and vessels.

OSHA's Construction Regulations also contain requirements dealing with confined space hazards in underground construction (Subpart S), underground electric transmission and distribution work (1926.956), excavations (Subpart P), and welding and cutting (Subpart J).

Further guidance may be obtained from ANSI Z117.1-1989, Safety Requirements for Confined Spaces. This standard provides minimum safety requirements to be followed while entering, exiting, and working in confined spaces at normal atmospheric pressure. This standard does not pertain to underground mining, tunneling, caisson work, or similar tasks that have established national consensus standards.

More specific guidance can be found in OSHA's General Industry Regulation, 1910.146, Permit-Required Confined Spaces. The regulation on confined space entry covers general industry workers including 1.6 million who enter confined spaces annually and an additional 10.6 million employed at the 240,000 worksites covered by the standard (29 CFR 1910.146). This standard is expected to prevent nearly 85 percent of deaths and injuries (i.e., 54 deaths and 10,949 injuries) each year.

Anatomy of Confined Spaces in Construction

Fatalities and injuries constantly occur among construction workers who during the course of their jobs are required to enter confined spaces. In some circumstances, these workers are exposed to multiple hazards, any of which may cause bodily injury, illness, or death. Newspaper and magazine articles abound with stories of workers injured and killed from a variety of atmospheric factors and physical agents. Throughout the construction job site, contractors and workers encounter both inherent and induced hazards within confined workspaces.

A confined space is defined as an area that:
- Has adequate size and configuration for employee entry;
- Has limited means of access or egress; and
- Is not designed for continuous employee occupancy.
- A permit-required confined space is a confined space that presents or has the potential for hazards related to atmospheric conditions (e.g., toxic, flammable, asphyxiating), engulfment, configuration or any other recognized serious hazard.
- A prohibited condition is defined as any condition not allowed by permit during entry operations.

Inherent Hazards

Inherent hazards, such as electrical, thermal, chemical, and mechanical, are associated with specific types of equipment and the interactions among them. Examples include:
- High voltage (e.g., shock or corona discharge and the resulting burns);
- Radiation generated by equipment;
- Defective design;
- Omission of protective features (e.g., no provision for grounding non-current-carrying conductive parts);
- High or low temperatures;
- High noise levels; and
- High-pressure vessels and lines (e.g., rupturing with resultant release of fragments, fluids, gases).
- Inherent hazards usually cannot be eliminated without degrading the system or equipment, or without making them inoperative. Therefore, emphasis must be placed on hazard control methods.

Induced Hazards

Induced hazards arise and are induced from a multitude of incorrect decisions and actions that occur during the actual construction process. Examples include:
- Omission of protective features;
- Physical arrangements that may cause unintentional worker contact with electrical energy sources;
- Oxygen-deficient atmospheres created at the bottom of pits or shafts;
- Lack of safety factors in structural strength; and
- Flammable atmospheres.

Typical Confined Spaces

Vaults

A variety of vaults are found on construction job sites. Workers often must enter these vaults to perform a number of functions. The restricted nature of vaults and their frequently below-grade location can create an assortment of safety and health problems.

Oxygen-deficient atmosphere. One of the major problems confronting construction workers while working in vaults is the ever-present possibility of an oxygen-deficient atmosphere.

Explosive or toxic gases, vapors, or fumes. While working in an electrical vault, workers may be exposed to the build-up of explosive gases such as those used for heating (propane). Welding and soldering produce toxic fumes that are confined in the limited atmosphere.

Electrical shock. Electrical shock is often encountered from power tools and line cords. In many instances, electrical shock results from the fact that the contractor has not provided an approved grounding system or the protection afforded by ground-fault circuit interrupters or low-voltage systems.

Purging. In some instances, purging agents such as nitrogen and argon may enter the vault from areas adjacent to it. These agents may displace the oxygen in the vault to the extent that it will asphyxiate workers almost immediately.

Materials falling in and on. A hazard normally considered a problem associated with confined spaces is material or equipment that may fall into the vault or onto workers as they enter and leave the vault. Vibration could cause the materials on top of the vault to roll off and strike workers. If the manhole covers were removed or if they were not installed in the first place, materials could fall into the vault, causing injury to the workers inside.

Condenser Pits

A common confined space found in the construction of nuclear power plants is the condenser pit. Because of their large size, they are often overlooked as potentially hazardous confined spaces. These below-grade areas create large containment areas for accumulating toxic fumes, gases, and so forth, or for creating oxygen-deficient atmospheres when purging with argon, freon, and other inert gases. Workers above who drop equipment, tools, and materials into the pit will create other hazards.

Manholes

Throughout the construction site, manholes are commonplace. As means of entry into and exit from vaults, tanks, pits, and so forth, manholes perform a necessary function. However, these confined spaces may present serious hazards that could cause injuries and fatalities. A variety of hazards are associated with manholes. With no cover, the manhole becomes a dangerous trap into which a worker could fall. Manhole covers are often removed and not replaced or else they are not provided in the first place.

Pipe Assemblies

One of the most frequently unrecognized types of confined spaces encountered throughout the construction site is the pipe assembly. Piping of 16 in. to 36 in. in diameter is commonly used in construction. For any number of reasons, workers will enter the pipe. Once inside, they are faced with potential oxygen-deficient atmospheres, often caused by purging with argon or another inert gas. Welding fumes generated by the worker in the pipe or by other workers operating outside the pipe at either end, subject the worker to toxic atmospheres. The generally restricted dimensions of the pipe provide little room for the workers to move about and gain any degree of comfort while performing their tasks. Once inside the pipe, communication is extremely difficult. In situations where the pipe bends, communication and extrication

become even more difficult. Electrical shock is another problem to which the worker can be exposed. Ungrounded tools and equipment or inadequate line cords are some of the causes. Heat generated within the pipe run may cause heat prostration.

Ventilation Ducts

Ventilation ducts, like pipe runs, are very common at construction sites. These sheet metal enclosures create a complex network that moves heated and cooled air and exhaust fumes to desired locations in the plant. Ventilation ducts may require that workers enter them to cut out access holes or install essential parts of the duct. Depending on where these ducts are located, oxygen deficiency could exist. They usually possess many bends, which create difficult entry and exit and make it difficult for workers inside the duct to communicate with those outside of it. Electrical shock and heat stress are other hazards associated with work inside ventilation ducts.

Tanks

Tanks are another type of confined workspace commonly found in construction. They are used for a variety of purposes, including the storage of water and chemicals. Tanks require entry for cleaning and repairs. Ventilation is always a problem. Oxygen-deficient atmospheres, along with toxic and explosive atmospheres created by the substances stored in the tanks, present hazards to workers. Heat, another problem in tanks, may cause heat prostration, particularly on a hot day. Because electrical line cords are often taken into the tank, the hazard of electrical shock usually is present. The nature of the tank's structure often dictates that workers must climb ladders to reach high places on the walls of the tank, which presents fall hazards.

Sumps

Sumps are commonplace. They are used as collection places for water and other liquids. Workers entering sumps may encounter an oxygen-deficient atmosphere. Also, because of the wet nature of the sump, electrical shock hazards are present when power tools are used inside. Sumps are often poorly illuminated.

Inadequate lighting also may heighten the potential for accidents.

Containment Cavities

These large below-grade areas are characterized by little or no air movement. Ventilation is always a problem. In addition, the possibility of oxygen deficiency exists. Also, welding and other gases may easily collect in these areas, creating toxic atmospheres. As these structures near completion, more confined spaces will exist as rooms are built off the existing structure.

Electrical Transformers

Electrical transformers are often located on job sites. They often contain a nitrogen purge or dry air. Before they are opened, they must be well vented by having air pumped in. Workers, particularly electricians and power plant operators, will enter through hatches on the top of the transformers for various work-related reasons. Testing for oxygen deficiency and for toxic atmospheres is mandatory.

Heat Sinks

These large pit areas hold cooling water in the event that there is a problem with the pumps located at a nuclear power plant's water supply (normally a river or lake) that would prevent cooling water from reaching the reactor core. When in the pits, workers are exposed to welding fumes and electrical hazards, particularly because water accumulates in the bottom of the sink. Generally, it is difficult to communicate with workers in the heat sink because the rebar in the walls of the structure deadens radio signals.

Confined Space within a Confined Space

By the very nature of construction, situations are created that illustrate one of the most hazardous confined spaces of all—a confined space within a confined space. This situation often occurs when there are tanks within pits or pipe assemblies or vessels within pits. In this situation, not only do the potential hazards associated with the outer confined space require testing, monitoring, and control, but those of the inner space require the procedures as well. A good example of a confined

space within a confined space is a vessel with a nitrogen purge inside a filtering water access pit. Workers entering the pit and/or the vessel should do so only after both spaces have been evaluated and proper control measures have been established.

Hazards in One Space Entering Another Space

During an examination of confined spaces in construction, one often encounters situations that are not easy to evaluate or control. For instance, a room or area that is classified as a confined space may be relatively safe for work. However, access passages from other areas outside or adjacent to the room could, at some point, allow the transfer of hazardous agents into this "safe" space. One such instance would be a pipe coming through a wall into a containment room. Welding fumes and other toxic materials generated in one room may easily travel through the pipe into another area, causing it to change from a safe to an unsafe workplace. A serious problem with a situation such as this is that workers working in the "safe" area are not aware of the hazards leaking into their area. Thus, they are not prepared to take action to avoid or control it.

Permit-Required Confined Space Program

The standard requires employers initially to evaluate their workplaces and determine if there are any permit-required confined spaces, inform employees through signs or other equally effective means, and prevent unauthorized entry.

The permit-required confined space program:
- Mandates a written program to:
  - prevent unauthorized entry;
  - identify and evaluate hazards; and
  - establish procedures and practices for safe entry, including testing and monitoring conditions;
- Calls for:
  - an attendant to be stationed outside permit spaces during entry;
  - procedures to summon rescuers and prevent unauthorized personnel from attempting rescue; and

- a system for preparing, issuing, using, and canceling entry permits; and
- Requires:
  - coordinated entry for more than one employer;
  - procedures for concluding entry operations and canceling entry permits; and
  - review of the permit program at least annually and additionally as necessary.

A permit system must be established that requires an entry supervisor to authorize entry, prepare and sign written permits, order corrective measures if necessary and cancel permits when work is completed. Permits must be available to all employees and extend only for the duration of the task. Permits must be retained for one year to facilitate review of the confined space program. Permits must include:

- Identification of space;
- Purpose of entry;
- Date and duration of permit;
- List of authorized entrants;
- Names of current attendants and entry supervisor;
- List of hazards in the permit space;
- List of measurements to isolate permit space and eliminate or control hazards;
- The acceptable entry conditions;
- Results of tests initialed by the person(s) performing tests;
- Rescue emergency services and means to summon;
- Communication procedures for attendants or entrants;
- Required equipment (e.g., respirators, communications, alarm);
- Any additional permits (e.g., for hot work).

Training mandates initial and refresher training (when duties change, hazards in space change or whenever evaluation determines inadequacies in an employee's knowledge) to provide employees' understanding, skills and knowledge to do the job safely. Employer certification of training must include employee's name, signature or initials of trainer and date of training.

Authorized entrants must know the hazards they may face, be able to recognize signs or symptoms of exposure and understand the consequences of exposure to hazards. Entrants must know how to use any needed equipment, communicate with attendants as necessary, alert attendants when a warning symptom or other hazardous condition exists and exit as quickly as possible whenever ordered or alerted to do so (by alarm, warning sign or prohibited condition).

Attendants must know the hazards of confined spaces, be aware of behavioral effects of potential exposures, maintain continuous count and identification of authorized attendants, remain outside space until relieved, communicate with entrants as necessary to monitor entrant status. Attendants also must monitor activities inside and outside the permit space and order exit if required, summon rescuers if necessary, prevent unauthorized entry into confined space, and perform non-entry rescues if required. They may not perform other duties that interfere with their primary duties to monitor and protect the safety of authorized entrants.

Entry supervisors must know hazards of confined spaces, verify that all tests have been conducted and all procedures and equipment are in place before endorsing permits, terminate entry and cancel permits and verify that rescue services are available and the means for summoning them are operable. Supervisors are to remove unauthorized individuals who enter confined space. They also must determine, at least when shifts and entry supervisors change, that acceptable conditions as specified in the permit continue.

Rescue teams may be on onsite or off-site. Rescue is to use employee retrieval systems whenever possible. Onsite teams must be properly equipped and receive the same training as authorized entrants plus training to use personal protective and rescue equipment and first aid, including CPR. They must practice simulated rescues at least once every 12 months. Outside rescue services must be made aware of hazards, receive access to comparable permit spaces to develop rescue plans and practice rescues. Employers must provide hospital or treatment facilities with any MSDSs or other information on a permit space hazard exposure situation that may aid in the treatment of rescued employees.

Host employers must provide information to contractors on permit spaces, the permit space program, and procedures and likely hazards that the contractor might encounter. Joint entries must be coordinated and the contractor debriefed at the conclusion of entry operations.

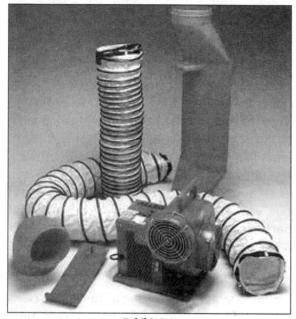

Exhibit 7-1.
Alternative protection procedures can be used when ventilation alone is sufficient to maintain safe entry.

Alternative Protection Procedures

For permit spaces where the only hazard is atmospheric and ventilation alone can control the hazard, employers may use alternative procedures for entry.

To qualify for alternative procedures employers must:

- Ensure that it is safe to remove the entrance cover;
- Determine that ventilation alone is sufficient to maintain the permit space safe for entry, and work to be performed within the permit-required space must introduce no additional hazards;
- Gather monitoring and inspection data to support the above two items;
- If entry is necessary to conduct initial data gathering, perform such entry under the full permit program; and
- Document the determinations and sup-

porting data and make them available to employees.

Entry can take place after:

- It has been determined safe to remove the entrance cover;
- Any openings have been guarded to protect against falling and falling objects;
- Internal atmospheric testing has been performed;
- Air remains without hazard whenever any employee is inside the space;
- Continuous forced air ventilation has eliminated any hazardous atmosphere; and
- The space is tested periodically.

Employees must exit immediately if a hazardous atmosphere is detected during entry Afterward. the space must be evaluated to determine how the hazardous atmosphere developed.

Permit-Required Confined Spaces for General Industry—1910.146

Many workplaces contain spaces that are considered to be "confined" because their configurations hinder the activities of any employees who must enter into, work in and exit from them. In many instances, employees who work in confined spaces also face an increased risk of exposure to serious physical injury from hazards such as entrapment, engulfment and hazardous atmospheric conditions. Confinement itself may pose entrapment hazards, and work in confined spaces may keep employees closer to hazards, such as an asphyxiating atmosphere, than they would be otherwise. For example, confinement, limited access and restricted airflow can result in hazardous conditions that would not arise in an open workplace.

A confined space has limited or restricted means of entry or exit, is large enough for an employee to enter and perform assigned work, and is not designed for continuous occupancy by the employee. These spaces may include, but are not limited to, underground vaults, tanks, storage bins, pits and diked areas, vessels and silos.

A permit-required confined space is one that meets the definition of a confined space and has one or more of the following characteristics:

- Contains or has the potential to contain a hazardous atmosphere;
- Contains a material that has the potential for engulfing an entrant;
- Has an internal configuration that might cause an entrant to be trapped or asphyxiated by inwardly converging walls or by a floor that slopes downward and tapers to a smaller cross-section; and/or
- Contains any other recognized serious safety or health hazards.

In general, employers must evaluate the workplace to determine if spaces are permit-required confined spaces. If there are permit spaces in the workplace, the employer must inform exposed employees of the existence, location and danger posed by the spaces. This can be accomplished by posting danger signs or by another equally effective means (See Exhibit 7-2.). The following language would satisfy the requirements for such a sign:

**DANGER-PERMIT
REQUIRED-CONFINED SPACE
AUTHORIZED ENTRANTS ONLY**

**Exhibit 7-2.
Permit-required confined spaces should
be clearly marked as dangerous.**

If employees are not to enter and work in permit spaces, employers must take effective measures to prevent their employees from entering the permit spaces.

If employees are to enter permit spaces, the employer must develop a written permit space program that shall be made available to employees or their representatives. Under certain conditions, the employer may use alternate procedures for worker entry into a permit space. For example, if employers can demonstrate with monitoring and inspection data that the only hazard is an actual or potential hazardous atmosphere that can be made safe for entry by the use of continuous forced-air ventilation, they may be exempted from some requirements, such as permits and attendants. Even in such circumstances, however, the internal atmosphere of the space must be tested first for oxygen content, second for flammable gases and vapors, and third for potential toxic air contaminants before any employee enters.

Written Program

The employer who allows employee entry must develop and implement a written program for permit-required confined spaces.

The OSHA standard requires the employer's program to:

- Identify and evaluate permit space hazards before allowing employee entry;
- Test conditions in the permit space before entry operations and monitor the space during entry;
- Perform appropriate testing for atmospheric hazards in the following order:
  - Oxygen;
  - Combustible gases or vapors; and
  - Toxic gases or vapors; and
- Implement necessary measures to prevent unauthorized entry;
- Establish and implement the means, procedures and practices, such as specifying acceptable entry conditions, isolating the permit space, providing barriers, verifying acceptable entry conditions, purging, making inert, flushing, or ventilation of the permit space to eliminate or control hazards necessary for safe permit-space entry operations;
- Identify employee job duties;
- Provide, maintain and require, at no cost to the employee, the use of personal protective equipment and any other equipment necessary for safe entry (e.g., testing, monitoring, ventilating, communications, and lighting equipment; barriers; shields and ladders);

- Ensure that at least one attendant is stationed outside the permit space for the duration of entry operations;
- Coordinate entry operations when employees of more than one employer are to be working in the permit space;
- Implement appropriate procedures for summoning rescue and emergency services;
- Establish, in writing, and implement a system for the preparation, issuance, use and cancellation of entry permits;
- Review established entry operations and annually revise the permit-space entry program; and
- When an attendant is required to monitor multiple spaces, implement the procedures to be followed during an emergency in one or more of the permit spaces being monitored.

If hazardous conditions are detected during entry, employees must immediately leave the space and the employer must evaluate the space to determine the cause of the hazardous atmospheres.

When entry to permit spaces is prohibited, the employer must take effective measures to prevent unauthorized entry. Non-permit confined spaces must be reevaluated when there are changes in their use or configuration and, where appropriate, must be reclassified.

If testing and inspection data prove that a permit-required confined space no longer poses hazards, that space may be reclassified as a non-permit confined space. If entry is required to eliminate hazards and to obtain the data, the employer must follow procedures as set forth under sections (d) through (k) of the standard. A certificate documenting the data must be made available to employees entering the space. The certificate must include the date, location of the space and the signature of the person making the certification.

Contractors must be informed of permit spaces and permit-space entry requirements, any identified hazards, the employer's experience with the space (i.e., the knowledge of hazardous conditions), and precautions or procedures to be followed when in or near permit spaces.

When employees of more than one employer are conducting entry operations, the affected employers must coordinate entry operations to ensure that affected employees are appropriately protected from permit space hazards. Contractors also must be given any other pertinent information regarding hazards and operations in permit spaces and be debriefed at the conclusion of entry operations.

Permit System

A permit must be posted at entrances or otherwise made available to entrants before they enter a permit space. The permit must be signed by the entry supervisor, who attests that pre-entry preparations have been completed and that the space is safe to enter.

The duration of entry permits must not exceed the time required to complete an assignment. Also, the entry supervisor must terminate entry and cancel permits when an assignment has been completed or when new conditions exist. New conditions must be noted on the canceled permit and used in revising the permit space program. The standard also requires the employer to keep all canceled entry permits for at least one year.

Entry Permits

Entry permits must include the following information:

- Test results;
- Tester's initials or signature;
- Name and signature of the supervisor who authorizes entry;
- Name of permit space to be entered, authorized entrant(s), eligible attendants and individual(s) authorized to be entry supervisor(s);
- Purpose of entry and known space hazards;
- Measures to be taken to isolate permit spaces and to eliminate or control space hazards (i.e., locking out or tagging of equipment and procedures for purging, making inert, ventilating and flushing permit spaces);
- Name and telephone numbers of rescue and emergency services;
- Date and authorized duration of entry;
- Acceptable entry conditions;
- Communication procedures and equipment to maintain contact during entry;
- Additional permit(s), such as for hot work, that have been issued to authorize work in the permit space;

- Special equipment and procedures, including personal protective equipment and alarm systems; and
- Any other information needed to ensure employee safety.

Training and Education

Before an initial work assignment begins, the employer must provide proper training for all workers who are required to work in permit spaces. Upon completing this training, employers must ensure that employees have acquired the understanding, knowledge and skills necessary for the safe performance of their duties. Additional training is required when: (1) the job duties change, (2) there is a change in the permit-space program or the permit-space operation presents a new hazard, and (3) when an employee's job performance shows deficiencies. Training also is required for rescue team members, including cardiopulmonary resuscitation (CPR) and first aid (see Emergencies). Employers must certify this training has been accomplished.

Upon completion of training, employees must receive a certificate of training that includes the employee's name, signature or initials of trainer(s), and dates of training. The certification must be made available for inspection by employees and their authorized representatives. In addition, the employer also must ensure that employees are trained in their assigned duties.

Authorized Entrant's Duties

An authorized entrant has specified duties. They must

- Know space hazards, including information on the mode of exposure (e.g., inhalation or dermal absorption), signs or symptoms and consequences of the exposure;
- Use appropriate personal protective equipment properly (e.g., face and eye protection and other forms of barrier protection such as gloves, aprons and coveralls);
- As necessary, maintain communication (i.e., telephone, radio, visual observation) with attendants to enable the attendant to monitor the entrant's status as well as to alert the entrant to evacuate;

- Exit from permit space as soon as possible when ordered by an authorized person, the entrant recognizes the warning signs or symptoms of exposure exist, a prohibited condition exists, or an automatic alarm is activated; and
- Alert the attendant when a prohibited condition exists or warning signs or symptoms of exposure exist.

Attendant's Duties

Attendants have different duties. They must

- Remain outside permit space during entry operations unless relieved by another authorized attendant;
- Perform no-entry rescues when specified by employer's rescue procedure;
- Know existing and potential hazards, including information on the mode of exposure, signs or symptoms, consequences of the exposure and their physiological effects;
- Maintain communication with and keep an accurate account of those workers entering the permit-required space;
- Order evacuation of the permit space when a prohibited condition exists, a worker shows signs of physiological effects of hazardous exposure, an emergency outside the confined space exists, or the attendant cannot effectively and safely perform required duties;
- Summon rescue and other services during an emergency;
- Ensure that unauthorized persons stay away from permit spaces or exit immediately if they have entered the permit space;
- Inform authorized entrants and entry supervisor of entry by unauthorized persons; and;
- Perform no other duties that interfere with the attendant's primary duties.

Entry Supervisor's Duties

The entry supervisor is responsible for particular tasks. They must

- Know space hazards, including information on the mode of exposure, signs or symptoms and consequences of exposure;
- Verify emergency plans and specified entry conditions such as permits, tests, procedures and equipment before allowing entry;

- Terminate entry and cancel permits when entry operations are completed or if a new condition exists;
- Take appropriate measures to remove unauthorized entrants; and
- Ensure that entry operations remain consistent with the entry permit and that acceptable entry conditions are maintained.

Emergencies

The standard requires the employer to ensure that rescue service personnel are provided with and trained in the proper use of personal protective and rescue equipment, including respirators; trained to perform assigned rescue duties; and have had authorized entrant's training. The standard also requires that rescuers be trained in first aid and CPR and, at a minimum, one rescue team member be currently certified in first aid and in CPR. The employer also must ensure that practice rescue exercises are performed annually, and that rescue services are provided access to permit spaces so they can practice rescue operations. Rescuers also must be informed of the hazards of the permit space.

When appropriate, authorized entrants who enter a permit space must wear a chest or full body harness with a retrieval line attached to the center of their backs near shoulder level or above their heads. Wristlets may be used if the employer can demonstrate that the use of a chest or full body harness is infeasible or creates a greater hazard. Also, the employer must ensure that the other end of the retrieval line is attached to a mechanical device or to a fixed point outside the permit space. A mechanical device must be available to retrieve personnel from vertical type permit spaces more than 5 ft. deep.

In addition, if an injured entrant is exposed to a substance for which a material safety data sheet (MSDS) or other similar written information is required to be kept at the worksite, that MSDS or other written information must be made available to the medical facility treating the exposed entrant.

Exhibit 7-3.
Rescue service personnel must be given access to practice rescue operations.

Permit-Required Confined Space Entry Quiz
(See appendix for answers.)

1. By definition, a confined space must be:
a. Large enough to enter, have restricted entry and be dangerous
b. Large enough to enter, be dangerous, have a confined space sign posted
c. Large enough to enter, restricted access, not be designed for continuous occupancy
d. Large enough to enter, be posted as a restricted area

2. The construction standard requires that workers entering a confined space:
a. Know about the hazards they will encounter
b. Be instructed on the hazards, what precautions must be taken and how to use PPE and emergency equipment
c. Wear a self-contained breathing apparatus
d. Be trained in permit-required entry rescue techniques

3. Examples of construction-related confined spaces are:
a. A tool shop, an enclosed trailer, and a sewage tank
b. A manhole, a building foundation, and the job shack,
c. A manhole, a condenser pit, and an underground vault
d. A classroom with no windows, a tool shop, and a job shack

4. Under the 1910 permit-required entry rules, entry into a permit-required confined space requires:
a. An authorized entrant, an attendant, a supervisor of the operation
b. An authorized entrant, a certified engineer, a supervisor of the operation
c. An authorized entrant, an attendant, a stand-by rescue team
d. An authorized entrant, a supervisor, a stand-by rescue team

5. The ANSI standard for entry into permit-required confined spaces is:
a. ANSI Z87.1
b. ANSI Z41
c. ANSI Z117.1
d. ANSI Z93.3

6. OSHA will enforce the rules for entry into permit-required confined spaces for construction workers using:
a. General Duty Clause and ANSI Z117.1
b. 29 CFR 1910.146
c. 29 CFR 1910.147
d. There are no rules for construction workers entering permit-required confined spaces

WELDING

Gas Welding and Cutting—1926.350

Valve protection caps shall be in place and secured.

When cylinders are hoisted, they shall be secured on a cradle, sling board, or pallet. They shall not be hoisted or transported by means of magnets or choker slings.

Cylinders shall be moved by tilting and rolling them on their bottom edges. They shall not be intentionally dropped, struck, or permitted to strike each other violently.

When powered vehicles transport cylinders, they shall be secured in a vertical position.

Valve protection caps shall not be used for lifting cylinders from one vertical position to another. Bars shall not be used under valves or valve protection caps to pry cylinders loose when frozen. Warm, not boiling, water shall be used to thaw cylinders loose.

Unless cylinders are firmly secured on a special carrier intended for this purpose, regulators shall be removed and valve protection caps put in place before cylinders are moved.

A suitable cylinder truck, chain, or other steadying device shall be used to keep cylinders from being knocked over while in use.

When work is finished, when cylinders are empty, or when cylinders are moved at any time, the cylinder valve shall be closed.

Compressed gas cylinders shall be secured in an upright position at all times, if necessary, for short periods of time while cylinders are actually being hoisted or carried.

Oxygen cylinders in storage shall be separated from fuel-gas cylinders or combustible materials (especially oil or grease), by a minimum distance of 20 ft. (6.1 m) or by a noncombustible barrier at least 5 ft. (1.5 m) high having a fire-resistance rating of at least one-half hour.

Inside of buildings, cylinders shall be stored in a well-protected, well-ventilated, dry location, at least 20 ft. (6.1 m) from highly combustible materials, such as oil or excelsior. Cylinders should be stored in definitely assigned places away from elevators, stairs, or gangways. Assigned storage places shall be located where cylinders will not be knocked over or damaged by passing or falling objects or subject to tampering.

The in-plant handling, storage, and use of all compressed gases in cylinders, portable tanks, rail tank cars, or motor vehicle cargo tanks shall be in accordance with Compressed Gas Association Pamphlet P-1-1965.

Placing Cylinders

Cylinders shall be kept far enough away from the actual welding or cutting operation so that sparks, hot slag, or flame will not reach them. When this is impractical, fire-resistant shields shall be provided.

Cylinders shall be placed where they cannot become part of an electrical circuit. Electrodes shall not be struck against a cylinder to strike an arc.

Fuel-gas cylinders shall be placed with *valve end* up whenever they are in use. They shall not be placed in a location where they would be subject to open flame, hot metal, or other sources of artificial heat.

Cylinders containing oxygen or acetylene or other fuel-gas shall not be taken into confined spaces.

Treatment of Cylinders

Cylinders, whether full or empty, shall not be used as rollers or supports.

No person other than the gas supplier shall attempt to mix gases in a cylinder. No one except the owner of the cylinder or person authorized by him or her shall refill a cylinder. No one shall use a cylinder's contents for purposes other than those intended by the supplier. All cylinders used shall meet the Department of Transportation requirements published in 49 CFR Part 178, Subpart C, Specification for Cylinders.

No damaged or defective cylinder shall be used.

Use of Fuel Gas

Fuel gas shall not be used from cylinders through torches or other devices that are equipped with shut-off valves without reducing the pressure through a suitable regulator attached to the cylinder valve or manifold.

Before a regulator to a cylinder valve is connected, the valve shall be opened slightly and closed immediately. (This action is generally termed "cracking" and is intended to clear the valve of dust or dirt that might otherwise enter the regulator.) The person cracking the valve shall stand to one side of the outlet, not in front of it. The valve of a fuel-gas cylinder shall not be cracked where the gas would reach welding work, sparks, flame, or other possible sources of ignition.

The cylinder valve shall always be opened slowly to prevent damage to the regulator. For quick closing, valves of fuel-gas cylinders shall not be opened more than 1½ turns. When a special wrench is required, it shall be left in position on the stem of the valve while the cylinder is in use so that the fuel-gas flow can be shut off quickly in case of an emergency. In the case of manifolded or coupled cylinders, at least one such wrench shall always be available for immediate use. Nothing shall be placed on top of a fuel-gas cylinder when in use, which may damage the safety device or interfere with the quick closing of the valve.

Before a regulator is removed from a cylinder valve, the cylinder valve shall always be closed and the gas released from the regulator.

If when the valve on a fuel-gas cylinder is opened, there is found to be a leak around the valve stem, the valve shall be closed and the gland nut tightened. If this action does not stop the leak, the use of the cylinder shall be discontinued and it shall be properly tagged and removed from the work area. In the event that fuel-gas leaks from the cylinder valve, rather than from the valve stem, and the gas cannot be shut off, the cylinder shall be properly tagged and removed from the work area. If a regulator attached to a cylinder valve will effectively stop a leak through the valve seat, the cylinder need not be removed from the work area.

If a leak should develop at a fuse plug or other safety device, the cylinder shall be removed from the work area.

Fuel-Gas and Oxygen Manifolds

Fuel-gas and oxygen manifolds shall bear the name of the substance they contain in letters at least 1-in. high and either be painted on the manifold or on a sign permanently attached to it. These manifolds shall be placed in safe, well-ventilated, accessible locations and not be located within enclosed spaces. Manifold hose connections, including both ends of the supply hose that lead to the manifold, shall be such that the hose cannot be interchanged between fuel-gas and oxygen manifolds and supply header connections. Adapters shall not be used to permit the interchange of hose. Hose connections shall be kept free of grease and oil. When not in use, manifold and header hose connections shall be capped. Nothing shall be placed on top of a manifold, when in use, that will damage the manifold or interfere with the quick closing of the valves.

Hose

Fuel-gas and oxygen hoses shall be easily distinguishable from each other. The contrast may be made by different colors or by surface characteristics readily distinguishable by the sense of touch. Oxygen and fuel-gas hoses shall not be interchangeable (See Exhibit 8-1.). A single hose having more than one gas passage shall not be used. When parallel sections of oxygen and fuel-gas hose are taped together, not more than 4 in. out of 12 in. shall be covered by tape.

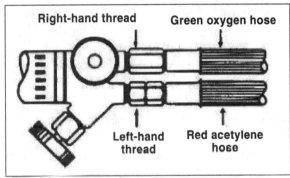

Exhibit 8-1.
Oxygen and fuel-gas hose connections must be separate.

All hose in use, carrying acetylene, oxygen, natural or manufactured fuel gas, or any gas or substance that may ignite or enter into combustion or be in any way harmful to employees shall be inspected at the beginning of each work shift. Defective hose shall be removed from service.

Hose that has been subject to flashback or shows evidence of severe wear or damage shall be tested to twice the normal pressure to which it is subject, but in no case less than 300 psi. Defective hose or hose in doubtful condition shall not be used.

Hose couplings shall be of the type that cannot be unlocked or disconnected by means of a straight pull without rotary motion.

Boxes used for the storage of gas hose shall be ventilated. Hoses, cables, and other equipment shall be kept clear of passageways, ladders, and stairs.

Torches

Clogged torch tip openings shall be cleaned with suitable cleaning wires, drills, or other devices designed for such purpose. Torches in use shall be inspected at the beginning of each work shift for leaking shut-off valves, hose couplings, and tip connections. Defective torches shall not be used. Torches shall be lighted by friction lighters or other approved devices, and not by matches or from hot work.

Regulators and Gauges

Oxygen and fuel-gas pressure regulators, including their related gauges, shall be in proper working order while in use.

Oil and Grease Hazards

Oxygen cylinders and fittings shall be kept away from oil or grease. Cylinders, caps and valves, couplings, regulators, hose and apparatus shall be kept free from oil or greasy substances. They shall not be handled with oily hands or oily gloves. Oxygen shall not be directed at oily surfaces, greasy clothing or within a fuel oil or storage tank or vessel.

Arc Welding—1926.351

Manual Electrode Holders

Only manual electrode holders that are specifically designed for arc welding and cutting and are of a capacity capable of safely handling the maximum rated current required by the electrodes shall be used.

Any current-carrying parts passing through the portion of the holder that the arc welder or cutter grips in his or her hand as well as the outer surfaces of the jaws of the holder shall be fully insulated against the maximum voltage, encountered to ground.

Welding Cables and Connectors

All arc welding and cutting cables shall be of the completely insulated, flexible type, capable of handling the maximum current requirements of the work in progress, taking into account the duty cycle under which the arc welder or cutter is working. Only cable free from repair or splices for a minimum distance of 10 ft. from the cable end to which the electrode holder is connected shall be used; however, cables with standard insulated connectors or with splices whose insulating quality is equal to that of the cable are permitted. Cables in need of repair shall not be used. When a cable, other than the cable lead referred to above, becomes worn to the extent of exposing bare conductors, the portion thus exposed shall be protected by means of rubber and friction tape or other equivalent insulation.

When it becomes necessary to connect or splice lengths of cable one to another, substantial insulated connectors of a capacity at least equivalent to that of the cable shall be used. If connections are affected by means of cable lugs, they shall be securely fastened together to give good electrical contact and the exposed metal parts of the lugs shall be completely insulated.

Ground Returns and Machine Grounding

A ground return cable shall have a safe current-carrying capacity equal to or exceeding the specified maximum output capacity of the arc welding or cutting unit that it services. When a single ground return cable services more than one unit, its safe current-carrying capacity shall equal or exceed the total specified maximum output capacities of all the units that it services.

Pipelines containing gases or flammable liquids or conduits containing electrical circuits, shall not be used as a ground return. When a structure or pipeline is employed as a ground return circuit, it shall be determined that the required electrical contact exists at all joints. The generation of an arc, sparks, or heat at any point shall cause rejection of the structures as a ground circuit. When a structure or pipeline is continuously employed as a ground return circuit, all joints shall be bonded, and periodic inspections shall be conducted to ensure that no condition of electrolysis or fire hazard exists by virtue of such use.

The frames of all arc welding and cutting machines shall be grounded either through a third wire in the cable containing the circuit conductor or through a separate wire which is grounded at the source of the current. Grounding circuits, other than by means of the structure, shall be checked to ensure that the circuit between the ground and the grounded power conductor has resistance low enough to permit sufficient current to flow to cause the fuse or circuit breaker to interrupt the current.

All ground connections shall be inspected to ensure that they are mechanically strong and electrically adequate for the required current.

Operating Instructions

Employers shall instruct employees in the safe means of arc welding and cutting as follows:

- When electrode holders are to be left unattended, the electrodes shall be removed and the holders shall be so placed or protected that they cannot make electrical contact with employees or conducting objects.
- Hot electrode holders shall not be dipped in water; to do so may expose the arc welder or cutter to electric shock.
- When the arc welder or cutter has occasion to leave his work or to stop work for any appreciable length of time, or when the arc welding or cutting machine is to be moved, the power supply switch to the equipment shall be opened.
- Any faulty or defective equipment shall be reported to the supervisor.
- A disconnecting means shall be provided in the supply circuit for each motor-generator arc welder, and for each AC transformer and DC rectifier arc welder that is not equipped with a disconnect mounted as an integral part of the welder.
- A switch or circuit breaker shall be provided by which each resistance welder and its control equipment can be isolated from the supply circuit. The ampere rating of this disconnecting means shall not be less than the supply conductor ampacity.

Shielding

Whenever practicable, all arc welding and cutting operations shall be shielded by noncombustible or flameproof screens that will protect the worker and others working in the vicinity from the direct rays of the arc.

Exhibit 8-2. Welding creates radiant energy hazards that require worker protection.

Fire Prevention—1926.352

When practical, objects to be welded, cut, or heated shall be moved to a designated safe location or if these objects cannot be readily moved, all movable fire hazards in the vicinity shall be taken to a safe place or otherwise protected. If these objects cannot be moved and if all the fire hazards cannot be removed, positive means shall be taken to confine the heat, sparks, and slag and to protect the immovable fire hazards from them.

No welding, cutting or heating shall be performed where the application of flammable paints, the presence of other flammable compounds, or heavy dust concentrations creates a hazard.

Suitable fire extinguishing equipment shall be immediately available in the work area and shall be maintained in a state of readiness for instant use.

When the welding, cutting, or heating operation is such that normal fire prevention precautions are not sufficient, additional personnel shall be assigned to guard against fire while the actual welding, cutting, or heating operation is being performed and for a sufficient period of time after completion of the work to ensure that no possibility of fire exists. Such personnel shall be instructed as to the specific anticipated fire hazards and how the firefighting equipment provided is to be used.

When welding, cutting, or heating is performed on walls, floors, and ceilings, the direct penetration of sparks or heat transfer may introduce a fire hazard to an adjacent area. Therefore, the same precautions shall be taken on the opposite side as are taken on the side on which the welding is being performed.

For the elimination of possible fire in enclosed spaces as a result of gas escaping through leaking or improperly closed torch valves, the gas supply to the torch shall be positively shut off at some point outside the enclosed space whenever the torch is not being used or whenever the torch is left unattended for a substantial period of time, such as during the lunch period. Overnight and at the change of shifts, the torch and hose shall be removed from the confined space. Open-end fuel-gas and oxygen hoses shall be immediately removed from enclosed spaces when they are disconnected.

Except when the contents are being removed or transferred, drums, pails, and other containers that contain or have contained flammable liquids shall be kept closed. Empty containers shall be removed to a safe area apart from hot work operations or open flames.

Drums, containers, or hollow structures that have contained toxic or flammable substances shall, before welding, cutting, or heating is undertaken on them, either be filled with water or thoroughly cleaned of such substances, ventilated, and tested.

Before heat is applied to a drum, container, or hollow structure, a vent or opening shall be provided for the release of any built-up pressure during the application of heat.

Ventilation and Protection in Welding, Cutting, and Heating—1926.353

Mechanical Ventilation

Mechanical ventilation shall consist of either general mechanical ventilation systems or local exhaust systems.

Ventilation shall be deemed adequate if it is of sufficient capacity and so arranged as to remove fumes and smoke at the source and keep their concentration in the breathing zone within safe limits as defined in Subpart D, Occupational Health and Environmental Controls.

Contaminated air exhausted from a working space shall be discharged clear of the source of intake air. All air replacing that withdrawn shall be clean and respirable.

Oxygen shall not be used for ventilation purposes, comfort cooling, blowing dust from clothing, or for cleaning the work area.

Welding, Cutting, and Heating in Confined Spaces

Except where airline respirators are required or allowed, adequate mechanical ventilation meeting the requirements described above shall be provided whenever welding, cutting, or heating is performed in a confined space.

When sufficient ventilation cannot be obtained without blocking the means of access, employees in the confined space shall be protected by airline respirators in accordance with the requirements of Subpart E, Personal Protective and Life Saving Equipment. An employee shall be assigned to stand outside of the confined space to maintain communication with those working within it and to aid them in an emergency.

Where a welder must enter a confined space through a small opening, means shall be provided for quickly removing him or her in case of an emergency. When safety belts and lifelines are used for this purpose, they shall be so attached to the welder's body that his or her body cannot be jammed in a small exit opening. An attendant with a pre-planned rescue procedure shall be stationed outside to observe the welder at all times and be capable of putting rescue operations into effect.

Welding, Cutting, or Heating of Metals of Toxic Significance

Welding, cutting, or heating in any enclosed space involving the following metals shall be performed with adequate mechanical ventilation as described previously:
- Zinc-bearing base or filler metals or metals coated with zinc-bearing materials;
- Lead base metals;
- Cadmium-bearing filler materials; or
- Chromium-bearing metals or metals coated with chromium-bearing materials.

Welding, cutting, or heating in any enclosed spaces involving the following metals shall be performed with adequate local exhaust ventilation as described previously or employees shall be protected by airline respirators in accordance with the requirements of Subpart E:
- Metals containing lead, other than as an impurity, or metals coated with lead-bearing materials;
- Cadmium-bearing or cadmium-coated base metals;
- Metal coated with mercury-bearing metals; or
- Beryllium-containing base or filler metals. Because of its high toxicity, work involving beryllium shall be performed with both local exhaust ventilation and airline respirators.

Employees performing such operations in the open air shall be protected by filter-type respirators in accordance with the requirements of Subpart E. However, the employees performing such operations on beryllium-containing base or filler metals shall be protected by airline respirators in accordance with the requirements of Subpart E. Other employees exposed to the same atmosphere as the welders or burners shall be protected in the same manner as the welder or burner.

Inert-Gas Metal-Arc Welding

Because the inert-gas metal-arc welding process involves the production of ultra-violet radiation of intensities of five to 30 times that produced during shielded metal-arc welding, the decomposition of chlorinated solvents by ultraviolet rays, and the liberation of toxic fumes and gases, employees shall not be permitted to engage in or be exposed to the process until the following special precautions have been taken:
- The use of chlorinated solvents shall be kept at least 200 ft., away, unless shielded, from the exposed arc and surfaces prepared with chlorinated solvents shall be thoroughly dry before welding is permitted on such surfaces;
- Filter lenses meeting the requirements of Subpart E shall protect employees in the area not protected from the arc by screening. When two or more welders are exposed to each other's arcs, filter lens goggles of a suitable type, meeting the requirements

of Subpart E, shall be worn under welding helmets. Hand shields to protect the welder against flashes and radiant energy shall be used when either the helmet is lifted or the shield is removed;

- Welders and other employees who are exposed to radiation shall be suitably protected so that the skin is covered completely to prevent burns and other damage by ultraviolet rays. Welding helmets and hand shields shall be free of leaks, openings, and highly reflective surfaces; and
- When inert-gas metal-arc welding is being performed on stainless steel, adequate local exhaust ventilation as described above or airline respirators as required by Subpart E shall be used to protect against dangerous concentrations of nitrogen dioxide.

General Welding, Cutting and Heating

Welding, cutting, or heating not involving hazardous conditions or toxic materials described above may normally be performed without mechanical ventilation or respiratory protective equipment. These protections shall be provided, however, where an unsafe accumulation of contaminants exists because of unusual physical or atmospheric conditions. Employees performing any type of welding, cutting, or heating shall be protected by suitable eye protective equipment in accordance with the requirements of Subpart E.

Welding, Cutting, and Heating in Way of Preservative Coatings—1926.354

Before welding, cutting, or heating is commenced on any surface covered by a preservative coating whose flammability is not known, a test shall be made by a competent person to determine its flammability. Preservative coatings shall be considered to be highly flammable when scrapings burn with extreme rapidity.

Precautions shall be taken to prevent ignition of highly flammable hardened preservative coatings. When coatings are determined to be highly flammable, they shall be stripped from the area to be heated to prevent ignition.

To protect workers from toxic preservative coatings:

- In enclosed spaces, all surfaces covered with toxic preservatives shall be stripped of all toxic coatings for a distance of at least 4 inches from the area of heat application, or the employees shall be protected by airline respirators that meet the requirements of Subpart E;
- In the open air, employees shall be protected by a respirator, in accordance with the requirements of Subpart E.
- The preservative coatings shall be removed a sufficient distance from the area to be heated to ensure that the temperature of the unstripped metal will not be appreciably raised. Artificial cooling of the metal surrounding the heating area may be used to limit the size of the area required to be cleaned.

Welding Health Hazards

I. Chemical Agents

Zinc

Zinc is used in large quantities in the manufacture of brass, galvanized metals, and various other alloys. Inhalation of zinc oxide fumes can occur when welding or cutting on zinc-coated metals. Exposure to these fumes is known to cause metal fume fever. Symptoms of metal fume fever are very similar to those of common influenza. They include fever (rarely exceeding 102°F), chills, nausea, dryness of the throat, cough, fatigue, and general weakness and aching of the head and body. The victim may sweat profusely for a few hours, after which the body temperature will begin to return to normal. The symptoms of metal fume fever have rarely, if ever, lasted beyond 24 hours. Subjects appear to be more susceptible to the onset of this condition on Mondays or on weekdays following a holiday than on other days.

Cadmium

Cadmium is used frequently as a rust-preventive coating on steel and also as an alloying element. Acute exposures to high concentrations of cadmium fumes can produce severe lung irritation, pulmonary edema (fluid in the lungs), and, in some cases, death. Long-term exposure to low levels of cadmium in the air can result in emphysema (a disease affecting the ability of the lung to absorb oxygen) and damage the kidneys. Cadmium is classified by OSHA, NIOSH, and EPA as a potential human carcinogen.

Beryllium

Beryllium is sometimes used as a alloying element with copper and other base metals. Acute exposure to high concentrations of beryllium can result in chemical pneumonia. Long-term exposure can result in shortness of breath, chronic cough, and significant weight loss, accompanied by fatigue and general weakness.

Iron Oxide

Iron is the principal alloying element in steel manufacture. During the welding process, iron oxide fumes arise from both the base metal and the electrode. The primary acute effect of this exposure is irritation of the nasal passages, throat, and lungs. Although long-term exposure to iron oxide fumes may result in iron pigmentation of the lungs, most authorities agree that these iron deposits in the lung are not dangerous.

Mercury

Mercury compounds are used to coat metals to prevent rust or inhibit foliage growth (e.g., marine paints). Under the intense heat of the arc or gas flame, mercury vapors will be produced. Exposure to these vapors may produce stomach pain, diarrhea, kidney damage, or respiratory failure. Long-term exposure may produce tremors, emotional instability, and hearing damage.

Lead

The welding and cutting of lead-bearing alloys or metals whose surfaces have been painted with lead-based paint can generate lead oxide fumes. Inhalation and ingestion of lead oxide fumes and other lead compounds can cause lead poisoning. Symptoms include metallic taste in the mouth, loss of appetite, nausea, abdominal cramps, and insomnia. In time, anemia and general weakness, chiefly in the muscles of the wrists, develop. Lead adversely affects the brain, central nervous system, circulatory system, reproductive system, kidneys, and muscles.

Fluorides

Fluoride compounds are found in the coatings of several types of fluxes used in welding. Exposure to these fluxes may irritate the eyes, nose, and throat. Repeated exposure to high concentrations of fluorides in the air over a long period may cause pulmonary edema (fluid in the lungs) and bone damage. Exposure to fluoride dusts and fumes also has produced skin rashes.

Chlorinated Hydrocarbon Solvents

Various chlorinated hydrocarbons are used in degreasing and other cleaning operations. The vapors of these solvents are a concern in welding and cutting because the heat and ultraviolet radiation from the arc will decompose the vapors and form highly toxic and irritating phosgene gas that destroys lung tissue (See also Phosgene.).

Phosgene

Phosgene is formed by the decomposition of chlorinated hydrocarbon solvents by ultraviolet radiation. It reacts with moisture in the lungs to produce hydrogen chloride, which in turn destroys lung tissue. For this reason, any use of chlorinated solvents should be well away from welding operations or any operation in which ultraviolet radiation or intense heat is generated.

Carbon Monoxide

Carbon monoxide is a gas usually formed by the incomplete combustion of fuels. Welding and cutting may produce significant amounts of carbon monoxide. In addition, welding operations that use carbon dioxide as the inert gas shield may produce hazardous concentrations of carbon monoxide in poorly ventilated areas. This is caused by a "breakdown" of shielding gas. Carbon monoxide is odorless, colorless and tasteless and often cannot be readily detected by the senses. Common symptoms of overexposure include pounding of the heart, a dull headache, flashes before the eyes, dizziness, ringing in the ears, and nausea.

Nitrogen Oxides

The ultraviolet light of the arc can produce nitrogen oxides (NO, NO_2), from the nitrogen (N) and oxygen (O_2) in the air. Nitrogen oxides are produced by gas metal-arc welding (GMAW or short-arc), gas tungsten-arc welding (GTAW or heli-arc), and plasma arc cutting. Even greater quantities are formed if the shielding gas contains nitrogen. Nitrogen dioxide (NO_2), one of the oxides formed, presents the greatest health risk. This gas is irritating to the eyes, nose and throat, but dangerous concentrations can be inhaled without any immediate discomfort. High concentrations can cause shortness of breath, chest pain, and pulmonary edema (fluid in the lungs).

Ozone

Ozone (O_3) is produced by ultraviolet light from the welding arc. Ozone is produced in greater quantities by gas metal-arc welding (GMAW or short-arc), gas tungsten-arc welding (GTAW or heli-arc), and plasma arc cutting. Ozone is a highly active form of oxygen and can cause great irritation to all of the mucous membranes. Symptoms of ozone exposure include headache, chest pain, and dryness of the upper respiratory tract. Excessive exposure can cause pulmonary edema (fluid in the lungs). Both nitrogen dioxide and ozone are thought to have long-term effects on the lungs.

II. Physical Agents

Ultraviolet Radiation

Ultraviolet radiation (UV) is generated by the electric arc in the welding process. Skin exposure to UV can result in severe burns, in many cases without prior warning. UV radiation can also damage the lens of the eye. Many arc welders are aware of the condition known as "arc-eye," a sensation of sand in the eyes. This condition is caused by excessive eye exposure to UV. Exposure to ultraviolet rays may also increase the effects some industrial chemicals (e.g., coal tar, cresol compounds) have on the skin.

Infrared Radiation

Exposure to infrared radiation (IR), produced by the electric arc and other flame cutting equipment may heat the skin surface and the tissues immediately below the surface. Except for this effect, which can progress to thermal burns in some situations, infrared radiation is not dangerous to welders. Most welders protect themselves from IR (and UV) with a welder's helmet (or glasses) and protective clothing.

Intense Visible Light

Exposure of the human eye to intense visible light can produce adaptation, pupillary reflex, and shading of the eyes. Such actions are protective mechanisms to prevent excessive light from being focused on the retina. In the arc welding process, eye exposure to intense visible light is prevented for the most part by the welder's helmet. However, some individuals have sustained retinal damage due to careless "viewing" of the arc. At no time should the arc be observed without eye protection.

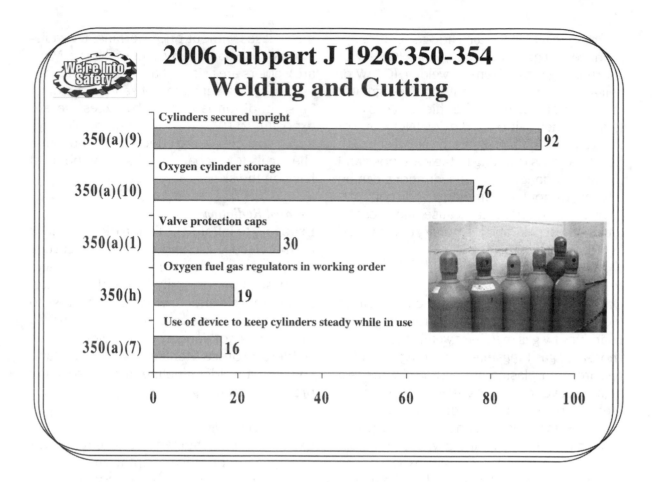

2006 Subpart J 1926.350-354
Welding and Cutting

ELECTRICAL

Electricity is a serious hazard on a construction site; workers and subcontractors are exposed to hazards such as electrical shock, fires, and explosions. Traditionally, experts have relied on the National Electric Code (NEC) for guidance in safeguarding construction workers from these hazards. OSHA recognized the importance of the NEC by including the entire 1971 NEC code in the construction regulations. In 1986 OSHA updated and simplified the electrical standard for construction by placing the NEC guidance directly into the standard, eliminating the need for the NEC to be incorporated into job safety by reference.

Performance language is used, superfluous specifications omitted, and changes in technology accommodated. The OSHA revision of the electrical standards has been made more flexible, eliminating the need for constant revision to keep pace with the NEC, which is revised every three years.

The NEC provisions directly related to employee safety are included in the body of the standard itself. Subpart K is divided into four major groups and a general definitions section:
- Installation Safety Requirements, 29 CFR 1926.402–1926.415
- Safety-Related Work Practices, 29 CFR 1926.416–1926.430
- Safety-Related Maintenance Considerations, 29 CFR 1926.431–1926.440
- Safety Requirements for Special Equipment, 29 CFR 1926.441–1926.448
- Definitions, 29 CFR 1926.449

Installation Safety Requirements

Part I of the standard is very comprehensive. Only some of the major topics and brief summaries of these requirements are included in this discussion. Sections 29 CFR 1926.402 through 1926.408 contain installation safety requirements for electrical equipment and installations used to provide electric power and light at the job site. These sections apply to installations, both temporary and permanent, used on the job site, but they do not apply to existing permanent installations that were in place before the construction activity commenced.

If an installation is made in accordance with the National Electric Code it will be considered to be in compliance with 1926.403 through 1926.408 except for:
- Ground Fault Protection for employees, 1926.401(b)(1)
- Protection on lamps for temporary wiring, 1926.405(a)(2)(ii)(e)
- Suspension of temporary lights by cords, 1926.405(a)(2)(ii)(f)
- Portable lighting used in wet or conductive locations, 1926.405(a)(2)(ii)(g)
- Extension cord sets and flexible cords, 1926.405(a)(2)(ii)(j)

Examination, Installation, and Use of Equipment

All electrical conductors and equipment used by the employer must be approved. The employer must ensure all electrical equipment is free from recognized hazards that are likely to cause death or serious physical harm to employees. The safety of the equipment must be determined by the following:

- Suitability for installation and use in conformity with the provisions of the standard;
- Suitability of equipment for an identified purpose may be evidenced by a listing, labeling, or certification for that identified purpose;
- Mechanical strength and durability. For parts designed to enclose and protect other equipment, this includes the adequacy of the protection thus provided;
- Electrical insulation;
- Heating effects under conditions of use;
- Arcing effects;
- Classification by type, size, voltage, current capacity, and specific use; and
- Other factors that contribute to the practical safeguarding of employees who use or are likely to come in contact with the equipment.

Guarding

Live parts of electric equipment operating at 50 volts or more must be guarded against accidental contact. Guarding of live parts must be accomplished as follows:

- Location in a cabinet, room, vault, or enclosure accessible only to qualified persons.
- Use of permanent, substantial partitions or screens to exclude unqualified persons.
- Location on a suitable balcony, gallery, or platform elevated and arranged to exclude unqualified persons.
- Elevation of 8 ft. or more above the floor.
- Entrance to rooms and other guarded locations containing exposed live parts must be marked with conspicuous warning signs forbidding unqualified persons to enter.

Electric installations that are more than 600 volts and are open to unqualified persons must be made with metal-enclosed equipment or enclosed in a vault or area controlled by a lock. In addition, equipment must be marked with appropriate caution signs.

To protect cords and cables run near a driveway or area where vehicles may run over them, a board may be constructed and placed over the cords or cables, and staked down to safeguard them (See Exhibit 9-1.).

Exhibit 9-1.
Electrical cords and cables may be protected from vehicles and other equipment by boards that are staked down over them.

Overcurrent Protection

The following requirements apply to overcurrent protection of circuits rated 600 volts, nominal, or less.

- Conductors and equipment must be protected from overcurrent in accordance with their ability to safely conduct current;
- Conductors also must have sufficient current-carrying capacity to carry the load;
- Overcurrent devices must not interrupt the continuity of the grounded conductor unless all conductors of the circuit are opened simultaneously, except for motor running overload protection;
- Overcurrent devices must be readily accessible and not located where they could create an employee safety hazard by being exposed to physical damage or located in the vicinity of easily ignitable material; and
- Fuses and circuit breakers must be so located or shielded that employees will not be burned or otherwise injured by their operation (e.g., arcing).

Grounding of Equipment Connected by Cord and Plug

Exposed noncurrent-carrying metal parts of cord- and plug-connected equipment that may become energized must be grounded in the following situations:
- When in a hazardous (classified) location;
- When operated at more than 150 volts to ground, except for guarded motors and metal frames of electrically heated appliances if the appliance frames are permanently and effectively insulated from ground; and
- When it is one of the types of equipment listed below:
  - Hand-held motor-operated tools;
  - Equipment used in damp or wet locations or by employees standing on the ground or on metal floors or working inside metal tanks or boilers;
  - Portable and mobile X-ray and associated equipment;
  - Tools likely to be used in wet and/or conductive locations;
  - Portable hand lamps, except tools that are likely to be used in wet and/or conductive locations do not need to be grounded if supplied through an isolating transformer with an ungrounded secondary of not more than 50 volts;

Listed or labeled portable tools and appliances protected by a system of double insulation, or its equivalent, need not be grounded. If such a system is employed, the equipment must be distinctively marked to indicate that the tool or appliance uses a system of double insulation.

Safety-Related Work Practices
Protection of Employees

The employer must not permit an employee to work near any part of an electric power circuit where he or she could contact in the course of work, unless the employee is protected against shock by de-energizing the circuit and grounding it or by guarding it effectively by insulation or other means. Where the exact location of underground electric power lines is unknown, employees using jackhammers or hand tools that may contact a line must be provided with insulated protective gloves.

Even before work is begun, the employer must determine by inquiry, observation, or instruments where any part of an exposed or concealed energized electric power circuit is located. This is necessary because a person, tool, or machine could come into physical or electrical contact with the electric power circuit. The employer is required to advise employees of the location of such lines, the hazards involved, and the protective measures to be taken. Employers also must post and maintain proper warning signs.

Passageways and Open Spaces

The employer must provide barriers or other means of guarding to ensure the workspace for electrical equipment will not be used as a passageway while energized parts of electrical equipment are exposed. Walkways and similar working spaces must be kept clear of electric cords. Other standards cover load ratings, fuses, cords, and cables.

Lockout and Tagging of Circuits

Tags must be placed on controls that are to be deactivated during the course of work on energized or de-energized equipment or circuits. Equipment or circuits that are de-energized must be rendered inoperative and have tags attached at all points where such equipment or circuits can be energized.

Safety-Related Maintenance and Environmental Considerations
Maintenance of Equipment

The employer must ensure that all wiring components and utilization equipment in hazardous locations are maintained in a dust-tight, dust-ignition-proof, or explosion-proof condition without loose or missing screws, gaskets, threaded connections, seals, or other impairments to a tight condition.

Environmental Deterioration of Equipment

Control equipment, utilization equipment, and busways approved for use in dry locations only must be protected against damage from the weather during building construction. Unless identified for use in the operating environment, no conductors or equipment can be located:

- In damp or wet locations;
- Where exposed to gases, fumes, vapors, liquids, or other agents having a deteriorating effect on the conductors or equipment; or
- Where exposed to excessive temperatures.

For protection against corrosion, metal raceways, cable armor, boxes, cable sheathing, cabinets, elbows, couplings, fittings, supports, and support hardware must be of materials appropriate for the environment in which they are installed.

Safety Requirements for Special Equipment

Batteries

Batteries of the unsealed type must be located in enclosures with outside vents or in well-ventilated rooms arranged to prevent the escape of fumes, gases, or electrolyte spray into other areas. Other provisions include the following:

- Ventilation—to ensure diffusion of the gases from the battery and to prevent the accumulation of an explosive mixture;
- Racks and trays—treated to make them resistant to the electrolyte;
- Floors—acid-resistant construction unless protected from acid accumulations;
- Face shields, aprons, and rubber gloves—for workers handling acids or batteries;
- Facilities for quick drenching of the eyes and body—within 25 ft. (7.62 m) of battery handling areas; and
- Facilities—for flushing and neutralizing spilled electrolytes and for fire protection.

Battery Charging

Battery charging installations must be located in areas designated for that purpose. When batteries are being charged, vent caps must be maintained in functioning condition and kept in place to avoid electrolyte spray. Also, the charging apparatus must be protected from damage by trucks.

Insulation and Grounding

Insulation and grounding are two recognized means of preventing injury during the operation of electrical equipment. Placing nonconductive material such as plastic around the conductor may provide conductor insulation. Grounding may be achieved through the use of a direct connection to a known ground such as a metal cold water pipe.

Consider, for example, the metal housing or enclosure around a motor or the metal box in which electrical switches, circuit breakers, and controls are placed. Such enclosures protect the equipment from dirt and moisture and prevent accidental contact with exposed wiring. However, there is a hazard associated with housings and enclosures. A malfunction within the equipment—such as deteriorated insulation—may create an electrical shock hazard. Many metal enclosures are connected to a ground to eliminate the hazard. If a "hot" wire contacts a grounded enclosure, a ground fault results that normally will trip a circuit breaker or blow a fuse. Connecting them with a wire going to ground usually grounds metal enclosures and containers; this wire is called an equipment-grounding conductor. Most portable electric tools and appliances are grounded by this means. There is one disadvantage to grounding: A break in the grounding system may occur without the user's knowledge.

Insulation may be damaged by hard usage on the job or simply by aging. If this damage causes the conductors to become exposed, the risk of shocks, burns, and fire will increase. Double insulation may be used as additional protection on the live parts of a tool, but double insulation does not provide protection against defective cords and plugs or against heavy moisture conditions.

Ground-Fault Circuit Interrupter (GFCI)

The use of a ground-fault circuit interrupter (GFCI) is one method used to overcome grounding and insulation deficiencies. The GFCI is a fast-acting circuit breaker that senses small imbalances in the circuit caused by current leakage to ground and, in a fraction of a second, shuts off the electricity. The GFCI continually matches the amount of current going to an electrical device against the amount of current returning from the device along the electrical path. Whenever the amount "going" differs from the amount "returning" by approximately 5 milliamps, the GFCI interrupts the electric power within as little as 1/40 of a second (See Exhibit 9-2.)

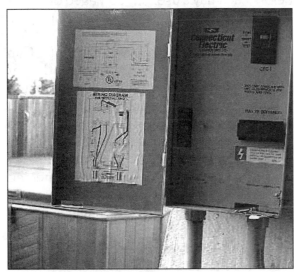

Exhibit 9-2.
A ground-fault circuit interrupter
can protect workers from electric shock.

However, the GFCI will not protect the employee from line-to-line contact hazards (e.g., a person holding two "hot" wires or a hot and a neutral wire in each hand). It does provide protection against the most common form of electrical shock hazard—the ground fault. It also provides protection against fires, overheating, and the destruction of insulation on wiring.

Portable Tool Hazards

With the wide use of portable tools on construction sites, the use of flexible cords is often necessary. Hazards are created when cords, cord connectors, receptacles, and cord- and plug-connected equipment are improperly used and maintained.

Generally, flexible cords are more vulnerable to damage than fixed wiring. Flexible cords must be connected to devices and to fittings so as to prevent tension at joints and terminal screws. Because a cord is exposed, flexible, and unsecured, joints and terminals become more vulnerable. Flexible cord conductors are finely stranded for flexibility, but the strands of one conductor may loosen from under terminal screws and touch another conductor, especially if the cord is subjected to stress or strain.

A flexible cord may be damaged by:
- Activities on the job;
- Door or window edges;
- Staples or fastenings;
- Abrasion from adjacent materials; or
- Aging.

If the electrical conductors become exposed, there is a danger of shocks, burns, or fire. A frequent hazard on a construction site is a cord assembly with improperly connected terminals.

When a cord connector is wet, hazardous leakage can occur to the equipment-grounding conductor and to humans who pick up that connector if they also provide a path to ground. Such leakage is not limited to the face of the connector but also at any wetted portion of it.

When the leakage current of tools is below 1 ampere, and the grounding conductor has a low resistance, no shock should be perceived. However, should the resistance of the equipment grounding conductor increase, the current through the body also will increase. Thus, if the resistance of the equipment-grounding conductor is significantly greater than 1 ohm, tools with even small leakages should be considered hazardous.

Preventing and Eliminating Hazards

GFCIs can be used successfully to reduce electrical hazards on construction sites. The tripping of GFCIs—interruption of current flow—is sometimes caused by wet connectors and tools. It is good practice to limit the exposure of connectors and tools to excessive moisture by using watertight or sealable connectors. Providing more GFCIs or shorter circuits can prevent tripping caused by the cumulative leakage from several tools or by leakages from extremely long circuits.

Employer Responsibility

OSHA ground-fault protection rules and regulations have been determined necessary and appropriate for employee safety and health. Therefore, it is the employer's responsibility to provide either:
- GFCIs on construction sites for receptacle outlets not part of the permanent wiring of the building or structure; or

- A scheduled and recorded assured equipment grounding conductor program on construction sites, covering all cord sets, receptacles that are not part of the permanent wiring of the building or structure, and equipment connected by cord and plug that are available for employee use or used by employees.

Ground-Fault Circuit Interrupters

The employer is required to provide approved ground-fault circuit interrupters for all 120-volt, single-phase, 15- and 20-ampere receptacle outlets on construction sites that are not a part of the permanent wiring of the building or structure and that are in use by employees. Receptacles on the ends of extension cords are not part of the permanent wiring and therefore must be protected by GFCIs whether or not the extension cord is plugged into permanent wiring. These GFCIs monitor the current to the load for leakage to ground. When the leakage exceeds 5 mA ± 1 mA, the GFCI interrupts the current. They are rated to trip quickly enough to prevent electrocution. This protection is required in addition to, not as a substitute for, the grounding requirements of OSHA safety and health rules and regulations, 29 CFR 1926.

Assured Equipment Grounding Conductor Program

The assured equipment grounding conductor program covers all cord sets, receptacles that are not a part of the permanent wiring of the building or structure, and equipment connected by cord and plug that are available for use or used by employees. The requirements that the program must meet are stated in 29 CFR 1926.404(b)(1)(iii), but employers may provide additional tests or procedures. OSHA requires that a written description of the employer's assured equipment grounding conductor program, including the specific procedures adopted, be kept at the job site. This program should outline the employer's specific procedures for the required equipment inspections, tests, and test schedules.

The required tests must be recorded, and the record maintained until it is replaced by a more current record. The written program description and the recorded tests must be made available, at the job site, to OSHA and to any affected employee upon request. The employer is required to designate one or more competent persons to implement the program.

Electrical equipment noted in the assured equipment grounding conductor program must be visually inspected for damage or defects before each day's use. Any damaged or defective equipment must not be used by employees until it is repaired.

OSHA requires two tests as part of an assured equipment grounding conductor program. One is a continuity test to ensure that the equipment-grounding conductor is electrically continuous. It must be performed on all cord sets, receptacles that are not part of the permanent wiring of the building or structure, and on cord- and plug-connected equipment that is required to be grounded. This test may be performed using a simple continuity tester, such as a lamp and battery, a bell and battery, an ohmmeter, or a receptacle tester.

The other test must be performed on receptacles and plugs to ensure that the equipment-grounding conductor is connected to its proper terminal. This test can be performed with the same equipment acceptable for use in the first test.

These tests are required before first use, after any repairs, after damage is suspected to have occurred, and at three-month intervals. Cord sets and receptacles that are essentially fixed and not exposed to damage must be tested at regular intervals not to exceed 6 months. Any equipment that fails to pass the required tests shall not be made available or used by employees.

Tests performed must be recorded. The test record shall identify each receptacle, cord set, and cord- and plug-connected equipment that passed the test and indicate the last date it was tested or the interval for which it was tested. This record shall be kept by means of logs, color-coding, or other effective means and shall be maintained until replaced by a more current record. The record shall be made available on the job site for inspection by OSHA and any affected employee.

Hazardous (Classified) Locations

The National Electrical Code (NEC) defines hazardous locations as those areas "where fire or explosion hazards may exist due to flammable gases or vapors, flammable liquids, combustible dust, or ignitable fibers or flyings."

A substantial part of the NEC is devoted to the discussion of hazardous locations because electrical equipment can become a source of ignition in these volatile areas. The writers of the NEC developed a shorthand method of describing areas classified as hazardous locations. They are classified in three ways: by type, condition, and nature.

Hazardous Location Types

Class I Locations
A Class I hazardous location is one that is created by the presence of flammable gases or vapors in the air, such as natural gas or gasoline vapor. When these materials are found in the atmosphere, a potential for explosion exists; the materials could be ignited if an electrical or other source of ignition is present. Some typical Class I locations are:
- Petroleum refineries and gasoline storage and dispensing areas;
- Dry cleaning plants (vapors from cleaning fluids);
- Spray-finishing areas;
- Aircraft hangars and fuel servicing areas; and
- Utility gas plants and operations involving storage and handling of liquefied petroleum gas or natural gas.

Class II Locations
A Class II location is made hazardous by the presence of combustible dust. Finely pulverized material suspended in the atmosphere can cause as powerful an explosion as one occurring at a petroleum refinery. Some typical Class II locations are:
- Grain elevators;
- Flour and feed mills;
- Plants that manufacture, use, or store magnesium or aluminum powders;
- Plants that produce plastics, medicines and fireworks;
- Plants that produce starches or candies;
- Spice-grinding plants, sugar plants and cocoa plants; and

- Coal preparation plants and other carbon-handling or processing areas.

Class III Locations
Class III hazardous locations are areas where there are easily ignitable fibers or flyings present, due to the types of materials being handled, stored, or processed. The fibers and flyings are not likely to be suspended in the air, but can collect around machinery, on lighting fixtures, and wherever heat, a spark, or hot metal could ignite them. Some typical Class III locations are:
- Textile mills and cotton gins;
- Cotton seed mills and flax processing plants; and
- Plants that shape, pulverize, or cut wood and create sawdust or flyings.

Hazardous Location Conditions
In addition to classifying hazardous locations, the National Electrical Code also defines the conditions under which these hazards are present: Division 1, normal, and Division 2, abnormal.

In a normal condition, the hazard is expected to be present in everyday production operations or during frequent repair and maintenance activity. When the hazardous material is expected to be confined within closed containers or closed systems and present only through accidental rupture, breakage, or unusual faulty operation, the situation would be called abnormal.

Good examples of Class I, Division 1 locations are the areas near open-dome loading facilities or adjacent to relief valves in a petroleum refinery because the hazardous material would be present during normal plant operations.

Closed storage drums containing flammable liquids in an inside storage room would not normally allow the hazardous vapors to escape into the atmosphere. If one of the containers had a leak, it would become a Class 1, Division 2 (i.e., abnormal) hazardous location.

Hazard Substances
The gases and vapors in Class I locations are broken into four groups by the NEC: A, B, C, and D. These materials are grouped according to the ignition temperature of the substance, its explosion pressure, and other flammable characteristics. The only substance in Group

A is acetylene, a gas with extremely high explosion pressures. Acetylene makes up only a very small percentage of hazardous locations. Consequently, little equipment is available for this type of location.

Group B is another relatively small segment of classified areas. This group includes hydrogen and other materials with similar characteristics. If employers follow certain specific NEC restrictions, some of these Group B locations (other than hydrogen) can be satisfied with Group C and Group D equipment.

Groups C and Group D are by far the most common Class I groups. Many of the most common flammable substances, such as butane, gasoline, natural gas, and propane, are listed in Group D.

Class II (dust) locations are broken into three groups: E, F, and G. These groups are classified according to the ignition temperature and the conductivity of the hazardous substance. Conductivity is an important consideration in Class II locations, especially with metal dusts.

Metal dusts are categorized in the Code as Group E. Included here are aluminum and magnesium dusts and other metal dusts of similar nature. Group F atmospheres contain such materials as carbon black, charcoal dust, coal, and coke dust. Group G contains grain dusts, flour, starch, cocoa, and similar types of materials.

EXAMPLE: How would a storage area where LP-Gas is contained in closed tanks be classified? LP-Gas is a Class I substance (gas or vapor). It is Division 2 because it would only enter the atmosphere if an accidental rupture or leakage occurred. It is a type of gas and thus is a Group D material.

Exhibit 9-3. Summarizes the various hazardous (classified) locations.

Summary of Class I, II, III Hazardous Locations			
		DIVISIONS	
CLASSES	**GROUPS**	**1**	**2**
I Gases, vapors, and liquids (Art. 501)	A: Acetylene B: Hydrogen, etc. C: Ether, etc. D: Hydrocarbons, fuels, solvents, etc.	Normally explosive and hazardous	Not normally present in an explosive concentration (but may accidentally exist)
II Dusts (Art. 502)	E: Metal dusts (conductive,* and explosive) F: Carbon dusts (some are conductive,* and all are explosive) G: Flour, starch, grain, combustible plastic or chemical dust (explosive)	Ignitable quantities of dust normally are or may be in suspension, or conductive dust may be present	Dust not normally suspended in an ignitable concentration (but may accidentally exist). Dust layers are present.
III Fibers and flyings (Art. 503)	Textiles, wood-working, etc. (easily ignitable, but not likely to be explosive)	Handled or used in manufacturing	Stored or handled in storage (exclusive of manufacturing)

* NOTE: Electrically conductive dusts are dusts with a resistivity less than 10^5 ohm-centimeter.

Hazardous Location Equipment

Sources of Ignition

Electrical equipment can become a source of ignition three ways:

1. Arcs and sparks produced by the normal operation of equipment, like motor starters, contactors, and switches, can ignite a hazardous location atmosphere.
2. The high temperatures of some heat-producing equipment, such as lamps and lighting fixtures, can ignite flammable atmospheres if they exceed the ignition temperature of the hazardous material.

The NEC requires special marking of heat-producing equipment with temperatures above 100°C (212°F).

3. Electrical equipment failure is another way an explosion could be set off. A burnout of a lamp socket or shorting of a terminal could spark a disaster in a hazardous location.

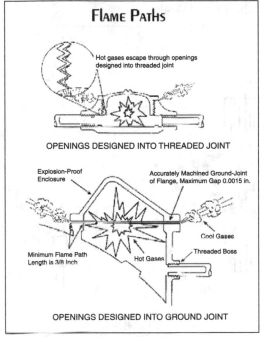

Exhibit 9-4.
Flame paths.

Equipment Design and Construction

Given the myriad types of materials, locations and conditions that workers may encounter, specific hardware has been designed and constructed to accomplish the job and protect the worker.

The first requirement for a Class I (gas and vapor) enclosure is strength. The enclosure must be strong enough to contain an explosion. The walls must be thick enough to withstand the internal strain. It has to be explosion proof in case gas or vapors get inside. It must function at a temperature below the ignition temperature of the surrounding atmosphere.

The equipment also must provide a way for the burning gases to escape as they expand during an internal explosion; but, only after they have been cooled off and their flames quenched. This escape route for the exploding gases is provided through several types of flame paths.

One type is the ground surface flame path. Here the surfaces are ground, mated, and

held to a tolerance of 15 ten-thousandths of an inch. This permits gases to escape, but only after they have been sufficiently *cooled*, so they will not ignite the volatile surrounding atmosphere.

Another kind of flame path is the threaded flame path. After an explosion, the gas travels out of the threaded joint, but as it does, it cools.

Exploded gases may also escape around the shafts of operators used in the enclosure. But, here again, close tolerances are used to quench the burning gas.

It is important to make certain that all flame paths are protected during installation and maintenance, and even during the handling, shipping, and storage of explosion-proof material. Even slight damage to a flame path can permit burning gases to escape, igniting the surrounding atmosphere. All cover bolts must be installed for the same reason; a single missing bolt could allow the release of flaming gases.

In designing equipment for Class I, Division 1 locations, it is assumed that the hazardous gases or vapors will be present and eventually seep into the enclosure, so there is a likely chance for an internal explosion to occur.

In the case of Class II, however, the assumptions are different and so the design is different. In Class II, the explosive dust is kept away from equipment housed within the enclosure so that no internal explosion can take place and there is no longer any need for heavy explosion-containing construction or flame paths. This difference explains why Class I, Division 1 equipment can be called explosion-proof and Class II equipment is called dust-ignition proof. Class II equipment has a different set of requirements:

- It must seal out the dust;
- It must operate below the ignition temperature of the hazardous substance; and
- It must allow for a dust blanket (i.e., the build-up of dust collecting on top of the device that can cause it to run "hot" and ignite the surrounding atmosphere).

For Class III equipment, there is very little difference in the design from Class II. Class

III equipment must minimize the entrance of fibers and flyings; prevent the escape of sparks, burning material, or hot metal particles resulting from the failure of equipment; and operate at a temperature that will prevent the ignition of fibers accumulated on the equipment.

There are many enclosures, devices, and fixtures suitable for all three classes. This simply means that it meets the specifications for each individual type. A Class I device that could contain an explosion of a specified gas would also have to prevent dust from entering the enclosure to be suitable for Class II. The close tolerance of the flame path that cools the burning gases is also close enough to exclude explosive dust so that a gasket would not be needed.

The proper installation of hazardous location equipment calls for the use of *seals*. Special fittings are required to keep hot gases from traveling through the conduit system and igniting other areas if an internal explosion occurs in a Class I device. They also are needed in certain situations to keep flammable dusts from entering dust-ignition-proof enclosures through the conduit. When arcs and sparks ignite flammable gases and vapors, the equipment contains the explosion and vents only cool gases into the surrounding hazardous area (See Exhibit 9-5.).

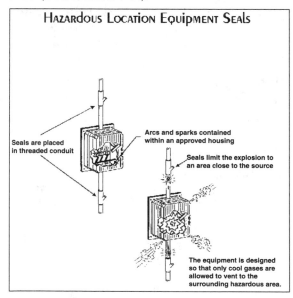

Exhibit 9-5.
Hazardous locations equipments seals.

Sealing fittings are designed to be filled with a chemical compound after the wires have been pulled. As the compound hardens, it seals passageways for dusts and gases. As shown in Exhibit 9-6, in each conduit run entering an enclosure for switches, circuit breakers, fuses, relays, resistors, or other apparatus that may produce arcs, sparks, or high temperatures within Class I locations, conduit seals shall be placed as close as practicable and in no case more than 18 in. (457 mm) from such enclosures. Consult the Code for specific rules for the use of seals.

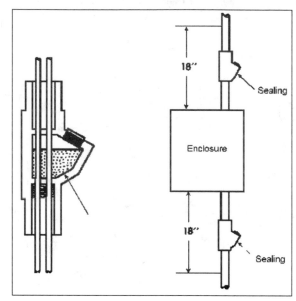

Exhibit 9-6.
Seals for Class I devices shall be placed no more than 18 in. from enclosures.

Rigorous standards for hazardous location equipment have been set. Nationally recognized testing laboratories conduct actual explosion tests under laboratory conditions. For each Class I enclosure, the laboratories experiment with different mixtures of gas and air—from very lean mixtures (a small percentage of gas) to very rich mixtures (a high percentage of gas)—until they find the one that creates the greatest explosion pressure. To pass inspection, the equipment must not only prevent the ignition of the surrounding atmosphere, but also be able to withstand a hydrostatic test where oil is pumped into the enclosure at high pressure to test the limits of its strength. The device will not pass unless it can resist rupture at four times the maximum pressure found in the explosion tests. For example, if explosion testing shows a maximum pressure for a junction box of 250 pounds per square inch (psi), to get approval, the box must be able to withstand 1,000 psi of hydrostatic pressure—*four times* the maximum anticipated pressure of 250 psi.

Regardless of the cause of a hazardous location, it is necessary that every precaution be taken to guard against ignition of the atmosphere. Electrical equipment can be a potential source of ignition through one of three ways:

1. Arcs and sparks;
2. High temperatures; or
3. Electrical equipment failure .

Hazardous location equipment is designed and constructed to eliminate the potential for ignition of the atmosphere. The National Electric Code is the authority for the electrical industry and is the basis for OSHA standard 1926.407 (Hazardous Locations). The NEC should be consulted as a supplement to the OSHA standards for additional background information concerning hazardous locations.

Protective Clothing Characteristics

Hazard/Risk Category	Clothing Description Number of Layers ( )	APTV Rating Cal/cm2
0	Untreated Cotton, Wool, Rayon, Silk, or Blend. Fabric weight >4.5oz/Yd2 (1)	N/A
1	FR Shirt and FR Pants or FR Coverall (1)	4
2	Cotton underwear plus FR shirt and FR pants (1 or 2)	8
3	Cotton underwear plus FR shirt and FR pants plus FR coverall, cotton underwear plus two FR Coveralls (2 or 3)	25
4	Cotton underwear plus FR shirt and FR pants plus multilayer flash suit (3 or more)	40

Electrical Safety Student Handout

Electricity is a powerful tool when used correctly. However, when accidents of this nature do occur, they happen with the speed of light.

Some citations that have been issued by OSHA in the electrical area include:

- No ground-fault circuit interrupter or assured equipment grounding program;
- Tools have no grounding conductor or the path to ground is not permanent and continuous;
- No signs or training when working near power lines; and
- Equipment not approved for classified locations.

Some key points about electrical systems that should be remembered are:

- Ground-fault circuit interrupters monitor between the hot and neutral conductors. They will interrupt the current if a leak of 5 milliamps is detected.
- Many sections of the electrical safe work practices section in the general industry standards apply to employees performing work on or near electrical equipment.
- Employers who use defective electrical wiring will most likely be cited if their employees

are exposed, whether or not the employer created the unsafe electrical condition. Common citations include:

- No ground-fault circuit interrupter or assured equipment-grounding program used for three wire tools. In the early 1970s, OSHA investigated more than 50 fatalities a year from electrocutions involving the use of power tools. The introduction and wide use of ground-fault circuit interrupters (GFCIs) has reduced the deaths to less than 10 a year in construction. Many companies have electrical contractors install GFCIs in the panel boxes to comply with the standard.
- Extension cords are frayed. This is commonly found when companies use extension cords that are not rated hard or extra hard for construction use.
- Equipment is ungrounded. When a tool or equipment shorts out or has a fault, the current will seek any path to earth. The grounding conductor will provide a low resistance path to earth that should protect the worker.
- Receptacles not mounted and secured. Most receptacles have wiring that is secured to the box by terminal screws. Having them

unsecured provides an opportunity for them to become lose and possibly shock an employee on contact.

- Panel boxes not covered. Boxes must be covered to prevent accidental contact with live parts. If the covers are off, some employees may assume that the power is not energized and make accidental contact.

Effects of the Amount of AC Current at 60 cycles

More than 3 mA*	A painful shock that can lead to indirect accidents
More than 10 mA	The person's muscles will contract and there is a danger that he or she will not be able to let go of the item.
More than 30 mA	Lung paralysis (usually temporary)
More than 50 mA	Possible ventricular fibrillation (heart dysfunction—usually fatal)
100 mA to 4 Amps	Certain ventricular fibrillation (fatal)
More than 4 Amps	Heart paralysis (may only be temporary) and severe burns (usually caused by more than 600 Volts)
*(1 mA = 1/1000 Amp)	

Fuses and Circuit Breakers

Overcurrent can occur when a worker attempts to use a 10 horsepower motor to do the work of a 12 horsepower motor. The circuits begin to overload as the motor pushes up to 150 percent of its normal current. When a fault occurs, the insulation fails in a circuit and the insulation becomes brittle and cracked. Fuses and circuit breakers will provide protection from an overcurrent situation. For example, when the current flowing through a fuse exceeds the rating of that fuse, the "heart" (that special metal strip or wire inside the fuse) of the fuse is designed to melt and blow out when the rated amperage is exceeded. The circuit breaker is an improvement over the fuse, in that when an overcurrent situation exists the circuit will open, but the worker need only fix the problem and then throw the circuit breaker switch. The fuse does not need to be replaced.

Grounding

In a simple circuit, the current is considered to flow through the black (ungrounded) wire to the load and returns to the source through the white (grounded) wire. If the current fails to return to the grounded wire, it will go somewhere else. Effective grounding means that the path to the ground is:

- Permanent and continuous;
- Of sufficient current-carrying capacity to conduct any current imposed on it; and

- Of sufficient impedance to limit the potential and to facilitate the operation of the overcurrent devices.

Effective grounding has no function unless and until there is electrical leakage from a current-carrying conductor to its enclosure. The risk of electrical shock needs to be reduced through grounding whenever possible. When a ground fault occurs, the grounding conductor:

- Prevents voltages from jumping between the electrical enclosure and other surroundings; and
- Provides a path for large amounts of fault or overload current to flow back to the service entrance, where it will blow the fuse or trip the circuit breaker.

Double Insulated Tools

Many portable hand tools are now manufactured with non-metallic cases and are referred to as being double insulated. While this design reduces the risk from grounding deficiencies, a danger of shock still exists. Workers often use these tools where there are considerably moist or wet conditions. If the water contacts the energized parts, a path will be provided from inside the housing to the outside of the tool, bypassing the double insulation. When a worker touches the wet portion of the tool, an electrical shock could result.

Ground-Fault Circuit Interrupter

A GFCI is *not* an overcurrent device. The GFCI opens the circuit if the current flowing to the load does not return by the prescribed route. The GFCI contains a special sensor that monitors the strength of the magnetic field around each wire in the circuit when the current is flowing. If the current around the two wires differs by more than 5 milliamps, the GFCI will quickly open the circuit. (Keep in mind that at 10 milliamps, a person's muscles contract and he or she will not be able to release the tool.)

There are several different types of GFCIs:

The circuit breaker type includes the functions of the circuit breaker with the additional functions of the GFCI and is usually installed in a panel board. This way it replaces the circuit breaker of the same rating and protects an entire branch circuit with multiple outlets.

The receptacle type is popular because it is low cost and incorporates one ore more receptacle outlets with GFCI protection. Most are of the duplex receptacle configuration and provide protection for receptacles connected "downstream" from the GFCI unit.

The permanently mounted type is frequently found around swimming pools, eye wash stations, bathrooms, and similar wet locations. They provide point protection at the site.

The portable type is common in construction because they are easily transported from one location to another. If they are exposed to rain, they must be listed as rain proof.

GFCIs must be tested on a regular basis. For permanent devices, a monthly test is recommended. Portable GFCIs must be tested each time before they are used. They have a built-in test circuit that imposes an artificial ground fault on the circuit for this purpose.

Assured Grounding Program

All electrical equipment shall be visually inspected for ground problems on a daily basis.

Equipment must be tested by a competent person who understands the OSHA rules regarding electrical safety and is authorized to take corrective action when an unsafe condition occurs.

The competent person will:

- Use a receptacle tester to ensure the plug is correctly connected to a ground;
- Use a continuity tester to ensure the path to the ground is continuous and without breaks. He or she should connect one end of the continuity tester to the ground prong and the other end to the equipment being tested. If the light goes on, or the buzzer sounds (whichever indicates a complete circuit), the path to the ground is complete; and
- Record the test in writing, including the equipment tested, the date of the test, the type of test performed, and the name of the person who conducted the test.

The test shall be done:

- Before the first use of the equipment;
- After any repair of cables or equipment;
- After any incident that creates damage or suspected damage; and
- At three-month intervals (every six months if the equipment is in a protected, fixed location).

The National Electrical Contractors Association (NECA) recommends using color codes for tape (See Exhibit 9-7.). Simply take the appropriate color tape and wrap it on one part of the cable when it has been tested it for the three-month period. That way, the worker will know if the cable has been tested. For example, if it is July and the cable is marked with a white tag, the worker will know that it has not been tested in the past 90 days.

Exhibit 9-7.
NECA-recommended color coding for tape.

January	White
February	White and yellow
March	White and blue
April	Green
May	Green and yellow
June	Green and blue
July	Red
August	Red and yellow
September	Red and blue
October	Orange
November	Orange and yellow
December	Orange and blue

Equipment to be repaired should be tagged brown.

The National Electric Code and the NFPA 70E

In 1881 Thomas Edison replied to a newspaper article in which the underwriters asked for information about the danger of fire from electric wires. Edison responded with "I beg to say that the system of lighting of the Edison Electric Light company is absolutely free from any possible danger from fire, even in connection with the most inflammable material."

Since electrical systems were a new development, no codes had been developed for safe installation. Installers had to make decisions based on their limited experience of this new technology. It is no wonder why electrical fires became prevalent throughout the United States. Eight years after Edison wrote his safety note about fires there were five different electrical installation codes in use in the United States. Each code was sufficiently different from the others that confusion reigned and the need for a uniform electrical code was recognized.

In 1896 a committee was formed by the American Society of Mechanical Engineers. This committee was given the task of selecting the most suitable rules from the five outstanding codes and developing a consensus through a review of their findings. The code was recognized by the National Board of Fire Underwriters and published as the "National Electrical Code of 1897."

In 1911 the work of periodically revising the National Electric Codes (NEC) was transferred to the Electrical Committee of the National Fire Protection Association (NFPA). This organization had been formed in 1896 to reduce fire and safety hazards. It has developed over two hundred articles (codes and standards). These codes cover a variety of topics from NFPA 10 "Standard for Portable Fire Extinguishers" to Article 70 which is the National Electric Code.

When the Williams-Steiger Occupational Safety and Health Act of 1970 created OSHA, the need for industrial regulation of electricity became apparent. OSHA adopted the most widely accepted electrical standard in the world, the National Fire Protection Association's Standard, NFPA 70. However, when the NEC was updated periodically, OSHA would have to go through an extensive legal process to adopt the new NEC edition and resolve conflicts between the adopted version and the updated version. The NEC only referred to electrical installation and OSHA needed a regulation that addressed operation, maintenance and repair as well.

How did OSHA solve this problem? Employers have a specific duty to follow the rules enacted by OSHA, and a general duty to provide a safe and healthy workplace. This "general duty" requires that each employer furnish to their workers a place that is free from recognized hazards. Generally, if there is a serious hazard that could result in death or serious injury, the hazard must be abated, regardless of whether or not OSHA has specifically addressed the hazard. An important example of recognized hazards that may not be covered by a specific standard drafted by OSHA is the national consensus standard. This type of standard is developed by the same persons it affects, is adopted by a nationally recognized organization and carries the same weight and is as enforceable as the OSHA regulations. NFPA 70E is a national consensus standard.

The most recent edition of the NFPA 70E was adopted in 2004. It reorganizes the article into the NEC format. There are four chapters and thirteen annexes to the article.

- Chapter 1 covers safety related work practices, qualified versus unqualified persons and training. This chapter calls for an electrical safety program that includes electrical hazard analysis for shock and flash, energized electrical work permits and lockout/tagout procedures. Personal protective equipment, protective clothing and approach boundaries are also discussed.
- The second chapter outlines safety related maintenance requirements necessary to ensure that electrical wiring, components and equipment are maintained in a safe condition.
- Chapter 3 discusses special equipment such as batteries, lasers, arc welding equipment, and other select equipment.
- Chapter 4 describes installation safety requirements and is a truncated version of the National Electrical Code.

While parts of the NFPA 70E have been around since 1981, only recently has OSHA begun to refer to the article in their documents and citations. This consensus standard covers electrical safety related work practices and procedures for employees who work on or near exposed energized electrical conductors or circuit parts. Relevant requirements include:

Power must be proven to be off
before performing work. This includes
- The safe interruption of the load & opening of the disconnect
- Visual verification/voltage testing to ensure deenergization

The potential electrical hazard
must be identified and documented
- Flash hazard analysis must be performed
- Flash protection boundaries must be determined

Appropriate steps must be taken
to protect persons working near live parts
or within the flash protection boundary.
- Personal Protective Equipment must be provided based on the relevant incident energy exposure levels (cal/cm2)
- Only properly qualified persons shall be allowed to perform work.

NFPA 70 (NEC) differs from NFPA 70E
The National Electrical Code is generally considered an electrical *installation* document and protects employees under normal circumstances. NFPA 70E is intended to provide guidance with respect to electrical *safe work practices*.

NFPA not incorporated by reference
OSHA does not enforce NFPA 70E since it is not incorporated by reference.

However, OSHA has several comparable requirements that are enforceable:
- **29 CFR 1910.132 (d)(1):** Requires employers perform a personal protective equipment (PPE) hazard assessment to determine necessary PPE;
- **29 CFR 1910.269 (l)(6)(iii):** Requires employers ensure each employee working at electric power generation, transmission, and distribution facilities who is exposed to the hazards of flames or electric arcs does not wear clothing that could increase the extent of injury when exposed to such a hazard;
- **29 CFR 1910.335 (a)(1)(i):** Employees working in areas where there are potential electrical hazards shall use electrical protective equipment appropriate for the specific parts of the body for the work being performed;
- **29 CFR 1910.335 (a)(1)(iv):** Requires employees wear nonconductive head protection whenever exposed to electric shock or burns due to contact with exposed energized parts;
- **29 CFR 1910.335 (a)(1)(v):** Employees shall wear protective equipment for the eyes or face wherever there is danger of injury to the eyes or face from electric arcs or flashes or from flying objects resulting from an electrical explosion;
- **29 CFR 1910.335 (a)(2):** Employees shall use insulated tools or handling equipment when working near exposed energized conductors or circuit parts;
- **29 CFR 1926.28 (a):** Employer shall require employees wear appropriate personal protective equipment (PPE) during construction work.

Boundaries for flash protection
NFPA 70E specifies boundaries within which flash protection is required as a means to reduce the extent of injuries. Protective equipment is also specified including flash resistant clothing and face shielding. Boundary distances vary depending on both the qualifications of the person being exposed and the voltage involved. Unqualified personnel must be accompanied by qualified personnel. All personnel within the defined boundaries must wear specified protective equipment.

The following boundary distances for flash protection have been established in NFPA 70E. For workers within the following approach distances, flash protection is required:

Voltage Flash Protection Boundary

up to 750V	3 feet
750V to 2kV	4 feet
2kV to 15kV	16 feet
15kV to 36kV	19 feet
over 36kV	Must be Calculated

Flash resistant personal protection equipment does not protect you from shock, but it will give substantial protection from the effects of flash, especially burns and eye damage. Flash protective clothing is specified by ASTM F1506 while eye protection must comply with ANSI Z87.1. Clothing coverage must be 100%, i.e., coveralls or shirt and trousers. NFPA 70E: 130.1 requires employers perform a flash hazard analysis to identify work tasks performed on energized electrical conductors. Appropriate flame retardant clothing (FRC), as well as voltage rated tools, may then be selected.

It is possible to protect an employee exposed to an electric arc incident from experiencing a burn that will cause irreversible tissue damage ~ a curable burn. This is a 2° burn where the skin temperature does not exceed 175° with a duration no longer than 0.1 second.

Although not specifically required by NFPA 70E, it is recommended that covered employees be provided FRC daily wear with an ATPV (Arc Thermal Performance Value) of at least 8. This satisfies the garment requirements for a Hazard Risk Classification 2 task.

The term "clearing time" is discussed under NFPA 70E: 130.3 (A). This refers to the time necessary for an electrical circuit breaker or disconnect to switch from an energized state to a deenergized state. A faster clearing time reduces the potential for an electric arc incident.

The Hazard Risk Category (HRC) classifications (0 ~ 4) listed in Table 130.7 (C)(9)(a) do not have a have a direct correlation to voltage. The hazard risk category (HRC) classifications are based upon estimated incident energy. Consider two work tasks with different voltages:

Task #1: Examination of insulated cable in open area 1,000 volts: **HRC 2 task**.

Task #2: Insertion or removal of 600 volt class individual starter buckets: **HRC 3 task.**

Although task #2 involves less voltage than task #1, it has a higher HRC.

The National Fire Protection Association (NFPA) published the seventh edition of the 70E Standard for Electrical Safety Requirements for Employee Workplaces in February 2004. The edition stresses safe work practices.

The issue of multi-employer relationships (110.4) is addressed. The addition of multi-employer relationships now makes the employer liable whenever outside contractors are engaged in activities covered by the scope and application of this standard. The employer and contractor must inform each other of existing hazards, personal protective equipment/clothing requirements, safe work practices, and emergency evacuation procedures applicable to the work to be performed. This coordination must include a meeting and documentation.

NFPA 70E covers the full range of electrical safety issues, including safety related work practices, maintenance, special equipment requirements, and installation. It focuses on protecting people and identifies requirements that are considered necessary to provide a workplace that is free of electrical hazards. OSHA bases its electrical safety mandates, found in Subpart S part 1910 and Subpart K part 1926, on the comprehensive information found in NFPA 70E. NFPA 70E is recognized as the tool that illustrates how an employer might comply with these OSHA standards. The relationship between the OSHA regulations and NFPA 70E can be described as OSHA is the "shall" and NFPA 70E the "how."

OSHA mandates that all services to electrical equipment be done in a de-energized state. Working live can only be under special circumstances. If it is necessary to work live (>50 volts to ground), the regulations outlined in NFPA 70E, Article 130 should be used as a tool to comply with OSHA mandates in Subpart S part 1910.333(a)(1).

- Shock hazard analysis (paragraph 130.2) : Determines the voltage to which personnel will be exposed, boundary requirements, and PPE necessary. Table 130.2(C) is used to determine boundary distances.
- Flash hazard analysis (paragraph 130.3): Determines the flash protection boundary and PPE needed within that boundary. The flash protection boundary is determined by methods found in 130.3(A) or Annex D of the standard. Protective clothing is determined by using tables 130.7(C)(9)(a), 130.7(C)(10), and 130.7(C)(11). See question and answer number 1 for more details.

Remember, OSHA only allows work on live electrical parts under two special circumstances: (1) when continuity of service is required, and (2) when de-energizing equipment would create additional hazards. In all other cases, lockout/tagout is the law.

Employers are also responsible for complying with the 2002 NEC 110.6 labeling requirements. This requires all switchboards, panel boards, industrial control panels, and motor control centers to be field marked. Any equipment installed after 2002 needs to be labeled. For equipment installed before 2002, labeling must be applied if ANY modifications or upgrades take place. Some of the labels listed below require boundary distances calculated in Article 130 of the standard. Examples of labels that meet this requirement are:

Each FR garment is assigned an ATPV rating by the manufacturer. The ATPV value represents the amount of incident energy that would cause the onset of second-degree burns. It also signifies the amount of protection the clothing affords when an electrical arc comes in contact with the fabric. Most of the industry falls into either Category 1 or 2 protection. Most uniforms already meet Category 1 or 2 requirements, but people who fall into this category typically are not covered by this standard. The employees addressed by this standard fall into Category 3 and 4. The garments must also be designed to withstand a cleaning process to remove soils and then be returned to service without damage to the protective characteristic of the fabric. The label on the garment must contain the following information: tracking ID number, meet ASTM spec F1506, name of manufacturer, size and care instructions, ATPV rating, and must meet ASTM spec f1506.

Summary of the New 2007 Electrical Standard

Changes to the electrical subpart of OSHA's 29 CFR 1910 standard were published in the **Federal Register** on February 14, 2007. To give firms time to comply with the changes, the effective date of the regulation is August 13, 2007.

The change clarifies some of the information that was in the electrical section and draws heavily on the 2002 National Electric Code. The section was originally drafted in the 1970's and stood the test of time. This updated version creates a more easily read and understood regulation while providing for changes in technology that make the workplace safer.

The following changes are effective in August 2007:

- **1910.303(a):** A reference to the Sec. 1910.399 definition of "approved" is added for clarification.
- **1910.303(b)(1)(III):** Adds wire-bending and connection space to the explicit list of things to consider when judging equipment.
- **1910.303(b)(3):** Adds a requirement for completed wiring to be free from short circuits and grounds other than those required in the standard.
- **1910.303(b)(4):** Adds requirements for equipment intended to interrupt current to have adequate interrupting ratings.
- **1910.303(b)(5):** Adds requirements for the coordination of over current protection for circuits and equipment.
- **1910.303(b)(6):** Adds a requirement for conductors and equipment to be identified for the purpose when installed in an environment containing deteriorating agents.
- **1910.303(b)(7):** Adds requirements for installing electric equipment in a neat and workmanlike manner.
- **1910.303(b)(8):** Adds requirements for equipment to be mounted securely and to allow for proper cooling.
- **1910.303(c)(1):** Adds requirements to ensure that electrical connections are secure and electrically safe.
- **1910.303(c)(2):** Adds requirements for connections at terminals and for the identification of terminals intended for connection to more than one conductor or to aluminum.
- **1910.303(c)(3)(ii):** Adds a requirement that wire connectors or splicing means installed on directly buried conductors be listed for such use.
- **1910.303(f)(4):** Adds a requirement for disconnecting means required by Subpart S to be capable of accepting a lock. This provision is added to make the Subpart S requirements on disconnecting means consistent with Sec. 1910.147(c)(2)(iii), which requires energy isolating devices (a generic term, which includes electrical disconnecting means) to be designed to accept a lockout device.
- **1910.303(f)(5):** Adds marking requirements for series combination ratings of circuit breakers or fuses.
- **1910.303(g)(1)(i):** Table S-1, Note 3: The final rule revises the language to clarify how wide and high the clear space must be. (See detailed explanation later in the preamble.)
- **1910.303(g)(1)(iv):** Adds a requirement for a second entrance on equipment rated 1200 amperes under certain conditions.
- **1910.303(g)(1)(iv):** Reduces the minimum width of the clear space to 762 mm.
- **1910.303(g)(1)(v):** Adds a prohibition against controlling illumination for working spaces by automatic means only.
- **1910.303(g)(1)(vi):** Increased the minimum height of the working space from 1.91m to 1.98m for new installations.
- **1910.303(g)(1)(vii):** Adds requirements for switchboards, panel boards, and distribution boards installed for the control of light and power circuits, and motor control centers to be installed in dedicated space and to be protected against damage.
- **1910.303(h)(2)(i) and (h)(2)(ii):** The minimum height of fences restricting access to electrical installations over 600 V is reduced from 2.44 m to 2.13 m.
- **1910.303(h)(2)(iii), (h)(2)(iv),(h)(2)(v), and (h)(5)(iii):** 1. The final rule organizes these requirements based on whether the installations are indoors or outdoors. (The existing standard organized them based on whether or not the installations were accessible to unqualified employees). 2. Adds requirements intended to prevent tampering by the general public. 3. Removes requirement to lock underground box covers weighing more than 45.4 kg.
- **1910.303(h)(5)(i), Table S-2, Note 3.:** The distances in Table S-2 for the Table S-2, Note 3 depth of working space in front of electrical equipment is increased for new installations to match the distances in NFPA 70E-2000.
- **1910.303(h)(5)(v):** The distances in Table S-3 for the elevations of unguarded live parts are increased for new installations to match the distances in NFPA 70E-2000.
- **1910.303(h)(4)(i):** The existing standard requires a second entrance to give access to the working space about switchboards and control panels over 600 V if the equipment exceeds 1.22 m in width if it is practical to install a second entrance. The final rule requires an entrance on each end of

switchboards and panel boards exceeding 1.83 m unless the working space permits a continuous and unobstructed way of travel or the working space is doubled. In addition, the final rule requires the lone entrance permitted under either of these exceptions to be at least the distance specified in Table S-2 from exposed live parts.

- **1910.303(h)(5)(ii):** Adds requirements for equipment operating at 600 V or less installed in rooms or enclosures containing exposed live parts or exposed wiring operating at more than 600 V.

- **1910.303(h)(5)(vi):** Adds requirements limiting the installation of pipes or ducts that are foreign to electrical installation operating at more than 600 V.

- **1910.304(b)(1):** Adds requirements for the identification of multiwire branch circuits.

- **1910.304(b)(2)(i):** Adds requirements that receptacles installed on 15- and 20-ampere circuits be of the grounding type and that grounding-type receptacles be installed in circuits within their rating.

- **1910.304(b)(2)(ii):** Adds a requirement for grounding contacts on receptacles to be effectively grounded.

- **1910.304(b)(2)(iii):** Adds requirements on the methods used to ground receptacles and cord connectors.

- **1910.304(b)(2)(iv):** Adds requirements on the replacement of receptacles.

- **1910.304(b)(2)(v):** Adds a requirement that receptacles installed on branch circuits having different voltages, frequencies, or types of current be noninterchangeable.

- **1910.304(b)(3):** Adds requirements for ground fault circuit interrupter protection. (These requirements are discussed in this section of the preamble to the final rule).

- **1910.304(b)(4)(i):** Adds requirements for ratings of lampholders.

- **1910.304(b)(4)(ii):** Adds requirements for ratings of receptacles.

- **1910.304(b)(5):** Adds requirements for receptacles to be installed wherever cords with attachment plugs are used.

- **1910.304(c)(1):** Adds a requirement for the separation of conductors on poles.

- **1910.304(c)(2):** Increases the minimum clearances for new installations of open

conductors and service drops to match those in NFPA 70E-2000.

- **1910.304(c)(3)(ii):** Adds restrictions for installing overhead service conductors near building openings through which materials may be moved.

- **1910.304(c)(4):** Adds an exception to the minimum clearance requirement for conductors attached to the side of a building. (The final rule also clarifies that paragraph (c)(2) applies to roof surfaces that are subject to pedestrian or vehicular traffic).

- **1910.304(e)(1)(iii):** Adds a requirement for service disconnecting means to be suitable for the prevailing conditions.

- **1910.304(f)(1)(iii):** The types of circuits that are allowed to have a single switch disconnect for multiple fuses are now specified in the standard.

- **1910.304(f)(1)(v):** Adds a requirement to clarify that handles of circuit breakers and similar moving parts also need to be guarded so that they do not injure employees.

- **1910.304(f)(1)(viii):** Adds circuit breakers used on 277-volt fluorescent lighting circuits to the types of breakers required to be marked "SWD."

- **1910.304(f)(1)(ix):** Adds a requirement to clarify ratings of circuit breakers.

- **1910.304(f)(2):** Adds specific requirements on how to protect feeders and branch circuits energized at more than 600 volts.

- **1910.304(g)(1)(v):** Adds an exception to the requirement to ground systems for high-impedance grounded systems of 480 V to 1000 V under certain conditions.

- **1910.304(g)(3):** Changes requirements for grounding portable and vehicle mounted generators so that the requirements are equivalent to those in OSHA's Construction Standards (Sec. 1926.404 (f)(3)). The sentence in the construction standard reading: "No other [nonneutral] conductor need be bonded to the generator frame" has been dropped from the general industry version.

- **1910.304(g)(4):** No longer allows employers to use a cold water pipe as a source of ground for installations made or modified after the effective date.

- **1910.304(g)(5):** Adds a requirement that the path to ground be effective.

- **1910.304(g)(6)(iv) and (g)(6)(v):** The exceptions for grounding fixed equipment operating at more than 150 V are extended to all fixed electric equipment regardless of voltage. Also, the final rule includes a new exception for double-insulated equipment.

- **1910.304(g)(6)(vi) and (g)(6)(vii):** Adds the following equipment to the list of cord- and plug-connected equipment required to be grounded: stationary and fixed motor-operated tools and light industrial motor-operated tools.

- **1910.304(g)(7):** Adds frames and tracks of electrically operated hoists to the list of Nonelectrical equipment required to be grounded.

- **1910.305(a)(1)(i):** Adds a requirement that equipment be bonded so as to provide adequate fault-current- carrying capability. Also, clarifies that nonconductive coatings need to be removed unless the fittings make this unnecessary.

- **1910.305(a)(1)(ii):** Adds an exception to the bonding requirement for the reduction of electrical noise.

- **1910.305(a)(2)(i)(A):** Removes demolition from the list of activities for which temporary wiring is permitted. Demolition is a form of construction work, which is not covered by the Subpart S installation requirements.

- **1910.305(a)(2)(i)(C):** Adds emergencies to the list of activities for which temporary wiring is permitted.

- **1910.305(a)(2)(iii):** Adds "construction-like activities" to the list of permitted uses for temporary electrical installations over 600 volts.

- **1910.305(a)(2)(iv):** Feeders may now only be run as single insulated conductors when accessible to qualified employees only and used for experiments, development work, or emergencies. (Individual requirements are placed in separate paragraphs).

- **1910.305(a)(2)(viii):** Adds a requirement that disconnecting means for a multiwire circuit simultaneously disconnect all ungrounded conductors of the circuit.

- **1910.305(a)(2)(ix):** This provision no longer allows installing fixtures or lampholders more than 2.1 meters above the working surface as a means of guarding. Also, the final rule adds a requirement for grounding metal-case sockets.

- **1910.305(a)(2)(xi):** Adds requirements for cable assemblies and flexible cords and cables to be adequately supported.

- **1910.305(a)(3)(ii):** Adds several types of cables and single insulated conductors to the list of types permitted in industrial establishments.

- **1910.305(a)(3)(iii):** Adds a requirement limiting the use of metallic cable trays as an equipment grounding conductor.

- **1910.305(a)(4)(ii):** Adds specific support requirements and limits the application of these requirements to conductors smaller than No. 8.

- **1910.305(b)(1)(iii):** Adds requirements for supporting cables entering cabinets, cutout boxes, and meter sockets.

- **1910.305(b)(2)(ii):** Adds a requirement for any exposed edge of a combustible ceiling finish at a fixture canopy or pan to be covered with noncombustible material.

- **1910.305(c)(3)(ii):** Adds a requirement for load terminals on switches to be deenergized when the switches are open except under limited circumstances.

- **1910.305(c)(4):** Adds a specific requirement for flush-mounted switches to have faceplates that completely cover the opening and that seat against the finished surface.

- **1910.305(c)(5):** Adds a requirement to ground faceplates for snap switches.

- **1910.305(e)(1):** Adds a requirement for metallic cabinets, cutout boxes, fittings, boxes, and panel board enclosures installed in damp or wet locations to have an air space between the enclosure and the mounting surface.

- **1910.305(g)(1)(i) and (g)(1)(ii):** Adds the following to the types of connections permitted for flexible cords and cables: Portable and mobile signs and connection of moving parts. The final rule also clarifies that flexible cords and cables may be used for temporary wiring as permitted in final Sec. 1910.305 (a) (2).

- **1910.305(g)(1)(v):** Permits additional cord types to be used in show windows and show cases.

- **1910.305(g)(2)(i):** Adds new types of cords to the list of those that must be marked with their type designation.

- **1910.305(g) (2) (ii):** Changes the minimum size of hard service and junior hard service cords that may be spliced from No. 12 to 14.

- **1910.305(h), introductory text, (h)(1), (h)(2), (h)(3), (h)(6), (h)(7), and (h)(8):** Permits the minimum introductory size of the insulated ground-check conductor of Type G-GC cables to be No. 10 rather than No. 8. (Individual requirements are placed in separate paragraphs).
- **1910.305(h)(4):** Adds a requirement for shields to be grounded.
- **1910.305(h)(5):** Adds minimum bending radii requirements for portable cables.
- **1910.305(i) (3):** Also permits fixture wire to be used in fire alarm circuits.
- **1910.305(j)(1)(iii):** Adds a requirement that the grounded circuit conductor, where present, be connected to the screw shell.
- **1910.305(j)(2)(i):** Adds requirements to ensure that attachment plugs and connectors have no exposed live parts.
- **1910.305(j)(2)(iii):** Clarifies that nongrounding-type receptacles may not be used with grounding-type attachment plugs.
- **1910.305(j)(2)(v), (j)(2)(vi), and (j)(2)(vii):** Adds requirements for receptacles outdoors to be installed in weatherproof enclosures appropriate for the use of the receptacle and for the location.
- **1910.305(j)(3)(ii):** Adds a requirement to group and identify disconnecting means for appliances supplied by more than one source.
- **1910.305(j)(3)(iii):** Adds requirements for marking frequency and required external overload protection for appliances.
- **1910.305(j)(3)(iv):** Clarifies that markings must be visible or easily accessible after installation.
- **1910.305(j)(6)(ii)(A) and (j)(6)(ii)(B):** Adds requirements to provide disconnecting means of adequate capacity for capacitors operating at more than 600 V.
- **1910.306(a)(1)(i), (a)(2)(i), and (a)(2)(ii):** Reorganized and clarified the requirements for disconnecting means for signs. The final rule does not apply these requirements to exit signs.
- **1910.306(a)(1)(ii):** Adds a requirement for the disconnects for signs located within fountains to be at least 1.52 m from the fountain wall.
- **1910.306(b)(1):** Adds specific requirements for the type and location of disconnecting means for runway conductors.

- **1910.306(c):** This paragraph now covers wheelchair lifts, and stairway chair lifts.
- **1910.306(c)(3)** Adds requirements for the type of disconnecting means.
- **1910.306(c)(4):** Adds requirements for the operation of disconnecting means.
- **1910.306(c)(5):** Adds requirements for the location of disconnecting means.
- **1910.306(c)(6):** Adds requirements for the identification of disconnecting means.
- **1910.306(c)(7):** Adds requirements for disconnecting means for single car and multicar installations supplied by more than one source.
- **1910.306(c)(9):** Adds requirements for warning signs for interconnected multicar controllers.
- **1910.306(c)(10):** Adds exceptions related to the location of motor controllers.
- **1910.306(d)(1):** Adds requirements for the type and rating of the disconnecting means.
- **1910.306(d)(2):** Clarifies that a supply circuit switch may be used as a disconnecting means if the circuit supplies only one welder.
- **1910.306(e):** Adds a requirement to group the disconnecting means for the HVAC systems serving information technology rooms with the disconnecting means for the information technology equipment. The final rule exempts integrated electrical systems covered by Sec. 1910.308(g). (The existing standard refers to this equipment as data processing equipment)
- **1910.306(f), introductory text:** Adds coverage of X-rays for dental or medical use.
- **1910.306(g)(1)(iii):** Adds a requirement for the installation of doors or detachable panels to provide access to internal parts. Adds a requirement that detachable panels not be readily removable.
- **1910.306(g)(1)(vi):** Adds a requirement to ensure adequate rating of disconnecting means. The final rule also clarifies when the supply circuit disconnecting means may be used as the disconnecting means for induction and dielectric heating equipment.
- **1910.306(h)(4)(i):** Adds requirements limiting primary and secondary voltage on isolating transformers supplying receptacles for ungrounded cord- and plug-connected equipment. Also, adds requirement for

overcurrent protection for circuits supplied by these transformers.

- **1910.306(i)(2):** Allows the disconnecting means for a center pivot irrigation machine to be located not more than 15.2 m (50 ft) from the machine if the disconnecting means is visible from the machine.
- **1910.306(j), introductory text:** Clarifies that hydro-massage bathtubs are covered by this paragraph.
- **1910.306(j)(1)(ii):** Extends the boundary within which receptacles require ground-fault circuit interrupter protection from 4.57 m (15 ft) to 6.08 m (20 ft) for new installations.
- **1910.306(j)(1)(iii):** Adds requirements for the installation of at least one receptacle near permanently installed pools at dwelling units.
- **1910.306(j)(2)(i):** Clarifies that ceiling suspended (paddle) fans are covered by this requirement.
- **1910.306(j)(4)(iii):** Adds a requirement to guard lighting fixtures facing upward.
- **1910.306(k):** Adds requirements for carnivals, circuses, fairs, and similar events. Sec. 1910.307 Hazardous (classified) locations.
- **1910.307(a):** Adds the Zone classification system for Class I locations. (See detailed discussion later in this section of the preamble).
- **1910.307(b):** Adds documentation requirements for hazardous locations classified using either the division or zone classification system.
- **1910.307(c)(2)(ii)(B):** Also permits fixtures approved for Class II, Division 2 locations to omit the group marking.
- **1910.307(c)(2)(ii)(E):** Adds a requirement that electric equipment suitable for an ambient temperature exceeding 40 [deg] C (104 [deg] F) be marked with the maximum ambient temperature.
- **1910.307(b)(3), Note:** The last sentence of the note is removed to make it clear that the OSHA standard does not incorporate the National Electrical Code by reference. The NEC continues to be a guideline that employers may reference in determining the type and design of equipment and installations that will meet the OSHA standard.
- **1910.307(f):** The final rule adds a list of specific protective techniques for electrical installations in hazardous locations classified under the division classification system.
- **1910.307(g):** Adds the zone classification system as an alternative method of installing electric equipment in hazardous locations. This paragraph sets the protective techniques and other requirements necessary for safe installation of electric equipment in hazardous locations classified under the zone classification system.
- **1910.308(a)(1)(i) and (a)(3)(ii):** Adds the following wiring methods to those acceptable for installations operating at more than 600 V: Electrical metallic tubing, rigid nonmetallic conduit, busways, and cable bus. The proposal also removes the specific requirement to support cables having a bare lead sheath or a braided outer covering in a manner to prevent damage to the braid or sheath. This hazard is covered by Sec. 1910.303(b)(1) and (b)(8)(i) and new Sec. 1910.308(a)(4).
- **1910.308(a)(2) and (a)(3)(i):** Adds requirements to ensure that high- voltage cables can adequately handle the voltage stresses placed upon them and to ensure that any coverings are flame retardant.
- **1910.308(a)(4):** Adds requirements for the protection of high-voltage cables against moisture and physical damage where the cable conductors emerge from a metal sheath.
- **1910.308(a)(5)(ii):** Adds requirements for fuses to protect each ungrounded conductor, for adequate ratings of fuses installed in parallel, and for the protection of employees from power fuses of the vented type.
- **1910.308(a)(5)(iii):** Clarifies that distribution cutouts are not suitable for installation in buildings or transformer vaults.
- **1910.308(a)(5)(iv):** Adds requirements for fused cutouts to either be capable of interrupting load current or be supplemented by a means of interrupting load current. In addition, a warning sign would be required for fused cutouts that cannot interrupt load current.
- **1910.308(a)(5)(v):** Adds a requirement for guarding nonshielded cables and energized parts of oil-filled cutouts.
- **1910.308(a)(5)(vi):** Adds requirements to ensure that load interrupting switches will be protected against interrupting fault current

and to provide for warning signs for back fed switches.

- **1910.308(a)(7)(ii):** Clarifies that multiconductor portable cable may supply mobile equipment.
- **1910.308(a)(7)(vi):** Limits the conditions under which switch or contactor enclosures may be used as junction boxes or raceways.
- **1910.308(b)(2):** Clarifies that emergency illumination includes all required means of egress lighting, illuminated exit signs, and all other lights necessary to provide required illumination.
- **1910.308(b)(3):** Adds requirements to provide signs indicating the presence and location of on-site emergency power sources under certain conditions.
- **1910.308(c)(1)(i), (c)(1)(ii), and (c)(1)(iii):** Clarifies the power limitations of Class 1, 2, and 3 remote control, signaling, and power-limited circuits based on equipment listing.
- **1910.308(c)(3):** Adds requirements for the separation of cables and conductors of Class 2 and Class 3 circuits from cables and conductors of other types of circuits.
- **1910.308(d)(2)(ii):** Adds a requirement for power-limited fire alarm circuit power sources to be listed and marked as such.
- **1910.308(d)(3)(ii), (d)(3)(iii), and (d)(3)(iv):** Clarifies the requirements for installing power-limited fire- protective signaling circuits with other types of circuits. (Individual requirements are placed in separate paragraphs).
- **1910.308(e)(1):** Clarifies the requirement for listed primary protectors to make it clear that circuits confined within a block do not need protectors.
- **1910.308(f):** Adds requirements to separate conductors of solar photovoltaic systems from conductors of other systems and to provide a disconnecting means for solar photovoltaic systems.
- **1910.308(g):** Adds an exception to the provisions on the location of over current protective devices for integrated electrical systems.

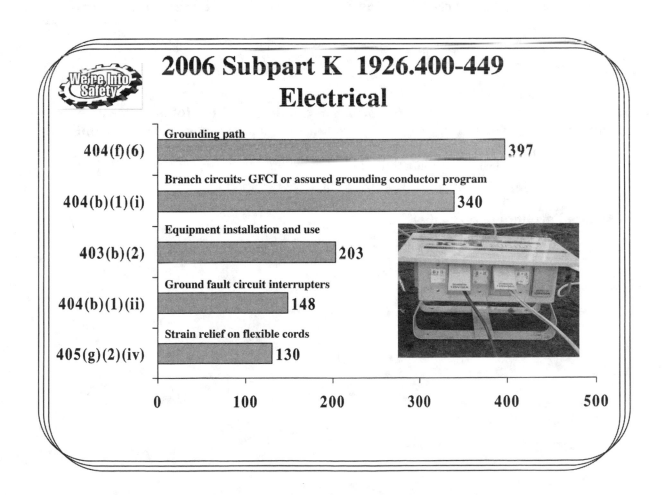

Sources for More Information

NFPA 70E Standard for Electrical Safety Requirements for Employee Workplaces, National Fire Protection Association, 1-617-770-3000.

Electrical Quiz
(See appendix for answers.)

1. Workers exposed to electrical shock on construction sites must be protected by:
a. Ground-fault circuit interrupter or an assured equipment grounding program
b. Grounding of all electrical systems
c. Low voltage tools
d. Ohm's Law

2. A ground-fault circuit interrupter is designed to trip at about:
a. 10 milliamps
b. 20 milliamps
c. 3 milliamps
d. 5 milliamps

3. Electrical conductors and equipment used in construction must be:
a. Approved for the type of use for which they will be used
b. Registered with the general contractor
c. Protected by a ground-fault circuit interrupter
d. Labeled with the name of the owner of the conductor or equipment

4. Using an assured protection program, all equipment must be tested by a competent person:
a. Before first use, after repairs, after suspected damage, and at least every 90 days
b. Before first use and every 90 days
c. Annually
d. As determined by the competent person

5. An assured equipment grounding program requires that the following tests be performed on all cord sets and receptacles that are not a permanent part of the building:
a. Continuity and proper insulation
b. Continuity and correct attachment of the cap or plug
c. Continuity and correct type of wiring for the use anticipated
d. Continuity and use of a ground-fault circuit interrupter

6. Assured grounding tests shall be:
a. Conducted daily
b. Recorded
c. Performed by a licensed electrician
d. Performed by an authorized individual

STAIRWAYS AND LADDERS

Stairways and ladders are a major source of injuries and fatalities among construction workers. OSHA estimates that there are 24,882 injuries and as many as 36 fatalities each year due to falls from stairways and ladders used in construction. Nearly half of these injuries are serious enough to require time off the job—11,570 lost workday injuries occur each year. This data demonstrates that work on and around ladders and stairways is hazardous. More importantly, it shows that compliance with OSHA's requirements for the safe use of ladders and stairways could have prevented many of these injuries.

Subpart X, 29 CFR 1926.1050 through 1926.1060 applies to all stairways and ladders used in construction, alteration, repair (including painting and decorating), and demolition of work sites covered by OSHA's construction safety and health standards. It also specifies when stairways and ladders must be provided. It does not apply to ladders that are specifically manufactured for scaffold access and egress, but does apply to job-made and manufactured portable ladders intended for general-purpose use and that are then used for scaffold access and egress.

General Requirements

A stairway or ladder must be provided at all worker points of access where there is a break in elevation of 19 in. (48 cm) or more and no ramp, runway, embankment, or personnel hoist is provided. When there is only one point of access between levels, it must be kept clear to permit free passage by workers. If free passage becomes restricted, a second point of access must be provided and used. In those instances where there are more than two points of access between levels, at least one point of access must be kept clear at all times.

All stairway and ladder fall protection systems required by this rule must be installed. All duties required by OSHA must be performed before employees may begin work that requires the use of stairways or ladders and their respective fall protection systems.

Stairways

The following general requirements apply to all stairways used during the process of construction:
- Stairways that will not be a permanent part of the structure on which construction work is performed must have landings at least 30 in. deep and 22 in. wide (76 x 56 cm) at every 12 ft. (3.7 m) or less of vertical rise.
- Stairways must be installed at no less than 30 degrees, and no more than 50 degrees, from the horizontal.

- Variations in riser height or stair tread depth must not exceed ¼ in. in any stairway system, including any foundation structure used as one or more treads of the stairs.
- Where doors or gates open directly onto a stairway, a platform must be provided that extends at least 20 in. (51 cm) in width beyond the swing of the door.
- Metal pan landings and metal pan treads must be secured in place before filling.
- All stairway parts must be free of dangerous projections such as protruding nails.
- Slippery conditions on stairways must be corrected.
- Workers may not use spiral stairways that will not be a permanent part of the structure.

The following requirements apply to stairs in temporary service during construction:
- Except during construction of the actual stairway, stairways with metal pan landings and treads must not be used where the treads and/or landings have not been filled in with concrete or other material, unless the pans of the stairs and/or landings are temporarily filled in with wood or other material.
- All treads and landings must be replaced when worn below the top edge of the pan.
- Except during construction of the actual stairway, skeleton metal frame structures and steps must not be used (where treads and/or landings are to be installed at a later date) unless the stairs are fitted with secured temporary treads and landings.
- Temporary treads must be made of wood or other solid material and installed the full width and depth of the stair.

Stairrails and Handrails
The following general requirements apply to all stair rails and handrails:
- Stairways having four or more risers or rising more than 30 in. (76 cm) in height, whichever is less, must have at least one handrail. A stair rail also must be installed along each unprotected side or edge. When the top edge of a stair rail system also serves as a handrail, the height of the top edge must not be more than 37 in. (94 cm) nor less than 36 in. (91.5 cm) from the upper surface of the stair rail to the surface of the tread.
- Winding or spiral stairways must be equipped with a handrail to prevent using areas where the tread width is less than 6 in. (15 cm).
- Stair rails installed after March 15, 1991, must not be less than 36 in. (91.5 cm) in height.
- Midrails, screens, mesh, intermediate vertical members, or equivalent intermediate structural members must be provided between the top rail and stairway steps of the stair rail system.
- Midrails, when used, must be located midway between the top of the stair rail system and the stairway steps.
- Screens or mesh, when used, must extend from the top rail to the stairway step and along the opening between top rail supports.
- Intermediate vertical members, such as balusters, when used, must not be more than 19 in. (48 cm) apart.
- Other intermediate structural members, when used, must be installed so that there are no openings of more than 19 in. (48 cm) wide.
- Handrails and the top rails of the stair rail systems must be capable of withstanding, without failure, at least 200 pounds (890 n) of weight applied within 2 in. (5 cm) of the top edge in any downward or outward direction, at any point along the top edge.
- The height of handrails must not be more than 37 in. (94 cm) nor less than 30 in. (76 cm) from the upper surface of the handrail to the surface of the tread.
- The height of the top edge of a stair rail system when used as a handrail must not be more than 37 in. (94 cm) nor less than 36 in. (91.5 cm) from the upper surface of the stair rail system to the surface of the tread.
- Stair rail systems and handrails must be surfaced to prevent injuries, such as punctures or lacerations, and to keep clothing from snagging.
- Handrails must provide an adequate handhold for employees to grasp to prevent falls.
- The ends of stair rail systems and handrails must be constructed to prevent dangerous projections, such as rails protruding beyond the end posts of the system.

- Temporary handrails must have a minimum clearance of 3 in. (8 cm) between the handrail and walls, stair rail systems, and other objects.
- Unprotected sides and edges of stairway landings must be provided with standard 42-in. guardrail systems.

Ladders

The following general requirements apply to all ladders, including job-made ladders:

- A double-cleated ladder or two or more ladders must be provided when ladders are the only way to enter or exit a work area having 25 or more employees or when a ladder serves simultaneous two-way traffic.
- Ladder rungs, cleats, and steps must be parallel, level, and uniformly spaced when the ladder is in position for use.
- Rungs, cleats, and steps of portable and fixed ladders (except as provided below) must not be spaced less than 10 in. (25 cm), nor more than 14 in. (36 cm), apart along the ladder's side rails.
- Rungs, cleats, and steps of step stools must not be less than 8 in. (20 cm), nor more than 12 in. (31 cm), apart between center lines of the rungs, cleats, and steps.
- Rungs, cleats, and steps at the base section of extension trestle ladders must not be less than 8 in. (20 cm), nor more than 18 in. (46 cm), apart between center lines of the rungs, cleats, and steps. The rung spacing on the extension section must not be less than 6 in. (15 cm) nor more than 12 in. (31 cm).
- When splicing side rails, the resulting side rail must be equivalent in strength to a one-piece side rail made of the same material.
- A metal spreader or locking device must be provided on each stepladder to hold the front and back sections in an open position when the ladder is being used.
- Ladders must not be tied or fastened together to create longer sections unless they are specifically designed for such use.
- Two or more separate ladders used to reach an elevated work area must be offset with a platform or landing between the ladders, except when portable ladders are used to gain access to fixed ladders.

- Ladder components must be surfaced to prevent injury from punctures or lacerations and prevent snagging of clothing.
- Wood ladders must not be coated with any opaque covering, except for identification or warning labels which may be placed on one face of a side rail.

Portable Ladders

Non-self-supporting and self-supporting portable ladders must support at least four times the maximum intended load; extra heavy-duty type 1A metal or plastic ladders must sustain 3.3 times the maximum intended load. The ability of a self-supporting ladder to sustain loads must be determined by applying the load to the ladder in a downward vertical direction. The ability of a non-self-supporting ladder to sustain loads must be determined by applying the load in a downward vertical direction when the ladder is placed at a horizontal angle of 75.5°. The minimum clear distance between side rails for all portable ladders must be 11.5 in. (29 cm). The rungs and steps of portable metal ladders must be corrugated, knurled, dimpled, coated with skid-resistant material, or treated to minimize slipping.

Fixed Ladders

A fixed ladder must be capable of supporting at least two loads of 250 lbs. (114 kg) each, concentrated between any two consecutive attachments. Fixed ladders also must support added anticipated loads caused by ice buildup, winds, rigging, and impact loads resulting from the use of ladder safety devices. Individual rung/step ladders must extend at least 42 in. (1.1 m) above the access level or landing platform either by the continuation of the rung spacing as horizontal grab bars or by providing vertical grab bars that have the same lateral spacing as the vertical legs of the ladder rails. Each step or rung of a fixed ladder must be capable of supporting a load of at least 250 lbs. (114 kg) applied in the middle of the step or rung.

The minimum clear distance between the sides of individual rung/step ladders and between the side rails of other fixed ladders must be 16 in. The rungs of individual rung/step ladders must be shaped to prevent workers from slipping off the end of the rungs. The rungs and steps of fixed metal ladders manufactured after January 14, 1991, must be corrugated, knurled, dimpled, coated with skid-resistant material, or treated to minimize slipping.

The minimum perpendicular clearance between fixed ladder rungs, cleats, and steps and any obstruction behind the ladder must be 7 in. However, the clearance for an elevator pit ladder must be 4.5 in. The minimum perpendicular clearance between the centerline of fixed ladder rungs, cleats, and steps and any obstruction on the climbing side of the ladder must be 30 in. If obstructions are unavoidable, clearance may be reduced to 24 in., provided that a deflection device is installed to guide workers around the obstruction.

The step-across distance between the center of the steps or rungs of fixed ladders and the nearest edge of a landing area must be no less than 7 in. and no more than 12 in. A landing platform must be provided if the step-across distance exceeds 12 in. Fixed ladders without cages or wells must have at least a 15-in. clear width to the nearest permanent object on each side of the centerline of the ladder.

Fixed ladders must be provided with cages, wells, ladder safety devices, or self-retracting lifelines where the length of climb is less than 24 ft., but the top of the ladder is at a distance greater than 24 ft. above the lower levels.

If the total length of a climb on a fixed ladder equals or exceeds 24 ft., the ladder must be equipped with either a:
- Ladder safety device;
- Self-retracting lifeline and rest platforms at intervals not to exceed 150 ft.; or
- Cage or well and multiple ladder sections, each ladder section not to exceed 50 ft. (15.2 m) in length. These ladder sections must be offset from adjacent sections and landing platforms must be provided at maximum intervals of 50 ft.

The side rails of through or side-step fixed ladders must extend 42 in. above the top level or landing platform served by the ladder. For a parapet ladder, the access level must be at the roof if the parapet is cut to permit passage through it. If the parapet is continuous, the access level is the top of the parapet.

Steps or rungs for through-fixed-ladder extensions must be omitted from the extension; and the extension of side rails must be flared to provide between 24 in. and 30 in. clearance between side rails. When safety devices are provided, the maximum clearance between side rail extensions must not exceed 36 in.

Exhibit 10-1.
A fixed ladder with a cage provides fall protection.

Cages for Fixed Ladders

Horizontal bands must be fastened to the side rails of rail ladders or directly to the structure, building, or equipment for individual-rung ladders. Vertical bars must be on the inside of the horizontal bands and must be fastened to them.

Cages must not extend less than 27 in. (68 cm) or more than 30 in. (76 cm) from the centerline of the step or rung and must not be less than 27 in. (68 cm) wide. The inside of the cage must be clear of projections.

Horizontal bands must be spaced at intervals not more than 4 ft. apart measured from centerline to centerline. Vertical bars must be spaced at intervals not more than 9.5 in. apart measured from centerline to centerline.

The bottom of the cage must be between 7 ft. and 8 ft. above the point of access to the bottom of the ladder. The bottom of the cage must be flared not less than 4 in. between the bottom horizontal band and the next higher band.

The top of the cage must be a minimum of 42 in. above the top of the platform or the point of access at the top of the ladder. Provisions must be made for access to the platform or other point of access.

Wells for Fixed Ladders

Wells must completely encircle the ladder and be free of projections. The inside face of the well on the climbing side of the ladder must extend between 27 in. and 30 in. from the centerline of the step or rung. The inside width of the well must be at least 30 in.

The bottom of the well above the point of access to the bottom of the ladder must be between 7 ft. and 8 ft.

Ladder Safety Devices and Related Support Systems for Fixed Ladders

All safety devices must be capable of withstanding, without failure, a drop test consisting of a 500-lb. weight dropping 18 in.

All safety devices must permit the worker to ascend or descend without continually having to hold, push, or pull any part of the device, leaving both hands free for climbing.

All safety devices must be activated within 2 ft. after a fall occurs and limit the descending velocity of an employee to 7 ft. per second or less.

The connection between the carrier or lifeline and the point of attachment to the body belt or harness must not exceed 9 in. in length.

Mounting Ladder Safety Devices for Fixed Ladders

Mountings for rigid carriers must be attached at each end of the carrier, with intermediate mountings spaced along the entire length of the carrier, to provide the necessary strength to stop workers' falls.

Mountings for flexible carriers must be attached at each end of the carrier. Cable guides for flexible carriers must be installed with spacing between 25 ft. and 40 ft. along the entire length of the carrier to prevent wind damage to the system.

The design and installation of mountings and cable guides must not reduce the strength of the ladder.

Side rails and steps or rungs for side-step fixed ladders must be continuous in extension.

Use of All Ladders (Including Job-Made Ladders)

When portable ladders are used for access to an upper landing surface, the side rails must extend at least 3 ft. above the upper landing surface. When such an extension is not possible, the ladder must be secured and a grasping device, such as a grab rail, must be provided to assist workers in mounting and dismounting the ladder. A ladder extension must not deflect under a load that would cause the ladder to slip off its support.

Ladders must be maintained free of oil, grease, and other slipping hazards. They must not be loaded beyond the maximum intended load for which they were built nor beyond their manufacturer's rated capacity. Ladders must be used only on stable and level surfaces unless they are secured to prevent accidental movement. Ladders must be used only for the purpose for which they were designed.

Non-self-supporting ladders must be used at an angle where the horizontal distance from the top support to the foot of the ladder is approximately one quarter of the working length of the ladder. Wood job-made ladders with spliced side rails must be used at an angle where the horizontal distance is one-eighth the working length of the ladder.

Fixed ladders must be used at a pitch no greater than 90 degrees from the horizontal, measured from the backside of the ladder.

Ladders must not be used on slippery surfaces unless they are secured or provided with slip-resistant feet to prevent accidental movement. Slip-resistant feet must not be used as a substitute for the care in placing, lashing, or holding a ladder upon slippery surfaces.

Ladders placed in areas such as passageways, doorways, or driveways, or where they can be displaced by workplace activities or traffic must be secured to prevent accidental movement or a barricade must be used to keep traffic or activities away from the ladder.

The top of a non-self-supporting ladder must be placed with two rails supported equally unless it is equipped with a single support attachment. Ladders must not be moved, shifted, or extended while in use. The area around the top and bottom of the ladders must be kept clear. The top or top step of a stepladder must not be used as a step.

Ladders must have nonconductive side rails if they are used where the worker or the ladder could contact exposed energized electrical equipment. Single-rail ladders must not be used.

Cross-bracing on the rear sections of stepladders must not be used for climbing unless the ladders are designed and provided with steps for climbing on both the front and rear sections.

Ladders must be inspected by a competent person for visible defects on a periodic basis and after any incident that could affect their safe use.

When ascending or descending a ladder, the worker must face the ladder. Each worker must use at least one hand to grasp the ladder when moving up or down the ladder. A worker on a ladder must not carry any object or load that could cause the worker to lose balance and fall.

Structural Defects

Portable ladders with structural defects such as broken or missing rungs, cleats, or steps; broken or split rails; corroded components; or other faulty or defective components must immediately be marked defective, or tagged with "Do Not Use" or similar language and withdrawn from service until repaired.

Fixed ladders with structural defects such as broken or missing rungs, cleats, or steps; broken or split rails; or corroded components must be withdrawn from service until repaired.

Defective fixed ladders are considered withdrawn from use when they are:

- Immediately tagged with "Do Not Use" or similar language;
- Marked in a manner that identifies them as defective; or
- Blocked (such as with a plywood attachment that spans several rungs).

Before a defective ladder can be returned to use, it must be restored to a condition meeting its original design criteria.

Training Requirements

Under the provisions of the standard, employers must provide a training program for employees who use ladders and stairways. The program must enable each employee to recognize the hazards related to ladders and stairways and to use proper procedures to minimize these hazards. For example, employers must ensure that each employee is trained by a competent person in the following areas, as applicable:

- The nature of fall hazards in the work area;
- The correct procedures for erecting, maintaining, and disassembling the fall protection systems to be used;
- The proper construction, use, placement, and care in handling of all stairways and ladders; and
- The maximum intended load-carrying capacities of ladders used.

In addition, retraining must be provided for each employee, as necessary, so that the employee maintains the understanding and knowledge acquired through the training, as required by the standard.

Common Citations for Walking and Working Surfaces

No Guardrails on Open-Sided Floors

This is a common problem on sites where materials must be loaded up stairs and the guardrail gets in the way. Guardrails are removed, but are not replaced after workers finish unloading the material. The controlling contractor has the responsibility to put up rails if they are missing.

Wire Rope Guardrails Deflect More than 3 in.

Most construction jobs that use these guardrails are going to have problems. Turnbuckles should be used to maintain the maximum deflection. One of the problems with wire rope is that it is not easy to tell if it meets this deflection requirement or is anchored at all without testing. This gives employees a false sense of security.

Floor Openings Not Guarded

Guardrails or covers must be used and in place. Securing covers is important because fatalities have occurred when covers have slipped and employees have fallen through the openings. Also, marking covers to indicate that they are for fall protection is necessary so that employees do not pick them up and walk into the openings. An opening of just a few in. is enough to cause an injury.

Summary

A stairway or ladder is needed any time an elevation changes by 19 in. In construction, temporary spiral stairways cannot be used. Access to ladders and stairways must be kept clear. Employers must provide safe ladder ways and stairways before employees may work at the elevated areas.

Stair rails are put on the stairs to provide some fall protection. Handrails are installed so workers can catch themselves and keep from slipping on stairs. The people who design, manufacture, and sell this equipment have detailed rules for the use of their equipment.

Cages on ladders do not prevent falls. Ladder climbing devices such as fall arrest systems are designed for that function and should be used. Most fatalities involve ladders that are at 10 ft. or lower.

Use the ¼ rule when setting up portable ladders. For every foot the ladder goes up, the base of the ladder should be ¼ that distance from the wall. For example, if there is a 20-ft. ladder up against a wall, the base should be 5 ft. away from the wall (20/4 = 5).

When using a temporary ladder, the edge of the ladder must extend 3 ft. beyond the top support. For example, in an excavation, the end of the ladder must stick up past the lip of the hole by 3 ft.

Ladders should not be tied or fastened together unless specifically designed that way. Wood ladders should never be varnished; it tends to conceal any cracks or faults.

Common citations have been issued from OSHA for:

- Stairs that have no handrails or guardrails;
- Ladders that have been set up within 10 ft. of power lines;
- Fixed ladders over 20 ft. that have no fall protection; and
- Ladders that have not been secured to prevent movement.

Loads Carried by Persons Climbing or Descending a Ladder—1926.1053(b)(22)

The following letter from Lydich-Hooks Roofing Company to OSHA's Lubbock Area Office requests a variance from the ladder use requirement of 29 CFR 1926.1053(b)(22). OSHA denied the request because this section allows an object or load to be carried by a person climbing or descending a ladder provided it is done safely (so as not to cause the employee to lose balance and fall). OSHA references the preamble of the final rule (55 FR 47682) to clarify which objects can be carried safely.

January 13, 1992

U.S. Department of Labor
Occupational Safety & Health Administration
Room 422
Federal Building
1205 Texas Avenue
Lubbock, Texas 79401

Re: 29 CFR 1926.1053(b)(22)

Gentlemen:

We hereby request a permanent variance from the above-referenced standard. The record will show that for our company the risks from the above-referenced hazard have been non-existent.

We take great care in training our personnel in ladder safety. The risks that we would incur in utilizing other methods of material conveyance seem to expose our employees to greater risk than simply carrying something up a ladder.

The statute as written seems a little vague. The working or the statute implies that there are objects or loads which could be carried safely. In short, this subpart seems to be judging. We submit that our employees should be allowed to occasionally carry materials up ladders without threat of citation.

Please let us know your views on our Variance Application.

Yours truly,

LYDICK-HOODS ROOFING COMPANY OF LUBBOCK, INC.

Randy Hooks
President

April 2, 1992

Mr. Randy Hooks, President
Lydich-Hooks Roofing Company
Post Office Box 2605
Lubbock, Texas 79408

Dear Mr. Hooks:

This is in response to your January 13 letter to the Occupational Safety and Health Administration's (OSHA) Lubbock Area Office requesting a variance from the ladder use requirement of 29 CFR 1926.1053(b)(22). Your request has been forwarded to this office for response. I apologize for the delay in responding to you.

OSHA is unable to grant your request for a variance from the requirements of 1926.1053(b)(22) because this section allows an object or load to be carried by a person climbing or descending a ladder provided it is done safely (so as not to cause the employee to lose balance and fall). In regard to which objects can be carried safely, please be guided by the following discussion from the preamble of the final rule (55 FR 47682) which was published on November 14, 1990:

"Although OSHA believes that small items such as hammers, pliers, measuring tapes, nails, paint brushes, and similar items should be carried in pouches, holsters, or belt loops, the language in the final rule would not preclude an employee from carrying such items while climbing a ladder so long as the items don't impede the employee's ability to maintain full control while climbing or descending the ladder. It is OSHA's belief that the employee's focus and attention while climbing up and/or down a ladder should be on making a safe ascent or descent and not on transporting items up and down the ladder. OSHA notes that an employee who needs to take a large or heavy object to a different level by means of a ladder can pull the object up or lower it with a handline."

If we can be of any further assistance, please contact Mr. Roy F. Gurnham or Mr. Dale Cavanaugh of my staff in the Office of Construction and Maritime Compliance Assistance at (202) 523 8136.

Sincerely,

Patricia K. Clark, Director
Directorate of Compliance Programs

Stairs and Ladders Quiz
(See appendix for answers.)

1. A stairway or ladder must be provided at all points of access where there is a break in elevation of:
a. 12 in.
b. 19 in.
c. 24 in.
d. 36 in.

2. Ladders must extend beyond the working surface by:
a. 1 ft.
b. 2 ft.
c. 3 ft.
d. 4 ft.

3. Ladders must be secured from movement and self supporting ladders must:
a. Have a 1:4 ratio: For every 4 ft. up, the base must come out 1 ft.
b. Be held by a competent person
c. Be made of fiberglass
d. Have a 1:3 ratio: For every 3 ft. up, the base must come out 1 ft.

4. Workers must be trained by a competent person on how to use ladders and stairways. This training must include:
a. Nature of hazards of falls, correct procedures for using the equipment, and maximum load
b. Nature of hazards of falls and the requirements of the OSHA regulation
c. The ANSI standard that governs ladder use
d. A written test that may be inspected by OSHA

5. Ladders that have structural defects such as missing rungs or steps:
a. May be used if they cannot be immediately repaired
b. Must be removed to the job trailer
c. Must be immediately marked defective or tagged with a "Do Not Use" sign
d. Must be repaired immediately

6. Around electrical lines:
a. Ladders may not be made of metal
b. Ladders must remain more than 30 ft. from power lines
c. Ladders must be protected with a coating of varnish
d. Ladders may come into contact with the insulation on the power lines

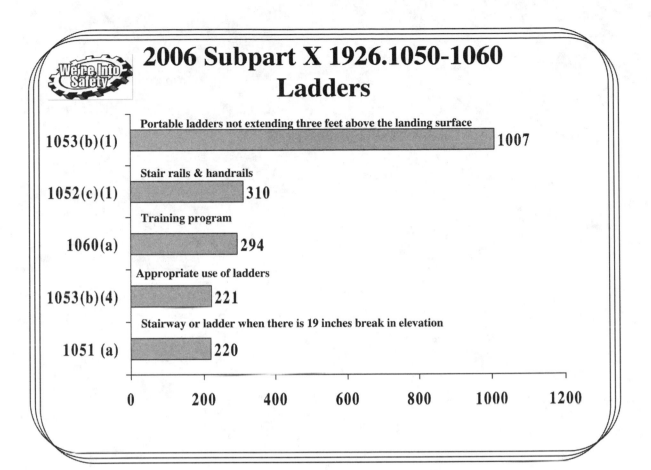

2006 Subpart X 1926.1050-1060
Ladders

Code	Description	Value
1053(b)(1)	Portable ladders not extending three feet above the landing surface	1007
1052(c)(1)	Stair rails & handrails	310
1060(a)	Training program	294
1053(b)(4)	Appropriate use of ladders	221
1051 (a)	Stairway or ladder when there is 19 inches break in elevation	220

Stairways and Ladders

FALL PROTECTION

Falls are the leading cause of worker fatalities in construction. Each year, on average, more than 200 workers are killed and more than 100,000 are injured as a result of falls at construction sites. There are several generally accepted methods of providing fall protection so that workers do not get injured when they fall from working surfaces. A hierarchy of fall protection has been used:

- Elimination of the hazard;
- Preventing the worker from falling over the edge;
- Use a system to arrest the fall;
- Use a warning line system to warn workers of the danger;
- Use a safety monitor to warn workers of the danger; and
- Use an administrative approach, such as detailed training.

OSHA recognizes that accidents involving falls are generally complex events frequently involving a variety of factors. The standard prescribes the duty to provide fall protection, sets the criteria and practices for fall protection systems, and requires training. It covers hazard assessment and fall protection and safety monitoring systems. Also addressed are controlled access zones, safety nets; and guardrail, personal fall arrest, warning line, and positioning device systems. Consequently, the standard for fall protection deals with both the human and equipment-related issues in protecting workers from fall hazards. For example, employers and employees need to do the following:

- Where protection is required, select a fall protection system appropriate for each situation;
- Properly construct and install safety systems;
- Supervise employees properly;
- Use safe work procedures; and
- Train workers in the proper selection, use, and maintenance of all protection systems.

The performance-oriented requirements make it easier for employers to provide the necessary protection. The rule covers most construction workers except those inspecting, investigating, or assessing workplace conditions prior to the actual start of work or after all work has been completed. The rule identifies areas or activities where fall protection is needed. These include, but are not limited to:

- Ramps, runways, and other walkways;
- Excavations;
- Hoist areas;
- Holes;
- Formwork and reinforcing steel;

- Leading edge work;
- Unprotected sides and edges;
- Overhand bricklaying and related work;
- Roofing work;
- Precast concrete erection;
- Wall openings;
- Residential construction; and
- Other walking/working surfaces.

The rule sets a uniform threshold height of 6 ft. (1.8 m), thereby providing consistent protection. This means that construction employers must protect their employees from fall hazards and falling objects whenever an affected employee is 6 ft. (1.8 m) or more above a lower level. Protection also must be provided for construction workers who are exposed to the hazard of falling into dangerous equipment.

Under the standard, employers are able to select fall protection measures compatible with the type of work being performed. Fall protection generally can be provided through the use of guardrail, safety net, personal fall arrest, positioning device, and warning line systems. The rule clarifies what an employer must do to provide fall protection for employees, such as identifying and evaluating fall hazards and providing specific training. Requirements to provide fall protection for workers on scaffolds and ladders and for workers engaged in steel erection of buildings are covered in other subparts of the OSHA regulations.

Employers are required to assess the workplace to determine whether the walking/working surfaces on which employees are to work have the strength and structural integrity to safely support workers. Employees are not permitted to work on those surfaces until it has been determined that the surfaces have the requisite strength and structural integrity to support the workers. Once employers have determined that the surface is safe for employees to work on, the employer must select one of the options listed for the work operation if a fall hazard is present.

For example, if an employee is exposed to falling 6 ft. or more from an unprotected side or edge, the employer must select a guardrail, safety net, or personal fall arrest system to protect the worker. Similar requirements are prescribed for other fall hazards.

Exhibit 11-1.
This site uses a guardrail with a top rail, midrail and toeband.

Guardrail Systems

If the employer chooses to use guardrail systems to protect workers from falls, the systems must meet the following criteria. Top rails and midrails of guardrail systems must be at least ¼ in. nominal diameter or thickness to prevent cuts and lacerations. If wire rope is used for top rails, it must be flagged at not more than 6-ft. intervals with high-visibility material. Steel and plastic banding cannot be used as top rails or midrails. Manila, plastic, or synthetic rope used for top rails or midrails must be inspected as frequently as necessary to ensure strength and stability.

The top edge height of top rails or (equivalent) guardrails must be 42 in. ± 3 in., above the walking/working level. When workers are using stilts, the top-edge height of the top rail, or equivalent member, must be increased by an amount equal to the height of the stilts.

Screens, midrails, mesh, intermediate vertical members, or equivalent intermediate structural members must be installed between the top edge of the guardrail system and the walking/working surface when there are no walls or parapet walls at least 21 in. high. When midrails are used, they must be installed at a height midway between the top edge of the guardrail system and the walking/working level. When screens and mesh are used, they must extend from the top rail to the walking/working level and along the entire opening between top-rail supports. Intermediate members, such as balusters, when used between posts, shall not be more than 19 in. apart.

Other structural members, such as additional midrails and architectural panels, shall be installed so that there are no openings in the guardrail system of more than 19 in.

The guardrail system must be capable of withstanding a force of at least 200 lbs. applied within 2 in. of the top edge in any outward or downward direction. When the 200-pound test is applied in a downward direction, the top edge of the guardrail must not deflect to a height less than 39 in. above the walking/working level.

Midrails, screens, mesh, intermediate vertical members, solid panels, and equivalent structural members shall be capable of withstanding a force of at least 150 lbs. applied in any downward or outward direction at any point along the midrail or other member.

Guardrail systems shall be surfaced to protect workers from punctures or lacerations and to prevent the snagging of clothing. The ends of top rails and midrails must not overhang terminal posts, except where such overhang does not constitute a projection hazard.

When guardrail systems are used at hoisting areas, a chain, gate, or removable guardrail section must be placed across the access opening between guardrail sections when hoisting operations are not taking place.

At holes, guardrail systems must be set up on all unprotected sides or edges. When holes are used for the passage of materials, the hole shall have not more than two sides with removable guardrail sections. When the hole is not in use, it must be covered or provided with guardrails along all unprotected sides or edges.

If guardrail systems are used around holes that are used as access points (e.g., ladder ways), gates must be used or the point of access must be offset to prevent accidental walking into the hole. If guardrails are used at unprotected sides or edges of ramps and runways, they must be erected on each unprotected side or edge.

Personal Fall Arrest Systems

These consist of an anchorage, connectors, and a body belt or body harness and may include a deceleration device, lifeline, or suitable combinations. If a personal fall arrest system is used for fall protection, it must do the following:

- Limit maximum arresting force on an employee to 900 lbs. when used with a body belt;
- Limit maximum arresting force on an employee to 1,800 lbs. when used with a body harness;
- Be rigged so that an employee can neither free fall more than 6 ft. nor contact any lower level;
- Bring an employee to a complete stop and limit maximum deceleration distance an employee travels to 3.5 ft.; and
- Have sufficient strength to withstand twice the potential impact energy of an employee free falling a distance of 6 ft. or the free fall distance permitted by the system, whichever is less.

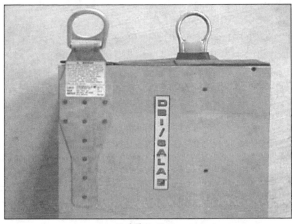

Exhibit 11-2.
Temporary anchor points.

It should be noted that the use of a body belt for fall arrest has been prohibited since 1998.

Personal fall arrest systems must be inspected prior to each use for wear damage and other deterioration. Defective components must be removed from service. Dee-rings and snaphooks must have a minimum tensile strength of 5,000 lbs. Dee-rings and snaphooks shall be proof-tested to a minimum tensile load of 3,600 lbs. without cracking, breaking, or suffering permanent deformation.

Snaphooks shall be sized to be compatible with the member to which they will be connected, or shall be of a locking configuration.

OSHA considers a hook to be compatible when the diameter of the Dee-ring to which the snaphook is attached is greater than the inside length of the snaphook when measured from the bottom (hinged end) of the snaphook keeper to the inside curve of the top of the snaphook. Thus, no matter how the Dee-ring is positioned or moved with the snaphook attached, the Dee-ring cannot touch the outside of the keeper thus depressing it open.

The use of nonlocking snaphooks also has been prohibited since 1998.

On suspended scaffolds or similar work platforms with horizontal lifelines that may become vertical lifelines, the devices used to connect to a horizontal lifeline shall be capable of locking in both directions on the lifeline.

Horizontal lifelines shall be designed, installed, and used under the supervision of a qualified person, as part of a complete personal fall arrest system that maintains a safety factor of at least 2. Lifelines shall be protected against being cut or abraded.

Self-retracting lifelines and lanyards that automatically limit free fall distance to 2 ft. (0.61 m) or less shall be capable of sustaining a minimum tensile load of 3,000 lbs. applied to the device with the lifeline or lanyard in the fully extended position.

Self-retracting lifelines and lanyards that do not limit free fall distance to 2 ft. (0.61 meters) or less, rip stitch lanyards, and tearing and deforming lanyards shall be capable of sustaining a minimum tensile load of 5,000 lbs. applied to the device with the lifeline or lanyard in the fully extended position.

Ropes and straps (webbing) used in lanyards, lifelines, and strength components of body belts and body harnesses shall be made of synthetic fibers.

Anchorages shall be designed, installed, and used under the supervision of a qualified person, as part of a complete personal fall arrest system that maintains a safety factor of at least two, i.e., capable of supporting at least twice the weight expected to be imposed upon it. Anchorages used to attach personal fall arrest systems shall be independent of any anchorage being used to support or suspend platforms and must be capable of supporting at least 5,000 lbs. (22.2 kN) per person attached.

Lanyards and vertical lifelines must have a minimum breaking strength of 5,000 lbs.

Positioning Device Systems

These body belt or body harness systems are to be set up so that workers can free fall no further than 2 ft. They shall be secured to an anchorage capable of supporting at least twice the potential impact load of an employee's fall or 3,000 lbs., whichever is greater. Requirements for snaphooks, Dee-rings, and other connectors used with positioning device systems must meet the same criteria as those for personal fall arrest systems.

Safety Monitoring Systems

When no other alternative fall protection has been implemented, the employer shall implement a safety monitoring system. Employers must appoint a competent person to monitor the safety of workers and ensure that the competent person:

- Is competent in the recognition of fall hazards;
- Is capable of warning workers of fall hazard dangers and in detecting unsafe work practices;
- Is operating on the same walking/working surfaces of the workers and can see them; and
- Is close enough to work operations to communicate orally with workers and has no other duties to distract him or her from the monitoring function.

Exhibit 11-3.
Roof work can be dangerous without some form of fall protection.

Mechanical equipment shall not be used or stored in areas where safety monitoring systems are being used to monitor employees engaged in roofing operations on low-sloped roofs.

No worker, other than one engaged in roofing work (on low-sloped roofs) or one covered by a fall protection plan, shall be allowed in an area where an employee is being protected by a safety monitoring system. All workers in a controlled access zone shall be instructed to promptly comply with fall hazard warnings issued by safety monitors.

Safety Net Systems

Safety nets must be installed as close as practicable under the walking/working surface on which employees are working and never more than 30 ft. below such levels. Defective nets shall not be used. Safety nets shall be inspected at least once a week for wear, damage, and other deterioration. The maximum size of each safety net mesh opening shall not exceed 36 sq. in. nor be longer than 6 in. on any side; the openings, measured center-to-center, of mesh ropes or webbing, also shall not exceed 6 in. All mesh crossings shall be secured to prevent enlargement of the mesh opening. Each safety net or section shall have a border rope for webbing with a minimum breaking strength of 5,000 lbs. Connections between safety net panels shall be as strong as integral net components and be spaced no more than 6 in. apart.

Safety nets shall be installed with sufficient clearance underneath to prevent contact with the surface or structure below. When nets are used on bridges, the potential fall area from the walking/working surface to the net shall be unobstructed.

Safety nets shall be capable of absorbing an impact force of a drop test consisting of a 400-pound bag of sand, 30 in. in diameter, dropped from the highest walking/working surface at which workers are exposed, but not from less than 42 in. above that level.

Items that have fallen into safety nets, including—but not restricted to, materials, scrap, equipment, and tools—must be removed as soon as possible and at least before the next work shift.

Exhibit 11-4. Safety Net Drop Distance

Vertical Distance	Horizontal Distance
Up to 5 ft.	8 ft.
Between 5 ft. and 10 ft.	10 ft.
More than 10 ft.	13 ft.

Warning Line Systems

Warning line systems consist of ropes, wires, or chains, and supporting stanchions and are set up as follows:

- Flagged at not more than 6-ft. intervals with high-visibility material;
- Rigged and supported so that the lowest point (including sag) is no less than 34 in. from the walking/working surface and its highest point is no more than 39 in. from the walking/working surface.
- Stanchions, after being rigged with warning lines, shall be capable of resisting, without tipping over, a force of at least 16 lbs. applied horizontally against the stanchion, 30 in. (0.8 m) above the walking/working surface, perpendicular to the warning line and in the direction of the floor, roof, or platform edge;
- The rope, wire, or chain shall have a minimum tensile strength of 500 lbs. and after being attached to the stanchions, must support without breaking, the load applied to the stanchions as prescribed above.
- Shall be attached to each stanchion in such a way that pulling on one section of the line between stanchions will not result in slack being taken up in the adjacent section before the stanchion tips over.

Warning lines shall be erected around all sides of roof work areas. When mechanical equipment is being used, the warning line shall be erected at least 6 ft. from the roof edge parallel to the direction of mechanical equipment operation, and at least 10 ft. from the roof edge perpendicular to the direction of mechanical equipment operation.

When mechanical equipment is not being used, the warning line must be erected at least 6 ft. from the roof edge.

Covers

Covers located in roadways and vehicular aisles must be able to support at least twice the maximum axle load of the largest vehicle to which the cover might be subjected. All other covers must be able to support at least twice the weight of employees, equipment, and materials that may be imposed on the cover at any one time. To prevent accidental displacement from wind, equipment, or workers' activities, all covers must be secured. All covers shall be color coded or bear the markings "HOLE" or "COVER."

Controlled Access Zones

A controlled access zone is a work area designated and clearly marked in which certain types of work (e.g., overhand bricklaying) may take place without the use of conventional fall protection systems. Because conventional fall protection systems are not in place (e.g., no guardrails), only authorized workers (e.g., masons) may enter the controlled access zone.

Controlled access zones, when created to limit entrance to areas where leading edge work and other operations are taking place, must be defined by a control line or by any other means that restricts access. Control lines shall consist of ropes, wires, tapes or equivalent materials, and supporting stanchions, and each must be:

- Flagged or clearly marked with highly visible material at intervals not more than 6 ft. apart;
- Rigged and supported in such a way that the lowest point is not less than 39 in. from the walking/working surface. The highest point must not be more than 45 in. from the walking/working surface. (When an overhand bricklaying operation is being conducted, the control line may be up to 50 in. from the walking/working surface; and
- Strong enough to sustain stress of not less than 200 lbs. Control lines shall extend along the entire length of the unprotected or leading edge and shall be approximately parallel to the unprotected or leading edge.

Control lines must be connected on each side to a guardrail system or a wall.

When control lines are used, they shall be erected between 6 ft. and 25 ft. from the unprotected or leading edge, except when precast concrete members are being erected. In those instances, the control line should be erected no less than 6 ft. nor more than 60 ft. or half the length of the member being erected from the leading edge, whichever is less.

When used to determine access to areas where overhand bricklaying and related work are taking place, controlled access zones are to be defined by a control line erected between 10 ft. and 15 ft. from the working edge. Additional control lines must be erected at each end to enclose the controlled access zone. Only employees engaged in overhand bricklaying or related work are permitted in controlled access zones.

On floors and roofs where guardrail systems are not in place prior to the beginning of overhand bricklaying operations, controlled access zones will be enlarged as necessary to enclose all points of access, material handling areas, and storage areas. On floors and roofs where guardrail systems are in place, but need to be removed to allow overhand bricklaying work or leading edge work to take place, only that portion of the guardrail necessary to accomplish that day's work shall be removed.

Other Fall Hazards

Excavations

Each employee at the edge of an excavation that is 6 ft. deep or more shall be protected from falling by guardrail systems, fences, barricades, or covers. If walkways are provided to permit employees to cross over excavations, the walkways must have guardrails if they are 6 ft. or more above the excavation.

Formwork and Reinforcing Steel

While moving vertically and/or horizontally on the vertical face of rebar assemblies built in place, fall protection is not required when employees are moving. OSHA considers the multiple hand holds and foot holds on rebar assemblies to provide similar protection as that provided by a fixed ladder; consequently, no fall protection is necessary while moving point to point for heights lower than 24 ft. An employee must be provided with fall protection when climbing or otherwise moving at a height of more than 24 ft., the same as for fixed ladders.

Hoist Areas

Each employee in a hoist area shall be protected from falling 6 ft. or more by guardrail or personal fall arrest systems. If guardrail systems (or chain gate or guardrail) or portions thereof must be removed to facilitate hoisting operations, as during the landing of materials, and a worker must lean through the access opening or out over the edge of the access opening to receive or guide equipment and materials, that employee must be protected by a personal fall arrest system.

Holes

Personal fall arrest systems, covers, or guardrail systems shall be erected around holes (including skylights) that are more than 6 ft. above lower levels.

Leading Edges

Each employee who is constructing a leading edge of 6 ft. or more above lower levels shall be protected by guardrail, safety net, or personal fall arrest systems. If the employer can demonstrate that it is infeasible or creates a greater hazard to implement these systems, it must develop and implement a fall protection plan that meets the requirements of 29 CFR 1926.502(k).

Overhand Bricklaying and Related Work

Each employee performing overhand bricklaying and related work 6 ft. or more above lower levels shall be protected by guardrail, safety net, or personal fall arrest systems or shall work in a controlled access zone. All employees reaching more than 10 in. below the level of a walking/working surface on which they are working shall be protected by a guardrail, safety net, or personal fall arrest system.

Precast Concrete Erection and Residential Construction

Each employee who is 6 ft. or more above lower levels while erecting precast concrete members and related operations, such as grouting of precast concrete members, and each employee who is engaged in residential construction shall be protected by guardrail, safety net, or personal fall arrest systems. Where the employer can demonstrate that it is infeasible or creates a greater hazard to use those systems, the employer must develop and implement a fall protection plan that meets the requirements of 29 CFR 1926.502(k).

Ramps, Runways, and Other Walkways

Each employee using ramps, runways, and other walkways shall be protected from falling 6 ft. or more by guardrail systems.

Roofing

Low-slope Roofs

Each employee engaged in roofing activities on low-slope roofs with unprotected sides and edges 6 ft. or more above lower levels shall be protected from falling by guardrail, safety net, personal fall arrest systems or a combination of a warning line system and guardrail system, warning line system and safety net system, warning line system and personal fall arrest system, or warning line system and safety monitoring system. On roofs 50 ft. or less in width, the use of a safety monitoring system without a warning line system is permitted.

Steep Roofs

Each employee on a steep roof with unprotected sides and edges 6 ft. or more above lower levels shall be protected by guardrail systems with toeboards, safety net systems, or personal fall arrest systems.

Wall Openings

Each employee working on, at, above, or near wall openings (including those with chutes attached) where the outside bottom edge of the wall opening is 6 ft. or more above lower levels and the inside bottom edge of the wall opening is less than 39 in. above the walking/working surface must be protected from falling by the use of a guardrail, a safety net, or a personal fall arrest system.

Protection From Falling Objects

When guardrail systems are used to prevent materials from falling from one level to another, any openings must be small enough to prevent the passage of potential falling objects. No materials or equipment except masonry and mortar shall be stored within 4 ft. of working edges. Excess mortar, broken or scattered masonry units, and all other materials and debris shall be kept clear of the working area by removal at regular intervals.

During roofing work, materials and equipment shall not be stored within 6 ft. of a roof edge unless guardrails are erected at the edge; materials piled, grouped, or stacked near a roof edge must be stable and self-supporting.

Canopies

When used as protection from falling objects, canopies must be strong enough to prevent collapse and to prevent penetration by any objects that may fall onto them.

Toeboards

When toeboards are used as protection from falling objects, they must be erected along the edges of the overhead walking/working surface for a distance sufficient to protect persons working below. Toeboards shall be capable of withstanding a force of at least 50 lbs. (222 N) applied in any downward or outward direction at any point along the toeboard. Toeboards shall be a minimum of 3.5 in. tall from their top edge to the level of the walking/working surface, have no more than 0.25 in. clearance above the walking/working surface, and be solid or have openings no larger than 1 in. in size.

Where tools, equipment, or materials are piled higher than the top edge of a toeboard, paneling or screening must be erected from the walking/working surface or toeboard to the top of a guardrail system's top rail or midrail, for a distance sufficient to protect employees below.

Training

Employers must provide a training program that teaches employees who might be exposed to fall hazards how to recognize such hazards and how to minimize them. Employees must be trained in the following areas:

- The nature of fall hazards in the work area;
- The correct procedures for erecting, maintaining, disassembling, and inspecting fall protection systems;
- The use and operation of controlled access zones and guardrail, personal fall arrest, safety net, warning line, and safety monitoring systems;
- The role of each employee in the safety monitoring system when the system is in use;

- The limitations on the use of mechanical equipment during the performance of roofing work on low-sloped roofs;
- The correct procedures for equipment and materials handling and storage and the erection of overhead protection; and
- Employees' role in fall protection plans.

Exhibit 11-5.
Employees must be trained if a fall protection harness is going to be used.

Employers must prepare a written certification that identifies the employee trained and the date of the training. The employer or trainer must sign the certification record. Retraining also must be provided when necessary.

Army Corps of Engineers Manual 385-1-1 (to be used on Federal Projects)

This manual prescribes the safety and health requirements for all Corps of Engineers activities and operations.

It applies to headquarters, U.S. Army COE elements, major subordinate commands, districts, centers, laboratories and field operating activities, as well as USACOE and Naval Facilities Engineering Command contracts. Applicability extends to occupational exposure for missions under the command of the Chief of Engineers, whether accomplished by military, civilian or contractor personnel.

21.A.15 Fall Protection

a. Employees exposed to fall hazards shall be protected by standard guardrail, catch platforms, temporary floors, safety nets, personal fall protection devices, or the equivalent, in the following situations:

(1) On accessways (excluding ladders), work platforms, or walking/working surfaces from which they may fall 6 ft. (1.8 m) or more;

(2) On accessways or work platforms over water, machinery, or dangerous operations;

(3) On runways from which they may fall 4 ft. (1.2 m) or more; and

(4) On installing or removing sheet pile, h-piles, cofferdams, or other interlocking materials from which they may fall 6 ft. (1.8 m) or more;

b. Every stairway and ladder way floor opening shall be guarded on all exposed sides, except the entrance opening, by securely anchored standard guardrail. Entrance openings shall be offset or provided with a gate to prevent anyone walking into the opening. ...

c. Platforms, except scaffolds, 4 ft. to 6 ft. (1.2 m to 1.8 m) in height, having a minimum horizontal dimension in either direction of less than 45 inches (114.3 cm) shall have standard railing installed on all open sides and ends of the platform or the workers shall use personal fall protection.

21.A.16 Training

a. Each employee who might be exposed to fall hazards shall be trained by a competent person qualified in the following areas in the safe use of accessways and fall protection systems and the recognition of hazards related to their use, including:

(1) The nature of access and fall hazards in the work area;

(2) The correct procedures for constructing, erecting, maintaining, using and dismantling accessways and fall protection systems;

(3) The maximum intended load-carrying capacities of accessways and fall protection systems; and

(4) All applicable requirements from this Section;

(5) The limitations on the use of mechanical equipment during the performance of roofing work on low-sloped roofs, the correct procedures for handling and storage of equipment and materials, and the erection of overhead protection; and

(6) Rescue equipment and procedures.

b. Retraining shall be provided as necessary for employees to maintain an understanding of these subjects.

c. The employer shall verify employee training by a written certification record that identifies the employee trained, the dates of the training, and the signature of the trainer.

Subpart M, Fall Protection

1926.500—Scope, application, and definitions applicable to this subpart.

This Subpart covers all fall hazards except when they are covered in other regulations:

- Subpart L, Scaffolds
- Subpart N, Cranes and Derricks
- Subpart R, Steel Erection
- Subpart S, Tunneling Operations
- Subpart V, Electric Transmission
- Subpart X, Stairways and Ladders

1926.501—Duty to have fall protection.

Protection is required for:

- Unprotected sides and edges
- Leading edges
- Holes
- Ramps, runways and other walkways
- Formwork and reinforcing steel
- Dangerous equipment
- Excavations, wells, pits, shafts
- Overhand bricklaying and related work
- Roofing work on low-slope roofs
- Precast concrete erection
- Residential construction

- Falling objects
- Hoist areas
- Wall openings
- Walking/working surfaces not addressed

1926.502—Fall protection systems criteria and practices.

Guardrails
- Top rail 42 in. (±3 in.) high
- No steel, plastic or banding material
- Mid-rails 21 in. high
- All rails ¼-in. diameter or greater
- Intermediate members—openings no greater than 19 in.
- Wire rope top rail flagged every 6 ft.
- Withstand 200 lbs. pressure Mid-rails 150 lbs. resistance
- Manila, plastic or synthetic rope rails—inspect them often

Safety Net Systems
- No defective nets
- Connections not more than 6 in. apart
- Weekly and after-impact inspections
- Border ropes 5,000 lbs. breaking strength
- No greater than 6 in. openings on any side
- Removal of objects daily or before next shift
- Installed no more than 30 ft. below walking/working surface

Personal Fall Arrest Systems
- Lifelines:
  - Horizontal lifelines that may become vertical require locking capability in both directions
  - Harness or body belt, lanyard and an attaching point are key elements
  - Horizontal lifelines installed by qualified person
  - Safety factor of at least 2
  - Free fall no more than 6 ft.
- Dee-rings, snaphooks:
  - 5,000 lb. tensile strength
  - Proof-tested to 3,600 lbs.
  - Sized or locking type
  - Must be self-closing and locking

Warning Line Systems
- Around all sides of roof work area 6 ft. from edge
- Roof access points to be guarded

- Flag with high visibility material.
- No lower than 34 in. nor higher than 39 in.

Safety Monitoring Systems
- Competent person to monitor
  - Close enough to communicate orally
  - On same level, in visual sight of workers
  - Can have no other duties
- Employees must comply with warnings
- No mechanical equipment to be used or stored in area
- Employees engaged in roofing or covered by fall protection plan

Protection from Falling Objects
- Toeboards 3½ in. tall
- Screens – install where needed
- Only masonry equipment/ materials within 4 ft. of edge
- Barricade areas and prohibit entry by employees
- No material stored within 6 ft. of edge unless guardrails have been installed and material is stable and self-supporting
- Canopies must be strong enough to not collapse and to prevent penetration of objects

Fall Protection Plans
- Must be at the job site and in writing
- Document why plan needed
- Include a written discussion of other measures to reduce or eliminate hazards
- Identify each location where plan needed
- Establish controlled access zone
- Implement safety monitoring system
- Investigate near misses
- Implement changes to correct deficiencies

Appendix E to Subpart M of Part 1926—Sample Fall Protection Plan

Non-Mandatory Guidelines for Complying With §1926.502(k)

Employers engaged in leading edge work, precast concrete construction work and residential construction work who can demonstrate that it is infeasible or creates a greater hazard to use conventional fall protection systems must develop and follow a fall protection plan. Below are sample fall protection plans developed for precast concrete construction and residential work that could be tailored to be site specific for other precast concrete or residential jobsite. This sample plan can be modified to be used for other work involving leading edge work. The sample plan outlines the elements that must be addressed in any fall protection plan. The reasons outlined in this sample fall protection plan are for illustrative purposes only and are not necessarily a valid, acceptable rationale (unless the conditions at the job site are the same as those covered by these sample plans) for not using conventional fall protection systems for a particular precast concrete or residential construction worksite. However, the sample plans provide guidance to employers on the type of information that is required to be discussed in fall protection plans.

Sample Fall Protection Plans

Fall Protection Plan For Precast/Prestress Concrete Structures

This Fall Protection Plan is specific for the following project:

Location of Job Erecting Company Date Plan Prepared or Modified Plan Prepared By Plan Approved By Plan Supervised By

The following Fall Protection Plan is a sample program prepared for the prevention of injuries associated with falls. A Fall Protection Plan must be developed and evaluated on a site by site basis. It is recommended that erectors discuss the written Fall Protection Plan with their OSHA Area Office prior to going on a jobsite.

I. Statement of Company Policy

(Company Name) is dedicated to the protection of its employees from on-the-job injuries. All employees of (Company Name) have the responsibility to work safely on the job. The purpose of this plan is: (a) To supplement our standard safety policy by providing safety standards specifically designed to cover fall protection on this job and; (b) to ensure that each employee is trained and made aware of the safety provisions which are to be implemented by this plan prior to the start of erection.

This Fall Protection Plan addresses the use of other than conventional fall protection at a number of areas on the project, as well as identifying specific activities that require non-conventional means of fall protection. These areas include:

a. Connecting activity (point of erection).
b. Leading edge work.
c. Unprotected sides or edge.
d. Grouting.

This plan is designed to enable employers and employees to recognize the fall hazards on this job and to establish the procedures that are to be followed in order to prevent falls to lower levels or through holes and openings in walking/working surfaces. Each employee will be trained in these procedures and strictly adhere to them except when doing so would expose the employee to a greater hazard. If, in the employee's opinion, this is the case, the employee is to notify the foreman of the concern and the concern is to be addressed before proceeding.

Safety policy and procedure on any one project cannot be administered, implemented, monitored and enforced by any one individual. The total objective of a safe, accident free work environment can only be accomplished by a dedicated, concerted effort by every individual involved with the project from management down to the last employee. Each employee must understand their value to the company; the costs of accidents, both monetary, physical, and emotional; the objective of the safety policy and procedures; the safety rules that apply to the safety policy and procedures; and what their individual role is in administering, implementing, monitoring, and compliance of their safety policy and procedures. This allows for a more personal approach to compliance through planning, training, understanding and cooperative effort, rather than by strict enforcement. If for any reason an unsafe act persists, strict enforcement will be implemented.

It is the responsibility of (name of competent person) to implement this Fall Protection Plan. (Name of Competent Person) is responsible for continual observational safety checks of their work operations and to enforce the safety policy and procedures. The foreman also is responsible to correct any unsafe acts or conditions immediately. It is the responsibility of the employee to understand and adhere to the procedures of this plan and to follow the instructions of the foreman. It is also the responsibility of the employee to bring to management's attention to any unsafe or hazardous conditions or acts that may cause injury to either themselves or any other employees. Any changes to this Fall Protection Plan must be approved by (name of Qualified Person).

II. Fall Protection Systems to Be Used on This Project

Where conventional fall protection is infeasible or creates a greater hazard at the leading edge and during initial connecting activity, we plan to do this work using a safety monitoring system and expose only a minimum number of employees for the time necessary to actually accomplish the job. The maximum number of workers to be monitored by one safety monitor is six (6). We are designating the following trained employees as designated erectors and they are permitted to enter the controlled access zones and work without the use of conventional fall protection.

- Safety monitor:
- Designated erector:
- Designated erector:
- Designated erector:
- Designated erector:
- Designated erector:
- Designated erector:

The safety monitor shall be identified by wearing an orange hard hat. The designated erectors will be identified by one of the following methods:

1. They will wear a blue colored arm band, or
2. They will wear a blue colored hard hat, or
3. They will wear a blue colored vest.

Only individuals with the appropriate experience, skills, and training will be authorized as designated erectors. All employees that will be working as designated erectors under the safety monitoring system shall have been trained and instructed in the following areas:

1. Recognition of the fall hazards in the work area (at the leading edge and when making initial connections—point of erection).
2. Avoidance of fall hazards using estab-

lished work practices which have been made known to the employees.
3. Recognition of unsafe practices or working conditions that could lead to a fall, such as windy conditions.
4. The function, use, and operation of safety monitoring systems, guardrail systems, body belt/harness systems, control zones and other protection to be used.
5. The correct procedure for erecting, maintaining, disassembling and inspecting the system(s) to be used.
6. Knowledge of construction sequence or the erection plan.

A conference will take place prior to starting work involving all members of the erection crew, crane crew and supervisors of any other concerned contractors. This conference will be conducted by the precast concrete erection supervisor in charge of the project. During the pre-work conference, erection procedures and sequences pertinent to this job will be thoroughly discussed and safety practices to be used throughout the project will be specified. Further, all personnel will be informed that the controlled access zones are off limits to all personnel other than those designated erectors specifically trained to work in that area.

Safety Monitoring System

A safety monitoring system means a fall protection system in which a competent person is responsible for recognizing and warning employees of fall hazards. The duties of the safety monitor are to:

1. Warn by voice when approaching the open edge in an unsafe manner.
2. Warn by voice if there is a dangerous situation developing which cannot be seen by another person involved with product placement, such as a member getting out of control.
3. Make the designated erectors aware they are in a dangerous area.
4. Be competent in recognizing fall hazards.
5. Warn employees when they appear to be unaware of a fall hazard or are acting in an unsafe manner.
6. Be on the same walking/working surface as the monitored employees and within

visual sighting distance of the monitored employees.

7. Be close enough to communicate orally with the employees.

8. Not allow other responsibilities to encumber monitoring. If the safety monitor becomes too encumbered with other responsibilities, the monitor shall (1) stop the erection process; and (2) turn over other responsibilities to a designated erector; or (3) turn over the safety monitoring function to another designated, competent person. The safety monitoring system shall not be used when the wind is strong enough to cause loads with large surface areas to swing out of radius, or result in loss of control of the load, or when weather conditions cause the walking-working surfaces to become icy or slippery.

Control Zone System

A controlled access zone means an area designated and clearly marked, in which leading edge work may take place without the use of guardrail, safety net or personal fall arrest systems to protect the employees in the area. Control zone systems shall comply with the following provisions:

1. When used to control access to areas where leading edge and other operations are taking place the controlled access zone shall be defined by a control line or by any other means that restricts access.

   When control lines are used, they shall be erected not less than 6 feet (1.8 m) nor more than 60 feet (18 m) or half the length of the member being erected, whichever is less, from the leading edge.

2. The control line shall extend along the entire length of the unprotected or leading edge and shall be approximately parallel to the unprotected or leading edge.

3. The control line shall be connected on each side to a guardrail system or wall.

4. Control lines shall consist of ropes, wires, tapes, or equivalent materials, and supporting stanchions as follows:

5. Each line shall be flagged or otherwise clearly marked at not more than 6-foot (1.8 m) intervals with high-visibility material.

6. Each line shall be rigged and supported in such a way that its lowest point (including sag) is not less than 39 inches (1 m) from the walking/working surface and its highest point is not more than 45 inches (1.3 m) from the walking/working surface.

7. Each line shall have a minimum breaking strength of 200 pounds (.88 kN).

Holes

All openings greater than 12 in.×12 in. will have perimeter guarding or covering. All predetermined holes will have the plywood covers made in the precasters' yard and shipped with the member to the jobsite. Prior to cutting holes on the job, proper protection for the hole must be provided to protect the workers. Perimeter guarding or covers will not be removed without the approval of the erection foreman.

Precast concrete column erection through the existing deck requires that many holes be provided through this deck. These are to be covered and protected. Except for the opening being currently used to erect a column, all opening protection is to be left undisturbed. The opening being uncovered to erect a column will become part of the point of erection and will be addressed as part of this Fall Protection Plan. This uncovering is to be done at the erection foreman's direction and will only occur immediately prior to "feeding" the column through the opening. Once the end of the column is through the slab opening, there will no longer exist a fall hazard at this location.

III. Implementation of Fall Protection Plan

The structure being erected is a multistory total precast concrete building consisting of columns, beams, wall panels and hollow core slabs and double tee floor and roof members.

The following is a list of the products and erection situations on this job:

Columns

For columns 10 ft to 36 ft long, employees disconnecting crane hooks from columns will work from a ladder and wear a body belt/harness with lanyard and be tied off when both hands are needed to disconnect. For tying off, a vertical lifeline will be connected to the lifting eye at the top of the column, prior to lifting, to be used with a manually operated or mobile rope grab. For columns too high for the use of a ladder, 36 ft and higher, an added cable will be used to reduce the height of the disconnecting point so that a ladder can be used. This cable will be left in place until a point in erection that it can be removed safely. In some cases, columns will be unhooked from the crane by using an erection tube or shackle with a pull pin which is released from the ground after the column is stabilized.

The column will be adequately connected and/or braced to safely support the weight of a ladder with an employee on it.

Inverted Tee Beams

Employees erecting inverted tee beams, at a height of 6 to 40 ft, will erect the beam, make initial connections, and final alignment from a ladder. If the employee needs to reach over the side of the beam to bar or make an adjustment to the alignment of the beam, they will mount the beam and be tied off to the lifting device in the beam after ensuring the load has been stabilized on its bearing. To disconnect the crane from the beam an employee will stand a ladder against the beam. Because the use of ladders is not practical at heights above 40 ft, beams will be initially placed with the use of tag lines and their final alignment made by a person on a manlift or similar employee positioning systems.

Spandrel Beams

Spandrel beams at the exterior of the building will be aligned as closely as possible with the use of tag lines with the final placement of the spandrel beam made from a ladder at the open end of the structure. A ladder will be used to make the initial connections and a ladder will be used to disconnect the crane. The other end of the beam will be placed by the designated erector from the double tee deck under the observation of the safety monitor.

The beams will be adequately connected and/or braced to safely support the weight of a ladder with an employee on it.

Floor and Roof Members

During installation of the precast concrete floor and/or roof members, the work deck continu-ously increases in area as more and more units are being erected and positioned. Thus, the unprotected floor/roof perimeter is constantly modified with the leading edge changing lo-cation as each member is installed. The fall protection for workers at the leading edge shall be assured by properly constructed and main-tained control zone lines not more than 60 ft away from the leading edge supplemented by a safety monitoring system to ensure the safety of all designated erectors working within the area defined by the control zone lines.

The hollow core slabs erected on the mason-ry portion of the building will be erected and grouted using the safety monitoring system. Grout will be placed in the space between the end of the slab and face shell of the concrete masonry by dumping from a wheelbarrow. The grout in the keyways between the slabs will be dumped from a wheelbarrow and then spread with long handled tools, allowing the worker to stand erect facing toward the unprotected edge and back from any work deck edge.

Whenever possible, the designated erec-tors will approach the incoming member at the leading edge only after it is below waist height so that the member itself provides protection against falls.

Except for the situations described below, when the arriving floor or roof member is within 2 to 3 inches of its final position, the designated erectors can then proceed to their position of erection at each end of the member under the control of the safety monitor. Crane hooks will be unhooked from double tee mem-bers by designated erectors under the direc-tion and supervision of the safety monitor.

Designated erectors, while waiting for the next floor or roof member, will be constantly under the control of the safety monitor for fall protection and are directed to stay a minimum of six (6) ft from the edge. In the event a des-ignated erector must move from one end of a member, which has just been placed at the leading edge, they must first move away from the leading edge a minimum of six (6) ft and then progress to the other end while maintaining the minimum distance of six (6) ft at all times.

Erection of double tees, where conditions require bearing of one end into a closed pocket and the other end on a beam ledge, restricting the tee legs from going directly into the pockets, require special considerations. The tee legs that are to bear in the closed pocket must hang lower than those at the beam bearing. The double tee will be "two-lined" in order to elevate one end higher than the other to allow for the low end to be ducked into the closed pocket using the following procedure.

The double tee will be rigged with a standard four-way spreader off of the main load line. An additional choker will be attached to the married point of the two-legged spreader at the end of the tee that is to be elevated. The double tee will be hoisted with the main load line and swung into a position as close as possible to the tee's final bearing elevation. When the tee is in this position and stabilized, the whip line load block will be lowered to just above the tee deck. At this time, two erectors will walk out on the suspended tee deck at midspan of the tee member and pull the load block to the end of the tee to be elevated and attach the additional choker to the load block. The possibility of entanglement with the crane lines and other obstacles during this two lining process while raising and lowering the crane block on that second line could be hazardous to an encumbered employee. Therefore, the designated erectors will not tie off during any part of this process. While the designated erectors are on the double tee, the safety monitoring system will be used. After attaching the choker, the two erectors then step back on the previously erected tee deck and signal the crane operator to hoist the load with the whip line to the elevation that will allow for enough clearance to let the low end tee legs slide into the pockets when the main load line is lowered. The erector, who is handling the lowered end of the tee at the closed pocket bearing, will step out on the suspended tee. An erection bar will then be placed between the end of the tee leg and the inside face of the pocketed spandrel member. The tee is barred away from the pocketed member to reduce the friction and lateral force against the pocketed member. As the tee is being lowered, the other erector remains on the tee which was previously erected to handle the other end. At this point the tee is slowly lowered by the crane to a point where the tee legs can freely slide into the pockets. The erector working the lowered end of the tee must keep pressure on the bar between the tee and the face of the pocketed spandrel member to very gradually let the tee legs slide into the pocket to its proper bearing dimension. The tee is then slowly lowered into its final erected position.

The designated erector should be allowed onto the suspended double tee, otherwise there is no control over the horizontal movement of the double tee and this movement could knock the spandrel off of its bearing or the column out of plumb. The control necessary to prevent hitting the spandrel can only be done safely from the top of the double tee being erected.

Loadbearing Wall Panels: The erection of the loadbearing wall panels on the elevated decks requires the use of a safety monitor and a controlled access zone that is a minimum of 25 ft and a maximum of 1/2 the length of the wall panels away from the unprotected edge, so that designated erectors can move freely and unencumbered when receiving the panels. Bracing, if required for stability, will be installed by ladder. After the braces are secured, the crane will be disconnected from the wall by using a ladder. The wall to wall connections will also be performed from a ladder.

Non-Loadbearing Panels (Cladding): The locating of survey lines, panel layout and other installation prerequisites (prewelding, etc.) for non-loadbearing panels (cladding) will not commence until floor perimeter and floor openings have been protected. In some areas, it is necessary because of panel configuration to remove the perimeter protection as the cladding is being installed. Removal of perimeter protection will be performed on a bay to bay basis, just ahead of cladding erection to minimize temporarily unprotected floor edges. Those workers within 6 ft of the edge, receiving and positioning the cladding when the perimeter protection is removed shall be tied off.

Detailing
Employees exposed to falls of six (6) feet or more to lower levels, who are not actively engaged in leading edge work or connecting activity, such as welding, bolting, cutting, bracing,

guying, patching, painting or other operations, and who are working less than six (6) ft from an unprotected edge will be tied off at all times or guardrails will be installed. Employees engaged in these activities but who are more than six (6) ft from an unprotected edge as defined by the control zone lines, do not require fall protection but a warning line or control lines must be erected to remind employees they are approaching an area where fall protection is required.

IV. Conventional Fall Protection Considered for the Point of Erection or Leading Edge Erection Operations

A. Personal Fall Arrest Systems

In this particular erection sequence and procedure, personal fall arrest systems requiring body belt/harness systems, lifelines and lanyards will not reduce possible hazards to workers and will create offsetting hazards during their usage at the leading edge of precast/prestressed concrete construction.

Leading edge erection and initial connections are conducted by employees who are specifically trained to do this type of work and are trained to recognize the fall hazards. The nature of such work normally exposes the employee to the fall hazard for a short period of time and installation of fall protection systems for a short duration is not feasible because it exposes the installers of the system to the same fall hazard, but for a longer period of time.

1. It is necessary that the employee be able to move freely without encumbrance in order to guide the sections of precast concrete into their final position without having lifelines attached which will restrict the employee's ability to move about at the point of erection.

2. A typical procedure requires 2 or more workers to maneuver around each other as a concrete member is positioned to fit into the structure. If they are each attached to a lifeline, part of their attention must be diverted from their main task of positioning a member weighing several tons to the task of avoiding entanglements of their lifelines or avoiding tripping over lanyards. Therefore, if these workers are attached to lanyards, more

fall potential would result than from not using such a device.

In this specific erection sequence and procedure, retractable lifelines do not solve the problem of two workers becoming tangled. In fact, such a tangle could prevent the lifeline from retracting as the worker moved, thus potentially exposing the worker to a fall greater than 6 ft. Also, a worker crossing over the lifeline of another worker can create a hazard because the movement of one person can unbalance the other. In the event of a fall by one person there is a likelihood that the other person will be caused to fall as well. In addition, if contamination such as grout (during hollow core grouting) enters the retractable housing it can cause excessive wear and damage to the device and could clog the retracting mechanism as the lanyard is dragged across the deck. Obstructing the cable orifice can defeat the device's shock absorbing function, produce cable slack and damage, and adversely affect cable extraction and retraction.

3. Employees tied to a lifeline can be trapped and crushed by moving structural members if the employee becomes restrained by the lanyard or retractable lifeline and cannot get out of the path of the moving load.

The sudden movement of a precast concrete member being raised by a crane can be caused by a number of factors. When this happens, a connector may immediately have to move a considerable distance to avoid injury. If a tied off body belt/harness is being used, the connector could be trapped. Therefore, there is a greater risk of injury if the connector is tied to the structure for this specific erection sequence and procedure.

When necessary to move away from a retractable device, the worker cannot move at a rate greater than the device locking speed typically 3.5 to 4.5 ft/sec. When moving toward the device it is necessary to move at a rate which does not permit cable slack to build up. This slack may cause cable retraction acceleration and cause a worker to lose their balance by applying a higher than normal jerking force on the body when the cable suddenly becomes taut after building up momentum. This slack can also cause damage to the internal spring-loaded drum, uneven coiling of cable on the drum, and possible cable damage.

The factors causing sudden movements for this location include:

(a) Cranes
  (1) Operator error.
  (2) Site conditions (soft or unstable ground).
  (3) Mechanical failure.
  (4) Structural failure.
  (5) Rigging failure.
  (6) Crane signal/radio communication failure.
(b) Weather Conditions
  (1) Wind (strong wind/sudden gusting)—particularly a problem with the large surface areas of precast concrete members.
  (2) Snow/rain (visibility).
  (3) Fog (visibility).
  (4) Cold—causing slowed reactions or mechanical problems.
(c) Structure/Product Conditions.
  (1) Lifting Eye failure.
  (2) Bearing failure or slippage.
  (3) Structure shifting.
  (4) Bracing failure.
  (5) Product failure.
(d) Human Error.
  (1) Incorrect tag line procedure.
  (2) Tag line hang-up.
  (3) Incorrect or misunderstood crane signals..
  (4) Misjudged elevation of member.
  (5) Misjudged speed of member.
  (6) Misjudged angle of member.

4. Anchorages or special attachment points could be cast into the precast concrete members if sufficient preplanning and consideration of erector's position is done before the members are cast. Any hole or other attachment must be approved by the engineer who designed the member. It is possible that some design restrictions will not allow a member to be weakened by an additional hole; however, it is anticipated that such situations would be the exception, not the rule. Attachment points, other than on the deck surface, will require removal and/or patching. In order to remove and/or patch these points, requires the employee to be exposed to an additional fall hazard at an unprotected perimeter. The fact that attachment points could be available anywhere on the structure does not eliminate the hazards of using these points for tying off as discussed above. A logical point for tying off on double tees would be using the lifting loops, except that they must be cut off to eliminate a tripping hazard at an appropriate time.

5. Providing attachment at a point above the walking/working surface would also create fall exposures for employees installing their devices. Final positioning of a precast concrete member requires it to be moved in such a way that it must pass through the area that would be occupied by the lifeline and the lanyards attached to the point above. Resulting entanglements of lifelines and lanyards on a moving member could pull employees from the work surface. Also, the structure is being created and, in most cases, there is no structure above the members being placed.

(a) Temporary structural supports, installed to provide attaching points for lifelines limit the space which is essential for orderly positioning, alignment and placement of the precast concrete members. To keep the lanyards a reasonable and manageable length, lifeline supports would necessarily need to be in proximity to the positioning process. A sudden shift of the precast concrete member being positioned because of wind pressure or crane movement could make it strike the temporary supporting structure, moving it suddenly and causing tied off employees to fall.

(b) The time in manhours which would be expended in placing and maintaining temporary structural supports for lifeline attaching points could exceed the expended manhours involved in placing the precast concrete members. No protection could be provided for the employees erecting the temporary structural supports and these supports would have to be moved for each successive step in the construction process, thus greatly increasing the employee's exposure to the fall hazard.

(c) The use of a cable strung horizontally between two columns to provide tie off lines for erecting or walking a beam for connecting work is not feasible and creates a greater hazard on this multi-story building for the following reasons:

(1) If a connector is to use such a line, it must be installed between the two columns. To perform this installation requires an erector to have more fall exposure time attaching the cable to the columns than would be spent to make the beam to column connection itself.

(2) If such a line is to be installed so that an erector can walk along a beam, it must be overhead or below him. For example, if a connector must walk along a 24 in. wide beam, the presence of a line next to the connector at waist level, attached directly to the columns, would prevent the connector from centering their weight over the beam and balancing themselves. Installing the line above the connector might be possible on the first level of a two-story column; however, the column may extend only a few feet above the floor level at the second level or be flush with the floor level. Attaching the line to the side of the beam could be a solution; however, it would require the connector to attach the lanyard below foot level which would most likely extend a fall farther than 6 ft.

(3) When lines are strung over every beam, it becomes more and more difficult for the crane operator to lower a precast concrete member into position without the member becoming fouled. Should the member become entangled, it could easily dislodge the line from a column. If a worker is tied to it at the time, a fall could be caused.

6. The ANSI A10.14–1991 American National Standard for Construction and Demolition Operations—Requirements for Safety Belts, Harnesses, Lanyards and Lifelines for Construction and Demolition Use, states that the anchor point of a lanyard or deceleration device should, if possible, be located above the wearer's belt or harness attachment. ANSI A10.14 also states that a suitable anchorage point is one which is located as high as possible to prevent contact with an obstruction below should the worker fall. Most manufacturers also warn in the user's handbook that the safety block/retractable lifeline must be positioned above the D-ring (above the work space of the intended user) and OSHA recommends that fall arrest and restraint equipment be used in accordance with the manufacturer's instructions.

Attachment of a retractable device to a horizontal cable near floor level or using the inserts in the floor or roof members may result in increased free fall due to the dorsal D-ring of the full-body harness riding higher than the attachment point of the snaphook to the cable or insert (e.g., 6 foot tall worker with a dorsal D-ring at 5 feet above the floor or surface, reduces the working length to only one foot, by placing the anchorage five feet away from the fall hazard). In addition, impact loads may exceed maximum fall arrest forces (MAF) because the fall arrest D-ring would be 4 to 5 feet higher than the safety block/retractable lifeline anchored to the walking-working surface; and the potential for swing hazards is increased.

Manufacturers also require that workers not work at a level where the point of snaphook attachment to the body harness is above the device because this will increase the free fall distance and the deceleration distance and will cause higher forces on the body in the event of an accidental fall.

Manufacturers recommend an anchorage for the retractable lifeline which is immovably fixed in space and is independent of the user's support systems. A moveable anchorage is one which can be moved around (such as equipment or wheeled vehicles) or which can deflect substantially under shock loading (such as a horizontal cable or very flexible beam). In the case of a very flexible anchorage, a shock load applied to the anchorage during fall arrest can cause oscillation of the flexible anchorage such that the retractable brake mechanism may undergo one or more cycles of locking/unlocking/locking (ratchet effect) until the anchorage deflection is dampened. Therefore, use of a moveable anchorage involves critical engineering and safety factors and should only be considered after fixed anchorage has been determined to be not feasible.

Horizontal cables used as an anchorage present an additional hazard due to amplification of the horizontal component of maximum arrest force (of a fall) transmitted to the points where the horizontal cable is attached to the structure. This amplification is due to the angle of sag of a horizontal cable and is most severe for small angles of sag. For a cable sag angle of 2 degrees the horizontal force on the points of cable attachment can be amplified by a factor of 15.

It is also necessary to install the retractable device vertically overhead to minimize swing falls. If an object is in the worker's swing path (or that of the cable) hazardous situations exist: (1) due to the swing, horizontal speed of the user may be high enough to cause injury when an obstacle in the swing fall path is struck by either the user or the cable; (2) the total vertical fall distance of the user may be much greater than if the user had fallen only vertically without a swing fall path.

With retractable lines, overconfidence may cause the worker to engage in inappropriate behavior, such as approaching the perimeter of a floor or roof at a distance appreciably greater than the shortest distance between the anchorage point and the leading edge. Though the retractable lifeline may arrest a worker's fall before he or she has fallen a few feet, the lifeline may drag along the edge of the floor or beam and swing the worker like a pendulum until the line has moved to a position where the distance between the anchorage point and floor edge is the shortest distance between those two points. Accompanying this pendulum swing is a lowering of the worker, with the attendant danger that he or she may violently impact the floor or some obstruction below.

The risk of a cable breaking is increased if a lifeline is dragged sideways across the rough surface or edge of a concrete member at the same moment that the lifeline is being subjected to a maximum impact loading during a fall. The typical 3/16 in. cable in a retractable lifeline has a breaking strength of from 3000 to 3700 lbs.

7. The competent person, who can take into account the specialized operations being performed on this project, should determine when and where a designated erector cannot use a personal fall arrest system.

B. Safety Net Systems
The nature of this particular precast concrete erection worksite precludes the safe use of safety nets where point of erection or leading edge work must take place.

1. To install safety nets in the interior high bay of the single story portion of the building poses rigging attachment problems. Structural members do not exist to which supporting devices for nets can be attached in the area where protection is required. As the erection operation advances, the location of point of erection or leading edge work changes constantly as each member is attached to the structure. Due to this constant change it is not feasible to set net sections and build separate structures to support the nets.

2. The nature of the erection process for the precast concrete members is such that an installed net would protect workers as they position and secure only one structural member. After each member is stabilized the net would have to be moved to a new location (this could mean a move of 8 to 10 ft or the possibility of a move to a different level or area of the structure) to protect workers placing the next piece in the construction sequence. The result would be the installation and dismantling of safety nets repeatedly throughout the normal work day. As the time necessary to install a net, test, and remove it is significantly greater than the time necessary to position and secure a precast concrete member, the exposure time for the worker installing the safety net would be far longer than for the workers whom the net is intended to protect. The time exposure repeats itself each time the nets and supporting hardware must

be moved laterally or upward to provide protection at the point of erection or leading edge.

3. Strict interpretation of §1926.502(c) requires that operations shall not be undertaken until the net is in place and has been tested. With the point of erection constantly changing, the time necessary to install and test a safety net significantly exceeds the time necessary to position and secure the concrete member.

4. Use of safety nets on exposed perimeter wall openings and opensided floors, causes attachment points to be left in architectural concrete which must be patched and filled with matching material after the net supporting hardware is removed. In order to patch these openings, additional numbers of employees must be suspended by swing stages, boatswain chairs or other devices, thereby increasing the amount of fall exposure time to employees.

5. Installed safety nets pose an additional hazard at the perimeter of the erected structure where limited space is available in which members can be turned after being lifted from the ground by the crane. There would be a high probability that the member being lifted could become entangled in net hardware, cables, etc.

6. The use of safety nets where structural wall panels are being erected would prevent movement of panels to point of installation. To be effective, nets would necessarily have to provide protection across the area where structural supporting wall panels would be set and plumbed before roof units could be placed.

7. Use of a tower crane for the erection of the high rise portion of the structure poses a particular hazard in that the crane operator cannot see or judge the proximity of the load in relation to the structure or nets. If the signaler is looking through nets and supporting structural devices while giving instructions to the crane operator, it is not possible to judge precise relationships between the load and the structure itself or to nets and supporting structural devices. This could cause the load to become entangled in the net or hit the structure causing potential damage.

C. Guardrail Systems

On this particular worksite, guardrails, barricades, ropes, cables or other perimeter guarding devices or methods on the erection floor will pose problems to safe erection procedures. Typically, a floor or roof is erected by placing 4 to 10 ft wide structural members next to one another and welding or grouting them together. The perimeter of a floor and roof changes each time a new member is placed into position. It is unreasonable and virtually impossible to erect guardrails and toe boards at the ever changing leading edge of a floor or roof.

1. To position a member safely it is necessary to remove all obstructions extending above the floor level near the point of erection. Such a procedure allows workers to swing a new member across the erected surface as necessary to position it properly without worrying about knocking material off of this surface.

Hollow core slab erection on the masonry wall requires installation of the perimeter protection where the masonry wall has to be constructed. This means the guardrail is installed then subsequently removed to continue the masonry construction. The erector will be exposed to a fall hazard for a longer period of time while installing and removing perimeter protection than while erecting the slabs.

In hollow core work, as in other precast concrete erection, others are not typically on the work deck until the precast concrete erection is complete. The deck is not complete until the leveling, aligning, and grouting of the joints is done. It is normal practice to keep others off the deck until at least the next day after the installation is complete to allow the grout to harden.

2. There is no permanent boundary until all structural members have been placed in the floor or roof. At the leading edge, workers are operating at the temporary edge of the structure as they work to position the next member in the sequence. Compliance with the standard would require a guardrail and toe board be installed along this edge. However, the presence of such a device would prevent

a new member from being swung over the erected surface low enough to allow workers to control it safely during the positioning process. Further, these employees would have to work through the guardrail to align the new member and connect it to the structure. The guardrail would not protect an employee who must lean through it to do the necessary work, rather it would hinder the employee to such a degree that a greater hazard is created than if the guardrail were absent.

3. Guardrail requirements pose a hazard at the leading edge of installed floor or roof sections by creating the possibility of employees being caught between guardrails and suspended loads. The lack of a clear work area in which to guide the suspended load into position for placement and welding of members into the existing structure creates still further hazards.

4. Where erection processes require precast concrete stairways or openings to be installed as an integral part of the overall erection process, it must also be recognized that guardrails or handrails must not project above the surface of the erection floor. Such guardrails should be terminated at the level of the erection floor to avoid placing hazardous obstacles in the path of a member being positioned.

V. Other Fall Protection Measures Considered for This Job

The following is a list and explanation of other fall protection measures available and an explanation of limitations for use on this particular jobsite. If during the course of erecting the building the employee sees an area that could be erected more safely by the use of these fall protection measures, the foreman should be notified.

A. Scaffolds are not used because:
1. The leading edge of the building is constantly changing and the scaffolding would have to be moved at very frequent intervals. Employees erecting and dismantling the scaffolding would be exposed to fall hazards for a greater length of time than they would by merely erecting the precast concrete member.

2. A scaffold tower could interfere with the safe swinging of a load by the crane.
3. Power lines, terrain and site do not allow for the safe use of scaffolding.

B. Vehicle mounted platforms are not used because:
1. A vehicle mounted platform will not reach areas on the deck that are erected over other levels.
2. The leading edge of the building is usually over a lower level of the building and this lower level will not support the weight of a vehicle mounted platform.
3. A vehicle mounted platform could interfere with the safe swinging of a load by the crane, either by the crane swinging the load over or into the equipment.
4. Power lines and surrounding site work do not allow for the safe use of a vehicle mounted platform.

C. Crane suspended personnel platforms are not used because:
1. A second crane close enough to suspend any employee in the working and erecting area could interfere with the safe swinging of a load by the crane hoisting the product to be erected.
2. Power lines and surrounding site work do not allow for the safe use of a second crane on the job.

VI. Enforcement

Constant awareness of and respect for fall hazards, and compliance with all safety rules are considered conditions of employment. The jobsite Superintendent, as well as individuals in the Safety and Personnel Department, reserve the right to issue disciplinary warnings to employees, up to and including termination, for failure to follow the guidelines of this program.

VII. Accident Investigations

All accidents that result in injury to workers, regardless of their nature, shall be investigated and reported. It is an integral part of any safety program that documentation take place as soon as possible so that the cause and means of prevention can be identified to prevent a reoccurrence.

In the event that an employee falls or there is some other related, serious incident occurring, this plan shall be reviewed to determine if additional practices, procedures, or training need to be implemented to prevent similar types of falls or incidents from occurring.

VIII. Changes to Plan

Any changes to the plan will be approved by (name of the qualified person). This plan shall be reviewed by a qualified person as the job progresses to determine if additional practices, procedures or training needs to be implemented by the competent person to improve or provide additional fall protection. Workers shall be notified and trained, if necessary, in the new procedures. A copy of this plan and all approved changes shall be maintained at the jobsite.

Sample Fall Protection Plan for Residential Construction

(Insert Company Name)

This Fall Protection Plan Is Specific For The Following Project:

Location of Job Date Plan Prepared or Modified Plan Prepared By Plan Approved By Plan Supervised By

The following Fall Protection Plan is a sample program prepared for the prevention of injuries associated with falls. A Fall Protection Plan must be developed and evaluated on a site by site basis. It is recommended that builders discuss the written Fall Protection Plan with their OSHA Area Office prior to going on a jobsite.

I. Statement of Company Policy

(Your company name here) is dedicated to the protection of its employees from on-the-job injuries. All employees of (Your company name here) have the responsibility to work safely on the job. The purpose of the plan is to supplement our existing safety and health program and to ensure that every employee who works for (Your company name here) recognizes workplace fall hazards and takes the appropriate measures to address those hazards.

This Fall Protection Plan addresses the use of conventional fall protection at a number of areas on the project, as well as identifies specific activities that require non-conventional means of fall protection. During the construction of residential buildings under 48 feet in height, it is sometimes infeasible or it creates a greater hazard to use conventional fall protection systems at specific areas or for specific tasks. The areas or tasks may include, but are not limited to:

 a. Setting and bracing of roof trusses and rafters;
 b. Installation of floor sheathing and joists;
 c. Roof sheathing operations; and
 d. Erecting exterior walls.

In these cases, conventional fall protection systems may not be the safest choice for builders. This plan is designed to enable employers and employees to recognize the fall hazards associated with this job and to establish the safest procedures that are to be followed in order to prevent falls to lower levels or through holes and openings in walking/working surfaces.

Each employee will be trained in these procedures and will strictly adhere to them except when doing so would expose the employee to a greater hazard. If, in the employee's opinion, this is the case, the employee is to notify the competent person of their concern and have the concern addressed before proceeding.

It is the responsibility of (name of competent person) to implement this Fall Protection Plan. Continual observational safety checks of work operations and the enforcement of the safety policy and procedures shall be regularly enforced. The crew supervisor or foreman (insert name) is responsible for correcting any unsafe practices or conditions immediately.

It is the responsibility of the employer to ensure that all employees understand and adhere to the procedures of this plan and follow the instructions of the crew supervisor. It is also the responsibility of the employee to bring to management's attention any unsafe or hazardous conditions or practices that may cause injury to either themselves or any other employees. Any changes to the Fall Protection Plan must be approved by (name of qualified person).

II. Fall Protection Systems To Be Used on This Job

Installation of roof trusses/rafters, exterior wall erection, roof sheathing, floor sheathing and joist/truss activities will be conducted by employees who are specifically trained to do this type of work and are trained to recognize the fall hazards. The nature of such work normally exposes the employee to the fall hazard for a short period of time. This Plan details how (Your company name here) will minimize these hazards.

Controlled Access Zones

When using the Plan to implement the fall protection options available, workers must be protected through limited access to high hazard locations. Before any non-conventional fall protection systems are used as part of the work plan, a controlled access zone (CAZ) shall be clearly defined by the competent person as an area where a recognized hazard exists. The demarcation of the CAZ shall be communicated by the competent person in a recognized manner, either through signs, wires, tapes, ropes or chains.

(Your company name here) shall take the following steps to ensure that the CAZ is clearly marked or controlled by the competent person:

- All access to the CAZ must be restricted to authorized entrants;
- All workers who are permitted in the CAZ shall be listed in the appropriate sections of the Plan (or be visibly identifiable by the competent person) prior to implementation;
- The competent person shall ensure that all protective elements of the CAZ be implemented prior to the beginning of work.

Installation Procedures for Roof Truss and Rafter Erection

During the erection and bracing of roof trusses/rafters, conventional fall protection may present a greater hazard to workers. On this job, safety nets, guardrails and personal fall arrest systems will not provide adequate fall protection because the nets will cause the walls to collapse, while there are no suitable attachment or anchorage points for guardrails or personal fall arrest systems.

On this job, requiring workers to use a ladder for the entire installation process will cause a greater hazard because the worker must stand on the ladder with his back or side to the front of the ladder. While erecting the truss or rafter the worker will need both hands to maneuver the truss and therefore cannot hold onto the ladder. In addition, ladders cannot be adequately protected from movement while trusses are being maneuvered into place. Many workers may experience additional fatigue because of the increase in overhead work with heavy materials, which can also lead to a greater hazard.

Exterior scaffolds cannot be utilized on this job because the ground, after recent backfilling, cannot support the scaffolding. In most cases, the erection and dismantling of the scaffold would expose workers to a greater fall hazard than erection of the trusses/rafters.

On all walls eight feet or less, workers will install interior scaffolds along the interior wall below the location where the trusses/rafters will be erected. "Sawhorse" scaffolds constructed of 46 inch sawhorses and 2 x 10 planks will often allow workers to be elevated high enough to allow for the erection of trusses and rafters without working on the top plate of the wall.

In structures that have walls higher than eight feet and where the use of scaffolds and ladders would create a greater hazard, safe working procedures will be utilized when working on the top plate and will be monitored by the crew supervisor. During all stages of truss/rafter erection the stability of the trusses/rafters will be ensured at all times.

(Your company name here) shall take the following steps to protect workers who are exposed to fall hazards while working from the top plate installing trusses/rafters:

- Only the following trained workers will be allowed to work on the top plate during roof truss or rafter installation:
- Workers shall have no other duties to perform during truss/rafter erection procedures;
- All trusses/rafters will be adequately braced before any worker can use the truss/rafter as a support;
- Workers will remain on the top plate using the previously stabilized truss/rafter

as a support while other trusses/rafters are being erected;

- Workers will leave the area of the secured trusses only when it is necessary to secure another truss/rafter;
- The first two trusses/rafters will be set from ladders leaning on side walls at points where the walls can support the weight of the ladder; and
- A worker will climb onto the interior top plate via a ladder to secure the peaks of the first two trusses/rafters being set.

The workers responsible for detaching trusses from cranes and/or securing trusses at the peaks traditionally are positioned at the peak of the trusses/rafters. There are also situations where workers securing rafters to ridge beams will be positioned on top of the ridge beam.

(Your company name here) shall take the following steps to protect workers who are exposed to fall hazards while securing trusses/rafters at the peak of the trusses/ridge beam:

- Only the following trained workers will be allowed to work at the peak during roof truss or rafter installation:
- Once truss or rafter installation begins, workers not involved in that activity shall not stand or walk below or adjacent to the roof opening or exterior walls in any area where they could be struck by falling objects;
- Workers shall have no other duties than securing/bracing the trusses/ridge beam;
- Workers positioned at the peaks or in the webs of trusses or on top of the ridge beam shall work from a stable position, either by sitting on a "ridge seat" or other equivalent surface that provides additional stability or by positioning themselves in previously stabilized trusses/rafters and leaning into and reaching through the trusses/rafters;
- Workers shall not remain on or in the peak/ridge any longer than necessary to safely complete the task.
- Roof Sheathing Operations

Workers typically install roof sheathing after all trusses/rafters and any permanent truss bracing is in place. Roof structures are unstable until some sheathing is installed, so workers installing roof sheathing cannot be protected from fall hazards by conventional fall protection systems until it is determined that the roofing system can be used as an anchorage point. At that point, employees shall be protected by a personal fall arrest system.

Trusses/rafters are subject to collapse if a worker falls while attached to a single truss with a belt/harness. Nets could also cause collapse, and there is no place to attach guardrails.

All workers will ensure that they have secure footing before they attempt to walk on the sheathing, including cleaning shoes/boots of mud or other slip hazards.

To minimize the time workers must be exposed to a fall hazard, materials will be staged to allow for the quickest installation of sheathing.

(Your company name here) shall take the following steps to protect workers who are exposed to fall hazards while installing roof sheathing:

- Once roof sheathing installation begins, workers not involved in that activity shall not stand or walk below or adjacent to the roof opening or exterior walls in any area where they could be struck by falling objects;
- The competent person shall determine the limits of this area, which shall be clearly communicated to workers prior to placement of the first piece of roof sheathing;
- The competent person may order work on the roof to be suspended for brief periods as necessary to allow other workers to pass through such areas when this would not create a greater hazard;
- Only qualified workers shall install roof sheathing;
- The bottom row of roof sheathing may be installed by workers standing in truss webs;
- After the bottom row of roof sheathing is installed, a slide guard extending the width of the roof shall be securely attached to the roof. Slide guards are to be constructed of no less than nominal 4" height capable of limiting the uncontrolled slide of workers.

Workers should install the slide guard while standing in truss webs and leaning over the sheathing;

- Additional rows of roof sheathing may be installed by workers positioned on previously installed rows of sheathing. A slide guard can be used to assist workers in retaining their footing during successive sheathing operations; and
- Additional slide guards shall be securely attached to the roof at intervals not to exceed 13 feet as successive rows of sheathing are installed. For roofs with pitches in excess of 9-in-12, slide guards will be installed at four-foot intervals.
- When wet weather (rain, snow, or sleet) are present, roof sheathing operations shall be suspended unless safe footing can be assured for those workers installing sheathing.
- When strong winds (above 40 miles per hour) are present, roof sheathing operations are to be suspended unless wind breakers are erected.

Installation of Floor Joists and Sheathing
During the installation of floor sheathing/joists (leading edge construction), the following steps shall be taken to protect workers:

- Only the following trained workers will be allowed to install floor joists or sheathing:
- Materials for the operations shall be conveniently staged to allow for easy access to workers,
- The first floor joists or trusses will be rolled into position and secured either from the ground, ladders or sawhorse scaffolds;
- Each successive floor joist or truss will be rolled into place and secured from a platform created from a sheet of plywood laid over the previously secured floor joists or trusses;
- Except for the first row of sheathing which will be installed from ladders or the ground, workers shall work from the established deck; and
- Any workers not assisting in the leading edge construction while leading edges still exist (e.g. cutting the decking for the installers) shall not be

permitted within six feet of the leading edge under construction.

Erection of Exterior Walls
During the construction and erection of exterior walls, employers shall take the following steps to protect workers:

- Only the following trained workers will be allowed to erect exterior walls:
- A painted line six feet from the perimeter will be clearly marked prior to any wall erection activities to warn of the approaching unprotected edge;
- Materials for operations shall be conveniently staged to minimize fall hazards; and
- Workers constructing exterior walls shall complete as much cutting of materials and other preparation as possible away from the edge of the deck.

III. Enforcement
Constant awareness of and respect for fall hazards, and compliance with all safety rules are considered conditions of employment. The crew supervisor or foreman, as well as individuals in the Safety and Personnel Department, reserve the right to issue disciplinary warnings to employees, up to and including termination, for failure to follow the guidelines of this program.

IV. Accident Investigations
All accidents that result in injury to workers, regardless of their nature, shall be investigated and reported. It is an integral part of any safety program that documentation take place as soon as possible so that the cause and means of prevention can be identified to prevent a reoccurrence.

In the event that an employee falls or there is some other related, serious incident occurring, this plan shall be reviewed to determine if additional practices, procedures, or training need to be implemented to prevent similar types of falls or incidents from occurring.

V. Changes to Plan
Any changes to the plan will be approved by (name of the qualified person). This plan shall be reviewed by a qualified person as

the job progresses to determine if additional practices, procedures or training needs to be implemented by the competent person to improve or provide additional fall protection. Workers shall be notified and trained, if necessary, in the new procedures. A copy of this plan and all approved changes shall be maintained at the jobsite.

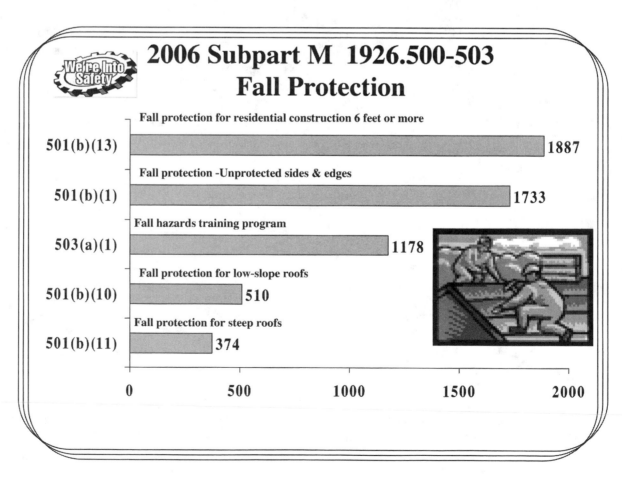

2006 Subpart M 1926.500-503
Fall Protection

Fall protection for residential construction 6 feet or more

501(b)(13) — 1887

Fall protection -Unprotected sides & edges

501(b)(1) — 1733

Fall hazards training program

503(a)(1) — 1178

Fall protection for low-slope roofs

501(b)(10) — 510

Fall protection for steep roofs

501(b)(11) — 374

0   500   1000   1500   2000

Fall Protection Quiz
(See appendix for answers.)

1. A general rule for all construction activities is that workers must be protected from falls at:
   a. 4 ft.
   b. 6 ft.
   c. 10 ft.
   d. 20 ft.

2. A personal fall arrest system consists of an:
   a. Anchor point, fall arrest harness, and shock-absorbing lanyard
   b. Anchor point, locking snap hooks, and shock-absorbing lanyard
   c. Anchor point, fall arrest harness, and locking snap hooks
   d. Anchor point, locking snap hooks, and guardrail

3. A body belt may be used for fall protection
   a. True
   b. False

4. Guardrails consist of a:
   a. Top rail, intermediate posts, and toeboard
   b. Top rail, intermediate posts, and fiber webbing
   c. Top rail, intermediate posts, and midrail
   d. Top rail, fiber webbing, and toeboard

5. A safety net that is placed 7 feet below the working deck must extend:
   a. 8 ft. horizontally
   b. 10 ft. horizontally
   c. 13 ft. horizontally
   d. 15 ft. horizontally

6. A positioning device, such as a body belt or harness, may allow free fall of:
   a. 1 ft.
   b. 2 ft.
   c. 6 ft.
   d. 10 ft.

SCAFFOLDING

In 1996 OSHA revised the scaffold standards found in Subpart L of 29 CFR 1926. Safety requirements for scaffolding also are discussed under the general industry standards at 1910.28.

No scaffold shall be erected, moved, dismantled, or altered except under the supervision of a competent person. There is a special definition for competent person as outlined by these definitions found in OSHA regulations:

- **Authorized person.** A person who is authorized by the employer to perform a task.
- **Qualified person.** A person who has the knowledge to perform that task through education, schooling, training or experience.
- **Competent person.** A person who is qualified and authorized to perform the task. A competent person must have the ability to identify hazardous conditions and have the authority to take action to maintain a safe workplace.

The footing or anchorage for scaffolds shall be sound, rigid, and capable of carrying the maximum intended load without settling or displacement. Unstable objects, such as barrels, boxes, loose brick, or concrete blocks shall not be used to support scaffolds or planks.

Guardrails and toeboards shall be installed on all open sides and ends of platforms more than 10 ft. above the ground or floor, except needle beam scaffolds and floats (see paragraphs (p) and (w) of this section). Scaffolds between 4 ft. and 10 ft. in height, having a minimum horizontal dimension in either direction of less than 45 in., shall have standard guardrails installed on all open sides and ends of the platform.

Guardrails shall be 2 in. × 4 in., or the equivalent, approximately 42 in. high, with a midrail, when required. Supports shall be at intervals not to exceed 8 ft. Toeboards shall be a minimum of 4 in. in height.

Where persons are required to work or pass under the scaffold, scaffolds shall be provided with a screen between the toeboard and the guardrail, extending along the entire opening, consisting of No. 18 gauge U.S. Standard wire ½-in. mesh, or the equivalent.

Scaffolds and their components shall be capable of supporting without failure at least four times the maximum intended load.

Any scaffold, including accessories such as braces, brackets, trusses, screw legs, and ladders, damaged or weakened from any cause shall be immediately repaired or replaced.

All load-carrying timber members of scaffold framing shall be a minimum of 1,500 fiber (Stress Grade) construction grade lumber. All dimensions are nominal sizes as provided in the American Lumber Standards, except that where rough sizes are noted, only rough or undressed lumber of the size specified will satisfy minimum requirements.

All planking shall be Scaffold Grade, or equivalent, as recognized by approved grading rules for the species of wood used. The maximum permissible spans for 2-in. × 9-in. or wider planks shall be used as shown in Exhibit 12-1.

Exhibit 12-1. Maximum Permissible Plank Span

	Material				
	Full thickness undressed lumber			Nominal thickness lumber	
Working load (psf)	25	50	75	25	50
Permissible span (ft.)	10	8	6	8	9

The maximum permissible span for 1¼-in. × 9-in. or wider plank of full thickness shall be 4 ft. with medium duty loading of 50 psf.

All planking of platforms shall be overlapped (minimum 12 in.) or secured from movement.

An access ladder or equivalent safe access shall be provided.

Scaffold planks shall extend over their end supports not less than 6 in. nor more than 12 in.

The poles, legs, or uprights of scaffolds shall be plumb, and securely and rigidly braced to prevent swaying and displacement.

Overhead protection shall be provided for employees on a scaffold who are exposed to overhead hazards. Slippery conditions on scaffolds shall be eliminated as soon as possible after they occur.

No welding, burning, riveting, or open-flame work shall be performed on any staging suspended by means of fiber or synthetic rope. Only treated or protected fiber or synthetic ropes shall be used for or near any work involving the use of corrosive substances or chemicals.

Wire or fiber rope used for scaffold suspension shall be capable of supporting at least six times the rated load. The use of shore or lean-to scaffolds is prohibited.

Lumber sizes, when used in this section, refer to nominal sizes except where otherwise stated. Materials being hoisted onto a scaffold shall have a tag line.

Employees shall not work on scaffolds during storms or high winds. Tools, materials, and debris shall not be allowed to accumulate in quantities to cause a hazard.

Wood Pole Scaffolds

Scaffold poles shall bear on a foundation of sufficient size and strength to spread the load from the pole over a sufficient area to prevent settlement. All poles shall be set plumb.

Where wood poles are spliced, the ends shall be squared and the upper section shall rest squarely on the lower section. Wood splice plates shall be:

- Provided on at least two adjacent sides and shall be not less than 4 ft. in length;
- Overlap the abutted ends equally;
- Have the same width; and
- Have a width that is not less than the cross-sectional area of the pole.

Splice plates or other materials of equivalent strength may be used.

Independent pole scaffolds shall be set as near to the wall of the building as practicable.

All pole scaffolds shall be securely guyed or tied to the building or structure. Where the height or length exceeds 25 ft., the scaffold shall be secured at intervals not greater than 25 ft. vertically and horizontally, and the ends shall be secured to prevent their dislodgment.

When a scaffold turns a corner, the platform planks shall be laid to prevent tipping. The planks that meet the corner putlog at an angle shall be laid first, extending over the diagonally placed putlog far enough to have a good safe bearing, but not far enough to involve any danger from tipping. The planking running in the opposite direction at an angle shall be laid so as to extend over and rest on the first layer of planking.

When moving platforms to the next level, the old platform shall be left undisturbed until the new putlogs or bearers have been set in place, ready to receive the platform planks.

Guardrails not less than 2 in. × 4 in. or the equivalent and not less than 36 in. or more than 42 in. high, with a midrail, when required, of 1 in. × 4-in. lumber or equivalent, and toeboards, shall be installed at all open sides on all scaffolds more than 10 ft. above the ground or floor. Toeboards shall be a minimum of 4 in. in height. Wire mesh shall be installed in accordance with 1910.28(a)(17).

All wood pole scaffolds 60 ft. or less in height shall be constructed and erected in accordance with Tables D-7 through D-12 in 1910.28. If they are more than 60 ft. in height they shall be designed by a registered professional engineer and constructed and erected in accordance with such design. A copy of the typical drawings and specifications shall be made available to the employer and for inspection purposes.

Tube and Coupler Scaffolds

A light-duty tube and coupler scaffold shall have all posts, bearers, runners, and bracing of nominal 2-in. O.D. steel tubing. The posts shall be spaced no more than 6 ft. apart by 10 ft. along the length of the scaffold. Other structural metals, when used, must be designed to carry an equivalent load. No dissimilar metals shall be used together.

A medium-duty tube and coupler scaffold shall have all posts, runners, and bracing of nominal 2-in. steel tubing. Posts spaced not more than 6 ft. apart by 8 ft. along the length of the scaffold shall have bearers of nominal 2½-in. O.D. steel tubing. Posts spaced not more than 5 ft. apart by 8 ft. along the length of the scaffold shall have bearers of nominal 2-in. O.D. steel tubing. Other structural metals, when used, must be designed to carry an equivalent load. No dissimilar metals shall be used together.

A heavy-duty tube and coupler scaffold shall have all posts, runners, and bracing of nominal 2-in. O.D. steel tubing, with posts spaced not more than 6 ft. × 6 ft., 6 in. Other structural metals, when used, must be designed to carry an equivalent load. No dissimilar metals shall be used together.

Tube and coupler scaffolds shall be limited in heights and working levels to those permitted in Tables D-13, 14, and 15, of 1910.28. Drawings and specification of all tube and coupler scaffolds above the limitations in Tables D-13, 14, and 15 of this section shall be designed by a registered professional engineer and copies made available to the employer and for inspection purposes.

All tube and coupler scaffolds shall be constructed and erected to support four times the maximum intended loads as set forth in Tables D-13, 14, and 15 of 1910.28, or as set forth in the specifications by a registered professional engineer, copies which shall be made available to the employer and for inspection purposes. Posts shall be accurately spaced, erected on suitable bases, and maintained plumb.

Runners shall be erected along the length of the scaffold, located on both the inside and the outside posts at even height. Runners shall be interlocked to the inside and the outside posts at even heights. Runners shall be interlocked to form continuous lengths and coupled to each post. The bottom runners shall be located as close to the base as possible. Runners shall be placed not more than 6 ft., 6 in. on centers.

Bearers shall be installed transversely between posts and shall be securely coupled to the posts bearing on the runner coupler. When coupled directly to the runners, the coupler must be kept as close to the posts as possible. Bearers shall be at least 4 in. but not more than 12 in. longer than the post spacing or runner spacing. Bearers may be cantilevered for use as brackets to carry not more than two planks.

Cross bracing shall be installed across the width of the scaffold at least every third set of posts horizontally and every fourth runner vertically. Such bracing shall extend diagonally from the inner and outer runners upward to the next outer and inner runners.

Longitudinal diagonal bracing on the inner and outer rows of poles shall be installed at approximately a 45° angle from near the base of the first outer post upward to the extreme top of the scaffold. Where the longitudinal length of the scaffold permits, such bracing shall be duplicated beginning at every fifth post. In a similar manner, longitudinal diagonal bracing also shall be installed from the last post extending back and upward toward the first post. Where conditions preclude the attachment of this bracing to the posts, it may be attached to the runners.

The entire scaffold shall be tied to and securely braced against the building at intervals not to exceed 30 ft. horizontally and 26 ft. vertically.

Guardrails not less than 2 in. × 4 in. or the equivalent and not less than 36 in. or more than 42 in. high, with a mid-rail, when required, of 1 in. × 4-in. lumber or equivalent, and toeboards, shall be installed at all open sides on all scaffolds more than 10 ft. above the ground or floor. Toeboards shall be a minimum of 4 in. in height. Wire mesh shall be installed in accordance with 1910.28(a)(17).

Tubular Welded Frame Scaffolds

Metal tubular frame scaffolds, including accessories such as braces, brackets, trusses, screw legs, and ladders, shall be designed, constructed, and erected to safely support four times the maximum rated load. Spacing of panels or frames shall be consistent with the loads imposed.

Scaffolds shall be properly braced by cross bracing or diagonal braces, or both, for securing vertical members together laterally, and the cross braces shall be of such length as will automatically square and align vertical members so that the erected scaffold is always plumb, square, and rigid. All brace connections shall be made secure.

Scaffold legs shall be set on adjustable bases or plain bases placed on mud sills or other foundations adequate to support the maximum rated load. The frames shall be placed one on top of the other with coupling or stacking pins to provide proper vertical alignment of the legs.

Where uplift may occur, panels shall be locked together vertically by pins or other equivalent suitable means.

Guardrails not less than 2 in. × 4 in. or the equivalent and not less than 36 in. or more than 42 in. high, with a mid-rail, when required, of 1 in. × 4-in. lumber or equivalent, and toeboards, shall be installed at all open sides on all scaffolds more than 10 ft. above the ground or floor. Toeboards shall be a minimum of 4 in. in height. Wire mesh shall be installed in accordance with 1910.28(a)(17).

All tubular metal scaffolds shall be constructed and erected to support four times the maximum intended loads. To prevent movement, the scaffold shall be secured to the building or structure at intervals not to exceed 30 ft. horizontally and 26 ft. vertically.

Maximum permissible spans or planking shall be in conformity with 1910.28(a)(9). Drawings and specifications for all frame scaffolds more than 125 ft. in height above the base plates shall be designed by a registered professional engineer and copies made available to the employer and for inspection purposes.

All tubular welded frame scaffolds shall be erected by competent and experienced personnel.

Frames and accessories for scaffolds shall be maintained in good repair and every defect, unsafe condition, or noncompliance with this section shall be immediately corrected before further use of the scaffold. Any broken, bent, excessively rusted, altered, or otherwise structurally damaged frames or accessories shall not be used.

Periodic inspections shall be made of all welded frames and accessories, and any maintenance, including painting, or minor corrections authorized by the manufacturer, shall be made before further use.

Manually Propelled Mobile Scaffolds

When freestanding mobile scaffold towers are used, the height shall not exceed four times the minimum base dimension.

Casters shall be properly designed for strength and dimensions to support four times the maximum intended load. All casters shall be provided with a positive locking device to hold the scaffold in position.

Scaffolds shall be properly braced by cross bracing and horizontal bracing conforming to paragraph (d)(3) of this section.

Platforms shall be tightly planked for the full width of the scaffold except for necessary entrance opening. Platforms shall be secured in place.

A ladder or stairway shall be provided for proper access and exit and shall be affixed or built into the scaffold and located so that when in use, it will not have a tendency to tip the scaffold. A landing platform must be provided at intervals not to exceed 35 ft.

The force necessary to move the mobile scaffold shall be applied near or as close to the base as practicable and provision shall be made to stabilize the tower during movement from one location to another. Scaffolds shall only be moved on level floors, free of obstructions and openings.

The employer shall not allow employees to ride on manually propelled scaffolds unless all of the following conditions exist:

- The floor or surface is within 3° of level and free from pits, holes, or obstructions;
- The minimum dimension of the scaffold base when ready for rolling is at least one-half of the height. Outriggers, if used, shall be installed on both sides of staging;
- The wheels are equipped with rubber or similar resilient tires; and
- All tools and materials are secured or removed from the platform before the mobile scaffold is moved.

Scaffolds in use by any persons shall rest upon a suitable footing and shall stand plumb. The casters or wheels shall be locked to prevent any movement.

Mobile scaffolds constructed of metal members also shall conform to applicable provisions of paragraphs (b), (c), or (d) of 1910.28, depending on the material of which they are constructed.

Guardrails made of lumber not less than 2 × 4 in. (or other material providing equivalent protection), approximately 42 in. high, with a midrail of 1 × 6 in. lumber (or other material providing equivalent protection) and toeboards shall be installed at all open sides and ends on all scaffolds more than 10 ft. above the ground or floor. Toeboards shall be a minimum of 4 in. in height. Wire mesh shall be installed in accordance with 1910.28(a)(17).

Elevating and Rotating Work Platforms

Applicable requirements of ANSI A92.2-1969, Vehicle Mounted Elevating and Rotating Work Platforms, shall be complied with for such equipment, as required by the provisions of 1926.556.

Outrigger Scaffolds

Outrigger beams shall extend not more than 6 ft. beyond the face of the building. The inboard end of outrigger beams, measured from the fulcrum point to anchorage point, shall be not less than 1½ times the outboard end in length. The beams shall rest on edge, the sides shall be plumb, and the edges shall be horizontal.

The fulcrum point of the beam shall rest on a secure bearing at least 6 in. in each horizontal dimension. The beam shall be secured in place against movement and shall be securely braced at the fulcrum point against tipping.

The inboard ends of outrigger beams shall be securely anchored by means of struts bearing against sills in contact with the overhead beams or ceiling by means of tension members secured to the floor joists underfoot, or both if necessary. The inboard ends of outrigger beams shall be secured against tipping, and the entire supporting structure shall be securely braced in both directions to prevent any horizontal movement.

Unless a registered professional engineer competent in this field designs outrigger scaffolds, they shall be constructed and erected in accordance with Table L-13. Outrigger scaffolds, designed by a registered professional engineer, shall be constructed and erected in accordance with such design. Planking shall be laid tight and extend to within 3 in. of the building wall. Planking shall be secured to the beams.

Guardrails made of lumber not less than 2 × 4 in. (or other material providing equivalent protection), approximately 42 in. high, with a midrail of 1 × 6 in. lumber (or other material providing equivalent protection) and toeboards shall be installed at all open sides and ends on all scaffolds more than 10 ft. above the ground or floor. Toeboards shall be a minimum of 4 in. in height. Wire mesh shall be installed in accordance with 1910.28(a)(17).

Masons' Adjustable Multiple-Point Suspension Scaffolds

The scaffold shall be capable of sustaining a working load of 50 lbs. per square foot and shall not be loaded in excess of that figure. The scaffold shall be provided with hoisting machines that meet the requirements of Underwriters' Laboratories or Factory Mutual Engineering Corporation. Wire ropes must be capable of supporting at least six times the intended load, suspended from overhead outrigger beams.

The scaffold outrigger beams shall consist of structural metal securely fastened or anchored to the frame or floor system of the building or structure. Each outrigger beam shall be equivalent in strength to at least a standard 7-in., 15.3-lb. steel I-beam, at least 15 ft. long and shall not project more than 6 ft., 6 in. beyond the bearing point.

Where the overhang exceeds 6 ft., 6 in., outrigger beams shall be composed of stronger beams or multiple beams and be installed under the supervision of a competent person.

All outrigger beams shall be set and maintained with their webs in a vertical position. A stop bolt shall be placed at each end of every outrigger beam. The outrigger beam shall rest on suitable wood bearing blocks.

The free end of the suspension wire ropes shall be equipped with proper size thimbles and secured by splicing or other equivalent means. The running ends shall be securely attached to the hoisting drum, and at least four turns of wire rope shall at all times remain on the drum. The use of fiber rope is prohibited. Where a single outrigger beam is used, the steel shackles or clevises with which the wire ropes are attached to the outrigger beams shall be placed directly over the hoisting drums.

The scaffold platform shall be equivalent in strength to at least 2-in. planking. (For maximum planking spans, see 1910.28(a)(11).)

When employees are at work on the scaffold and an overhead hazard exists, overhead protection shall be provided on the scaffold not more than 9 ft. above the platform, consisting of 2-in. planking, or material of equivalent strength, laid tight, and extending not less than the width of the scaffold.

Each scaffold shall be installed or relocated under the supervision of a competent person.

Guardrails made of lumber not less than 2 × 4 in. (or other material providing equivalent protection), approximately 42 in. high, with a midrail of 1 × 6 in. lumber (or other material providing equivalent protection) and toeboards shall be installed at all open sides and ends on all scaffolds more than 10 ft. above the ground or floor. Toeboards shall be a minimum of 4 in. in height. Wire mesh shall be installed in accordance with 1910.28(a)(17).

Two-Point Suspension (Swinging Scaffolds)

Two-point suspension scaffold platforms shall not be less than 20 in. nor more than 36 in.

wide overall. The platform shall be securely fastened to the hangers by U-bolts or other equivalent means.

The hangers of two-point suspension scaffolds shall be made of mild steel, or other equivalent materials, having a cross-sectional area capable of sustaining four times the maximum rated load, and shall be designed with a support for guardrail, intermediate rail, and toeboard.

When hoisting machines are used on two-point suspension scaffolds, such machines shall be of a design tested and approved by Underwriters' Laboratories or Factory Mutual Engineering Corporation.

The roof irons or hooks shall be of mild steel, or other equivalent material, of proper size and design, and securely installed and anchored. Tiebacks of ¾-in. manila rope, or the equivalent, shall serve as a secondary means of anchorage, installed at right angles to the face of the building, whenever possible, and secured to a structurally sound portion of the building.

Two-point suspension scaffolds shall be suspended by wire, synthetic, or fiber ropes capable of supporting at least six times the rated load. All other components shall be capable of supporting at least four times the rated load.

The sheaves of all blocks, consisting of at least one double and one single block, shall fit the size and type of rope used.

All wire ropes, fiber and synthetic ropes, slings, hangers, platforms, and other supporting parts shall be inspected before every installation. Periodic inspections shall be made while the scaffold is in use.

On suspension scaffolds designed for a working load of 500 lbs., no more than two employees shall be permitted to work at one time. On suspension scaffolds with a working load of 750 lbs., no more than three employees shall be permitted to work at one time. Each employee shall be protected by an approved safety life belt attached to a lifeline. The lifeline shall be securely attached to substantial members of the structure (not scaffold) or to securely rigged lines that will safely suspend the employee in case of a fall. To keep the lifeline continuously attached to a fixed structure, with a minimum of slack, the attachment point of the lifeline shall be appropriately changed as the work progresses.

Two-point suspension scaffolds shall be securely lashed to the building or structure to prevent them from swaying. Window cleaners' anchors shall not be used for this purpose.

The platform of every two-point suspension scaffold shall be one of the following types:

Ladder-type platforms. The side stringer shall be of clear straight-grained spruce or materials of equivalent strength and durability. The rungs shall be of straight-grained oak, ash, or hickory, at least 1 1/8-in. in diameter, with 7/8-in. tenons mortised into the side stringers at least 7/8 in. The stringers shall be tied together with tie rods not less than 1/4 in. in diameter, passing through the stringers and riveted up tight against washers on both ends. The flooring strips shall be spaced not more than 5/8 in. apart except at the side rails where the space may be 1 in. Ladder-type platforms shall be constructed in accordance with Table D-17 of 1910.28.

Plank-type platforms. Plank-type platforms shall be composed of no less than nominal 2-in. × 10-in. unspliced planks, properly cleated together on the underside, starting 6 in. from each end; intervals in between shall not exceed 4 ft. The plank-type platform shall not extend beyond the hangers more than 12 in. A bar or other effective means shall be securely fastened to the platform at each end to prevent it from slipping off of the hanger. The span between hangers for plank-type platforms shall not exceed 8 ft.

Beam-type platforms. Beam platforms shall have side stringers of lumber not less than 2 in. × 6 in. set on edge. The span between hangers shall not exceed 12 ft. when beam platforms are used. The flooring shall be supported on 2-in. × 6-in. cross beams, laid flat, and set into the upper edge of the stringers with a snug fit, at intervals of no more than 4 ft., and securely nailed in place. The flooring shall be of 1-in. × 6-in. material properly nailed. Floorboards shall not be spaced more than 1/2 in. apart.

Light metal-type platforms. Light metal-type platforms shall be tested and listed according to Underwriters' Laboratories or Factory Mutual Engineering Corporation.

Each scaffold shall be installed or relocated under the supervision of a competent person.

Guardrails not less than 2 in. × 4 in. or the equivalent and not less than 36 in. or more than 42 in. high, with a mid-rail, when required, of 1-in. × 4-in. lumber or equivalent, and toeboards, shall be installed at all open sides on all scaffolds more than 10 ft. above the ground or floor. Toeboards shall be a minimum of 4 in. in height. Wire mesh shall be installed in accordance with 1910.28(a)(17).

Stone Setters' Adjustable Multiple-Point Suspension Scaffolds

The scaffold shall be capable of sustaining a working load of 25 lbs. per square foot and shall not be overloaded. Scaffolds shall not be used to store stone or other heavy materials. When used, the hoisting machine and its supports shall be of a type tested and listed by Underwriters' Laboratories or Factory Mutual Engineering Corporation.

The platform shall be securely fastened to the hangers by U-bolts or other equivalent means. For materials and spans, see subdivision (ii) of paragraph (i)(10), Plank-Type Platforms, and Table L-14 of this section.

The scaffold unit shall be suspended from metal outriggers, iron brackets, wire rope slings, or iron hooks. Outriggers, when used, shall be set with their webs in a vertical position, securely anchored to the building or structure, and provided with stop bolts at each end. The scaffold shall be supported by wire rope capable of supporting at least six times the rated load. All other components shall be capable of supporting at least four times the rated load.

The free ends of the suspension wire ropes shall be equipped with proper size thimbles, and secured by splicing or other equivalent means. The running ends shall be securely attached to the hoisting drum and at least four turns of wire rope shall remain at the drum at all times.

When two or more scaffolds are used on a building or structure, they shall not be bridged one to the other, but shall be maintained at even height with platforms abutting closely.

Guardrails not less than 2 in. × 4 in. or the equivalent and not less than 36 in. or more than 42 in. high, with a mid-rail, when required, of 1-in. × 4-in. lumber or equivalent, and toe-boards, shall be installed at all open sides on all scaffolds more than 10 ft. above the ground or floor. Toeboards shall be a minimum of 4 in. in height. Wire mesh shall be installed in accordance with 1910.28(a)(17).

Single-Point Adjustable Suspension Scaffolds

The scaffolding, including power units or manu-ally operated winches, shall be of a type tested and listed by Underwriters' Laboratories or Factory Mutual Engineering Corporation.

The power units may be either electrically or air motor driven. All power-operated gears and brakes shall be enclosed. In addition to the normal operating brake, all power-driven units shall have an emergency brake that en-gages automatically when the normal speed of descent is exceeded.

The hoisting machines, cables, and equipment shall be regularly serviced and inspected.

The units may be combined to form a two-point suspension scaffold.

The supporting cable shall be vertical for its entire length, and the basket shall not be swayed nor the cable fixed to any intermediate points to change the original path of travel.

Suspension methods shall conform to applicable provisions of paragraphs (f) and (g) of 1910.28.

Guardrails not less than 2 in. × 4 in. or the equivalent and not less than 36 in. or more than 42 in. high, with a mid-rail, when required, of 1-in. × 4-in. lumber or equivalent, and toe-boards, shall be installed at all open sides on all scaffolds more than 10 ft. above the ground or floor. Toeboards shall be a minimum of 4 in. in height. Wire mesh shall be installed in accordance with 1910.28(a)(17).

For additional details not covered in this paragraph, applicable technical portions of ANSI A120.1-1970, Power-Operated Devices for Exterior Building Maintenance Powered Platforms, shall be used.

Boatswains' Chairs

The chair seat shall not be less than 12 in. × 24 in. and 1-in. thick. The seat shall be reinforced on the underside by securely fastened cleats to prevent the board from splitting.

The two fiber rope seat slings shall be of 5/8-in. diameter, reeved through the four seat holes so as to cross each other on the under-side of the seat.

Seat slings shall be of at least 5/8-in. wire rope when an employee is conducting a heat-producing process, such as gas or arc welding. The employee shall be protected by a safety belt and lifeline in accordance with 1926.104. The attachment point of the lifeline to the structure shall be appropriately changed as the work progresses.

The tackle shall consist of correct size ball bearing or bushed blocks and properly spliced 5/8-in. diameter first-grade manila rope, or equivalent.

The roof irons, hooks, or the object to which the tackle is anchored shall be securely in-stalled. Tiebacks, when used, shall be installed at right angles to the face of the building and securely fastened.

Carpenters' Bracket Scaffolds

The brackets shall consist of a triangular wood frame not less than 2 in. × 3 in. in cross section, or of metal of equivalent strength. Each member shall be properly fitted and securely joined.

Each bracket shall be attached to the struc-ture by means of one of the following:

- A bolt no less than 5/8 in. in diameter that shall extend through to the inside of the building wall;
- A metal stud attachment device that extends from the bottom of each square to the top of the next square shall be provided on both front and rear sides of the scaffold; or
- Platform planks of at least 2-in. × 10-in. nominal size. The ends of the planks shall overlap the bearers of the squares and each plank shall be supported by not less than three squares.

Bricklayers' square scaffolds shall not exceed three tiers in height and shall be so constructed and arranged that one square shall rest directly above the other. The upper tiers shall stand on a continuous row of planks laid across the next lower tier and be nailed down or otherwise se-cured to prevent displacement.

Scaffolds shall be level and set upon a firm foundation.

Horse Scaffolds

Horse scaffolds shall not be constructed or arranged more than two tiers or 10 ft. in height.

The members of the horses shall be not less than those specified in Table D-19. Horses shall be spaced not more than 5 ft. for medium duty and not more than 8 ft. for light duty. When arranged in tiers, each horse shall be placed directly over the horse in the tier below.

On all scaffolds arranged in tiers, the legs shall be nailed down or otherwise secured to the planks to prevent displacement or thrust, and each tier shall be substantially cross-braced.

Horses or parts that have become weak or defective shall not be used.

Guardrails not less than 2 in. × 4 in. or the equivalent and not less than 36 in. or more than 42 in. high, with a mid-rail, when required, of 1-in. × 4-in. lumber or equivalent, and toeboards, shall be installed at all open sides on all scaffolds more than 10 ft. above the ground or floor. Toeboards shall be a minimum of 4 in. in height. Wire mesh shall be installed in accordance with 1910.28(a)(17).

Needle Beam Scaffold

Wood needle beams shall be not less than 4 in. × 6 in. in size, with the greater dimension placed in a vertical direction. Metal beams or the equivalent, conforming to paragraphs (a)(8) and (10) of this section, may be used and shall not be altered or moved horizontally while they are in use.

Ropes or hangers shall be provided for supports. The span between supports on the needle beam shall not exceed 10 ft. for 4-in. × 6-in. timbers. Rope supports shall be equivalent in strength to 1-in. diameter first-grade manila rope.

The ropes shall be attached to the needle beams by a scaffold hitch or a properly made eye splice. The loose end of the rope shall be tied by a bowline knot or by a round turn and a half hitch. The scaffold hitch shall be arranged so as to prevent the needle beam from rolling or becoming otherwise displaced.

The platform span between the needle beams shall not exceed 8 ft. when using 2-in. scaffold plank. For spans greater than 8 ft., platforms shall be designed based on design requirements for the special span. The overhang of each end of the platform planks shall be between 6 in. and 12 in.

When needle beam scaffolds are used, the planks shall be secured against slipping. All unattached tools, bolts, and nuts used on needle beam scaffolds shall be kept in suitable containers, and properly secured. One end of a needle beam scaffold may be supported by a permanent structural member conforming to paragraphs (a)(8) and (10) of this section.

Each employee working on a needle beam scaffold shall be protected by a safety belt and lifeline in accordance with 1926.104.

Plasterers', Decorators', and Large Area Scaffolds

Plasterers, lathers, and ceiling workers inside scaffolds shall be constructed in accordance with paragraphs (a), (b), or (c) of this section, as appropriate.

All platform planks shall be laid with the edges close together.

When independent pole scaffold platforms are erected in sections, such sections shall be provided with connecting runways equipped with substantial guardrails.

Guardrails not less than 2 in. × 4 in. or the equivalent and not less than 36 in. or more than 42 in. high, with a mid-rail, when required, of 1-in. × 4-in. lumber or equivalent, and toeboards, shall be installed at all open sides on all scaffolds more than 10 ft. above the ground or floor. Toeboards shall be a minimum of 4 in. in height. Wire mesh shall be installed in accordance with 1910.28(a)(17).

Interior Hung Scaffolds

An interior hung scaffold shall be hung or suspended from the roof structure or ceiling beams.

The suspending wire or fiber rope shall be capable of supporting at least six times the rated load. The rope shall be wrapped at least twice around the supporting members and twice around the bearers of the scaffold, with each end of the wire rope secured by at least three properly installed standard wire-rope clips.

For hanging wood scaffolds, the following minimum nominal size material shall be used:

- Supporting bearers 2 in. × 10 in. on edge; and
- Planking 2 in. × 10 in., with maximum span 7 ft. for heavy duty and 10 ft. for light duty or medium duty.

Steel tube and coupler members may be used for hanging scaffolds with both types of scaffold designed to sustain a uniform distributed working load up to heavy-duty scaffold loads with a safety factor of 4.

Guardrails made of lumber, not less than 2 x 4 in. (or other material providing equivalent protection), approximately 42 in. high, with a midrail of 1 x 6 in. lumber (or other material providing equivalent protection), and toeboards, shall be installed at all open sides and ends on all scaffolds more than 10 ft. above the ground or floor. Toeboards shall be a minimum of 4 in. in height. Wire mesh shall be installed in accordance with paragraph (a)(6) of this section.

Ladder Jack Scaffolds

All ladder jack scaffolds shall be limited to light duty and shall not exceed a height of 20 ft. above the floor or ground. All ladders used in connection with ladder jack scaffolds shall be heavy-duty ladders and shall be designed and constructed in accordance with ANSI A14.1-1968, Safety Code for Portable Wood Ladders, and A14.2-1968, Safety Code for Portable Metal Ladders. Cleated ladders shall not be used for this purpose.

The ladder jack shall be so designed and constructed that it will bear on the side rails in addition to the ladder rungs or, if bearing on rungs only, the bearing area shall be at least 10 in. on each rung.

Ladders used in conjunction with ladder jacks shall be placed, fastened, held, or equipped with devices so as to prevent slipping.

The wood platform planks shall be not less than 2 in. nominal in thickness. Both metal and wood platform planks shall overlap the bearing surface not less than 12 in. The span between supports for wood shall not exceed 8 ft. Platform width shall be not less than 18 in. No more than two employees shall occupy any given 8 ft. of any ladder jack scaffold at any one time.

Window Jack Scaffolds

Window jack scaffolds shall be used only for the purpose of working at the window opening through which the jack is placed. Window jack scaffolds shall be provided with guardrails unless a safety belt with lifeline is attached and is provided for the employee.

Window jacks shall not be used to support planks placed between one window jack and another or for other elements of scaffolding. No more than one employee shall occupy a window jack scaffold at any one time.

Roofing Brackets

Roofing brackets shall be constructed to fit the pitch of the roof. Brackets shall be secured in place by nailing, in addition to the pointed metal projections. When it is impractical to nail brackets, rope supports shall be used. When rope supports are used, they shall consist of first-grade manila or equivalent.

A catch platform shall be installed below the working area of roofs more than 16 ft. from the ground to eaves with a slope greater than 4 in. in 12 in. without a parapet. In width, the platform shall extend 2 ft. beyond the protection of the eaves and shall be provided with a guardrail, midrail, and toeboard. This provision shall not apply where employees engaged in work upon such roofs are protected by safety belts attached to lifelines.

Crawling Boards or Chicken Ladders

Crawling boards shall be not less than 10 in. wide and 1 in. thick and have cleats 1 in. × 1½ in. The cleats shall be equal in length to the width of the board and spaced at equal intervals not to exceed 24 in. Nails shall be driven through and clinched on the underside. The crawling board shall extend from the ridgepole to the eaves when used in connection with roof construction, repair, or maintenance.

Exhibit 12-2.
A crawling board with cleats of improper length.

A firmly fastened lifeline shall be strung beside each crawling board for a handhold. Crawling boards shall be secured to the roof by means of adequate ridge hooks or other effective means.

Float or Ship Scaffolds

Float or ship scaffolds shall not be used to support more than three men and a few light tools, such as those needed for riveting, bolting, and welding. They shall be constructed as designed in paragraphs (w)(2) through (6) of this section unless substitute designs and materials provide equivalent strength, stability, and safety.

The platform shall be not less than 3 ft. × 6 ft., made of ¾-in. plywood, equivalent to American Plywood Association Grade B-B, Group I, Exterior, or other similar material.

Under the platform, there shall be two supporting bearers made from 2-in. × 4-in., or 1-in × 10-in., rough "selected lumber," or better. The bearers shall be free of knots or other flaws and project 6 in. beyond the platform on both sides. The ends of the platform shall extend 6 in. beyond the outer edges of the bearers. Each bearer shall be securely fastened to the platform.

An edging of wood not less than ¾ in. × 1½ in. or equivalent shall be placed around all sides of the platform to prevent tools from rolling off.

Supporting ropes shall be 1-in. diameter manila rope or equivalent and free of deterioration, chemical damage, flaws, or other imperfections. Rope connections shall be such that the platform cannot shift or slip. If two ropes are used with each float, they shall be arranged so as to provide four ends that can be securely fastened to an overhead support. Each of the two supporting ropes shall be hitched around one end of bearer and pass under the platforms to the other end of the bearer where it is hitched again, leaving sufficient rope at each end for the supporting ties. Each employee shall be protected by an approved safety lifebelt and lifeline, in accordance with 1926.104.

Form Scaffolds

Form scaffolds shall be constructed of wood or other suitable material, such as steel or aluminum, with known strength characteristics. All scaffolds shall be designed and erected with a minimum safety factor of 4, computed on the basis of the maximum rated load.

All scaffold planking shall be a minimum of 2-in. × 10-in. nominal Scaffold Grade, as recognized by approved grading rules for the species of lumber used, or equivalent material. Maximum permissible spans shall not exceed 8 ft. on centers for 2-in. × 10-in. nominal planking. Scaffold planks shall be nailed or bolted to the ledgers or of such length that they overlap the ledgers by at least 6 in. Unsupported projecting ends of scaffolding planks shall be limited to a maximum overhang of 12 in.

Scaffolds shall not be loaded in excess of the working load for which they have been designed.

Figure-Four Form Scaffolds

Figure-four form scaffolds are intended for light duty and shall not be used to support loads exceeding 25 lbs. per square foot unless specifically designed for heavier loading.

Figure-four form scaffold frames shall be spaced not more than 8 ft. on centers and constructed from sound lumber, as follows:

- The outrigger ledger shall consist of two pieces of 1-in. × 6-in. or heavier material nailed on opposite sides of the vertical form support.
- Ledgers shall project not more than 3 ft., 6 in. from the outside of the form support and shall be substantially braced and secured to prevent tipping or turning.

- The knee or angle brace shall intersect the ledger at least 3 ft. from the form at an angle of approximately 45°, and the lower end shall be nailed to a vertical support.
- The platform shall consist of two or more 2-in. × 10-in. planks, which shall be of such length that they extend at least 6 in. beyond ledgers at each end unless secured to the ledgers.
- When planks are secured to the ledgers (nailed or bolted), a wood filler strip shall be used between the ledgers.
- Unsupported projecting ends of planks shall be limited to an overhang of 12 in.

Metal Bracket Form Scaffolds

Metal brackets or scaffold jacks that are an integral part of the form shall be securely bolted or welded to the form. Folding type brackets shall be bolted or secured with a locking-type pin when extended for use.

"Clip-on" or "hook-over" brackets may be used, provided the form walers are bolted to the form or secured by snap ties that extend through the form and are securely anchored. Metal brackets shall be spaced not more than 8 ft. on centers.

Scaffold planks shall be bolted to the metal brackets or of such length that they overlap the brackets at each end by at least 6 in. Unsupported projecting ends of scaffold planks shall be limited to a maximum overhang of 12 in.

Metal bracket form scaffolds shall be equipped with wood guardrails, intermediate rails, toeboards, and scaffold planks meeting the minimum dimensions shown in Table L-18. (Metal may be substituted for wood, providing it affords equivalent or greater design strength.)

Wooden Bracket Form Scaffolds

Wooden bracket form scaffolds shall be an integral part of the form panel. The minimum design criteria set forth herein and in Table L-19 cover scaffolding intended for light duty and shall not be used to support loads exceeding 25 lbs. per square foot, unless specifically designed for heavier loading.

Scaffold planks shall be nailed or bolted to the ledgers or of such length that they overlap the ledgers at each end by at least 6 in. Unsupported projecting ends of scaffold planks shall be limited to a maximum overhang of 12 in.

Guardrails and toeboards shall be installed on all open sides and ends of platforms and scaffolding more than 10 ft. above floor or ground. Guardrails shall be made of lumber 2 in. × 4 in. nominal dimension (or other material providing equivalent protection), approximately 42 in. high, and supported at intervals not to exceed 8 ft. Guardrails shall be equipped with midrails constructed of 1 in. × 6 in. nominal lumber (or other material providing equivalent protection). Toeboards shall extend not less than 4 in. above the scaffold plank.

Pump Jack Scaffolds

Pump jack scaffolds shall not carry a working load that exceeds 500 lbs. and be capable of supporting, without failure, at least four times the maximum intended load. The manufactured components however shall not be loaded in excess of the manufacturer's recommended limits.

Pump jack brackets, braces, and accessories shall be fabricated from metal plates and angles. Each pump jack bracket shall have two positive gripping mechanisms to prevent any failure or slippage.

The platform bracket shall be fully decked and the planking secured. Planking, or equivalent, shall conform to paragraph (a) of this section.

When wood scaffold planks are used as platforms, poles used for pump jacks shall not be spaced more than 10 ft. center to center. When fabricated platforms are used that fully comply with all other provisions of this paragraph, pole spacing may exceed 10 ft. center to center. Poles shall not exceed 30 ft. in height.

Poles shall be secured to the work wall by rigid triangular bracing, or equivalent, at the bottom, top, and other points as necessary, to provide a maximum vertical spacing of not more than 10 ft. between braces. Each brace shall be capable of supporting a minimum of 225 lbs. tension or compression.

For the pump jack bracket to pass bracing already installed, an extra brace shall be used approximately 4 ft. above the one to be passed until the original brace is reinstalled. All poles shall bear on mudsills or other adequate firm foundations.

Pole lumber shall be two 2 × 4s, of Douglas fir, or equivalent; straight-grained; clear;

and free of cross-grain, shakes, large loose or dead knots, and other defects that might impair strength.

When poles are constructed of two continuous lengths, they shall be 2 × 4s, spiked together, with the seam parallel to the bracket, with 10d common nails, no more than 12 in. center to center, staggered uniformly from opposite outside edges.

If 2 × 4s are spliced to make up the pole, the splices shall be so constructed as to develop the full strength of the member.

A ladder, in accordance with 1926.1053, shall be provided for access to the platform during use.

No more than two persons shall be permitted at one time upon a pump jack scaffold between any two supports.

Pump jacks scaffolds shall be provided with standard guardrails as defined in 1926.451(a)(5), but no guardrail is required when safety belts with lifelines are provided for employees.

When a workbench is used at an approximate height of 42 in., the top guardrail may be eliminated if the workbench is fully decked, has secured planking, and is capable of withstanding 200 lbs. force in any direction.

Employees shall not be permitted to use a workbench as a scaffold platform.

Manually Propelled Mobile Ladder Stands and Scaffolds (Towers)

Working Loads

Work platforms and scaffolds shall be capable of carrying the design load under varying circumstances depending upon the conditions of use. Therefore, all parts and appurtenances necessary for their safe and efficient utilization must be integral parts of the design.

Specific design and construction requirements are not a part of this section because of the variety of materials and design possibilities. However, the design shall be such as to produce a mobile ladder stand or scaffold that will safely sustain the specified loads. The material selected shall be of sufficient strength to meet the test requirements and shall be protected against corrosion or deterioration.

The design working load of ladder stands shall be calculated on the basis of one or more 200-lb. persons together with 50 lbs. of equipment each.

The design load of all scaffolds shall be calculated on the basis of:

- Light—Designed and constructed to carry a working load of 25 lbs. per square foot.
- Medium—Designed and constructed to carry a working load of 50 lbs. per square foot.
- Heavy—Designed and constructed to carry a working load of 75 lbs. per square foot.

All ladder stands and scaffolds shall be capable of supporting at least four times the design working load. The materials used in mobile ladder stands and scaffolds shall be of standard manufacture and conform to standard specifications of strength, dimensions, and weights and shall be selected to safely support the design working load.

Nails, bolts, or other fasteners used in the construction of ladders, scaffolds, and towers shall be of adequate size and in sufficient numbers at each connection to develop the designed strength of the unit. Nails shall be driven full length. (All nails should be immediately withdrawn from dismantled lumber.) All exposed surfaces shall be free from sharp edges, burrs, or other safety hazards.

Work Levels

The maximum work level height shall not exceed four times the minimum or least base dimensions of any mobile ladders or scaffolds. Where the basic mobile unit does not meet this requirement, suitable outrigger frames shall be employed to achieve this least base dimension, or provisions shall be made to guy or brace the unit against tipping. The minimum platform width for any work level shall not be less than 20 in. for mobile scaffolds (towers). Ladder stands shall have a minimum step width of 16 in. The supporting structure for the work level shall be rigidly braced, using adequate cross bracing or diagonal bracing with rigid platforms at each work level. The steps of ladder stands shall be fabricated from slip-resistant treads.

The work level platform of scaffolds (towers) shall be wood, aluminum, or plywood planking, steel or expanded metal, for the full width of the scaffold, except for necessary openings. Work platforms shall be secured in place. All planking shall be 2-in. (nominal) scaffold grade minimum 1,500 f. (stress grade) construction grade lumber or equivalent.

All scaffold work levels 10 ft. or higher above the ground or floor shall have a standard (4-in. nominal) toeboard. All work levels 10 ft. or higher above the ground or floor shall have a guardrail of 2-in. × 4-in. nominal or the equivalent installed no less than 36 in. or more than 42 in. high, with a midrail, when required, of 1-in. × 4-in. nominal lumber or equivalent. A climbing ladder or stairway shall be provided for proper access and egress, and shall be affixed or built into the scaffold and so located that its use will not have a tendency to tip the scaffold. A landing platform shall be provided at intervals not to exceed 30 ft.

Wheels or Casters

Wheels or casters shall be properly designed for strength and dimensions to support four times the design working load. All scaffold casters shall be provided with a positive wheel and/or swivel lock to prevent movement. Ladder stands shall have at least two of the four casters and shall be of the swivel type. Where leveling of the elevated work platform is required, screw jacks or other suitable means for adjusting the height shall be provided in the base section of each mobile unit.

Mobile Tubular Welded Sectional Folding Scaffolds

An integral stairway and work platform shall be incorporated into the structure of each sectional folding stairway scaffold. An integral set of pivoting and hinged folding diagonal and horizontal braces and a detachable work platform shall be incorporated into the structure of each sectional folding ladder scaffold.

Sectional Folding Stairway Scaffolds

Sectional folding stairway scaffolds shall be designed as medium-duty scaffolds except for high clearance. These special base sections shall be designed as light-duty scaffolds. When upper sectional folding stairway scaffolds are used with a special high clearance base, the load capacity of the entire scaffold shall be reduced accordingly. The width of a sectional folding stairway scaffold shall not exceed 4 ft.). The maximum length of a sectional folding stairway scaffold shall not exceed 6 ft.

Sectional Folding Ladder Scaffolds

Sectional folding ladder scaffolds shall be designed as light-duty scaffolds, including special base (open end) sections that are designed for high clearance. For certain special applications, the 6 ft. folding ladder scaffolds, except for special high clearance base sections, shall be designed for use as medium-duty scaffolds. The width of a sectional folding ladder scaffold shall not exceed 4 ft. The maximum length of a sectional folding ladder scaffold shall not exceed 6 ft., 6 in. for a 6 ft.-long unit, 8 ft., 6 in. for an 8 ft.-long unit or 10 ft., 6 in. for a 10 ft.-long unit. The end frames of sectional ladder and stairway scaffolds shall be designed so that the horizontal bearers provide supports for multiple planking levels.

Only the manufacturer of the scaffold or its qualified designated agent shall be permitted to erect or supervise the erection of scaffolds exceeding 50 ft. in height above the base, unless such structure is approved in writing by a licensed professional engineer or erected in accordance with instructions furnished by the manufacturer.

Aerial Lift Trucks

Unless otherwise provided in this section, aerial lifts acquired for use on or after January 22, 1973, shall be designed and constructed in conformance with the applicable requirements of ANSI A92.2-1969, Vehicle Mounted Elevating and Rotating Work Platforms, including the appendix. Aerial lifts acquired before January 22, 1973, may not be used unless they shall have been modified so as to conform with the applicable design and construction requirements of ANSI A92.2-1969.

Aerial lifts include the following types of vehicle-mounted aerial devices used to elevate personnel to job-sites above ground:
- Extensible boom platforms;
- Aerial ladders;
- Articulating boom platforms;
- Vertical towers; and
- A combination of any such devices.

Aerial equipment may be made of metal, wood, fiberglass reinforced plastic (FRP), or other material; may be powered or manually operated; and are deemed to be aerial lifts whether or not they are capable of rotating about a substantially vertical axis.

Aerial lifts may be "field modified" for uses other than those intended by the manufacturer provided the modification has been certified in writing by the manufacturer or by any other equivalent entity, such as a nationally recognized testing laboratory, to be in conformity with all applicable provisions of ANSI A92.2-1969 and this section and to be at least as safe as the equipment was before modification.

Specific requirements

Ladder Trucks And Tower Trucks

Aerial ladders shall be secured in the lower traveling position by the locking device on top of the truck cab, and the manually operated device at the base of the ladder before the truck is moved for highway travel.

Extensible And Articulating Boom Platforms

Lift controls shall be tested each day prior to use to determine that such controls are in safe working condition.

Only authorized persons shall operate an aerial lift.

Belting off to an adjacent pole, structure, or equipment while working from an aerial lift shall not be permitted.

Employees shall always stand firmly on the floor of the basket, and shall not sit or climb on the edge of the basket or use planks, ladders, or other devices for a work position.

A body belt shall be worn and a lanyard attached to the boom or basket when working from an aerial lift.

NOTE. As of January 1, 1998, Subpart M (1926.502(d)) provides that body belts are not acceptable as part of a personal fall arrest system. The use of a body belt in a tethering system or in a restraint system is acceptable and is regulated under 1926.502(e).

Boom and basket load limits specified by the manufacturer shall not be exceeded.

The brakes shall be set and when outriggers are used; they shall be positioned on pads or a solid surface. Wheel chocks shall be installed before using an aerial lift on an incline, provided they can be safely installed.

An aerial lift truck shall not be moved when the boom is elevated in a working position with workers in the basket, except for equipment that is specifically designed for this type of operation in accordance with the provisions of 1926.435(a)(1) and (2).

Articulating boom and extensible boom platforms, primarily designed as personnel carriers, shall have both platform (upper) and lower controls. Upper controls shall be in or beside the platform within easy reach of the operator. Lower controls shall provide for overriding the upper controls. Controls shall be plainly marked as to their function. Lower level controls shall not be operated unless permission has been obtained from the employee in the lift, except in case of emergency.

Climbers shall not be worn while performing work from an aerial lift.

The insulated portion of an aerial lift shall not be altered in any manner that might reduce its insulating value.

Before moving an aerial lift for travel, the boom(s) shall be inspected to see that it is properly cradled and outriggers are in stowed position except as provided in 1926.453(b)(2)(viii).

Electrical Tests

All electrical tests shall conform to the requirements of ANSI A92.2-1969, Section 5. However equivalent DC voltage tests may be used in lieu of the AC voltage specified in A92.2-1969. DC voltage tests that are approved by the equipment manufacturer or equivalent entity shall be considered an equivalent test for the purpose of this paragraph (b)(3).

Bursting Safety Factor

The provisions of ANSI A92.2-1969, Section 4.9, Bursting Safety Factor, shall apply to all critical hydraulic and pneumatic components. Critical components are those in which a failure would result in a free fall or free rotation of the boom. All noncritical components shall have a bursting safety factor of at least 2 to 1.

Welding Standards

All welding shall conform to the following standards as applicable:

- Standard Qualification Procedure, AWS B3.0-41.

- Recommended Practices for Automotive Welding Design, AWS D8.4-61.
- Standard Qualification of Welding Procedures and Welders for Piping and Tubing, AWS D10.9-69.
- Specifications for Welding Highway and Railway Bridges, AWS D2.0-69.

Common Citations Regarding Scaffolds

Falls from scaffolding continue to be a large producer of injuries. In other words, more people have fallen from scaffolds than from any other platform. Some things to look for:

- Guardrails on scaffolds—a complete guardrail with a midrail and toeboard;
- Pins to prevent uplift when workers are on the scaffolds;
- Unsafe access to scaffolds;
- Poor footing for scaffolds;
- Scaffolds that are fully planked;
- There should be a 4:1 ratio of height to width; and
- Wheels on mobile scaffolds must be locked to prevent moving.

No Guardrails on Scaffolds

This is consistently a problem with all types of scaffolds. This is more prevalent with smaller employers because equipment has not been purchased with guardrails. Manufacturers will sell guardrails with all sales or rental of metal scaffolds. Many construction sites have been inspected on a referral basis because an OSHA compliance officer on the street observed this condition in passing.

Defective Wood Planks

This is becoming an increasing citation item as more OSHA compliance officers are now inspecting wood planks for rot, saw marks, and cracks through the whole board.

Unsafe Access to Scaffold

This occurs on sites that often do not have guardrail protection. Instead of providing stairs or a ladder, many employers require the employee to climb the cross brace or scaffold frames. This is a fall hazard in that many frames were not designed as a ladder and the scaffold may tip over.

No Fall Arrest Equipment on Two-Point Suspended Scaffolds

Problems occur on sites where the general contractor does not require subcontractors to provide 100 percent fall protection on the site. Tuck pointers, brick cleaners, and window installers are common operations where this is commonly cited.

Cross Bracing Not Adequate

Most manufacturers of scaffolds will require full cross bracing on all sections. If the standard cross bracing cannot be used, then horizontal braces from the manufacturer must be used. Cross bracing is not acceptable as a guardrail unless the manufacturer of the scaffold has strict written guidelines on their use.

Exhibit 12-3.
Do not let your scaffold crew become complacent.
How many citations can you spot?

General Requirements for Scaffolds

- The footing or anchorage for scaffolds shall be sound, rigid and capable of carrying the maximum intended load without settling or displacement. Unstable objects such as barrels, boxes, loose brick or concrete blocks shall not be used to support scaffolds or planks.
- Scaffolds and their components shall be capable of supporting, without failure, at least four times the maximum intended load.

- Scaffolds shall be maintained in a safe condition and shall not be altered or moved horizontally while they are in use or occupied.
- Damaged or weakened scaffolds shall be immediately repaired and shall not be used until repairs have been completed.
- An access ladder or equivalent safe access shall be provided to gain entry to the working platform.

- Overhead protection shall be provided for personnel on a scaffold who are exposed to overhead hazards.
- Guardrails, midrails and toeboards shall be installed on all open sides and ends of platforms more than 10 ft. above the ground or floor.
January 28, 1994

MEMORANDUM FOR: BYRON R. CHADWICK

Regional Administrator - VIII
FROM: ROGER A. CLARK, Director
Directorate of Compliance Programs
SUBJECT: Morgen Scaffold Access

This is in response to your July 7 memorandum in which you expressed your concerns with the use of Morgen scaffold towers as ladders and the position taken by Michael Best and Friedreich that OSHA's requirement to use conventional ladders resulted in one fatality. I apologize for the delay in responding to your memo.

We agree with your determination that the use of conventional ladders for access to Morgen scaffolds was not the cause of the fatality in California. That accident, we believe, would have been prevented if the California standard equivalent to 29 CFR 1926.451(a)(3) had been followed. That is, had a competent person supervised the moving of the scaffold, then the ladder problem would have been noticed and corrected. Furthermore, since the potential for this problem exists every time the platform is raised, it should have been anticipated and proper measures taken to reset the ladder.

With respect to the use of the Morgen tower itself as a ladder, we agree that there are problems with the rung length, nonuniform spacing of the "rungs," obstructions caused by tower plates, and obstructions caused by the diagonal bracing, all of which are violations of OSHA's minimum standards which are intended to prevent falls from ladders. Recognizing that conventional portable ladders are limited in height and that scaffold stair towers may not line up properly with the working levels of the Morgen scaffold, it may be that tower access is the most feasible way of climbing to the working level. However, because of all the above mentioned deficiencies in the Morgen system and similar problems which might be present in similar scaffold systems, a ladder climbing device or rope grab safety system must be provided in order for Morgen towers and other similar systems to be considered as providing "equivalent safe access."

If you have any questions, please do not hesitate to call Mr. Roy Gurnham of my staff in the Office of Construction and Maritime Compliance Assistance at (202) 219-8136.

Scaffolding

July 7, 1993

MEMORANDUM FOR: ROGER A. CLARK, DIRECTOR
DIRECTORATE OF COMPLIANCE PROGRAMS

FROM: BYRON R. CHADWICK
REGIONAL ADMINISTRATOR – VIII
SUBJECT: Transmittal of Standard Interpretation – Morgen Scaffolding

Over the past year we have had several inquiries from the Morgen Scaffold Company regarding Region VIII and the issue of "equivalent safe access." We informed the Morgen Scaffold Company that we had several concerns that would indicate that their scaffold did not provide for "equivalent safe access"; however, a decision on whether a citation would be warranted or be deemed de minimis could only be made on a case-by-case basis.

The first concern that we had was the nonuniform spacing of their horizontal scaffold members at the locations of the plates used for to join the tower sections. Second, these plates obstruct the horizontal members and block the normal location for foot insertion. Lastly, the towers sides (3) that are used for climbing have one side that is 4 inches wide and the other two sides are 8 inches wide. The 8-inch sides have diagonal cross bracing which disrupts the openings and spacings. Using the 4-inch side is limited to smaller climbers, for instance, a size 13 work boot is approximately 4.5 inches wide and it also has the obstruction of cross bracing. In either instance, none of the sides meet the ANSI requirement of a minimum of 10 in. (ANSI A10.8 1988).

The latest correspondence from Morgen dated June 3, 1993, is attempting to blame OSHA for an employee death when an extension ladder was used for access instead of climbing the scaffold towers. The fatality occurred in the state of California on May 5, 1993. A ladder was secured at the scaffold platform. As the platform was raised, it dragged the ladder up, dislodging the ladder base leaving it hanging in midair. When employees attempted to use the ladder to down climb, the ladder became dislodged and one employee fell to his death.

The concern that the Morgen Scaffold Company now has with the use of ladders is that the platform of the scaffold raises slowly over time dragging the ladder with it. When 30 - 40 ft. up the employees often cannot see if the ladder base is secured. They also stated that to safely use a ladder would require an additional employee on site to adjust the ladder after all scaffold movement. It is interesting to note that the Morgen brochure shows the use of a ladder. The obvious problem with this practice is not in the use of a ladder but in the improper use. If this practice is becoming common because companies do not want to assign anyone to ensure that the ladder is secured prior to use, this type of accident may reoccur. Perhaps a national hazard alert would be in order.

Since the issue of Morgen Scaffolding and "equivalent safe access" is of national concern, I am forwarding this matter to you. Attached are copies of all correspondence that we have had with the Morgen Scaffold Company, the CAL/OSHA case file, and copies of Commission decisions on this issue. It is my understanding that other regions, including some states, have been also contacted by Morgen Scaffold Company, and similar types of correspondence may exist.

OSHA Instruction CPL 2-1.23
January 7, 1997
Directorate of Construction

SUBJECT: Inspection Procedures for Enforcing Subpart L, Scaffolds Used in Construction –
29 CFR 1926.450-454.

A. **Purpose.** This instruction establishes inspection procedures and provides clarification to ensure uniform enforcement of the scaffold standards for construction.

B. **Scope.** This instruction applies OSHA-wide.

C. **References.**
   1. Construction Safety and Health Standards, Subpart L, 29 CFR 1926.450, .451, .452, .453, and .454.
   2. OSHA Instruction CPL 2.103, the Field Inspection Reference Manual (FIRM).
   3. **Federal Register,** Vol. 61, No. 170, August 29, 1996, pages 46026 – 46131, Safety Standards for Scaffolds Used in the Construction Industry.

D. **Cancellation.** OSHA Instruction STD 3-14.1, October 30, 1978, Citation Policy - Specific Scaffold Requirements, is canceled, as are all interpretations issued prior to this date which are in conflict with the standard or the directive.

E. **Action.** Regional Administrators and Area Directors shall ensure that the guidelines in this instruction are followed and that compliance officers are familiar with the contents of the standard.

F. **Federal Program Change.** This instruction describes a Federal program change which affects State programs. Each Regional Administrator shall:
   1. Ensure that this change is promptly forwarded to each State designee using a format consistent with the Plan Change Two-way Memorandum in Appendix P, OSHA Instruction STP 2.22A, State Plans Policies and Procedures Manual (SPM).
   2. Explain to each State designee as requested the technical content of the change and the State designee as requested.
   3. Ensure that the State designees acknowledge receipt of this Federal program change in writing to the Regional Administrator when the State's intention is known, but not later than 70 calendar days after the issuance (10 days for mailing and 60 days for response). This acknowledgment must include a statement indicating whether the State will follow the guidelines in this instruction or develop alternative guidance.
   4. Ensure that State designees submit a plan supplement in accordance with OSHA Instruction STP 2.22A, CH-3, as appropriate, following the established schedule that is agreed upon by the State and Regional Administrator to submit non-field Operations Manual/OSHA Technical Manual Federal program changes.
   a. The State plan supplement should be in the form of a State directive or policy/procedure document, which details procedures for implementing the safety guidelines in the State.
   b. The State's acknowledgment of the Plan Changes Two-Way Memorandum may fulfill the plan supplement requirement if the appropriate documentation is provided.
   5. The Regional Administrator shall review policies, instruction and guidelines issued by the State to determine that this change has been communicated to the State.

G. **Effective Date.** The effective date for the Scaffold Standard is November 29, 1996, except that

1. 1926.453(a)(2) will not take effect until an OMB control number will have been received and displayed for this "collection of information." The National Office will inform the Regional Administrators when clearance is received.

2. 1926.451(e)(9) and 1926.451(g)(2) are delayed until September 2, 1997.

H. **Background.** The Occupational Safety and Health Administration has issued a revised standard for Scaffolds Used in the Construction Industry (Subpart L to 29 CFR 1926).

1. On November 25, 1986, OSHA issued a notice of proposed rulemaking on scaffolds (51 FR 4268). The comment period was extended or reopened several times (most recently closing on March 18, 1994) and OSHA convened an informal public hearing on March 23, 1988 (53 FR 2048, January 26, 1988).

2. Proposed Subpart L was reviewed by the Advisory Committee on Construction Safety and Health (ACCSH). Many of the revisions made to the proposal reflect recommendations from ACCSH and from other interested parties.

3. The final rule resolves many issues raised in earlier attempts to regulate this activity within the construction industry.

   a. This rule establishes one set of requirements which is applicable to all scaffolds used in construction, except that 1926.451 does not apply to aerial lifts (covered by 1926.453).

   b. Where provisions of Subpart L are intended to cover only one type of scaffold, the final rule makes that clear.

4. Any questions involving enforcement, including compliance concerns raised by employers, should be promptly reported to the Office of Construction Standards and Compliance Assistance at (202) 219-7207.

I. Overview of Subpart L – Scaffolds

1. Paragraph (a) of 1926.450 states that this standard does not apply to Crane- or Derrick-Suspended Personnel Platforms.

   a. The standards applicable to aerial lifts are set out **exclusively** in 1926.453. b. Paragraph (b) of 1926.450 provides definitions for particular terms used in Subpart L.

2. Section 1926.451 sets general requirements that apply to all scaffolds, with variations for some specific types of scaffolds or work situations.

   a. The standard distinguishes between supported scaffolds (paragraph 1926.451(c)) and suspension scaffolds (paragraph 1926.451(d)).

   b. This section references criteria in Appendix A that the qualified person may consult when designing scaffolds to meet capacity requirements.

3. Section 1926.452 sets additional requirements for 23 specific types of scaffolds. Section 1926.452 includes references to Appendix A, which provides technical criteria to be used by the employer in designing, installing, and loading these specified types of scaffolds and related guardrail systems.

4. Section 1926.453 covers requirements for aerial lifts, and refers to Non-mandatory Appendix C of the standard, which lists the consensus standards related to aerial lifts.

   a. This standard is solely a renumbering of the previous standards for aerial lifts to bring them under Subpart L and does not change substantively any requirements previously covered under 1926.556 or 1926.451(f).

   b. General requirements for scaffolds contained in 1926.451 do not apply to aerial lifts covered by 1926.453.c. Compliance with the pertinent ANSI A92 standard for any of the newer, specialized types of equipment (as listed in Non-mandatory Appendix C) will provide employee protection equivalent to that provided through the application of ANSI A92.2-1969, which is referenced in 1926.453.

5. Section 1926.454 covers training requirements and refers to Non-mandatory Appendix D for additional information related to training for employees engaged in the erecting and dismantling of scaffolds.

6. The appendices, which are non-mandatory, provide important compliance guidance, examples of acceptable mea-

sures, and specific information for the compliance officer's and the employer's understanding of Subpart L.

J. **Compliance Guidelines for Significant General Issues In Subpart L.** The following information provides guidance that will aid in understanding the overall requirements in the revised standard for scaffolds.

1. **Competent Person.** Although Subpart L provides employers with flexibility in the design of scaffolds and the selection of fall protection, the employer is required to have a competent person who has the training and experience necessary to make determinations as to fall protection, integrity of scaffolds and that the scaffold is maintained and used in a safe manner. NOTE: OSHA recognizes that an employer may have more than one competent person on the worksite to deal with different aspects of scaffolding.

   a. The compliance officer shall determine the identity of the competent person and assess the training and experience qualifications of that person at an early stage of any inspection.

   b. Appendix A of this directive provides guidance for the compliance officer and the employer in evaluating compliance with requirements pertaining to competent person and qualified person responsibilities.

2. Safe Access and Fall Protection During the Erection and Dismantling of Supported Scaffolds. (NOT EFFECTIVE UNTIL SEPTEMBER 2, 1997.) The prior standard did not require that employers provide safe access and fall protection during erection or dismantling operations.

   a. OSHA recognizes that compliance may not be feasible during certain scaffold erection and dismantling operations. However, employers will be required to determine at each stage of erection and dismantling if safe access and fall protection can be provided and, if so, to comply with the pertinent requirements.

   b. The employer has the responsibility to evaluate whether providing access and fall protection for employees is feasible

and safer (i.e., does not create a greater hazard.)

   (1) A competent person who has the knowledge and experience necessary must be used to make the appropriate determination.

   (2) This evaluation shall include a determination whether, alternatively, partial compliance may be feasible and safer under the circumstances present at the site.

   c. Provisions for safe access during erecting and dismantling of supported scaffolds are contained in 1926.451(e)(9).

   (1) Failure of the employer to have the operation initially evaluated by a competent person or failure to use fall protection during erecting and dismantling when it is feasible and safer to do so is a violation of 1926.451(g)(2).

   (2) The CSHO shall document specific worksite factors and compliance considerations encountered by the competent person when evaluating the feasibility of providing safe access or fall protection during these operations for use in developing and updating Appendix B.

   d. The CSHO shall ascertain whether employees engaged in erecting and dismantling scaffolds have been trained in these activities and in the hazards specific to the types of scaffolds involved. Training guidelines are addressed in Appendix D of the standard.

3. **Fall Protection Requirements.** Fall protection is required for employees when working 10' or more above the next lower level.

   a. The employer has the option, in many instances, of providing a guardrail system or of having each employee use a personal fall arrest system. Exceptions are provided in 1926.451(g)(1)(i) through (vi), and are discussed below.

   b. Fall protection must be provided on all supported and suspended scaffolds.

   (1) In most instances on supported scaffolds, this will be a guardrail system.

   (2) However, there may be some unique situations in which a personal fall arrest system may be necessary on a supported system. In such cases the requirements in section 1926.502 for

safe anchorage of the system must be met.

c. For some types of scaffolds (such as single-point or two-point adjustable suspension scaffolds), both a guardrail system and personal fall protection are required.

d. On some types of scaffolds, only personal fall arrest systems are required (catenary, float and needle beam scaffolds, boatswains' chairs, roof bracket scaffolds and ladder jack scaffolds). Therefore, the employer must provide personal fall arrest systems for fall protection on these types of scaffolds.

e. When employees are installing suspension scaffold support systems employers must provide fall protection meeting the requirements of Subpart M - Fall Protection.

f. The fall protection to be provided for employees working on aerial lifts will vary according to the type of aerial lift involved.

(1) Some lifts are intended to be used with guardrails, while others are designed to be used by employees protected by personal fall arrest systems.

(2) The consensus standards listed in Nonmandatory Appendix C indicate what fall protection would be appropriate for particular types of aerial lifts.

K. **Inspection Guidance and Compliance Procedures for Selected Scaffold Requirements.** This section highlights changes from the previous scaffold standard and clarifies certain issues to assist in compliance with Subpart L.

1. **Capacity Requirements — 1926.451(a).**

a. Paragraph (a)(1) states that the scaffold must be capable of supporting four times the maximum **intended** load (not the rated load).

(1) The intended load includes all personnel, equipment, and supply loads.

(2) The intended load will often be less than the rated load but should never exceed the rated load unless such design is approved by an engineer and the manufacturer.

(3) The requirement not to overload the scaffold is found in subparagraph .451(f)(1).

b. Paragraph (a)(2) requires that direct connections and counterweights used to balance adjustable suspension scaffolds be capable of resisting at least four times the tipping moment of the scaffold, including stall loads.

(1) CSHOs are not expected to perform these calculations in the field but shall ensure that the competent person directing the rigging of the suspended scaffold has performed them.

(2) The competent person's duty to supervise and direct the rigging of the scaffold is set out in 1926.451(f)(7).

NOTES: 1. The stall load of the suspension hoist equipment referenced in 1926.451(a)(2), (4) and (5) means the load at which the hoist motor of a power-operated hoist stalls or automatically disconnects its power when overloaded or obstructed.

2. If the stall load (not to exceed 3 times the rated load) is not listed or labeled for the scaffold in use, the CSHO shall determine whether

(a) The qualified person has determined the stall load of the scaffold hoist prior to the lift or

(b) The scaffold is counter-balanced by at least 4 times the rated load of the hoist.

c. Paragraph 1926.451(a)(6) requires that scaffolds be designed by a qualified person. This requirement is discussed in depth in Appendix A of this Instruction. Information to assist the employer in complying with capacity requirements is also contained in Appendix A of the standard.

2. **Scaffold Platform Construction – 1926.451(b)**

a. Paragraph (b)(1) allows exceptions to the full planking of platforms but requires that the platform be planked or decked "as fully as possible." Employers may leave an opening between uprights and planking but the opening may not exceed 9 1/2 inches.

b. Paragraph (b)(2) requires that scaffold platforms be at least 18" wide, but exceptions are provided in paragraphs (b)(2)(i) and (ii).

c. Paragraph 1926.451(b)(11) is meant to ensure that dissimilar metal components that could cause galvanic action are not used together at the job without evaluation by the competent person.

(1) If the competent person believes that significant galvanic action may result from the use of dissimilar metal components and that this galvanic reaction can reduce the strength of any scaffold component to below the requirements of subpart L, corrective action must be taken promptly.

(2) If the competent person cannot make this evaluation, scaffold parts of dissimilar metals cannot be used. The competent person may, of course, rely upon the manufacturer's recommendations.

3. **Criteria for Supported Scaffolds – 1926.451**

a. Paragraph (c)(1) requires vertical and horizontal tie-ins on all supported scaffolds with a height to base ratio of more than four times the minimum base width.

(1) Vertical and horizontal tie-ins are to be installed to keep a scaffold from falling into and away from the structure.

(2) Scaffold tie-ins, as with all other scaffold component designs, must be designed by a **qualified** person to keep the scaffold steady and capable of resisting pushing and pulling forces created by wind and load conditions.

b. Paragraph (c)(2) requires the use of both base plates **and** mud sills or other adequate firm foundations.

(1) Base plates are always required.

(2) However, a concrete slab would be considered a firm foundation, and therefore, mud sills would not be necessary.

c. Paragraph (c)(2)(iv) states that front-end loaders and similar type equipment may not be used to support scaffolds, **unless** specifically designed by the manufacturer for such use. The CSHO may ask the employer to produce the manufacturer's literature demonstrating that the equipment has been designed for this use.

d. Paragraph (c)(2)(v) provides that fork lifts may only be used if the entire platform is attached to the forks. "Attached" does not mean merely placing the platform on the forks. A positive means of attachment, such as bolting, must be present.

e. When these types of equipment are used to support scaffolds, all other requirements of 1926.451 (capacity, construction, access, use and fall protection, etc.) must be met.

NOTE: These types of equipment are not considered aerial lifts unless the employer can demonstrate that they are primarily designed and used to position personnel **and** they meet all other requirements for aerial lifts.

4. **Criteria for Suspension Scaffolds – 1926.451(d)**

a. Paragraph (d)(3)(ii) prohibits the use of flowable material as counterweights, such as sandbags or water buckets, which are easily displaced or may leak. Solid materials, such as **large** blocks of concrete specifically designed for use as counterweights, or **large** ingots of metal (such as lead) are examples of acceptable counterweights.

b. The use of 3/4" inch manila rope or equivalent as a secondary means of anchorage is no longer acceptable. See (d)(3)(vii).

5. **Access – 1926.451(e)**

a. Under paragraph (e)(1) the use of cross bracing as a means of access is prohibited.

b. The revised standard does not specifically prohibit climbing over or through a guardrail.

(1) There is no consensus with regard to climbing over or through guardrails; therefore, OSHA has not adopted a rule prohibiting the practice.

(2) Gates, removable rails or chains across the point of access are preferred.

c. 1926.451(e)(1) and (e)(8) both address direct access.

(1) Paragraph (e)(1) addresses vertical access, and paragraph (e)(8) addresses direct access both vertically and horizontally.

(2) Compliance officers should cite (e)(1) when the direct access is more than 24

inches away vertically and (e)(8) when direct access is more than 14 inches away horizontally.

d. 1926.451(e)(2) is not intended to require the use of ladder climbing devices or cages on scaffolds.

e. 1926.451(e)(5) requires that ramps and walkways 6 feet or more above a lower level shall have guardrail systems which comply with subpart M.

f. See paragraph K.7.b. of this instruction for walkways which are located within the framing of scaffold units.

6. **Use of Scaffolds – 1926.451(f).**

a. Paragraph (f)(7) requires that the employer ensure that a competent person having the required training, knowledge, and experience on the type of scaffold system used, **is at the site** directing and supervising the work during all erecting, dismantling, alteration, and moving of the scaffold.

b. Employees engaged in this activity must also be trained in accordance with 1926.454 and selected by the competent person.

c. Paragraph (f)(15) allows the use of ladders only on "large area scaffolds." Ladders may not be used on other types of scaffold platforms to increase the working height.

d. Paragraph (f)(16) is intended to apply only to wood scaffold planks.

7. **Fall Protection – 1926.451(g)**

a. 1926.451(g)(1)(iv) requires personal fall arrest systems in addition to guardrail systems for employees whenever a self-contained adjustable scaffold is supported only by ropes with no safety catch to support the platform in the event of rope failure. The standard applies whenever the platform is at a work level or is being raised or lowered.

b. Under paragraph (g)(1)(v), walkways which are within a scaffold, such as inside the frame of a fabricated frame scaffold, have to be guarded on at least one side of the walkway, and the guardrail system must be within 9 1/2" of the walkway. (See paragraph K.5.d. above for walkways which are not an integral part of the scaffold.)

c. Paragraph 1926.451(g)(3) permits lanyards attached to personal fall arrest systems to be attached to vertical lifelines, horizontal life lines or scaffold structural members.

(1) This decision is at the discretion of the competent person.

(2) If the lanyard is attached to a supported scaffold structural member, the scaffold must be properly braced and tied-in to the structure before being used as an anchorage point and must meet the requirements of 1926.502(d), which defines the criteria for anchorage points and other components of a personal fall arrest system.

d. Paragraph (g)(4) covers criteria for guardrail systems and components. Appendix A of the standard provides specifications for certain types of scaffolds, to assist in determining whether the guardrails meet the strength requirements of the standard.

e. Paragraph (g)(4)(ii) covers the required minimum and maximum height of the top rails.

(1) Note that the requirements for top rail height of guardrails on supported scaffolds have been changed from 36 to 45 inches to between 38 to 45 inches. However, this new provision applies only to scaffolds manufactured or placed into service after January 1, 2000.

(2) Also, for platforms where personal fall arrest systems are required as the primary type of fall protection, such as for suspended systems, the top rail minimum height remains at 36 inches. As with subpart M, guardrail toprails can exceed 45 inches only if all other pertinent provisions of 1926.502(b) are followed.

f. While the previous standard was silent on the use of cross bracing for guard rails, paragraph (g)(4)(xv) states that cross bracing is acceptable in place of either the top rail or the midrail on a scaffold system, **but not both,** when the crossing point is at the specified height.

8. **Falling Object Protection – 1926.451(h)**

a. Paragraph (h)(1) clarifies that hard hats shall not be the sole means of protecting employees from overhead falling objects.

b. The use or non-use of hard hats by employees shall be documented by compliance officers whenever it could affect the gravity of a violation of this standard, for failure to institute any of the additional protective measures mandated.

9. **Additional Requirements for Specific Types of Scaffolds – 1926.452**

a. Item 2(z) of Appendix A provides guidance regarding the use of tank builder's scaffolds, a type of scaffold which is covered only by the general requirements of 1926.451, and which has no additional specific provisions within 1926.452.

b. Scissors lifts are addressed by 1926.453 - Aerial Lifts, not by 1926.452(w), mobile scaffolds.

10. **Aerial lifts – 1926.453**

a. Paragraph 1926.453(b)(2)(v) requires a body belt and lanyard attached to the boom or basket. As of January 1, 1998, Subpart M (1926.502(d)) provides that body belts will no longer be acceptable as part of a personal fall arrest system.

b. The use of a body belt in a tether system (i.e., to keep the employee from going over the guardrail) is acceptable, however, and is regulated under 1926.502(e).

11. **Training Requirements – 1926.454.**

a. In accordance with paragraph (a), each employee working on a scaffold must be trained regarding the requirements of Subpart L that are associated with the type of work that employee is performing. Specifically, training in associated hazards, methods of protection, and the maximum intended load and load-carrying capacities of the scaffold must be included, as applicable.

b. Training is particularly important for employees engaged in erecting and dismantling operations. Paragraph (b) specifies the training needed for those employees.

(1) Non-mandatory Appendix E of Subpart L provides specific training topics for employees engaged in erecting and dismantling scaffolds.

(2) The CSHO shall interview those employees engaged in erecting and dismantling operations to ascertain whether they have received the necessary training required under 1926.454(b)(1)-(4).

c. The standard does not specify criteria for training employees who have responsibilities as a competent person.

(1) If the compliance officer determines that an employee (or management official) who has been serving in the capacity of a competent person does not have the necessary knowledge to carry out those responsibilities, violations of the requirements addressing specific competent person duties under Sections 451 and 452 of Subpart L would also exist.

(2) Refer to **Appendix A** of this Instruction for additional guidance in assessing the capabilities of the competent person.

d. Section 1926.454 does not require certification, or other documentation, of training. Compliance officers shall evaluate compliance with the training requirements through observation of work practices, inspections of rigging, correct utilization of scaffold equipment, and interviews with employees and management representatives.

e. If training has been conducted but employees do not understand or are not adhering to the requirements of Subpart L, a violation of 454(c), which requires retraining to maintain proficiency, may exist.

APPENDIX A
COMPETENT/QUALIFIED PERSON

Under the scaffold standards, "competent persons" and "qualified persons" have specified responsibilities. This Appendix summarizes the provisions in Subpart L using those terms.

I. Competent Person.

A. **Definition.** "Competent person" is defined at 29 CFR 1926.450(b) as one who is capable of identifying existing and predictable hazards in the surroundings or working conditions which are unsanitary, hazardous, or dangerous to employees, and who has authorization to take prompt corrective measures to eliminate them. 29 CFR 1926.450(b).

1. A competent person must be knowledgeable about the requirements of this standard and have sufficient training or knowledge to identify and correct hazards encountered in scaffold work.

   a. For the purposes of this Subpart, a competent person must have had specific training in and be knowledgeable regarding the structural integrity of scaffolds and the procedures needed to maintain them.

   b. For example, a competent person must be able to evaluate the effects of such potentially damage-causing occurrences as a dropped load or a truck backing into a support leg.

2. By definition, the competent person must have the authority to take prompt corrective measures to abate potentially hazardous work site conditions. The exercise, or lack thereof, of this authority may frequently be the deciding factor in assessing whether a particular individual is in fact a competent person under Subpart L.

B. **Duties of the Competent Person.**

1. 29 CFR 1926.451(b)(10). Only a competent person can permit the modification of scaffold components manufactured by different manufacturers when they are used in conjunction with each other, and must ensure that the resulting scaffold is structurally sound.

2. 29 CFR 1926.451(b)(11). Scaffold components made of dissimilar metals are not to be used together unless a competent person has determined that galvanic action will not reduce the strength of any component to a level below that which is required by 1926.451(a)(1), i.e., capable of supporting, without failure, its own weight and at least four times the maximum intended load applied or transmitted to it.

3. These two preceding provisions reflect that, unless adequate precautions are taken, an unsafe condition could be created by the intermingling of differing scaffold components, or by the occurrence of galvanic action.

   a. If scaffold components of different manufacturers or of different metals are used together, the competent person must carefully evaluate the scaffold to ensure structural soundness and the absence of galvanic action.

   b. OSHA expects a competent person to be able to identify the causes and significance of any deterioration present in scaffold components and take the necessary corrective actions.

   c. With respect to both these issues, the manufacturer's recommendations should be reviewed and may be relied upon by the competent person.

4. 29 CFR 1926.451(d)(3)(i) requires that direct connections on suspension scaffolds be evaluated by a competent person before the scaffold is used to confirm that the surfaces are capable of supporting the loads to be imposed.

   a. OSHA anticipates that compliance with this provision will ensure that roof or floor decks are capable of supporting the loads to be imposed as well as ensuring that those connections are properly designed and made.

   b. The competent person must have the ability to identify any problems with the direct connections and the authority to make any necessary corrections.

5. 29 CFR 1926.451(d)(10) requires the competent person to inspect all ropes used in suspension scaffolds for defects prior to each work shift and after every occurrence which could affect a rope's integrity.

   a. Paragraph (d)(10) goes on to require the replacement of damaged, kinked, or abraded rope, as well as to specify other conditions requiring replacement.

   b. This paragraph adopts the ANSI standard provisions describing damaged and defective rope as representing good industry practice. See ANSI A10.8-1988, Par. 6.7.10.

6. 29 CFR 1926.451(d)(18). A competent person is also required to evaluate multi-point suspension scaffolds to determine whether they need to be tied or otherwise secured to prevent them from swaying.

7. 29 CFR 1926.451(e)(9)(i). For employees erecting or dismantling supported scaffolds, a competent person will have to determine the feasibility and safety of using a "safe means of access," based on, for example, site conditions and the type of scaffold being erected or dismantled.

a. OSHA has determined that, while there may be some situations where providing safe access for scaffold erectors and dismantlers is difficult, employers who carefully evaluate their scaffold operations can provide safe access or, at least minimize employee exposure to hazards.

b. The competent person, therefore, will be expected to determine the appropriate means of access for erectors/dismantlers based on a site-specific analysis of the workplace conditions.

8. 29 CFR 1926.451(f)(3). The competent person is also required to inspect the scaffold and its components for visible defects before each work shift and after any occurrence which could affect the scaffold's structural integrity.

a. However, on very large frame systems, the inspection is only required for areas to be used that work shift by employees.

b. The standard does not require that the competent person document the inspection findings.

9. In addition, 29 CFR 1926.451(g)(4)(xiv) requires that any manila or synthetic rope being used for top rails or midrails be inspected by the competent person as often as necessary (daily and/or prior to use) to ensure that it continues to meet the strength requirements of 29 CFR 1926.451(g).

10. 29 CFR 1926.451(f)(7). A competent person qualified in scaffold erection, moving, dismantling or alteration is required to supervise and direct all scaffold erection, moving, alteration or dismantling activities.

a. Such activities are to be performed only by trained and experienced employees selected by the competent person.

b. The standard makes clear that, for these activities, the competent person must actually be on site and directing the work.

11. 29 CFR 1926.451(g)(2). For each scaffold erection and dismantling operation, the competent person will have to determine the feasibility of providing fall protection.

a. Employers must provide fall protection to scaffold erectors and dismantlers unless there are valid reasons not to.

b. The standard does not require that these reasons be documented.

c. Compliance officers shall evaluate the employer's claims of infeasibility or greater hazard and document on-site observations and interviews with the competent person and other affected workers relating to any such claim.

12. 29 CFR 1926.451(f)(12). During storms or high winds, work on or from scaffolds is prohibited unless a competent person has determined that it is safe and that employees on the scaffold are protected by a personal fall arrest system or wind screens. High winds are any wind conditions that adversely affect the stability of the scaffold or the safety of the employees. Rather than setting a specific wind speed limit, the standard directs the competent person, after analysis of all pertinent information, to ensure that the scaffold is safe under high wind conditions, that protective measures have been instituted, and that work may safely be done from the scaffold.

C. **Compliance Issues for Competent Persons.**

1. A CSHOs determination of the employer's compliance with requirements involving a competent person will involve judgments on complex issues. The compliance officer must evaluate all the factors associated with competent person requirements.

2. The duties of the competent person may be shared among several individuals.

a. However, each must possess the qualifications related to his or her area of responsibility, and each must have the ability and authority to take corrective action.

(1) For example, an individual designated as the competent person for the erecting of the scaffold might not be

the same individual who inspects the scaffold before each work shift.

(2) Also, different individuals may be designated competent persons depending on the type of scaffold used.

b. An individual who has competent person responsibilities for supported scaffolds would not need to have knowledge of requirements related to suspended scaffolds on the work site, if another individual were assigned those responsibilities.

3. The employer may rely on the expertise of persons who are not employees, such as consultants and scaffold systems representatives, to design, erect and dismantle scaffolds.

a. This may be acceptable if that individual actually supervises the work being done and has authority to correct hazards. Additionally, contractors on a multi-employer site may rely on employees of the general contractor or another subcontractor to fulfill competent person responsibilities, if all the qualification criteria are met.

b. The compliance officer would need to determine whether, for the specific site and operation in question, the employer has effectively complied by designating another employer's employee as the competent person.

4. When more than one employer erects and uses a scaffold, the compliance officer will need to determine who the controlling and exposing employers are and document factors related to OSHA's multi-employer citation policy.

a. The compliance officer must exercise professional judgment in these situations and a variety of case-by-case factors will need to be considered.

b. Information contained in the general contractor's and the subcontractors' safety programs and contract requirements, as well as copies of safety meeting minutes, written correspondence between contractors, and employer and employee interviews will be helpful in determining responsibility for violations.

II. **Qualified Person.**

A. **Definition** A "qualified" person means "one who, by possession of a recognized degree, certificate, or professional standing, or by extensive knowledge, training, and experience, has successfully demonstrated his/her ability to solve or resolve problems related to the subject matter, the work, or the project". 29 CFR 1926.450(b).

B. **Duties**

1. Section 29 CFR 1926.451(a)(6) requires that scaffolds be designed by a qualified person. Non-mandatory Appendix A contains examples of criteria to guide an employer in designing scaffold systems. With certain exceptions carried over from the previous rule, the qualified person designing the scaffold need not be an engineer. Those exceptions are found in the following provisions:

a. 1926.451(d)(3)(i). Scaffold connections for masons' adjustable multi-point suspension scaffolds must be designed by an engineer "experienced in such scaffold design."

b. 1926.452(a)(10), (b)(10), (i)(8). Pole scaffolds over 60', tube and coupler scaffolds over 125', and outrigger scaffolds must be designed by a "registered professional engineer" and constructed and loaded in accordance with that design. Appendix A of the standard contains examples of criteria that will enable the employer to comply with the design and loading requirements.

c. 1926.452(c)(6). Fabricated frame scaffolds over 125 feet in height above their base plate must be designed by a "registered professional engineer" and constructed and loaded in accordance with that design. In addition, brackets used to support cantilevered loads on such scaffolds shall be used only to support personnel unless the scaffold has been designed for other loads by a "qualified engineer" and is built to withstand the tipping forces generated by such loads. See 29 CFR 1926.452(c)(5)(iii).

2. Other designs required by a qualified person include the following:

a. 29 CFR 1926.452(o)(2)(i) requires the supporting rope on single-point adjustable suspension scaffolds be kept vertical unless, among other requirements, the rigging has been designed by a qualified person.

b. 29 CFR 1926.452(p)(1) requires that platforms on two-point adjustable suspension scaffolds (swing stages) shall not be more than 36 inches wide unless designed by a "qualified" person to prevent unstable conditions.

NOTE: Paragraph (p)(1) does not apply to two-point adjustable suspension scaffolds used as masons' or stone setters' scaffolds. See 29 CFR 1926.452(q).

c. 29 CFR 1926.454(a) requires the employer to have each employee who performs work while on a scaffold trained by a person qualified in the subject matter to recognize the hazards associated with the type of scaffold being used and to understand the procedures to control or minimize those hazards.

Joseph A. Dear Assistant Secretary

DISTRIBUTION: National, Regional, and Area Offices All Compliance Officers State Designees NIOSH Regional Program Directors 7(C)(1) Project Managers

Scaffolding Quiz
(See appendix for answers.)

1. During assembly or disassembly of a scaffold, what fall protection standard applies?
   a. Scaffold section rules
   b. Fall protection rules
   c. Stairways and ladders rules
   d. General Duty Clause

2. Assembly or disassembly of a scaffold must be supervised by:
   a. A qualified supervisor
   b. An authorized supervisor
   c. A competent supervisor
   d. A professionally licensed engineer

3. When the scaffold is correctly built and used, fall protection is provided by:
   a. Training of the users on the scaffold
   b. Personal fall arrest systems on the users
   c. The competent person conducting periodic work site inspections
   d. The guardrail and midrail system of the scaffold

4. Mobile scaffolds may be moved while occupied when:
   a. The competent person says it is OK to do so
   b. All abutting ends of the scaffold are tied with No. 200 wire
   c. Flooring planks are secured
   d. Never

5. Planking on scaffolds must be of scaffold grade lumber and:
   a. Complete with no openings of more than 6 in.
   b. Complete with no openings at all
   c. Should provide a safe working platform as determined by the competent person
   d. Should be secured to the scaffold at all times with No. 200 wire

6. The base of scaffolds should rest on:
   a. The steel leg of the scaffold placed on a cement block
   b. The steel leg of the scaffold placed on the 4 in. metal base
   c. The steel leg of the scaffold placed on the 4 in. metal base that rests on a mudsill
   d. A sound and secure surface, such as dry soil

2006 Subpart L 1926.450-454
Scaffolds

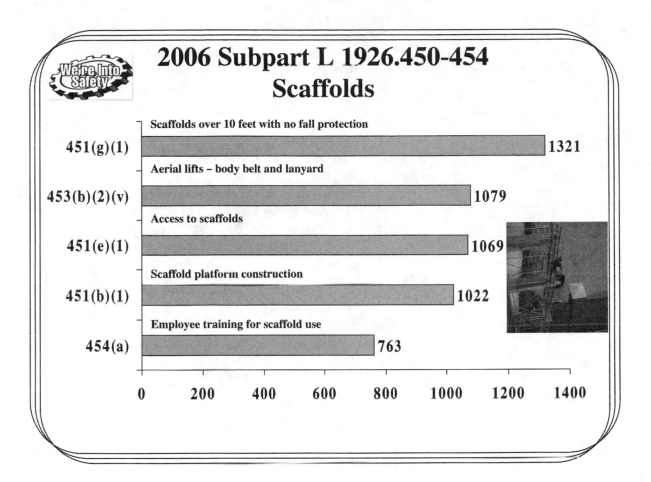

Scaffolds over 10 feet with no fall protection

451(g)(1) 1321

Aerial lifts – body belt and lanyard

453(b)(2)(v) 1079

Access to scaffolds

451(e)(1) 1069

Scaffold platform construction

451(b)(1) 1022

Employee training for scaffold use

454(a) 763

0   200   400   600   800   1000   1200   1400

STEEL ERECTION

Steel Erection – Subpart R

Iron workers create the skyscrapers and metal buildings that house our centers of commerce. Structures where steel erection occurs include single and multi-story buildings, systems-engineered metal buildings, lift slab/tilt-up structures, auditoriums, malls, bridges, even amusement park structures and rides are examples of steel erection. Every year about 35 construction iron workers are killed and over two thousand are injured.

This industry is unique and has special considerations that must be met. The basic fall protection rules of "tie off at six feet" may create a more hazardous situation for these workers. Imagine what could happen if a workers fall protection lanyard was snagged by an iron girder that was being lifted into position. As a result of these concerns the Steel Erection Negotiated Rule-making Advisory Committee (SENRAC) was formed in 1994. This committed met over an eighteen month period and developed a standard that has innovative provisions that will save lives and reduce injuries in the steel erection industry.

The standard addresses hazards that have been identified as the major causes of injuries and fatalities in the steel erection industry.

A portion of the regulation with a delayed effective date requires slip resistance of skeletal structural steel to be determined. Section 1926.754 (c)(3) prohibits workers from walking on any coated steel member unless the coating has been certified or documented to have a slip resistance of .50 when measured with an English XL tribometer. These results must be available on site and to the steel erector. This section 1926.754(c)(3) will not take effect until July 18, 2006.

As in any regulatory situation the a priority is to determine which standard applies. Some activities such as work on electrical transmission, communication towers or tanks is excluded from this standard.

The flowchart shown here provides guidance as to whether the construction activity is covered by Subpart R (Steel Erection) or Subpart M (Fall Protection) or some other standard.

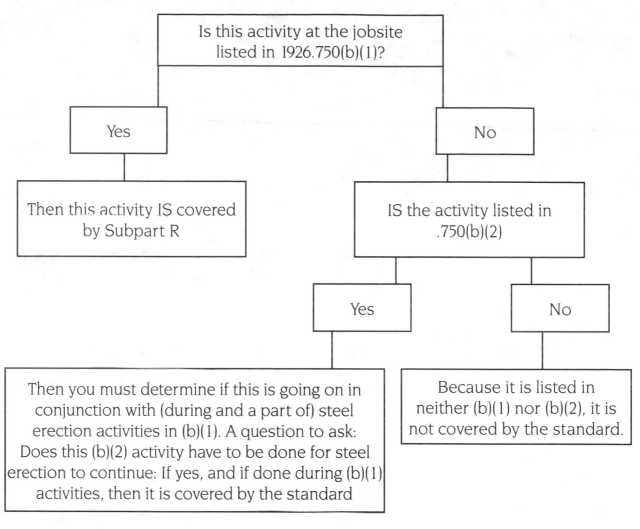

Exhibit 13-1.
Determining which standard applies.

Covered activities listed at 1926.750(b)(1) include such primary activities as:

- Hoisting;
- Laying out;
- Placing;
- Connecting;
- Welding;
- Burning;
- Guying;
- Bracing;
- Bolting;
- Plumbing and decking;
- Curtain walls;
- Window walls;
- Siding systems;
- Miscellaneous metals, ornamental iron and similar materials; and
- Moving point to point while performing these activities.

Covered activities listed at 1926.750(b)(2) include ancillary activities that may be covered when they occur during and are part of steel erection activities. Such activities include:

- Rigging;
- Hoisting;
- Connecting;
- Guying;
- Bracing;
- Welding;
- Bolting;
- Grinding; and
- All related activities for construction, alteration, and/or repair.

Concepts Addressed by the Standard

Site Layout and Construction Sequence

Requires certification of proper curing of concrete in footings, piers, etc. for steel columns.

Requires controlling contractor to provide erector with a safe site layout including pre-planning routes for hoisting loads.

Site-Specific Erection Plan

Requires pre-planning of key erection elements, including coordination with controlling contractor before erection begins, in certain circumstances.

Hoisting and Rigging

Provides additional crane safety for steel erection.

Minimizes employee exposure to overhead loads through pre-planning and work practice requirements.

Prescribes proper procedure for multiple lifts ("christmas-treeing" or "suitcasing").

Exhibit 13-2.
There are specific requirements to follow when "Christmas-treeing" a lift.

Structural Steel Assembly

Provides safer walking/working surfaces by eliminating tripping hazards and minimizes slips through new slip resistance requirements.

Provides specific work practices regarding safely landing deck bundles and promoting

the prompt protection from fall hazards in interior openings.

Exhibit 13-3.
Tribometer measuring friction coefficient.

Exhibit 13-4.
Tribometer.

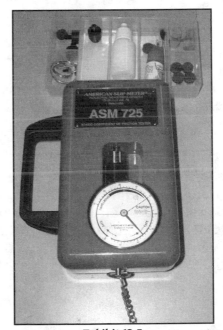

Exhibit 13-5.
Tribometers measure the coefficient of friction of painted surfaces.

Column Anchorage

Requires 4 anchor bolts per column along with other column stability requirements.

Requires procedures for adequacy of anchor bolts that have been modified in the field

Beams and Columns

Eliminates extremely dangerous collapse hazards associated with making double connections at columns.

Open Web Steel Joists

Requirements minimizing collapse of lightweight steel joists by addressing need for erection bridging and method of attachment.

Requirements for bridging terminus anchors with illustrations and drawings in a non-mandatory appendix (provided by SJI).

New requirements to minimize collapse in placing loads on steel joists.

Systems-Engineered Metal Buildings

Requirements to minimize collapse in the erection of these specialized structures which account for a major portion of steel erection in this country.

Falling Object Protection

Performance provisions that address hazards of falling objects in steel erection.

Fall Protection

Controlled decking zone (CDZ) provisions to prevent decking fatalities.

Deckers in a CDZ and connectors must be protected at heights greater than two stories

or 30 feet. Connectors between 15 and 30 feet must wear fall arrest or restraint equipment and be able to be tied off or be provided another means of fall protection.

Requires fall protection for all others engaged in steel erection at heights greater than 15 feet.

Exhibit 13-6.
Fall arrest or restraint equipment is required
for connectors between 15 ft. and 30 ft.

Training

Requires qualified person to train exposed workers in fall protection.

Requires qualified person to train exposed workers engaged in special, high risk activities

Inspection Policy and Procedures

Compliance Directive on the Inspection policy and procedures for OSHA's steel erection standards for construction based on 29CFR1926, dated March 22, 2002.

BACKGROUND

Purpose. This instruction describes OSHA's inspection policy and procedures and provides clarification to ensure uniform enforcement by field enforcement personnel of the steel erection standards for construction.

Scope. This instruction applies OSHA-wide.

Cancellation. All interpretations (including letters of interpretation and memoranda) regarding the previous version of Subpart R issued prior to January 18, 2001 are cancelled.

Significant Changes. The new standard's provisions that are significantly different from the previous steel erection standard include:

Site layout and construction sequence.

Requires notification of proper curing of concrete in footings, piers, etc. for steel columns.

Requires controlling contractor to provide erector with a safe site layout.

Site-specific erection plan.

Requires pre-planning of key erection elements, including coordination with controlling contractor before erection begins, in certain circumstances.

Hoisting and rigging.

Provides additional crane safety for steel erection.

Minimizes employee exposure to overhead loads through pre-planning and work practice requirements.

Prescribes proper procedure for multiple lifts (Christmas-treeing).

Structural steel assembly.
Provides safer walking/working surfaces by eliminating tripping hazards and minimizing slips through new slip resistance requirements (effective July 18, 2006).

Provides specific work practices regarding safely landing deck bundles and protecting against fall hazards from interior openings.

Column anchorage.
Requires 4 anchor bolts per column along with other column stability requirements.

Requires procedures to ensure adequacy of anchor bolts that have been modified in the field.

Beams and columns.
Eliminates collapse hazards associated with making double connections at columns.

Open web steel joists.
Erection bridging and attachment requirements to minimize risk of collapse of lightweight steel joists.

Requirements for bridging terminus anchors, with illustrations and drawings in a non-mandatory appendix.

Requirements addressing how to place loads on steel joists to minimize risk of collapse.

Systems-engineered metal buildings.
Requirements to minimize collapse in the erection of these specialized structures.

Falling object protection.
Performance provisions that address hazards of falling objects in steel erection.

Fall protection.
Deckers in a Controlled Decking Zone (CDZ) and connectors must be protected at heights greater than two stories or 30 feet.

Connectors between 15 feet and two stories or 30 feet must wear fall arrest or restraint equipment and be able to be tied off or be pro-vided another means of fall protection. Deckers working between 15 feet and two stories or 30 feet may be protected by a CDZ.

Requires fall protection for all others engaged in steel erection at heights greater than 15 feet.

Training.
Requires qualified person to train exposed workers in fall protection.

Requires qualified person to train exposed workers engaged in special, high risk activities.

References.
Construction Safety and Health Standards, Subpart R, 29 CFR 1926.750-761 and Subpart M, 1926.502.

Federal Register, Vol. 66, No. 12, January 18, 2001, pages 5196-5280, Final Rule; Safety Standards for Steel Erection.

Federal Register, Vol. 66, No. 137, July 17, 2001, pages 37137-37139, Final Rule; Delay of Effective Date.

OSHA Instruction CPL 2.103, Field Inspection Reference Manual (FIRM)

Occupational Safety and Health Act of 1970, Section 5(a)(1).

Application. This instruction applies to construction, alteration and/or repair involving steel erection activities.

Action Information.
Responsible Office. Directorate of Construction (DOC)

Action Offices. Regional Offices, Area Offices, State Plan States

Information Offices. Information copies of this Instruction are provided to OSHA Directorate heads and the Solicitor of Labor (SOL)

Action. Regional Administrators and Area Directors shall ensure that compliance officers are familiar with the contents of this instruction and that the enforcement guidelines are followed. This instruction will be re-evaluated after one year.

Federal Program Change. This instruction describes a Federal program change for which

State adoption is not required. States were notified on July 18, 2001 of the requirement to adopt a standard equivalent to the Federal standard for steel erection by January 18, 2002.

NOTE: In order to effectively enforce safety and health standards, guidance to compliance staff is necessary. Although adoption of this instruction is not required, States are expected to have standards, enforcement policies and procedures which are at least as effective as those of Federal OSHA.

Phase-in of certain requirements.

Component requirements. Component requirements are provisions that address the safety of certain structural members. These are provisions that: prohibit shear connectors on members before they are erected (§1926.754(c)(1)(i)); require all columns to be anchored by a minimum of 4 anchor bolts, which must meet specified strength requirements (§1926.755(a)) (there is a comparable requirement for systems-engineered metal buildings, §1926.758(b)); set requirements for double connections (§1926.756(c)(1)) (there is a comparable requirement for systems-engineered metal buildings §1926.758(e)); require column splices to be at a specified height and meet a strength requirement (§1926.756(d)); require perimeter columns to have holes or other devices for perimeter safety cables (§1926.756(e)); in some instances require a vertical stabilizer plate to stabilize steel joists (§1926.757(a)(1)(i)); require certain joists to be strong enough to allow one employee to release the hoisting cable without the need for erection bridging (§1926.757(a)(3)), and require certain joists to be fabricated to allow for field bolting during erection (§1926.757(a)(8)(i)).

For building construction, the component requirements of the final rule will not be applied: (1) where the building permit was obtained prior to January 18, 2001, or (2) where steel erection began on or before September 16, 2001 (see volume 66 of the Federal Register, page 37137-37139).

For bridge construction, the component requirements of the final rule will not be applied where: (1) the bridge project has a contract date before January 18, 2001; or (2) steel erection began on or before September 16, 2001.

Column joist requirements in §1926.757(a)(3).

Until July 18, 2003, for all joists at or near columns that span 60 feet or less, employers will be considered to be in compliance with §1926.757(a)(3) if they erect these joists either by: (1) installing bridging or otherwise stabilizing the joist prior to releasing the hoisting cable, or (2) releasing the cable without having a worker on the joists. This will allow the joist industry the necessary time to develop joists that will meet the requirement.

General Schedule Inspection Delay.

The Agency will not conduct general schedule inspections of steel erection until March 18, 2002.

STANDARD OVERVIEW

This section is a quick overview of the subjects addressed in the new standard. References to sections of the standard that pertain to these subjects are included.

§1926.750 Scope of coverage for Subpart R, Steel Erection, Final Rule (§1926.750-761 and Appendices A-H).

Defines what activities are always covered by Subpart R [§.750(b)(1)]

Provides examples of job activities that are covered only when they occur during and as a part of steel erection [§.750(b)(2)]

Lists specific activities that are not covered [§.750(a)]

Defines the duties of the controlling contractor as including, but not limited to, the duties specified in §§1926.752(a) and (c), 1926.755(b)(2), 1926.759(b), and 1926.760(e). [§.750(c)]

§1926.751 Definitions.

Key terms used throughout the standard are defined in this section.

§1926.752 Site layout and construction sequence.

Prior to commencement of steel erection:

Controlling contractor must ensure that the steel erector is provided with written notification that concrete has attained sufficient strength for steel erection activities [§.752(a)(1)]

Note: The steel erector is prohibited from erecting steel until it receives written notification that the concrete has cured enough to support steel erection [§.752(b)]

Controlling contractor must ensure that the steel erector is provided with written notification of any repairs, replacements and modifications to anchor bolts.[§.752(a)(2)] — *requirements are also found in #167; .755(b)*

Controlling contractor must ensure that the worksite has adequate access and storage areas [§.752(c)]

Hoisting operations must be pre-planned to reduce employee exposures to overhead loads [§.752(d)]

Allows **Site-specific erection plans** as substitute for certain requirements **(Appendix A contains sample plans)** [§.752(e)].

Safety latches on hooks activated [§.753(c)(5)]

Setting joists 60'+ at/near columns in tandem [§.757(a)(4)]

Landing decking on steel joists [§.757(e)(4)]

§1926.753 Hoisting and rigging.

Crane safety: All provisions of §1926.550 apply to hoisting and rigging with the exception of §1926.550(g)(2). In addition, §1926.753(c) through (e) contain additional hoisting and rigging requirements. [§.753]

Pre-shift inspection requirements

Pre-shift inspection must be done by a competent person [§.753(c)]

Qualified rigger (rigger who is also a qualified person) must inspect the rigging prior to each shift. [§.753(c)(2)]

Responsibilities during crane operations

Safety latches on hooks may not be deactivated unless a qualified rigger determines it is safer to place purlins and joists without them, or equivalent protection is provided in a site specific erection plan [§.753(c)(5)]

The standard allows employees engaged in initial steel erection or hooking/unhooking to work under loads in some specific instances. When that occurs, the load must be rigged by a qualified rigger [§.753(d)]

Operators are responsible for operations under their control and have the authority to stop and refuse to handle loads until safety has been assured [§.753(c)(2)(iv)]

Rules for crane operations

Prohibits the use of cranes to hoist personnel unless all provisions of §1926.550 are met except §1926.550(g)(2) [§.753(c)(4)]

When employees work under loads (allowed in specified instances), requirements in this section must be followed [§.753(d)]

Multiple lift rigging ("Christmas Treeing") is permitted as long as the requirements in this section are met [§.753(e)]

§1926.754 Structural steel assembly and stability.

Stability requirements

Structural stability must be maintained at all times during the erection process [§.754(a)]. This section contains a number of specific requirements for stability (Note: Requirement for four anchor bolts found in §1926.755(a)(1))

Additional requirements for multi-story structures [§.754(b)]

Requirements applicable when plumbing up [§.754(d)]

Decking requirements

Requirements for hoisting, landing, and placing metal decking [§.754(e)(1)]

Requirements for installing metal decking at roof and floor holes/openings [§.754(e)(2)]

Other requirements

Requirements for skeletal steel walking surfaces [§.754(c)] (NOTE: These do not go into effect until July 18, 2006).

§1926.755 Column anchorage.

General requirements for stability

Minimum of 4 anchor bolts required on columns [§.755(a)(1)]

Requirement to withstand 300 pound load [§.755(a)(2)]

All columns must be evaluated by competent person [§.755(a)(4)]

Repair, replacement, or field modification of anchor rods/bolts

Approval required by the project structural engineer [§.755(b)(1)]

Written notification to steel erector [§.755(b)(2)]

§1926.756 Beams and columns.

This section of the standard focuses on increasing safety for employees involved in connecting solid web beams and columns.

Requires that solid web structural members remain attached to the hoisting line until members are secured with at least two bolts per connection drawn up wrench tight [§.756(a)(1)]

Competent person shall determine if more than two bolts are necessary to ensure the stability of cantilevered members [§.756(a)(2)]

Solid web structural members used as diagonal bracing shall be secured by at least one bolt per connection drawn up wrench tight [§.756(b)]

Requires that one wrench-tight bolt or a seat (or seat equivalent) secure the first member and column throughout the entire double connection process [§.756(c)]

Requires column splices to be designed to resist a minimum eccentric gravity load of 300 pounds (136.3 kg) [§.756(d)]

Sets requirements for the erection of perimeter columns [§.756(e)]

§1926.757 Open web steel joists.

This section focuses on increasing safety for employees involved in connecting open web steel joists. (Some requirements may be modified through a site-specific erection plan [§§.757(a)(4) and .757(e)(4)])

Requirements for stabilizing steel joists and girders before releasing hoisting cables [§.757(a)]

Requirements for attaching steel joists and steel joist girders (includes requirements for "K," "LH," and "DLH" series steel joists) [§.757(b)]

Requirements for the erection of steel joists (short span and long span) [§.757(c)]

Requirements for the erection of erection bridging (short span and long span) [§.757(d)]

Requirements for landing and placing loads on joists [§.757(e)]

§1926.758 Systems-engineered metal buildings.

All the requirements of the standard apply to the erection of systems-engineered metal buildings except §1926.755 (column anchorage) and §1926.757 (open web steel joist). In addition:

All columns are to have a minimum of four anchor rods/bolts [§.758(b)]

The rigid frames must have 50$ of their bolts or the number specified by manufacturer (whichever is greater) installed and tightened before the hoisting equipment is released [§.758(c)]

Construction loads prohibited unless the framework is adequately secured [§.758(d)]

Requirements for girt and eave-to-strut connections [§.758(e)]

Steel joists must be secured before releasing hoisting cables, allowing employees on the joist, or placing construction loads on the joists. [§.758(f)]

Purlins and girts are not to be used as anchorages for fall arrest systems unless written approval is obtained from a qualified person [§.758(g)]

Only after permanent bridging has been installed and fall protection provided can purlins be used as a walking/working surface when installing safety systems [§.758(h)]

Limitations on placing construction loads on joists [§.758(i)]

§1926.759 Falling object protection

All materials, equipment, and tools that are not being used must be secured against accidental displacement [§.759(a)]

The controlling contractor must bar other construction processes below steel erection unless overhead protection is provided for the employees working below [§.759(b)]

§1926.760 Fall protection

All employees must be protected at 15 feet, except for deckers in controlled decking zones and connectors [§.760(a)]

Exception for connectors — protected at 30 feet or two stories, whichever is less [§.760(b)]

Controlled decking zone requirements [§.760(c)]

Exception for deckers in controlled decking zones - protected at 30 feet or two stories above lower deck, whichever is less [§.760(c)(1)]

Criteria for fall protection [§.760(d)]

Responsibility of controlling contractors to choose whether to accept responsibility for fall protection equipment [§.760(e)]

§1926.761 Training.

Requirements found in this section supplement those found in §1926.21

Training conducted by qualified person(s) [§.761(a)]

Requirements that must be included in training [§.761(b)]

Special training programs required for multiple lift rigging, connectors, and controlled decking zones [§.761(c)(1) through (3)(ii)]

COMPLIANCE OFFICER GUIDE AND INSPECTION TIPS

INTRODUCTION.

This section is designed to assist compliance officers in the practical aspects of conducting enforcement inspections under the new Steel Erection rule. The suggestions below should be considered helpful hints.

The new steel erection rule addresses a wide range of issues related to steel erection safety. The new standard not only addresses fall protection for iron workers, but places a heavy emphasis on maintaining the structural integrity of the building during the erection process.

NOTE On Effective Date: See Steel Erection Delay Notice (Federal Register #66 pages 37137-37139) to determine if component requirements of the new standard are in effect for a particular project. A number of provisions in the final rule address the safety of certain structural components. These provisions ("component requirements") contain requirements for these components to help ensure that the structure can be erected safely. There are provisions that: prohibit shear connectors on members before they are erected (§1926.754(c)(1)(i)); require all columns to be anchored by a minimum of 4 anchor bolts, which must meet specified strength requirements (§1926.755(a)) (there is a comparable requirement for systems-engineered metal buildings, §1926.758(b)); set requirements for double connections (§1926.756(c)(1)) (there is a comparable requirement for systems-engineered metal buildings §1926.758(e)); require column splices to be at a specified height and meet a strength requirement (§1926.756(d)); require perimeter columns to have holes or other devices for perimeter safety cables (§1926.756(e)); in some instances require a vertical stabilizer plate to stabilize steel joists (§1926.757(a)(1)(i)); require certain joists to be strong enough to allow one employee to release the hoisting cable without the need for

erection bridging (§1926.757(a)(3)), and require certain joists to be fabricated to allow for field bolting during erection (§1926.757(a)(8)(i)).

For building construction, the component requirements of the final rule will not be applied: (1) where the building permit was obtained prior to January 18, 2001, or (2) where steel erection began on or before September 16, 2001 (see volume 66 of the Federal Register, page 37137-37139).

For bridge construction, the component requirements of the final rule will not be applied where: (1) the bridge project has a contract date before January 18, 2001; or (2) steel erection began on or before September 16, 2001.

The Agency will not conduct general schedule inspections of steel erection until March 18, 2002.

OPENING CONFERENCE.

Consider obtaining the information outlined below at the opening conference and during the initial observations of the steel erection site. Note that a number of the tips suggest asking for various documents. This does not mean that those documents are required by the standard. **While it is advisable to obtain the documents mentioned below, the only documents an employer is required to have are those specified in Subpart R or other standards.**

During the opening conference with the controlling contractor, consider doing the following:

Obtain a copy of the blueprints and consult with someone knowledgeable in blueprint reading (engineer). Note the name of the structural engineer of record from the blueprints.

Find out when the steel erection began and on what date they obtained the permits for the job. (This information will only be important during the first few months after the standard becomes effective.)

Ask for a copy of the written notification to the steel erector that the concrete in the footings, piers and walls and the mortar in the masonry piers and walls has attained the required strength [.752(a)(1)]. You will also want to find out when the concrete was poured, how long after the pour they waited before allowing steel erection to begin, and what compressive strength of concrete was required.

Ask if there have been any changes to anchor bolts. Ask for a copy of the written notifications of repairs/replacements/modifications.

Determine if, prior to the erection of columns, they provided written notification to the steel erector if any repairs, replacements and modifications to the anchor bolts were conducted. [§§.752(a)(2) and .755(b)]. Were these repairs, replacements and modifications performed with approval of the project structural engineer of record? If so, obtain a copy.

Was the fall protection provided by the steel erector left in the area where steel erection activity has been completed for use by other trades?

If yes, ask the following: Did you or your authorized representative direct the steel erector to leave the fall protection in place? Have you or your authorized representative inspected and accepted control and responsibility of the fall protection prior to authorizing persons other than steel erectors to work in the area? (the answer to both of these questions must be yes to be in compliance with §1926.760(e))

If no, the controlling contractor is not required to take any further action with regard to this section.

During the opening conference with the steel erector, consider doing the following:

- Determine if they are using open web joists (also known as bar joists).
- Determine the current stage of the erection process.
- Ask for a copy of the lift procedure (if kept).
- Determine who is the competent person and qualified rigger.

- Determine if they are using a site specific steel erection plan (a plan is only required in some circumstances. See Chapter 2, Section I, Paragraph C).

STANDARD SECTIONS.

The following is a section-by-section description of observations the CSHO should make and questions the CSHO should ask while performing a steel erection inspection.

SCOPE - §1926.750.

Subpart R does **NOT** cover - precast concrete, electrical transmission towers, communication and broadcast towers, or tanks. NOTE on tanks: a tank is defined as a container for holding gases, liquids, or solids. Subpart R **does** apply to the construction of the steel structure that supports a tank. Construction of the tank would be covered under Subpart E - 1926.105.

The CSHO must initially determine if the activity being inspected is covered by Subpart R. The first question to ask: Is this activity listed in §1926.750(b)(1)? If so, then it is covered by the standard.

If the activity is listed only in §1926.750(b)(2), then you must determine if it is going on in conjunction with ("during and [is] a part of") steel erection activities listed in §1926.750(b)(1). A question also to ask: Does this (b)(2) activity have to be done for the steel erection to continue? The following flow chart may help:

NOTE: *Paragraph .750(b)(2) lists a number of activities that are covered by subpart R when they occur during and are a part of the steel erection activities described in paragraph (b)(1). Paragraph (b)(2) explicitly states that coverage depends on whether an activity occurs during and is a part of steel erection. For example, there are standing seam metal roofing systems that incorporate a layer of insulation under the metal roof. In the installation process, a row of insulation is installed, which is then covered by a row of metal roofing. Once that row of roofing is attached, the process is repeated, row by row, until the roof is completed. The installation of the row of insulation is a part of the installation of the metal roofing (which is steel erection), and so the installation of the insulation is covered by Subpart R.*

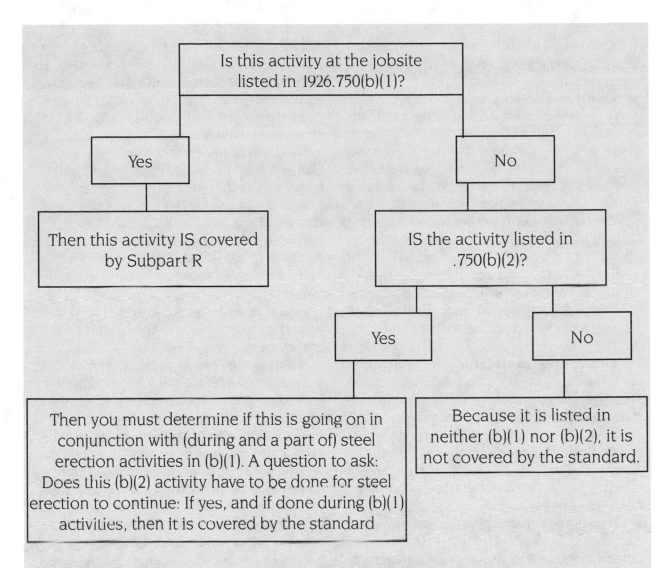

Is this activity at the jobsite listed in 1926.750(b)(1)?

Yes → Then this activity IS covered by Subpart R

No → IS the activity listed in .750(b)(2)?

Yes → Then you must determine if this is going on in conjunction with (during and a part of) steel erection activities in (b)(1). A question to ask: Does this (b)(2) activity have to be done for steel erection to continue: If yes, and if done during (b)(1) activities, then it is covered by the standard

No → Because it is listed in neither (b)(1) nor (b)(2), it is not covered by the standard.

DEFINITIONS - §1926.751.

The following definitions, which are in the standard, should be helpful when conducting the walk around inspection (see photos in Chapter 5):

Anchored bridging means that the steel joist bridging is connected to a bridging terminus point.

Bolted diagonal bridging means diagonal bridging that is bolted to a steel joist or joists.

Bridging clip means a device that is attached to the steel joist to allow the bolting of the bridging to the steel joist.

Bridging terminus point means a wall, a beam, tandem joists (with all bridging installed and a horizontal truss in the plane of the top chord) or other element at an end or intermediate point(s) of a line of bridging that provides an anchor point for the steel joist bridging.

Choker means a wire rope or synthetic fiber rigging assembly that is used to attach a load to a hoisting device.

Cold forming means the process of using press brakes, rolls, or other methods to shape steel into desired cross sections at room temperature.

Column means a load-carrying vertical member that is part of the primary skeletal framing system. Columns do not include posts.

Competent person (also defined in §1926.32) means one who is capable of identifying existing and predictable hazards in the surroundings or working conditions which are unsanitary, hazardous, or dangerous to employees, and who has authorization to take prompt corrective measures to eliminate them.

Connector means an employee who, working with hoisting equipment, is placing and connecting structural members and/or components.

Constructibility means the ability to erect structural steel members in accordance with Subpart R without having to alter the overall structural design.

Construction load (for joist erection) means any load other than the weight of the employee(s), the joists and the bridging bundle.

Controlled decking zone (CDZ) means an area in which certain work (for example, initial installation and placement of metal decking) may take place without the use of guardrail systems, personal fall arrest systems, fall restraint systems, or safety net systems and where access to the zone is controlled.

Controlled load lowering means lowering a load by means of a mechanical hoist drum device that allows a hoisted load to be lowered with maximum control using the gear train or hydraulic components of the hoist mechanism. Controlled load lowering requires the use of the hoist drive motor, rather than the load hoist brake, to lower the load.

Controlling contractor means a prime contractor, general contractor, construction manager or any other legal entity which has the overall responsibility for the construction of the project – its planning, quality and completion.

Critical lift means a lift that (1) exceeds 75 percent of the rated capacity of the crane or derrick, or (2) requires the use of more than one crane or derrick.

Decking hole means a gap or void more than 2 inches (5.1 cm) in its least dimension and less than 12 inches (30.5 cm) in its greatest dimension in a floor, roof or other walking/working surface. Pre-engineered holes in cellular decking (for wires, cables, etc.) are not included in this definition.

Derrick floor means an elevated floor of a building or structure that has been designated to receive hoisted pieces of steel prior to final placement.

Double connection means an attachment method where the connection point is intended for two pieces of steel which share common bolts on either side of a central piece.

Double connection seat means a structural attachment that, during the installation of a double connection, supports the first member while the second member is connected.

Erection bridging means the bolted diagonal bridging that is required to be installed prior to releasing the hoisting cables from the steel joists.

Fall restraint system means a fall protection system that prevents the user from falling any distance. The system is comprised of either a body belt or body harness, along with an anchorage, connectors and other necessary equipment. The other components typically include a lanyard, and may also include a lifeline and other devices.

Final interior perimeter means the perimeter of a large permanent open space within a building such as an atrium or courtyard. This does not include openings for stairways, elevator shafts, etc.

Girt (in systems-engineered metal buildings) means a "Z" or "C" shaped member formed from sheet steel spanning between primary framing and supporting wall material.

Headache ball means a weighted hook that is used to attach loads to the hoist load line of the crane.

Hoisting equipment means commercially manufactured lifting equipment designed to lift and position a load of known weight to a location at some known elevation and horizontal distance from the equipment's center of rotation. "Hoisting equipment" includes but is not limited to cranes, derricks, tower cranes, barge-mounted derricks or cranes, gin poles and gantry hoist systems. A "come-a-long" (a mechanical device, usually consisting of a chain or cable attached at each end, that is used to facilitate movement of materials through leverage) is not considered "hoisting equipment."

Leading edge means the unprotected side and edge of a floor, roof, or formwork for a floor or other walking/working surface (such as deck) which changes location as additional floor, roof, decking or formwork sections are placed, formed or constructed.

Metal decking means a commercially manufactured, structural grade, cold rolled metal panel formed into a series of parallel ribs; for this subpart, this includes metal floor and roof decks, standing seam metal roofs, other metal roof systems and other products such as bar gratings, checker plate, expanded metal panels, and similar products. After installation and proper fastening, these decking materials serve a combination of functions including, but not limited to: a structural element designed in combination with the structure to resist, distribute and transfer loads, stiffen the structure and provide a diaphragm action; a walking/working surface; a form for concrete slabs; a support for roofing systems; and a finished floor or roof.

Multiple lift rigging means a rigging assembly manufactured by wire rope rigging suppliers that facilitates the attachment of up to five independent loads to the hoist rigging of a crane (Note: Under §1926.753(e)(2), components from several manufacturers may be assembled by a qualified rigger. See Question and Answer #18).

Opening means a gap or void 12 inches (30.5 cm) or more in its least dimension in a floor, roof or other walking/working surface. For the purposes of this subpart, skylights and smoke domes that do not meet the strength requirements of §1926.754(e)(3) shall be regarded as openings (Note: The definition of "opening" in subpart R is different than the definition of "opening" in subpart M).

Permanent floor means a structurally completed floor at any level or elevation (including slab on grade).

Personal fall arrest system means a system used to arrest an employee in a fall from a working level. A personal fall arrest system consists of an anchorage, connectors, a body harness and may include a lanyard, deceleration device, lifeline, or suitable combination of these. The use of a body belt for fall arrest is prohibited.

Positioning device means a body belt or body harness rigged to allow an employee to be supported on an elevated, vertical surface, such as a wall or column and work with both hands free while leaning.

Post means a structural member with a longitudinal axis that is essentially vertical, that: (1) weighs 300 pounds or less and is axially loaded (a load presses down on the top end), or (2) is not axially loaded, but is laterally restrained by the above member. Posts typically support stair landings, wall framing, mezzanines and other substructures.

Project structural engineer of record means the registered, licensed professional responsible for the design of structural steel framing and whose seal appears on the structural contract documents.

Purlin (in systems-engineered metal buildings) means a "Z" or "C" shaped member formed from sheet steel spanning between primary framing and supporting roof material.

Qualified person (also defined in §1926.32) means one who, by possession of a recognized degree, certificate, or professional standing, or who by extensive knowledge, training, and experience, has successfully demonstrated the ability to solve or resolve problems relating to the subject matter, the work, or the project.

Safety deck attachment means an initial attachment that is used to secure an initially placed sheet of decking to keep proper alignment and bearing with structural support members.

Shear connector means headed steel studs, steel bars, steel lugs, and similar devices which are attached to a structural member for the purpose of achieving composite action with concrete.

Steel erection means the construction, alteration or repair of steel buildings, bridges and other structures, including the installation of metal decking and all planking used during the process of erection.

Steel joist means an open web, secondary load-carrying member of 144 feet (43.9 m) or less, designed by the manufacturer, used for the support of floors and roofs. This does not include structural steel trusses or cold-formed joists.

Steel joist girder means an open web, primary load-carrying member, designed by the manufacturer, used for the support of floors and roofs. This does not include structural steel trusses.

Steel truss means an open web member designed of structural steel components by the project structural engineer of record. For the purposes of this subpart, a steel truss is considered equivalent to a solid web structural member.

Structural steel means a steel member, or a member made of a substitute material (such as, but not limited to, fiberglass, aluminum or composite members). These members include, but are not limited to, steel joists, joist girders, purlins, columns, beams, trusses, splices, seats, metal decking, girts, and all bridging, and cold formed metal framing which is integrated with the structural steel framing of a building.

Systems-engineered metal building means a metal, field-assembled building system consisting of framing, roof and wall coverings. Typically, many of these components are cold-formed shapes. These individual parts are fabricated in one or more manufacturing facilities and shipped to the job site for assembly into the final structure. The engineering design of the system is normally the responsibility of the systems-engineered metal building manufacturer.

Tank means a container for holding gases, liquids or solids.

Unprotected sides and edges means any side or edge (except at entrances to points of access) of a walking/working surface, for example a, floor, roof, ramp or runway, where there is no wall or guardrail system at least 39 inches (1.0 m) high.

SITE LAYOUT, SITE-SPECIFIC ERECTION PLAN AND CONSTRUCTION SEQUENCE - §1926.752.

This section of the standard sets forth OSHA's requirements for communication between the controlling contractor and the steel erector prior to the beginning of steel erection, and pre-planning by the steel erector to minimize overhead exposure during hoisting operations.

During an inspection, visually determine the following:
- Did the controlling contractor provide adequate road access on the site for the delivery and movement of derricks, cranes, trucks, steel erection materials and other equipment? (Note: This requirement does not apply to roads outside of the construction site.) [§.752(c)(1)]
- Did the controlling contractor provide means and methods for pedestrian and vehicular control? [§.752(c)(1)]
- Did the controlling contractor provide a firm, properly graded, drained area, readily accessible to the work with adequate space for the safe storage of materials and safe operation of the erectors' equipment? [§.752(c)(2)]
- Did the controlling contractor either bar other construction processes below steel erection or provide overhead protection for the employees below? (This relates only to protection from falling objects other than materials being hoisted.) [§.759(b)]

Site-specific erection plan [§.752(e)]. A site-specific erection plan is required only when the contractor has decided to use alternative means to protect employees from three specific hazards:

- When safety latches on hooks are being de-activated or made inoperable. [§.753(c)(5)]
- When joists (which span more than 60 feet) at or near columns are not being set in tandem with all bridging installed. [§.757(a)(4)]
- When bundles of decking are being placed on steel joists before all bridging has been installed and anchored and all joist bearing ends attached. [§.757(e)(4)]

If it is determined that any of the above three conditions exist, a site-specific erection plan is required. The employer may use Appendix A as a framework for the plan. Methods for providing alternative worker protection from the above three conditions must be specified in the plan.

Determine if there is a plan available at the site. (Note: The plan does not need to be in writing - only §1926.757(e)(4)) requires a written plan.

HOISTING AND RIGGING - §1926.753.

The requirements of §1926.753 supplement the existing crane and rigging standards in §1926.251 and §1926.550. The requirements of Subpart R cover every type of crane. All the provisions of §1926.550 apply to hoisting and rigging with the exception of §1926.550(g)(2).

Questions to ask the steel erector:
- Who is the qualified rigger?
- Did they do a pre-shift inspection of the rigging?
- Who is the competent person assigned to inspect the crane?

Questions to ask the crane operator and/or qualified rigger:
- Do they have load charts, operator manual or riggers' handbook?
- Has the heaviest anticipated lift been calculated?

(Note: See the June 1994 booklet "Mobile Crane Inspection Guidelines for OSHA Compliance Officers")

Paragraph(c)(2) requires the qualified rigger inspect the below-hook rigging before each shift. Section 1926.251 inspection procedures will be applied for each type of rigging equipment to be used during the shift. In addition, paragraph (c)(5)(i) allows the safety latch on hoisting hooks to be deactivated when the qualified rigger makes a determination that it is safer for the connectors during the placement of purlins and single joists (Note that a safety latch is required to be used only where: (1) the manufacturer has equipped the hook with a latch, or (2) when working under suspended loads pursuant to §1926.753(d)).

Observe hooks with deactivated safety latches for anything other than single joists or purlins.

Refer to the site-specific erection plan for equivalent protection.

Talk to the qualified rigger.

Paragraph (d) addresses the hazards associated with overhead loads. Specifically, these hazards include failure of the lifting device, which would create a crushing hazard, and items falling from the load, which creates a struck-by and crushing hazard, among others. Given the nature of the loads used in steel erection, either of these events could result in serious injury or death.

See if employees are exposed to overhead loads. If you see employees working under loads, determine if the route was pre-planned (and exposure minimized) by interviewing the competent person, crane operator, etc. (The exception being connectors doing initial connection; or riggers hooking or unhooking of the load. These employees may work under the load.)

MULTIPLE LIFT RIGGING PROCEDURE (MLRP).

Paragraph (e)(1) lists the prerequisite conditions for multiple lift procedures (MLRP assembly, maximum of 5 pieces of steel per lift, only beams or similar structural members allowed, only by specifically trained employees, and the crane manufacturer must allow.)

If the steel erector is performing multiple-lifts:
(1) Request a copy of their multiple-lift procedure (if kept).
(2) Determine the number of pieces being lifted (no more than 5 are allowed).
(3) Check for certification of the rigging assembly from the qualified rigger (whether a manufacturer supplied rigging or the qualified rigger assembled it) and inspect the rigging equipment.

(4) Review the rigging chart and calculate the total load.
(5) Check the crane for controlled load lowering capability.
(6) Assure that the rigging is 7 feet or more apart.

The MLRP rigging assembly must be specifically designed for the structural steel members to be lifted. The design must incorporate the maximum anticipated load for each component part as it will be used in the assembly.

On a manufacturer-assembled rig, check for a tag or other means to specify the limits of the rig.

On a qualified rigger-assembled rig, check that the qualified rigger certified the maximum loading of the assembly and its component parts.

STRUCTURAL STEEL ASSEMBLY - §1926.754.

Paragraph (a): This paragraph requires that structural stability be maintained throughout the structural steel erection process. While guy wires (steel cable) are not specifically required, they are often used for this purpose. (See also §.755(a)(4)). These guy wires may also be used to plumb the building and add support to resist wind conditions.

Look for guying and bracing and see if any apparent problems exist.

Paragraph (c)(1): Shear connectors and similar devices. The standard requires that, where used, shear connectors must be field-installed rather than shop-installed.

Check steel beams for shear connectors. There should not be any shear connectors on beams without the decking or other walking/working surface in place, unless conventional fall protection is used (see Q & A # 25).

Ask the steel erector if they field-install shear connectors and what procedures are followed.

Paragraph (c)(3): **THIS PROVISION ONLY APPLIES AFTER JULY 18, 2006**. Once in effect, this will require documented or certified slip resistance of any painted or coated structural steel that an employee would walk on.

After July 18, 2006, observe the following conditions: Does the site have any painted or coated steel? If so, ask the steel erector for documentation or certification of slip resistance. This would probably be something the steel erector would obtain from the steel fabricator and/or paint manufacturer certifying the slip resistance of the paint.

Paragraph (d)(1): Plumbing-up.
Look for plumbing-up equipment. Guy wires (steel cable) and turnbuckles are generally used to plumb structures. Check for proper installation -- see if the wire rope components (U clips) were installed according to the manufacturers' requirements.

Paragraph (e)(1)(i) (general prohibition against using bundle packaging and strapping for hoisting): This hazard usually occurs while unloading trucks, when the metal decking bundles are tightly packed together and the rigging is difficult to attach and the end of the bundle is lifted with the bundles banding straps.
Ask the steel erector or observe if these straps are marked as approved for lifting.

Paragraph (e)(1)(iii)-(iv)(requirements for landing metal decking bundles). Generally, the competent person (foreman) will layout specific locations for the placement of bundles of decking for the ease of installation.
Look for metal decking landed on joists. Climb the ladder and ensure that bridging is installed and all joist ends are attached. Check the placement of the decking bundles. Refer to §1926.757(e)(4) for specific requirements.
Look for metal decking landed on solid web framing members. Check placement and support of bundles.

Paragraph (e)(2): Roof and floor holes and openings.
Look for any "decking holes" and "openings" on the site. Framed openings in metal decking must have structural members turned down. Any openings (as defined in the standard) that do exist because of constructibility or design constraints must be covered or employees protected by fall protection [.760(a)(1)].

Paragraph (e)(3): Covers for roof and floor openings. Look for any covers on the site. If covers exist:
- Are they secured?
- Are they painted, or marked visibly with "HOLE" or "COVER"?

COLUMN ANCHORAGE - §1926.755.
Paragraph (a) contains requirements to ensure that columns remain stable during the erection process.

Paragraph (a)(1) requires 4 anchor rods/bolts on all columns. However, this requirement does not include posts. The standard defines these terms as follows: A column is a load-carrying vertical member that is part of the primary skeletal framing system. A post is a structural member with a longitudinal axis that is essentially vertical, that: (1) is axially loaded (a load presses down on the top end) and weighs 300 pounds or less, or (2) is not axially loaded, but is laterally restrained by the above member. Posts typically support stair landings, wall framing, mezzanines and other structures.

Determine whether a vertical member is a column. If it is, check if it has the required 4 anchor rods/bolts. Remember that a post can have less than 4.

Paragraph (a)(2) requires that columns be able to withstand a specified load.

Check for unusually small bolts, insufficient length or failure.

Request documentation of the design criteria from the contractor.

Paragraph (a)(3) is intended to ensure that the column is properly set.

If leveling nuts are used, make sure the weight of the column rests on all 4 nuts. If shims are used, look for loose shims or instances where only a few shims are supporting the load.

Paragraph (a)(4) requires that a competent person evaluate the columns to determine whether guying or bracing is needed. If guying or bracing is needed, it must be provided. All columns need to be evaluated; in some instances the 4 anchor bolts/rods may not provide sufficient stability.

Ask the contractor who their competent person is and ask the competent person if and how this evaluation was performed.

Paragraph (b) requires that all anchor bolt/rod repairs be approved by the project structural engineer of record and that all such repairs be communicated in writing to the steel erector.

Ask for a copy of the notification when it is suspected that anchorage bolts/rods have been damaged, repaired, replaced or field-modified.

BEAMS AND COLUMNS - §1926.756.

Paragraph (c)(1): Double connections at columns and /or at beam webs over columns.

Ask the steel erector's representative/competent person if the structure's design includes double connections at columns and/or beam webs over columns. If the answer is yes, you should observe the double connection operation.

Ask the employer the following questions on how the connectors are being protected during this type operation:

(1) Are the connectors able to maintain at least 1-bolt and nut at least wrench tight at a common connection hole at all times? Among the ways of doing this are to use clipped end connections or staggered connections.

(2) If not, is the erector using seats or equivalent connection devices that were supplied with the member?

(3) If a seat or equivalent device is used, is it attached to both the supporting member and the first member before the nuts on the shared bolts are removed?

(4) If a seat or equivalent device is used, has it been adequately bolted or welded to both a supporting member and the first member **before** the nuts on the shared bolts are removed to make the double connection?

Paragraph (d): Column splices.

If a need arises to determine if column splices were designed to resist a minimum eccentric gravity load of 300 pounds located 18 inches from the extreme outer face of the column in each direction at the top of the column shaft, ask the project structural engineer of record.

The perimeter columns must extend a minimum of 48 inches above the finish floor and have holes or other devices attached to them at 42 - 45 inches above the finish floor (and also at the mid-point) to permit the installation of perimeter safety cables. If this requirement is not met, and the employer claims that constructibility does not allow meeting the requirement, ask the employer why constructibility does not allow this and what the employer is doing

in the mean time to provide protection to the employees exposed to the perimeter.

OPEN WEB STEEL JOISTS - §1926.757.

Some of the most serious risks facing the ironworker are encountered during the erection of open web steel joists, particularly from landing loads on unbridged joists and improperly placing loads on joists.

Questions to ask the steel erector and the ironworkers with regard to steel joists:

- What type of joists are you installing?
- What's the elevation?
- Are you installing joists in bays? If so, how many joists per bay and how many bays?
- What are the spans of the joists and are there different types of joists being installed?
- Are you familiar with the Steel Joist Institute and/or OSHA's requirements for the safe installation of steel joists?
- Can I see the steel erection drawings and can you explain the joist pattern?
- Are you following a site specific erection plan? If so, may I see a copy?
- How are you bracing/bridging the joists? Diagonal and/or horizontal?
- What bridging is required? What type of bridging is being used?
- When is the erection bridging installed and by whom is it installed?
- How much and what type of erection bridging is required by the plans?
- At what point during the installation process is the erection bridging installed?
- Is all the erection bridging designated in the drawings being installed? If not, why not?
- How are you lifting the joists?
- What are the qualifications of the crane operator?
- How are the joists rigged? Is a qualified rigger being used?
- Is the erection bridging installed before or after releasing the joist from the crane?
- How are the joists released from the crane? (Open hooks? Remote release? Ironworker walks the joists? From an aerial lift?)
- Are the joist connections bolted or welded? If welded, do welds meet the standard's requirements [.757(b)]?
- Are joists in bays of 40 feet or more bolted? If not, why not? If the employer claims that

constructibility does not allow field-bolting, ask its basis for making that claim.

- What type of fall protection is being used during joist installation and during the installation of erection bridging?
- Are you setting joists in tandem?
- How are you securing your joists - are both sides of the seat at one end of the joist secured?
- Have there been any stability problems? Problems with anchor bolts or wall pockets?
- Have there been any change orders? May I see the change log (if kept)?
- Are you field bolting your joists at the columns?
- Are the columns framed in at least two directions?
- When landing joists, how are you securing them against accidental displacement?
- What kind of bridging terminus points are you using? Please identify them.
- Are you placing any loads on the joists? If so, what are they (e.g., bundles of bridging or deck or joists)? How much load is being placed on the joists and across how many joists is the load spread?

SYSTEMS-ENGINEERED METAL BUILDINGS - §1926.758.

When performing an inspection on a systems-engineered metal building, be aware that all the requirements in subpart R apply to these structures except for §1926.755 (column anchorage) and §1926.757 (steel joist erection).

Check column base plates for four anchor bolts/rods [§.758(b)]

Check for any double connections on the structure and ensure that either a seat or similar connection device is being used for double connections.

If joists are being installed, observe the operation to ensure that joists are fully bolted or welded prior to release of the hoisting cable, allowing an employee on the joists or placing any construction load on the joist.

FALLING OBJECT PROTECTION - §1926.759.

Under paragraph (b), when it is necessary to have work performed below on-going steel erection activities (other than hoisting), effective overhead protection must be provided to those workers to prevent injuries from falling objects.

If this protection is not provided, work by other trades is not to be permitted below steel erection work ~ the controlling contractor must institute measures to keep employees out of the area below the steel erection activities.

Check the site for unsecured materials, tools and equipment that are not in use [§.759(a)].

If you see workers below where steel erection activities are being performed, ask some of the employees if they know of any tools or other materials that have fallen from the worksite above. If they have, look into what falling hazards are present and what has and is being done to protect the employees.

FALL PROTECTION - §1926.760.

Paragraph (a): The first thing that needs to be determined is if the activity is covered by Subpart R (see §1926.750(b)) or by Subpart M.

Ask the general contractor about their fall protection program and what they require their subcontractors to follow. Then ask the erectors. Check to see if the employers are effectively communicating and enforcing the standard. If the erector allows employees to work unprotected between 15 and 30 feet, make sure that the unprotected workers meet the connector definition or are working on the leading edge of a decking operation in a CDZ (see definitions of connector, leading edge, and controlled decking zone).

Establish by observation and asking employees the following:

(1) What fall protection system are you using?
(2) Who are the connectors? (Note: Come-a-longs and chain-falls are not hoisting equipment, so employees cannot be considered connectors simply on the basis of using these to move steel into place.)
(3) How often do you inspect your fall protection equipment?
(4) For decking operations between 15 and 30 feet/2 stories, are you using fall protection or CDZs?
(5) Are all employees over 30feet/2 stories protected by conventional fall protection?

Paragraph (c): Controlled decking zone
If the employer is using a CDZ between 15 and 30 feet/2 stories, observe the operation to

determine if the employer is complying with the requirements of §1926.760(c).

Physically inspect CDZ from outside the zone if possible. Measure the size and ask employees working in the zone about their training and what activities are performed in the zone.

Paragraph (a)(2): Perimeter cables

Look at the perimeter cables. Do they meet the criteria of §1926.502(g)? Are the perimeter cables being installed as soon as the metal decking is completed?

TRAINING - §1926.761.

Section 1926.761 supplements §1926.21(b)(2) training requirements. Failure to train on hazards not covered by this section should be cited under §1926.21(b)(2) (for example: training on falling objects, bolting, impalement hazards from rebar). Subpart R does not require a certification that training has been conducted.

Employees must be provided the training prior to exposure to the hazard.

Ask the employer whether it trained the employees or relied on a third-party trainer. If a third-party trainer was used, ask how the employer determined that the training meets the standard.

Subpart R does not include a testing requirement. However, an effective training program necessarily involves some means of determining whether the instruction was understood. Ask the employer how it makes this determination (this can be done in a variety of ways, such as formal oral, or written tests, observation, or through discussion). Also, ask employees about their training.

Section (a): Requires that all training required by this section be provided by a qualified person.

A qualified person, is defined in §1926.751 as one who by possession of a recognized degree, certificate, or professional standing, or by extensive knowledge, training, and experience has successfully demonstrated the ability to solve or resolve problems relating to the subject matter, the work, or the project.

QUESTIONS AND ANSWERS

Note: Several questions and answers that appeared in the draft version of this directive have been removed pending further consideration.

GENERAL GUIDANCE.

Question 1: What is the effective date of the standard?

Answer: The effective date for the final rule has been changed to January 18, 2002. Note also that the effective date of §1926.754(c)(3)(slip resistance requirement for coated skeletal structural steel) is July 18, 2006.

Question 2: On February 1, 2002, a contractor receives the columns at the site to be erected. They have only 2 anchor bolts, and column splice locations do not meet the standard's requirements. The design and/or fabrication of these columns was done prior to the new effective date (January 18, 2002) of the final rule. Is the contractor required to comply with §1926.755 (a)(1)(requirement for 4 anchor bolts) and §1926.756(d) (requirement for column splice height)?

Answer: In two situations the component requirements (provisions that address the safety of certain structural members) of the final rule will not be applied: (1) where the building permit was obtained prior to January 18, 2001, or (2) where steel erection began on or before September 16, 2001 (see volume 66 of the Federal Register, page 37137-37139). Steel erection begins when a steel erection activity covered by the standard begins.

In this scenario, the answer depends on when the building permit was obtained and when steel erection began. If the building permit was obtained before January 18, 2001 (the date the final rule was published), these component requirements would not be applied to these columns. If steel erection began on or before September 16, 2001, the component requirements would not apply, irrespective of when the building permit was obtained. Otherwise, the requirements would apply.

For bridge construction, OSHA will exempt a bridge project from the component requirements of the new steel erection standard if: (1) the project has a contract date before January 18, 2001; or (2) steel erection began on or before September 16, 2001.

Question 3: Which provisions in the standard are considered "component requirements"?

Answer: A number of provisions in the final rule address the safety of certain structural components. These provisions contain design requirements for these components to help ensure that the structure can be erected safely. For example, there are provisions that prohibit shear connectors on members before they are erected (§1926.754(c)(1)(i)); require all columns to be anchored by a minimum of 4 anchor bolts, which must meet specified strength requirements (§1926.755(a)) (there is a comparable requirement for systems-engineered metal buildings, §1926.758(b)); set requirements for double connections (§1926.756(c)(1)) (there is a comparable requirement for systems-engineered metal buildings §1926.758(e)); require column splices to be at a specified height and meet a strength requirement (§1926.756(d)); require perimeter columns to have holes or other devices for perimeter safety cables (§1926.756(e)); in some instances require a vertical stabilizer plate to stabilize steel joists (§1926.757(a)(1)(i)); require certain joists to be strong enough to allow one employee to release the hoisting cable without the need for erection bridging (§1926.757(a)(3)), and require certain joists to be fabricated to allow for field bolting during erection (§1926.757(a)(8)(i)).

SECTION 1926.750-SCOPE.

Question 4(a): The structural steel and decking has been completed on floor 4. Structural steel is being erected for floor 6. Is the installation of an item listed only in §1926.750(b)(2) on floor 4 considered steel erection?

Answer: No. The activities listed in §1926.750(b)(1) are covered by the standard. The activities listed in §1926.750(b)(2) are covered by the standard only if they are installed "during and are a part of" steel erection activities listed in (b)(1).

In this scenario no (b)(1) activities are taking place on the 4th floor, the ongoing steel erection activities have progressed to the 6th floor, and the installation of the (b)(2) item is not part of the work on floor 6. The work on floor 4 is not covered by Subpart R.

Question 4(b): Some structural steel work (listed in (b)(1)) is taking place in the northeast corner

of floor 5. In the southwest corner of floor 5, some work listed in (b)(2) is taking place. Is the installation of the (b)(2) item covered by subpart R?

Answer: No. As long as the §1926.750(b)(1) activities can proceed irrespective of the progress on the §1926.750(b)(2) activities, the (b)(2) activities are excluded from coverage under Subpart R.

Question 5: When a tank is to be supported by a structure that falls under the scope of Subpart R, does construction of the tank also fall within the scope of Subpart R?

Answer: No. 1926.750(a) excludes tank construction from the scope of Subpart R. It is excluded because it is considered to be a specialized industry based upon its unique use of cylindrical construction techniques. The construction of the tank itself would not be steel erection even though the structure supporting the tank is covered by subpart R.

Question 6: When installing an integrated metal roof decking system, which includes the metal banding, insulation, and screw down clips, is the entire process considered steel erection?

Answer: Yes. These operations take place in a repeating sequence of steps. Once the banding is in place, a row of insulation is put down, metal decking is laid over it and then secured with clips. The metal decking forms both the structural and weather-proofing roof surface. Working from that completed row, the next row of insulation and decking is then installed and the process repeated across the building.

The installation of the metal roof decking is covered by subpart R under 1926.750(b)(1). Because the metal banding, insulation and screw-down clips are installed "during and [as] a part of" the installation of the metal decking, these activities are covered by subpart R under 1926.750(b)(2).

Question 7: Is the construction of a house framed with metal studs within subpart R?

Answer: No. Metal studs are not mentioned in §1926.750, and while the installation of "structural steel" is covered, the definition of structural steel in §1926.751 includes metal studs only where those studs are "integrated with the structural steel framing of a building." Since such a house has no such structural steel framing, but simply the cold-formed metal studs, a house framed with metal studs is not covered by subpart R. The use of one or several hot-formed I-beams in such a structure would not constitute "structural steel framing" [emphasis added], so their use in such a house would not change the answer; subpart R would apply only to the installation of the hot-formed I-beams.

Question 8: When would the installation of metal studs be covered by subpart R?

Answer: The installation of metal studs is covered by subpart R when the studs are "integrated with the structural steel framing of a building." For example, in some buildings, the skeletal frame is composed of hot-formed columns and beams. However, the filler walls and roof structure, which are attached to that frame, are constructed with metal studs. In that case, the installation of the metal studs are covered by subpart R.

Question 9: Is the installation of metal stairways, and the installation of an iron fence and gate outside a completed building, considered "miscellaneous metals" and covered by subpart R?

Answer: Yes. The activities listed in §1926.750(b)(1), which are covered by Subpart R, include installing "miscellaneous metals, [and] ornamental iron . . ." An iron fence and gate have traditionally been considered ornamental iron, and so are covered. Metal stairways have also traditionally been considered miscellaneous metals and would be covered by the standard.

Question 10: Scenario: A prefabricated tank is installed on a pad. The tank has connection points for a catwalk pre-installed by the manufacturer. The catwalk will be installed by a crane crew after the tank is installed. Do the fall protection requirements of Subpart R apply to the installation of the catwalk?

Answer: Yes, the installation of the catwalk on a completed tank is covered by Subpart R. Catwalks traditionally have been considered "miscellaneous metals." The installation of miscellaneous metals are covered by Subpart R pursuant to §1926.750(b)(1). Therefore, fall protection by use of a guardrail system, safety net system, personal fall arrest system, posi-

tioning device system or fall restraint system is required by §1926.760 (a)(1) at heights more than 15 feet above a lower level.

Question 11: Subpart R does not apply to transmission towers. Some power lines are supported with steel poles. Is the installation of these steel poles covered by subpart R?

Answer: No. Although such poles are not "towers," 1926 Subpart V (Power Transmission and Distribution) is a more specifically applicable standard. Under 1926.950(a), Subpart V applies to "the construction of electric transmission and distribution lines and equipment." "Equipment" is defined in §1926.960(s) as including "fittings, devices, appliances, fixtures, apparatus, and the like, used as part of, or in connection with, an electrical power transmission and distribution system, or communication systems." Steel poles used to support power lines meet this definition. Therefore, the installation of these poles is covered by 1926 Subpart V, not Subpart R.

SECTION 1927.752-SITE LAYOUT, SITE-SPECIFIC ERECTION PLAN AND CONSTRUCTION SEQUENCE.

Question 12: Before any steel erection begins, who is responsible for performing the test to determine whether the concrete has cured to 75% of the intended minimum compressive design strength or cured enough so that it can support the loads imposed during steel erection?

Answer: The controlling contractor must ensure that written notification is given to the steel erector that the concrete has cured to the level required by the standard. The standard does not require any specific entity to perform the test. The choice of who will do the test is left to the controlling contractor. Since it is the controlling contractor's responsibility to ensure that the notification is given to the steel erector, the controlling contractor must select an entity that has the expertise to perform the test. The controlling contractor may do the test itself if it has the expertise to do so. In the preamble of the final rule (page 5206), OSHA stated:

In the proposed rule, the controlling contractor would have had to provide the ASTM test results to the steel erector. The final rule has been changed to reflect that the controlling contractor must ensure that the test results are provided to the steel erector. This rephrasing will allow the controlling contractor to have a contractor familiar with the ASTM test methods perform the test and provide the results to the steel erector.

Question 13: Can the controlling contractor contract with subcontractors to perform the work required by §1926.752(a)? If so, is the controlling contractor still responsible for these duties after subcontracting them out?

Answer: Under §1926.752 (a), the controlling contractor "shall ensure that the steel erector is provided" with written notification that the concrete has cured to the specified degree. While the controlling contractor may contract with subcontractors to do the requisite tests and provide the written notification, the controlling contractor remains responsible for ensuring that the subcontractor does that work. If the subcontractor fails to do the test and provide the notification, the controlling contractor may be cited for a violation under §1926.752(a).

Question 14: Section 1926.752(a)(1) requires the controlling contractor to ensure that the steel erector is provided with written notifications that the concrete and masonry meet certain specified strength requirements. To what extent is the controlling contractor responsible for the accuracy of the strength assessments in the written notifications?

Answer: As explained in Q&A # 12, the controlling contractor can choose to either: (1) conduct the tests itself, if it has the expertise to do so; or (2) select an entity that has the expertise to do the test. If the controlling contractor does the tests itself, it is responsible for the accuracy of the tests.

If the controlling contractor selects someone else to do the tests, it is responsible for exercising reasonable care in the selection of the testing entity. As long as it has a reasonable basis for believing that the testing entity is competent and capable of doing the work, and the controlling contractor has no actual knowledge that the tests results are wrong, erroneous test results will not constitute a violation of 1926.752(a).

Question 15: Section 1926.752(a)(1) and (b) require that an appropriate ASTM standard test method be used to determine that field-cured concrete/mortar testing samples have attained 75% of the intended minimum compressive strength or sufficient strength to support loads imposed during steel erection before that erection begins. Can I rely on cure time instead of doing such a test?

Answer: No. The standard does not provide that cure time may be used instead of the ASTM test. Because of the many factors that influence cure rates (temperature, humidity, ingredient ratios, etc.), cure time is an unreliable means of assessing how much the concrete has cured.

Question 16(a): Does the written notification from the controlling contractor to the steel erector about concrete footings, etc. in §1926.752(a) and (b) have to be maintained on site?

Answer: Once the written notification is given to the erector, there is no requirement that it be maintained at the site.

Question 16(b): Does the anchor bolt repair, replacement or field-modification approval from the Structural Engineer of Record (SER) required by §1926.755(b)(1) have to be maintained on site?

Answer: No. Where an anchor bolt repair, replacement or field-modification is made, §1926.752(a)(2) requires that the controlling contractor ensure that the steel erector is provided with written notification that the requirements in §1926.755(b) were met. Section 1926.755(b)(1) requires that, prior to erection, the repair, replacement or field-modification must be approved by the SER. Once the written notification is given to the erector under §1926.752(a)(2), there is no requirement that it be maintained at the site. Also, there is no requirement that a record of the SER's approval be maintained at the site.

SECTION 1926.753-HOISTING AND RIGGING.

Question 17: Section 1926.753(e)(4) requires the members be rigged at least 7 feet apart on a multiple lift rigging assembly (Christmas tree rig). If they are rigged 7' apart and the connector needs to slacken the line to unhook the lower beam, the beam above now has less than

7' of clearance. Does a 7' clearance need to be maintained at all times?

Answer: No. The 7 feet specifically refers to the distance as rigged.

Question 18: Does the standard permit a qualified rigger to design and assemble a "multiple lift rigging" assembly on the jobsite by mixing components from one rigging supplier or by mixing components from several rigging suppliers?

Answer: Yes. In §1926.751, "Multiple lift rigging" is defined as "a rigging assembly manufactured by wire rope rigging suppliers . . . ." The use of the plural "suppliers" reflects that an assembly may be made from components from more than one manufacturer. This is also reflected in the fact that §1926.753(e)(2) allows a qualified rigger to certify the capacity of an assembly instead of a manufacturer: "Components of the multiple lift rigging assembly shall be specifically designed and assembled with a maximum capacity for total assembly and for each individual attachment point. This capacity, certified by the manufacturer or a qualified rigger, shall be based on the manufacturer's specifications with a 5 to 1 safety factor for all components." [Emphasis added].

The preamble to the final rule also shows that an assembly may be either put together from separately produced manufactured components, or obtained as a single, manufactured unit: "[t]he rigging must be certified by the qualified rigger who assembles it or the manufacturer who provides the entire assembly to ensure that the assembly can support the whole load . . . ." (Volume 66 of the Federal Register at page 5211). The provision, then, permits a qualified rigger to assemble the multiple lift rigging from manufactured components. These may be from either a single or multiple suppliers.

Question 19: How often must the multiple lift rigging assembly be inspected?

Answer: In §1926.753(c)(2), the standard requires a qualified rigger to inspect the rigging before every shift in accordance with §1926.251, Rigging equipment for material handling. Additional inspections of the rigging assembly where service conditions warrant are required under §1926.251(a)(6).

Question 20: Section 1926.753(c)(1)(i) requires a pre-shift visual inspection of cranes to be done by a competent person. Section 1926.753(c)(1)(iv) states that "the [crane] operator shall be responsible for those operations under the operator's direct control. Whenever there is any doubt as to safety, the operator shall have the authority to stop and refuse to handle loads until safety has been assured."

Scenario: The crane is rented, and the operator is supplied by the crane rental company. The steel erector designates the operator as the competent person for purposes of the pre-shift inspection requirements. Is the steel erector still responsible for compliance with the pre-shift inspection requirements? Is the steel erector responsible for crane operations under the direct control of the operator?

Answer: Under §1926.750(a), "the requirements of [subpart R] apply to employers engaged in steel erection unless otherwise specified." Section 1926.753 (c)(1)(iv) specifies the operator as responsible for operations that are "under the operator's direct control." However, those are only operations involving the actual operation of the crane.

While an operator may be designated as a competent person for purposes of the pre-shift inspection, §1926.753(c)(1)(i) does not specify who is responsible for compliance with the pre-shift inspection requirements. Therefore, a designation by the steel erector of the crane owner's operator as the competent person would not absolve the steel erector of responsibility for making sure that the pre-shift inspection was done (Note, though, that the steel erector is not expected to have the same level of expertise regarding those inspections as either the crane owner or the competent person).

Question 21: Does §1926.753(e) permit beams of different sizes to be lifted in a multiple lift?
Answer: Yes.

Question 22: Section 1926.753(e)(2) requires that the capacity of each multiple lift rigging component and the total assembly be certified by the manufacturer or qualified rigger. Does that certification have to be in writing?

Answer: Yes, a certification is a written document.

SECTION 1926.754-STRUCTURAL STEEL ASSEMBLY.

Question 23: Section 1926.754 (b)(3) requires a "fully planked or decked floor or nets" within two stories or 30 feet, whichever is less. Can an employer's requirement that workers be protected by fall arrest equipment at all times above 15 feet (or less) take the place of nets and temporary floors?
Answer: Yes. Where an employer establishes, communicates and enforces a requirement to be protected by fall arrest equipment at all times above 15 feet (or less), the failure to comply with §1926.754(b)(3) is considered a de minimis violation and will not be cited.

Question 24: Prior to installation of a bridge girder, a contractor welds a limited number of shear connectors (the minimum needed for a fall protection system) on the top flange of the girder. Each shear connector is encapsulated by a split collar, a tee joint and line post/anchor post (or a round pipe). These are designed to serve as supports for horizontal lifelines in a fall protection system. Is this a violation of §1926.754(c)(1)(i)?
Answer: In this scenario, the spacing and height requirements for the supports would essentially eliminate the tripping hazards. Since the shear studs will be encapsulated by a fall protection anchor device, prior to the beam being erected, the provision in §1926.754(c)(1)(i) regarding shear connectors does not apply. Section 1926.753(c)(1)(i) does not apply when: (1) the shear connector studs are encapsulated by the line post or anchor post prior to erecting the member; and (2) the encapsulated studs serve as an integral part of the fall protection system's fixed anchor point.

Question 25: I have beams with shop-installed shear connectors at 20 feet. If the employer requires the use of fall protection for all workers, including connectors and deckers, would the presence of the shop-installed shear connectors on these beams still be a violation under 1926.754(c)(1)?
Answer: No. If an employer requires that all workers, including those engaged in connect-ing and in decking (as well as deckers in a CDZ), be protected from falls by conventional fall protection, then the failure to meet the requirements of §1926.754(c)(1) would be considered de minimis and no citation would be issued.

Question 26: If a roof void is 11 inches by 25 feet, does it need to be covered for steel erection purposes (§1926.754(e)(3) and definition of "opening").
Answer: No. The definition of "opening" in §1926.751 refers to a gap or void whose least dimension is 12 inches (30.5 cm) or more. Thus a roof void whose least dimension is 11 inches would not be an "opening" under subpart R and would not need to be covered during steel erection. Note that this void is too large to be considered a "decking hole" (a term that is also defined in §1926.751) under subpart R since its greatest dimension is more than 12 inches.

Question 27: Is §1926.754(b)(3)(fully planked floor or nets) a form of interior fall protection?
Answer: This provision requires that fully planked or decked floors or nets be maintained within two stories or 30 feet, whichever is less. Use of nets to meet the provision would provide interior fall protection. Use of decked floors does not provide the equivalent of fall protection (such floors do limit interior fall distances as workers ascend to or descend from their work locations).

Question 28: Are bundle packaging and strapping that have been designed for hoisting purposes marked accordingly? If not, who is responsible under §1926.754(e)(1)(i) for determining whether they are designed for hoisting? How is this determination to be made?
Answer: Under §1926.754(e)(1)(i), employers engaged in steel erection are responsible for ensuring that bundle packaging and strapping, if used for hoisting, are specifically designed for hoisting purposes. Some manufacturers design metal decking bundle packaging and strapping, applied at the factory to keep bundles together, to be used as a lifting device. However, subpart R does not require that they be so marked. We are not aware that the manufacturers mark these bundles uniformly or consistently.

When bundle packaging/strapping is used for hoisting, it is considered rigging. Under

§1926.753(c)(2), a qualified rigger must inspect the rigging prior to each shift in accordance with §1926.251. Therefore, the employer would use a qualified rigger in making this determination.

SECTION 1926.755-COLUMN ANCHORAGE.

Question 29: To make a field repair to an anchor rod (anchor bolt), must there be a written order from the project's engineer of record?
Answer: Section 1926.755(b)(1) prohibits such repairs "without the approval of the project structural engineer of record." While the standard requires approval, it does not require the approval to be in writing.

Question 30: The requirements in §1926.755(b) apply to the "repair, replacement or field modification of anchor rods (anchor bolts)." Is hitting an anchor bolt with a hammer to line it up with the base plate holes considered a modification?
Answer: Generally, hitting an anchor bolt with a hammer to line it up with the base plate holes would not be considered a modification, since those minor adjustments do not normally affect the structural integrity of the rod or the concrete. However, unbending a bolt is considered a modification since that will weaken it.

SECTION 1926.757-OPEN WEB STEEL JOISTS.

Question 31: Is it acceptable to use a forklift to raise and set in place roof joists?
Answer: Yes. It is acceptable to use a forklift to raise and set joists in steel erection provided all the necessary safety requirements for landing and placing loads contained in §1926.757(e) are followed. In addition, the employer must comply with the requirements of §1926.602 - Material handling equipment - for the use and operation of the forklift equipment itself.

Question 32: Section 1926.757(a)(3) requires: "where steel joists at or near columns span 60 feet or less, the joist shall be designed with sufficient strength to allow one employee to release the hoisting cable without the need for erection bridging." Joist manufacturers have stated that, for some lengths, there are no existing joist designs that would provide the necessary stability (even with the stabilizer plate). These are primarily joists in the 55-60 foot length range. The manufacturers state that it will take a period of time to develop a formula, build the formula into the design of these joists and have the joists manufactured for use in construction. How will OSHA enforce this provision during this period?
Answer: Until July 18, 2004 or until a new directive is issued, for all joists at or near columns that span 60 feet or less, employers will be considered to be in compliance with §1926.757(a)(3) if they erect these joists either by: (1) installing bridging or otherwise stabilizing the joist prior to releasing the hoisting cable, or (2) releasing the cable without having a worker on the joists. This will allow the joist industry the necessary time to develop joists that will meet the requirement.

Question 33: Is installation of "erection bridging" considered connecting?
Answer: Yes.

Question 34: If workers are on a one story building that is 20' tall (top of steel) and the joists require horizontal bridging, is fall protection is required for employees installing this bridging?
Answer: Normally, yes. Fall protection by use of a guardrail system, safety net system, personal fall arrest system, positioning device system or fall restraint system is required by §1926.760 (a)(1) to be provided at heights more than 15 feet above a lower level. The requirements in §1926.760(a)(1) apply irrespective of whether the building is single or multi-story. The connector exception will not normally apply in situations like this. Horizontal bridging is not erection bridging. These workers typically will not be working with hoisting equipment when installing horizontal bridging. So, employees installing horizontal bridging at a height of 20 feet, on a single story building, working without hoisting equipment, would be required to have fall protection in accordance with §1926.760(a)(1).

Question 35: Section 1926.757(c)(2) requires that joists over 60 feet be attached in accordance with §1926.757(b). Section 1926.757(b) allows either bolting or welding of the joist ends.

However, §1926.757(a)(8) requires that all joists over 40 feet be bolted (with an exception for constructibility). Do these provisions conflict?

Answer: No. Section 1926.757(b)(2) refers to the final connection of the member; §1926.757(a)(8) refers to the initial connection of the member. They work together as follows:

Under §1926.757(c)(2), there are several requirements that must be met before the hoisting cables can be released from these joists. One of these requirements is that the joist be attached as specified in §1926.757(b)(2). Under that provision, the **final** connection can be either a bolted or welded connection.

In contrast, §1926.757(a)(8) refers to the **initial** connection of certain members. Under this provision, these members must be initially bolted (unless constructability does not allow). However, the final connection can be either bolted or welded. The initial bolting is typically done with an erection bolt, which would either be replaced with a high-strength bolt for the final connection or the final connection would be welded.

So, §1926.757(c)(2)'s requirement that joists over 60 feet be attached in accordance with §1926.757(b) means that there must be a final connection -- whether bolted or welded -- that meets the §1926.757(b) requirements before the hoisting cable is released. While these joists had to be initially bolted, the final connection could be either by bolting or welding.

Question 36(a): Section 1926.757(c)(3) and (d) contain requirements that refer to Table A (Erection Bridging for Short Span Joists) and Table B (Erection Bridging for Long Span Joists). How do I read these tables?

Answer: Joists are manufactured in a variety of types and lengths. Some types need no erection bridging at any length. Other types need bridging if they are a certain length or greater.

Each table has two columns. The left-hand column, titled "Joist," identifies specific types of joists. The right-hand column, titled "Span," indicates at what length erection bridging is required. Many of the joists have "NM" (for "not mandatory") marked in the Span column. That means that the type of joist designated does not require erection bridging, irrespective of its length. (**NOTE: the definition of "NM" printed in the Tables is incorrect** -- it says

"NM=diagonal bolted bridging not mandatory for joists under 40 feet." The clause "for joists under 40 feet" was mistakenly taken from the proposed rule, and was not supposed to be included in the final rule. Please disregard that clause; it will be removed in later printings).

Other joists have numbers marked in the Span column. For example, in Table A, Joist 12K1 has "23-0" marked in the Span column. That means that 12K1 joists that are 23 feet 0 inches in length or longer require erection bridging. Shorter lengths of this type of joist do not require erection bridging.

In Table B, joist 32LH06 has "47-0 through 60-0" in the Span column. That means that 32LH06 joists 47 feet long, up through 60 feet long, require erection bridging.

Also in Table B, joist 32LH09 has "NM through 60-0" in the Span column. That means that erection bridging is not required for lengths through 60 feet. However, lengths over 60 feet 0 inches do require erection bridging.

Once it is determined that erection bridging is required, the erection bridging must be installed in accordance with §1926.757(d).

Questions 36(b): Section 1926.757(c)(3) states that, "[o]n steel joists that do not require erection bridging under Tables A and B, only one employee shall be allowed on the joist until all bridging is installed and anchored." If a joist does not require erection bridging under the Tables, what bridging is required under this provision before allowing additional employees on the joist?

Answer: Under this provision, if a steel joist does not require erection bridging (bolted diagonal bridging) under §1926.757(c)(3), bridging that is called for in the erection drawings must be installed prior to additional employees going out on the joist. This includes any horizontal bridging or bolted diagonal bridging that is specified in the drawings.

Question 37: Section 1926.757(a)(6) requires that, "[w]hen steel joists are landed on a structure, they shall be secured to prevent unintentional displacement prior to installation." Do all joists remaining in a bundle have to be re-secured each time a joist is removed to be installed?

Answer: In the preamble to the final rule, OSHA stated that this provision:

"*addresses the hazard that arises when a single steel joist or a bundle of joists are placed on the structure and then left unattended and unattached. . . [T]he bundles must remain intact prior to installation until the time comes for them to be set. This paragraph also prevents those ironworkers who are shaking out the filler joists from getting too far ahead of those workers welding the joists, a practice that leaves many joists placed but unattached. Paragraph (b)(3) of this section . . . requires that at least one end of each steel joist be attached immediately upon placement in its final erection position and before additional joists are placed. Another example of a situation addressed by this paragraph is if the exact dimensions of a piece of mechanical equipment to be installed in the decking are not known. A common practice, when this occurs, is to leave a joist unattached until the dimension is known. This paragraph requires such a joist to be secured . . .pending its final attachment.*" (Volume 66 of the Federal Register at page 5231).

The joists remaining in the bundle do not have to be re-secured while workers are in the process of removing them from the bundle and installing them. However, if, for example, an erector lands all of the joist bundles for a section of a building and will not install the joists until the following day, the joists must be secured to prevent unintentional displacement.

SECTION 1926.759-FALLING OBJECT PROTECTION.

Question 38: An 80 foot long beam has been initially connected, if ironworkers are now bolting-up the beam, is the controlling contractor required to protect (or bar) operations under the beam in areas where the ironworkers are not working in accordance with §1926.759(b)? For example, if an ironworker is working at one end of a beam bolting-up, and another is bolting-up the other end (80 feet away), do operations below the middle of the beam have to be protected or barred?

Answer: As stated in the preamble to the final rule (page 5243), the intent of this provision is to protect employees from falling objects. If there are no tools or materials located at the middle of the beam that could be displaced, then employees working below the middle of the beam would not be subjected to the hazard of falling objects. In that case, protection/bar-

ring of operations would not be required below the middle area of the beam.

SECTION 1926.760-FALL PROTECTION.

Question 39: Section 1926.760(c) says that employees in a CDZ can work unprotected up to 30 feet. However, in 1926.760(c)(1), it requires employees at the leading edge to be protected from fall hazards of "more than two stories or 30 feet, whichever is less." At which height, 30 feet or two stories, is conventional fall protection required to be used to protect deckers?

Answer: The answer depends on whether the building is single or multi-story, and, if multi-story, whether two stories is less than 30 feet. Under paragraph §1926.760(c), a CDZ "may" be established up to 30 feet and used as a substitute for fall protection required in 1926.760(a), depending on certain prerequisites being met. Under 1926.760(c)(1), one of the prerequisites for using a CDZ instead of fall protection as high as 30 feet is that, if the building is multi-story, two stories must be 30 feet. Otherwise, where two stories are less than 30 feet, the CDZ may be used as a substitute for fall protection only up to two stories. In a single story structure, the prerequisite is automatically met—the CDZ can be used as a fall protection substitute up to 30 feet.

Question 40: Does some decking need to be in place for a CDZ to begin?

Answer: A CDZ can be implemented in an area where metal decking is being installed and forms the leading edge of the work surface. One or more panels will normally need to be installed before the control line is erected. These panels can be installed while workers are positioned on ladders, elevated platforms, protected by conventional fall protection, or otherwise protected from falling.

Question 41: A CDZ is defined as an area where certain work may take place "without the use of guardrail systems, personal fall arrest systems, fall restraint systems, or safety net systems . . ." Are employees required to use a positioning device when working in a CDZ?

Answer: No. Positioning device systems, as defined in the standard, are systems used on

Steel Erection

STEEL ERECTION

vertical surfaces, such as walls or columns. In a CDZ, workers are installing the horizontal surface on which they will be standing and working. No mention was made of positioning device systems in the CDZ definition since (as defined) they are not to be used while on a horizontal surface.

Question 42: A connector initially connects one end of a beam. Do OSHA standards allow the connector to then walk across the beam to connect the other end while the beam remains suspended from the crane?

Answer: Yes; this practice is allowed in steel erection. At the time of the SENRAC negotiations, it was a common industry practice to have the ironworker walk across the beam while it is still connected to the crane. This is evidenced by the American National Standard Institute's 1989 consensus standard for Steel erection Safety Requirements (ANSI A10.13-1989), section 9.2 and 9.4. Section 9.2 states: "When connectors are working at the same connecting point, they shall connect one end of the structural member before going out to connect the other end . . .".

It is also reflected in the Steel Joist Institute's 1994 manual for steel joists, section 105 A.2., which specifically recognizes that two erectors may be on certain joists if the joist is "stabilized by the hoisting cables . . ." For example, in section 105 A. 2. (for LH and DLH series joists), it states that "a maximum weight of two erectors shall be allowed on any unbridged joist if 1) the joist is stabilized by the hoisting cable(s) . . .".

In view of the industry history recognizing this as a safe practice, where a connector initially connects one end of a beam and then walks across to connect the other end while the beam remains suspended from the crane, the violation of 1926.550 for being on a crane load is considered *de minimis* and no citation will be issued.

Question 43: Does a connector have to be tied off above 15 feet while moving to an initial beam connection location and while moving to or from subsequent beam connection locations if the crane is busy getting the next piece?

Answer: No. The process of connecting includes moving on the steel to and from initial

and subsequent points at which these connections are made.

Question 44: Under §1926.760 (c)(2), only those employees involved in "leading edge work" are allowed to have access to the CDZ. The rule defines the term "leading edge" but not "leading edge work." What constitutes leading edge work in a CDZ?

Answer: In a CDZ, leading edge work consists of the placement and initial installation (by safety deck attachments, which typically are tack welds) of decking to create a deck. The leading edge of the deck changes location as this work progresses.

Question 45: At what height are connectors required to be protected from falls? Is there a conflict between §§1926.760(b)(1) and 1926.760(b)(3)?

Answer: There is not a conflict between §1926.760(b)(1) and §1926.760(b)(3). Section 1926.760(b)(3) requires that at all times between 15 and 30 feet, an employee must be provided with fall protection equipment and be able to tie-off. This provision addresses circumstances under which an employer must provide fall protection, whereas, §1926.760(b)(1) addresses when an employee must use the fall protection equipment.

For clarification, under the requirements of §1926.760(b)(1), connectors working on a single story structure do not need to tie-off until they are above 30 feet since the 2-story criteria would not apply. Furthermore, connectors working on a multi-story structure do not need to tie-off until they are above 2 stories or 30 feet, whichever is less.

Question 46: Section 1926.760(c)(2) states that "access to a CDZ shall be limited to only those employees engaged in leading edge work." Installation of perimeter fall protection does not meet the standard's definition of leading edge work. Are workers prohibited from installing perimeter fall protection in a CDZ?

Answer: Installation of perimeter cables inside a CDZ will be considered a *de minimis* violation of 1926.760(c)(2) where **all** of the following conditions are met: (1) the workers installing the perimeter cables are protected by conventional fall protection; (2) their work does not interfere with the deckers, and (3) they have been trained on the hazards associated with decking. In a situation where all three conditions are met, the violation will be considered *de minimis* and a citation for that provision will not be issued

Question 47: Section 1926.760(c)(2) requires that access to a CDZ be limited to those engaged in leading edge work. Typically one crew lays down the metal decking and another crew comes behind and tack welds the sheets in place. Can the tack weld work be done in a CDZ?

Answer: Yes. Tack welding, if done for safety deck attachments, can be done in a CDZ. Section 1926.760(c)(6) gives criteria for performing safety deck attachments in the CDZ and states that they shall be performed from the leading edge back. However, 1926.760(c)(7) does not allow final deck attachments to be performed in a CDZ.

Question 48: Section 1926.760(c)(3) & Appendix D: The suggested example in the appendix states that "any other means that restricts access" may be used instead of control lines. What are some examples of other means?

Answer: Section 1926.760(c)(3) requires that the boundaries of the CDZ be marked "by the use of control lines or the equivalent." In a CDZ, the control line restricts access by visually warning employees of an unprotected area (66 FR 5247). Control lines can be made of rope, wire, tape, or other equivalent materials, but they must clearly designate the CDZ. Examples of other acceptable methods would be a perimeter wall, guardrail system, or even a restraint system rigged so that non-leading edge workers could not access the area. In contrast, a line painted on the floor would not be considered to be equivalent to control lines since it would be less visible than a control line.

Question 49: When do perimeter cables have to be installed?

Answer: Section 1926.760(a)(2) requires perimeter safety cables to be installed in multi-story structures. Under this provision, they must be installed "as soon as the metal decking has been installed." Employers may choose to install them earlier.

Question 50: Section 1926.760: Can controlling contractors require connectors to tie off between 15 and 30 feet?

Answer: Yes. The standard does not prohibit controlling contractors from imposing stricter requirements than those in the standard.

Question 51: Section 1926.760(d)(2) states that "fall arrest system components shall be used in fall restraint systems and shall conform to the criteria in §1926.502 . . . either body belts or body harnesses shall be used in fall restraint systems." Section 1926.502 prohibits the use of body belts. Is this section internally inconsistent?

Answer: No. Section 1926.502(d) prohibits the use of body belts "as part of a personal fall arrest system." A fall restraint system, as defined in §1926.751, is a system that "prevents the user from falling any distance;" rather than arresting a fall towards a lower level, it prevents it. Therefore, body belts are permitted to be used in restraint systems.

Question 52: Section 1926.760(e) requires that fall protection provided by the steel erector remain in place after steel erection in that area has been completed to be used by other trades only if the controlling contractor directs the steel erector to leave it and inspects and accepts responsibility for it. What, if any, documentation does OSHA require when the steel erector leaves and the fall protection is left in place under this provision?

Answer: No written documentation is required by the standard.

SECTION 1926.761-TRAINING.

Question 53: Can third-party training be used to comply with §1926.761? Can an employer be cited for deficiencies in the third party training of employees?

Answer: Third party training can be used to comply with the requirements of §1926.761. The preamble to this section states:

The employer can choose the provider, method, and frequency of training that is appropriate for the employees being trained. The provider may be an outside, professional training organization or other qualified entity, or the employer may develop and conduct the training in-house [Volume 66 Federal Register at page 5152].

The preamble also states that "*the program must meet the requirements of this section, and each employee must be provided the training prior to exposure to the hazard.*" [same Federal Register page as above]. It is the responsibility of the employer to take reasonable steps to assess the third party trainer's ability to adequately train the employees in accordance with this section. For example, discussing the curriculum and instructors' qualifications with the third party trainer to determine if they were sufficient, coupled with evaluating the employee's knowledge after completing the training, would be considered reasonable steps.

If a third party training program is deficient, and an employer failed to take reasonable steps to assess it, or used it knowing that it was deficient, the employer may be cited.

Question 54: Does a steel erector need to provide refresher training to its employees? When would an employee have to be given additional training?

Answer: There is no specific requirement for scheduled retraining. However, where technologies or techniques of steel erection have changed, resulting in new hazards, the employee would have to be trained regarding the new technologies, techniques, and associated hazards. Training in the recognition and avoidance of any new hazards, including unique, site-specific hazards, would be required under §1926.21(b)(2). Page 5251 of the preamble to the final steel erection standard states:

> While retraining/refresher training is not specifically addressed, the employer is responsible for making sure that it has programs necessary to comply with the training requirements in §1926.21(b)(2): 'The employer shall instruct each employee in the recognition of unsafe conditions and the regulations applicable to his work environment to control or eliminate any hazards or other exposure to illness or injury.' Steel erection involves progressive sequences of erection, so that the work environment on any one day may involve entirely different or unique new hazards than the day before and that new employees may enter into the erection process when it is already underway. In order to apply §1926.21 during steel erection activities, an employer would have to assess the type of

> training needed on a continuing basis as the environment and changes in personnel occur. It is the employer's responsibility to determine if an employee needs retraining in order to strengthen skills required to safely perform the assigned job duties and whenever the work environment changes to include newly recognized or encountered hazards. This is a key element in the employer's accident prevention program. [Volume 66 Federal Register at page 5152]

Question 55: Is receiving training through union apprenticeship programs the only way to meet the requirements of this standard?

Answer: No. Appendix E of the final rule states that "the training requirements of §1926.761 will be deemed to have been met if employees have completed a training course on steel erection . . . that has been approved by the U.S. Department of Labor Bureau of Apprenticeship." Union apprenticeship programs are mentioned in the preamble as an example of an option an employer might choose for training its employees. However, union apprenticeship programs are not the only way to provide employee training.

An employer may elect to identify a qualified person (in or out of the employer's organization) or a third party organization whose training program meets the requirements of section §1926.761 to train those employees. The new steel erection standard defines a qualified person in section §1926.751 (definitions) as:

> ..[o]ne who, by possession of a recognized degree, certificate, or professional standing, or who by extensive knowledge, training, and experience, has successfully demonstrated the ability to solve or resolve problems relating to the subject matter, the work, or the project.

As discussed in the answer to Question 53, the employer is responsible for assessing the third party organization's or qualified person's qualifications and experience as they relate to the training program requirements and subject areas described in section 1926.761. The proficiency of the employees in their work activities as determined by the employer is important evidence of an effective training program. [see page 5152 of January 18, 2001 FR]

Question 56: Does any required training under §1926.761 have to be documented? Does the employer have to keep a record of employee training?

Answer: No.

[NOTE: I need to get clarification whether what follows is part of the above document or something Joe created. If it is Joe's, then gray shading ends before this section starts. I will need to assign Exhibit #s. If it is OSHA's, then gray shading continues and there will not be exhibit numbers to assign. But we may have to use a gray box outline since the pix won't show well on top of gray screen background.

DEFINITIONS AND PHOTOS

The photographs and illustrations in this section are simply examples, for illustrative purposes only. They are not intended to be comprehensive depictions. While we hope that they are helpful in understanding some of the standard's terms and provisions, they are not to be viewed as modifying the standard.

Anchored bridging
Steel joist bridging is connected to a bridging terminus point.

Bolted diagonal bridging
Diagonal bridging that is bolted to a steel joist or joists.

Bridging clip
A device that is attached to the steel joist to allow the bolting of the bridging to the steel joist.

Choker
A wire rope or synthetic fiber rigging assembly that is used to attach a load to a hoisting device.

Column
A load-carrying vertical member that is part of the primary skeletal framing system. (Columns do not include posts)

Connector
An employee who, working with hoisting equipment, is placing and connecting structural members and/or components.

Controlled load lowering
Lowering a load by means of a mechanical hoist drum device that allows a hoisted load to be lowered with a maximum control using the gear train or hydraulic components of the hoist mechanism. Controlled load lowering requires the use of the hoist drive motor, rather than the load hoist brake, to lower the load.

Controlled decking zone (CDZ)
An area in which certain work may take place without the use of guardrail systems, personal fall arrest systems, fall restraint systems, or safety net systems and where access to the zone is controlled. (For example, initial installation and placement of metal decking)

Critical lift
A lift that (1) exceeds 75 percent of the rated capacity of the crane or derrick, or (2) requires the use of more than one crane or derrick.

293

Double connection
Attachment method where the connection point is intended for two pieces of steel which share common bolts on either side of a central piece.

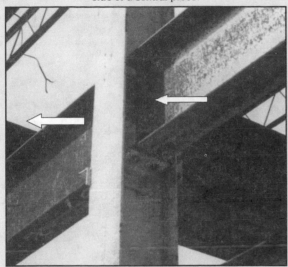

Double connection seat
A structural attachment that, during the installation of a double connection, supports the first member while the second member is connected.

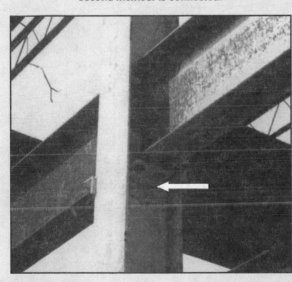

Girt
In systems-engineered metal buildings, a "Z" or "C" shaped member formed from sheet steel spanning between primary framing and supporting wall materials.

"Z" shaped girt

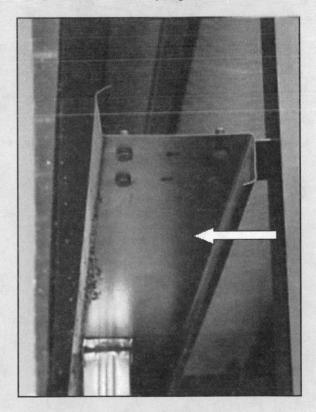

Headache ball
A weighted hook that is used to attach loads to the hoist load line of the crane.

Hoisting equipment
Commercially manufactured lifting equipment designed to lift and position a load of known weight to a location at some known elevation and horizontal distance from the equipment's center of rotation.

A "come-a-long" (a mechanical device usually consisting of a chain or cable attached at each end, that is used to facilitate movement of materials through leverage) is NOT considered "hoisting equipment."

Leading edge
An unprotected side and edge of a floor, roof, or formwork for a floor or other walking/working surface which changes location as additional floor, roof, decking or formwork sections are placed, formed or constructed.

Metal decking
Commercially manufactured, structural grade, cold rolled metal panel formed into a series of parallel ribs. (Metal decking includes metal floor and roof decks, standing seam metal roofs, other metal roof systems and other products such as bar gratings, checker plate, expanded metal panels, and similar products)

Multiple lift rigging
A rigging assembly manufactured by wire rope rigging suppliers that facilitates the attachment of up to five independent loads to the hoist rigging of a crane.

Multiple lift rigging procedure (MLRP) ("Christmas Treeing")

Opening
A gap or void 12 inches or more in its least dimension in a floor, roof or other walking/working surface. (Skylights and smoke domes that do not meet the strength requirements of a cover, are considered openings)

Personal fall arrest system

A system used to arrest an employee in a fall from a working level. System consists of an anchorage, connectors, a body harness and may include a lanyard, deceleration device, lifeline or suitable combination of these. (The use of a body belt for fall arrest is prohibited.)

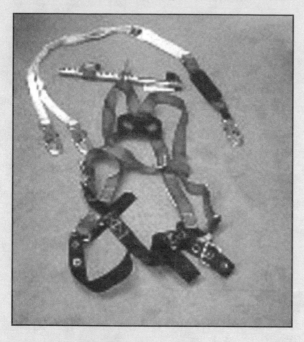

Positioning device

A body belt or body harness rigged to allow an employee to be supported on an elevated, vertical surface, such as a wall or column and work with both hands free while leaning.

Post

A structural member with a longitudinal axis that is essentially vertical, that: (1) is axially loaded (a load presses down on the top end) and weighs 300 pounds or less, or (2) is not axially loaded, but is laterally restrained by the above member. Posts typically support stair landings, wall framing, mezzanines and other substructures.

Purlin

In systems-engineered metal buildings, a "Z" or "C" shaped member formed from sheet steel spanning between primary framing and supporting roof material.

Safety deck attachment
An initial attachment that is used to secure an initially placed sheet of decking to keep proper alignment and bearing with structural support members.

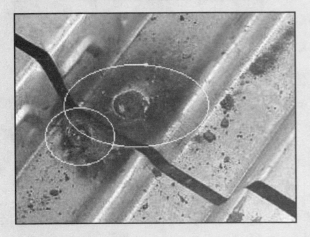

Shear connector
Steel bars, steel lugs, headed steel studs, and similar devices that are attached to a structural member for the purpose of achieving composite action with concrete.

Steel joist
An open web, secondary load-carrying member of 144 feet or less, designed by the manufacturer, used for the support of floors and roofs. (This does not include structural steel trusses or cold-formed joists)

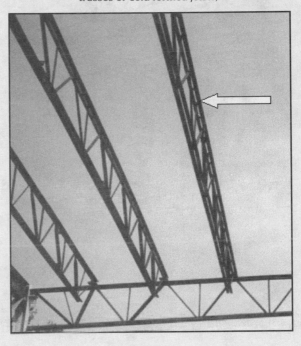

Steel joist girder
An open web, primary load carrying member, designed by a manufacturer, used for the support of floors and roofs. (This does not include structural steel trusses or cold-formed joists)

Steel Erection

Systems-engineered metal building
Field-assembled building system consisting of framing, roof and wall coverings.

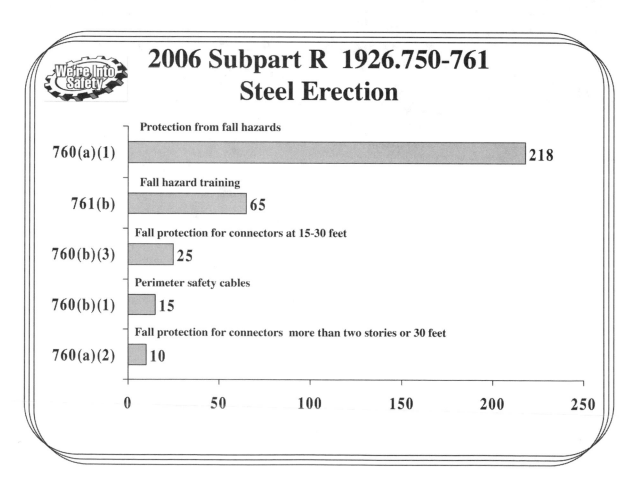

2006 Subpart R 1926.750-761
Steel Erection

Protection from fall hazards

760(a)(1) — 218

Fall hazard training

761(b) — 65

Fall protection for connectors at 15-30 feet

760(b)(3) — 25

Perimeter safety cables

760(b)(1) — 15

Fall protection for connectors more than two stories or 30 feet

760(a)(2) — 10

0   50   100   150   200   250

Cranes, Derricks, Hoists, Elevators, and Conveyors

Cranes and Derricks—1926.550

The employer shall comply with the manufacturer's specifications and limitations applicable to the operation of any and all cranes and derricks. Where manufacturer's specifications are not available, the limitations assigned to the equipment shall be based on the determinations of a qualified engineer competent in this field and such determinations will be appropriately documented and recorded. Attachments used with cranes shall not exceed the capacity, rating, or scope recommended by the manufacturer.

Crane operators must:
- Know the capacity of the crane they are using;
- Know the weight of the load they are lifting;
- Guard their machine against accidental power line contact;
- Check for proper footing on their machine;
- Use outriggers as required;
- Conduct inspections on the crane and rigging frequently;
- Use correct hand signals;
- Guard the counterweight swing radius; and
- Follow the lift plan.

Rated load capacities, and recommended operating speeds, special hazard warnings, or instruction, shall be conspicuously posted on all equipment. Instructions or warnings shall be visible to the operator while he is at his control station.

Hand signals to crane and derrick operators shall be those prescribed by the applicable ANSI standard for the type of crane in use. An illustration of the signals shall be posted at the job site.

The employer shall designate a competent person who shall inspect all machinery and equipment prior to each use, and during use, to make sure it is in safe operating condition. Any deficiencies shall be repaired, or defective parts replaced, before continued use.

A thorough, annual inspection of the hoisting machinery shall be made by a competent person, or by a government or private agency recognized by the U.S. Department of Labor. The employer shall maintain a record of the dates and results of inspections for each hoisting machine and piece of equipment.

Wire rope shall be taken out of service when any of the following conditions exist:

- In running ropes, six randomly distributed broken wires in one lay or three broken wires in one strand in one lay;
- Wear of one-third the original diameter of outside individual wires.
- Kinking, crushing, bird caging, or any other damage resulting in distortion of the rope structure;
- Evidence of any heat damage from any cause;
- Reductions from nominal diameter of more than 1/64 in. for diameters up to and including 5/16 in.; 1/32 in. for diameters 3/8 in. to and including ½ in.; 3/64 in. for diameters 9/16 in. to and including ¾ in.; 1/16 in. for diameters 7/8 in. to 1 1/8 in. inclusive; 3/32 in. for diameters 1¼ to 1½ in. inclusive;
- In standing ropes, more than two broken wires in one lay in sections beyond end connections or more than one broken wire at an end connection.
- Wire rope safety factors shall be in accordance with American National Standards Institute B30.5-1968 or SAE J959-1966.

Belts, gears, shafts, pulleys, sprockets, spindles, drums, fly wheels, chains, or other reciprocating, rotating, or other moving parts or equipment shall be guarded if such parts are exposed to contact by employees, or otherwise create a hazard. Guarding shall meet the requirements of the American National Standards Institute B15.1-1958 Rev., Safety Code for Mechanical Power Transmission Apparatus.

Accessible areas within the swing radius of the rear of the rotating superstructure of the crane, either permanently or temporarily mounted, shall be barricaded in such a manner as to prevent an employee from being struck or crushed by the crane.

All exhaust pipes shall be guarded or insulated in areas where contact by employees is possible in the performance of normal duties.

Whenever internal combustion engine powered equipment exhausts in enclosed spaces, tests shall be made and recorded to see that employees are not exposed to unsafe concentrations of toxic gases or oxygen deficient atmospheres.

All windows in cabs shall be of safety glass, or equivalent, that introduces no visible distortion that will interfere with the safe operation of the machine.

Where necessary for rigging or service requirements, a ladder, or steps, shall be provided to give access to a cab roof.

Guardrails, handholds, and steps shall be provided on cranes for easy access to the car and cab, conforming to American National Standards Institute B30.5.

Platforms and walkways shall have anti-skid surfaces.

Fuel tank filler pipes shall be located in such a position, or protected in such manner, as to not allow spill or overflow to run onto the engine, exhaust, or electrical equipment of any machine being fueled.

An accessible fire extinguisher of 5BC rating, or higher, shall be available at all operator stations or cabs of equipment.

All fuels shall be transported, stored, and handled to meet the rules of subpart F of this part. When fuel is transported by vehicles on public highways, Department of Transportation rules contained in 49 CFR Parts 177 and 393 concerning such vehicular transportation are considered applicable.

Except where electrical distribution and transmission lines have been deenergized and visibly grounded at point of work or where insulating barriers, not a part of or an attachment to the equipment or machinery, have been erected to prevent physical contact with the lines, equipment or machines shall be operated proximately to power lines only in accordance with the following:

- For lines rated 50 kV. or below, minimum clearance between the lines and any part of the crane or load shall be 10 ft.;
- For lines rated over 50 kV., minimum clearance between the lines and any part of the crane or load shall be 10 ft. plus 0.4 in. for each 1 kV. over 50 kV., or twice the length of the line insulator, but never less than 10 ft.;
- In transit with no load and boom lowered, the equipment clearance shall be a minimum of 4 ft. for voltages less than 50 kV., and 10 ft. for voltages over 50 kV., up to and including 345 kV., and 16 ft. for voltages up to and including 750 kV.

- A person shall be designated to observe clearance of the equipment and give timely warning for all operations where it is difficult for the operator to maintain the desired clearance by visual means;
- Cage-type boom guards, insulating links, or proximity warning devices may be used on cranes, but the use of such devices shall not alter the requirements of any other regulation of this part even if such device is required by law or regulation;
- Any overhead wire shall be considered to be an energized line unless and until the person owning such line or the electrical utility authorities indicate that it is not an energized line and it has been visibly grounded;
- Prior to work near transmitter towers where an electrical charge can be induced in the equipment or materials being handled, the transmitter shall be de-energized or tests shall be made to determine if electrical charge is induced on the crane. The following precautions shall be taken when necessary to dissipate induced voltages:
  - The equipment shall be provided with an electrical ground directly to the upper rotating structure supporting the boom; and
  - Ground jumper cables shall be attached to materials being handled by boom equipment when electrical charge is induced while working near energized transmitters. Crews shall be provided with nonconductive poles having large alligator clips or other similar protection to attach the ground cable to the load.
  - Combustible and flammable materials shall be removed from the immediate area prior to operations.

No modifications or additions which affect the capacity or safe operation of the equipment shall be made by the employer without the manufacturer's written approval. If such modifications or changes are made, the capacity, operation, and maintenance instruction plates, tags, or decals, shall be changed accordingly. In no case shall the original safety factor of the equipment be reduced.

The employer shall comply with Power Crane and Shovel Association Mobile Hydraulic Crane Standard No. 2.

Sideboom cranes mounted on wheel or crawler tractors shall meet the requirements of SAE J743a–1964.

All employees shall be kept clear of loads about to be lifted and of suspended loads.

Crawler, Locomotive, and Truck Cranes

All jibs shall have positive stops to prevent their movement of more than 5° above the straight line of the jib and boom on conventional type crane booms. The use of cable type belly slings does not constitute compliance with this rule.

All crawler, truck, or locomotive cranes in use shall meet the applicable requirements for design, inspection, construction, testing, maintenance and operation as prescribed in the ANSI B30.5-1968, Safety Code for Crawler, Locomotive and Truck Cranes. However, the written, dated, and signed inspection reports and records of the monthly inspection of critical items prescribed in section 5-2.1.5 of the ANSI B30.5-1968 standard are not required. Instead, the employer shall prepare a certification record which includes the date the crane items were inspected; the signature of the person who inspected the crane items; and a serial number, or other identifier, for the crane inspected. The most recent certification record shall be maintained on file until a new one is prepared.

Hammerhead Tower Cranes

Adequate clearance shall be maintained between moving and rotating structures of the crane and fixed objects to allow the passage of employees without harm.

Each employee required to perform duties on the horizontal boom of hammerhead tower cranes shall be protected against falling by guardrails or by a personal fall arrest system in conformance with subpart M of this part.

Buffers shall be provided at both ends of travel of the trolley.

Cranes mounted on rail tracks shall be equipped with limit switches limiting the travel of the crane on the track and stops or buffers at each end of the tracks.

Cranes, Derricks, Hoists, Elevators, and Conveyors

All hammerhead tower cranes in use shall meet the applicable requirements for design, construction, installation, testing, maintenance, inspection, and operation as prescribed by the manufacturer.

Overhead and Gantry Cranes

The rated load of the crane shall be plainly marked on each side of the crane, and if the crane has more than one hoisting unit, each hoist shall have its rated load marked on it or its load block, and this marking shall be clearly legible from the ground or floor.

Bridge trucks shall be equipped with sweeps which extend below the top of the rail and project in front of the truck wheels.

Except for floor-operated cranes, a gong or other effective audible warning signal shall be provided for each crane equipped with a power traveling mechanism.

All overhead and gantry cranes in use shall meet the applicable requirements for design, construction, installation, testing, maintenance, inspection, and operation as prescribed in the ANSI B30.2.0-1967, Safety Code for Overhead and Gantry Cranes.

Derricks

All derricks in use shall meet the applicable requirements for design, construction, installation, inspection, testing, maintenance, and operation as prescribed in American National Standards Institute B30.6-1969, Safety Code for Derricks.

Mobile Cranes Mounted on Barges

When a mobile crane is mounted on a barge, the rated load of the crane shall not exceed the original capacity specified by the manufacturer.

A load rating chart, with clearly legible letters and figures, shall be provided with each crane, and securely fixed at a location easily visible to the operator. When load ratings are reduced to stay within the limits for list of the barge with a crane mounted on it, a new load rating chart shall be provided.

Mobile cranes on barges shall be positively secured.

Permanently Mounted Floating Cranes and Derricks

When cranes and derricks are permanently installed on a barge, the capacity and limitations of use shall be based on competent design criteria.

A load rating chart with clearly legible letters and figures shall be provided and securely fixed at a location easily visible to the operator.

Floating cranes and floating derricks in use shall meet the applicable requirements for design, construction, installation, testing, maintenance, and operation as prescribed by the manufacturer.

Protection of Employees Working on Barges

The employer shall comply with the applicable requirements for protection of employees working onboard marine vessels specified in 1926.605.

Crane Inspections

Initial Inspections

New or altered cranes must be inspected by a "qualified inspector" as designated by the owner of the crane. Every initial inspection will include a load test to verify the cranes structural integrity ratings.

Periodic Inspections

This type of inspection may be scheduled on a regular basis depending on the use of the crane. They are usually conducted monthly, quarterly or annually, but must not exceed an annual inspection. The schedule is determined by the crane owner based on the usage of the crane. They may be performed by either a qualified operator or an inspector depending on the length of the interval and the intensity of the inspection.

Frequent (Pre-Use) Inspections

These inspections are performed daily prior to the use of the crane, during the operation or at the beginning of each shift. A strict program of preventive maintenance, daily service and thorough pre-operation checks will result in proper operation, safer equipment and lower operating costs. The operator is required to know the condition of the equipment and must not knowingly operate any crane or equipment that is unsafe or hazardous.

Exhibit 14-1.
Daily and Monthly Crane Safety Inspection Log
Daily Crane Safety Inspection—Keep This Form on the Crane

Crane: _____ Equipment # _____

I have inspected the cranes equipment and machinery before operation. It is in safe operating condition. My initials below verify that I have done a visual inspection consisting of checking at least the following items:

Month: _____

- Safety devices are present and operable
- Fire extinguishers are present and operable
- Crane is on proper, solid foundation
- No broken or cracked glass
- Boom, sheaves, nuts and bolts are OK
- Pins properly fastened
- Wire rope, pendant lines are OK
- Slings and rigging are OK
- No air, oil, fuel, or water leakage
- Proper lubrication
- Control mechanisms operate properly
- No damaged or missing guards or covers
- No cracked or broken parts
- Capacity chart and hand signal charts are posted
- Areas within the swing radius of rear of crane are barricaded

1. ____	11. ____	21. ____
2. ____	12. ____	22. ____
3. ____	13. ____	23. ____
4. ____	14. ____	24. ____
5. ____	15. ____	25. ____
6. ____	16. ____	26. ____
7. ____	17. ____	27. ____
8. ____	18. ____	28. ____
9. ____	19. ____	29. ____
10. ____	20. ____	30. ____
31. ____		

Month: _____

1. ____	11. ____	21. ____
2. ____	12. ____	22. ____
3. ____	13. ____	23. ____
4. ____	14. ____	24. ____
5. ____	15. ____	25. ____
6. ____	16. ____	26. ____
7. ____	17. ____	27. ____
8. ____	18. ____	28. ____
9. ____	19. ____	29. ____
10. ____	20. ____	30. ____
31. ____		

Helicopters—1926.551

Helicopter cranes shall be expected to comply with any applicable regulations of the Federal Aviation Administration.

Prior to each day's operation a briefing shall be conducted. This briefing shall set forth the plan of operation for the pilot and ground personnel.

Slings and Tag Lines

Loads shall be properly slung. Tag lines shall be of a length that will not permit their being drawn up into rotors. Pressed sleeve, swedged eyes, or equivalent means shall be used for all freely suspended loads to prevent hand splices from spinning open or cable clamps from loosening.

Cargo Hooks

All electrically operated cargo hooks shall have the electrical activating device so designed and installed as to prevent inadvertent operation. In addition, these cargo hooks shall be equipped with an emergency mechanical control for releasing the load. The hooks shall be tested prior to each day's operation to determine that the release functions properly, both electrically and mechanically.

Personal Protective Equipment

Personal protective equipment for employees receiving the load shall consist of complete eye protection and hard hats secured by chin-straps. Loose-fitting clothing likely to flap in the downwash, and thus be snagged on hoist line, shall not be worn.

Loose Gear and Objects

Every practical precaution shall be taken to provide for the protection of the employees from flying objects in the rotor downwash. All loose gear within 100 ft. of the place of lifting the load, depositing the load, and all other areas susceptible to rotor downwash shall be secured or removed. Good housekeeping shall be maintained in all helicopter loading and unloading areas.

Operator Responsibility

The helicopter operator shall be responsible for size, weight, and manner in which loads are connected to the helicopter. If, for any reason, the helicopter operator believes the lift cannot be made safely, the lift shall not be made.

Hooking and Unhooking Loads

When employees are required to perform work under hovering craft, a safe means of access shall be provided for employees to reach the hoist line hook and engage or disengage cargo slings. Employees shall not perform work under hovering craft except when necessary to hook or unhook loads.

Static Charge

Static charge on the suspended load shall be dissipated with a grounding device before ground personnel touch the suspended load, or protective rubber gloves shall be worn by all ground personnel touching the suspended load.

Weight Limitation

The weight of an external load shall not exceed the manufacturer's rating.

Ground Lines

Hoist wires or other gear, except for pulling lines or conductors that are allowed to "pay out" from a container or roll off a reel, shall not be attached to any fixed ground structure, or allowed to foul on any fixed structure.

Visibility

When visibility is reduced by dust or other conditions, ground personnel shall exercise special caution to keep clear of main and stabilizing rotors. Precautions shall also be taken by the employer to eliminate as far as practical reduced visibility.

Signal Systems. Signal systems between aircrew and ground personnel shall be understood and checked in advance of hoisting the load. This applies to either radio or hand signal systems. Hand signals shall be as shown in Figure N-1.

Exhibit 14-2. Figure N-1. Helicopter Hand Signal

Approach Distance

No unauthorized person shall be allowed to approach within 50 ft. of the helicopter when the rotor blades are turning.

Approaching Helicopter

Whenever approaching or leaving a helicopter with blades rotating, all employees shall remain in full view of the pilot and keep in a crouched position. Employees shall avoid the area from the cockpit or cabin rearward unless authorized by the helicopter operator to work there.

Personnel

Sufficient ground personnel shall be provided when required for safe helicopter loading and unloading operations.

Communications

There shall be constant reliable communication between the pilot, and a designated employee of the ground crew who acts as a signalman during the period of loading and unloading. This signalman shall be distinctly recognizable from other ground personnel.

Fires

Open fires shall not be permitted in an area that could result in such fires being spread by the rotor downwash.

Material Hoists, Personnel Hoists, and Elevators—1926.552

General Requirements

The employer shall comply with the manufacturer's specifications and limitations applicable to the operation of all hoists and elevators. Where manufacturer's specifications are not available, the limitations assigned to the equipment shall be based on the determinations of a professional engineer competent in the field.

Rated load capacities, recommended operating speeds, and special hazard warnings or instructions shall be posted on cars and platforms.

Wire rope shall be removed from service when any of the following conditions exists:

- In hoisting ropes, six randomly distributed broken wires in one rope lay or three broken wires in one strand in one rope lay;
- Abrasion, scrubbing, flattening, or peening, causing loss of more than one-third of the original diameter of the outside wires;
- Evidence of any heat damage resulting from a torch or any damage caused by contact with electrical wires;
- Reduction from nominal diameter of more than 3/64 in. for diameters up to and including 3/4 in.; 1/16 in. for diameters 7/8 in. to 1 1/8 in.; and 3/32 in. for diameters 1¼ in. to 1½ in.

Hoisting ropes shall be installed in accordance with the wire rope manufacturers' recommendations.

The installation of live booms on hoists is prohibited.

The use of endless belt-type manlifts on construction shall be prohibited.

Material Hoists

Operating rules shall be established and posted at the operator's station of the hoist. Such rules shall include a signal system and allowable line speed for various loads. Rules and notices shall be posted on the car frame or crosshead in a conspicuous location, including the statement "No Riders Allowed."

No person shall be allowed to ride on material hoists except for the purposes of inspection and maintenance.

All entrances of the hoistways shall be protected by substantial gates or bars which shall guard the full width of the landing entrance. All hoistway entrance bars and gates shall be painted with diagonal contrasting colors, such as black and yellow stripes.

Bars shall be not less than 2-in. × 4-in. wooden bars or the equivalent, located 2 ft. from the hoistway line. Bars shall be located not less than 36 in. nor more than 42 in. above the floor.

Gates or bars protecting the entrances to hoistways shall be equipped with a latching device.

Overhead protective covering of 2-in. planking, ¾-in. plywood, or other solid material of equivalent strength, shall be provided on the top of every material hoist cage or platform.

The operator's station of a hoisting machine shall be provided with overhead protection equivalent to tight planking not less than 2 in. thick. The support for the overhead protection shall be of equal strength.

Hoist towers may be used with or without an enclosure on all sides. However, whichever alternative is chosen, the following applicable conditions shall be met:

- When a hoist tower is enclosed, it shall be enclosed on all sides for its entire height with a screen enclosure of ½-in. mesh, No. 18 U.S. gauge wire or equivalent, except for landing access.
- When a hoist tower is not enclosed, the hoist platform or car shall be totally enclosed (caged) on all sides for the full height between the floor and the overhead protective covering with ½-in. mesh of No. 14 U.S. gauge wire or equivalent. The hoist platform enclosure shall include the required gates for loading and unloading. A 6-ft. high enclosure shall be provided on the unused sides of the hoist tower at ground level.

Car arresting devices shall be installed to function in case of rope failure.

All material hoist towers shall be designed by a licensed professional engineer.

All material hoists shall conform to the requirements of ANSI A10.5-1969, Safety Requirements for Material Hoists.

Personnel Hoists

Hoist towers outside the structure shall be enclosed for the full height on the side or sides used for entrance and exit to the structure. At the lowest landing, the enclosure on the sides not used for exit or entrance to the structure shall be enclosed to a height of at least 10 ft. Other sides of the tower adjacent to floors or scaffold platforms shall be enclosed to a height of 10 ft. above the level of such floors or scaffolds.

Towers inside of structures shall be enclosed on all four sides throughout the full height.

Towers shall be anchored to the structure at intervals not exceeding 25 ft. In addition to tie-ins, a series of guys shall be installed. Where tie-ins are not practical the tower shall be anchored by means of guys made of wire rope at least ½ in. in diameter, securely fastened to anchorage to ensure stability.

Hoistway doors or gates shall be not less than 6 ft., 6 in. high and shall be provided with mechanical locks which cannot be operated from the landing side, and shall be accessible only to persons on the car.

Cars shall be permanently enclosed on all sides and the top, except sides used for entrance and exit which have car gates or doors.

A door or gate shall be provided at each entrance to the car which shall protect the full width and height of the car entrance opening.

Overhead protective covering of 2-in. planking, ¾-in. plywood or other solid material or equivalent strength shall be provided on the top of every personnel hoist.

Doors or gates shall be provided with electric contacts which do not allow movement of the hoist when door or gate is open.

Safeties shall be capable of stopping and holding the car and rated load when traveling at governor tripping speed.

Cars shall be provided with a capacity and data plate secured in a conspicuous place on the car or crosshead.

Internal combustion engines shall not be permitted for direct drive.

Normal and final terminal stopping devices shall be provided.

An emergency stop switch shall be provided in the car and marked "Stop."

Ropes

The minimum number of hoisting ropes used shall be three for traction hoists and two for drum-type hoists.

The minimum diameter of hoisting and counterweight wire ropes shall be ½-in. Minimum factors of safety for suspension wire ropes are available at 1926.552(c)(14)(iii) (See Exhibit 14-3.).

Exhibit 14-3. Minimum Factors of Safety for Suspension Wire Ropes

Rope speed in feet per minute	Minimum factor of safety
50	7.60
75	7.75
100	7.95
125	8.10
150	8.25
175	8.40
200	8.60
225	8.75
250	8.90
300	9.20
350	9.50
400	9.75
450	10.00
500	10.25
550	10.45
600	10.70

Following assembly and erection of hoists, and before being put in service, an inspection and test of all functions and safety devices shall be made under the supervision of a competent person. A similar inspection and test is required following major alteration of an existing installation. All hoists shall be inspected and tested at not more than 3-month intervals. The employer shall prepare a certification record which includes the date the inspection and test of all functions and safety devices was performed, the signature of the person who performed the inspection and test; and a serial number, or other identifier, for the hoist that was inspected and tested. The most recent certification record shall be maintained on file.

All personnel hoists used by employees shall be constructed of materials and components which meet the specifications for materials, construction, safety devices, assembly, and structural integrity as stated in the American National Standard A10.4-1963, Safety Requirements for Workmen's Hoists. The requirements of 1926.552(c)(16) do not apply to cantilever type personnel hoists.

Personnel hoists used in bridge tower construction shall be approved by a registered professional engineer and erected under the supervision of a qualified engineer competent in this field. When a hoist tower is not enclosed, the hoist platform or car shall be totally enclosed (caged) on all sides for the full height between the floor and the overhead protective covering with ¾-in. mesh of No. 14 U.S. gauge wire or equivalent. The hoist platform enclosure shall include the required gates for loading and unloading.

These hoists shall be inspected and maintained on a weekly basis. Whenever the hoisting equipment is exposed to winds exceeding 35 mph it shall be inspected and put in operable condition before reuse. Wire rope shall be taken out of service when any of the following conditions exist:

- In running ropes, six randomly distributed broken wires in one lay or three broken wires in one strand in one lay;
- Wear of one-third the original diameter of outside individual wires. Kinking, crushing, bird caging, or any other damage resulting in distortion of the rope structure;
- Evidence of any heat damage from any cause;
- Reductions from nominal diameter of more than 3/64 in. for diameters to and including ¾ in., 1/16 in. for diameters 7/8 in. to 1 1/8 in. inclusive, 3/32 in. for diameters 1¼ to 1½ in. inclusive;
- In standing ropes, more than two broken wires in one lay in sections beyond end connections or more than one broken wire at an end connection.

Permanent elevators under the care and custody of the employer and used by employees for work covered by this Act shall comply with the requirements of American National Standards Institute A17.1-1965 with addenda A17.1a-1967, A17.1b-1968, A17.1c-1969, A17.1d-1970, and inspected in accordance with A17.2-1960 with addenda A17.2a-1965, A17.2b-1967.

Base-Mounted Drum Hoists—1926.553

Exposed moving parts such as gears, projecting screws, setscrews, chain, cables, chain sprockets, and reciprocating or rotating parts, which constitute a hazard, shall be guarded.

All controls used during the normal operation cycle shall be located within easy reach of the operator's station.

Electric motor-operated hoists shall be provided with:

- A device to disconnect all motors from the line upon power failure and not permit any motor to be restarted until the controller handle is brought to the "off" position;
- Where applicable, an overspeed preventive device;
- A means whereby remotely operated hoists stop when any control is ineffective.

All base-mounted drum hoists in use shall meet the applicable requirements for design, construction, installation, testing, inspection, maintenance, and operations, as prescribed by the manufacturer.

Overhead Hoists—1926.554

The safe working load of the overhead hoist, as determined by the manufacturer, shall be indicated on the hoist, and this safe working load shall not be exceeded.

The supporting structure to which the hoist is attached shall have a safe working load equal to that of the hoist. The support shall be arranged so as to provide for free movement of the hoist and shall not restrict the hoist from lining itself up with the load.

The hoist shall be installed only in locations that will permit the operator to stand clear of the load at all times.

Air hoists shall be connected to an air supply of sufficient capacity and pressure to safely operate the hoist. All air hoses supplying air shall be positively connected to prevent their becoming disconnected during use.

All overhead hoists in use shall meet the applicable requirements for construction, design, installation, testing, inspection, maintenance, and operation, as prescribed by the manufacturer.

Conveyors—1926.555

Means for stopping the tmotor or engine shall be provided at the operator's station. Conveyor systems shall be equipped with an audible warning signal to be sounded immediately before starting up the conveyor.

If the operator's station is at a remote point, similar provisions for stopping the motor or engine shall be provided at the motor or engine location.

Emergency stop switches shall be arranged so that the conveyor cannot be started again until the actuating stop switch has been reset to running or "on" position.

Screw conveyors shall be guarded to prevent employee contact with turning flights.

Where a conveyor passes over work areas, aisles, or thoroughfares, suitable guards shall be provided to protect employees required to work below the conveyors.

All crossovers, aisles, and passageways shall be conspicuously marked by suitable signs, as required by subpart G of this part.

Conveyors shall be locked out or otherwise rendered inoperable, and tagged out with a "Do Not Operate" tag during repairs and when operation is hazardous to employees performing maintenance work.

All conveyors in use shall meet the applicable requirements for design, construction, inspection, testing, maintenance, and operation, as prescribed in the ANSI B20.1-1957, Safety Code for Conveyors, Cableways, and Related Equipment.

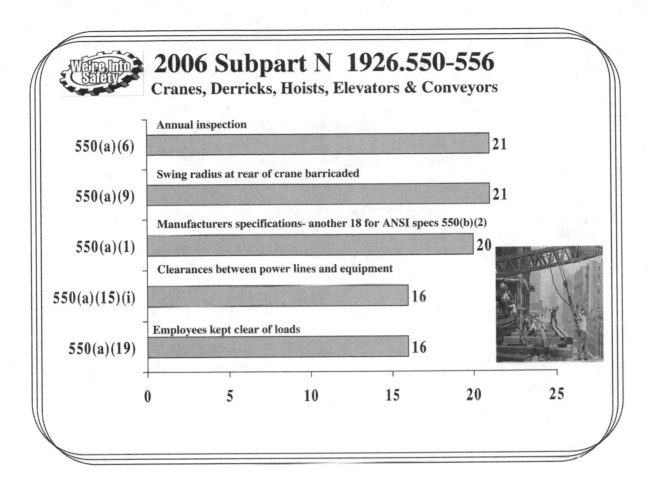

2006 Subpart N 1926.550-556
Cranes, Derricks, Hoists, Elevators & Conveyors

Annual inspection
550(a)(6) — 21

Swing radius at rear of crane barricaded
550(a)(9) — 21

Manufacturers specifications- another 18 for ANSI specs 550(b)(2)
550(a)(1) — 20

Clearances between power lines and equipment
550(a)(15)(i) — 16

Employees kept clear of loads
550(a)(19) — 16

MATERIALS HANDLING AND STORAGE

Potential Hazards

Handling and storing materials involves diverse operations such as hoisting tons of steel with a crane; driving a truck loaded with concrete blocks; manually carrying bags and material; and stacking drums, barrels, kegs, lumber, or loose bricks.

The efficient handling and storing of materials is vital to industry. These operations provide a continuous flow of raw materials, parts, and assemblies through the workplace and help ensure materials are available when needed. Yet, the improper handling and storing of materials can cause costly injuries.

Workers frequently cite the weight and bulkiness of objects being lifted as major contributing factors to their injuries. In 1990, back injuries resulted in 400,000 workplace accidents. The second factor frequently cited by workers as contributing to their injuries was body movement. Bending, followed by twisting and turning, were the more commonly cited movements that caused back injuries. Back injuries accounted for more than 20 percent of all occupational illnesses, according to data from the National Safety Council.

In addition, workers can be injured by falling objects, improperly stacked materials, or by various types of equipment. When manually moving materials, however, workers should be aware of potential injuries, including the following:

■ Strains and sprains from improperly lifting loads or from carrying loads that are either too large or too heavy;

■ Fractures and bruises caused by being struck by materials or by being caught in pinch points; and

■ Cuts and bruises caused by falling materials that have been improperly stored or by incorrectly cutting ties or other securing devices.

Because numerous injuries can result from improperly handling and storing materials, it is important to be aware of accidents that may occur from unsafe or improperly handled equipment and improper work practices and to recognize the methods for eliminating, or at least minimizing, the occurrence of those accidents. Consequently, employers and employees can and should examine their workplaces to detect any unsafe or unhealthful conditions, practices, or equipment and take the necessary steps to correct them.

Methods of Prevention

General safety principles can help reduce workplace accidents. These include work practices, ergonomic principles, and training and education. Whether moving materials manually or mechanically, employees should be aware of the potential hazards associated with the task at hand and know how to exercise control over their workplaces to minimize the danger.

Moving, Handling, and Storing Materials

When manually moving materials, employees should seek help when a load is so bulky it cannot be properly grasped or lifted, when they cannot see around or over it, or when a load cannot be safely handled.

When an employee is placing blocks under raised loads, the employee should ensure that the load is not released until his or her hands are clearly removed from the load. Blocking materials and timbers should be large and strong enough to support the load safely. Materials with evidence of cracks, rounded corners, splintered pieces, or dry rot should not be used for blocking.

Handles and holders should be attached to loads to reduce the chances of getting fingers pinched or smashed. Workers also should use appropriate personal protective equipment. For loads with sharp or rough edges, employees should wear gloves or other hand and forearm protection. To avoid injuries to the hands and eyes, employees should use gloves and eye protection. When the loads are heavy or bulky, the mover also should wear steel-toed safety shoes or boots to prevent foot injuries if the worker slips or accidentally drops a load.

When mechanically moving materials, workers can avoid overloading the equipment by letting the weight, size, and shape of the material being moved dictate the type of equipment used for transporting it. All materials handling equipment has rated capacities that determine the maximum weight the equipment can safely handle and the conditions under which it can handle those weights. The equipment-rated capacities must be displayed on each piece of equipment and must not be exceeded except for load testing.

When picking up items with a powered industrial truck, the load must be centered on the forks and as close to the mast as possible to minimize the potential for the truck tipping or the load falling. A lift truck must never be overloaded because it would be hard to control and could easily tip over. Extra weight must not be placed on the rear of a counterbalanced forklift to offset an overload. The load must be at the lowest position for traveling, and the truck manufacturer's operational requirements must be followed. All stacked loads must be correctly piled and cross-tiered, where possible. Precautions also should be taken when stacking and storing material.

Stored materials must not create a hazard. Storage areas must be kept free from accumulated materials that may cause tripping, fires, or explosions, or that may contribute to the harboring of rats and other pests. When stacking and piling materials, it is important to be aware of such factors as:

- The materials' height and weight;
- How accessible the stored materials are to the user; and
- The condition of the containers where the materials are being stored.

All bound material should be stacked, placed on racks, blocked, interlocked, or otherwise secured to prevent it from sliding, falling, or collapsing. A load greater than that approved by a building official may not be placed on any floor of a building or other structure. Where applicable, load limits approved by the building inspector should be conspicuously posted in all storage areas.

When stacking materials, height limitations should be observed. For example, lumber must be stacked no more than 16 ft. high if it is handled manually and no more than 20 ft. if a forklift is used. For quick reference, walls or posts may be painted with stripes to indicate maximum stacking heights.

Used lumber must have all nails removed before stacking. Lumber must be stacked and leveled on solidly supported bracing. The stacks must be stable and self-supporting. Stacks of loose bricks should not be more than 7 ft. in height. When these stacks reach a height of 4 ft., they should be tapered back 2 in. for every foot of height above the 4-ft. level. When masonry blocks are stacked higher than 6 ft., the stacks should be tapered back one-half block for each tier above the 6-ft. level.

Bags and bundles must be stacked in interlocking rows to remain secure. Bagged material must be stacked by stepping back the layers and cross-keying the bags at least every 10 layers. To remove bags from the stack, workers should start from the top row first. Baled paper and rags stored inside a building must not be closer than 18 in. to the walls, partitions, or sprinkler heads. Boxed materials must be banded or held in place using crossties or shrink plastic fiber.

Drums, barrels, and kegs must be stacked symmetrically. If stored on their sides, the bottom tiers must be blocked to keep them from rolling. When stacked on end, workers should put planks, sheets of plywood dunnage, or pallets between each tier to make a firm, flat, stacking surface. When stacking materials two or more tiers high, the bottom tier must be chocked on each side to prevent shifting in either direction.

When stacking, workers should consider the need for availability of the material. Material that cannot be stacked due to size, shape, or fragility can be safely stored on shelves or in bins. Structural steel, bar stock, poles, and other cylindrical materials, unless in racks, must be stacked and blocked to prevent spreading or tilting. Pipes and bars should not be stored in racks that face main aisles; this could create a hazard to passers-by when supplies are being removed.

To reduce potential accidents associated with workplace equipment, employees must be trained in the proper use and limitations of the equipment they operate. This training must include teaching employees how to effectively use equipment such as conveyors, cranes, and slings.

Conveyors

When using conveyors, workers' hands may be caught in nip points where the conveyor runs over support members or rollers; workers may be struck by material falling off the conveyor or become caught on or in the conveyor, being drawn into the conveyor path.

To reduce the severity of an injury, an emergency button or pull cord designed to stop the conveyor must be installed at the employee's workstation. Continuously accessible conveyor belts should have an emergency stop cable that extends the entire length of the conveyor belt so that the cable can be accessed from any location along the belt. The emergency stop switch must be designed to be reset before the conveyor can be restarted. Before restarting a conveyor that has stopped due to an overload, appropriate personnel must inspect the conveyor and clear the stoppage before restarting. Employees must never ride on a materials handling conveyor. Where a conveyor passes over work areas or aisles, guards must be provided to keep employees from being struck by falling material. If the crossover is low enough for workers to run into it, it must be guarded to protect employees and marked with a warning sign or painted a bright color.

Screw conveyors must be completely covered except at loading and discharging points. At those points, guards must protect employees against contacting the moving screw. The guards must be movable and be interlocked to prevent conveyor movement when not in place.

Cranes

Only thoroughly trained and competent persons are permitted to operate cranes. Operators should know what they are lifting and what it weighs. The rated capacity of a mobile crane varies with the length of the boom and the boom radius. When a crane has a telescoping boom, a load may be safe to lift at a short boom length and/or a short boom radius, but the same load may overload the crane when the boom is extended and the radius increases.

All movable cranes must be equipped with a boom angle indicator; those cranes with telescoping booms must be equipped with some means to determine the boom length, unless the load rating is independent of the boom length. Load rating charts must be posted in the cab of cab-operated cranes. All mobile cranes do not have uniform capacities for the same boom length and radius in all directions around the chassis of the vehicle.

Operators should always check the crane's load chart to ensure the crane is not going to be overloaded for the conditions under which it will be used. Operators also should plan lifts before starting them to ensure they are safe. Employees should take additional precautions and exercise extra care when operating cranes around power lines.

Some mobile cranes cannot operate with outriggers in the traveling position. When used, the outriggers must rest on firm ground, on timbers, or be sufficiently cribbed to spread the weight of the crane and the load over a large enough area. This prevents the crane from tipping during use. Hoisting chains and ropes must always be free of kinks or twists and must never be wrapped around a load. Loads should be attached to the load hook by slings, fixtures, or other devices that have the capacity to support the load on the hook. Sharp edges of loads should be padded to prevent cutting slings. Proper sling angles shall be maintained so that slings are not loaded in excess of their capacity.

Persons thoroughly familiar with the cranes and the methods of inspecting the cranes, must inspect all cranes frequently and know what can make the cranes unserviceable. Crane activity, the severity of use, and environmental conditions should determine inspection schedules. Critical parts, such as crane operating mechanisms, hooks, air or hydraulic system components, and other load-carrying components, should be inspected daily for any maladjustment, deterioration, leakage, deformation, or other damage.

Slings

Employers must ensure that slings are visually inspected before use and during operation, especially if used under heavy stress. Riggers or other knowledgeable employees should conduct or assist in the inspection because they are aware of how the sling is used and what makes a sling unserviceable. Damaged or defective slings must be removed from service.

Slings must not be shortened with knots or bolts or other makeshift devices; sling legs that have been kinked must not be used. Slings

must not be loaded beyond their rated capacity, as specified in the manufacturer's instructions. Suspended loads must be kept clear of all obstructions, and crane operators should avoid sudden starts and stops when moving suspended loads. Employees also must remain clear of loads about to be lifted and suspended. All shock loading is prohibited.

Powered Industrial Trucks

Workers who must handle and store materials often use fork trucks, platform lift trucks, motorized hand trucks, and other specialized industrial trucks powered by electrical motors or internal combustion engines. Affected workers, should be aware of the safety requirements pertaining to fire protection and the design, maintenance, and use of these trucks.

All new powered industrial trucks, except vehicles intended primarily for earth moving or over-the-road hauling, shall meet the design and construction requirements for powered industrial trucks established in the American National Standard for Powered Industrial Trucks, Part II, ANSI B56.1-1969. Approved trucks also shall bear a label or some other identifying mark indicating acceptance by a nationally recognized testing laboratory.

Companies may not make any modification or additions that affect capacity and safe operation of the trucks to a forklift without the manufacturer's prior written approval. Capacity, operation, and maintenance instruction plates and tags or decals must be changed to reflect the new information. If the truck is equipped with front-end attachments that are not factory installed, the truck must be marked to identify these attachments and show the truck's approximate weight, including the installed attachment, when it is at maximum elevation with its load laterally centered.

There are 11 types of industrial trucks or tractors. There also are designated conditions and locations under which the vast range of industrial-powered trucks can be used. For example, powered industrial trucks must not be used in atmospheres containing hazardous concentrations of the following substances:

- Acetylene;
- Butadiene;
- Ethylene oxide;

- Hydrogen (or gases or vapors equivalent in hazard to hydrogen, such as manufactured gas);
- Propylene oxide;
- Acetaldehyde;
- Cyclopropane;
- Dimethyl ether;
- Ethylene;
- Isoprene; and
- Unsymmetrical dimethyl hydrazine.

Industrial trucks are not to be used in atmospheres containing hazardous concentrations of metal dust, including aluminum, magnesium, and other metals of similarly hazardous characteristics, or in atmospheres containing carbon black, coal, or coke dust. Where dust of magnesium, aluminum, or aluminum bronze dusts may be present, the fuses, switches, motor controllers, and circuit breakers of trucks must be enclosed with enclosures approved for these substances.

There also are powered industrial trucks or tractors that are designed, constructed, and assembled for use in atmospheres containing flammable vapors or dusts. These include industrial-powered trucks equipped with:

- Additional safeguards to their exhaust, fuel, and electrical systems;
- No electrical equipment, including the ignition;
- Temperature-limitation features; and
- Completely enclosed electric motors and all other electrical equipment.

These specially designed powered industrial trucks may be used in locations where volatile flammable liquids or flammable gases are handled, processed, or used. The liquids, vapors, or gases should, among other things, be confined within closed containers or closed systems from which they cannot escape.

Powered industrial trucks that are powered electrically by liquefied petroleum gas or by a gasoline or diesel engine may be used on piers and wharves that handle general cargo.

Safety precautions the user can observe when operating or maintaining powered industrial trucks include:

- High-lift rider trucks must be fitted with an overhead guard, unless operating conditions do not permit it.

- Fork trucks must be equipped with a vertical load backrest extension, according to manufacturer's specifications, if the load presents a hazard. Those personnel on the loading platform must have the means to shut off power to the truck.
- Battery-charging installations must be located in areas designated for that purpose and facilities be provided for flushing and neutralizing spilled electrolytes when changing or recharging a battery. Ventilation must be adequate.
- Conveyors, overhead hoists, or equivalent materials handling equipment must be provided for handling batteries. Trucks whose electrical systems are in need of repair must have the battery disconnected prior to such repairs.
- Auxiliary directional lighting must be provided on the truck where general lighting is less than 2 lumens per square foot.
- Arms and legs must not be placed between the uprights of the mast or outside the running lines of the truck.
- Brakes must be set and wheel blocks or other adequate protection be in place to prevent the movement of trucks, trailers, or railroad cars when using trucks to load or unload materials onto train boxcars.
- Sufficient headroom must be provided under overhead installations, lights, pipes, and sprinkler systems.
- Dock boards or bridge plates must be properly secured so they will not move when equipment moves over them. Only stable or safely arranged loads may be handled and caution must be exercised when handling loads.
- Replacement parts of any industrial truck must be equivalent in safety to the original parts.

Forklift operators must be trained by a qualified instructor to operate the forklift. This training must consist of a classroom-type session with a written examination and a hands-on demonstration of the operator's competency. This training must be certified in a document that contains the name of the operator, the date of training, and the name of the qualified instructor. Such training must take place every three years or whenever a forklift operator demonstrates incompetency with the forklift.

Simply showing a forklift safety video does not constitute training. The qualified instructor must be available to answer questions from the operator-student. Computer-assisted training and lectures can be augmented by safety videos. Some of the topics that must be covered in the training are as follows:

- The types of forklifts and their power plants;
- The concept of the center of gravity and stability triangle;
- Common characteristics of the forklift;
- How to handle the load safely;
- Dynamic forces; and
- Driving conditions.

Ergonomic Principles

Ergonomics is defined as the study of work and is based on the principle that the job should be adapted to fit the person, rather than forcing the person to fit the job. Ergonomics focuses on the work environment and items such as design and function of workstations, controls, displays, safety devices, tools, and lighting to fit the employees' physical requirements and to ensure their health and well being.

Ergonomics includes restructuring or changing workplace conditions to make the job easier and reducing stressors that cause cumulative trauma disorders and repetitive motion injuries. In the area of materials handling and storing, ergonomic principles may require controls such as reducing the size or weight of the objects lifted, installing a mechanical lifting aid, or changing the height of a pallet or shelf.

Although no approach has been found for totally eliminating back injuries resulting from lifting materials, lifting injuries can be reduced by implementing an effective ergonomics program and by training employees in appropriate lifting techniques.

In addition to using ergonomic controls, there are some basic safety principles that can be employed to reduce injuries resulting from handling and storing materials. These include taking general fire safety precautions and keeping aisles and passageways clear.

In adhering to fire safety precautions, employees should note that flammable and combustible materials must be stored according to their fire characteristics. Flammable liquids, for example, must be separated from other material by a firewall. Also, other combustibles must be stored in an area where smoking and using an open-flame or a spark-producing device is prohibited. Dissimilar materials that are dangerous when they come into contact with each other must be stored apart from one another.

When using aisles and passageways to move materials mechanically, sufficient clearance must be allowed for aisles at loading docks, through doorways, wherever turns must be made, and in other parts of the workplace. Providing sufficient clearance for mechanically moved materials will prevent workers from being pinned between the equipment and fixtures in the workplace, such as walls, racks, posts, or other machines. Sufficient clearance also will prevent the load from striking an obstruction and falling on an employee.

All passageways used by employees should be kept clear of obstructions and tripping hazards. Materials in excess of supplies needed for immediate operations should not be stored in aisles or passageways, and permanent aisles and passageways must be marked appropriately.

OSHA recommends using a formal training program to reduce materials handling hazards. Instructors should be well versed in matters that pertain to safety engineering and materials handling and storing. The content of the training should emphasize those factors that will contribute to reducing workplace hazards, including the following:

- Alerting the employee to the dangers of lifting without proper training;
- Showing the employee how to avoid unnecessary physical stress and strain;
- Teaching workers to become aware of what they can comfortably handle without undue strain;
- Instructing workers on the proper use of equipment; and
- Teaching workers to recognize potential hazards and how to prevent or correct them.

Because of the high incidence of back injuries, safe lifting techniques for manual lifting should be demonstrated and practiced at the work site by supervisors as well as by employees. A training program to teach proper lifting techniques should cover the following topics:

- Awareness of the health risks to improper lifting— citing organizational case histories;
- Knowledge of the basic anatomy of the spine, the muscles, and the joints of the trunk, and the contributions of intra-abdominal pressure while lifting. Recognition of the physical factors that might contribute to an accident and how to avoid the unexpected;
- Awareness of individual body strengths and weaknesses—determining one's own lifting capacity. Knowledge of body responses—warning signals—to be aware of when lifting;
- Use of safe lifting postures and timing for smooth, easy lifting and the ability to minimize the load-moment effects; and
- Use of handling aids such as stages, platforms, steps, trestles, shoulder pads, handles, and wheels.

A campaign using posters to draw attention to the need to do something about potential accidents, including lifting and back injuries, is one way to increase awareness of safe work practices and techniques. To have an effective materials handling and storing safety and health program, managers must take an active role in its development. First-line supervisors must be convinced of the importance of controlling hazards associated with materials handling and storing and must be held accountable for employee training. An on-going safety and health program should be used to motivate employees to continue to use necessary protective equipment and to observe proper job procedures.

Sling Safety

Whenever possible, mechanical means should be used to move materials in order to avoid employee injuries such as muscle pulls, strains, and sprains. In addition, many loads are too heavy and/or bulky to be safely moved manually. Therefore, several types of equipment have been designed specifically to aid in the movement of materials, including cranes, derricks, hoists, powered industrial trucks, and conveyors. Because cranes, derricks, and hoists rely upon slings to hold their suspended loads, slings are the most commonly used piece of materials-handling apparatus.

Sling Types

The dominant characteristics of a sling are determined by the components of that sling. For example, the strengths and weaknesses of a wire rope sling are essentially the same as the strengths and weaknesses of the wire rope of which it is made.

Slings are generally one of six types:
- Chain,
- Wire rope,
- Metal mesh,
- Natural fiber rope,
- Synthetic fiber rope, or
- Synthetic web.

In general, use and inspection procedures tend to place these slings into three groups:
- Chain;
- Wire rope and mesh; and
- Fiber rope web.

Each type has its own particular advantages and disadvantages. Factors that should be taken into consideration when choosing the best sling for the job include the size, weight, shape, temperature and sensitivity of the material to be moved, as well as the environmental conditions under which the sling will be used.

Chains

Chains are commonly used because of their strength and ability to adapt to the shape of the load. Care should be taken, however, when using alloy chain slings because they are subject to damage by sudden shocks. Misuse of chain slings could damage the sling, resulting in sling failure and possible injury to an employee.

Chain slings are the best choice for lifting materials that are very hot. They can be heated to temperatures of up to 1000°F; however, when alloy chain slings are consistently exposed to service temperatures in excess of 600°F, operators must reduce the working load limits in accordance with the manufacturer's recommendations.

All sling types must be visually inspected prior to use. When inspecting alloy steel chain slings, pay special attention to any stretching, wear in excess of the allowances made by the manufacturer, and nicks and gouges. These are all indications that the sling may be unsafe and should immediately be removed from service.

Wire Rope

A second type of sling is made of wire rope. Wire rope is composed of individual wires that have been twisted to form strands (See Exhibit 15-1.). The strands are then twisted to form a wire rope. When wire rope has a fiber core, it is usually more flexible but less resistant to environmental damage. Conversely, a core that is made of a wire rope strand tends to have greater strength and be more resistant to heat damage.

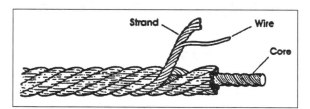

Exhibit 15-1.
Wipe rope is composed of individual wires twisted around a core.

Rope Lay

Wire rope may be further defined by the "lay." The lay of a wire rope can mean any of three things:

1. **One complete wrap of a strand around the core.** One rope lay is one complete wrap of a strand around the core (See Exhibit 15-2.).

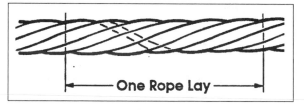

Exhibit 15-2.
An example of one rope lay.

2. **The direction the strands are wound around the core.** Wire rope is referred to as *right lay or left lay.* A right lay rope is one in which the strands are wound in a right-hand direction like a conventional screw thread (See Exhibit 15-3.). A left lay rope is just the opposite.

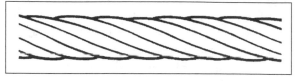

Exhibit 15-3.
An example of right lay rope.

3. **The direction the wires are wound in the strands in relation to the direction of the strands around the core.** In regular lay rope, the wires in the strands are laid in one direction, while the strands in the rope are laid in the opposite direction. In lang lay rope, the wires are twisted in the same direction as the strands. (See Exhibit 15-4.)

In regular lay ropes, the wires in the strands are laid in one direction, while the strands in the rope are laid in the opposite direction. The result is that the wire crown runs approximately parallel to the longitudinal axis of the rope. These ropes have good resistance to kinking and twisting and are easy to handle. They are also able to withstand considerable crushing and distortion due to the short length of exposed wires. This type of rope has the widest range of applications.

Lang lay (where the wires are twisted in the *same* direction as the strands) is recommended for such excavating, construction and mining applications, including draglines, hoist lines, dredge lines and other similar lines.

Lang lay ropes are more flexible and have greater wearing surface per wire than regular lay ropes. In addition, because the outside wires in lang lay rope lie at an angle to the rope axis, internal stress due to bending over sheaves and drums is reduced, causing lang lay ropes to be more resistant to bending fatigue.

A **left lay rope** is one in which the strands form a left-hand helix similar to the threads of a left-hand screw thread. Left lay rope has its greatest use in oil fields on rod and tubing lines, blast hole rigs and spudders where rotation of right lay would loosen couplings. The rotation of a left lay rope tightens a standard coupling.

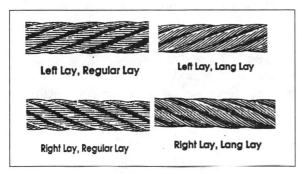

Exhibit 15-4.
Examples of regular lay and lang lay ropes.

Wire Rope Sling Selection

When selecting a wire rope to give the best service, there are four characteristics to consider:

- Strength;
- Ability to bend without distortion;
- Ability to withstand abrasive wear; and
- Ability to withstand abuse.

Strength. The strength of a wire rope is a function of its size, grade and construction. It must be sufficient to accommodate the maximum load that will be applied. The maximum load limit is determined by means of an appropriate multiplier. This multiplier is the number by which the ultimate strength of a wire rope is divided to determine the working load limit. Thus, a wire rope sling with the strength of 10,000 lbs. and a total working load of 2,000 lbs. has a design factor (multiplier) of 5. New wire rope slings have a design factor of 5. As a sling suffers from the rigors of continued service; however, both the design factor and the sling's ultimate strength will be proportionately reduced. If a sling is loaded beyond its ultimate strength, it will fail. For this reason, older slings must be more rigorously inspected to ensure that rope conditions adversely affecting the strength of the sling are considered when determining whether a wire rope sling should be allowed to continue in service.

Fatigue. A wire rope must have the ability to withstand repeated bending without the failure of the wires from fatigue. Fatigue failure of the wires in a wire rope is the result of the development of small cracks under repeated applications of bending loads (See Exhibit 15-5.). It occurs when ropes make small radius bends. The best means of preventing fatigue failure of wire rope slings is to use blocking or padding to increase the radius of the bend.

Exhibit 15-5.
Example of Wire rope fatigue failure.

Abrasive Wear. The ability of a wire rope to withstand abrasion is determined by the size, number of wires and construction of the rope. Smaller wires bend more readily and therefore offer greater flexibility but are less able to withstand abrasive wear. Conversely, the larger wires of less flexible ropes are better able to withstand abrasion than smaller wires of more flexible ropes.

Abuse. All other factors being equal, misuse or abuse of wire rope will cause a wire rope sling to become unsafe long before any other factor. Abusing a wire rope sling can cause serious structural damage to the wire rope, such as kinking or bird caging, which reduces the strength of the wire rope. (In bird caging, the wire rope strands are forcibly untwisted and become spread outward (See Exhibit 15-6.).) Therefore, to prolong the life of the sling and protect the lives of employees, the manufacturer's suggestion for safe and proper use of wire rope slings must be strictly followed.

Exhibit 15-6.
Example of Wire rope "bird cage."

Wire Rope Life. Many operating conditions affect wire rope life, including bending, stresses, loading conditions, speed of load application, jerking, abrasions, corrosion, sling design, materials handled, environmental conditions and history of previous use.

In addition to the above operating conditions, the weight, size and shape of the loads to be handled also affect the service life of a wire rope sling. Flexibility is also a factor. Generally, more flexible ropes are selected when smaller radius bending is required. Less flexible ropes should be used when the rope must move through or over abrasive materials.

Wire Rope Sling Inspection. Wire rope slings must be visually inspected before each use. The operator should check the twists or lay of the sling. If 10 randomly distributed wires in one lay are broken or five wires in one strand of a rope lay are damaged, the sling must not be used. It is not sufficient, however, to check only the condition of the wire rope. End fittings and other components should also be inspected for any damage that could make the sling unsafe.

To ensure safe sling usage between scheduled inspections, all workers must participate in a safety awareness program. Each operator must keep a close watch on the slings he or she is using. If any accident involving the movement of materials occurs, the operator must immediately shut down the equipment and report the accident to a supervisor. The cause of the accident must be determined and corrected before operations can resume.

Field Lubrication. Although every rope sling is lubricated during manufacture, to lengthen its useful service life it must also be lubricated in the field. There is no set rule on how much or how often this should be done. It depends on the conditions under which the sling is used; the more adverse the conditions under which the sling operates, the more frequently lubrication will be required.

Storage. Wire rope slings should be stored in a well-ventilated, dry building or shed. They should never be stored on the ground or continuously exposed to the elements because this will make them vulnerable to corrosion and rust. If it is necessary to store wire rope slings outside, they must be set off the ground and protected.

Note: Using the sling several times a week, even at a light load, is a good practice. Records show that slings that are used frequently or continuously give useful service far longer than those that are idle.

Discarding Slings. Wire rope slings can provide a margin of safety by showing early signs of failure. Factors requiring that a wire sling be discarded include:

- Severe corrosion;
- Localized wear (shiny worn spots) on the outside;
- A one-third reduction in outer wire diameter;
- Damage or displacement of end fittings, hooks, rings, links or collars by overload or misapplication;
- Distortion, kinking, bird caging or other evidence of damage to the wire rope structure; or
- Excessive broken wires.

Fiber Rope and Synthetic Web

Fiber rope and synthetic web slings are used primarily for temporary work, such as construction and painting jobs, and in marine operations. They are also the best choice for use on expensive loads, highly finished parts, fragile parts and delicate equipment.

Fiber Rope

Fiber rope slings are preferred for some applications because they are pliant, grip the load well and do not mar the surface of the load. They should be used only on light loads, however, and must not be used on objects that have sharp edges capable of cutting the rope or in applications where the sling will be exposed to high temperatures, severe abrasion or acids.

The choice of rope type and size will depend upon the application, the weight to be lifted and the sling angle. Before lifting any load with a fiber rope sling, the sling should be inspected carefully because they deteriorate far more rapidly than wire rope slings and their actual strength is very difficult to estimate.

When inspecting a fiber rope sling prior to using it, look first at its surface. Look for dry, brittle, scorched or discolored fibers. If any of these conditions are found, the supervisor must be notified and a determination made regarding the safety of the sling. If the sling is found to be unsafe, it must be discarded.

Next, check the interior of the sling. It should be as clean as when the rope was new. A build-up of powder-like sawdust on the inside of the fiber rope indicates excessive internal wear and is an indication that the sling is unsafe.

Finally, scratch the fibers with a fingernail. If the fibers come apart easily, the fiber sling has suffered some kind of chemical damage and must be discarded.

Synthetic Web Slings

Synthetic web slings offer a number of advantages for rigging purposes. The most commonly used synthetic web slings are made of nylon, dacron and polyester. They have the following properties in common:

- **Strength:** can handle load of up to 300,000 lbs.;
- **Convenience:** can conform to any shape;
- **Safety:** will adjust to the load contour and hold it with a tight, nonslip grip;
- **Load protection:** will not mar, deface, or scratch highly polished or delicate surfaces;
- **Long life:** are unaffected by mildew, rot, or bacteria; resist some chemical action and have excellent abrasion resistance;
- **Economy:** have low initial cost plus long service life;
- **Shock absorbency:** can absorb heavy shocks without damage; and
- **Temperature resistance:** are unaffected by temperatures up to 180° F.

Each synthetic material has its own unique properties. Nylon must be used wherever alkaline or greasy conditions exist. It is also preferable when neutral conditions prevail and resistance to chemicals and solvents is important. Dacron must be used where high concentrations of acid solutions, such as sulfuric, hydrochloric, nitric and formic acids, and high-temperature bleach solutions are prevalent. (Nylon will deteriorate under these conditions.) Dacron should not be used in alkaline conditions because it will deteriorate; nylon or polypropylene should be used instead. Polyester must be used where acids or bleaching agents are present and is also ideal for applications where a minimum of stretching is important.

Possible Defects. Synthetic web slings must be removed from service if any of the following defects exist:

- Acid or caustic burns;
- Melting or charring of any part of the surface;
- Snags, punctures, tears or cuts;
- Broken or worn stitches;
- Wear or elongation exceeding the amount recommended by the manufacturer; or
- Distortion of fittings.

Safe Lifting Practices

After the sling has been selected (based upon the characteristics of the load and the environmental conditions surrounding the lift) and inspected prior to use, it can be used—safely. There are four primary factors to take into consideration when safely lifting a load:

- The size, weight and center of gravity of the load;
- The number of legs and the angle the sling makes with the horizontal line;
- The rated capacity of the sling; and
- The history of the care and use of the sling.

Size, Weight and Center of Gravity

The center of gravity of an object is that point at which the entire weight may be considered as concentrated. In order to make a level lift, the crane hook must be directly above this point. While slight variations are usually permissible, if the crane hook is too far to one side of the center of gravity, dangerous tilting will result, causing unequal stresses in the different sling legs. This imbalance must be compensated for at once.

Number of Legs and Angle with the Horizontal

As the angle formed by the sling leg and the horizontal line decreases, the rated capacity of the sling also decreases. In other words, the smaller the angle between the sling leg and the horizontal, the greater the stress on the sling leg and the smaller (lighter) the load the sling can safely support. Larger (heavier) loads can be safely moved if the weight of the load is distributed among more sling legs.

Rated Capacity of the Sling

The rated capacity of a sling varies depending upon the shape of sling, the size of the sling and the type of hitch. Operators must know the capacity of the sling. Charts or tables that contain this information generally are available from sling manufacturers. However, the values given are for *new* slings; older slings must be used with additional caution. Under no circumstances shall a sling's rated capacity be exceeded.

History of Care and Usage

The mishandling and misuse of slings are the leading causes of accidents involving their use. The majority of injuries and accidents, however, can be avoided by becoming familiar with the essentials of proper sling care and use.

Proper care and usage are essential for maximum service and safety. Slings must be protected from sharp bends and cutting edges by means of cover saddles, burlap padding or wood blocking, as well as from unsafe lifting procedures such as overloading.

Before making a lift, check to be certain that the sling is properly secured around the load and that the weight and balance of the load have been accurately determined if the load is on the ground. Do not allow the load to drag along the ground; this could damage the sling if the load is already resting on the sling. Then ensure that there is no sling damage prior to making the lift.

Next, position the hook directly over the load and seat the sling squarely within the hook bowl. This gives the operator maximum lifting efficiency without bending the hook or overstressing the sling.

Wire rope slings are also subject to damage resulting from contact with sharp edges of the loads being lifted. These edges can be blocked or padded to minimize damage to the sling. After the sling is properly attached to the load, there are a number of good lifting techniques that are common to all slings:

- Make sure the load is not lagged, clamped or bolted to the floor.
- Guard against shock loading by taking up the slack in the sling slowly.
- Apply power cautiously so as to prevent jerking at the beginning of the lift and accelerate or decelerate slowly.
- Check the tension on the sling.

- Raise the load a few inches, stop, and check for proper balance and that all items are clear of the path of travel.
- Never allow anyone to ride on the hood or load.
- Keep all personnel clear while the load is being raised, moved or lowered.
- Crane or hoist operators should watch the load at all times when it is in motion. Obey the following "nevers":
- Never allow more than one person to control a lift;
- Never allow more than one person to give signals to a crane operator;
- Never raise the load more than necessary;
- Never leave the load suspended in the air; and
- Never work under a suspended load or allow anyone else to.

Once the lift has been completed, clean the sling, check it for damage and store it in a clean, dry, airy place. It is best to hang it on a rack or wall. Safe and proper use and storage of slings will increase their service life.

Maintenance of Slings

Chains

Chain slings must be cleaned prior to each inspection, as dirt or oil may hide damage. The operator must be certain to inspect the total length of the sling, periodically looking for stretching, binding, wear, or nicks and gouges. If a sling has stretched so that it is now more than 3 percent longer than it was when new, it is unsafe and must be discarded.

Binding is the term used to describe the condition that exists when a sling has become deformed to the extent that its individual links cannot move within each other freely. It is also an indication that the sling is unsafe. Generally, wear occurs on the load bearing inside ends of the links. Pushing links together so that the inside surface becomes clearly visible is the best way to check for this type of wear. Wear may also occur, however, on the outside of links when the chain is dragged along abrasive surfaces or pulled out from under heavy loads. Either type of wear weakens slings and makes accidents more likely.

Heavy nicks and gouges must be filed smooth, measured with calipers, and then compared with the manufacturer's minimum allowable safe dimensions. When in doubt or in borderline situations, do not use the sling. In addition, never attempt to repair the welded components on a sling. If the sling needs repair of this nature, the supervisor must be notified.

Wire Rope

Wire rope slings, like chain slings, must be cleaned prior to each inspection because they are also subject to damage hidden by dirt or oil. In addition, they must be lubricated according to the manufacturer's instructions. Lubrication prevents or reduces corrosion and wear due to friction and abrasion. Before applying any lubricant, however, the sling user should make certain that the sling is dry. Applying lubricant to a wet or damp sling traps moisture against the metal and hastens corrosion, which deteriorates wire rope. Pitting may indicate it, but it is sometimes hard to detect. Therefore, if a wire rope sling shows any sign of significant deterioration, that sling must be removed until a person who is qualified to determine the extent of the damage can examine it.

Fiber Ropes and Synthetic Webs

In general, fiber ropes and synthetic webs should be discarded rather than serviced or repaired. Operators must always follow manufacturer's recommendations.

Summary

There are good practices to follow to protect employees while using slings to move materials. First, an employee should learn as much as he or she can about the materials with which he or she will be working. Slings come in many different types; analyze the load to be moved—in terms of size, weight, shape, temperature and sensitivity — then choose the sling which best meets those needs. Next, always inspect all the equipment before and after a move. Always be sure to give equipment the "in service" maintenance it may need. Finally, use safe lifting practices. Use the proper lifting technique for the type of sling and the type of load

2006 Subpart H 1926.250.252
Materials Handling, Storage, Use & Disposal

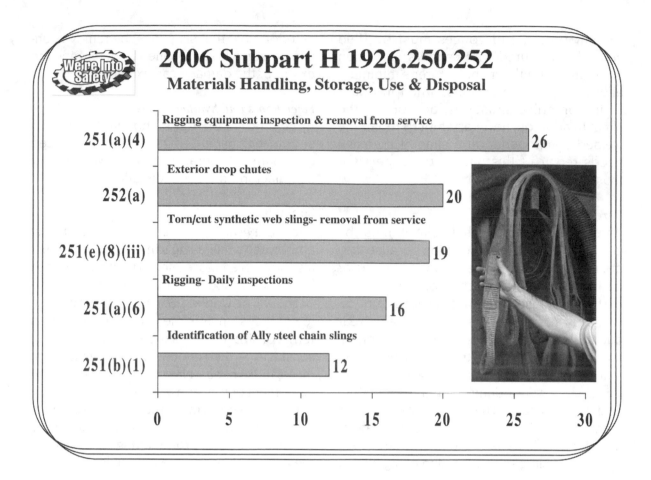

Rigging equipment inspection & removal from service
251(a)(4) — 26

Exterior drop chutes
252(a) — 20

Torn/cut synthetic web slings- removal from service
251(e)(8)(iii) — 19

Rigging- Daily inspections
251(a)(6) — 16

Identification of Ally steel chain slings
251(b)(1) — 12

(0, 5, 10, 15, 20, 25, 30)

2006 Powered Industrial Truck 1910.178 cited in construction!

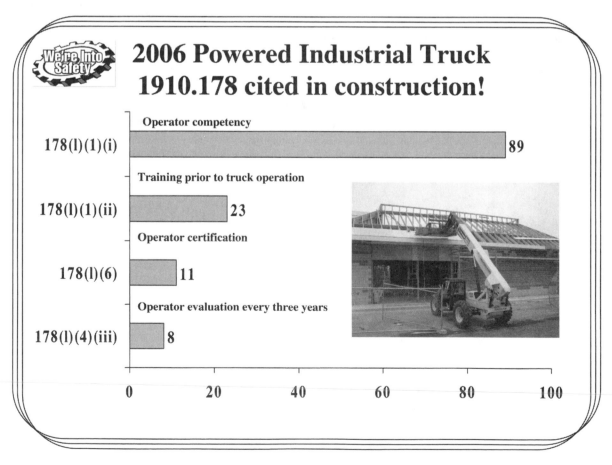

Operator competency
178(l)(1)(i) — 89

Training prior to truck operation
178(l)(1)(ii) — 23

Operator certification
178(l)(6) — 11

Operator evaluation every three years
178(l)(4)(iii) — 8

(0, 20, 40, 60, 80, 100)

CONCRETE AND MASONRY

The Occupational Safety and Health Administration's standard, Subpart Q sets forth requirements with which construction employers must comply to protect construction workers from accidents and injuries resulting from the premature removal of formwork, the failure to brace masonry walls, the failure to support precast panels, the inadvertent operation of equipment, and the failure to guard reinforcing steel. OSHA's revised standard includes the following important changes:

- Expands and toughens protection against masonry wall collapses by requiring bracing and a limited access zone prior to the construction of a wall
- Permits employers to use several more recently developed methods of testing concrete instead of just the formerly recognized method; and
- Sets and clarifies requirements for both cast-in-place concrete and precast concrete during construction.

Subpart Q is divided into the following major groups, each of which is discussed in more detail in the following paragraphs:

- Scope, application, and definitions (29 CFR 1926.700);
- General requirements (29 CFR 1926.701);
- Equipment and tools (29 CFR 1926.702);
- Cast-in-place concrete (29 CFR 1926.703);
- Precast concrete (29 CFR 1926.704);
- Lift-slab construction (29 CFR 1926.705); and
- Masonry construction (29 CFR 1926.706).

The standard, Subpart Q, prescribes performance-oriented requirements designed to help protect all construction workers from the hazards associated with concrete and masonry construction operations at construction, demolition, alteration, and repair worksites.

Employers must not place construction loads on a concrete structure or portion of a concrete structure unless the employer determines, based on information received from a person who is qualified in structural design, that the structure or portion of the structure is capable of supporting the intended loads.

All protruding reinforcing steel, onto and into which employees could fall, must be guarded to eliminate the hazard of impalement. Employees (except those essential to the post-tensioning operations) must not be permitted to be behind a jack during tensioning operations.

Signs and barriers must be erected to limit employee access to the post-tensioning area during tensioning operations. Employees must not be permitted to ride concrete buckets.

Working under Loads

Employees must not be permitted to work under concrete buckets while the buckets are being elevated or lowered into position. To the extent practicable, elevated concrete buckets must be routed so that no employee or the fewest employees possible are exposed to the hazards associated with falling concrete buckets.

Personal Protective Equipment

Employees must not be permitted to apply a cement, sand, and water mixture through a pneumatic hose unless they are wearing protective head and face equipment. Employees must not be permitted to place or tie reinforcing steel more than 6 ft. above any adjacent working surfaces unless they are protected by the use of a safety belt or equivalent fall protection meeting the criteria in OSHA standards on Personal Protective and Life Saving Equipment.

Equipment and Tools

The standard also includes requirements for the following equipment and operations:

- Bulk cement storage;
- Concrete mixers;
- Power concrete trowels;
- Concrete buggies;
- Concrete pumping systems;
- Concrete buckets;
- Tremies;
- Bull floats;
- Masonry saws; and
- Lockout/tagout procedures.

Cast-in-Place Concrete

General Requirements for Formwork

Formwork must be designed, fabricated, erected, supported, braced, and maintained so that it will be capable of supporting without

failure all vertical and lateral loads that might be applied to the formwork. As indicated in the appendix to the standard, formwork that is designed, fabricated, erected, supported, braced, and maintained in conformance with Sections 6 and 7 of the American National Standard for Construction and Demolition Operations—Concrete and Masonry Work (ANSI A10.9-1983) also meets the requirements of this paragraph.

Drawings or Plans

Drawings and plans, including all revisions for the jack layout, formwork (including shoring equipment), working decks, and scaffolds, must be available at the jobsite.

Shoring and Reshoring

All shoring equipment, including equipment used in reshoring operations, must be inspected prior to erection to determine that the equipment meets the requirements specified in the formwork drawings.

Damaged shoring equipment must not be used for shoring. Erected shoring equipment must be inspected immediately prior to, during, and immediately after concrete placement. Shoring equipment that is found to be damaged or weakened after erection must be immediately reinforced.

If single-post shores are used on top of one another (tiered), then additional shoring requirements must be met. The shores must be:

- Designed by a qualified designer (erected shoring must be inspected by an engineer qualified in structural design);
- Vertically aligned;
- Spliced to prevent misalignment; and
- Adequately braced in two mutually perpendicular directions at the splice level.

In addition, each tier must be diagonally braced in the same two directions.

Adjustments of single-post shores to raise formwork must not be made after the placement of concrete. Reshoring must be erected, as the original forms and shores are removed, whenever the concrete is required to support loads in excess of its capacity.

Vertical Slip Forms

The steel rods or pipes on which jacks climb or by which the forms are lifted must be specifically designed for that purpose and adequately braced where not encased in concrete. Forms must be designed to prevent excessive distortion of the structure during the jacking operation. Jacks and vertical supports must be positioned in such a manner that the loads do not exceed the rated capacity of the jacks.

The jacks or other lifting devices must be provided with mechanical dogs or other automatic holding devices to support the slip forms whenever a failure of the power supply or lifting mechanisms occurs.

The form structure must be maintained within all design tolerances specified for plumbness during the jacking operation. All vertical slip forms must be provided with scaffolds or work platforms where employees are required to work or pass.

The predetermined safe rate of lift must not be exceeded.

Reinforcing Steel

Reinforcing steel for walls, piers, columns, and similar vertical structures must be adequately supported to prevent overturning and collapse.

Employers must take measures to prevent unrolled wire mesh from recoiling. Such measures may include, but are not limited to, securing each end of the roll or turning over the roll.

Removal of Formwork

Forms and shores (except those used for slabs on grade and slip forms) must not be removed until the employer determines that the concrete has gained sufficient strength to support its weight and superimposed loads. Such determination must be based on compliance with one of the following:

- The plans and specifications stipulate conditions for the removal of forms and shores, and such conditions have been followed; or
- The concrete has been properly tested with an appropriate American Society for Testing and Materials (ASTM) standard test method that is designed to indicate the concrete compressive strength, and the test results

indicate that the concrete has gained sufficient strength to support its weight and superimposed loads.

Reshoring must not be removed until the concrete being supported has attained adequate strength to support its weight and all loads in place upon it.

Precast Concrete

Precast concrete wall units, structural framing, and tilt-up wall panels must be adequately supported to prevent overturning and to prevent collapse until permanent connections are completed.

Lifting inserts that are embedded or otherwise attached to tilt-up wall panels must be capable of supporting at least two times the maximum intended load applied or transmitted to them; lifting inserts for other precast members must be capable of supporting four times the load. Only essential employees are permitted under precast concrete that is being lifted or tilted into position.

Lift-Slab Operations

Lift-slab operations must be designed and planned by a registered professional engineer who has experience in lift-slab construction. Such plans and designs must be implemented by the employer and must include detailed instructions and sketches that indicate the prescribed method of erection. The plans and designs also must include provisions for ensuring the lateral stability of the building or structure during construction.

Jacking equipment must be capable of supporting at least two and one-half times the load being lifted during jacking operations; the equipment must not be overloaded. For the purpose of this provision, jacking equipment includes any load-bearing component that is used to carry out the lifting operation(s). Such equipment includes, but is not limited to, the following:

- Threaded rods;
- Lifting attachments;
- Lifting nuts;
- Hook-up collars;
- T-caps;
- Shear heads;

- Columns; and
- Footings.

No employee, except those essential to the jacking operation, must be permitted in the building or structure while any jacking operation is taking place unless the building or structure has been sufficiently reinforced to ensure its integrity during erection. The phrase "reinforced sufficiently to ensure its integrity" used in this paragraph means that a registered professional engineer, independent of the engineer who designed and planned the lifting operation, has determined from the plans that if there is a loss of support at any jack location, that loss will be confined to that location and the structure as a whole will remain stable.

Under no circumstances must any employee who is not essential to the jacking operation be permitted immediately beneath a slab while it is being lifted.

Masonry Construction

Whenever a masonry wall is being constructed, employers must establish a limited access zone prior to the start of construction. The limited access zone shall:
- Be equal to the height of the wall to be constructed plus 4 ft.;
- Run the entire length of the wall;
- Be on the side of the wall that will be unscaffolded;
- Be restricted to entry only by employees actively engaged in constructing the wall; and
- Be kept in place until the wall is adequately supported to prevent overturning and collapse unless the height of wall is more than 8 ft. and unsupported; in which case, it must be braced. The bracing must remain in place until permanent supporting elements of the structure are in place.

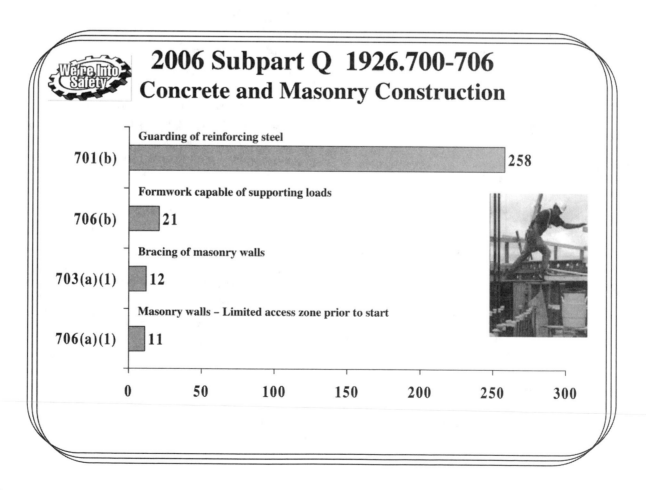

FIRE PROTECTION AND PREVENTION

The employer shall be responsible for the development of a fire protection program to be followed throughout all phases of the construction and demolition work and shall provide for firefighting equipment as specified in this subpart. As fire hazards occur, there shall be no delay in providing the necessary equipment. Access to all available firefighting equipment shall be maintained at all times. All firefighting equipment provided by the employer shall be conspicuously located. All firefighting equipment shall be periodically inspected and maintained in operating condition. Defective equipment shall be immediately replaced. As warranted by the project, the employer shall provide a trained and equipped firefighting organization (Fire Brigade) to ensure adequate protection to life.

Exhibit 17-1. Common Ignition Temperatures and Sources of Heat.

Common Ignition Temperatures		Common Sources of Heat	
Material	**Ignition Temperature**	**Source**	**Temperature**
Newsprint	446°F	Match head	2000°F
Filter paper	450°F	Electric Arc	2000°–6000°F
Cotton batting	450°F	Welding Arc	10,000°F
Gasoline	500°–850°F	Cigarette (no wind)	550°F
Polystyrene	900°–950°F	Cigarette (wind)	1,350°F
Sawdust	400°–500°F	Spark from Steel Wool	2000°F
		Steam 14.7 psi	212°F
		Steam 25 psi	267°F

Water Supply

A temporary or permanent water supply of sufficient volume, duration, and pressure necessary to properly operate the firefighting equipment shall be made available as soon as combustible materials accumulate. Where underground water mains are to be provided, they shall be installed, completed, and made available for use as soon as practicable.

Portable Firefighting Equipment

Fire Extinguishers and Small Hose Lines

A fire extinguisher, rated not less than 2A, shall be provided for each 3,000 sq. ft. of the protected building area, or major fraction thereof. Travel distance from any point of the protected area to the nearest fire extinguisher shall not exceed 100 ft. One 55-gal. open drum of water with two fire pails may be substituted for a fire extinguisher with a 2A rating.

A ½-in. diameter garden-type hose line, not to exceed 100 ft. in length and equipped with a nozzle, may be substituted for a 2A-rated fire extinguisher, providing it is capable of discharging a minimum of 5 gal. per minute with a minimum hose stream range of 30 ft. horizontally. The garden-type hose lines shall be mounted on conventional racks or reels. The number and location of hose racks or reels shall be such that at least one hose stream can be applied to all points in the area.

One or more fire extinguishers, rated not less than 2A, shall be provided on each floor. In multi-story buildings, at least one fire extinguisher shall be located adjacent to stairway.

Extinguishers and water drums that are subject to freezing shall be protected from freezing.

A fire extinguisher, rated not less than 10B, shall be provided within 50 ft. of wherever more than 5 gal. of flammable or combustible liquids or 5 lbs. of flammable gas are being used on the job site. This requirement does not apply to the integral fuel tanks of motor vehicles.

Carbon tetrachloride and other toxic vaporizing liquid fire extinguishers are prohibited.

Portable fire extinguishers shall be inspected periodically and maintained in accordance with NFPA No. 10A-1970, Maintenance and Use of Portable Fire Extinguishers. Fire extinguishers that have been listed or approved by a nationally recognized testing laboratory shall be used to meet the requirements of this subpart. Table F-1 in 1926.150(c)(1)(x) may be used as a guide for selecting the appropriate portable fire extinguishers (See Exhibit 17-2.).

Fire Hose and Connections

One hundred feet or less of 1½-in. hose, with a nozzle capable of discharging water at 25 gal. or more per minute, may be substituted for a fire extinguisher rated not more than 2A in the designated area, provided that the hose line can reach all points in the area.

If fire hose connections are not compatible with local firefighting equipment, the contrac-

Exhibit 17-2.
Fire Extinguishers Data.

	WATER TYPE				FOAM	CARBON DIOXIDE	DRY CHEMICAL			
							SODIUM OR POTASSIUM BICARBONATE		MULTI-PURPOSE ABC	
	STORED PRESSURE	CARTRIDGE OPERATED	WATER PUMP TANK	SODA ACID	FOAM	CO²	CARTRIDGE OPERATED	STORED PRESSURE	STORED PRESSURE	CARTRIDGE OPERATED
CLASS A FIRES WOOD, PAPER, TRASH HAVING GLOWING EMBERS (ORDINARY COMBUSTIBLES)	YES	YES	YES	YES	YES	NO (But will control small surface fires)	NO (But will control small surface fires)	NO (But will control small surface fires)	YES	YES
CLASS B FIRES FLAMMABLE LIQUIDS, GASOLINE, OIL, PAINTS GREASE, ETC. (FLAMMABLE LIQUIDS)	NO	NO	NO	NO	YES	YES	YES	YES	YES	YES
CLASS C FIRES ELECTRICAL EQUIPMENT (ELECTRICAL EQUIPMENT)	NO	NO	NO	NO	NO	YES	YES	YES	YES	YES
CLASS D FIRES COMBUSTIBLE METALS (COMBUSTIBLE METALS)	SPECIAL EXTINGUISHING AGENTS APPROVED BY RECOGNIZED TESTING LABORATORIES									
METHOD OF OPERATION	PULL PIN-SQUEEZE HANDLE	TURN UPSIDE DOWN AND BUMP	PUMP HANDLE	TURN UPSIDE DOWN	TURN UPSIDE DOWN	PULL PIN-SQUEEZE LEVER	RUPTURE CARTRIDGE SQUEEZE LEVER	PULL PIN-SQUEEZE HANDLE	PULL PIN-SQUEEZE HANDLE	RUPTURE CARTRIDGE SQUEEZE LEVER
RANGE	30'-40'	30'-40'	30'-40'	30'-40'	30'-40'	3'-8'	5'-20'	5'-20'	5'-20'	5'-20'
MAINTENANCE	CHECK AIR PRESSURE GAUGE MONTHLY	WEIGH GAS CARTRIDGE ADD WATER IF REQUIRED ANNUALLY	DISCHARGE AND FILL WITH WATER ANNUALLY	DISCHARGE ANNUALLY-RECHARGE	DISCHARGE ANNUALLY-RECHARGE	WEIGH SEMI-ANNUALLY	WEIGH GAS CARTRIDGE-CHECK CONDITION OF DRY CHEMICAL ANNUALLY	CHECK PRESSURE GAUGE AND CONDITION OF DRY CHEMICAL ANNUALLY	CHECK PRESSURE GAUGE AND CONDITION OF DRY CHEMICAL ANNUALLY	WEIGH GAS CARTRIDGE-CHECK CONDITION OF DRY CHEMICAL ANNUALLY

tor shall provide adapters, or the equivalent, to permit connections. During demolition involving combustible materials, charged hose lines, supplied by hydrants; water tank trucks with pumps; or the equivalent, shall be made available.

Fixed Firefighting Equipment

Sprinkler Protection
If the facility being constructed includes the installation of automatic sprinkler protection, the installation shall closely follow the construction and be placed in service upon completion of each story, as applicable laws permit.

During demolition or alterations, existing automatic sprinkler installations shall be retained in service as long as reasonable. Only properly authorized persons shall permit the operation of sprinkler control valves. Modification of sprinkler systems to permit alterations or additional demolition should be expedited so the automatic protection may be returned to service as quickly as possible. Sprinkler control valves shall be checked daily at the close of work to ensure the system is in service.

Standpipes
In structures where standpipes are required or where standpipes exist in structures being altered, they shall be brought up as soon as applicable laws permit and be maintained as construction progresses in such a manner that they are always ready for fire protection use. The standpipes shall be provided with Siamese fire department connections on the outside of the structure at the street level and shall be conspicuously marked. There shall be at least one standard hose outlet at each floor.

Fire Alarm Devices
An alarm system (e.g., telephone system, siren) shall be established by the employer whereby employees on the site and the local fire department can be alerted during an emergency. The alarm code and reporting instructions shall be conspicuously posted at phones and at employee entrances.

Fire Cutoffs
Fire walls and exit stairways, which are required in completed buildings, shall be given construction priority. Fire doors with automatic closing devices shall be hung on openings as soon as practicable. Fire cutoffs shall be retained in buildings undergoing alterations or demolition until operations necessitate their removal.

Fire Prevention—1926.151

Ignition Hazards
Electrical wiring and equipment for light, heat, or power purposes shall be installed in compliance with the requirements of Subpart K, Electrical. Smoking shall be prohibited at or in the vicinity of operations that constitute a fire hazard and shall have signs conspicuously posted that read: "No Smoking" or "Open Flame."

Internal combustion engine-powered equipment shall be located so the exhausts are well away from combustible materials. When the exhausts are piped to outside the building under construction, a clearance of at least 6 in. shall be maintained between such piping and combustible material.

Portable battery-powered lighting equipment used in connection with the storage, handling, or use of flammable gases or liquids, shall be of the type approved for the hazardous locations.

The nozzle of air, inert gas, and steam lines or hoses, when used in the cleaning or ventilation of tanks and vessels that contain hazardous concentrations of flammable gases or vapors, shall be bonded to the tank or vessel shell. Bonding devices shall not be attached or detached in hazardous concentrations of flammable gases or vapors.

Temporary Buildings
No temporary building shall be erected where it will adversely affect any means of exit.

When temporary buildings are located within another building or structure, they shall be of either noncombustible construction or of combustible construction having a fire resistance of not less than one hour.

Temporary buildings, located other than inside another building and not used for the storage, handling, or use of flammable or combustible liquids, flammable gases, explosives, or blasting agents, or similar hazardous occupancies, shall be located at a distance of not less than 10 ft. from another building or structure. Groups of temporary buildings not exceeding 2,000 sq. ft. in aggregate, shall, for the purposes of this part, be considered a single temporary building.

Open Yard Storage

Combustible materials shall be piled with due regard to the stability of piles and in no case higher than 20 ft.

Driveways between and around combustible storage piles shall be at least 15 ft. wide and maintained free from the accumulation of rubbish, equipment, or other articles or materials. Driveways shall be so spaced that a maximum grid system unit of 50 ft. × 150 ft. is produced.

The entire storage site shall be kept free from the accumulation of unnecessary combustible materials. Weeds and grass shall be kept down and a regular procedure provided for the periodic cleanup of the entire area. When there is a danger of an underground fire, that land shall not be used for combustible or flammable storage.

The method of piling shall be solid wherever possible and in orderly and regular piles. No combustible material shall be stored outdoors within 10 ft. of a building or structure.

Portable fire extinguishing equipment, suitable for the fire hazard involved, shall be provided at convenient, conspicuously accessible locations in the yard area. Portable fire extinguishers, rated not less than 2A, shall be placed so the maximum travel distance to the nearest unit does not exceed 100 ft.

Indoor Storage

Storage shall not obstruct, or adversely affect, means of exit. All materials shall be stored, handled, and piled with due regard to their fire characteristics. Incompatible materials, which may create a fire hazard, shall be segregated by a barrier that has a fire resistance of at least one hour.

Material shall be piled to minimize the spread of fire internally and to permit convenient access for firefighting. Stable piling shall be maintained at all times. Aisle space shall be maintained to safely accommodate the widest vehicle that may be used within the building for

firefighting purposes. Clearance of at least 36 in. shall be maintained between the top level of the stored material and the sprinkler deflectors. Clearance shall be maintained around lights and heating units to prevent the ignition of combustible materials.

A clearance of 24 in. shall be maintained around the path of travel of fire doors unless a barricade is provided, in which case no clearance is needed. Material shall not be stored within 36 in. of a fire door opening.

Flammable and Combustible Liquids—1926.152

General Requirements

Only approved containers and portable tanks shall be used for the storage and handling of flammable and combustible liquids. Approved metal safety cans shall be used for the handling and use of flammable liquids in quantities greater than one gallon; however, this does not apply to those flammable liquid materials that are highly viscid (i.e., extremely hard to pour), which may be used and handled in their original shipping containers. For quantities of one gallon or less, only the original container or an approved metal safety can shall be used for the storage, use, and handling of flammable liquids.

Flammable or combustible liquids shall not be stored in areas that are used for exits, stairways, or normally used for the safe passage of people.

Indoor Storage of Flammable and Combustible Liquids

No more than 25 gal. of flammable or combustible liquids shall be stored in a room outside of an approved storage cabinet. For storage of liquefied petroleum gas, see 1926.153.

Quantities of flammable and combustible liquid in excess of 25 gal. shall be stored in an acceptable or approved cabinet meeting the following requirements:

- Acceptable wooden storage cabinets shall be constructed in the following manner, or equivalent:
  - The bottom, sides, and top shall be constructed of an exterior grade of plywood

at least 1 in. in thickness, which shall not break down or delaminate under standard fire test conditions.

- All joints shall be rabbeted and shall be fastened in two directions with flathead wood screws.
- When more than one door is used, there shall be a rabbeted overlap of not less than 1 in.
- Steel hinges shall be mounted in such a manner as to not lose their holding capacity due to loosening or burning out of the screws when subjected to fire.
- Such cabinets shall be painted inside and out with fire-retardant paint.

- Approved metal storage cabinets will be acceptable.
- Cabinets shall be labeled in conspicuous lettering, "Flammable—Keep Fire Away."

Not more than 60 gal. of flammable or 120 gal. of combustible liquids shall be stored in any one storage cabinet. Not more than three such cabinets may be located in a single storage area. Quantities in excess of this shall be stored in an inside storage room.

Inside storage rooms shall be constructed to meet the required fire-resistive rating for their use. Such construction shall comply with the test specifications set forth in NFPA 251-1969, Standard Methods of Fire Test of Building Construction and Material.

Where an automatic extinguishing system is provided, the system shall be designed and installed in an approved manner. Openings to other rooms or buildings shall be provided with noncombustible liquid-tight raised sills or ramps at least 4 in. in height or the floor in the storage area shall be at least 4 in. below the surrounding floor. Openings shall be provided with approved self-closing fire doors. The room shall be liquid tight where the walls join the floor. A permissible alternate to the sill or ramp is an open-grated trench inside of the room that drains to a safe location. Where other portions of the building or other buildings are exposed, windows shall be protected as set forth in NFPA No. 80-1970, Standard for Fire Doors and Windows (for Class E or F openings). Wood of at least 1-in. nominal thickness may be used for shelving,

racks, dunnage, scuff boards, floor overlay, and similar installations.

Materials that will react with water and create a fire hazard shall not be stored in the same room with flammable or combustible liquids. Storage in inside storage rooms shall comply with Table F-2 (See Exhibit 17-3.).

Exhibit 17-3. Table F-2. Guidelines for storage inside of storage rooms.

Fire Protection Provided	Fire Resistance	Maximum Size	Total Allowable Quantities (gal./sq. ft./floor area)
Yes	2 hrs.	500 sq. ft.	10
No	2 hrs.	500 sq. ft.	4
Yes	1 hr.	150 sq. ft.	5
No	1 hr.	150 sq. ft.	2

Note: Fire protection system shall be sprinkler, water spray, carbon dioxide or other system approved by a nationally recognized testing laboratory for this purpose.

Electrical wiring and equipment located in inside storage rooms shall be approved for Class I, Division 1, Hazardous Locations.

Every inside storage room shall be provided with either a gravity or a mechanical exhausting system. Such system shall commence not more than 12 in. above the floor and be designed to provide for a complete change of air within the room at least six times per hour. If a mechanical exhausting system is used, a switch located outside of the door shall control it. The same switch shall operate the ventilating equipment and any lighting fixtures. An electric pilot light shall be installed adjacent to the switch if flammable liquids are dispensed within the room. Where gravity ventilation is provided, the fresh air intake, as well as the exhausting outlet from the room, shall be on the exterior of the building in which the room is located.

In every inside storage room there shall be maintained one clear aisle at least 3 ft. wide. Containers with more than a 30-gal. capacity shall not be stacked upon one other. Flammable and combustible liquids in excess of that permitted in inside storage rooms shall be stored outside of buildings in accordance with paragraph "Storage Outside Buildings" of this section.

The quantity of flammable or combustible liquids kept in the vicinity of spraying operations shall be the minimum required for operations and should ordinarily not exceed a supply for one day or one shift. The bulk storage of portable containers of flammable or combustible liquids shall be in a separate constructed building that is detached from other important buildings or cut off in a standard manner.

Storage Outside Buildings

The storage of containers (not more than 60 gal. each) shall not exceed 1,100 gal. in any one pile or area. Piles or groups of containers shall be separated by a 5-ft. clearance. Piles or groups of containers shall not be closer than 20 ft. to a building.

Within 200 ft. of each pile of containers, there shall be a 12-ft.-wide access way to permit the approach of fire control apparatus.

The storage area shall be graded in a manner to divert possible spills away from buildings or other exposures or shall be surrounded by a curb or earth dike at least 12 in. high. When curbs or dikes are used, provisions shall be made for draining off accumulations of ground or rainwater or spills of flammable or combustible liquids. Drains shall terminate at a safe location and shall be accessible to operation under fire conditions.

Outdoor Portable Tank Storage

Portable tanks shall not be stored within 20 ft. of any building. When storing, two or more portable tanks together that have a combined capacity in excess of 2,200 gal., they shall be separated by a 5-ft.-clear area. A 5-ft.-clear area shall separate individual portable tanks exceeding 1,100 gal.

Within 200 ft. of each portable tank, there shall be a 12-ft.-wide access way to permit the approach of fire control apparatus.

Storage areas shall be kept free of weeds, debris, and other combustible material not necessary to the storage. Portable tanks not exceeding 660 gal. shall be provided with emergency venting and other devices, as required by Chapters III and IV of NFPA 30-1969, The Flam-

mable and Combustible Liquids Code. Portable tanks, in excess of 660 gallons, shall have emergency venting and other devices, as required by Chapters II and III of NFPA 30-1969.

Fire Control for Flammable or Combustible Liquid Storage

At least one portable fire extinguisher, having a rating of not less than 20-B units, shall be located outside of, but not more than 10 ft. from, the door opening into any room used for the storage of more than 60 gal. of flammable or combustible liquids.

At least one portable fire extinguisher having a rating of not less than 20-B units shall be located not less than 25 ft., nor more than 75 ft., from any flammable liquid storage area located outside. At least one portable fire extinguisher having a rating of not less than 20-B:C units shall be provided on all tank trucks or other vehicles used for transporting and/or dispensing flammable or combustible liquids. When sprinklers are provided, they shall be installed in accordance with the NFPA 13-1969, Standard for the Installation of Sprinkler Systems.

Dispensing Liquids

Areas in which flammable or combustible liquids in quantities greater than 5 gal. are transferred at one time from one tank or container to another tank or container shall be separated from other operations by a 25-ft. distance or by construction having a fire resistance of at least one hour. Drainage or other means shall be provided to control spills. Adequate natural or mechanical ventilation shall be provided to maintain the concentration of flammable vapor at or below 10 percent of the lower flammable limit.

The transfer of flammable liquids from one container to another shall be performed only when containers are electrically interconnected or bonded.

Flammable or combustible liquids shall be drawn from or transferred into vessels, containers, or tanks within a building or outside only through a closed piping system, from safety cans, by means of a device drawing through the top, or from a container, or portable tanks, by gravity or pump, through an approved self-closing valve. Transferring by means of air pressure on the container or portable tanks is prohibited.

The dispensing units shall be protected against collision damage. Dispensing devices and nozzles for flammable liquids shall be of an approved type.

Handling Liquids at Point of Final Use

Flammable liquids shall be kept in closed containers when not actually in use. Leakage or spillage of flammable or combustible liquids shall be disposed of promptly and safely.

Flammable liquids may be used only where there are no open flames or other sources of ignition within 50 ft. of the operation, unless conditions warrant greater clearance.

Service and Refueling Areas

Flammable or combustible liquids shall be stored in approved closed containers, tanks located underground, or above-ground portable tanks. The dispensing hose shall be an approved type and the dispensing nozzle shall be an approved automatic-closing type without a latch-open device. The tank trucks shall comply with the requirements covered in NFPA No. 385-1966, Standard for Tank Vehicles for Flammable and Combustible Liquids. Underground tanks shall not be abandoned.

Clearly identified and easily accessible switch(es) shall be provided at a location remote from dispensing devices to shut off the power to all dispensing devices in the event of an emergency.

Heating equipment of an approved type may be installed in the lubrication or service area where there is no dispensing or transferring of flammable liquids, provided the bottom of the heating unit is at least 18 in. above the floor and is protected from physical damage.

Heating equipment installed in lubrication or service areas where flammable liquids are dispensed, shall be of an approved type for garages and shall be installed at least 8 ft. above the floor.

There shall be no smoking or open flames in the areas used for fueling, servicing fuel systems for internal combustion engines, or receiving or dispensing flammable or combustible liquids. Conspicuous and legible signs prohibiting smoking shall be posted.

The motors of all equipment being fueled shall be shut off during fueling operations.

Each service or fueling area shall be provided with at least one fire extinguisher having a rating of not less than 20-B:C located within 75 ft. of each pump, dispenser, underground fill pipe opening, or lubrication or service area.

Liquified Petroleum Gas (LP-Gas) —1926.153

Approval of Equipment and Systems

Each system shall have containers, valves, connectors, manifold valve assemblies, and regulators of an approved type. All cylinders shall meet the Department of Transportation specification identification requirements published in 49 CFR Part 178, Shipping Container Specifications. As used in this section, "Containers" are defined as all vessels, such as tanks, cylinders, or drums, that are used for the transportation or storage of liquefied petroleum gases.

LP-Gas Prohibitions

Storage of LP-Gas within buildings is prohibited. Welding is prohibited on containers.

Container Valves and Container Accessories

Valves, fittings, and accessories connected directly to the container, including primary shut-off valves, shall have a rated working pressure of at least 250 psig and shall be of material and design suitable for LP-Gas service. Connections to containers, except safety relief connections, liquid level gauging devices, and plugged openings, shall have shut-off valves located as close to the container as practicable.

Safety Devices

Every container and every vaporizer shall be provided with one or more approved safety relief valves or devices. These valves shall be arranged to afford free vent to the outer air with discharge not less than 5 ft. horizontally away from any opening into a building that is below such discharge. A shut-off valve shall not be installed between the safety relief device and the container, equipment or piping to which the safety relief device is connected, except that a shut-off valve may be used where the arrangement of this valve is such that full required capacity flow through the safety relief device is always afforded.

Container safety relief devices and regulator relief vents shall be located not less than 5 ft. in any direction from air openings into sealed combustion system appliances or mechanical ventilation air intakes.

Dispensing

The filling of fuel containers for trucks or motor vehicles from bulk storage containers shall be performed not less than 10 ft. from the nearest masonry-walled building, not less than 25 ft. from the nearest building or other construction and, in any event, not less than 25 ft. from any building opening. The filling of portable containers or containers mounted on skids from storage containers shall be performed not less than 50 ft. from the nearest building.

Requirements for Appliances

Any appliance that was originally manufactured for operation with a gaseous fuel other than LP-Gas and is in good condition may be used with LP-Gas only after it is properly converted, adapted, and tested for performance with LP-Gas. Containers shall be placed upright upon firm foundations or otherwise firmly secured. A flexible connection or special fitting shall guard against the possible effect on the outlet piping of settling.

Containers and Equipment Used Inside of Buildings or Structures

When operational requirements make portable use of containers necessary and their location outside of buildings or structures is impracticable, containers and equipment shall be permitted to be used inside of buildings or structures in accordance with 1926.153(h)(2) through 1926.153(11). "Containers in use" means connected for use.

Systems using containers having a water capacity greater than 2½ lbs. (nominal 1 lb.

LP-Gas capacity) shall be equipped with excess flow valves. Excess flow valves shall be integral with the container valves or in the connections to the container valve outlets.

Regulators shall either be directly connected to the container valves or to manifolds connected to the container valves. The regulator shall be suitable for use with LP-Gas. Manifolds and fittings connecting containers to pressure regulator inlets shall be designed for at least 250 psig service pressure. Valves on containers having a water capacity of greater than 50 lbs. (nominal 20 lbs. LP-Gas capacity) shall be protected from damage while in use or storage. Aluminum piping or tubing shall not be used.

Hose shall be designed for a working pressure of at least 250 psig. Design, construction, and performance of hose, and hose connections shall have their suitability determined by listing by a nationally recognized testing agency. The hose length shall be as short as practicable. Hoses shall be long enough to permit compliance with the spacing provisions of 1926.153(h)(1) through 1926.153(13), without kinking or straining, or causing hose to be so close to a burner as to be damaged by heat.

Portable heaters, including salamanders, shall be equipped with an approved automatic device to shut off the flow of gas to the main burner and pilot, if used, in the event of flame failure. Heaters having inputs of more than 50,000 BTU per hour shall be equipped with a pilot, which must be lighted and proved before the main burner can be turned on, or an electrical ignition system.

Container valves, connectors, regulators, manifolds, piping, and tubing shall not be used as structural supports for heaters. Containers, regulating equipment, manifolds, pipe, tubing, and hose shall be located so as to minimize exposure to high temperatures or physical damage.

Containers having a water capacity of greater than 2½ lb. (nominal 1 lb. LP-Gas capacity) that are connected for use shall stand on firm, substantially level surfaces and, when necessary, shall be secured in an upright position. The maximum water capacity of an individual container shall be 245 lbs. (nominal 100 lbs. LP-Gas capacity).

For temporary heating, heaters (other than integral heater-container units) shall be located at least 6 ft. from any LP-Gas container. The use of heaters specifically designed for attachment to the container or to a supporting standard is acceptable, provided they are designed and installed so as to prevent direct or radiant heat application from the heater onto the containers. Blower and radiant-type heaters shall not be directed toward any LP-Gas container within 20 ft.

If two or more heater-container units, of either the integral or nonintegral type, are located in an unpartitioned area on the same floor, the container or containers of each unit shall be separated from the container or containers of any other unit by at least 20 ft. When heaters are connected to containers for use in an unpartitioned area on the same floor, the total water capacity of containers, manifolded together for connection to a heater or heaters, shall not be greater than 735 lbs. (nominal 300 lbs. LP-Gas capacity). Such manifolds shall be separated by at least 20 ft.

Multiple Container Systems

Valves in the assembly of multiple container systems shall be arranged so containers can be replaced without shutting off the flow of gas in the system. This provision is not to be construed as requiring an automatic change-over device. Heaters shall be equipped with an approved regulator in the supply line between the fuel cylinder and the heater unit. Cylinder connectors shall be provided with an excess flow valve to minimize the flow of gas in the event the fuel line becomes ruptured. Regulators and low-pressure relief devices shall be rigidly attached to the cylinder valves, cylinders, supporting standards, the building walls, or otherwise rigidly secured, and shall be so installed or protected from the elements.

Storage Outside of Buildings

Containers shall be in a suitable ventilated enclosure or otherwise protected against tampering. If containers awaiting use are stored outside of buildings, they shall be located the specified number of feet from the nearest

building or group of buildings as stated in Table F-3 (See Exhibit 17-4.).

Exhibit 17-4. Table F-3. Distance of stored LP-Gas from nearest building.

Quantity of LP-Gas Stored (lbs.)	Distance (ft.)
500 or less	0
501 to 6,000	10
6,001 to 10,000	20
More than 10,000	25

Fire Protection

Storage locations shall be provided with at least one approved portable fire extinguisher having a rating of not less than 20-B:C.

Systems Using Containers Other than DOT Containers

This paragraph applies specifically to systems using storage containers other than those constructed in accordance with DOT specifications. Paragraph (b) of 1926.153 applies to this paragraph unless otherwise noted in paragraph (b). Storage containers shall be designed and classified in accordance with Table F-31 of 1926.153(m)(2).

Containers with foundations attached (portable or semi-portable containers with suitable steel "runners" or "skids," often called "skid tanks") shall be designed, installed, and used in accordance with these rules subject to the following provisions:

- If they are to be used at a given general location for a temporary period not to exceed 6 months they need not have fire-resisting foundations or saddles, but shall have adequate ferrous metal supports.
- They shall not be located with the outside bottom of the container shell more than 5 ft. (1.52 m) above the surface of the ground unless fire-resisting supports are provided.
- The bottom of the skids shall not be less than 2 in. (5.08 cm) or more than 12 in. (30.48 cm) below the outside bottom of the container shell.
- Flanges, nozzles, valves, fittings, and the like, having communication with the interior of the container, shall be protected against physical damage.

- When not permanently located on fire-resisting foundations, piping connections shall be sufficiently flexible to minimize the possibility of breakage or leakage of the connections if the container settles, moves, or is otherwise displaced.
- Skids, or lugs for attachment of skids, shall be secured to the container in accordance with the code or rules under which the container is designed and built (with a minimum factor of safety of 4) to withstand loading in any direction equal to four times the weight of the container and attachments when filled to the maximum permissible loaded weight.

Field welding where necessary shall be made only on saddle plates or brackets that were applied by the manufacturer of the tank.

Marking of Gas Cylinders

When LP-Gas and one or more other gases are stored or used in the same area, the containers shall be marked to identify their content. Marking shall be in compliance with ANSI Z48.1-1954, Method of Marking Portable Compressed Gas Containers to Identify the Material Contained.

Damage from Vehicles

When damage to LP-Gas systems from vehicular traffic is a possibility, precautions against such damage shall be taken.

Temporary Heating Devices—1926.154

Ventilation

Fresh air shall be supplied in sufficient quantities to maintain the health and safety of workers. Where natural means of fresh air supply is inadequate, mechanical ventilation shall be provided. When heaters are used in confined spaces, special care shall be taken to provide sufficient ventilation to ensure proper combustion, maintain the health and safety of workers, and limit temperature rise in the area.

Clearance and Mounting

Temporary heating devices shall be installed to provide clearance to combustible material not less than the amount shown in Table F-4 (See Exhibit 17-5.). Temporary heating devices, which are listed for installation with lesser clearances than specified in Table F-4, may be installed in accordance with their approval.

Exhibit 17-5. Table F-4. Clearance for temporary heating devices.

Heating appliances	Minimum clearance (in.)		
	Sides	Rear	Chimney Connector
Room heater, circulating type	12	12	18
Room heater, radiant type	36	36	18

Heaters not suitable for use on wood floors shall not be set directly upon them or other combustible materials. When such heaters are used, they shall rest on suitable heat insulating material or at least 1-in. concrete, or equivalent. The insulating material shall extend beyond the heater 2 ft. or more in all directions.

Heaters used in the vicinity of combustible tarpaulins, canvas, or similar coverings shall be located at least 10 ft. from the coverings. The coverings shall be securely fastened to prevent ignition or upsetting of the heater due to wind action on the covering or other material. Heaters, when in use, shall be set horizontally level, unless otherwise permitted by the manufacturer's markings.

Solid Fuel Salamanders

Solid fuel salamanders are prohibited in buildings and on scaffolds.

Oil-Fired Heaters

Flammable liquid-fired heaters shall be equipped with a primary safety control to stop the flow of fuel in the event of flame failure. Barometric or gravity oil feed shall not be considered a primary safety control. Heaters designed for barometric or gravity oil feed shall be used only with the integral tanks. Heaters specifically designed and approved for use with separate supply tanks may be directly connected for gravity feed, or an automatic pump, from a supply tank.

Fire Protection and Prevention

There are four types of fires that may occur and three types of fire extinguishers used to fight these fires. Employers must provide and train workers to use the correct fire extinguisher for the fire being fought. The four types of fires are:

- A. Trash fire. Burning wood and paper products. Usually extinguished with a water type extinguisher

- B. Liquid fire. Perhaps gasoline or a grease fire. If water is used as an extinguisher, the fire may spread.

- C. Electrical fire. If water is used as an extinguisher, the electricity may travel up the water stream to the employee.

- D. Special metal fire. Metals such as magnesium produce heat, hydrogen, and oxygen as by-products.

Exhibit 17-6. The table summarizes the types of extinguishers and the corresponding construction standard.

Standards for Fire Extinguishers in Construction	
Type of Fire Extinguisher	OSHA Standard
Type 2A	
Within 100 ft. of the workers in a building	150(c)(1)(i)
On each floor	150(c)(1)(iv)
Adjacent to the stairway (two story building)	150(c)(1)(iv)
Within 100 ft. of workers in open storage yards	151(c)(6)
Type 10B	
Within 50 ft. of 5 lbs. of flammable gas	150(c)(1)(vi)
Within 50 ft. of 5 gal. of flammable liquid	150(c)(1)(vi)
Type 20-B	
Within 10 ft., outside a flammable storage area	152(d)(2)
Type 5-B:C	
Crane cabs or at operator's station	550(a)(14)(i)
Type 20-B:C	
Within 75 ft. of service/fuel area	152(g)(11)
On vehicles transporting flammable liquid	152(d)(4)

Fatalities as a Result of Noncompliance

Violation: Tipping the asphalt roofing kettle on a roofing job; the spigot stuck.
Standard: Combustible liquids must be drawn through approved containers; transfer via air pressure is prohibited (1926.152(e)(3)).
Violation: Welding and cutting on pipes near an underground storage tank while the welder was in an underground vault
Standard: Object to be cut must be at a safe location (1926.352(a)).
Violation: Torpedo type heater was being used to dry out water in an underground vault. The heater exploded.
Standard: Portable heaters must have an automatic shut-off device to stop the flow of gas to the main burner and pilot. (1926.153(h)(8)).

Violation: Worker was in a 200,000-gal. tank applying a coating when there was an explosion.
Standard: Flammable liquids cannot be used within 50 ft. of an ignition source (1926.152(f)(3)).
Violation: Worker was cutting on a fuel storage tank when it exploded.
Standard: Drums that contained toxic materials must be cleaned, ventilated, and tested or filled with water before cutting (1926.352(i)).
Violation: Worker was cutting a pipe for removal that was not empty of diesel vapors.
Standard: Pipes must be surveyed to determine whether they previously contained hazardous chemicals, and be purged and tested, as necessary (1926.850(e)).

CONTACT: Frank Kane   FOR RELEASE: 2:00 P.M. EST
OFFICE: (202) 219-8151   Wednesday, Feb. 8, 1995

OSHA DELIVERS NOTICES TO THE FOREST SERVICE AND BUREAU OF LAND MANAGEMENT FOLLOWING DEATH OF 14 FIREFIGHTERS

The Occupational Safety and Health Administration (OSHA) today cited the Bureau of Land Management (BLM) and the U.S. Forest Service (USFS) for unsafe conditions that led to the deaths of 14 firefighters in a wild land fire near Glenwood Springs, Colo.

The 14, including 13 Forest Service firefighters and one from Bureau of Land Management, were killed when the fire raged out of control at South Canyon on July 6, 1994.

Assistant Secretary of Labor for Occupational Safety and Health Joseph A. Dear said, "Based on evidence collected from on-site observations, document reviews and numerous interviews, OSHA has determined that BLM and USFS violated standard firefighting procedures. They also failed to recognize and respond in a timely manner to numerous factors that, together, clearly identified the South Canyon fire as highly hazardous to firefighting personnel."

"OSHA's investigation indicated that this was a management failure," Dear said. "Our investigation, which took almost seven months to complete, was designed to identify the causes of this tragedy and to recommend corrective actions to avoid another South Canyon tragedy. We want to assist the agencies in making firefighting safer."

The Notices of Unsafe Conditions issued to BLM and USFS cited one alleged willful and one alleged serious violation.

Dear said the alleged willful violation was based on a finding that the management of the two agencies demonstrated "plain indifference" to the safety and health of their employees. "Management officials were aware of the conditions and practices at the site of the fire but failed to determine the extent of danger and thus did not take the necessary corrective actions."

The alleged willful citation said that in fighting the South Canyon fire the agency management did not enforce the safety provisions of the National Wildfire Coordination Group Fireline Handbook:

a) The identity of the Incident Commander was not effectively communicated to firefighters.
b) Adequate safety zones and escape routes were not established for and identified to employees.
c) Available weather forecasts and expected fire behavior information were not provided to employees.
d) Adequate fire lookouts were not used on the fire.
e) Hazardous downhill fireline construction did not follow established safe practices and proper safety precautions.

The alleged serious citation said the agencies failed to provide sufficient management oversight to ensure that existing safe firefighting practices were followed:

a) Management failed to provide firefighters with comprehensive fire behavior information to include fuel type/moisture, topography and local weather forecasts.
b) Management failed to ensure that the evolution of the Incident Command system was commensurate with the fire threat.
c) Even though fires in the surrounding area (the Bunniger Fire and the Paonia Fire), with similar fuels, were exhibiting extreme fire behavior, management failed to follow the safety practices for blow-up conditions.
d) Management failed to conduct adequate workplace inspections of firefighting operations to include on-site, front-line evaluations.

In issuing the citations, OSHA recommended several feasible and acceptable methods of abating the hazards. OSHA believes that the joint investigation of the fire conducted earlier by the BLM and USFS was thorough.

Following the release of the joint investigation team's Aug. 17, 1994 report, the five federal wild land firefighting agencies undertook a comprehensive management review. The results of that review highlighted the importance of management involvement and accountability in ensuring the health and safety of wild land firefighters. The review team also developed a detailed corrective action plan, most of which will be implemented before the 1995 Western fire season. OSHA believes that this interagency management review team report was an excellent report and blueprint for change.

OSHA has no authority to propose monetary penalties for other federal agencies. The agencies have 15 working days in which to request an informal conference with the Denver Area OSHA Director in which they may present any evidence or views that they believe might support an adjustment to the notice. In such a conference, they also are required to bring supporting documentation of existing conditions as well as any abatement steps they have taken.

If the results of an informal conference are not satisfactory to the agencies, they can make a formal appeal of the notice to the Regional Administrator in Denver. Further appeals, if necessary, can be made to OSHA's Office of Federal Agency Programs in Washington.

An Example of a Flammability Fatality

Workers in Puerto Rico were cleaning a large storage tank in a refinery. Since the last time that it had been cleaned, the tank had been used to store various oils, such as gasoline, gas oil, and light and heavy crude oils. The employer expected that the tank would contain some residue from these liquids.

All of the equipment, tools, and procedures to be used for entry into the tank were prescribed by an entry permit that had been prepared by the parent company, not by the refinery. Workers were required to use air-supplied respirators, lifelines, explosion-proof lighting and to test the atmosphere for flammable conditions before and during entry. However, no one at the refinery had been made accountable for compliance with the permit.

Employee accounts of the incident indicate that refinery management had originally followed the prescribed procedures. However, on the day of the incident, the permit requirements were generally ignored. For example, even though it was known that the work could generate an explosive atmosphere and that only explosion-proof lighting was allowed, only two of the 12 lamps used to illuminate the inside of the tank were explosion proof. No lifelines were available and no atmospheric testing was performed.

Five employees were in the tank when it exploded. The fires burned out in just seconds; nonetheless, four of the workers were killed. Workers outside the tank were unable to help them. The fifth entrant died later of massive respiratory injuries.

Fire Protection Quiz
(See appendix for answers.)

1. For every 3,000 sq. ft. of a building, there must be:
   a. A fire extinguisher with a rating of at least 2A
   b. A Type C fire extinguisher
   c. A Type B fire extinguisher
   d. A garden hose

2. Flammable and combustible liquids must be stored in a storage cabinet:
   a. If the amount is more than 15 gal.
   b. If the amount is more than 25 gal.
   c. If the amount is more than 35 gal.
   d. If the flash point is below 65°

3. When pouring 10 gal. of gasoline from one tank to another, the area must be separated by:
   a. 25 ft. from other operations
   b. A construction with a one-hour fire rating
   c. Both of the above
   d. Either of the above
   e. None of the above

4. On a multiple story building, fire extinguishers must be located:
   a. At the base of the stairway
   b. On each floor
   c. Within 200 ft. of flammable gas
   d. Based on the operation taking place

5. Temporary heating devices, such as torpedo heaters, must:
   a. Have sufficient fresh air supply and be used according to manufacturer's directions
   b. Be set on solid wood flooring
   c. Be directly plumbed to the gas source
   d. Be located at least 25 ft. from coverings such as canvas or tarps

6. Which statement is not correct?
   a. Fire extinguishers must be within 100 ft. of workers
   b. Fire extinguishers must be on vehicles that transport flammables
   c. Fire extinguishers must be within 100 ft. of open storage yards
   d. Fire extinguishers must be within 100 ft. of a service/fuel area

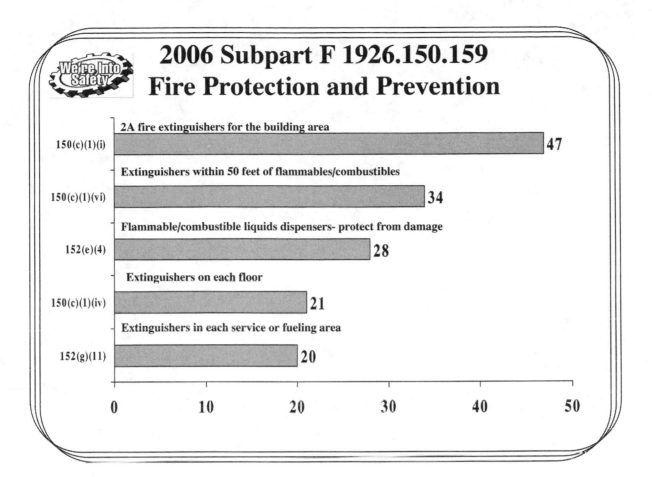

Motor Vehicles, Mechanized Equipment, and Marine Operations Equipment

All equipment left unattended at night, adjacent to a highway in normal use or adjacent to construction areas where work is in progress shall have appropriate lights, reflectors, or barricades equipped with appropriate lights and reflectors to identify the location of the equipment. A safety tire rack, cage, or equivalent protection shall be provided and used when inflating, mounting or dismounting tires installed on split rims or rims equipped with locking rings or similar devices.

Heavy machinery, equipment, or parts thereof that are suspended or held aloft by the use of slings, hoists, or jacks shall be substantially blocked or cribbed to prevent falling or shifting before employees are permitted to work under or between them. Bulldozer and scraper blades, end-loader buckets, dump bodies and similar equipment shall be fully lowered or blocked when being repaired or not in use. All controls shall be in a neutral position, with the motors stopped and brakes set, unless work being performed requires otherwise.

Whenever the equipment is parked, the parking brake shall be set. Equipment parked on inclines shall have the wheels chocked and the parking brake set.

The use, care, and charging of all batteries shall conform to the requirements of Subpart K, Electrical.

All cab glass shall be safety glass (or equivalent) that introduces no visible distortion affecting the safe operation of any machine covered by this subpart. All equipment shall comply with the requirements of 1926.550(a)(15), Cranes and Derricks, when working or being moved in the vicinity of power lines or energized transmitters.

Derail and/or bumper blocks shall be provided on spur railroad tracks where a rolling car could contact other cars being worked on or enter a building, work, or traffic area.

Motor Vehicles—1926.601

Motor vehicles covered by this section are those that operate within an off-highway jobsite that is not open to public traffic. This section does not apply to equipment that is governed by 1926.602 (e.g., bulldozers, scrapers, industrial and agricultural tractors).

General Requirements

All vehicles shall have a service brake system, an emergency brake system, and a parking brake system. These systems may use common components and shall be maintained in operable condition.

Whenever visibility conditions warrant additional light, all vehicles or combinations of vehicles in use shall be equipped with at least two headlights and two taillights that are in operable condition.

All vehicles shall be equipped with brake lights in operable condition and an adequate audible warning device at the operator's station in operable condition.

Any operating vehicle with an obstructed view to the rear must have a reverse signal alarm that can be heard above the surrounding noise level and an observer to guide the vehicle (a ground guide).

All vehicles with cabs shall be equipped with windshields and powered wipers. Cracked and broken glass shall be replaced. Vehicles operating in areas or under conditions that cause fogging or frosting of the windshields shall be equipped with operable defogging or defrosting devices.

All haulage vehicles whose pay load is loaded by means of cranes, power shovels, loaders or similar equipment shall have a cab shield and/or canopy adequate to protect the operator from shifting or falling materials. Tools and material shall be secured to prevent movement when transported in the same compartment with employees.

Vehicles used to transport employees shall have seats firmly secured and adequate for the number of employees to be carried.

Seat belts and anchorages that meet the Department of Transportation Federal Motor Vehicle Safety Standards (49 CFR 571) shall be installed in all motor vehicles. All rubber-tired motor vehicle equipment shall be equipped with fenders. Mud flaps may be used in lieu of fenders when the motor vehicle equipment is not designed for fenders.

Trucks with dump bodies shall be equipped with a positive means of support that is permanently attached and capable of being locked in position to prevent the accidental lowering of the body while maintenance or inspection work is being performed.

Operating levers controlling hoisting or dumping devices on haulage bodies shall be equipped with a latch or other device that will prevent the mechanism from accidental starting or tripping. Trip handles on the tailgates of dump trucks shall be located so the operator will be in the clear when the load is dumped.

All vehicles in use shall be checked at the beginning of each shift to ensure all equipment and accessories are in safe operating condition and free of apparent damage that could cause failure while in use. All defects shall be corrected before the vehicle is placed in service.

The following is a list of items that must be inspected before a vehicle may be put into service.

- Service brakes (including trailer brake connections);
- Parking system (hand brakes);
- Emergency stopping system (brakes);
- Tires;
- Horn;
- Steering mechanism;
- Coupling devices;
- Seat belts;
- Operating controls; and
- Safety devices.

When required to be present, the following also shall be inspected:

- Lights;
- Reflectors;
- Windshield wipers;
- Defroster; and
- Fire extinguisher.

Material Handling Equipment— 1926.602

Earthmoving Equipment—General

These rules apply to the following types of earthmoving equipment:

- Scrapers;
- Loaders;
- Crawler or wheel tractors;
- Bulldozers;
- Off-highway trucks;
- Graders; and
- Agricultural and industrial tractors.

Seat Belts

Seat belts shall be provided on all equipment covered by this section and shall meet the requirements of the Society of Automotive Engineers, J386-1969, Seat Belts for Construction Equipment. Seat belts for agricultural and light industrial tractors shall meet the seat belt requirements of the Society of Automotive Engineers J333a-1970, Operator Protection for Agricultural and Light Industrial Tractors. Seat belts need not be provided for equipment that is designed only for stand-up operation or equipment that does not have rollover protective structure (ROPS) or adequate canopy protection.

Access Roadways and Grades

No employer shall move or cause to be moved, construction equipment or vehicles upon any access roadway or grade unless the access roadway or grade is constructed and maintained to safely accommodate the movement of the equipment and vehicles involved. Every emergency access ramp and berm used by an employer shall be constructed to restrain and control runaway vehicles.

Brakes

All earthmoving equipment mentioned earlier in this section shall have a service braking system capable of stopping and holding the equipment fully loaded as specified in Society of Automotive Engineers SAE-J237, Loader Dozer-1971, J236, Graders-1971, and J319b, Scrapers-1971. Brake systems for self-propelled, rubber-tired off-highway equipment manufactured after January 1, 1972, shall meet the applicable minimum performance criteria set forth by the following Society of Automotive Engineers Recommended Practices:

- SAEJ319b-1971, Self-Propelled Scrapers;
- SAEJ23-1971, Self-Propelled Graders;
- SAEJ166-1971, Trucks and Wagons; and
- SAEJ237-1971, Front-End Loaders and Dozers.

Fenders

Pneumatic-tired earth-moving haulage equipment (e.g., trucks, scrapers, tractors, trailing units) whose maximum speed exceeds 15 miles per hour shall be equipped with fenders on all wheels to meet the requirements of the Society of Automotive Engineers SAE J321a-1970, Fenders for Pneumatic-Tired Earthmoving Haulage Equipment. An employer may request a variance from safety and health standards under 29 CFR 1926.2 to demonstrate that the uncovered wheels present no hazard to personnel from flying materials.

Audible Alarms

All bi-directional machines shall be equipped with a horn that is distinguishable from the surrounding noise level. The horn shall be maintained in an operative condition and shall be operated as needed when the machine is moving in either direction. This applies to:

- Rollers;
- Compacters;
- Front-end loaders;
- Bulldozers; and
- Similar equipment.

No employer shall permit earthmoving or compacting equipment that has an obstructed view to the rear to be used in reverse gear unless the equipment has an operational reverse signal alarm that is distinguishable from the surrounding noise level. Ground guides also may be used to signal the operator that it is safe to proceed.

Scissor Points

Scissor points on all front-end loaders that constitute a hazard to the operator during normal operations shall be guarded.

Excavating and Other Equipment

Tractors covered under this section shall have seat belts as required for the operators when seated in the normal seating arrangement for tractor operation, even though backhoe, brakers, or other similar attachments are used on these machines for excavating or other work.

Industrial trucks shall meet the requirements of 29 CFR 1926.602 and the following:

- Lift trucks, stackers, etc. shall have the rated capacity clearly posted on the vehicle so as to be clearly visible to the operator. When the manufacturer provides auxiliary removable counterweights, corresponding alternate-rated capacities shall be clearly shown on the vehicle as well. These ratings shall not be exceeded.

- No modifications or additions that affect the capacity or safe operation of the equipment shall be made without the manufacturer's written approval. If such modifications or changes are made, the capacity, operation, and maintenance instruction plates, tags, or decals shall be changed accordingly. In no case shall the original safety factor of the equipment be reduced.

- If a load is lifted by two or more trucks working in unison, the proportion of the total load carried by any one truck shall not exceed that truck's capacity.

- Steering or spinner knobs shall not be attached to the steering wheel unless the steering mechanism is of a type that prevents road reactions from causing the steering hand wheel to spin. The steering knob shall be mounted within the periphery of the wheel.

- All industrial trucks in use shall meet the applicable requirements of design, construction, stability, inspection, testing, maintenance, and operation established by the American National Standards Institute. High lift rider industrial trucks shall be equipped with overhead guards that meet the configuration and structural requirements as defined in ANSI B56.1-1969, Safety Standards for Powered Industrial Trucks, ¶421.

- Unauthorized personnel shall not be permitted to ride on powered industrial trucks. A safe place to ride shall be provided when the riding of trucks is authorized.

- Whenever a truck is equipped with vertical only, or vertical and horizontal controls elevatable with the lifting carriage or forks for lifting personnel, the following precautions must be taken for the personnel being elevated:
  - Use of a safety platform firmly secured to the lifting carriage and/or forks;
  - Means shall be provided whereby personnel on the platform can shut off power to the truck; and
  - Protection from falling objects, as indicated necessary by the operating conditions, shall be provided.

Pile-Driving Equipment—1926.603

Boilers and piping systems that are a part of or used with pile driving equipment shall meet the applicable requirements of the American Society of Mechanical Engineers, Power Boilers (Section I).

All pressure vessels that are a part of or used with pile-driving equipment shall meet the applicable requirements of the American Society of Mechanical Engineers, Pressure Vessels (Section VIII).

Overhead protection that will not obscure the vision of the operator and that meets the requirements of Subpart N (Cranes, Derricks, Hoists, Elevators and Conveyors) shall be provided. Protection shall be the equivalent of a 2-in. planking or other solid material of equivalent strength.

Stop blocks shall be provided for the leads to prevent the hammer from being raised against the head block. A blocking device capable of safely supporting the weight of the hammer shall be provided for placement in the leads under the hammer at all times while employees are working under the hammer.

When the leads must be included in the driving of batter piles, provisions shall be made to stabilize the leads. Fixed leads shall be provided with ladder and adequate rings or similar attachment points so that the loft worker may engage his or her safety belt lanyard to the leads. If the leads are provided with loft platform(s), standard guardrails shall protect such platform(s).

Guards shall be provided across the top of the head block to prevent the cable from jumping out of the sheaves.

Site Clearing—1926.604

Employees engaged in site clearing shall be protected from hazards of irritant and toxic plants and suitably instructed in the first-aid treatment available.

All equipment used in site-clearing operations shall be equipped with rollover guards that meet the requirements of this subpart. In addition, rider-operated equipment shall be equipped with an overhead and rear canopy guard that meets the following requirements:

- The overhead covering on this canopy structure shall be of not less than 1/8-in. steel plate or 1/4-in. woven wire mesh with openings no greater than 1 in., or equivalent.
- The opening in the rear of the canopy structure shall be covered with not less than ¼-in. woven wire mesh with openings no greater than 1 in.

Marine Operations and Equipment—1926.605

Material Handling Operations

Operations fitting the definition of "material handling" shall be performed in conformance with applicable requirements of Part 118, "Safety and Health Regulations for Long Shoring." The term "longshoring operations" means the loading, unloading, moving, or handling of construction materials, equipment, and supplies into, in, on, or out of any vessel from a fixed structure or shore-to-vessel, vessel-to-shore, or vessel-to-vessel structure.

Access to Barges

Ramps for access of vehicles to or between barges shall be of adequate strength, provided with sideboards, well maintained, and properly secured. Unless employees can step safely to or from the wharf, float, barge, or river towboat, a ramp or a safe walkway shall be provided that meets the requirements established above.

Jacob's ladders shall be of the double rung or flat tread type. They shall be well maintained, properly secured, and either hang without slack from their lashings or be pulled up entirely.

When the upper end of the means of access rests on or is flush with the top of the bulwark, substantial steps properly secured and equipped with at least one substantial hand rail approximately 33 in. in height shall be provided between the top of the bulwark and the deck. Obstructions shall not be laid on or across the gangway. The means of access shall be adequately illuminated for its full length. Unless the structure makes it impossible, the means of access shall be so located that the load will not pass over employees.

Working Surfaces of Barges

Employees shall not be permitted to walk along the sides of covered lighters or barges with coamings more than 5 ft. high unless there is a 3-ft. clear walkway or a grab rail or taut handline is provided. Decks and other working surfaces shall be maintained in a safe condition.

Employees shall not be permitted to pass in front of or back of, over, or around deckloads unless there is a safe passageway. Employees shall not be permitted to walk over deck loads from rail to coaming unless there is a safe passageway. If it is necessary to stand at the outboard or inboard edge of the deck load where less than 24 in. of bulwark, rail, coaming, or other protection exists, employees shall be provided with a suitable means of protection against falling from the deck load.

First-Aid and Life-Saving Equipment

Provisions for rendering first aid and medical assistance shall be in accordance with Subpart D, Occupational Health and Environmental Controls.

The employer shall ensure that there is in the vicinity of each barge in use at least one U.S. Coast Guard-approved, 30-in. life ring with not less than 90 ft. of line attached and at least one portable or permanent ladder that will reach from the top of the apron to the surface of the water. If the above equipment is not available at the pier, the employer shall furnish it during the time its employees are working on the barge.

Employees walking or working on the unguarded decks of barges shall be protected with U.S. Coast Guard-approved work vests or buoyant vests.

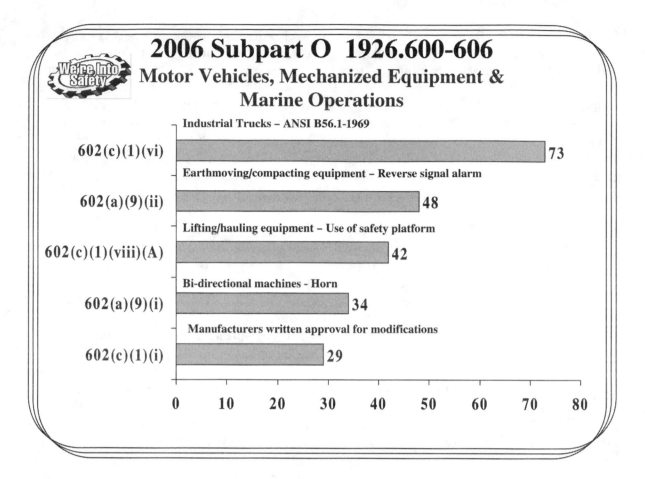

2006 Subpart O 1926.600-606
Motor Vehicles, Mechanized Equipment & Marine Operations

- Industrial Trucks – ANSI B56.1-1969 — 602(c)(1)(vi) — 73
- Earthmoving/compacting equipment – Reverse signal alarm — 602(a)(9)(ii) — 48
- Lifting/hauling equipment – Use of safety platform — 602(c)(1)(viii)(A) — 42
- Bi-directional machines - Horn — 602(a)(9)(i) — 34
- Manufacturers written approval for modifications — 602(c)(1)(i) — 29

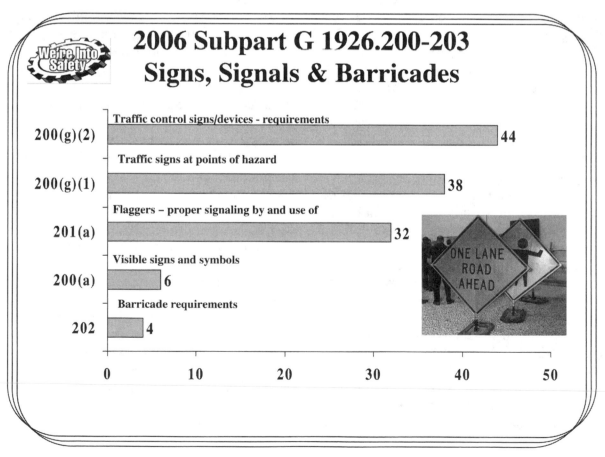

2006 Subpart G 1926.200-203
Signs, Signals & Barricades

- Traffic control signs/devices - requirements — 200(g)(2) — 44
- Traffic signs at points of hazard — 200(g)(1) — 38
- Flaggers – proper signaling by and use of — 201(a) — 32
- Visible signs and symbols — 200(a) — 6
- Barricade requirements — 202 — 4

EXCAVATIONS

OSHA issued its first Excavation and Trenching Standard in 1971 to protect workers from excavation hazards. Since then OSHA has amended the standard several times to increase worker protection and reduce the frequency and severity of excavation accidents and injuries. Despite these efforts, excavation-related accidents that result in injuries and fatalities continue to occur.

One appendix in the regulation provides a consistent method of soil classification. Others provide sloping and benching requirements, pictorial examples of shoring and shielding devices, timber tables, hydraulic shoring tables, and selection charts that provide a graphic summary of the requirements contained in the standard.

OSHA's revised rule applies to all open excavations made in the earth's surface, which includes trenches. According to the OSHA construction safety and health standards, a *trench* is a narrow excavation made below the surface of the ground in which the depth is greater than the width—the width not exceeding 15 ft. An *excavation* is any man-made cut, cavity, trench, or depression in the earth's surface formed by earth removal. This can include excavations for anything from cellars to highways.

Many on-the-job accidents are a direct result of inadequate initial planning. Correcting mistakes in shoring and/or sloping after work has begun slows down the operation, adds to the cost, and increases the possibility of an excavation failure. The contractor should build safety into the pre-bid planning in the same way all other pre-bid factors are considered. OSHA requires that an individual be identified as the competent person during excavation work.

Trenches vs. Excavations

A trench is less than 15 feet wide and is generally deeper than it is wide. It has two sides and is usually open for less than 24 hours. An excavation, on the other hand, normally has a width of 15 ft. or more and is wider than it is deep. Excavations normally have one or more sides and are open for long periods of time. Each worker in an excavation must be protected from the hazards of a cave-in by an adequate protective system that meets OSHA requirements. This system may consist of a method of sloping the soil away from the edge of the excavation, shoring the sides of the excavation to withstand cave-ins, or using a shielding system. Excavations do not need to be protected by these systems only if they are made entirely in stable rock, or if the excavation is less than 5 ft. deep and the competent person examines the excavation and determines there is no indication of a potential cave-in. A competent person must conduct soil classification tests and make his or her determination based on at least one visual and one manual test of the soil.

Protective Systems for Excavations

To be a competent person, the worker must have the ability to recognize and predict hazards in the excavation site and must have the authority to correct those hazards. The competent person will conduct inspections of the trench or excavation each day prior to work and as conditions change, such as vibrations in the ground or rainstorms that affect the ground condition.

Prior to excavating, firms must call underground utilities to locate the wires and pipes that criss-cross the area and identify hazards in the area that will be dug.

While the excavation is in use, a ladder, ramp, stairway, or other means of egress must be located not more than 25 ft. away from the workers when the trench is greater than 4 ft. deep. A system of fall protection must be provided for any walkway that passes over the excavation, such as guardrails. The edges of the excavation also must be protected by using a warning system, such as barricades, mechanical signals, or stop logs. Material or equipment must be kept at least 2 ft. away from the edge of the trench unless they are restrained from falling into the trench. Water must be kept from accumulating in the trench or excavation.

There is a special definition for a competent person as outlined by the OSHA regulations:

- **Authorized Person** – A person who is authorized by the employer to perform a task.
- **Qualified Person** – A person who has the knowledge to perform that task through education, schooling, training, or experience.
- **Competent Person** – A person who is qualified and authorized to perform the task. A competent person must have the ability to identify hazardous conditions and have the authority to take action to maintain a safe workplace.
  - 1926.650 (b) One who is capable of identifying existing and predictable hazards in the surroundings or working conditions that are unsanitary, hazardous, or dangerous to employees, and who has the authorization to eliminate them.
  - Must have training in and be knowledgeable about soils analysis, the use of protective systems, and the requirements of the OSHA standard. "One who does not

have such training or knowledge cannot possibly be capable of identifying existing and predictable hazards in work or taking prompt corrective measures."

It is a good idea for the competent person to develop safety checklists before working on excavations to make certain there is adequate information about the job site and all needed items are on hand. These checklists should incorporate elements of the relevant OSHA standards as well as other information necessary for safe operations. Before preparing a bid, these specific site conditions should be taken into account:

- Traffic;
- Nearness of structures and their conditions;
- Soil;
- Surface and ground water;
- The water table;
- Overhead and underground utilities; and
- Weather.

These and other conditions can be determined by job site studies, observations, test borings for soil type or conditions, and consultations with local officials and utility companies.

Before any excavation actually begins, the standard requires the employer to determine the estimated location of utility installations (e.g., sewer, telephone, fuel, electric, water lines, or any other underground installations) that may be encountered during digging. Before starting the excavation, the contractor must contact the utility companies or owners involved and inform them, within established or customary local response times, of the proposed work. The contractor also must ask the utility companies or owners to find the exact location of the underground installations. If they cannot respond within 24 hours (unless the period required by state or local law is longer), or if they cannot find the exact location of the utility installations, the contractor may proceed with caution. To find the exact location of underground installations, workers must use safe and acceptable means. If underground installations are exposed, OSHA regulations also require that they be removed, protected, or properly supported.

When all the necessary specific information about the job site is assembled, the contractor will be ready to determine the amount, kind, and cost of the safety equipment needed. A careful inventory of the safety items on hand should be made before deciding what additional safety material must be acquired. No matter how many trenching, shoring, and back-filling jobs have been done in the past, each job should be approached with the utmost care and preparation.

Before Beginning the Job

It is important, before beginning the job, for the contractor to establish and maintain a safety and health program for the work site that provides adequate systematic policies, procedures, and practices to protect employees from, and allow them to recognize, job-related safety and health hazards.

An effective program includes provisions for the systematic identification, evaluation, and prevention or control of general workplace hazards, specific job hazards, and potential hazards that may arise from foreseeable conditions. The program may be written or verbal, but it should reflect the unique characteristics of the job site.

To be sure safety policies are implemented effectively, there must be cooperation among supervisors, employee groups, including unions, and individual employees. Each supervisor must understand the degree of responsibility and authority he or she holds in a particular area. For effective labor support, affected unions should be notified of construction plans and asked to cooperate.

It is also important, before beginning work, for employers to provide employees who will be exposed to public vehicular traffic with warning vests or other suitable garments marked with or made of reflectorized or high-visibility material and ensure that they wear them. Workers must also be instructed to remove or neutralize surface encumbrances that may create a hazard. In addition, no employee should operate a piece of equipment without first being properly trained to handle it and fully alerted to its potential hazards.

On-the-Job Evaluation

The standard requires that a competent person inspect, on a daily basis, excavations and the adjacent areas for possible cave-ins, failures of protective systems and equipment, hazardous atmospheres, or other hazardous conditions. If these conditions are encountered, exposed employees must be removed from the hazardous area until the necessary safety precautions have been taken. Inspections also are required after natural (e.g., heavy rains) or man-made events, such as blasting, that may increase the potential for hazards.

Larger and more complex operations should have a full-time safety official who makes recommendations to improve the implementation of the safety plan. In a smaller operation, the safety official may be part-time; usually it is a supervisor.

Supervisors are the contractor's representatives on the job. Supervisors should conduct inspections, investigate accidents, and anticipate hazards. They should ensure that employees receive on-the-job safety and health training. They should also review and strengthen overall safety and health precautions to guard against potential hazards, get the necessary worker cooperation in safety matters, and make frequent reports to the contractor.

It is important that managers and supervisors set the example for safety at the job site. It is essential that when visiting the job site, all managers, regardless of status, wear the prescribed personal protective equipment, such as safety shoes, safety glasses, hard hats, and other necessary gear (see CFR 1926.100 and 102).

Employees must also take an active role in job safety. The contractor and supervisor should make certain that workers have been properly trained in the use and fit of the prescribed protective gear and equipment, that they are wearing and using the equipment correctly, and that they are using safe work practices.

Cave-Ins and Protective Support Systems

Mechanics of a Cave-In

An open excavation is an unnatural situation. The average landscape shows no vertical or near vertical slopes. Soil or dirt is a very heavy material. A cubic foot can easily weigh 114 lbs. and a cubic yard can be as heavy as a pick-up truck.

Consider a column of soil that is 1 ft. × 1 ft. and several feet high. At 1 ft. of depth, a horizontal plane 1 ft. × 1 ft. is carrying the cubic foot that lies over it. The stress, or load per unit area is 100 lbs. per square foot (psf). At a depth of 2 ft., the horizontal plane is carrying 2 cu. ft. or 200 psf. At a depth of 5 ft., the vertical stress is 500 psf, and so on.

The column described would soon collapse if not supported by similar adjacent columns. Stresses are developed which act horizontally on the column. These lateral stresses can be considered half as large as the vertical stresses. At a depth of 5 ft., the vertical stress is 500 psf and the lateral, or horizontal stress is 250 psf.

Undisturbed soil may be visualized as an infinite number of columns of soil adjoining and supporting one another. The system is in equilibrium and is perfectly stable.

When an excavation is cut, the system is disturbed. Lateral stresses that existed on the excavation wall are removed as the excavation is done. The soil in the excavation wall will immediately begin to move, however slowly, into the excavation.

At the same time, the surface of the ground next to the excavation will subside, creating an unnatural situation. The surface of the ground will be in tension and some of the weight of the soil in the excavation wall will be transferred to the soil back away from the wall face by a phenomenon called shear.

The combination of tension in the ground surface and shear stress causes cracks to form back from the edge of the excavation. Cracks occur from the edge of the excavation. Cracks occur from about to of the depth of the excavation back from its edge. For example, if an excavation 10 ft. deep is dug, the cracks may be found somewhere between 3 ft. to 7 ft. back from the excavation edge. There may be several

cracks. They are usually vertical and may be half of the depth of the excavation.

When cracks develop, the weight of the soil in the excavation wall is no longer partly carried by the soil back from the excavation's face. Then the lower part of the excavation wall fails under the great stress from the weight of the soil above it. There is no lateral stress to prevent the failure.

When the bottom of the excavation fails, or "kicks," into the excavation, the support for the upper part of the excavation wall is now essentially hanging only by shear and tension forces. Failure occurs.

A third cave-in quickly follows. Soil, like concrete, is normally strong in compression, but not at all strong in tension. Reinforced concrete makes use of the compressive strength of concrete and the tensile strength of steel; there is no steel in the soil. See Exhibit 19-1 for an illustration of this multiple cave-in process.

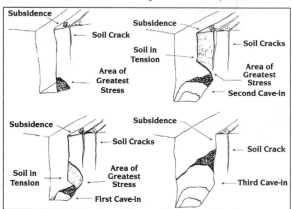

Exhibit 19-1.
Cave-ins are caused by tension and stress and usually occur in multiples.

Cave-ins generally come in multiples. If the first one does not harm workers, the second one may, and the third is always a possibility.

This example of the mechanics of a cave-in identifies some of the forces involved in such accidents. By no means does it consider all of the forces that may be involved in such an occurrence. Weathering, water, vibration and superimposed loads may add to the hazardous conditions leading to a cave-in.

It is critical that supervisors understand the mechanics of a cave-in and why it is so important to protect workers in a trench. This standard was revised in 1989 and fatalities have decreased since the changes have been instituted. Still, the collapse of trench walls is still the leading cause of death in trenching operations.

When building a trench of more than 20 ft. in depth, a registered professional engineer is required to oversee the protection systems used. A competent person (one who has knowledge of the soil mechanics and operation at hand as well as the authority to stop the operation) is required to be on the site during trenching operations.

The competent person will consider the effects of street and ground vibration, cracks, and water in the classification of soil type. Sources of vibrations that may cause a cave-in include:

- Railroad operations;
- Vehicular traffic;
- Heavy equipment operations;
- Jack hammers; and
- Tamping machine operations.

Types of Soil

The competent person also must ensure that the slope is at the correct angle for the soil type being disturbed. Soil is classified into the following types:

- Type A soil is a cohesive soil that is usually composed of clay, silty clay, sandy clay, or loam. It has a maximum permitted slope of 0.75:1 (53° slope). Soil cannot be considered to be Type A if:
  - The soil is fissured;
  - It is subject to vibration by pile driving or heavy traffic; or
  - It has been previously disturbed.
- Type B soil is a granular cohesion-less soils, including angular gravel, similar to crushed rock, silt, and silt loam or sandy loam. Type A that is fissured is reclassified as Type B soil. This type of soil has a maximum permitted slope of 1:1 (45° slope).
- Type C soil is a granular soil that includes gravel, sand, and loamy sand. It is often submerged soil or soil from which water is freely seeping. This type of soil has a maximum permitted slope of 1.5:1 (34° slope).

If the classification of soil is Type B, and there are vibrations from a nearby road or the area has been previously disturbed, the competent person should downgrade the type of soil classification to Type C. This will change the way the workers are protected from cave-ins.

Exhibit 19-2. Field Method for Identification of Soil Texture.

Soil Texture	Visual Detection of Particle Size and General Appearance of the Soil	Squeezed in hand and pressure released When air dry	When Moist	Soil ribboned between thumb and finger when moist
Sand	Soil has a granular appearance in which the individual grain sizes can be detected. It is free-flowing when in a dry condition.	Will not form a cast and will fall apart when pressure is released.	Forms a cast which will crumble when lightly touched.	Can not be ribboned.
Sandy Loam	Essentially a granular soil with sufficient silt and clay to make it somewhat coherent. Sand characteristics predominate.	Forms a cast which readily falls apart when lightly touched.	Forms a cast which will bear careful handling without breaking.	Can not be ribboned.
Loam	A uniform mixture of sand, silt and clay. Grading of sand fraction quite uniform from coarse to fine. It is mellow, has somewhat gritty feel, yet is fairly smooth and slightly plastic.	Forms a cast which will bear careful handling without breaking.	Forms a cast which can be handled freely without breaking.	Can not be ribboned.
Silt Loam	Contains a moderate amount of the finer grades of sand and only a small amount of clay. Over half of the particles are silt. When dry it may appear quite cloddy which readily can be broken and pulverized to a powder.	Forms a cast which can be freely handled. Pulverized it has a soft flourlike feel.	Forms a cast which can be freely handled. When wet, soil runs together and puddles.	It will not ribbon but it has a broken appearance, feels smooth and may be slightly plastic.
Silt	Contains over 80% of silt particles with very little fine sand and clay. When dry, it may be cloddy, readily pulverizes to powder with a soft flourlike feel.	Forms a cast which can be handled without breaking.	Forms a cast which can freely be handled. When wet, it readily puddles.	It has a tendency to ribbon with a broken appearance, feels smooth.
Clay Loam	Fine textured soil breaks into very hard lumps when dry. Contains more clay than silt loam. Resembles clay in a dry condition; identification is made on physical behavior of moist soil.	Forms a cast which can be freely handled without breaking.	Forms a cast which can be handled freely without breaking. It can be worked into a dense mass.	Forms a thin ribbon which readily breaks, barely sustaining its own weight.
Clay	Fine textured soil breaks into very hard lumps when dry. Difficult to pulverize into a soft flourlike powder when dry. Identification based on cohesive properties of the moist soil.	Forms a cast which can be freely handled without breaking.	Forms a cast which can be handled freely without breaking.	Forms long, thin flexible ribbons. Can be worked into a dense, compact mass. Considerable plasticity.
Organic Soils	Identification based on the high organic content. Muck consists of thoroughly decomposed organic material with considerable amount of mineral soil finely divided with some fibrous remains. When considerable fibrous material is present, it may be classified as peat. The plant remains or sometimes the woody structure can easily be recognized. Soil color ranges from brown to black. They occur in lowlands, in swamps or swales. They have high shrinkage upon drying.			

Support Systems

Excavation workers are exposed to many hazards, but the chief hazard is the danger of a cave-in. OSHA requires that in all excavations, employees exposed to potential cave-ins must be protected by sloping or benching the sides of the excavation, supporting the sides of the excavation, or placing a shield between the side of the excavation and the work area.

Designing a protective system can be complex because of the number of factors involved:

- Soil classification;
- Depth of cut;
- Water content of soil;
- Changes due to weather and climate; and
- Other operations in the vicinity.

The standard, however, provides several methods and approaches (e.g., four for sloping, four for shoring) for designing protective systems that will protect workers from cave-ins and meet OSHA requirements.

One method of ensuring the safety and health of workers in an excavation is to slope the sides to an angle not steeper than one and one-half horizontal to one vertical (34° measured from the horizontal) (See Exhibit 18-3.). These slopes must be excavated to form configurations that are in accordance with those for Type C soil found in Appendix B of the standard.

A second design method, which can be applied for both sloping and shoring, involves using tabulated data, such as tables and charts, approved by a registered professional engineer. This data must be in writing and must include sufficient explanatory information to enable the user to make a selection, including the criteria for determining the selection and the limits on the use of the data. At least one copy of the information, including the identity of the registered professional engineer who approved the data, must be kept at the work site during construction of the protective system. Upon completion of the system, the data may be stored away from the job site, but a copy must be made available, upon request, to the OSHA inspector.

Contractors also may use a trench box or shield that is either designed or approved by a registered professional engineer or is based on tabulated data prepared or approved by a registered professional engineer. Timber, aluminum, or other suitable materials may also be used. OSHA standards permit the use of a trench shield (also known as a welder's hut) as long as the protection it provides is equal to or greater than the protection that would be provided by the appropriate shoring system.

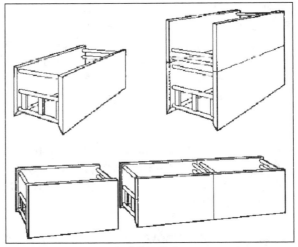

Exhibit 19-4.
Examples of trench boxes.

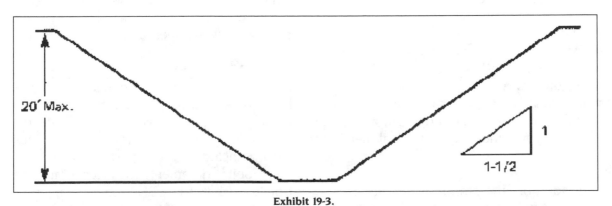

Exhibit 19-3.
A slope angle no steeper than 1½ horizontal to 1 vertical will provide adequate cave-in protection.

The employer is free to choose the most practical design approach for any particular circumstance. Once an approach has been selected, however, the required performance criteria must be met by that system.

The standard does not require the installation and use of a protective system when an excavation is:

- Made entirely in stable rock; or
- Is less than 5 ft. deep and a competent person has examined the ground and found no indication of a potential cave-in.

Safety Precautions

The standard requires the employer to provide support systems such as shoring, bracing, or underpinning to ensure the stability of adjacent structures such as buildings, walls, sidewalks, and pavements.

The standard prohibits excavation below the level of the base or footing of any foundation or retaining wall unless:

- A support system such as underpinning is provided;
- The excavation is in stable rock; or
- A registered professional engineer determines that the structure has been sufficiently removed from the excavation and that excavation will not pose a hazard to employees.

Excavations under sidewalks and pavements are also prohibited unless an appropriately designed support system is provided or another effective method is used.

Installation and Removal of Protective Systems

When installing support systems, employers must protect employees by:

- Securely connecting members of support systems;
- Safely installing support systems;
- Never overloading members of support systems; and
- Installing other structural members to carry loads imposed on the support system when temporary removal of individual members is necessary.

In addition, the standard permits excavations of 2 ft. or less below the bottom of the members of a support or shield system of a trench if: (1) the system is designed to resist the forces calculated for the full depth of the trench; and (2) there are no indications of a possible cave-in below the bottom of the support system while the trench is open. Also, the installation of support systems must be closely coordinated with the excavation of trenches.

As soon as work is completed, the excavation should be back-filled as the protective system is dismantled. After the excavation has been cleared, workers should slowly remove the protective system from the bottom up, taking care to release members slowly.

Materials and Equipment

The employer is responsible for the safe condition of materials and equipment used for protective systems. Defective and damaged materials and equipment can result in the failure of a protective system and cause excavation hazards.

To avoid possible failure of a protective system, the employer must ensure that:

- Materials and equipment are free from damage or defects;
- Manufactured materials and equipment are used and maintained in a manner consistent with the recommendations of the manufacturer and in a way that will prevent employee exposure to hazards; and
- While in operation, damaged materials and equipment are examined by a competent person to determine if they are suitable for continued use.

If materials and equipment are not safe for use, they must be removed from service. These materials cannot be returned to service without the evaluation and approval of a registered professional engineer.

Falls and Equipment

In addition to cave-in hazards and secondary hazards related to cave-ins, there are other hazards from which workers must be protected during excavation-related work. These hazards include exposure to falls, falling loads, and mobile equipment. To protect employees from these hazards, OSHA requires employers to take the following precautions:

- Keep materials or equipment that might fall or roll into an excavation at least 2 ft. from the edge of the excavation, install retaining devices, or both;
- Provide warning systems, such as mobile equipment, barricades, hand or mechanical signals, or stop logs, to alert operators of the edge of an excavation. If possible, keep the grade away from the excavation;
- Provide scaling to remove loose rock or soil or install protective barricades and other equivalent protection to protect employees against falling rock, soil, or materials;
- Prohibit employees from working on faces of sloped or benched excavations at levels above other employees unless employees at lower levels are adequately protected from the hazard of falling, rolling, or sliding material or equipment; and
- Prohibit employees under loads that are handled by lifting or digging equipment. To avoid being struck by any spillage or falling materials, require employees to stand away from vehicles being loaded or unloaded. If the cabs of vehicles provide adequate protection from falling loads during loading and unloading operations, the operators may remain in them.

Water Accumulation

The standard prohibits employees from working in excavations where water has accumulated or is accumulating unless adequate protection has been taken. If water removal equipment is used to control or prevent water from accumulating, a competent person must monitor the equipment and operations of the equipment to ensure proper use.

OSHA standards also require that diversion ditches, dikes, or other suitable means be used to prevent surface water from entering an excavation and to provide adequate drainage of the area adjacent to the excavation. Also, a competent person must inspect excavations that are subject to runoffs from heavy rains.

Hazardous Atmospheres

Under this provision, a competent person must test excavations greater than 4 ft. in depth as well as ones where an oxygen-deficient or hazardous atmosphere exists or could reasonably be expected to exist before an employee enters the excavation. If hazardous conditions exist, controls such as proper respiratory protection or ventilation must be provided. Also, controls used to reduce atmospheric contaminants to acceptable levels must be tested regularly. Where adverse atmospheric conditions exist or develop in an excavation, the employer also must provide and ensure that emergency rescue equipment (e.g., breathing apparatus, safety harness and line, basket stretcher) is readily available. This equipment must be attended when used.

When an employee enters bell-bottom pier holes and similar deep, confined footing excavations, the employee must wear a harness with a lifeline. The lifeline must be securely attached to the harness and must be separate from any line used to handle materials. While the employee wearing the lifeline is in the excavation, an observer must be present to ensure that the lifeline is working properly and to maintain communication with the employee.

Access and Egress

Under the standard, the employer must provide safe access and egress to all excavations. According to OSHA regulations, when employees are required to be in trench excavations 4 ft. deep or more, adequate means of exit, such as ladders, steps, ramps or other safe means of egress, must be provided and be within 25 ft. of lateral travel. If structural ramps are used as a means of access or egress, a competent person must design them. If used as a means of access or egress by vehicles, a competent person qualified in structural design must design them. Also, structural members used for ramps or runways must be uniform in thickness and joined in a manner to prevent tripping or displacement.

Trenching and excavation work presents serious risks to all workers involved. The greatest risk, and one of primary concern, is that of a cave-in. Furthermore, when cave-in accidents occur, they are much more likely to result in worker fatalities than other excavation-related accidents. Strict compliance with all sections of the standard however will prevent or greatly reduce the risk of cave-ins as well as other excavation-related accidents.

In the event of a trench collapse, rescue workers will begin to search at the base of the ladder since they assume the worker will have attempted to get out of the trench during the collapse. Ladders should be no more than 25 ft. from workers at all times.

Exhibit 19-5.
A ladder placed within 25ft. of a worker's lateral travel provides a means of access or egress.

Common Citations for Excavations

Not Sloping to the Proper Angle
If sloping is chosen as the method of protection, the employer must follow the charts in the OSHA standard or have the data tabulated by a professional engineer. Type C soil is usually sloped 1½ ft. per side for every 1 ft. of excavation. So, a 5-ft. deep trench must be open at the top by at least 15 ft. across. If the work area in the bottom of the trench is 2-ft. wide, this must be added to the top measurement:

(7½ ft. + 7½ ft. + 2 ft. = 17 ft. at the top measurement for a 5-ft. trench)

No Competent Person On site
OSHA requires a competent person to be on site to observe changing conditions and take corrective action as necessary. The competent person must know how to perform manual and visual tests as well as how to classify soil. The failure to meet these basic requirements has resulted in many citations. Competent persons usually have specialized training and carry ID cards that identify them as such. Again, they must be on site at all times.

Allowing Water in Trenches
Water is a hazard to soil in that it weakens the soil layer and causes undercutting of the trench walls. Water must be pumped out as it enters the trench and the protection provided must be for Type C soil.

Unacceptable Means of Egress from the Trench

Most citations occur when employees must crawl out the end of the trench. Ladders should be used if employees are exposed to hazards while exiting a trench box. Workers should not have to move more than 25 ft. laterally to reach a ladder. Ladders must extend 3 ft. beyond the top of the trench.

Storage of Material at Edge
Surface encumbrances must be protected from rolling at the edge. Materials commonly cited are pipe, wood, and cylinders. Materials must not be kept within 2 ft. of the edge of a trench.

Excavation Standard Violation Exercise

Standard Violation	Condition	Yes	No
26.651(a)	Surface encumbrances	❑	❑
26.651(b)(1)	Underground utilities located	❑	❑
26.651(c)(2)	Egress ladder, stairway or ramp	❑	❑
26.651(d)	"Orange" vests if traffic	❑	❑
26.651(e)	Loads suspended over employees	❑	❑
26.651(r)	Stop logs or hand signals	❑	❑
26.651(h)(1)	Water accumulation in trench	❑	❑
26.651(i)(2)	Excavating below adjacent footings	❑	❑
26.651(j)(l)	Loose rock on excavation face	❑	❑
26.651(j)(2)	Spoil, material less than 2 ft. from edge	❑	❑
26.651(k)(1)	Daily inspections conducted	❑	❑
26.651(k)(1)	Competent person inspecting	❑	❑
26.651(1)(2)	Remote pits, shafts barricaded	❑	❑
26.652(a)(1)	Employees protected from cave-ins	❑	❑
26.652(b)(1)	Lack of classification, slope	❑	❑
26.652(b)(2)	Correct slope per soil class	❑	❑
26.652(b)(3)(i)	Correct slope per tabulated data	❑	❑
26.652(b)(4)(i)	Correct slope per professional engineer	❑	❑
26.652(c)(1)	Adequate shoring per appendices	❑	❑
26.652(c)(2)	Support system per manufacturer's data	❑	❑
26.652(c)(3)	Support per tabulated data	❑	❑
26.652(c)(4)	Trench box or support per professional engineer	❑	❑
26.652(d)(1)	Trench box, support without defects	❑	❑
26.652(g)(1)(iii)	Employees ever outside trench box	❑	❑

Classification Exercise

	Yes	No
Is soil cemented?		
The particles are held together by a chemical agent such that a hand-sized sample cannot be crushed into powder or individualsoil particles by finger pressure.	❑	❑
Is soil cohesive?		
Clay (finely grained soil) or soil with a high clay content that has cohesive strength, does not crumble, can be excavated with vertical side slopes, is plastic when moist, is hard to break up when dry, and exhibits significant cohesion when submerged.	❑	❑
Is soil dry?		
Does not exhibit visible signs of moisture content.	❑	❑
Is soil fissured?		
Soil material that has a tendency to break along definite planes of fracture with little resistance or material that exhibits open cracks such as tension cracks in an exposed surface	❑	❑
Is soil granular?		
Gravel, sand, or silt (coarse grained soil) with little or no clay content, no cohesive strength.	❑	❑
Some moist granular soils exhibit apparent cohesion.	❑	❑
Granular soil cannot be molded when moist and crumbles easily when dry.	❑	❑
Is soil layered?		
Two or more distinctly different soil or rock types arranged in layers.	❑	❑
Micaceous seams or weakened planes in rock or shale are layers.	❑	❑
Is soil moist?		
Soil looks and feels damp. Moist cohesive soil can easily be shaped into a ball and rolled into small diameter threads before crumbling.	❑	❑
Moist granular soil that contains some cohesive material will exhibit signs of cohesion between particles.	❑	❑
Is soil plastic?		
Soil can be deformed or molded without cracking or appreciable volume change.	❑	❑
Is soil saturated?		
The voids in the soil are filled with water. Saturation does not require flow.	❑	❑
Is soil submerged?		
Soil that is under water or is freely seeping.	❑	❑

Exhibit 19.6.
When the bottom of the excavation "kicks"
into the excavation, a failure in the upper part
of the wall is likely to follow.

Trenching and Excavation Practical Exercise

(See appendix for answers.)

1. Regarding trenching and excavations, what are the requirements to be considered a "competent person"?

2. Prior to beginning a dig at a construction site, who should be called and why?

3. While digging a trench, how close to the edge of the trench may materials be placed?

4. Workers in a trench must be protected by an adequate protective system whenever a trench is more than _____ ft. deep.

5. Workers in a trench must have a ladder, stairway, or ramp within how many feet of them?

6. A shield system for a trench box must be built to manufacturer's specifications or be designed by _____.

7. The trench has been dug in soil classified as Class C soil. The competent person decides to slope the trench. What should the angle of the slope be?

8. How often must the competent person inspect the trench?

9. A walkway is built over a trench that is 10 ft. deep. What must the walkway have?

10. Class B soil is being dug, but there is water seeping freely from the bottom of the excavation. What must the competent person do?

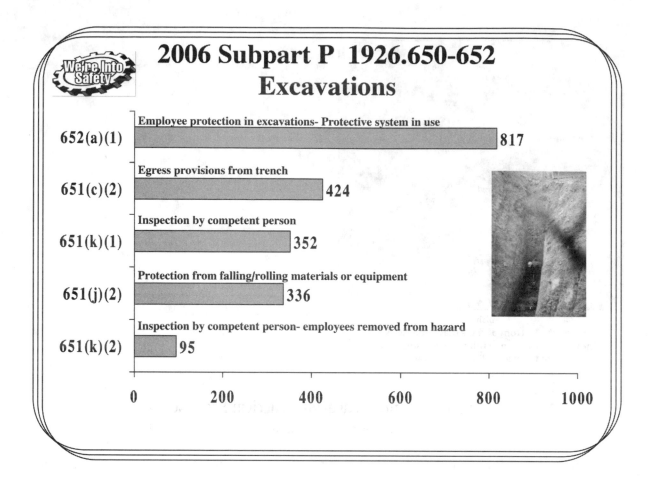

2006 Subpart P 1926.650-652
Excavations

We're Into Safety

Employee protection in excavations- Protective system in use
652(a)(1) — 817

Egress provisions from trench
651(c)(2) — 424

Inspection by competent person
651(k)(1) — 352

Protection from falling/rolling materials or equipment
651(j)(2) — 336

Inspection by competent person- employees removed from hazard
651(k)(2) — 95

0   200   400   600   800   1000

HAND AND POWER TOOLS

Tools are such a common part of our lives that it is easy to forget that they pose hazards. All tools are manufactured with safety in mind, but serious accidents often occur because users have not taken the time to learn about potential hazards and how to avoid them.

Hand Tools

Hand tools are manually operated. They include anything from axes to wrenches. The greatest hazards posed by hand tools result from misuse and improper maintenance. Some examples include:

- Using a screwdriver as a chisel, which may cause the tip of the screwdriver to break and fly, hitting the user or another employee;
- If a wooden handle on a tool such as a hammer or an axe is loose, splintered, or cracked, the head of the tool may fly off and strike the user or another employee;
- Using a wrench with its jaws sprung may cause the wrench to slip; and
- Impact tools such as chisels, wedges, or drift pins are unsafe if they have mushroomed heads. The heads might shatter on impact, sending sharp fragments flying.

The employer is responsible for the safe condition of tools and equipment used by employees, but the employees have the responsibility for properly using and maintaining the tools. Employers should caution employees that saw blades, knives, and other tools be directed away from aisle areas and other employees working in close proximity. Knives and scissors must be sharp; dull tools can be more hazardous than sharp ones.

Appropriate personal protective equipment (e.g., safety goggles, gloves,) should be worn to protect against hazards that may be encountered while using portable power tools and hand tools. Safety requires that floors be kept as clean and dry as possible to prevent accidental slips with or around dangerous hand tools. Around flammable substances, sparks produced by iron and steel hand tools can be a dangerous ignition source. Where this hazard exists, spark-resistant tools made from brass, plastic, aluminum, or wood will provide for safety.

Power Tool Precautions

Power tools can be hazardous when improperly used. There are several types of power tools, based on the power source: electric, pneumatic, liquid fuel, hydraulic, and powder-actuated. Employees should be trained in the use of all tools—not just power tools. They should understand the hazards as well as the precautions to prevent those hazards from occurring.

Power tool users should observe the following general precautions:

- Never carry a tool by its cord or hose.
- Never yank the cord or the hose to disconnect it from the receptacle or outlet.
- Keep cords and hoses away from heat, oil, and sharp edges.
- Disconnect tools when not in use, before servicing, and when changing accessories such as blades, bits, and cutters.
- Ensure that all power tools are grounded, double insulated or battery powered.
- Secure work with clamps or a vise to free both hands to operate the tool.
- Avoid accidental starting. Never hold a finger on the switch button while carrying a plugged-in tool.
- Tools should be maintained with care; they should be kept sharp and clean for the best performance. Follow the instructions in the user's manual for lubricating and changing accessories.
- Be sure to keep good footing and maintain good balance when operating hand or power tools.
- The proper apparel should be worn. Loose clothing, ties, and jewelry can become caught in moving parts and therefore should not be worn.
- All portable electric tools that are damaged shall be removed from use and tagged "Do Not Use."

Guards

Hazardous moving parts of a power tool need to be safeguarded. For example, belts, gears, shafts, pulleys, sprockets, spindles, drums, fly wheels, chains, or other reciprocating, rotating, or moving parts of equipment must be guarded if such parts may come into contact with employees.

Guards, as necessary, should be provided to protect the operator and others from the following:

- Point of operation;
- In-running nip points;
- Rotating parts; and
- Flying chips and sparks.

Safety guards must never be removed when a tool is being used. For example, portable circular saws must be equipped with guards. An upper guard must cover the entire blade of the saw. A retractable lower guard must cover the teeth of the saw, except when it makes contact with the work material. The lower guard must automatically return to the covering position as the tool is being withdrawn from the work.

Safety Switches

The following hand-held power tools must be equipped with a momentary contact "on-off" control switch: drills, tappers, fastener drivers, horizontal, vertical, and angle grinders with wheels larger than 2 in. in diameter, disc and belt sanders, reciprocating saws, and saber saws. These tools also may be equipped with a lock-on control, provided that a single motion of the same finger or fingers that turn it on can turn it off.

The following hand-held powered tools may be equipped with only a positive "on-off" control switch:

- All hand-held powered platen sanders, grinders with discs 2 in. or less in diameter;
- Routers, planers, laminate trimmers, nibblers, shears, scroll saws and jigsaws with blade shanks ¼-in. wide or less.

Other hand-held power tools, such as circular saws having a blade diameter greater than 2 in., chain saws, and percussion tools, without positive accessory holding means must be equipped with a constant pressure switch that will shut off the power when the pressure is released.

Electric Tools

Employees using electric tools must be aware of several dangers; the most serious is the possibility of electrocution.

Among the chief hazards of electric-powered tools are burns and slight shocks that can lead to injuries or even heart failure. Under certain conditions, even a small amount of current can result in fibrillation of the heart and eventual death. A shock also can cause the user to fall off a ladder or other elevated work surface.

To protect the user from shock, tools must either have:

- A three-wire cord with ground and be grounded;
- Be double insulated; or
- Be powered by a low-voltage isolation transformer.

Three-wire cords contain two current-carrying conductors and a grounding conductor. One end of the grounding conductor connects to the tool's metal housing. The other end is grounded through a prong on the plug. Anytime an adapter is used to accommodate a two-hole receptacle, the adapter wire must be attached to a known ground. The third prong should never be removed from the plug.

Double insulation is more convenient and provides the user and tools protection in two ways: by normal insulation on the wires inside and by a housing that cannot conduct electricity to the operator in the event of a malfunction.

These general practices should be followed when using electric tools:

- Electric tools should be operated within their design limitations;
- Gloves and safety footwear are recommended during the use of electric tools;
- When not in use, tools should be stored in a dry place;
- Electric tools should not be used in damp or wet locations; and
- Work areas should be well lighted.

Powered Abrasive Wheel Tools

Powered abrasive grinding, cutting, polishing, and wire buffing wheels create special safety problems because they may throw off flying fragments.

Before an abrasive wheel is mounted, it should be inspected closely and sound- or ring-tested to be sure that it is free from cracks or defects. To test, wheels should be tapped gently with a light non-metallic instrument. If the wheels sound cracked or dead, there is a possibility they could fly apart in operation and therefore must not be used. A sound and undamaged wheel will give a clear metallic tone or "ring."

To prevent the wheel from cracking, the user should be sure it fits freely on the spindle. The spindle nut must be tightened enough to hold the wheel in place, without distorting the flange. Care must be taken to ensure that the spindle wheel will not exceed the abrasive wheel specifications. The manufacturer's recommendations should always be followed.

Because a wheel may disintegrate, or explode, during start-up, the employee should never stand directly in front of the wheel as it accelerates to full operating speed. Portable grinding tools need to be equipped with safety guards to protect workers not only from the moving wheel surface, but also from flying fragments in case of breakage.

In addition, when using a powered grinder workers should:

- Always use eye protection;
- Turn off the power when not in use; and
- Never clamp a hand-held grinder in a vise.

Pneumatic Tools

Pneumatic tools are powered by compressed air and include chippers, drills, hammers, and sanders. There are several dangers presented by pneumatic tools. The main one is the danger of getting hit by one of the tool's attachments or by a fastener the worker is using with the tool. Eye protection is required and face protection is recommended for employees who work with pneumatic tools. Noise is another hazard. Working with noisy tools such as jackhammers requires proper, effective use of hearing protection.

When using pneumatic tools, employees must check to ensure the tools are fastened securely to their hoses to help prevent accidental disconnection. A short wire or positive locking device attaching the air hose to the tool will serve as an added safeguard. A safety clip or retainer must be installed to prevent attachments, such as chisels on a chipping hammer, from being unintentionally shot from the barrel. Screens must be set up to protect nearby workers from being struck by flying fragments around chippers, riveting guns, staplers, and air drills.

Compressed air guns should never be pointed toward anyone. Users should never "dead-end" the tools against themselves or anyone else.

Powder-Actuated Tools

Powder-actuated tools operate like a loaded gun and should be treated with the same respect and precautions. In fact, they are so dangerous that only specially trained employees should operate them.

Safety precautions to remember include the following:

- These tools should not be used in an explosive or flammable atmosphere;
- Before using the tool, the worker should inspect it to ensure it is clean, all moving parts operate freely, and the barrel is free from obstructions;
- The tool should never be pointed at anybody;
- The tool should not be loaded unless it is to be used immediately. A loaded tool should not be left unattended, especially where it would be available to unauthorized persons;
- Hands should be kept clear of the barrel end. To prevent the tool from firing accidentally, two separate motions are required for firing: one to bring the tool into position and another to pull the trigger. The tools must not be able to operate until they are pressed against the work surface with a force of at least 5 pounds greater than the total weight of the tool;
- If a powder-actuated tool misfires, the employee should wait at least 30 seconds before trying to fire it again. If it still will not fire, the user should wait another 30 seconds so the faulty cartridge is less likely to explode, then carefully remove the load. The bad cartridge should be put in water; and
- Suitable eye and face protection should always be worn when using a powder-actuated tool.
- The muzzle end of the tool must have a protective shield or guard centered perpendicularly on the barrel to confine any flying fragments or particles that might otherwise create a hazard when the tool is fired. The tool must be designed so that it will not fire unless it has this kind of safety device.
- All powder-actuated tools must be designed for varying powder charges so the user can select a powder level necessary to perform a given task without using excessive force. If the tool develops a defect during use, it should immediately be tagged and removed from service until it is properly repaired.

Fasteners

When using powder-actuated tools to apply fasteners, there are additional precautions to consider. Fasteners must not be fired into material that would let them pass through to the other side. Fasteners must not be driven into materials like brick or concrete any closer than 3 in. to an edge or corner. In steel, fasteners must not come any closer than $1/2$ in. from a corner or edge. Fasteners must not be driven into very hard or brittle materials that might chip or splatter or make the fastener ricochet.

An alignment guide must be used when shooting a fastener into an existing hole. A fastener must not be driven into a spalled area caused by an unsatisfactory fastening.

Hydraulic Power Tools

The fluid used in hydraulic power tools must be an approved fire-resistant fluid and must retain its operating characteristics at the most extreme temperatures to which it will be exposed.

The manufacturer's recommended safe operating pressure for hoses, valves, pipes, filters, and other fittings must not be exceeded.

Jacks

All jacks—lever and ratchet jacks, screw jacks, and hydraulic jacks—must have a device that stops them from jacking up too high. Also, the manufacturer's load limit must be permanently marked in a prominent place on the jack and should not be exceeded.

A jack should never be used to support a lifted load. Once the load has been lifted, it must immediately be blocked up.

If the jack needs to be leveled and secured, wooden blocking should be placed under the base. If the lift surface is metal, a 1-in.-thick hardwood block or equivalent may be placed between the lift surface and the metal jack head to reduce the danger of slippage.

When setting up a jack, workers should make certain of the following:

- The base rests on a firm level surface;
- The jack is correctly centered;
- The jack head bears against a level surface; and
- The lift force is applied evenly.

The proper maintenance of jacks is essential for safety. All jacks must be inspected before each use and lubricated regularly. If a jack is subjected to an abnormal load or shock, it should be thoroughly examined afterward to make sure it has not been damaged.

Hydraulic jacks exposed to freezing temperatures must be filled with an adequate antifreeze liquid.

General Safety Precautions

Employees who use hand and power tools and are exposed to the hazards of falling, flying, abrasive, and splashing objects or to harmful dusts, fumes, mists, vapors, or gases must be provided with the appropriate personal protective equipment necessary to protect them from the hazard.

Employees and employers have a responsibility to work together to establish safe working procedures. If a hazardous situation is encountered, it should be brought to the attention of the proper individual immediately. Following five basic safety rules can protect workers from all hazards involved in the use of power tools:

- Keep all tools in good condition with regular maintenance;
- Use the right tool for the job;
- Examine each tool for damage before use;
- Operate according to the manufacturer's instructions; and
- Provide and use the proper protective equipment.

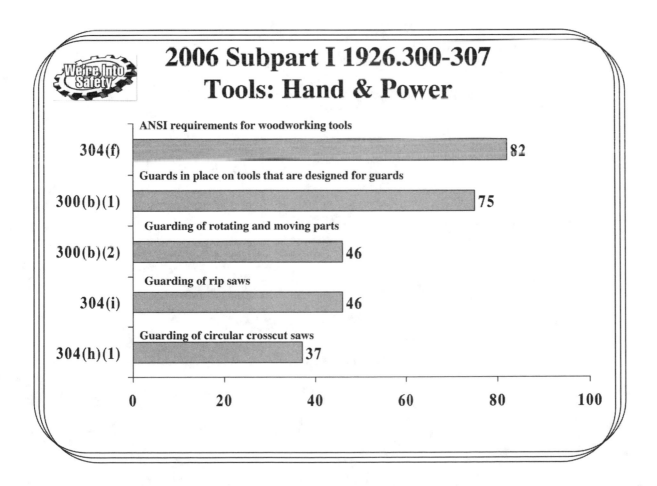

2006 Subpart I 1926.300-307
Tools: Hand & Power

DEMOLITION

Preparatory Operations

Before the start of every demolition job, the demolition contractor should take a number of steps to safeguard the health and safety of workers at the job site. These preparatory operations involve the overall planning of the demolition job, including the methods to be used to bring the structure down, the equipment necessary to do the job, and the measures to be taken to perform the work safely. Planning for a demolition job is as important as actually doing the work. Therefore a competent person experienced in all phases of the demolition work to be performed should perform all planning work.

Engineering Survey

The American National Standards Institute (ANSI) in ANSI A10.6-1983, Safety Requirements For Demolition Operations, states:

> No employee shall be permitted in any area that can be adversely affected when demolition operations are being performed. Only those employees necessary for the performance of the operations shall be permitted in these areas.

OSHA Standard 1926.850(a) requires that before any demolition operations begin, a competent person must conduct an engineering survey of the structure. The purpose of this survey is to determine the condition of the framing, floors, and walls so that measures can be taken, if necessary, to prevent the premature collapse of any portion of the structure. When indicated as advisable, any adjacent structure(s) or improvements also should be similarly checked. The demolition contractor must maintain a written copy of this survey. Photographing existing damage in neighboring structures also is advisable.

The engineering survey provides the demolition contractor with the opportunity to evaluate the job in its entirety. The contractor should plan for the wrecking of the structure, the equipment to do the work, manpower requirements, and the protection of the public. The safety of all workers on the job site should be a prime consideration. During the preparation of the engineering survey, the contractor should plan for potential hazards, such as fires and cave-ins as well as injuries.

If the structure to be demolished has been damaged by fire, flood, explosion, or some other cause, appropriate measures, including the bracing and shoring of walls and floors, shall be taken to protect workers and any adjacent structures. It shall also be determined if any type of hazardous chemicals, gases, explosives, flammable material, or similar dangerous substances have been used or stored on the site. If the nature of a substance cannot be easily determined, samples should be taken and analyzed by a qualified person prior to demolition.

During the planning stage of the job, all safety equipment needs should be determined. The required number and type of respirators, lifelines, warning signs, safety nets, special face and eye protection, hearing protection, and other worker protection devices should be determined during the preparation of the engineering survey. A comprehensive plan is necessary for any confined space entry.

Utility Location

One of the most important elements of the pre-job planning is the location of all utility services. All electric, gas, water, steam, sewer, and other services lines should be shut off, capped, or otherwise controlled, at or outside the building before demolition work is started. In each case, any utility company that is involved should be notified in advance and its approval or services, if necessary, shall be obtained.

If it is necessary to maintain any power, water, or other utilities during demolition, such lines shall be temporarily relocated as necessary and/or protected. The location of all overhead power sources also should be determined, as they can prove especially hazardous during any machine demolition. All workers should be informed of the location of any existing or relocated utility service.

Medical Services and First Aid

Prior to starting work, provisions should be made for prompt medical attention in case of serious injury. The nearest hospital, infirmary, clinic, or physician shall be located as part of the engineering survey. The job supervisor should be provided with directions for the most direct route to these facilities. Proper equipment for prompt transportation of an injured worker, as well as a communication system to contact any necessary ambulance service, must be available at the job site. The telephone numbers of the hospitals, physicians, and emergency services shall be conspicuously posted.

In the absence of an infirmary, clinic, hospital, or physician that is reasonably accessible

in terms of time and distance to the work site, a person who has a valid certificate in first-aid training from the U.S. Bureau of Mines, the American Red Cross, or equivalent, should be available at the work site to render first aid.

A properly stocked first-aid kit, as determined by an occupational physician, must be available at the job site. The first aid kit should contain individually sealed, approved supplies in a weatherproof container. It also should include rubber gloves to prevent the transfer of infectious diseases. Provisions also should be made to provide for the quick drenching or flushing of the eyes should any person be working near corrosive materials. Eye flushing must be done with water containing no additives. The contents of the kit shall be checked before being sent out on each job and at least weekly to ensure all expended items have been replaced.

Police and Fire Contact

The telephone numbers of the local police and fire departments and emergency services should be available at each job site. This information can prove useful to the job supervisor in the event of any traffic problems, such as the movement of equipment to the job, uncontrolled fires, or other police or fire matters. The police number also may be used to report any vandalism, unlawful entry to the job site, or accidents that require police assistance.

Fire Prevention and Protection

A "fire plan" should be established before beginning a demolition job. This plan should outline the assignments of key personnel in the event of a fire and provide an evacuation plan for workers on the site.

Common sense should be the general rule in all fire-prevention planning as well as the following:

- All potential sources of ignition should be evaluated and the necessary corrective measures taken.
- Electrical wiring and equipment for providing light, heat, or power should be installed by a competent person and inspected regularly.
- Equipment powered by an internal combustion engine should be located so that the exhausts discharge well away from combustible materials and away from workers.

- When the exhausts are piped outside the building, a clearance of at least 6 in. should be maintained between such piping and combustible material.
- All internal combustion equipment should be shut down prior to refueling. Fuel for this equipment should be stored in a safe location.
- Sufficient firefighting equipment should be located near any flammable or combustible liquid storage area.
- Only approved containers and portable tanks should be used for the storage and handling of flammable and combustible liquids.

Heating devices should be situated so they are not likely to overturn and shall be installed in accordance with their listing, including clearance to combustible material or equipment. Competent personnel should maintain temporary heating equipment when it is used.

Smoking should be prohibited at or in the vicinity of hazardous operations or materials. Where smoking is permitted, safe receptacles shall be provided for smoking materials.

Roadways between and around combustible storage piles should be at least 15 ft. wide and maintained free from accumulation of rubbish, equipment, or other materials.

When storing debris or combustible material inside a structure, such storage shall not obstruct or adversely affect the means of exit.

A suitable location at the job site should be designated and provided with plans, emergency information, and equipment, as necessary. Access for heavy firefighting equipment should be provided on the immediate job site at the start of the job and maintained until the job is completed.

Free access from the street to fire hydrants and to outside connections for standpipes, sprinklers, or other fire extinguishing equipment, whether permanent or temporary, should be provided and maintained at all times. Pedestrian walkways should not be so constructed as to impede access to hydrants. No material or construction should interfere with access to hydrants, Siamese connections, or fire extinguishing equipment.

A temporary or permanent water supply with the sufficient volume, duration, and pressure required to properly operate the firefighting equipment should be made available.

Standpipes with outlets should be provided on large multi-story buildings to provide for fire protection on upper levels. If the water pressure is insufficient, a pump also should be provided.

An ample number of fully charged portable fire extinguishers should be provided throughout the work site. All motor-driven equipment should be equipped with an approved fire extinguisher.

An alarm system (e.g., telephone system, siren, two-radio) shall be established in such a way that employees on the site and the local fire department can be alerted in the event of an emergency. The alarm code and reporting instructions shall be conspicuously posted, and the alarm system shall be in service during the entire demolition process. Fire cut-offs shall be retained in the buildings undergoing alterations or demolition until operations necessitate their removal.

Special Structures Demolition

Special consideration must be given and safe work practices followed when demolishing a chimney, stack, silo, or cooling tower.

Inspection and Planning

When preparing to demolish any chimney, stack, silo, or cooling tower, the first step must be a careful, detailed inspection of the structure by an experienced person. If possible, architectural and engineering drawings should be consulted.

Particular attention should be paid to the condition of chimneys and stacks. Workers should be on the lookout for any structural defects such as weak or acid-laden mortar joints and any cracks or openings. The interior brickwork in some sections of industrial chimney shafts can be extremely weak. If the stack has been banded with steel straps, these bands shall be removed from the top down and only as the work progresses. Sectioning of the chimney by water, etc. should be considered.

Safe Work Practices

When hand demolition is required, it should be carried out from a working platform.

Experienced personnel must install a self-supporting tubular scaffold, suspended platform, or knee-braced scaffolding around a chimney.

Particular attention should be paid to the design, support, and tie-in (braces) of the scaffold.

A competent person should be present at all times during the erection of the scaffold.

It is essential that there be adequate working clearance between the chimney and the work platform.

Access to the top of the scaffold should be provided by means of portable walkways.

The platforms should be decked solid and the area from the work platform to wall bridged with a minimum of 2-in. thick lumber.

A back rail 42 in. above the platform with a midrail covered with canvas or mesh should be installed around the perimeter of the platform to prevent injury to workers below. Debris netting may be installed below the work platform.

Excess canvas or plywood attachments can form a wind sail that could cause collapse of the scaffold.

When working on the platform, all personnel should wear hard hats; long-sleeve shirts; eye or face protection, such as goggles and face shields; respirators; and safety belts, as required.

Care should be taken that the proper number of workers are assigned to the task; too many people on a small work platform can lead to accidents.

An alternative to the erection of a self-supporting tubular steel scaffold is to "climb" the structure with a creeping bracket scaffold. A competent person must carefully inspect the masonry and determine the safety of this alternative. It is essential that the masonry of the chimney be in good enough condition to support the bracket scaffold.

The area around the chimney should be secured by being roped off or barricaded. Appropriate warning signs also should be posted. No unauthorized entry should be permitted to this area. It is also good practice to keep a worker (e.g., a supervisor, operating engineer, another worker, or "safety person") on the ground with a way to communicate to the workers above.

Special attention should be paid to weather conditions when working on a chimney. No work should be done during inclement weather such as lightning or high winds. The work site should be wetted down, as needed, to control dust.

Debris Clearance

If debris is dropped inside the shaft, it can be removed through an opening in the chimney at grade level. The opening at grade must be kept relatively small so as not to weaken the structure. If a larger opening is desired, a professional engineer should be consulted.

When removing debris by hand, an overhead canopy of adequate strength should be provided. If machines are used for the removal of debris, proper overhead protection for the operator should be used.

Excessive debris should not be allowed to accumulate inside or outside the shaft of the chimney because the excess weight of the debris can impose pressure on the wall of the structure and may cause the shaft to collapse.

The foreman should determine when debris is to be removed, halt all demolition during debris removal, and ensure the area is clear of clean-up workers before demolition continues.

Demolition by Deliberate Collapse

Another method of demolishing a chimney or stack is by deliberate collapse (e.g., with explosives). Deliberate collapse requires extensive planning and experienced personnel, and should be used only when conditions are favorable. There must be a clear space for the fall of the structure of at least 45° on each side of the intended fall line and 1½ times the total height of the chimney. Considerable vibration may occur when the chimney falls, so there should be no sewers or underground services on the line of the fall. Lookouts must be posted on the site and warning signals must be arranged. The public and non-essential workers at the job site must be kept well back from the fall area as well as cleared from the entire work area if explosives are going to be used.

Demolition of Pre-Stressed Concrete Structures

The different forms of construction used in a number of more or less conventional structures built during the last few decades will give rise to a variety of problems when the time comes for them to be demolished. Pre-stressed concrete structures fall in this general category. The most important aspect of demolishing a pre-stressed concrete structure takes place during the engineering survey. During the survey, a qualified person should determine if the structure to be demolished contains any pre-stressed members.

It is the responsibility of the demolition contractor to inform all workers on the demolition job site of the presence of pre-stressed concrete members within the structure. They also should instruct workers in the safe work practices that must be followed to safely perform the demolition. Workers should be informed of the hazards of deviating from the prescribed procedures and the importance of following their supervisor's instructions.

Exhibit 21-1.
Categories of Pre-Stressed Construction

There are four main categories of pre-stressed members. The category, or categories, should be determined before attempting demolition, bearing in mind that any pre-stressed structure may contain elements of more than one category.

Category 1. Members pre-stressed before the application of the superimposed loads and having all cables or tendons fully bonded to the concrete or grouted within ducts.

Category 2. As Category 1, but having the tendons left ungrouted. This type of construction can sometimes be recognized from the access points which may have been provided for inspection of the cables and anchors. More recently, unbonded tendons have been used in the construction of beams, slabs, and other members; these tendons are protected by grease and surrounded by plastic sheathing, instead of the usual metal duct.

Category 3. Members that are pre-stressed progressively as the building construction proceeds and the dead load increases, using bonded tendons, as category 1.

Category 4. As category 3, but using unbonded tendons, as Category 2.

Examples of construction using members of Categories 3 or 4 are relatively rare up to this time. However, they may be found, for example, in the podium of a tall building or some types of bridges. They require that particular care be taken in demolition.

Pre-tensioned Members

These usually do not have any end anchors, the wires being embedded or bonded within the length of the member. Simple pre-tensioned beams and slabs of spans up to about 23 ft. (7 m) can be demolished in a manner similar to ordinary reinforced concrete. Pre-tensioned beams and slabs may be lifted and lowered to the ground as complete units after the removal of any composite concrete covering to the tops and ends of the units. To facilitate breaking up, the members should be turned on their sides. Lifting from the structure should generally be done from points near the ends of the units or from lifting-point positions. Reuse of lifting eyes, if in good condition, is recommended whenever possible. When units are too large to be removed, consideration should be given to temporary supporting arrangements.

Before breaking up pre-cast units that are stressed separately from the main frames of the structure, with end anchors and grouted and ungrouted ducts, they should be lowered to the ground, if possible. It is advisable to seek the counsel of a professional engineer before carrying out this work, especially where there are ungrouted tendons. In general, this is true because grouting is not always 100 percent efficient. After lowering, the units can be turned on their side with the ends up on blocks after any composite concrete is removed. This may suffice to break the unit and release the pre-stress; if not, a sandbag screen, timbers, or a blast mat as a screen should be erected around the ends before demolition. It should be kept in mind that the end blocks may be heavily reinforced and therefore difficult to break up.

Monolithic Structures

The advice of a professional engineer experienced in pre-stressed work should be sought before any attempt is made to expose the tendons or anchorages of structures in which two or more members have been stressed together. It will usually be necessary for temporary supports to be provided so the tendons and the anchorage can be cautiously exposed. In these circumstances, it is essential that indiscriminate attempts to expose and de-stress the tendons and anchorages are not made.

Progressively Pre-Stressed Structures

In the case of progressively pre-stressed structures, it is essential to obtain the advice of a professional engineer and to demolish the structure in strict accordance with the engineer's recommended method of demolition. The stored energy in this type of structure is large. In some cases, the inherent properties of the stressed section may delay failure for some time, but the presence of these large pre-stressing forces may cause sudden and complete collapse with little warning.

Safe Work Practices when Working in Confined Spaces

Demolition contractors often come in contact with confined spaces when demolishing structures at industrial sites. These confined spaces can be generally categorized in two major groups:

1. Those with open tops and a depth that restricts the natural movement of air; and
2. Enclosed spaces with very limited openings for entry.

Examples of these spaces include storage tanks, vessels, degreasers, pits, vaults, casings, and silos.

The hazards encountered when entering and working in confined spaces are capable of causing bodily injury, illness, and death. Accidents often occur because workers fail to recognize that a confined space is a potential hazard. It should therefore be considered that the most unfavorable situation exists in every case and that the danger of explosion, poisoning, and asphyxiation will be present at the onset of entry.

Safe Blasting Procedures

Blasting Survey and Site Preparation

Before blasting any structure or a portion thereof, a complete written survey must be made by a qualified person of all adjacent improvements and underground utilities. When there is a possibility of excessive vibration due to blasting operations, seismic or vibration tests should be taken to determine the proper safety limits to prevent damage to adjacent or nearby buildings, utilities, or other property.

The preparation of a structure for demolition by explosives may require the removal of structural columns, beams, or other building components. A structural engineer or a qualified competent person should direct the removal of these structural elements. Extreme caution must be taken during this preparatory work to prevent the weakening and premature collapse of the structure.

The use of explosives to demolish smokestacks, silos, cooling towers, or similar structures should only be permitted if there is a minimum of 90° of open space extended for at least 150 percent of the height of the structure or if an explosives specialist can demonstrate consistent previous performance with tighter constraints at the site.

Fire Precautions

The presence of fire near explosives presents a severe danger. Every effort should be made to ensure that fires or sparks do not occur near explosive materials. Smoking, matches, firearms, open-flame lamps, other fires, flame- or heat-producing devices, and sparks must be prohibited in or near explosive magazines or in areas where explosives are being handled, transported, or used. In fact, persons working near explosives should not even carry matches, lighters, or other sources of sparks or flame. Open fires or flames should be prohibited within 100 ft. of any explosive materials. In the event of a fire that is in imminent danger of contact with explosives, all employees must be removed to a safe area.

Electrical detonators can be inadvertently triggered by stray radio frequency (RF) signals from two-way radios. RF signal sources should be restricted from or near the demolition site if electrical detonators are used.

Personnel Selection

A blaster is a competent person who uses explosives. A blaster must be qualified by reason of training, knowledge, or experience in the field of transporting, storing, handling, and using explosives. In addition, the blaster should have a working knowledge of state and local regulations that pertain to explosives. Training courses are often available from manufacturers of explosives, and blasting safety manuals are offered by the Institute of Makers of Explosives (IME) as well as other organizations.

Blasters shall be required to furnish satisfactory evidence of competency in handling explosives and in safely performing the type of blasting required. A competent person should always be in charge of explosives and should be held responsible for enforcing all recommended safety precautions in connection with them.

Transportation of Explosives

Vehicles used for transporting explosives shall be strong enough to carry the load without difficulty and shall be in good mechanical condition. All vehicles used for the transportation of explosives shall have tight floors, and any exposed spark-producing metal on the inside of the body shall be covered with wood or some other non-sparking material. Vehicles or conveyances transporting explosives shall only be driven by, and shall be under the supervision of, a licensed driver familiar with the local, state, and federal regulations governing the transportation of explosives. No passengers should be allowed in any vehicle transporting explosives.

Explosives, blasting agents, and blasting supplies shall not be transported with other materials or cargo. Blasting caps shall not be transported with other materials or cargo. Blasting caps shall not be transported in the same vehicle with other explosives. If an open-bodied truck is used, the entire load should be completely covered with a fire- and water-resistant tarpaulin to protect it from the elements. Vehicles carrying explosives should not be loaded beyond the manufacturer's safe capacity rating, and in no case should the explosives be piled higher than the closed sides and ends of the body.

Every motor vehicle or conveyance used for transporting explosives shall be marked or placarded with warning signs as required by OSHA and the Department of Transportation. Each vehicle used for transportation of explosives shall be equipped with an Underwriters Laboratory-approved fire extinguisher of not less than 10-ABC rating. All drivers should be trained in the use of the extinguishers on their vehicle. When transporting explosives, congested traffic and high density population areas should be avoided, where possible, and no unnecessary stops should be made. Vehicles carrying explosives, blasting agents, or blasting supplies shall not be taken inside a garage or shop for repairs or servicing. No motor vehicle transporting explosives shall be left unattended.

Storage of Explosives

Inventory Handling and Safe Handling
All explosives must be accounted for at all times and those not being used must be kept in a locked magazine. A complete detailed inventory of all explosives received and placed in, removed from, and returned to the magazine should be maintained at all times. Appropriate authorities must be notified of any loss, theft, or unauthorized entry into a magazine.

Manufacturers' instructions for the safe handling and storage of explosives are ordinarily enclosed in each case of explosives. The specifics of storage and handling are best referred to these instructions and the aforementioned IME manuals; they should be carefully followed. Packages of explosives should not be handled roughly. Sparking metal tools should not be used to open wooden cases. Metallic slitters may be used for opening fiberboard cases, provided the metallic slitter does not come in contact with the metallic fasteners of the case.

The oldest stock should always be used first to minimize the chance of deterioration from long storage. Loose explosives or broken, defective, or leaking packages can be hazardous and should be segregated and properly disposed of in accordance with the specific instructions of the manufacturer. If the explosives are in good condition, it may be advisable to repack them. In this case, the explosives supplier should be contacted. Explosives cases should not be opened or explosives packed or repacked while in a magazine.

Storage Conditions
Providing a dry, well-ventilated place for the storage of explosives is one of the most important and effective safety measures. Exposure to weather damages most kinds of explosives, especially dynamite and caps. Ev-

ery precaution should be taken to keep them dry and relatively cool. Dampness or excess humidity may cause misfires, which could result in injury or loss of life. Explosives should be stored in properly constructed fire- and bullet-resistant structures, located according to the IME American Table of Distances, and kept locked at all times, except when opened for use by an authorized person. Explosives should not be left, kept, or stored where children, unauthorized persons, or animals have access to them, nor should they be stored in or near a residence.

Detonators should be stored in a separate magazine located according to the IME American Table of Distances. **Detonators should never be stored in the same magazine with any other kind of explosives.**

Ideally, arrangements should be made whereby the supplier delivers the explosives to the job site in quantities that will be used during that workday. An alternative would be for the supplier to return to pick up the unused explosives. If it is necessary for the contractor to store his or her explosives, he or she should be familiar with all local requirements for such storage.

Proper Use of Explosives

Blasting operations shall be conducted between sunrise and sunset, whenever possible. Adequate signs should be posted to alert to the hazard presented by blasting. Blasting mats or other containment should be used where there is danger of rocks or other debris being thrown into the air or where there are buildings or transportation systems nearby. Care should be taken to ensure the mats and other means of protection do not disturb the connections to electrical blasting caps.

Supervision and Signaling of Blast

After loading is completed, there should be as little delay as possible before firing. Each blast should be fired under the direct supervision of the blaster, who should inspect all connections before firing and personally see that all persons are in the clear before giving the order to fire.

Standard signals that indicate a blast is about to be fired and a later all-clear signal should be used. It is important that everyone working in the area be familiar with these signals and that they be strictly obeyed.

Inspection after the Blast

Immediately after the blast has been fired, the firing line shall be disconnected from the blasting machine and short-circuited. Where power switches are used, they shall be locked open or in the off position. Sufficient time shall be allowed for dust, smoke, and fumes to leave the blasted area before returning to the spot. An inspection of the area and the surrounding rubble shall be made by the blaster to determine if all charges have been exploded before employees are allowed to return to the work site. The blaster also should trace all wires and search for unexploded cartridges.

Additional Precautions for Electrical Blasting Caps

Radio, television, and radar transmitters create fields of electrical energy that can, under exceptional circumstances, detonate electric blasting caps. Therefore, certain precautions must be taken to prevent the accidental discharge of electric blasting caps from current induced by radar, radio transmitters, lightning, adjacent power lines, dust storms, or other sources of extraneous or static electricity. These precautions shall include:

- Ensuring mobile radio transmitters on the job site that are less than 100 ft. from electric blasting caps, in other-than-original containers, shall be de-energized and effectively locked;
- Prominently displaying of adequate signs that warn against the use of mobile radio transmitters on all roads within 1,000 ft. of the blasting operations;
- Maintaining the minimum distances recommended by the IME between the nearest transmitter and electric blasting caps; and
- Suspending all blasting operations and removing all persons from the blasting area during the approach and progress of an electric storm.

Disposal of Explosives

Explosives, blasting agents, and blasting supplies that are obviously deteriorated or damaged should not be used; they should be properly disposed of. Explosives distributors will usually take back old stock. Local fire marshals or representatives of the U.S. Bureau of Mines also may arrange for their disposal. Under no circumstances should any explosives be abandoned.

Wood, paper, fiber, or other materials that have previously contained high explosives should not be used again for any purpose, but should be destroyed by burning. These materials should not be burned in a stove, fireplace, or other confined space. Rather, they should be burned at an isolated outdoor location, at a safe distance from thoroughfares, magazines, and other structures. It is important to check that the containers are entirely empty before burning. While burning, the area should be adequately protected from intruders and all persons kept at least 100 ft. from the fire.

Underground Construction (Tunneling)

The OSHA regulation for underground construction (29 CFR 1926.800, Tunnels and Shafts) was originally issued under the Construction Safety Act of 1969 as 29 CFR Part 1518. These regulations were adopted and redesignated by OSHA in 1971. In 1974 and 1983, OSHA proposed revisions to the regulations in an effort to increase worker protection in underground construction activities. A final rule issued on June 2, 1989, added new protective measures and provided performance-oriented language to mitigate the hazards of underground construction. Many provisions have been revised to give the employer the flexibility to select from a variety of appropriate and effective methods of controlling workplace hazards in underground construction. In addition, an integral part of the standard is a safety program that focuses on instructing workers in topics relevant and appropriate to the specific jobsite.

The final rule applies to the construction of underground tunnels, shafts, chambers, and passageways. It also applies to cut-and-cover excavations, both those physically connected to ongoing underground construction tunnels and those that create conditions characteristic of underground construction. These hazards include:

- Reduced natural ventilation and light;
- Difficult and limited access and egress; and

- Exposure to air contaminants, fire, and explosion.

Workers in this industry traditionally have had a higher accident and injury rate than other workers in the heavy construction industry.

Competent Person

The revisions in the final rule give additional duties and responsibilities to a "competent person."

A competent person is one who is capable of identifying existing and predictable hazards in the workplace and is authorized to take corrective action to eliminate them ([29 CFR 1926.32(f)). Under the standard, a competent person is responsible for:

- Determining whether air contaminants are present in sufficient quantities to be dangerous to life;
- Testing the atmosphere for flammable limits before restoring power and equipment and before returning to work after a ventilation system has been shut down due to hazardous levels of flammable gas or methane;
- Inspecting the work area for ground stability; for inspecting all drilling equipment prior to each use; and
- Inspecting hauling equipment before each shift and visually checking all hoisting machinery, equipment, anchorages, and rope at the beginning of each shift and during hoisting, as necessary.

Safety Instruction

The standard requires that employees be taught to recognize and avoid hazards associated with underground construction. The training shall include the following topics, as appropriate for the job site:

- Air monitoring;
- Ventilation and illumination;
- Communications;
- Flood control;
- Mechanical and personal protective equipment;
- Explosives;
- Fire prevention and protection; and
- Emergency procedures (e.g., evacuation plans and check-in and checkout procedures).

Access and Egress

Under this provision, the employer must provide safe access to and egress from all workstations and prevent any unauthorized entry underground. Completed or unused sections of an underground work area must be barricaded. Unused openings must be covered, fenced off, or posted with warning signs that read "Keep Out" or similar language. Completed or unused sections of the underground facility shall be barricaded.

Check-in/Check-out

The employer is required to maintain a check-in/check-out procedure that ensures aboveground personnel have an accurate count of the number of persons underground in an emergency. At least one designated person is to be on duty aboveground whenever anyone is working underground. This person is also responsible for securing immediate aid for and keeping an accurate count of employees underground in case of an emergency.

A check-in/check-out procedure is not required, however, when the underground construction is sufficiently completed so that permanent environmental controls are effective and when remaining construction activity will not cause an environmental hazard or structural failure of the construction.

Hazardous Classifications

The standard provides classification criteria for gassy or potentially gassy operations and identifies additional requirements for work in gassy operations.

Potentially Gassy Operations

Potentially gassy operations occur when:

- Air monitoring shows 10 percent or more of the lower explosive limit (LEL) for methane or other flammable gases measured at 12 in. (304.8 mm) ±0.25 in. (6.35 mm) from the roof, face, floor, or walls in any underground work area for more than a 24-hour period; or
- The geological formation or history of the area shows that 10 percent or more of the LEL for methane or other flammable gases is likely to be encountered in the underground operation.

Gassy Operations

Gassy operations occur when:

- Air monitoring shows 10 percent or more of the lower explosive limit (LEL) for methane or other flammable gases measured at 12 in. (304.8 mm) ±0.25 in. (6.35 mm) from the roof, face, floor, or walls in any underground work area for three consecutive days; or
- Methane or other flammable gases emanating from the strata have ignited, indicating the presence of such gases; or
- The underground operation is connected to a currently gassy underground work area and is subject to a continuous course of air containing a flammable gas concentration.

When a gassy operation exists, additional safety precautions are required. These include:

- Using more stringent ventilation requirements;
- Using diesel equipment only if it is approved for use in gassy operations;
- Posting each entrance with warning signs, prohibiting smoking and personal sources of ignition;
- Maintaining a fire watch when hot work is performed; and
- Suspending all operations in the affected area until all special requirements are met or the operation is declassified.

Additional air monitoring also is required during gassy and potentially gassy conditions (see below).

Air Monitoring

Under the standard, employers are required to assign a competent person to perform all air monitoring required to determine proper ventilation and quantitative measurements of potentially hazardous gases. In instances where monitoring of airborne contaminants is required by the standard to be conducted "as often as necessary," this individual is responsible for determining which substances to monitor and how frequently, taking into consideration factors such as job site location, geology, history, work practices, and conditions.

The atmosphere in all underground areas shall be tested quantitatively for carbon monoxide, nitrogen dioxide, hydrogen sulfide, and other toxic gases, dusts, vapors, mists, and fumes as often as necessary to ensure that prescribed limits (as set by 29 CFR 1926.55) are met. Quantitative tests for methane also shall be performed to determine whether an operation is gassy or potentially gassy and to comply with other sections of the standard. A record of all air quality tests (including location, date, time, substances, and amount monitored) is to be kept aboveground at the worksite and shall be made available to the Secretary of Labor upon request.

Oxygen

Testing is to be performed as often as necessary to ensure the atmosphere at normal atmospheric pressure contains between 19.5 percent and 22 percent oxygen.

Hydrogen Sulfide

When air monitoring indicates the presence of 5 parts per million (ppm) or more of hydrogen sulfide, testing is to be conducted in the affected area at the beginning and midpoint of each shift until the concentration of hydrogen sulfide has been less than 5 ppm for three consecutive days. Continuous monitoring shall be performed when hydrogen sulfide is present above 10 ppm. Employees must be notified when the concentration of hydrogen sulfide is above 10 ppm. At concentrations of 20 ppm, an alarm (visual and aural) must signal to indicate that additional measures might be required (e.g., respirators, increased ventilation, evacuation) to maintain the proper exposure levels.

Other Precautions

When the competent person determines that there are contaminants present that are dangerous to life, the employer must post notices of the condition at all entrances to underground work areas and must ensure the necessary precautions are taken.

In cases where 5 percent or more of the LEL for these gases is present, steps must be taken to increase ventilation air volume to reduce the concentration to less than 5 percent of the LEL (except when operating under gassy or potentially gassy requirements).

When 10 percent or more of the LEL for methane or other flammable gases is detected where welding, cutting, or other hot work is being performed, work shall be suspended until the concentration is reduced to less than 10 percent of the LEL.

Where there is a concentration of 20 percent or more LEL, all employees shall be immediately withdrawn to a safe location aboveground, except those necessary to eliminate the hazard. Electrical power, except for acceptable pumping and ventilating equipment, shall be cut off to the endangered area until the concentration of the gas is less than 20 percent of the LEL.

As previously stated, gassy and potentially gassy conditions require additional air monitoring. These include testing for oxygen in the affected work areas; using flammable gas monitoring equipment (continuous automatic when using rapid excavation machines; manual as needed to monitor prescribed limits); performing local gas tests prior to performing, and continuously while performing, any hot work; testing continuously for flammable gas when employees are working underground using drill and blast methods, and prior to reentry after blasting.

Ventilation

There are a number of requirements for ventilation in underground construction work areas. In general, fresh air must be supplied to all underground work areas in sufficient amounts to prevent any dangerous or harmful accumulation of dusts, fumes, mists, vapors, or gases. A minimum of 200 cu. ft. of fresh air per minute is to be supplied for each employee underground. Mechanical ventilation, with reversible airflow, is to be provided in all of these work areas, except where natural ventilation is demonstrably sufficient. Where blasting or drilling is performed or other types of work operations that may cause harmful amounts of dust, fumes, vapors, etc., the velocity of airflow must be at least 30 ft. per minute.

For gassy or potentially gassy operations, ventilation systems must meet additional requirements. Ventilation systems used during gassy operations also must have controls located aboveground for reversing airflow.

Illumination

As in all construction operations, the standard requires that proper illumination be provided during tunneling operations, as specified in 29 CFR 1926.56. When explosives are handled, only acceptable portable lighting equipment shall be used within 50 ft. of any underground heading.

Fire Prevention and Control

In addition to the requirements of Subpart F, Fire Protection and Prevention, open flames and fires are prohibited in all underground construction activities, except for hot work operations. Smoking is allowed only in areas free of fire and explosion hazards, and the employer is required to post signs prohibiting smoking and open flames where these hazards exist. Various work practices also are identified as preventive measures. For example, there are limitations on the piping of diesel fuel from the surface to an underground location. Also, the pipe or hose system used to transfer fuel from the surface to the storage tank must remain empty except when transferring the fuel. Gasoline is not to be used, stored, or carried underground. Gases such as acetylene, liquefied petroleum, and methyl acetylene propadiene (stabilized) may be used underground only for hot work operations. Leaks and spills of flammable or combustible fluids must be cleaned up immediately. The standard also requires fire prevention measures regarding fire-resistant barriers and hydraulic fluids, the location and storage of combustible materials near openings or access to underground operations, electrical installations underground, lighting fixtures, and fire extinguishers.

Hot Work

During hot work operations such as welding, noncombustible barriers must be installed below work being performed in or over a shaft or raise. As mentioned previously, during these operations, only the amount of fuel-gas and oxygen cylinders necessary to perform welding, cutting, or other hot work over the next 24-hour period shall be kept underground. When work is completed, gas and oxygen cylinders shall be removed from the underground work area.

Cranes and Hoists

The standard contains provisions applicable to hoisting that are unique to underground construction. The standard incorporates by reference 1925.550 with respect to cranes; 1926.550(g) with respect to crane-hoisting of personnel, except that the limitations in paragraph (g)(2) do not apply to the routine access of employees to the underground via a shaft; 1926.552(a) and (b) with respect to requirements for material hoists and 1926.552(a), (c) and (d) with respect to requirements of personnel hoists and elevators. The provisions for underground construction include the following:

- Securing or stacking materials, tools, etc., being raised or lowered in a way to prevent the load from shifting, snagging, or from falling into the shaft;
- Using a flashing warning light for employees at the shaft bottom and subsurface shaft entrances whenever a load is above these locations or is being moved in the shaft;
- Following procedures for the proper lowering of loads when a hoist way is not fully enclosed and employees are at the shaft bottom;
- Informing and instructing employees of maintenance and repair work that is to commence in a shaft served by a cage, skip, or bucket;
- Providing a warning sign at the shaft collar, the operator's station, and each underground landing for work being performed in the shaft;
- Using connections between the hoisting rope and cage or skip that are compatible with the wire rope used for hoisting;
- Using cage, skip, and load connections that will not disengage from the force of the hoist pull, vibration, misalignment, release of lift force, or impact;
- Maintaining spin-type connections in a clean condition; and
- Ensuring that wire rope wedge sockets, when used, are properly seated.

Additional requirements for cranes include the use of limit switches, or anti-two-block devices. These operational aids are to be used only to limit travel of loads when operational controls malfunction and not as a substitute for other operational controls.

Emergencies

At work sites where 25 or more employees work underground at one time, employers are required to provide rescue teams or rescue services that include at least two five-person teams (one on the job site or within 30 minutes travel time and one within two hours travel time). Where there are fewer than 25 employees underground at one time, the employer shall provide or make available in advance one five-person rescue team on site or within 30 minutes travel time.

Rescue team members have to be qualified in rescue procedures and in the use of firefighting equipment and breathing apparatus. Their qualifications must be reviewed annually. The employer must ensure that rescue teams are familiar with the job site conditions. Rescue team members are required to practice donning and using self-contained breathing apparatus on a monthly basis for job sites where flammable or noxious gases are encountered or anticipated in hazardous quantities.

As part of emergency procedures, the employer shall provide self-rescuers (currently approved by the National Institute for Occupational Safety and Health and Mine Safety and Health Administration) to be immediately available to all employees at underground workstations who might be trapped by smoke or gas. The selection, use, and care of respirators shall be in accordance with 1926.103(b) and 1926.103(c).

A designated, or authorized, person shall be responsible for securing immediate aid for workers and keeping an accurate count of employees underground. Emergency lighting, such as a portable hand or cap lamp, shall be provided to all underground workers in their work areas to provide adequate light for escape.

Recordkeeping

Under the General Industry Standards at 29 CFR 1910.1020, records of exposure to toxic substances and data analyses based on these records are to be kept for 30 years. Medical records are to be kept for at least the duration of employment plus 30 years. Background data for exposure records, such as laboratory reports and worksheets, need to be kept only for one year. Records of employees who have worked for less than one year need not be retained after employment, but the employer must provide these records to the employee upon termination of employment. First-aid records of one-time treatment need not be retained for any specified period.

Three months before disposing of records, employers must notify the Director of the National Institute for Occupational Safety and Health.

Blasting and Explosives—General Provisions—1926.900

(a) The employer shall permit only authorized and qualified persons to handle and use explosives.

(b) Smoking, firearms, matches, open flame lamps, and other fires, flame or heat producing devices and sparks shall be prohibited in or near explosive magazines or while explosives are being handled, transported or used.

(c) No person shall be allowed to handle or use explosives while under the influence of intoxicating liquors, narcotics, or other dangerous drugs.

(d) All explosives shall be accounted for at all times. Explosives not being used shall be kept in a locked magazine, unavailable to persons not authorized to handle them. The employer shall maintain an inventory and use record of all explosives. Appropriate authorities shall be notified of any loss, theft, or unauthorized entry into a magazine.

(e) No explosives or blasting agents shall be abandoned.

(f) No fire shall be fought where the fire is in imminent danger of contact with explosives. All employees shall be removed to a safe area and the fire area guarded against intruders.

(g) Original containers, or Class II magazines, shall be used for taking detonators and other explosives from storage magazines to the blasting area.

(h) When blasting is done in congested areas or in proximity to a structure, railway, or highway, or any other installation that may be damaged, the blaster shall take special precautions in the loading, delaying, initiation, and confinement of each blast with mats or other methods so as to control the throw of fragments, and thus prevent bodily injury to employees.

(i) Employees authorized to prepare explosive charges or conduct blasting operations shall use every reasonable precaution including, but not limited to, visual and audible warning signals, flags, or barricades, to ensure employee safety.

(j) Insofar as possible, blasting operations above ground shall be conducted between sunup and sundown.

(k) Due precautions shall be taken to prevent accidental discharge of electric blasting caps from current induced by radar, radio transmitters, lightning, adjacent power lines, dust storms, or other sources of extraneous electricity. These precautions shall include:

(1) Detonators shall be short-circuited in holes which have been primed and shunted until wired into the blasting circuit.

(2) The suspension of all blasting operations and removal of persons from the blasting area during the approach and progress of an electric storm;

(3)(i) The prominent display of adequate signs, warning against the use of mobile radio transmitters, on all roads within 1,000 feet of blasting operations. Whenever adherence to the 1,000-foot distance would create an operational handicap, a competent person shall be consulted to evaluate the particular situation, and alternative provisions may be made which are adequately designed to prevent any premature firing of electric blasting caps. A description of any such alternatives shall be reduced to writing and shall be certified as meeting the purposes of this subdivision by the competent person consulted. The description shall be maintained at the construction site during the duration of the work, and shall be available for inspection by representatives of the Secretary of Labor.

(ii) Specimens of signs which would meet the requirements of paragraph (k)(3) of this section are the following:

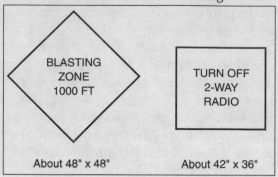

(4) Ensuring that mobile radio transmitters which are less than 100 feet away from electric blasting caps, in other than original containers, shall be deenergized and effectively locked;

(5) Compliance with the recommendations of The Institute of the Makers of Explosives with regard to blasting in the vicinity of radio transmitters as stipulated in Radio Frequency Energy—A Potential Hazard in the Use of Electric Blasting Caps, IME Publication No. 20, March 1971.

(l) Empty boxes and paper and fiber packing materials, which have previously contained high explosives, shall not be used again for any purpose, but shall be destroyed by burning at an approved location.

(m) Explosives, blasting agents, and blasting supplies that are obviously deteriorated or damaged shall not be used.

(n) Delivery and issue of explosives shall only be made by and to authorized persons and into authorized magazines or approved temporary storage or handling areas.

(o) Blasting operations in the proximity of overhead power lines, communication lines, utility services, or other services and structures shall not be carried on until the operators and/or owners have been notified and measures for safe control have been taken.

(p) The use of black powder shall be prohibited.

(q) All loading and firing shall be directed and supervised by competent persons thoroughly experienced in this field.

(r) All blasts shall be fired electrically with an electric blasting machine or properly designed electric power source, except as provided in §1926.906 (a) and (r).

(s) Buildings used for the mixing of blasting agents shall conform to the requirements of this section.

(1) Buildings shall be of noncombustible construction or sheet metal on wood studs.

(2) Floors in a mixing plant shall be of concrete or of other nonabsorbent materials.

(3) All fuel oil storage facilities shall be separated from the mixing plant and located in such a manner that in case of tank rupture, the oil will drain away from the mixing plant building.

(4) The building shall be well ventilated.

(5) Heating units which do not depend on combustion processes, when properly designed and located, may be used in the building. All direct sources of heat shall be provided exclusively from units located outside the mixing building.

(6) All internal-combustion engines used for electric power generation shall be located outside the mixing plant building, or shall be properly ventilated and isolated by a firewall. The exhaust systems on all such engines shall be located so any spark emission cannot be a hazard to any materials in or adjacent to the plant.

(t) Buildings used for the mixing of water gels shall conform to the requirements of this subdivision.

(1) Buildings shall be of noncombustible construction or sheet metal on wood studs.

(2) Floors in a mixing plant shall be of concrete or of other nonabsorbent materials.

(3) Where fuel oil is used all fuel oil storage facilities shall be separated from the mixing plant and located in such a manner that in case of tank rupture, the oil will drain away from the mixing plant building.

(4) The building shall be well ventilated.

(5) Heating units that do not depend on combustion processes, when properly designed and located, may be used in the building. All direct sources of heat shall be provided exclusively from units located outside of the mixing building.

(6) All internal-combustion engines used for electric power generation shall be located outside the mixing plant building, or shall be properly ventilated and isolated by a firewall. The exhaust systems on all such engines shall be located so any spark emission cannot be a hazard to any materials in or adjacent to the plant.

Blaster Qualifications—1926.901

(a) A blaster shall be able to understand and give written and oral orders.

(b) A blaster shall be in good physical condition and not be addicted to narcotics, intoxicants, or similar types of drugs.

(c) A blaster shall be qualified, by reason of training, knowledge, or experience, in the field of transporting, storing, handling, and use of explosives, and have a working knowledge of state and local laws and regulations which pertain to explosives.

(d) Blasters shall be required to furnish satisfactory evidence of competency in handling explosives and performing in a safe manner the type of blasting that will be required.

(e) The blaster shall be knowledgeable and competent in the use of each type of blasting method used.

Surface Transportation of Explosives—1926.902

(a) Transportation of explosives shall meet the provisions of Department of Transportation regulations contained in 46 CFR parts 146–149, Water Carriers; 49 CFR parts 171–179, Highways and Railways; 49 CFR part 195, Pipelines; and 49 CFR parts 390–397, Motor Carriers.

(b) Motor vehicles or conveyances transporting explosives shall only be driven by, and be in the charge of, a licensed driver who is physically fit. He shall be familiar with the local, state, and federal regulation governing the transportation of explosives.

(c) No person shall smoke, or carry matches or any other flame-producing device, nor shall firearms or loaded cartridges be carried while in or near a motor vehicle or conveyance transporting explosives.

(d) Explosives, blasting agents, and blasting supplies shall not be transported with other materials or cargoes. Blasting caps (including electric) shall not be transported in the same vehicle with other explosives.

(e) Vehicles used for transporting explosives shall be strong enough to carry the load without difficulty, and shall be in good mechanical condition.

(f) When explosives are transported by a vehicle with an open body, a Class II magazine or original manufacturer's container shall be securely mounted on the bed to contain the cargo.

(g) All vehicles used for the transportation of explosives shall have tight floors and any exposed spark-producing metal on the inside of the body shall be covered with wood, or other nonsparking material, to prevent contact with containers of explosives.

(h) Every motor vehicle or conveyance used for transporting explosives shall be marked or placarded on both sides, the front, and the rear with the word "Explosives" in red letters, not less than 4 inches in height, on white background. In addition to such marking or placarding, the motor vehicle or conveyance may display, in such a manner that it will be readily visible from all directions, a red flag 18 inches by 30 inches, with the word "Explosives" painted, stamped, or sewed thereon, in white letters, at least 6 inches in height.

(i) Each vehicle used for transportation of explosives shall be equipped with a fully charged fire extinguisher, in good condition. An Underwriters Laboratory-approved extinguisher of not less than 10-ABC rating will meet the minimum requirement. The driver shall be trained in the use of the extinguisher on his vehicle.

(j) Motor vehicles or conveyances carrying explosives, blasting agents, or blasting supplies, shall not be taken inside a garage or shop for repairs or servicing.

(k) No motor vehicle transporting explosives shall be left unattended.

Underground Transportation of Explosives—1926.903

(a) All explosives or blasting agents in transit underground shall be taken to the place of use or storage without delay.

(b) The quantity of explosives or blasting agents taken to an underground loading area shall not exceed the amount estimated to be necessary for the blast.

(c) Explosives in transit shall not be left unattended.

(d) The hoist operator shall be notified before explosives or blasting agents are transported in a shaft conveyance.

(e) Trucks used for the transportation of explosives underground shall have the electrical system checked weekly to detect any failures which may constitute an electrical hazard. A certification record which includes the date of the inspection; the signature of the person who performed the inspection; and a serial number, or other identifier, of the truck inspected shall be prepared and the most recent certification record shall be maintained on file.

(f) The installation of auxiliary lights on truck beds, which are powered by the truck's electrical system, shall be prohibited.

(g) Explosives and blasting agents shall be hoisted, lowered, or conveyed in a powder car. No other materials, supplies, or equipment shall be transported in the same conveyance at the same time.

(h) No one, except the operator, his helper, and the powderman, shall be permitted to ride on a conveyance transporting explosives and blasting agents.

(i) No person shall ride in any shaft conveyance transporting explosives and blasting agents.

(j) No explosives or blasting agents shall be transported on any locomotive. At least two car lengths shall separate the locomotive from the powder car.

(k) No explosives or blasting agents shall be transported on a man haul trip.

(l) The car or conveyance containing explosives or blasting agents shall be pulled, not pushed, whenever possible.

(m) The powder car or conveyance especially built for the purpose of transporting explosives or blasting agents shall bear a reflectorized sign on each side with the word "Explosives" in letters, not less than 4 inches in height; upon a background of sharply contrasting color.

(n) Compartments for transporting detonators and explosives in the same car or conveyance shall be physically separated by a distance of 24 inches or by a solid partition at least 6 inches thick.

(o) Detonators and other explosives shall not be transported at the same time in any shaft conveyance.

(p) Explosives, blasting agents, or blasting supplies shall not be transported with other materials.

(q) Explosives or blasting agents, not in original containers, shall be placed in a suitable container when transported manually.

(r) Detonators, primers, and other explosives shall be carried in separate containers when transported manually.

Storage of Explosives and Blasting Agents—1926.904

(a) Explosives and related materials shall be stored in approved facilities required under the applicable provisions of the Bureau of Alcohol, Tobacco and Firearms regulations contained in 27 CFR part 55, Commerce in Explosives.

(b) Blasting caps, electric blasting caps, detonating primers, and primed cartridges shall not be stored in the same magazine with other explosives or blasting agents.

(c) Smoking and open flames shall not be permitted within 50 feet of explosives and detonator storage magazine.

(d) No explosives or blasting agents shall be permanently stored in any underground operation until the operation has been developed to the point where at least two modes of exit have been provided.

(e) Permanent underground storage magazines shall be at least 300 feet from any shaft, adit, or active underground working area.

(f) Permanent underground magazines containing detonators shall not be located closer than 50 feet to any magazine containing other explosives or blasting agents.

Loading of Explosives or Blasting Agents—1926.905

(a) Procedures that permit safe and efficient loading shall be established before loading is started.

(b) All drill holes shall be sufficiently large to admit freely the insertion of the cartridges of explosives.

(c) Tamping shall be done only with wood rods or plastic tamping poles without exposed metal parts, but nonsparking metal connectors may be used for jointed poles. Violent tamping shall be avoided. The primer shall never be tamped.

(d) No holes shall be loaded except those to be fired in the next round of blasting. After loading, all remaining explosives and detonators shall be immediately returned to an authorized magazine.

(e) Drilling shall not be started until all remaining butts of old holes are examined for unexploded charges, and if any are found, they shall be refired before work proceeds.

(f) No person shall be allowed to deepen drill holes which have contained explosives or blasting agents.

(g) No explosives or blasting agents shall be left unattended at the blast site.

(h) Machines and all tools not used for loading explosives into bore holes shall be removed from the immediate location of holes before explosives are delivered. Equipment shall not be operated within 50 feet of loaded holes.

(i) No activity of any nature other than that which is required for loading holes with explosives shall be permitted in a blast area.

(j) Powerlines and portable electric cables for equipment being used shall be kept a safe distance from explosives or blasting agents being loaded into drill holes. Cables in the proximity of the blast area shall be deenergized and locked out by the blaster.

(k) Holes shall be checked prior to loading to determine depth and conditions. Where a hole has been loaded with explosives but the explosives have failed to detonate, there shall be no drilling within 50 feet of the hole.

(l) When loading a long line of holes with more than one loading crew, the crews shall be separated by practical distance consistent with efficient operation and supervision of crews.

(m) No explosive shall be loaded or used underground in the presence of combustible gases or combustible dusts.

(n) No explosives other than those in Fume Class 1, as set forth by the Institute of Makers of Explosives, shall be used; however, explosives complying with the requirements of Fume Class 2 and Fume Class 3 may be used if adequate ventilation has been provided.

(o) All blast holes in open work shall be stemmed to the collar or to a point which will confine the charge.

(p) Warning signs, indicating a blast area, shall be maintained at all approaches to the blast area. The warning sign lettering shall not be less than 4 inches in height on a contrasting background.

(q) A bore hole shall never be sprung when it is adjacent to or near a hole that is loaded. Flashlight batteries shall not be used for springing holes.

(r) Drill holes which have been sprung or chambered, and which are not water-filled, shall be allowed to cool before explosives are loaded.

(s) No loaded holes shall be left unattended or unprotected.

(t) The blaster shall keep an accurate, up-to-date record of explosives, blasting agents, and blasting supplies used in a blast and shall keep an accurate running inventory of all explosives and blasting agents stored on the operation.

(u) When loading blasting agents pneumatically over electric blasting caps, semiconductive delivery hose shall be used and the equipment shall be bonded and grounded.

Initiation of Explosive Charges— Electric Blasting—1926.906

(a) Electric blasting caps shall not be used where sources of extraneous electricity make the use of electric blasting caps dangerous. Blasting cap leg wires shall be kept short-circuited (shunted) until they are connected into the circuit for firing.

(b) Before adopting any system of electrical firing, the blaster shall conduct a thorough survey for extraneous currents, and all dangerous currents shall be eliminated before any holes are loaded.

(c) In any single blast using electric blasting caps, all caps shall be of the same style or function, and of the same manufacture.

(d) Electric blasting shall be carried out by using blasting circuits or power circuits in accordance with the electric blasting cap manufacturer's recommendations, or an approved contractor or his designated representative.

(e) When firing a circuit of electric blasting caps, care must be exercised to ensure that an adequate quantity of delivered current is available, in accordance with the manufacturer's recommendations.

(f) Connecting wires and lead wires shall be insulated single solid wires of sufficient current-carrying capacity.

(g) Bus wires shall be solid single wires of sufficient current-carrying capacity.

(h) When firing electrically, the insulation on all firing lines shall be adequate and in good condition.

(i) A power circuit used for firing electric blasting caps shall not be grounded.

(j) In underground operations when firing from a power circuit, a safety switch shall be placed in the permanent firing line at intervals. This switch shall be made so it can be locked only in the "Off" position and shall be provided with a short-circuiting arrangement of the firing lines to the cap circuit.

(k) In underground operations there shall be a "lightning" gap of at least 5 feet in the firing system ahead of the main firing switch; that is, between this switch and the source of power. This gap shall be bridged by a flexible jumper cord just before firing the blast.

(l) When firing from a power circuit, the firing switch shall be locked in the open or "Off" position at all times, except when firing. It shall be so designed that the firing lines to the cap circuit are automatically short-circuited when the switch is in the

"Off" position. Keys to this switch shall be entrusted only to the blaster.

(m) Blasting machines shall be in good condition and the efficiency of the machine shall be tested periodically to make certain that it can deliver power at its rated capacity.

(n) When firing with blasting machines, the connections shall be made as recommended by the manufacturer of the electric blasting caps used.

(o) The number of electric blasting caps connected to a blasting machine shall not be in excess of its rated capacity. Furthermore, in primary blasting, a series circuit shall contain no more caps than the limits recommended by the manufacturer of the electric blasting caps in use.

(p) The blaster shall be in charge of the blasting machines, and no other person shall connect the leading wires to the machine.

(q) Blasters, when testing circuits to charged holes, shall use only blasting galvanometers or other instruments that are specifically designed for this purpose.

(r) Whenever the possibility exists that a leading line or blasting wire might be thrown over a live powerline by the force of an explosion, care shall be taken to see that the total length of wires are kept too short to hit the lines, or that the wires are securely anchored to the ground. If neither of these requirements can be satisfied, a nonelectric system shall be used.

(s) In electrical firing, only the man making leading wire connections shall fire the shot. All connections shall be made from the bore hole back to the source of firing current, and the leading wires shall remain shorted and not be connected to the blasting machine or other source of current until the charge is to be fired.

(t) After firing an electric blast from a blasting machine, the leading wires shall be immediately disconnected from the machine and short-circuited.

Use of Safety Fuse—1926.907

(a) Safety fuse shall only be used where sources of extraneous electricity make the use of electric blasting caps dangerous. The use of a fuse that has been hammered or injured in any way shall be forbidden.

(b) The hanging of a fuse on nails or other projections which will cause a sharp bend to be formed in the fuse is prohibited.

(c) Before capping safety fuse, a short length shall be cut from the end of the supply reel so as to assure a fresh cut end in each blasting cap.

(d) Only a cap crimper of approved design shall be used for attaching blasting caps to safety fuse. Crimpers shall be kept in good repair and accessible for use.

(e) No unused cap or short capped fuse shall be placed in any hole to be blasted; such unused detonators shall be removed from the working place and destroyed.

(f) No fuse shall be capped, or primers made up, in any magazine or near any possible source of ignition.

(g) No one shall be permitted to carry detonators or primers of any kind on his person.

(h) The minimum length of safety fuse to be used in blasting shall be as required by State law, but shall not be less than 30 inches.

(i) At least two men shall be present when multiple cap and fuse blasting is done by hand lighting methods.

(j) Not more than 12 fuses shall be lighted by each blaster when hand lighting devices are used. However, when two or more safety fuses in a group are lighted as one by means of igniter cord, or other similar fuse-lighting devices, they may be considered as one fuse.

(k) The so-called "drop fuse" method of dropping or pushing a primer or any explosive with a lighted fuse attached is forbidden.

(l) Cap and fuse shall not be used for firing mudcap charges unless charges are separated sufficiently to prevent one charge from dislodging other shots in the blast.

(m) When blasting with safety fuses, consideration shall be given to the length and burning rate of the fuse. Sufficient time, with a margin of safety, shall always be provided for the blaster to reach a place of safety.

Use of Detonating Cord—1926.908

(a) Care shall be taken to select a detonating cord consistent with the type and physical condition of the bore hole and stemming and the type of explosives used.

(b) Detonating cord shall be handled and used with the same respect and care given other explosives.

(c) The line of detonating cord extending out of a bore hole or from a charge shall be cut from the supply spool before loading the remainder of the bore hole or placing additional charges.

(d) Detonating cord shall be handled and used with care to avoid damaging or severing the cord during and after loading and hooking-up.

(e) Detonating cord connections shall be competent and positive in accordance with approved and recommended methods. Knot-type or other cord-to-cord connections shall be made only with detonating cord in which the explosive core is dry.

(f) All detonating cord trunklines and branchlines shall be free of loops, sharp kinks, or angles that direct the cord back toward the oncoming line of detonation.

(g) All detonating cord connections shall be inspected before firing the blast.

(h) When detonating cord millisecond-delay connectors or short-interval-delay electric blasting caps are used with detonating cord, the practice shall conform strictly to the manufacturer's recommendations.

(i) When connecting a blasting cap or an electric blasting cap to detonating cord, the cap shall be taped or otherwise attached securely along the side or the end of the detonating cord, with the end of the cap containing the explosive charge pointed in the direction in which the detonation is to proceed.

(j) Detonators for firing the trunkline shall not be brought to the loading area nor attached to the detonating cord until everything else is in readiness for the blast.

Firing the Blast—1926.909

(a) A code of blasting signals equivalent to Table U-1, shall be posted on one or more conspicuous places at the operation, and all employees shall be required to familiarize themselves with the code and conform to it. Danger signs shall be placed at suitable locations.

(b) Before a blast is fired, a loud warning signal shall be given by the blaster in charge, who has made certain that all surplus explosives are in a safe place and all employees, vehicles, and equipment are at a safe distance, or under sufficient cover.

(c) Flagmen shall be safely stationed on highways which pass through the danger zone so as to stop traffic during blasting operations.

(d) It shall be the duty of the blaster to fix the time of blasting.

(e) Before firing an underground blast, warning shall be given, and all possible entries into the blasting area, and any entrances to any working place where a drift, raise, or other opening is about to hole through, shall be carefully guarded. The blaster shall make sure that all employees are out of the blast area before firing a blast.

Table U–1

Warning Signal—A 1-minute series of long blasts 5 minutes prior to blast signal.
Blast Signal—A series of short blasts 1 minute prior to the shot.
All Clear Signal—A prolonged blast following the inspection of blast area.

Inspection after Blasting—1926.910

(a) Immediately after the blast has been fired, the firing line shall be disconnected from the blasting machine, or where power switches are used, they shall be locked open or in the off position.

(b) Sufficient time shall be allowed, not less than 15 minutes in tunnels, for the smoke and fumes to leave the blasted area before returning to the shot. An inspection of the area and the surrounding rubble shall be made by the blaster to determine if all charges have been exploded before employees are allowed to return to the operation, and in tunnels, after the muck pile has been wetted down.

Misfires—1926.911

(a) If a misfire is found, the blaster shall provide proper safeguards for excluding all employees from the danger zone.

(b) No other work shall be done except that necessary to remove the hazard of the misfire and only those employees necessary to do the work shall remain in the danger zone.

(c) No attempt shall be made to extract explosives from any charged or misfired hole; a new primer shall be put in and the hole reblasted. If refiring of the misfired hole presents a hazard, the explosives may be removed by washing out with water or, where the misfire is under water, blown out with air.

(d) If there are any misfires while using cap and fuse, all employees shall remain away from the charge for at least 1 hour. Misfires shall be handled under the direction of the person in charge of the blasting. All wires shall be carefully traced and a search made for unexploded charges.

(e) No drilling, digging, or picking shall be permitted until all missed holes have been detonated or the authorized representative has approved that work can proceed.

Underwater Blasting—1926.912

(a) A blaster shall conduct all blasting operations, and no shot shall be fired without his approval.

(b) Loading tubes and casings of dissimilar metals shall not be used because of possible electric transient currents from galvanic action of the metals and water.

(c) Only water-resistant blasting caps and detonating cords shall be used for all marine blasting. Loading shall be done through a nonsparking metal loading tube when tube is necessary.

(d) No blast shall be fired while any vessel under way is closer than 1,500 feet to the blasting area. Those on board vessels or craft moored or anchored within 1,500 feet shall be notified before a blast is fired.

(e) No blast shall be fired while any swimming or diving operations are in progress in the vicinity of the blasting area. If such operations are in progress, signals and arrangements shall be agreed upon to assure that no blast shall be fired while any person is in the water.

(f) Blasting flags shall be displayed.

(g) The storage and handling of explosives aboard vessels used in underwater blasting operations shall be according to provisions outlined herein on handling and storing explosives.

(h) When more than one charge is placed under water, a float device shall be attached to an element of each charge in such manner that it will be released by the firing. Misfires shall be handled in accordance with the requirements of §1926.911.

Blasting in Excavation Work under Compressed Air—1926.913

(a) Detonators and explosives shall not be stored or kept in tunnels, shafts, or caissons. Detonators and explosives for each round shall be taken directly from the magazines to the blasting zone and immediately loaded. Detonators and explosives left over after loading a round shall be removed from the working chamber before the connecting wires are connected up.

(b) When detonators or explosives are brought into an air lock, no employee except the powderman, blaster, lock tender and the employees necessary for carrying, shall be permitted to enter the air lock. No other material, supplies, or equipment shall be locked through with the explosives.

(c) Detonators and explosives shall be taken separately into pressure working chambers.

(d) The blaster or powderman shall be responsible for the receipt, unloading, storage, and on-site transportation of explosives and detonators.

(e) All metal pipes, rails, air locks, and steel tunnel lining shall be electrically bonded together and grounded at or near the portal or shaft, and such pipes and rails shall be cross-bonded together at not less than 1,000-foot intervals throughout the length of the tunnel. In addition, each low air supply pipe shall be grounded at its delivery end.

(f) The explosives suitable for use in wet holes shall be water-resistant and shall be Fume Class 1.

(g) When tunnel excavation in rock face is approaching mixed face, and when tunnel excavation is in mixed face, blasting shall be performed with light charges and with light burden on each hole. Advance drilling shall be performed as tunnel excavation in rock face approaches mixed face, to determine the general nature and extent of rock cover and the remaining distance ahead to soft ground as excavation advances.

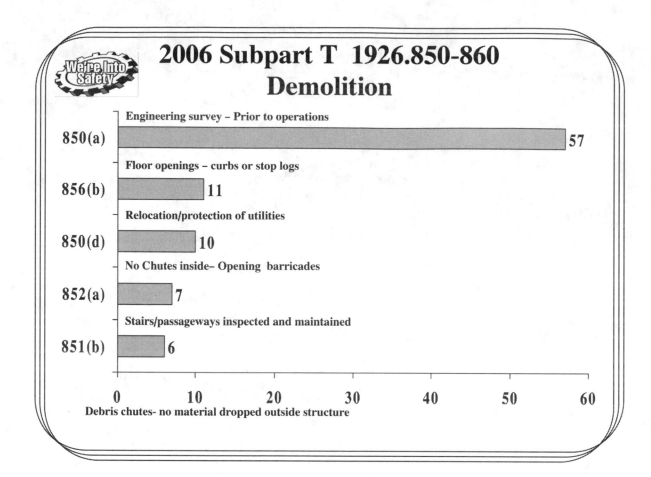

2006 Subpart T 1926.850-860
Demolition

Engineering survey – Prior to operations

850(a) — 57

Floor openings – curbs or stop logs

856(b) — 11

Relocation/protection of utilities

850(d) — 10

No Chutes inside– Opening barricades

852(a) — 7

Stairs/passageways inspected and maintained

851(b) — 6

0   10   20   30   40   50   60

Debris chutes- no material dropped outside structure

RECORDING AND REPORTING OCCUPATIONAL INJURIES AND ILLNESSES

The following is an abstract of Section VII, Summary and Explanation of the Final Rule, of 29 CFR 1904, Occupational Injury and Illness Recording and Reporting Requirements (66 Fed. Reg. 5916). Subparts covered include:

A. Purpose
B. Scope
C. Recordkeeping Forms and Recording Criteria
D. Other OSHA Injury and Illness Recordkeeping Requirements
E. Reporting Fatality, Injury and Illness Information to the Government.
F. Transition From the Former Rule
G. Definitions

No attempt has been made to discuss every detail of the regulation. Readers are encouraged to consult the *Federal Register* for the complete text. The corresponding page numbers of major paragraphs as they appear in the *Federal Register* are provided throughout this document to facilitate further reading.

A list of major changes to the recordkeeping rule, released by the Occupational Safety and Health Administration, also is included.

Major Changes To OSHA's Recordkeeping Rule

This document provides a list of the major changes from OSHA's old 1904 recordkeeping rule to the new rule employers began using in 2002. This list summarizes the major differences between the old and new recordkeeping rules to help people who are familiar with the old rule to learn the new rule quickly.

Scope

- The list of service and retail industries that are partially exempt from the rule has been updated. Some establishments that were covered under the old rule are not required to keep OSHA records under the new rule and some formerly exempted establishments will now have to keep records. (§1904.2)
- The new rule continues to provide a partial exemption for employers who had 10 or fewer workers at all times in the previous calendar year. (§1904.1)

Forms

- The new OSHA Form 300 (Log of Work-Related Injuries and Illnesses) has been simplified and can be printed on smaller legal-sized paper.
- The new OSHA Form 301 (Injury and Illness Incident Report) includes more data about how the injury or illness occurred.
- The new OSHA Form 300A (Summary of Work-Related Injuries and Illnesses) provides additional data to make it easier for employers to calculate incidence rates.
- Maximum flexibility has been provided so employers can keep all the information on computers, at a central location, or on alternative forms, as long as the information is compatible and the data can be produced when needed. (§1904.29 and §1904.30)

Work-related

- A "significant" degree of aggravation is required before a preexisting injury or illness becomes work-related. (§1904.5(a))
- Additional exceptions have been added to the geographic presumption of work relationship; cases arising from eating and drinking of food and beverages, blood donations, exercise programs, etc., no longer need to be recorded. Common cold and flu cases also no longer need to be recorded. (§1904.5(b)(2))
- Criteria for deciding when mental illnesses are considered work-related have been added. (§1904.5(b)(2))
- Sections have been added clarifying work relationship when employees travel or work out of their home. (§1904.5(b)(6) and §1904.5(b)(7))

Recording criteria

- Different criteria for recording work-related injuries and work-related illnesses are eliminated; one set of criteria is used for both. (The former rule required employers to record all illnesses, regardless of severity). (§1904.4)
- Employers are required to record work-related injuries or illnesses if they result in one of the following: death; days away from work; restricted work or transfer to another job; medical treatment beyond first aid; loss of consciousness; or diagnosis of a significant injury/illness by a physician or other licensed health care professional. (§1904.7(a))
- New definitions are included for medical treatment and first aid. First aid is defined by treatments on a finite list. All treatment not on this list is medical treatment. (§1904.7(b)(5))
- The recording of "light duty" or restricted work cases is clarified. Employers are required to record cases as restricted work cases when the injured or ill employee only works partial days or is restricted from performing their "routine job functions" (defined as work activities the employee regularly performs at least once weekly). (§1904.7(b)(4))
- Employers are required to record all needle-stick and sharps injuries involving contamination by another person's blood or other potentially infectious material. (§1904.8)
- Musculoskeletal disorders (MSDs) are treated like all other injuries or illnesses: they must be recorded if they result in days away, restricted work, transfer to another job, or medical treatment beyond first aid.
- Special recording criteria are included for cases involving the work-related transmission of tuberculosis or medical removal under OSHA standards. (§1904.9 and §1904.11)

Day counts

- The term "lost workdays" is eliminated and the rule requires recording of days away, days of restricted work, or transfer to another job. Also, new rules for counting that rely on calendar days instead of workdays are included. (§1904.7(b)(3))
- Employers are no longer required to count days away or days of restriction beyond 180 days. (§1904.7(b)(3))
- The day on which the injury or illness occurs is not counted as a day away from work or a day of restricted work. (§1904.7(b)(3) and §1904.7(b)(4))

Annual Summary

- Employers must review the 300 Log information before it is summarized on the 300A form. (§1904.32(a))
- The new rule includes hours worked data to make it easier for employers to calculate incidence rates. (§1904.32(b)(2))
- A company executive is required to certify the accuracy of the summary. (§1904.32(b)(3))
- The annual summary must be posted for three months instead of one. (§1904.32(b)(6))

Employee involvement

- Employers are required to establish a procedure for employees to report injuries and illnesses and to tell their employees how to report. (§1904.35(a))
- The new rule informs employers that the OSH Act prohibits employers from discriminating against employees who do report. (§1904.36)
- Employees are allowed to access the 301 forms to review records of their own injuries and illnesses. (§1904.35(b)(2))
- Employee representatives are allowed to access those parts of the OSHA 301 form relevant to workplace safety and health. (§1904.35(b)(2))

Protecting privacy

- Employers are required to protect employee's privacy by withholding an individual's name on Form 300 for certain types of sensitive injuries/illnesses (e.g., sexual assaults, HIV infections, mental illnesses, etc.). (§1904.29(b)(6) to §1904.29(b)(8))
- Employers are allowed to withhold descriptive information about sensitive injuries in cases where not doing so would disclose the employee's identity. (§1904.29(b)(9))
- Employee representatives are given access only to the portion of Form 301 that contains information about the injury or illness, while personal information about the employee and his or her health care provider is withheld. (§1904.35(b)(2))
- Employers are required to remove employees' names before providing injury and illness data to persons who do not have access rights under the rule. (§1904.29(b)(10))

Reporting information to the government

- Employers must call in all fatal heart attacks occurring in the work environment. (§1904.39(b)(5))
- Employers do not need to call in public street motor vehicle accidents except those in a construction work zone. (§1904.39(b)(3))
- Employers do not need to call in commercial airplane, train, subway or bus accidents. (§1904.39(b)(4))
- Employers must provide records to an OSHA compliance officer who requests them within 4 hours. (§1904.40(a))

VII. Summary and Explanation [p. 5932]

The following sections discuss the contents of the final 29 CFR Part 1904 and section 1952.4 regulations. OSHA has written these regulations using the plain language guidance set out in a Presidential Memo to the heads of executive departments and agencies on June 1, 1998. The Agency also used guidance from the Plain Language Action Network (PLAN), which is a government-wide group working to improve communications from the Federal government to the public, with the goals of increasing trust in government, reducing government costs, and reducing the burden on the public. For more information on PLAN, see their Internet site at http://www.plainlanguage.gov/. The plain language concepts encourage government agencies to adopt a first person question and answer format, which OSHA used for the Part

1904 rule. The rule contains several types of provisions. Requirements are described using the "you must * * *" construction, prohibitions are described using "you may not * * *", and optional actions that are not requirements or prohibitions are preceded by "you may * * *." OSHA has also included provisions to provide information to the public in the rule.

Subpart A. Purpose [p. 5933]

The Purpose section of the final rule explains why OSHA is promulgating this rule. The Purpose section contains no regulatory requirements and is intended merely to provide information. A Note to this section informs employers and employees that recording a case on the OSHA recordkeeping forms does not indicate either that the employer or the employee was at fault in the incident or that an OSHA rule has been violated. Recording an injury or illness on the Log also does not, in and of itself, indicate that the case qualifies for workers' compensation or other benefits. Although any specific work-related injury or illness may involve some or all of these factors, the record made of that injury or illness on the OSHA recordkeeping forms only shows three things: (1) that an injury or illness has occurred; (2) that the employer has determined that the case is work-related (using OSHA's definition of that term); and (3) that the case is non-minor, i.e., that it meets one or more of the OSHA injury and illness recording criteria. OSHA has added the Note to this first subpart of the rule because employers and employees have frequently requested clarification on these points.

The following paragraphs describe the changes OSHA has made to the Purpose provisions in Subpart A of the final rule, and discusses the Agency's reasons for these changes.

[The final rule's Purpose paragraph states "The purpose of this rule (Part 1904) is to require employers to record and report work-related fatalities, injuries and illnesses." It clearly and succinctly states OSHA's reasons for issuing the final rule.]

Employers have frequently asked OSHA to explain the relationship between workers' compensation reporting systems and the OSHA injury and illness recording and reporting requirements. As NYNEX

(Ex. 15: 199) noted,

[t]he issue of confusion between OSHA recordkeeping and workers' compensation/insurance requirements cannot be totally eliminated as the workers' compensation criteria vary somewhat from state to state. There will always be some differences between OSHA recordability and compensable injuries and illnesses. The potential consequences of these differences can be minimized, however, if all stakeholders in the recordkeeping process (i.e., employers, employees, labor unions, OSHA compliance officials) are well informed that OSHA recordability does not equate to compensation eligibility. This can be facilitated by printed reminders on all of the OSHA record-keeping documents (e.g., forms, instructions, pamphlets, compliance directives, etc.).

As NYNEX observed, employers must document work-related injuries and illnesses for both OSHA recordkeeping and workers' compensation purposes. Many cases that are recorded in the OSHA system are also compensable under the State workers' compensation system, but many others are not. However, the two systems have different purposes and scopes. The OSHA recordkeeping system is intended to collect, compile and analyze uniform and consistent nationwide data on occupational injuries and illnesses. The workers' compensation system, in contrast, is not designed primarily to generate and collect data but is intended primarily to provide medical coverage and compensation for workers who are killed, injured or made ill at work, and varies in coverage from one State to another.

Although the cases captured by the OSHA system and workers' compensation sometimes overlap, they often do not. For example, many injuries and illnesses covered by workers' compensation are not required to be recorded in the OSHA records. Such a situation would arise, for example, if an employee were injured on the job, sent to a hospital emergency room, and was examined and x-rayed by a physician, but was then told that the injury was minor and required no treatment. In this case, the employee's medical bills would be covered by workers' compensation insurance, but the case would not be recordable under Part 1904.

Conversely, an injury may be recordable for OSHA's purposes but not be covered by workers' compensation. For example, in some states, workers' compensation does not cover certain types of injuries (e.g., certain musculoskeletal disorders) and certain classes of workers (e.g., farm workers, contingent workers). However, if the injury meets OSHA recordability criteria it must be recorded even if the particular injury would not be compensable or the worker not be covered. Similarly, some injuries, although technically compensable under the state compensation system, do not result in the payment of workers' compensation benefits. For example, a worker who is injured on the job, receives treatment from the company physician, and returns to work without loss of wages would generally not receive workers' compensation because the company would usually absorb the costs. However, if the case meets the OSHA recording criteria, the employer would nevertheless be required to record the injury on the OSHA forms.

As a result of these differences between the two systems, recording a case does not mean that the case is compensable, or vice versa. When an injury or illness occurs to an employee, the employer must independently analyze the case in light of both the OSHA recording criteria and the requirements of the State workers' compensation system to determine whether the case is recordable or compensable, or both.

The American Federation of Labor and Congress of Industrial Organizations (AFL-CIO) urged OSHA to emphasize the no-fault philosophy of the Agency's recordkeeping system.

...

OSHA believes that the note to the Purpose paragraph of the final rule will allay any fears employers and employees may have about recording injuries and illnesses, and thus will encourage more accurate reporting. Both the Note to Subpart A of the final rule and the new OSHA Form 300 expressly state that recording a case does not indicate fault, negligence, or compensability.

...

OSHA has rejected the suggestion made by these commenters to limit the admissibility of the forms as evidence in a court proceeding. Such action is beyond the statutory authority of the agency, because OSHA has no authority over the courts, either Federal or State.

...

OSHA notes that many circumstances that lead to a recordable work-related injury or illness are "beyond the employer's control," at least as that phrase is commonly interpreted. Nevertheless, because such an injury or illness was caused, contributed to, or significantly aggravated by an event or exposure at work, it must be recorded on the OSHA form (assuming that it meets one or more of the recording criteria and does not qualify for an exemption to the geographic presumption). This approach is consistent with the no-fault recordkeeping

system OSHA has adopted, which includes work-related injuries and illnesses, regardless of the level of employer control or non-control involved. The issue of whether different types of cases are deemed work-related under the OSHA recordkeeping rule is discussed in the Legal Authority section, above, and in the work-relationship section (section 1904.5) of this preamble.

Subpart B. Scope [p. 5935]

The coverage and partial exemption provisions in Subpart B of the final rule establish which employers must keep OSHA injury and illness records at all times, and which employers are generally exempt but must keep records under specific circumstances. This subpart contains sections 1904.1 through 1904.3 of the final rule.

OSHA's recordkeeping rule covers many employers in OSHA's jurisdiction but continues to exempt many employers from the need to keep occupational injury and illness records routinely. This approach to the scope of the rule is consistent with that taken in the former recordkeeping rule. Whether a particular employer must keep these records routinely depends on the number of employees in the firm and on the Standard Industrial Classification, or SIC code, of each of the employer's establishments. Employers with 10 or fewer employees are not required to keep OSHA records routinely. In addition, employers whose establishments are classified in certain industries are not required to keep OSHA records under most circumstances. OSHA refers to establishments exempted by reason of size or industry classification as "partially exempt," for reasons explained below.

The final rule's size exemption and the industry exemptions listed in non-mandatory Appendix A to Subpart B of the final rule do not relieve employers with 10 or fewer employees or employers in these industries from all of their recordkeeping obligations under 29 CFR Part 1904. Employers qualifying for either the industry exemption or the employment size exemption are not routinely required to record work-related injuries and illnesses occurring to their employees, that is, they are not normally required to keep the OSHA

398

Log or OSHA Form 301. However, as sections 1904.1(a)(1) and 1904.2 of this final recordkeeping rule make clear, these employers must still comply with three discrete provisions of Part 1904. First, all employers covered by the Act must report work-related fatalities or multiple hospitalizations to OSHA under Sec. 1904.39. Second, under Sec. 1904.41, any employer may be required to provide occupational injury and illness reports to OSHA or OSHA's designee upon written request. Finally, under Sec. 1904.42, any employer may be required to respond to the Survey of Occupational Injuries and Illnesses conducted by the Bureau of Labor Statistics (BLS) if asked to do so. Each of these requirements is discussed in greater detail in the relevant portion of this summary and explanation.

Section 1904.1 Partial Exemption for Employers With 10 or Fewer Employees [p. 5935]

In Sec. 1904.1 of the final rule, OSHA has retained the former rule's size-based exemption, which exempts employers with 10 or fewer employees in all industries covered by OSHA from most recordkeeping requirements. Section 1904.1, "Partial exemption for employers with 10 or fewer employees," states that:

(a) Basic requirement.
  (1) If your company had ten (10) or fewer employees at all times during the last calendar year, you do not need to keep OSHA injury and illness records unless OSHA or the BLS informs you in writing that you must keep records under Sec. 1904.41 or Sec. 1904.42. However, as required by Sec. 1904.39, all employers covered by the OSH Act must report to OSHA any workplace incident that results in a fatality or the hospitalization of three or more employees.
  (2) If your company had more than ten (10) employees at any time during the last calendar year, you must keep OSHA injury and illness records unless your establishment is classified as a partially exempt industry under Sec. 1904.2.

(b) Implementation.
  (1) Is the partial exemption for size based on the size of my entire company or on the size of an individual business establishment?
    The partial exemption for size is based on the number of employees in the entire company.
  (2) How do I determine the size of my company to find out if I qualify for the partial exemption for size?
  To determine if you are exempt because of size, you need to determine your company's peak employment during the last calendar year. If you had no more than 10 employees at any time in the last calendar year, your company qualifies for the partial exemption for size.

The Size-Based Exemption in the Former Rule
The final rule published today maintains the former rule's partial exemption for employers in all covered industries who have 10 or fewer employees. Under the final rule (and the former rule), an employer in any industry who employed no more than 10 employees at any time during the preceding calendar year is not required to maintain OSHA records of occupational illnesses and injuries during the current year unless requested to do so in writing by OSHA (under Sec. 1904.41) or the BLS (under Sec. 1904.42). If an employer employed 11 or more people at a given time during the year, however, that employer is not eligible for the size-based partial exemption.

[Size Exemption Threshold for Construction Companies]
In the final rule, OSHA has decided to continue the Agency's longstanding practice of partially exempting employers with 10 or fewer employees from most recordkeeping requirements, but not to extend the exemption to non-construction businesses with 19 or fewer employees, as was proposed.

Section 1904.2 Partial Exemption for Establishments in Certain Industries [p. 5939]

Section 1904.2 of the final rule partially exempts employers with establishments classified in certain lower-hazard industries. The final rule updates the former rule's listing of partially exempted lower-hazard industries. Lower-hazard industries are those Standard Industrial Classification (SIC) code industries within SICs 52-89 that have an average Days Away, Restricted, or Transferred (DART) rate at or below 75% of the national average DART rate. The former rule also contained such a list based on data from 1978-1980. The final rule's list differs from that of the former rule in two respects: (1) the hazard information supporting the final rule's lower-hazard industry exemptions is based on the most recent three years of BLS statistics (1996, 1997, 1998), and (2) the exception is calculated at the 3-digit rather than 2-digit level.

The changes in the final rule's industry exemptions are designed to require more employers in higher-hazard industries to keep records all of the time and to exempt employers in certain lower-hazard industries from keeping OSHA injury and illness records routinely. For example, compared with the former rule, the final rule requires many employers in the 3-digit industries within retail and service sector industries that have higher rates of occupational injuries and illnesses to keep these records but exempts employers in 3-digit industries within those industries that report a lower rate of occupational injury and illness. Section 1904.2 of the final rule, "Partial exemption for establishments in certain industries," states:

(a) Basic requirement.
  (1) If your business establishment is classified in a specific low hazard retail, service, finance, insurance or real estate industry listed in Appendix A to this Subpart B, you do not need to keep OSHA injury and illness records unless the government asks you to keep the records under Sec. 1904.41 or Sec. 1904.42. However, all employers must report to OSHA any workplace incident that results in a fatality or the hospitalization of three or more employees (see Sec. 1904.39).
  (2) If one or more of your company's establishments are classified in a non-exempt industry, you must keep OSHA injury and illness records for all of such establishments unless your company is partially exempted because of size under Sec. 1904.1.

(b) Implementation.
  (1) Does the partial industry classification exemption apply only to business establishments in the retail, services, finance, insurance or real estate industries (SICs 52-89)?
Yes. Business establishments classified in agriculture; mining; construction; manufacturing; transportation; communication, electric, gas and sanitary services; or wholesale trade are not eligible for the partial industry classification exemption.

  (2) Is the partial industry classification exemption based on the industry classification of my entire company or on the classification of individual business establishments operated by my company?
The partial industry classification exemption applies to individual business establishments. If a company has several business establishments engaged in different classes of business activities, some of the company's establishments may be required to keep records, while others may be exempt.

  (3) How do I determine the Standard Industrial Classification code for my company or for individual establishments?
You determine your Standard Industrial Classification (SIC) code by using the Standard Industrial Classification Manual, Executive Office of the President, Office of Management and Budget. You may contact your nearest OSHA office or State agency for help in determining your SIC.

Employers with establishments in those industry sectors shown in Appendix A are not required routinely to keep OSHA records for their establishments. They must, however, keep records if requested to do so by the Bureau of Labor Statistics in connection with its Annual Survey (section 1904.42) or by OSHA in connection with its Data Initiative (section 1904.41). In addition, all employers covered by the OSH Act must report a work-related fatality, or an accident that results in the hospitalization of three or more employees, to OSHA within 8 hours (section 1904.39).

...

Evaluating industries at the 3-digit level allows OSHA to identify 3-digit industries with high LWDI rates (DART rates in the terminology of the final rule) that are located within 2-digit industries with relatively low rates. Conversely, use of this approach allows OSHA to identify lower-hazard 3-digit industries within a 2-digit industry that have relatively high LWDI (DART) rates. Use of LWDI (DART) rates at the more detailed level of SIC coding increases the specificity of the targeting of the exemptions and makes the rule more equitable by exempting workplaces in lower-hazard industries and requiring employers in more hazardous industries to keep records.

...

For multi-establishment firms, the industry exemption is based on the SIC code of each establishment, rather than the industrial classification of a firm as a whole. For example, some larger corporations have establishments that engage in different business activities. Where this is the case, each establishment could fall into a different SIC code, based on its business activity. The Standard Industrial Classification manual states that the establishment, rather than the firm, is the appropriate unit for determining the SIC code. Thus, depending on the SIC code of the establishment, one establishment of a firm may be exempt from routine recordkeeping under Part 1904, while another establishment in the same company may not be exempt.

...

For those States with OSHA-approved State plans, the state is generally required to adopt Federal OSHA rules, or a State rule that is at least as effective as the Federal OSHA rule. States with approved plans do not need to exempt employers from recordkeeping, either by employer size or by industry classification, as the final Federal OSHA rule does, although they may choose to do so. For example, States with approved plans may require records from a wider universe of employers than Federal OSHA does. These States cannot exempt more industries or employers than Federal OSHA does, however, because doing so would result in a State rule that is not as effective as the Federal rule. A larger discussion of the effect on the State plans can be found in Section VIII of this preamble, State Plans.

Recordkeeping Under the Requirements of Other Federal Agencies

Section 1904.3 of the final rule provides guidance for employers who are subject to the occupational injury and illness recording and reporting requirements of other Federal agencies. Several other Federal agencies have similar requirements, such as the Mine Safety and Health Administration (MSHA), the Department of Energy (DOE), and the Federal Railroad Administration (FRA). The final rule at section 1904.3 tells the employer that OSHA will accept those records in place of the employer's Part 1904 records under two circumstances: (1) if OSHA has entered into a memorandum of understanding (MOU) with that agency that specifically accepts the other agency's records, the employer may use them in place of the OSHA records, or (2) if the other agency's records include the same information required by Part 1904, OSHA would consider them an acceptable substitute.

...

Subpart C. Recordkeeping Forms and Recording Criteria [p. 5945]

Subpart C of the final rule sets out the requirements of the rule for recording cases in the recordkeeping system. It contains provisions directing employers to keep records of the recordable occupational injuries and illnesses experienced by their employees, describes the forms the employer must use, and establishes the criteria that employers must follow to determine which work-related injury and illness cases must be entered onto the forms. Subpart C contains sections 1904.4 through 1904.29.

Section 1904.4 provides an overview of the requirements in Subpart C and contains a flowchart describing the recording process. How employers are to determine whether a given injury or illness is work-related is set out in section 1904.5. Section 1904.6 provides the requirements employers must follow to determine whether or not a work-related injury or illness is a new case or the continuation of a previously recorded injury or illness. Sections 1904.7 through 1904.12 contain the recording criteria for determining which new work-related injuries and illnesses must be recorded on the

OSHA forms. Section 1904.29 explains which forms must be used and indicates the circumstances under which the employer may use substitute forms.

Section 1904.4 Recording Criteria [p. 5945]

Section 1904.4 of the final rule contains provisions mandating the recording of work-related injuries and illnesses that must be entered on the OSHA 300 (Log) and 301 (Incident Report) forms. It sets out the recording requirements that employers are required to follow in recording cases.

Paragraph 1904.4(a) of the final rule mandates that each employer who is required by OSHA to keep records must record each fatality, injury or illness that is work-related, is a new case and not a continuation of an old case, and meets one or more of the general recording criteria in section 1904.7 or the additional criteria for specific cases found in sections 1904.8 through 1904.12. Paragraph (b) contains provisions implementing this basic requirement.

Paragraph 1904.4(b)(1) contains a table that points employers and their recordkeepers to the various sections of the rule that determine which work-related injuries and illnesses are to be recorded. These sections lay out the requirements for determining whether an injury or illness is work-related, if it is a new case, and if it meets one or more of the general recording criteria. In addition, the table contains a row addressing the application of these and additional criteria to specific kinds of cases (needlestick and sharps injury cases, tuberculosis cases, hearing loss cases, medical removal cases, and musculoskeletal disorder cases). The table in paragraph 1904.4(b)(1) is intended to guide employers through the recording process and to act as a table of contents to the sections of Subpart C.

Paragraph (b)(2) is a decision tree, or flowchart, that shows the steps involved in determining whether or not a particular injury or illness case must be recorded on the OSHA forms. It essentially reflects the same information as is in the table in paragraph 1904.4(b)(1), except that it presents this information graphically.

...

Section 1904.5 Determination of Work-Relatedness [p. 5946]

This section of the final rule sets out the requirements employers must follow in determining whether a given injury or illness is work-related. Paragraph 1904.5(a) states that an injury or illness must be considered work-related if an event or exposure in the work environment caused or contributed to the injury or illness or significantly aggravated a pre-existing injury or illness. It stipulates that, for OSHA recordkeeping purposes, work relationship is presumed for such injuries and illnesses unless an exception listed in paragraph 1904.5(b)(2) specifically applies.

Implementation requirements are set forth in paragraph (b) of the final rule. Paragraph (b)(1) defines "work environment" for recordkeeping purposes and makes clear that the work environment includes the physical locations where employees are working as well as the equipment and materials used by the employee to perform work.

Paragraph (b)(2) lists the exceptions to the presumption of work-relatedness permitted by the final rule; cases meeting the conditions of any of the listed exceptions are not considered work-related and are therefore not recordable in the OSHA recordkeeping system.

This section of the preamble first explains OSHA's reasoning on the issue of work relationship, then discusses the exceptions to the general presumption and the comments received on the exceptions proposed, and then presents OSHA's rationale for including paragraphs (b)(3) through (b)(7) of the final rule, and the record evidence pertaining to each.
...

Final Rule's Exceptions to the Geographic Presumption

Paragraph 1904.5(b)(2) of the final rule contains eight exceptions to the work environment presumption that are intended to exclude from the recordkeeping system those injuries and illnesses that occur or manifest in the work environment, but have been identified by OSHA, based on its years of experience with recordkeeping, as cases that do not provide information useful to the identification of occupational injuries and illnesses and would thus tend to skew national injury and illness statistics. These eight exceptions are the only exceptions to the presumption permitted by the final rule.

(i) Injuries or illnesses will not be considered work-related if, at the time of the injury or illness, the employee was present in the work environment as a member of the general public rather than as an employee. This exception, which is codified at paragraph 1904.5(b)(2)(i), is based on the fact that no employment relationship is in place at the time an injury or illness of this type occurs. A case exemplifying this exception would occur if an employee of a retail store patronized that store as a customer on a non-work day and was injured in a fall. This exception allows the employer not to record cases that occur outside of the employment relationship when his or her establishment is also a public place and a worker happens to be using the facility as a member of the general public. In these situations, the injury or illness has nothing to do with the employee's work or the employee's status as an employee, and it would therefore be inappropriate for the recordkeeping system to capture the case.

...

(ii) Injuries or illnesses will not be considered work-related if they involve symptoms that surface at work but result solely from a non-work-related event or exposure that occurs outside the work environment. OSHA's recordkeeping system is intended only to capture cases that are caused by conditions or exposures arising in the work environment. It is not designed to capture cases that have no relationship with the work environment. For this exception to apply, the work environment cannot have caused, contributed to, or significantly aggravated the injury or illness. This exception is consistent with the position followed by OSHA for many years and reiterated in the final rule: that any job-related contribution to the injury or illness makes the incident work-related, and its corollary—that any injury or illness to which work makes no actual contribution is not work-related. An example of this

type of injury would be a diabetic incident that occurs while an employee is working. Because no event or exposure at work contributed in any way to the diabetic incident, the case is not recordable. This exception allows the employer to exclude cases where an employee's non-work activities are the sole cause of the injury or illness.

...

(iii) Injuries and illnesses will not be considered work-related if they result solely from voluntary participation in a wellness program or in a medical, fitness, or recreational activity such as blood donation, physical, flu shot, exercise classes, racquetball, or baseball. This exception allows the employer to exclude certain injury or illness cases that are related to personal medical care, physical fitness activities and voluntary blood donations. The key words here are "solely" and "voluntary." The work environment cannot have contributed to the injury or illness in any way for this exception to apply, and participation in the wellness, fitness or recreational activities must be voluntary and not a condition of employment. This exception allows the employer to exclude cases that are related to personal matters of exercise, recreation, medical examinations or participation in blood donation programs when they are voluntary and are not being undertaken as a condition of work. For example, if a clerical worker was injured while performing aerobics in the company gymnasium during his or her lunch hour, the case would not be work-related. On the other hand, if an employee who was assigned to manage the gymnasium was injured while teaching an aerobics class, the injury would be work-related because the employee was working at the time of the injury and the activity was not voluntary. Similarly, if an employee suffered a severe reaction to a flu shot that was administered as part of a voluntary inoculation program, the case would not be considered work-related; however, if an employee suffered a reaction to medications administered to enable the employee to travel overseas on business, or the employee had an illness reaction to a medication administered to treat a work-related injury, the case would be considered work-related.

...

(iv) Injuries and illnesses will not be considered work-related if they are solely the result of an employee eating, drinking, or preparing food or drink for personal consumption (whether bought on the premises or brought in). This exception responds to a situation that has given rise to many letters of interpretation and caused employer concern over the years. An example of the application of this exception would be a case where the employee injured himself or herself by choking on a sandwich brought from home but eaten in the employer's establishment; such a case would not be considered work-related under this exception. On the other hand, if the employee was injured by a trip or fall hazard present in the employer's lunchroom, the case would be considered work-related. In addition, a note to the exception makes clear that if an employee becomes ill as a result of ingesting food contaminated by workplace contaminants such as lead, or contracts food poisoning from food items provided by the employer, the case would be considered work-related. As a result, if an employee contracts food poisoning from a sandwich brought from home or purchased in the company cafeteria and must take time off to recover, the case is not considered work related. On the other hand, if an employee contracts food poisoning from a meal provided by the employer at a business meeting or company function and takes time off to recover, the case would be considered work related. Food provided or supplied by the employer does not include food purchased by the employee from the company cafeteria, but does include food purchased by the employer from the company cafeteria for business meetings or other company functions. OSHA believes that the number of cases to which this exception applies will be few.

...

(v) Injuries and illnesses will not be considered work-related if they are solely the result of employees doing personal tasks (unrelated to their employment) at the establishment outside of their assigned working hours. This exception, which responds to inquiries received over the years, allows employers limited flexibility to exclude from the recordkeeping system situations where the employee is using the employer's establishment for purely personal reasons during his or her off-shift time. For example, if an employee were using a meeting room at the employer's establishment outside of his or her assigned working hours to hold a meeting for a civic group to which he or she belonged, and slipped and fell in the hallway, the injury would not be considered work-related. On the other hand, if the employee were at the employer's establishment outside his or her assigned working hours to attend a company business meeting or a company training session, such a slip or fall would be work-related. OSHA also expects the number of cases affected by this exception to be small.

...

(vi) Injuries and illnesses will not be considered work-related if they are solely the result of personal grooming, self-medication for a non-work-related condition, or are intentionally self-inflicted. This exception allows the employer to exclude from the Log cases related to personal hygiene, self-administered medications and intentional self-inflicted injuries, such as attempted suicide. For example, a burn injury from a hair dryer used at work to dry the employee's hair would not be work-related. Similarly, a negative reaction to a medication brought from home to treat a non-work condition would not be considered a work-related illness, even though it first manifested at work. OSHA also expects that few cases will be affected by this exception.

...

(vii) Injuries will not be considered work-related if they are caused by motor vehicle accidents occurring in company parking lots or on company access roads while employees are commuting to or from work. This exception allows the employer to exclude cases where an employee is injured in a motor vehicle accident while commuting from work to home or from home to work or while on a personal errand. For example, if an employee was injured in a car accident while arriving at work or while leaving the company's property at the end of the day, or while driving on his or her lunch hour to run an errand, the case would not be considered work-related. On the other hand, if an employee was injured in a car accident while leaving the property to purchase supplies for the employer, the case would be work-related. This exception represents a change from the position taken under the former rule, which was that no injury or illness occurring in a company parking lot was considered work-related. As explained further below, OSHA has concluded, based on the evidence in the record, that some injuries and illnesses that occur in company parking lots are clearly caused by work conditions or activities—e.g., being struck by a car while painting parking space indicators on the pavement of the lot, slipping on ice permitted to accumulate in the lot by the employer—and by their nature point to conditions that could be corrected to improve workplace safety and health.

(viii) Common colds and flu will not be considered work-related. Paragraph 1904.5(b)(2)(viii) allows the employer to exclude cases of common cold or flu, even if contracted while the employee was at work. However, in the case of other infectious diseases such as tuberculosis, brucellosis, and hepatitis C, employers must evaluate reports of such illnesses for work relationship, just as they would any other type of injury or illness.

(ix) Mental illness will not be considered work-related unless the employee voluntarily provides the employer with an opinion from a physician or other licensed health care professional with appropriate training and experience (psychiatrist, psychologist, psychiatric nurse practitioner, etc.) stating that the employee has a mental illness that is work-related.

...

OSHA agrees that recording work-related mental illnesses involves several unique issues, including the difficulty of detecting, diagnosing and verifying mental illnesses; and the sensitivity and privacy concerns raised by mental illnesses. Therefore, the final rule requires employers to record only those mental illnesses verified by a health care professional with appropriate training and experience in the treatment of mental illness, such as a psychiatrist, psychologist, or psychiatric nurse practitioner. The employer is under no obligation to seek out information on mental illnesses from its employees, and employers are required to consider mental illness cases only when an employee voluntarily presents the employer with an opinion from the health care professional that the employee has a mental illness and that it is work related. In the event that the employer does not believe the reported mental illness is work-related, the employer may refer the case to a physician or other licensed health care professional for a second opinion.

OSHA also emphasizes that work-related mental illnesses, like other illnesses, must be recorded only when they meet the severity criteria outlined in Sec. 1904.7. In addition, for mental illnesses, the employee's identity must be protected by omitting the employee's name from the OSHA 300 Log and instead entering "privacy concern case" as required by Sec. 1904.29.

...

Determining Whether the Precipitating Event or Exposure Occurred in the Work Environment or Elsewhere

Paragraph 1904.5(b)(3) of the final rule provides guidance on applying the geographic presumption when it is not clear whether the event or exposure that precipitated the injury or illness occurred in the work environment or elsewhere. If an employee reports pain and swelling in a joint but cannot say whether the symptoms first arose during work or during recreational activities at home, it may be difficult for the employer to decide whether the case is work-related. The same problem arises when an employee reports symptoms of a contagious disease that affects the public at large, such as a staphylococcus infection ("staph" infection) or Lyme disease, and the workplace is only one possible source of the infection. In these situations, the employer must examine the employee's work duties and environment to determine whether it is more likely than not that one or more events or exposures at work caused or contributed to the condition. If the employer determines that it is unlikely that the precipitating event or exposure occurred in the work environment, the employer would not record the case. In the staph infection example given above, the employer would consider the case work-related, for example, if another employee with whom the newly infected employee had contact at work had been out with a staph infection. In the Lyme disease example, the employer would determine the case to be work-related if, for example, the employee was a groundskeeper with regular exposure to outdoor conditions likely to result in contact with deer ticks.

In applying paragraph 1904.5(b)(3), the question employers must answer is whether the precipitating event or exposure occurred in the work environment. If an event, such as a fall, an awkward motion or lift, an assault, or an instance of horseplay, occurs at work, the geographic presumption applies and the case is work-related unless it otherwise falls within an exception. Thus, if an employee trips while walking across a level factory floor, the resulting injury is considered work-related under the geographic presumption because the precipitating event—the tripping accident—occurred in the workplace.

The case is work-related even if the employer cannot determine why the employee tripped, or whether any particular workplace hazard caused the accident to occur. However, if the employee reports an injury at work but cannot say whether it resulted from an event that occurred at work or at home, as in the example of the swollen joint, the employer might determine that the case is not work-related because the employee's work duties were unlikely to have caused, contributed to, or significantly aggravated such an injury.

Significant Workplace Aggravation of a Pre-existing Condition

In paragraph 1904.5(b)(4), the final rule makes an important change to the former rule's posi-

tion on the extent of the workplace aggravation of a preexisting injury or illness that must occur before the case is considered work-related. In the past, any amount of aggravation of such an injury or illness was considered sufficient for this purpose. The final rule, however, requires that the amount of aggravation of the injury or illness that work contributes must be "significant," i.e., non-minor, before work-relatedness is established. The preexisting injury or illness must be one caused entirely by non-occupational factors.

...

Paragraph 1904.5(b)(4) of the final rule defines aggravation as significant if the contribution of the aggravation at work is such that it results in tangible consequences that go beyond those that the worker would have experienced as a result of the preexisting injury or illness alone, absent the aggravating effects of the workplace. Under the final rule, a preexisting injury or illness will be considered to have been significantly aggravated, for the purposes of OSHA injury and illness recordkeeping, when an event or exposure in the work environment results in: (i) Death, providing that the preexisting injury or illness would likely not have resulted in death but for the occupational event or exposure; (ii) Loss of consciousness, providing that the preexisting injury or illness would likely not have resulted in loss of consciousness but for the occupational event or exposure; (iii) A day or days away from work or of restricted work, or a job transfer that otherwise would not have occurred but for the occupational event or exposure; or (iv) Medical treatment where no medical treatment was needed for the injury or illness before the workplace event or exposure, or a change in the course of medical treatment that was being provided before the workplace event or exposure. OSHA's decision not to require the recording of cases involving only minor aggravation of preexisting conditions is consistent with the Agency's efforts in this rulemaking to require the recording only of non-minor injuries and illnesses; for example, the final rule also no longer requires employers to record minor illnesses on the Log.

Preexisting Conditions

Paragraph 1904.5(b)(5) stipulates that pre-existing conditions, for recordkeeping purposes, are conditions that resulted solely from a non-work-related event or exposure that occurs outside the employer's work environment. Pre-existing conditions also include any injury or illness that the employee experienced while working for another employer.

Off Premises Determinations

Employees may be injured or become ill as a result of events or exposures away from the employer's establishment. In these cases, OSHA proposed to consider the case work-related only if the employee was engaged in a work activity or was present as a condition of employment (61 FR 4063). In the final rule, (paragraph 1904.5(b)(1)) the same concept is carried forward in the definition of the work environment, which defines the environment as including the establishment and any other location where one or more employees are working or are present as a condition of their employment.

Thus, when employees are working or conducting other tasks in the interest of their employer but at a location away from the employer's establishment, the work-relatedness of an injury or illness that arises is subject to the same decision making process that would occur if the case had occurred at the establishment itself. The case is work-related if one or more events or exposures in the work environment either caused or contributed to the resulting condition or significantly aggravated a pre-existing condition, as stated in paragraph 1904.5(a). In addition, the exceptions for determining work relationship at paragraph 1904.5(b)(2) and the requirements at paragraph 1904.5(b)(3) apply equally to cases that occur at or away from the establishment.

As an example, the work-environment presumption clearly applies to the case of a delivery driver who experiences an injury to his or her back while loading boxes and transporting them into a building. The worker is engaged in a work activity and the injury resulted from an event—loading/unloading—occurring in the work environment. Similarly, if an employee is injured in an automobile accident while running errands for the company or traveling to make a speech on behalf of the company, the employee is present at the scene as a condition of employment, and any resulting injury would be work-related.

Employees on Travel Status

The final rule continues (at Sec. 1904.5(b)(6)) OSHA's longstanding practice of treating injuries and illnesses that occur to an employee on travel status as work-related if, at the time of the injury or illness, the employee was engaged in work activities "in the interest of the employer." Examples of such activities include travel to and from customer contacts, conducting job tasks, and entertaining or being entertained if the activity is conducted at the direction of the employer.

The final rule contains three exceptions for travel-status situations. The rule describes situations in which injuries or illnesses sustained by traveling employees are not considered work-related for OSHA recordkeeping purposes and therefore do not have to be recorded on the OSHA 300 Log. First, when a traveling employee checks into a hotel, motel, or other temporary residence, he or she is considered to have established a "home away from home." At this time, the status of the employee is the same as that of an employee working at an establishment who leaves work and is essentially "at home". Injuries and illnesses that occur at home are generally not considered work related. However, just as an employer may sometimes be required to record an injury or illness occurring to an employee working in his or her home, the employer is required to record an injury or illness occurring to an employee who is working in his or her hotel room (see the discussion of working at home, below).

Second, if an employee has established a "home away from home" and is reporting to a fixed worksite each day, the employer does not consider injuries or illnesses work-related if they occur while the employee is commuting between the temporary residence and the job location. These cases are parallel to those involving employees commuting to and from work when they are at their home location, and do not have to be recorded, just as injuries and illnesses that occur during normal commuting are not required to be recorded.

Third, the employer is not required to consider an injury or illness to be work-related if it occurs while the employee is on a personal detour from the route of business travel. This exception allows the employer to exclude injuries and illnesses that occur when the worker has taken a side trip for personal reasons while on a business trip, such as a vacation or sightseeing excursion, to visit relatives, or for some other personal purpose.

...

Working at Home

The final rule also includes provisions at Sec. 1904.5(b)(7) for determining the work-relatedness of injuries and illnesses that may arise when employees are working at home. When an employee is working on company business in his or her home and reports an injury or illness to his or her employer, and the employee's work activities caused or contributed to the injury or illness, or significantly aggravated a pre-existing injury, the case is considered work-related and must be further evaluated to determine whether it meets the recording criteria. If the injury or illness is related to non-work activities or to the general home environment, the case is not considered work-related.

...

OSHA has recently issued a compliance directive (CPL 2-0.125) containing the Agency's response to many of the questions raised by this commenter. That document clarifies that OSHA will not conduct inspections of home offices and does not hold employers liable for employees' home offices. The compliance directive also notes that employers required by the recordkeeping rule to keep records "will continue to be responsible for keeping such records, regardless of whether the injuries occur in the factory, in a home office, or elsewhere, as long as they are work-related, and meet the recordability criteria of 29 CFR Part 1904."

With more employees working at home under various telecommuting and flexible workplace arrangements, OSHA believes that it is important to record injuries and illnesses attributable to work tasks performed at home. If these cases are not recorded, the Nation's injury and illness statistics could be skewed. For example, placing such an exclusion in the final rule would make it difficult to determine if a decline in the overall number or rate of occupational injuries and illnesses is attributable to a trend toward working at home or to a change in the Nation's actual injury and illness experience. Further, excluding these work-related injuries and illnesses from the recordkeeping system could potentially obscure previously unidentified causal connections between events or exposures in the work environment and these incidents. OSHA is unwilling to adopt an exception that would have these potential effects.

...

Section 1904.6 Determination of New Cases [p. 5962]

Employers may occasionally have difficulty in determining whether new signs or symptoms are due to a new event or exposure in the workplace or whether they are the continuation of an existing work-related injury or illness. Most occupational injury and illness cases are fairly discrete events, i.e., events in which an injury or acute illness occurs, is treated, and then resolves completely. For example, a worker may suffer a cut, bruise, or rash from a clearly recognized event in the workplace, receive treatment, and recover fully within a few weeks. At some future time, the worker may suffer another cut, bruise or rash from another workplace event. In such cases, it is clear that the two injuries or illnesses are unrelated events, and that each represents an injury or illness that must be separately evaluated for its recordability.

However, it is sometimes difficult to determine whether signs or symptoms are due to a new event or exposure, or are a continuance of an injury or illness that has already been recorded. This is an important distinction, because a new injury or illness requires the employer to make a new entry on the OSHA 300 Log, while a continuation of an old recorded case requires, at most, an updating of the original entry.

Section 1904.6 of the final rule being published today explains what employers must do to determine whether or not an injury or illness is a new case for recordkeeping purposes.

The basic requirement at Sec. 1904.6(a) states that the employer must consider an injury or illness a new case to be evaluated for recordability if (1) the employee has not previously experienced a recorded injury or illness of the same type that affects the same part of the body, or (2) the employee previously experienced a recorded injury or illness of the same type that affected the same part of the body but had recovered completely (all signs and symptoms of the previous injury or illness had disappeared) and an event or exposure in the work environment caused the injury or illness, or its signs or symptoms, to reappear.

The implementation question at Sec. 1904.6(b)(1) addresses chronic work-related cases that have already been recorded once and distinguishes between those conditions that will progress even in the absence of workplace exposure and those that are triggered by events in the workplace. There are some conditions that will progress even in the absence of further exposure, such as some occupational cancers, advanced asbestosis, tuberculosis disease, advanced byssinosis, advanced silicosis, etc. These conditions are chronic; once the disease is contracted it may never be cured or completely resolved, and therefore the case is never "closed" under the OSHA recordkeeping system, even though the signs and symptoms of the condition may alternate between remission and active disease.

However, there are other chronic work-related illness conditions, such as occupational asthma, reactive airways dysfunction syndrome (RADs), and sensitization (contact) dermatitis, that recur if the ill individual is exposed to the agent (or agents, in the case of cross-reactivities or RADs) that triggers the illness again. It is typical, but not always the case, for individuals with these conditions to be symptom-free if exposure to the sensitizing or precipitating agent does not occur.

The final rule provides, at paragraph (b)(1), that the employer is not required to record as a new case a previously recorded case of chronic work-related illness where the signs or symptoms have recurred or continued in the absence of exposure in the workplace. This paragraph recognizes that there are occupational illnesses that may be diagnosed at some stage of the disease and may then progress without regard to workplace events or exposures. Such diseases, in other words, will progress without further workplace exposure to the toxic substance(s) that caused the disease. Examples of such chronic work-related diseases are silicosis, tuberculosis, and asbestosis. With these conditions, the ill worker will show signs (such as a positive TB skin test, a positive chest roentgenogram, etc.) at every medical examination, and may experience symptomatic bouts as the disease progresses.

Paragraph 1904.6(b)(2) recognizes that many chronic occupational illnesses, however, such as occupational asthma, RADs, and contact dermatitis, are triggered by exposures in the workplace. The difference between these conditions and those addressed in paragraph 1904.6(b)(1) is that in these cases exposure triggers the recurrence of symptoms and signs, while in the chronic cases covered in the previous paragraph, the symptoms and signs recur even in the absence of exposure in the workplace.

Paragraph 1904.6(b)(3) addresses how to record a case for which the employer requests a physician or other licensed health care professional (HCP) to make a new case/continuation of an old case determination. Paragraph (b)(3) makes clear that employers are to follow the guidance provided by the HCP for OSHA recordkeeping purposes. In cases where two or more HCPs make conflicting or differing recommendations, the employer is required to base his or her decision about recordation based on the most authoritative (best documented, best reasoned, or most persuasive) evidence or recommendation.

...

Section 1904.7 General Recording Criteria [p. 5968]

Section 1904.7 contains the general recording criteria for recording work-related injuries and illnesses. This section describes the recording of cases that meet one or more of the following six criteria: death, days away from work, restricted work or transfer to another job, medical treatment beyond first aid, loss of consciousness, or diagnosis as a significant injury or illness by a physician or other licensed health care professional.

Paragraph 1904.7(a)

Paragraph 1904.7(a) describes the basic requirement for recording an injury or illness in the OSHA recordkeeping system. It states that employers must record any work-related injury or illness that meets one or more of the final rule's general recording criteria. There are six such criteria: death, days away from work, days on restricted work or on job transfer, medical treatment beyond first aid, loss of consciousness, or diagnosis by a physician or other licensed heath care professional as a significant injury or illness. Although most cases are recorded because they meet one of these criteria, some cases may meet more than one criterion as the case continues. For example, an injured worker may initially be sent home to recuperate (making the case recordable as a "days away" case) and then subsequently return to work on a restricted ("light duty") basis (meeting a second criterion, that for restricted work). (see the discussion in Section 1904.29 for information on how to record such cases.)

Paragraph 1904.7(b)

Paragraph 1904.7(b) tells employers how to record cases meeting each of the six general recording criteria and states how each case is to be entered on the OSHA 300 Log. Paragraph 1904.7(b)(1) provides a simple decision table listing the six general recording criteria and the paragraph number of each in the final rule. It is included to aid employers and recordkeepers in recording these cases.

1904.7(b)(2) Death

Paragraph 1904.7(b)(2) requires the employer to record an injury or illness that results in death by entering a check mark on the OSHA 300 Log in the space for fatal cases. This paragraph also directs employers to report work-related fatalities to OSHA within 8 hours and cross references the fatality and catastrophe reporting requirements in Sec. 1904.39 of the final rule, Reporting fatalities and multiple hospitalizations to OSHA. Paragraph 1904.7(b)(2) implements the OSH Act's requirements to record all cases resulting in work-related deaths.
...

Paragraph 1904.7(b)(3) Days Away From Work

Paragraph 1904.7(b)(3) contains the requirements for recording work-related injuries and illnesses that result in days away from work and for counting the total number of days away associated with a given case. Paragraph 1904.7(b)(3) requires the employer to record an injury or illness that involves one or more days away from work by placing a check mark on the OSHA 300 Log in the space reserved for day(s) away cases and entering the number of calendar days away from work in the column reserved for that purpose. This paragraph also states that, if the employee is away from work for an extended time, the employer must update the day count when the actual number of days away becomes known. This requirement continues the day counting requirements of the former rule and revises the days away requirements in response to comments in the record.

Paragraphs 1904.7(b)(3)(i) through (vi) implement the basic requirements. Paragraph 1904.7(b)(3)(i) states that the employer is not to count the day of the injury or illness as a day away, but is to begin counting days away on the following day. Thus, even though an injury or illness may result in some loss of time on the day of the injurious event or exposure because, for example, the employee seeks treatment or is sent home, the case is not considered a days-away-from-work case unless the employee does not work on at least one subsequent day because of the injury or illness. The employer is to begin counting days away on the day following the injury or onset of illness. This policy is a continuation of OSHA's practice under the former rule, which also excluded the day of injury or onset of illness from the day counts.

Paragraphs 1904.7(b)(3)(ii) and (iii) direct employers how to record days-away cases when a physician or other licensed health care professional (HCP) recommends that the injured or ill worker stay at home or that he or she return to work but the employee chooses not to do so. As these paragraphs make clear, OSHA requires employers to follow the physician's or HCP's recommendation when recording the case.

Further, whether the employee works or not is in the control of the employer, not the employee. That is, if an HCP recommends that the employee remain away from work for one or more days, the employer is required to record the injury or illness as a case involving days away from work and to keep track of the days; the employee's wishes in this case are not relevant, since it is the employer who controls the conditions of work. Similarly, if the HCP tells the employee that he or she can return to work, the employer is required by the rule to stop counting the days away from work, even if the employee chooses not to return to work. These policies are a continuation of OSHA's previous policy of requiring employees to follow the recommendations of health care professionals when recording cases in the OSHA system. OSHA is aware that there may be situations where the employer obtains an opinion from a physician or other health care professional and a subsequent HCP's opinion differs from the first. (The subsequent opinion could be that of an HCP retained by the employer or the employee.) In this case, the employer is the ultimate record-keeping decision-maker and must resolve the differences in opinion; he or she may turn to a third HCP for this purpose, or may make the recordability decision himself or herself.

Paragraph 1904.7(b)(3)(iv) specifies how the employer is to account for weekends, holidays, and other days during which the employee was unable to work because of a work-related injury or illness during a period in which the employee was not scheduled to work. The rule requires the employer to count the number of calendar days the employee was unable to work because of the work-related injury or illness, regardless of whether or not the employee would have been scheduled to work on those calendar days. This provision will ensure that a measure of the length of disability is available, regardless of the employee's work schedule. This requirement is a change from the former policy, which focused on scheduled workdays missed due to injury or illness and excluded from the days away count any normal days off, holidays, and other days the employee would not have worked.

Paragraph 1904.7(b)(3)(v) tells the employer how to count days away for a case where the employee is injured or becomes ill on the last day of work before some scheduled time off, such as on the Friday before the weekend or the day before a scheduled vacation, and returns to work on the next day that he or she was scheduled to work. In this situation, the employer must decide if the worker would have been able to work on the days when he or she was not at work. In other words, the employer is not required to count as days away any of the days on which the employee would have been able to work but did not because the facility was closed, the employee was not scheduled to work, or for other reasons unrelated to the injury or illness. However, if the employer determines that the employee's injury or illness would have kept the employee from being able to work for part or all of time the employee was away, those days must be counted toward the days away total.

Paragraph 1904.7(b)(3)(vi) allows the employer to stop counting the days away from work when the injury or illness has resulted in 180 calendar days away from work. When the injury or illness results in an absence of more than 180 days, the employer may enter 180 (or 180+) on the Log. This is a new provision of the final rule; it is included because OSHA believes that the "180" notation indicates a case of exceptional severity and that counting days away beyond that point would provide little if any additional information.

Paragraph 1904.7(b)(3)(vii) specifies that employers whose employees are away from work because of a work-related injury or illness and who then decide to leave the company's employ or to retire must determine whether the employee is leaving or retiring because of the injury or illness and record the case accordingly. If the employee's decision to leave or retire is a result of the injury or illness, this paragraph requires the employer to estimate and record the number of calendar days away or on restricted work/job transfer the worker would have experienced if he or she had remained on the employer's payroll. This provision also states that, if the employee's decision was unrelated to the injury or illness, the employer is not required to continue to count and record days away or on restricted work/job transfer.

Paragraph 1904.(b)(3)(viii) directs employers how to handle a case that carries over from one year to the next. Some cases occur in one calendar year and then result in days away from work in the next year.

For example, a worker may be injured on December 20th and be away from work until January 10th. The final rule directs the employer only to record this type of case once, in the year that it occurred. If the employee is still away from work when the annual summary is prepared (before February 1), the employer must either count the number of days the employee was away or estimate the total days away that are expected to occur, use this estimate to calculate the total days away during the year for the annual summary, and then update the Log entry later when the actual number of days is known or the case reaches the 180-day cap allowed in Sec. 1904.7(b)(3)(v).

...

Final Rule's Restricted Work and Job Transfer Provisions, and OSHA's Reasons for Adopting Them

Paragraph 1904.7(b)(4) contains the restricted work and job transfer provisions of the final rule. These provisions clarify the definition of restricted work in light of the comments received and continue, with a few exceptions, most of the former rule's requirements with regard to these kinds of cases. OSHA finds, based on a review of the record, that these provisions of the final rule will increase awareness among employers of the importance of recording restricted work activity and job transfer cases and make the recordkeeping system more accurate and the process more efficient.

OSHA believes that it is even more important today than formerly that the definition of restricted work included in the final rule be clear and widely understood, because employers have recently been relying on restricted work (or "light duty") with increasing frequency, largely in an effort to encourage injured or ill employees to return to work as soon as possible. According to BLS data, this category of cases has grown by nearly 70% in the last six years. In 1992, for example, 9% of all injuries and illnesses (or a total of 622,300 cases) recorded as lost workday cases were classified in this way solely because of restricted work days, while in 1998, nearly 18% of all injury and illness cases (or a total of 1,050,200 cases) were recorded as lost workday cases only because they involved restricted work [BLS Press Release 99-358, 12-16-99]. The return-to-work programs increasingly being relied on by employers (often at the recommendation of their workers' compensation insurers) are designed to prevent exacerbation of, or to allow recuperation from, the injury or illness, rehabilitate employees more effectively, reintegrate injured or ill workers into the workplace more rapidly, limit workers' compensation costs, and retain productive workers. In addition, many employees are eager to accept restricted work when it is available and prefer returning to work to recuperating at home.

The final rule's requirements in paragraph 1904.10(b)(4) of the final rule state:

(4) How do I record a work-related injury or illness that involves restricted work or job transfer? When an injury or illness involves restricted work or job transfer but does not involve death or days away from work, you must record the injury or illness on the OSHA 300 Log by placing a check mark in the space for job transfer or restricted work and entering the number of restricted or transferred days in the restricted work column.

(i) How do I decide if the injury or illness resulted in restricted work? Restricted work occurs when, as the result of a work-related injury or illness:

(A) You keep the employee from performing one or more of the routine functions of his or her job, or from working the full workday that he or she would otherwise have been scheduled to work; or

(B) A physician or other licensed health care professional recommends that the employee not perform one or more of the routine functions of his or her job, or not work the full workday that he or she would otherwise have been scheduled to work.

(ii) What is meant by "routine functions"? For recordkeeping purposes, an employee's routine functions are those work activities the employee regularly performs at least once per week.

(iii) Do I have to record restricted work or job transfer if it applies only to the day on which the injury occurred or the illness began?

No. You do not have to record restricted work or job transfers if you, or the physician or other licensed health care professional, impose the restriction or transfer only for the day on which the injury occurred or the illness began.

(iv) If you or a physician or other licensed health care professional recommends a work restriction, is the injury or illness automatically recordable as a "restricted work" case?

No. A recommended work restriction is recordable only if it affects one or more of the employee's routine job functions. To determine whether this is the case, you must evaluate the restriction in light of the routine functions of the injured or ill employee's job. If the restriction from you or the physician or other licensed health care professional keeps the employee from performing one or more of his or her routine job functions, or from working the full workday the injured or ill employee would otherwise have worked, the employee's work has been restricted and you must record the case.

(v) How do I record a case where the worker works only for a partial work shift because of a work-related injury or illness?

A partial day of work is recorded as a day of job transfer or restriction for recordkeeping purposes, except for the day on which the injury occurred or the illness began.

(vi) If the injured or ill worker produces fewer goods or services than he or she would have produced prior to the injury or illness but otherwise performs all of the activities of his or her work, is the case considered a restricted work case?

No. The case is considered restricted work only if the worker does not perform all of the routine functions of his or her job or does not work the full shift that he or she would otherwise have worked.

(vii) How do I handle vague restrictions from a physician or other licensed health care professional, such as that the employee engage only in "light duty" or "take it easy for a week"?

If you are not clear about a physician or other licensed health care professional's recommendation, you may ask that person whether the employee can perform all of his or her routine job functions and work all of his or her normally assigned work shift. If the answer to both of these questions is "Yes," then the case does not involve a work restriction and does not have to be recorded as such. If the answer to one or both of these questions is "No," the case involves restricted work and must be recorded as a restricted work case. If you are unable to obtain this additional information from the physician or other licensed health care professional who recommended the restriction, record the injury or illness as a case involving job transfer or restricted work.

(viii) What do I do if a physician or other licensed health care professional recommends a job restriction meeting OSHA's definition but the employee does all of his or her routine job functions anyway?

You must record the injury or illness on the OSHA 300 Log as a restricted work case. If a physician or other licensed health care professional recommends a job restriction, you should ensure that the employee complies with that restriction. If you receive recommendations from two or more physicians or other licensed health care providers, you may make a decision as to which recommendation is the most authoritative, and record the case based upon that recommendation.

...

As the regulatory text for paragraph (b)(4) makes clear, the final rule's requirements for the recording of restricted work cases are similar in many ways to those pertaining to restricted work under the former rule. First, like the former rule, the final rule only requires employers to record as restricted work cases those cases in which restrictions are imposed or recommended as a result of a work-related injury or illness. A work restriction that is made for another reason, such as to meet reduced production demands, is not a recordable restricted work case. For example, an employer might "restrict" employees from entering the area in which a toxic chemical spill has occurred or make an accommodation for an employee who is disabled as a result of a non-work-related injury or illness. These cases would not be recordable as restricted work cases because they are not associated with a work-related injury or illness. However, if an employee has a work-related injury or illness, and that employee's work is restricted by the employer to prevent exacerbation of, or to allow recuperation from, that injury or illness, the case is recordable as a restricted work case because the restriction was necessitated by the work-related injury or illness. In some cases, there may be more than one reason for imposing or recommending a work restriction, e.g., to prevent an injury or illness from becoming worse or to prevent entry into a contaminated area. In such cases, if the employee's work-related illness or injury played any role in the restriction, OSHA considers the case to be a restricted work case.

Second, for the definition of restricted work to apply, the work restriction must be decided on by the employer, based on his or her best judgment or on the recommendation of a physician or other licensed health care professional. If a work restriction is not followed or implemented by the employee, the injury or illness must nevertheless be recorded on the Log as a restricted case. This was also the case under the former rule.

Third, like the former rule, the final rule's definition of restricted work relies on two components: whether the employee is able to perform the duties of his or her pre-injury job, and whether the employee is able to perform those duties for the same period of time as before.

The principal differences between the final and former rules' concept of restricted work cases are these: (1) the final rule permits employers to cap the total number of restricted work days for a particular case at 180 days, while the former rule required all restricted days for a given case to be recorded; (2) the final rule does not require employers to count the restriction of an employee's duties on the day the injury occurred or the illness began as restricted work, providing that the day the incident occurred is the only day on which work is restricted; and (3) the final rule defines work as restricted if the injured or ill employee is restricted from performing any job activity the employee would have regularly performed at least once per week before the injury or illness, while the former rule counted work as restricted if the employee was restricted in performing any activity he or she would have performed at least once per year.

In all other respects, the final rule continues to treat restricted work and job transfer cases in the same manner as they were treated under the former rule, including the counting of restricted days. Paragraph 1904.7(b)(4)(xi) requires the employer to count restricted days using the same rules as those for counting days away from work, using Sec. 1904.7(b)(3)(i) to (viii), with one exception. Like the former rule, the final rule allows the employer to stop counting restricted days if the employee's job has been permanently modified in a manner that eliminates the routine functions the employee has been restricted from performing. Examples of permanent modifications would include reassigning an employee with a respiratory allergy to a job where such allergens are not present, or adding a mechanical assist to a job that formerly required manual lifting. To make it clear that employers may stop counting restricted days when a job has been permanently changed, but not to eliminate the count of restricted work altogether, the rule makes it clear that at least one restricted workday must be counted, even if the restriction is imposed immediately. A discussion of the desirability of counting days of restricted work and job transfer at all is included in the explanation for the OSHA 300 form and the Sec. 1904.29 requirements. The revisions to this category of cases that have been made in the final rule reflect the views of commenters, suggestions made by the Keystone report (Ex. 5), and OSHA's experience in enforcing the former recordkeeping rule.

RECORDING AND REPORTING OCCUPATIONAL INJURIES AND ILLNESSES

Paragraph 1904.7(b)(5) Medical Treatment Beyond First Aid

The definitions of first aid and medical treatment have been central to the OSHA recordkeeping scheme since 1971, when the Agency's first recordkeeping rule was issued. Sections 8(c)(2) and 24(a) of the OSH Act specifically require employers to record all injuries and illnesses other than those "requiring only first aid treatment and which do not involve medical treatment, loss of consciousness, restriction of work or motion, or transfer to another job." Many injuries and illnesses sustained at work do not result in death, loss of consciousness, days away from work or restricted work or job transfer. Accordingly, the first aid and medical treatment criteria may be the criteria most frequently evaluated by employers when deciding whether a given work-related injury must be recorded.

In the past, OSHA has not interpreted the distinction made by the Act between minor (i.e., first aid only) injuries and non-minor injuries as applying to occupational illnesses, and employers have therefore been required to record all occupational illnesses, regardless of severity. As a result of this final rule, OSHA will now apply the same recordability criteria to both injuries and illnesses (see the discussion of this issue in the Legal Authority section of this preamble). The Agency believes that doing so will simplify the decision-making process that employers carry out when determining which work-related injuries and illnesses to record and will also result in more complete data on occupational illness, because employers will know that they must record these cases when they result in medical treatment beyond first aid, regardless of whether or not a physician or other licensed health care professional has made a diagnosis.

The former recordkeeping rule defined first aid as "any one-time treatment and any follow-up visit for the purpose of observation, of minor scratches, cuts, burns, splinters, and so forth, which do not ordinarily require medical care." Medical treatment was formerly defined as "treatment administered by a physician or by registered professional personnel under the standing orders of a physician."

To help employers determine the recordability of a given injury, the Recordkeeping Guidelines, issued by the Bureau of Labor Statistics (BLS) in 1986, provided numerous examples of medical treatments and of first aid treatments (Ex. 2). These examples were published as mutually exclusive lists, i.e., a treatment listed as a medical treatment did not also appear on the first-aid list. Thus, for example, a positive x-ray diagnosis (fractures, broken bones, etc.) was included among the treatments generally considered medical treatment, while a negative x-ray diagnosis (showing no fractures) was generally considered first aid. Despite the guidance provided by the Guidelines, OSHA continued to receive requests from employers for interpretations of the recordability of specific cases, and a large number of letters of interpretation addressing the distinction between first aid and medical treatment have been issued.

...

[The final rule] includes a list of first-aid treatments that is inclusive, and defines as medical treatment any treatment not on that list. OSHA recognizes, as several commenters pointed out, that no one can predict how medical care will change in the future. However, using a finite list of first aid treatments—knowing that it may have to be amended later based on new information—helps to limit the need for individual judgment about what constitutes first aid treatment. If OSHA adopted a more open-ended definition or one that relied on the judgment of a health care professional, employers and health care professionals would inevitably interpret different cases differently, which would compromise the consistency of the data. Under the system adopted in the final rule, once the employer has decided that a particular response to a work-related illness or injury is in fact treatment, he or she can simply turn to the first aid list to determine, without elaborate analysis, whether the treatment is first aid and thus not recordable.

OSHA finds that this simple approach, by providing clear, unambiguous guidance, will reduce confusion for employers and improve the accuracy and consistency of the data.

...

Final Rule

The final rule, at Sec. 1904.7(b)(5)(i), defines medical treatment as the management and care of a patient for the purpose of combating disease or disorder. For the purposes of Part 1904, medical treatment does not include:

(A) Visits to a physician or other licensed health care professional solely for observation or counseling;

(B) The conduct of diagnostic procedures, such as x-rays and blood tests, including the administration of prescription medications used solely for diagnostic purposes (e.g., eye drops to dilate pupils); or

(C) "first aid" as defined in paragraph (b)(5)(ii) of this section.

The final rule, at paragraph (b)(5)(ii), defines first aid as follows:

(A) Using a nonprescription medication at nonprescription strength (for medications available in both prescription and non-prescription form, a recommendation by a physician or other licensed health care professional to use a non-prescription medication at prescription strength is considered medical treatment for recordkeeping purposes).

(B) administering tetanus immunizations (other immunizations, such as hepatitis B vaccine or rabies vaccine, are considered medical treatment).

(C) Cleaning, flushing or soaking wounds on the surface of the skin;

(D) Using wound coverings, such as bandages, Band-Aids, gauze pads, etc.; or using butterfly bandages or Steri-Strips (other wound closing devices, such as sutures, staples, etc. are considered medical treatment);

(E) Using hot or cold therapy;

(F) Using any non-rigid means of support, such as elastic bandages, wraps, non-rigid back belts, etc. (devices with rigid stays or other systems designed to immobilize parts of the body are considered medical treatment for recordkeeping purposes);

(G) Using temporary immobilization devices while transporting an accident victim (e.g. splints, slings, neck collars, back boards, etc.)

(H) Drilling of a fingernail or toenail to relieve pressure, or draining fluid from a blister;

(I) Using eye patches;

(J) Removing foreign bodies from the eye using only irrigation or a cotton swab;

(K) Removing splinters or foreign material from areas other than the eye by irrigation, tweezers, cotton swabs, or other simple means;

(L) Using finger guards;

(M) Using massages (physical therapy or chiropractic treatment are considered medical treatment for recordkeeping purposes);

(N) Drinking fluids for relief of heat stress.

This list of first aid treatments is comprehensive, i.e., any treatment not included on this list is not considered first aid for OSHA recordkeeping purposes. OSHA considers the listed treatments to be first aid regardless of the professional qualifications of the person providing the treatment; even when these treatments are provided by a physician, nurse, or other health care professional, they are considered first aid for recordkeeping purposes.

...

The three listed exclusions from the definition—visits to a health care professional solely for observation or counseling; diagnostic procedures, including prescribing or administering of prescription medications used solely for diagnostic purposes; and procedures defined in the final rule as first aid—clarify the applicability of the definition and are designed to help employers in their determinations of recordability.

...

In making its decisions about the items to be included on the list of first aid treatments, OSHA relied on its experience with the former rule, the advice of the Agency's occupational medicine and occupational nursing staff, and a thorough review of the record comments. In general, first aid treatment can be distinguished from medical treatment as follows:

First aid is usually administered after the injury or illness occurs and at the location (e.g., workplace) where the injury or illness occurred.

First aid generally consists of one-time or short-term treatment.

First aid treatments are usually simple and require little or no technology.

First aid can be administered by people with little training (beyond first aid training) and even by the injured or ill person.

First aid is usually administered to keep the condition from worsening, while the injured or ill person is awaiting medical treatment.

The final rule's list of treatments considered first aid is based on the record of the rulemaking, OSHA's experience in implementing the recordkeeping rule since 1986, a review of the BLS Recordkeeping Guidelines, letters of interpretation, and the professional judgment of the Agency's occupational physicians and nurses.

...

In the final rule, OSHA has not included prescription medications, whether given once or over a longer period of time, in the list of first aid treatments. The Agency believes that the use of prescription medications is not first aid because prescription medications are powerful substances that can only be prescribed by a licensed health care professional, and for the majority of medications in the majority of states, by a licensed physician. The availability of these substances is carefully controlled and limited because they must be prescribed and administered by a highly trained and knowledgeable professional, can have detrimental side effects, and should not be self-administered.

...

OSHA has decided to retain its long-standing policy of requiring the recording of cases in which a health care professional issues a prescription, whether that prescription is filled or taken or not. The patient's acceptance or refusal of the treatment does not alter the fact that, in the health care professional's judgment, the case warrants medical treatment. In addition, a rule that relied on whether a prescription is filled or taken, rather than on whether the medicine was prescribed, would create administrative difficulties for employers, because such a rule would mean that the employer would have to investigate whether a given prescription had been filled or the medicine had actually been taken. Finally, many employers and employees might well consider an employer's inquiry about the filling of a prescription an invasion of the employee's privacy. For these reasons, the final rule continues OSHA's longstanding policy of considering the giving of a prescription medical treatment. It departs from former

practice with regard to the administration of a single dose of a prescription medicine, however, because there is no medical reason for differentiating medical treatment from first aid on the basis of the number of doses involved. This is particularly well illustrated by the recent trend toward giving a single large dose of antibiotics instead of the more traditional pattern involving several smaller doses given over several days.

Yet another issue raised by commenters about medications involved the use of non-prescription medications at prescription strength. In recent years, many drugs have been made available both as prescription and "over-the-counter" medications, depending on the strength or dosage of the product. Some examples include various non-steroidal anti-inflammatory drugs (NSAIDs), such as ibuprofen, and cortisone creams.

...

The final rule does not consider the prescribing of non-prescription medications, such as aspirin or over-the-counter skin creams, as medical treatment. However, if the drug is one that is available both in prescription and nonprescription strengths, such as ibuprofen, and is used or recommended for use by a physician or other licensed health care professional at prescription strength, the medical treatment criterion is met and the case must be recorded. There is no reason for one case to be recorded and another not to be recorded simply because one physician issued a prescription and another told the employee to use the same medication at prescription strength but to obtain it over the counter. Both cases received equal treatment and should be recorded equally. This relatively small change in the recordkeeping rule will improve the consistency and accuracy of the data on occupational injuries and illnesses and simplify the system as well.

...

OSHA believes that cleaning, flushing or soaking of wounds on the skin surface is the initial emergency treatment for almost all surface wounds and that these procedures do not rise to the level of medical treatment. This relatively simple type of treatment does not require technology, training, or even a visit to a health care professional. More serious wounds will be captured as recordable cases because they will meet other recording criteria, such as prescription medications, sutures, restricted work, or days away from work. Therefore, OSHA has included cleaning, flushing or soaking of wounds on the skin surface as an item on the first aid list. As stated previously, OSHA does not believe that multiple applications of first aid should constitute medical treatment; it is the nature of the treatment, not how many times it is applied, that determines whether it is first aid or medical treatment.

...

In the final rule, OSHA has included hot and cold treatment as first aid treatment, regardless of the number of times it is applied, where it is applied, or the injury or illness to which it is applied. The Agency has decided that hot or cold therapy must be defined as either first aid or medical treatment regardless of the condition being treated, a decision that departs from the proposal. It is OSHA's judgment that hot and cold treatment is simple to apply, does not require special training, and is rarely used as the only treatment for any significant injury or illness. If the worker has sustained a significant injury or illness, the case almost always involves some other form of medical treatment (such as prescription drugs, physical therapy, or chiropractic treatment); restricted work; or days away from work. Therefore, there is no need to consider hot and cold therapy to be medical treatment, in and of itself. Considering hot and cold therapy to be first aid also clarifies and simplifies the rule, because it means that employers will not need to consider whether to record when an employee uses hot or cold therapy without the direction or guidance of a physician or other licensed health care professional.

...

In the final rule, OSHA has included hot and cold treatment as first aid treatment, regardless of the number of times it is applied, where it is applied, or the injury or illness to which it is applied.

The Agency has decided that hot or cold therapy must be defined as either first aid or medical treatment regardless of the condition being treated, a decision that departs from the proposal. It is OSHA's judgment that hot and cold treatment is simple to apply, does not require special training, and is rarely used as the only treatment for any significant injury or illness. If the worker has sustained a significant injury or illness, the case almost always involves some other form of medical treatment (such as prescription drugs, physical therapy, or chiropractic treatment); restricted work; or days away from work. Therefore, there is no need to consider hot and cold therapy to be medical treatment, in and of itself. Considering hot and cold therapy to be first aid also clarifies and simplifies the rule, because it means that employers will not need to consider whether to record when an employee uses hot or cold therapy without the direction or guidance of a physician or other licensed health care professional.

...

[OSHA believes] that the use of these devices during an emergency to stabilize an accident victim during transport to a medical facility is not medical treatment. In this specific situation, a splint or other device is used as temporary first aid treatment, may be applied by non-licensed personnel using common materials at hand, and often does not reflect the severity of the injury. OSHA has included this item as G on the first aid list: "[u]sing temporary immobilization devices while transporting an accident victim (e.g. splints, slings, neck collars, etc.)"

...

[Item H on the first aid list is the "drilling of a fingernail or toenail to relieve pressure, or draining fluid from a blister."] These are both one time treatments provided to relieve minor soreness caused by the pressure beneath the nail or in the blister. These are relatively minor procedures that are often performed by licensed personnel but may also be performed by the injured worker. More serious injuries of this type will continue to be captured if they meet one or more of the other recording criteria. OSHA has specifically mentioned finger nails and toenails to provide clarity. These treatments are now included as item H on the first aid list.

...

In the final rule, OSHA has included the use of eye patches as first aid in item I of the first aid list. Eye patches can be purchased without a prescription, and are used for both serious and non-serious injuries and illnesses. OSHA believes that the more serious injuries to the eyes will that NIOSH refers to require medical treatment, such as prescription drugs or removal of foreign material by means other than irrigation or a cotton swab, and will thus be recordable.

...

In the final rule, OSHA has included as item J "Removing foreign bodies from the eye using only irrigation or a cotton swab." OSHA believes that it is often difficult for the health care professional to determine if the object is embedded or adhered to the eye, and has not included this suggested language in the final rule. In all probability, if the object is embedded or adhered, it will not be removed simply with irrigation or a cotton swab, and the case will be recorded because it will require additional treatment.

...

OSHA believes that it is appropriate to exclude those cases from the Log that involve a foreign body in the eye of a worker that can be removed from the eye merely by rinsing it with water (irrigation) or touching it with a cotton swab. These cases represent minor injuries that do not rise to the level requiring recording. More significant eye injuries will be captured by the records because they involve medical treatment, result in work restrictions, or cause days away from work.

...

[OSHA has included as item K "Removal of splinters or foreign material from areas other than the eyes by irrigation, tweezers, cotton swabs or other simple means."] The inclusion of the phrase "other simple means" will provide some flexibility and permit simple means other than those listed to be considered first aid. Cases involving more complicated removal procedures will be captured on the Log because they will require medical treatment such as prescription drugs or stitches or will involve restricted work or days away from work.

...

Paragraph 1904.7(b)(6) Loss of Consciousness

The final rule, like the former rule, requires the employer to record any work-related injury or illness resulting in a loss of consciousness. The recording of occupational injuries and illnesses resulting in loss of consciousness is clearly required by Sections 8(c) and 24 of the OSH Act. The new rule differs from the former rule only in clearly applying the loss of consciousness criterion to illnesses as well as injuries. Since the former rule required the recording of all illnesses, illnesses involving loss of consciousness were recordable, and thus OSHA expects that this clarification will not change recording practices. Thus, any time a worker becomes unconscious as a result of a workplace exposure to chemicals, heat, an oxygen deficient environment, a blow to the head, or some other workplace hazard that causes loss of consciousness, the employer must record the case.

...

Paragraph 1904.7(b)(7) Recording Significant Work-Related Injuries and Illnesses Diagnosed by a Physician or Other Licensed Health Care Professional

Paragraph 1904.7(b)(7) of this final rule requires the recording of any significant work-related injury or illness diagnosed by a physician or other licensed health care professional. Paragraph 1904.7(b)(7) clarifies which significant, diagnosed work-related injuries and illnesses OSHA requires the employer to record in those rare cases where a significant work-related injury or illness has not triggered recording under one or more of the general recording criteria, i.e., has not resulted in death, loss of consciousness, medical treatment beyond first aid, restricted work or job transfer, or days away from work. Based on the Agency's prior recordkeeping experience, OSHA believes that the great majority of significant occupational injuries and illnesses will be captured by one or more of the other general recording criteria in Section 1904.7. However, OSHA has found that there is a limited class of significant work-related injuries and illnesses that may not be captured under the other Sec. 1904.7 criteria. Therefore, the final rule stipulates at paragraph 1904.7(b)(7) that any significant work-related occupational injury or illness that is not captured by any of the general recording criteria but is diagnosed by a physician or other licensed health care professional be recorded in the employer's records.

Under the final rule, an injury or illness case is considered significant if it is a work-related case involving occupational cancer (e.g., mesothelioma), chronic irreversible disease (e.g., chronic beryllium disease), a fractured or cracked bone (e.g., broken arm, cracked rib), or a punctured eardrum. The employer must record such cases within 7 days of receiving a diagnosis from a physician or other licensed health care professional that an injury or illness of this kind has occurred. As explained in the note to paragraph 1904.7(b)(7), OSHA believes that the great majority of significant work-related injuries and illnesses will be recorded because they meet one or more of the other recording criteria listed in Sec. 1904.7(a): death, days away from work, restricted work or job transfer, medical treatment beyond first aid, or loss of consciousness. However, there are some significant injuries, such as a punctured eardrum or a fractured toe or rib, for which neither medical treatment nor work restrictions may be administered or recommended.

There are also a number of significant occupational diseases that progress once the disease process begins or reaches a certain point, such as byssinosis, silicosis, and some types of cancer, for which medical treatment or work restrictions may not be recommended at the time of diagnosis, although medical treatment and loss of work certainly will occur at later stages. This provision of the final rule is designed to capture this small group of significant work-related cases. Although the employer is required to record these illnesses even if they manifest themselves after the employee leaves employment (assuming the illness meets the standards for work-relatedness that apply to all recordable incidents), these cases are less likely to be recorded once the employee has left employment. OSHA believes that work-related cancer, chronic irreversible diseases, fractures of bones or teeth and punctured eardrums are generally recognized as constituting significant diagnoses and, if the condition is work-related, are appropriately recorded at the time of initial diagnosis even if, at that time, medical treatment or work restrictions are not recommended.

As discussed in the Legal Authority section, above, OSHA has modified the Agency's prior position so that, under the final rule, minor occupational illnesses no longer are required to be recorded on the Log. The requirement pertaining to the recording of all significant diagnosed injuries and illnesses in this paragraph of the final rule, on the other hand, will ensure that all significant (non-minor) injuries and illnesses are in fact captured on the Log, as required by the OSH Act. Requiring significant cases involving diagnosis to be recorded will help to achieve several of the goals of this rulemaking. First, adherence to this requirement will produce better data on occupational injury and illness by providing for more complete recording of significant occupational conditions. Second, this requirement will produce more timely records because it provides for the immediate recording of significant disorders on first diagnosis. Many occupational illnesses manifest themselves through gradual onset and worsening of the condition. In some cases, a worker could be diagnosed with a significant illness, such as an irreversible respiratory disorder, not be given medical treatment because no effective treatment was available, not lose time from work because the illness was not debilitating at the time, and not have his or her case recorded on the Log because none of the recording criteria had been met. If such a worker left employment or changed employers before one of the other recording criteria had been met, this serious occupational illness case would never be recorded. The requirements in paragraph 1904.7(b)(7) remedy this deficiency and will thus ensure the capture of more complete and timely data on these injuries and illnesses.

...

Section 1904.8 Additional Recording Criteria for Needlestick and Sharps Injuries [p. 5998]

Section 1904.8 of the final rule being published today deals with the recording of a specific class of occupational injuries involving punctures, cuts and lacerations caused by needles or other sharp objects contaminated or reasonably anticipated to be contaminated with blood or other potentially infectious materials that may lead to bloodborne diseases, such as Acquired Immunodeficiency Syndrome (AIDS), hepatitis B or hepatitis C. The final rule uses the terms "contaminated," "other potentially infectious material," and "occupational exposure" as these terms are defined in OSHA's Bloodborne Pathogens standard (29 CFR 1910.1030). These injuries are of special concern to healthcare workers because they use needles and other sharp devices in the performance of their work duties and are therefore at risk of bloodborne infections caused by exposures involving contaminated needles and other sharps. Although healthcare workers are at particular risk of bloodborne infection from these injuries, other workers may also be at risk of contracting potentially fatal bloodborne disease. For example, a worker in a hospital laundry could be stuck by a contaminated needle left in a patient's bedding, or a worker in a hazardous waste treatment facility could be occupationally exposed to bloodborne pathogens if contaminated waste from a medical facility was not treated before being sent to waste treatment.

Section 1904.8(a) requires employers to record on the OSHA Log all work-related needlestick and sharps injuries involving objects contaminated (or reasonably anticipated to be contaminated) with another person's blood or other potentially infectious material (OPIM). The rule prohibits the employer from entering the name of the affected employee on the Log to protect the individual's privacy; employees are understandably sensitive about others knowing that they may have contracted a bloodborne disease. For these cases, and other types of privacy concern cases, the employer simply enters "privacy concern case" in the space reserved for the employee's name. The employer then keeps a separate, confidential list of privacy concern cases with the case number from the Log and the employee's name; this list is used by the employer to keep track of the injury or illness so that the Log can later be updated, if necessary, and to ensure that the information will be available if a government representative needs information about injured or ill employees during a workplace inspection (see Sec. 1904.40). The regulatory text of Sec. 1904.8 refers recordkeepers

and others to Sec. 1904.29(b)(6) through Sec. 1904.29(b)(10) of the rule for more information about how to record privacy concern cases of all types, including those involving needlesticks and sharps injuries. The implementation section of Sec. 1904.8(b)(1) defines "other potentially infectious material" as it is defined in OSHA's Bloodborne Pathogens Standard (29 CFR Sec. 1910.1030, paragraph (b)). Other potentially infectious materials include (i) human bodily fluids, human tissues and organs, and (ii) other materials infected with the HIV or hepatitis B (HBV) virus such as laboratory cultures or tissues from experimental animals. (For a complete list of OPIM, see paragraph (b) of 29 CFR 1910.1030.)

Although the final rule requires the recording of all workplace cut and puncture injuries resulting from an event involving contaminated sharps, it does not require the recording of all cuts and punctures. For example, a cut made by a knife or other sharp instrument that was not contaminated by blood or OPIM would not generally be recordable, and a laceration made by a dirty tin can or greasy tool would also generally not be recordable, providing that the injury did not result from a contaminated sharp and did not meet one of the general recording criteria of medical treatment, restricted work, etc. Paragraph (b)(2) of Sec. 1904.8 contains provisions indicating which cuts and punctures must be recorded because they involve contaminated sharps and which must be recorded only if they meet the general recording criteria.

Paragraph (b)(3) of Sec. 1904.8 contains requirements for updating the OSHA 300 Log when a worker experiences a wound caused by a contaminated needle or sharp and is later diagnosed as having a bloodborne illness, such as AIDS, hepatitis B or hepatitis C. The final rule requires the employer to update the classification of such a privacy concern case on the OSHA 300 Log if the outcome of the case changes, i.e., if it subsequently results in death, days away from work, restricted work, or job transfer. The employer must also update the case description on the Log to indicate the name of the bloodborne illness and to change the classification of the case from an injury (i.e., the needlestick) to an illness (i.e., the illness that resulted from the needlestick). In no case may the employer enter the employee's name on the Log itself, whether when initially recording the needlestick or sharp injury or when subsequently updating the record.

The privacy concern provisions of the final rule make it possible, for the first time, for the identity of the bloodborne illness caused by the needlestick or sharps injury to be included on the Log. By excluding the name of the injured or ill employee throughout the recordkeeping process, employee privacy is assured. This approach will allow OSHA to gather valuable data about the kinds of bloodborne illnesses healthcare and other workers are contracting as a result of these occupational injuries, and will provide the most accurate and informative data possible, including the seroconversion status of the affected worker, the name of the illness he or she contracted, and, on the OSHA 301 Form for the original case, more detailed information about how the injury occurred, the equipment and materials involved, and so forth. Use of the privacy case concept thus meets the primary objective of this rulemaking, providing the best data possible, while simultaneously ensuring that an important public policy goal—the protection of privacy about medical matters—is met. OSHA recognizes that requiring employers to treat privacy cases differently from other cases adds some complexity to the recordkeeping system and imposes a burden on those employers whose employees experience such injuries and illnesses, but believes that the gain in data quality and employee privacy outweigh these disadvantages considerably.

The last paragraph (paragraph (c)) of Sec. 1904.8 deals with the recording of cases involving workplace contact with blood or other potentially infectious materials that do not involve needlesticks or sharps, such as splashes to the eye, mucous membranes, or non-intact skin. The final recordkeeping rule does not require employers to record these incidents unless they meet the final rule's general recording criteria (i.e., death, medical treatment, loss of consciousness, restricted work or motion, days away from work, diagnosis by an HCP) or the employee subsequently develops an illness caused by bloodborne pathogens. The final

rule thus provides employers, for the first time, with regulatory language delineating how they are to record injuries caused by contaminated needles and other sharps, and how they are to treat other exposure incidents (as defined in the Bloodborne Pathogens standard) involving blood or OPIM. "Contaminated" is defined just as it is in the Bloodborne Pathogens standard: "Contaminated means the presence or the reasonably anticipated presence of blood or other potentially infectious materials on an item or surface."

...

Section 1904.9 Additional Recording Criteria for Cases Involving Medical Removal Under OSHA Standards [p. 6003]

The final rule, in paragraph 1904.9(a), requires an employer to record an injury or illness case on the OSHA 300 Log when the employee is medically removed under the medical surveillance requirements of any OSHA standard. Paragraph 1904.9(b)(1) requires each such case to be recorded as a case involving days away from work (if the employee does not work during the medical removal) or as a case involving restricted work activity (if the employee continues to work but in an area where exposures are not present.) This paragraph also requires any medical removal related to chemical exposure to be recorded as a poisoning illness.

Paragraph 1904.9(b)(2) informs employers that some OSHA standards have medical removal provisions and others do not. For example, the Bloodborne Pathogen Standard (29 CFR 1910.1030) and the Occupational Noise Standard (29 CFR 1910.95) do not require medical removal. Many of the OSHA standards that contain medical removal provisions are related to specific chemical substances, such as lead (29 CFR 1901.1025), cadmium (29 CFR 1910.1027), methylene chloride (29 CFR 1910.1052), formaldehyde (29 CFR 1910.1048), and benzene (29 CFR 1910.1028). Paragraph 1904.9(b)(3) addresses the issue of medical removals that are not required by an OSHA standard. In some cases employers voluntarily rotate employees from one job to another to reduce exposure to hazardous substances; job rotation is an administrative method of reducing exposure that is permitted in some OSHA standards. Removal (job transfer) of an asymptomatic employee for administrative exposure control reasons does not require the case to be recorded on the OSHA 300 Log because no injury or illness—the first step in the recordkeeping process—exists. Paragraph 1904.9(b)(3) only applies to those substances with OSHA mandated medical removal criteria. For injuries or illnesses caused by exposure to other substances or hazards, the employer must look to the general requirements of paragraphs 1910.7(b)(3) and (4) to determine how to record the days away or days of restricted work.

The provisions of Sec. 1904.9 are not the only recording criteria for recording injuries and illnesses from these occupational exposures. These provisions merely clarify the need to record specific cases, which are often established with medical test results, that result in days away from work, restricted work, or job transfer. The Sec. 1904.9 provisions are included to produce more consistent data and provide needed interpretation of the requirements for employers. However, if an injury or illness results in the other criteria of Sec. 1904.7 (death, medical treatment, loss of consciousness, days away from work, restricted work, transfer to another job, or diagnosis as a significant illness or injury by a physician or other licensed health care professional) the case must be recorded whether or not the medical removal provisions of an OSHA standard have been met.

...

OSHA has therefore included section 1904.9 in the final rule to provide a uniform, simple method for recording a variety of serious disorders that have been addressed by OSHA standards. The Sec. 1904.9 provisions of the final rule cover all of the OSHA standards with medical removal provisions, regardless of whether or not those provisions are based on medical tests, physicians' opinions, or a combination of the two. Finally, by relying on the medical removal provisions in any OSHA standard, section 1904.9 of the final rule establishes recording criteria for future standards, and avoids the need to amend the recordkeeping rule whenever OSHA issues a standard containing a medical removal level.

...

Section 1904.10 Recording Criteria for Cases Involving Occupational Hearing Loss [p. 6004]

[The Department of Labor has proposed that the criteria for recording work-related hearing loss not be implemented for one year pending further investigation into the level of hearing loss that should be recorded as a "significant" health condition. Paragraph 1904.10(b)(1) of the final rule had required that a standard threshold shift of an average of 10 decibels (dB) or more at 2000, 3000, or 4000 hertz in one or both ears would be recordable.

Until more information is obtained, a standard threshold shift of 25 decibels, as required by the former regulation, is to be recorded.]

Section 1904.11 Additional Recording Criteria for Work-Related Tuberculosis Cases [p. 6013]

Section 1904.11 of the final rule being published today addresses the recording of tuberculosis (TB) infections that may occur to workers occupationally exposed to TB. TB is a major health concern, and nearly one-third of the world's population may be infected with the TB bacterium at the present time. There are two general stages of TB, tuberculosis infection and active tuberculosis disease. Individuals with tuberculosis infection and no active disease are not infectious; tuberculosis infections are asymptomatic and are only detected by a positive response to a tuberculin skin test. Workers in many settings are at risk of contracting TB infection from their clients or patients, and some workers are at greatly increased risk, such as workers exposed to TB patients in health care settings. Outbreaks have also occurred in a variety of workplaces, including hospitals, prisons, homeless shelters, nursing homes, and manufacturing facilities (62 FR 54159).

The text of Sec. 1904.11 of the final rule states:

(a) **Basic requirement.** If any of your employees has been occupationally exposed to anyone with a known case of active tuberculosis (TB), and that employee subsequently develops a tuberculosis infection, as evidenced by a positive skin test or diagnosis by a physician or other licensed health care professional, you must record the case on the OSHA 300 Log by checking the "respiratory condition" column.

(b) Implementation.

(1) Do I have to record, on the Log, a positive TB skin test result obtained at a pre-employment physical?

No, because the employee was not occupationally exposed to a known case of active tuberculosis in your workplace.

(2) May I line-out or erase a recorded TB case if I obtain evidence that the case was not caused by occupational exposure?

Yes. you may line-out or erase the case from the Log under the following circumstances:

(i) The worker is living in a household with a person who has been diagnosed with active TB;

(ii) The Public Health Department has identified the worker as a contact of an individual with a case of active TB unrelated to the workplace; or

(iii) A medical investigation shows that the employee's infection was caused by exposure to TB away from work, or proves that the case was not related to the workplace TB exposure.

Section 1904.12 Recording Criteria for Cases Involving Work-Related Musculoskeletal Disorders [p. 6017]

[This section provides requirements for recording work-related musculoskeletal disorders (MSDs). OSHA has proposed to delay for one year the definition of MSD and the requirement to check the MSD column. However, the same recording criteria applies to musculoskeletal disorders (MSDs) as to all other injuries and illnesses.]

Section 1904.29 Forms [p. 6022]

Section 1904.29, titled "Forms," establishes the requirements for the forms (OSHA 300 Log, OSHA 300A Annual Summary, and OSHA 301 Incident Report) an employer must use to keep OSHA Part 1904 injury and illness records, the time limit for recording an injury or illness case, the use of substitute forms, the use of computer equipment to keep the records, and privacy protections for certain information recorded on the OSHA 300 Log.

Paragraph 1904.29(a) sets out the basic requirements of this section. It directs the employer to use the OSHA 300 (Log), 300A (Summary), and 301 (Incident Report) forms, or equivalent forms, to record all recordable occupational injuries and illnesses. Paragraph 1904.29(b) contains requirements in the form of questions and answers to explain how employers are to implement this basic requirement. Paragraph 1904.29(b)(1) states the requirements for: (1) Completing the establishment information at the top of the OSHA 300 Log, (2) making a one- or two-line entry for each recordable injury and illness case, and (3) summarizing the data at the end of the year. Paragraph 1904.29(b)(2) sets out the requirements for employers to complete the OSHA 301 Incident Report form (or equivalent) for each recordable case entered on the OSHA 300 Log. The requirements for completing the annual summary on the Form 300A are found at Section 1904.32 of the final rule.

Required Forms

In addition to establishing the basic requirements for employers to keep records on the OSHA 300 Log and OSHA 301 Incident Report and providing basic instructions on how to complete these forms, this section of the rule states that employers may use two lines of the OSHA 300 Log to describe an injury or illness, if necessary.

...

OSHA believes that most injury and illness cases can be recorded using only one line of the Log. However, for those cases requiring more space, this addition to the Log makes it clear that two lines may be used to describe the case. The OSHA 300 Log is designed to be a scannable document that employers, employees and government representatives can use to review a fairly large number of cases in a brief time, and OSHA believes that employers will not need more than two lines to describe a given case. Employers should enter more detailed information about each case on the OSHA 301 form, which is designed to accommodate lengthier information.

Deadline for Entering a Case

Paragraph 1904.29(b)(3) establishes the requirement for how quickly each recordable injury or illness must be recorded into the records. It states that the employer must enter each case on the OSHA 300 Log and OSHA 301 Form within 7 calendar days of receiving information that a recordable injury or illness has occurred. In the vast majority of cases, employers know immediately or within a short time that a recordable case has occurred. In a few cases, however, it may be several days before the employer is informed that an employee's injury or illness meets one or more of the recording criteria.

...

Accordingly, paragraphs 1904.29(b)(4) and (b)(5) of the final rule make clear that employers are permitted to record the required information on electronic media or on paper forms that are different from the OSHA 300 Log, provided that the electronic record or paper forms are equivalent to the OSHA 300 Log. A form is deemed to be "equivalent" to the OSHA 300 Log if it can be read and understood as easily as the OSHA form and contains at least as much information as the OSHA 300 Log. In addition, the equivalent form must be completed in accordance with the instructions used to complete the OSHA 300 Log. These provisions are intended to balance OSHA's obligation, as set forth in Section 8(d) of the OSH Act, to reduce information collection burdens on employers as much as possible, on the one hand, with the need, on the other hand, to maintain uniformity of the data recorded and provide employers flexibility in meeting OSHA's recordkeeping requirements. These provisions also help to achieve one of OSHA's goals for this rulemaking: to allow employers to take full advantage of modern technology and computers to meet their OSHA recordkeeping obligations.

...

The final rule does not include a requirement that certain questions on an equivalent form be asked in the same order and be phrased in language identical to that used on the OSHA 301 form. Instead, OSHA has decided, based on a review of the record evidence, that employers may use any substitute form that contains the same information and follows the same recording directions as the OSHA 301 form, and the final rule clearly allows this. Although the consistency of the data on the OSHA 301 form might be improved somewhat if the questions asking for further details were phrased and positioned in an identical way on all employers' forms, OSHA has concluded that the additional burden such a requirement would impose on employers and workers' compensation agencies outweighs this consideration.

...

Handling of Privacy Concern Cases

Paragraphs 1904.29(b)(6) through (b)(10) of the final rule arc ncw and are designed to address privacy concerns raised by many commenters to the record. Paragraph 1904.29(b)(6) requires the employer to withhold the injured or ill employee's name from the OSHA 300 Log for injuries and illnesses defined by the rule as "privacy concern cases" and instead to enter "privacy concern case" in the space where the employee's name would normally be entered if an injury or illness meeting the definition of a privacy concern case occurs. This approach will allow the employer to provide OSHA 300 Log data to employees, former employees and employee representatives, as required by Sec. 1904.35, while at the same time protecting the privacy of workers who have experienced occupational injuries and illnesses that raise privacy concerns. The employer must also keep a separate, confidential list of these privacy concern cases, and the list must include the employee's name and the case number from the OSHA 300 Log. This separate listing is needed to allow a government representative to obtain the employee's name during a workplace inspection in case further investigation is warranted and to assist employers to keep track of such cases in the event that future revisions to the entry become necessary.

Paragraph 1904.29(b)(7) defines "privacy concern cases" as those involving: (i) An injury or illness to an intimate body part or the reproductive system; (ii) an injury or illness resulting from a sexual assault; (iii) a mental illness; (iv) a work-related HIV infection, hepatitis case, or tuberculosis case; (v) needlestick injuries and cuts from sharp objects that are contaminated with another person's blood or other potentially infectious material, or (vi) any other illness, if the employee independently and voluntarily requests that his or her name not be entered on the log. Paragraph 1904.29(b)(8) establishes that these are the only types of occupational injuries and illnesses that the employer may consider privacy concern cases for recordkeeping purposes.

Paragraph 1904.29(b)(9) permits employers discretion in recording case information if the employer believes that doing so could compromise the privacy of the employee's identity, even though the employee's name has not been entered. This clause has been added because OSHA recognizes that, for specific situations, coworkers who are allowed to access the log may be able to deduce the identity of the injured or ill worker and obtain inappropriate knowledge of a privacy-sensitive injury or illness. OSHA believes that these situations are relatively infrequent, but still exist. For example, if knowing the department in which the employee works would inadvertently divulge the person's identity, or recording the gender of the injured employee would identifying that person (because, for example, only one woman works at the plant), the employer has discretion to mask or withhold this information both on the Log and Incident Report.

The rule requires the employer to enter enough information to identify the cause of the incident and the general severity of the injury or illness, but allows the employer to exclude details of an intimate or private nature. The rule includes two examples; a sexual assault case could be described simply as "injury from assault," or an injury to a reproductive organ could be described as "lower abdominal injury." Likewise, a work-related diagnosis of post traumatic stress disorder could be described as "emotional difficulty." Reproductive disorders, certain cancers, contagious diseases and other disorders that are intimate and private in nature may also be described in a general way to avoid privacy concerns. This allows the employer to avoid overly graphic descriptions that may be offensive, without sacrificing the descriptive value of the recorded information.

Paragraph 1904.29(b)(10) protects employee privacy if the employer decides voluntarily to disclose the OSHA 300 and 301 forms to persons other than those who have a mandatory right of access under the final rule. The paragraph requires the employer to remove or hide employees' names or other personally identifying information before disclosing the forms to persons other than government representatives, employees, former employees or authorized representatives, as required by paragraphs 1904.40 and 1904.35, except in three cases. The employer may disclose the forms, complete with personally identifying information, (2) only: (i) to an auditor or consultant hired by the employer to evaluate the safety and health program; (ii) to the extent necessary for processing a claim for workers' compensation or other insurance benefits; or (iii) to a public health authority or law enforcement agency for uses and disclosures for which consent, an authorization, or opportunity to agree or object is not required under section 164.512 of the final rule on Standards for Privacy of Individually Identifiable Health Information, 45 CFR 164.512.

These requirements have been included in Sec. 1904.29 rather than in Sec. 1904.35, which establishes requirements for records access, because waiting until access is requested to remove identifying information from the OSHA 300 Log could unwittingly compromise the injured or ill worker's privacy and result in unnecessary delays. The final rule's overall approach to handling privacy issues is discussed more fully in the preamble discussion of the employee access provisions in Sec. 1904.35.

The Treatment of Occupational Illness and Injury Data on the Forms

The treatment of occupational injury and illness data on the OSHA forms is a key issue in this rulemaking. Although the forms themselves are not printed in the Code of Federal Regulations (CFR), they are the method OSHA's recordkeeping regulation uses to meet the Agency's goal of tracking and reporting occupational injury and illness data. As such, the forms are a central component of the recordkeeping system and mirror the requirements of the Part 1904 regulation. The final Part 1904 rule requires employers to use three forms to track occupational injuries and illnesses: the OSHA 300, 300A, and 301 forms, which replace the OSHA 200 and 101 forms called for under the former recordkeeping rule, as follows:

1. The OSHA Form 300, Log of Work-Related Injuries and Illnesses, replaces the Log portion of the former OSHA Form 200 Log and Summary of Occupational Injuries and Illnesses. The OSHA 300 Log contains space for a description of the establishment name, city and state, followed by a one-line space for the entry for each recordable injury and illness.

2. The OSHA Form 300A, Summary of Work-Related Injuries and Illnesses, replaces the Summary portion of the former OSHA Form 200 Log and Summary of Occupational Injuries and Illnesses. The Form 300A is used to summarize the entries from the Form 300 Log at the end of the year and is then posted from February 1 through April 30 of the following year so that employees can be aware of the occupational injury and illness experience of the establishment in which they work. The form contains space for entries for each of the columns from the Form 300, along with information about the establishment, and the average number of employees who worked there the previous year, and the recordkeeper's and corporate officer's certification of the accuracy of the data recorded on the summary. (These requirements are addressed further in Section 1904.32 of the final rule and its associated preamble.)

3. The OSHA Form 301, Injury and Illness Report, replaces the former OSHA 101 Form. Covered employers are required to fill out a one-page form for each injury and illness recorded on the Form 300. The form contains space for more detailed information about the injured or ill employee, the physician or other health care professional who cared for the employee (if medical treatment was necessary), the treatment (if any) of the employee at an emergency room or hospital, and descriptive information telling what the employee was doing when injured or ill, how the incident occurred, the specific details of the injury or illness, and the object or substance that harmed the employee. (Most employers use a workers' compensation form as a replacement for the OSHA 301 Incident Report.)

...

The OSHA recordkeeping forms required by the final Part 1904 recordkeeping rule are printed on legal size paper ($8\frac{1}{2}$" x 14"). The former rule's Log was an 11 by 17-inch form, the equivalent of two standard $8\frac{1}{2}$ by 11-inch pages. The former 200 Log was criticized because it was unwieldy to copy and file and contained 12 columns for recording occupational injury and occupational illness cases.

Accordingly, OSHA has redesigned the OSHA 300 Log to fit on a legal size ($8\frac{1}{2}$ x 14 inches) piece of paper and to clarify that employers may use two lines to enter a case if the information does not fit easily on one line. The OSHA forms 300A and 301, and the remainder of the recordkeeping package, have also been designed to fit on the same-size paper as the OSHA 300 Log. For those employers who use computerized systems (where handwriting space is not as important) equivalent computer-generated forms can be printed out on $8\frac{1}{2}$ x 11 sheets of paper if the printed copies are legible and are as readable as the OSHA forms.

...

Defining Lost Workdays

In the final rule, OSHA has eliminated the term "lost workdays" on the forms and in the regulatory text. The use of the term has been confusing for many years because many people equated the terms ``lost workday" with "days away from work" and failed to recognize that the former OSHA term included restricted days. OSHA finds that deleting this term from the final rule and the forms will improve clarity and the consistency of the data.

The 300 Log has four check boxes to be used to classify the case: death, day(s) away from work, days of restricted work or job transfer; and case meeting other recording criteria. The employer must check the single box that reflects the most severe outcome associated with a given injury or illness. Thus, for an injury or illness where the injured worker first stayed home to recuperate and then was assigned to restricted work for several days, the employer is required only to check the box for days away from work (column I). For a case with only job transfer or restriction, the employer must check the box for days of restricted work or job transfer (Column H). However, the final

Log still allows employers to calculate the incidence rate formerly referred to as a "lost workday injury and illness rate" despite the fact that it separates the data formerly captured under this heading into two separate categories. Because the OSHA Form 300 has separate check boxes for days away from work cases and cases where the employee remained at work but was temporarily transferred to another job or assigned to restricted duty, it is easy to add the totals from these two columns together to obtain a single total to use in calculating an injury and illness incidence rate for total days away from work and restricted work cases.

Counting Days of Restricted Work or Job Transfer

Although the final rule does not use the term "lost workday" (which formerly applied both to days away from work and days of restricted or transferred work), the rule continues OSHA's longstanding practice of requiring employers to keep track of the number of days on which an employee is placed on restricted work or is on job transfer because of an injury or illness.

...

In the final rule, OSHA has decided to require employers to record the number of days of restriction or transfer on the OSHA 300 Log. From the comments received, and based on OSHA's own experience, the Agency finds that counts of restricted days are a useful and needed measure of injury and illness severity. OSHA's decision to require the recording of restricted and transferred work cases on the Log was also influenced by the trend toward restricted work and away from days away from work. In a recent article, the BLS noted that occupational injuries and illnesses are more likely to result in days of restricted work than was the case in the past. From 1978 to 1986, the annual rate in private industry for cases involving only restricted work remained constant, at 0.3 cases per 100 full-time workers. Since 1986, the rate has risen steadily to 1.2 cases per 100 workers in 1997, a fourfold increase. At the same time, cases with days away from work declined from 3.3 in 1986 to 2.1 in 1997 (Monthly Labor Review, June 1999, Vol. 122. No. 6, pp. 11-17). It is clear that employers have caused this shift by modifying their return-to-work policies and offering more restricted work opportunities to injured or ill employees. Therefore, in order to get an accurate picture of the extent of occupational injuries and illnesses, it is necessary for the OSHA Log to capture counts of days away from work and days of job transfer or restriction.

The final rule thus carries forward OSHA's longstanding requirement for employers to count and record the number of restricted days on the OSHA Log. On the Log, restricted work counts are separated from days away from work counts, and the term "lost workday" is no longer used. OSHA believes that the burden on employers of counting these days will be reduced somewhat by the simplified definition of restricted work, the counting of calendar days rather than work days, capping of the counts at 180 days, and allowing the employer to stop counting restricted days when the employees job has been permanently modified to eliminate the routine job functions being restricted (see the preamble discussion for 1904.7 General Recording Criteria).

Separate 300 Log Data on Occupational Injury and Occupational Illness

OSHA proposed (61 FR 4036-4037) to eliminate any differences in the way occupational injuries, as opposed to occupational illnesses, were recorded on the forms.

After a thorough review of the comments in the record, however, OSHA has concluded that the proposed approach, which would have eliminated for recording purposes, the distinction between work-related injuries and illnesses, is not workable in the final rule. The Agency finds that there is a continuing need for separately identifiable information on occupational illnesses and injuries, as well as on certain specific categories of occupational illnesses. The published BLS statistics have included separate estimates of the rate and number of occupational injuries and illnesses for many years, as well as the rate and number of different types of occupational illnesses, and employers, employees, the government, and the public have found this information useful and worthwhile. Separate illness and injury data are particularly useful at the establishment level, where employers and employees can use them to evaluate the establishment's health experience and compare it to the national experience or to the experience of other employers in their industry or their own prior experience. The data are also useful to OSHA personnel performing worksite inspections, who can use this information to identify potential health hazards at the establishment.

Under the final rule, the OSHA 300 form has therefore been modified specifically to collect information on five types of occupational health conditions: musculoskeletal disorders, skin diseases or disorders, respiratory conditions, poisoning, and hearing loss. There is also an "all other illness" column on the Log. To record cases falling into one of these categories, the employer simply enters a check mark in the appropriate column, which will allow these cases to be separately counted to generate establishment-level summary information at the end of the year.

...

In the final rule, two of the illness case columns on the OSHA 300 Log are identical to those on the former OSHA Log: a column to capture cases of skin diseases or disorders and one to capture cases of systemic poisoning. The single column for respiratory conditions on the new OSHA Form 300 will capture data on respiratory conditions that were formerly captured in two separate columns, i.e., the columns for respiratory conditions due to toxic agents (formerly column 7c) and for dust diseases of the lungs (formerly column 7b). Column 7g of the former OSHA Log provided space for data on all other occupational illnesses, and that column has also been continued on the new OSHA 300 Log. On the other hand, column 7e from the former OSHA Log, which captured cases of disorders due to physical agents, is not included on the new OSHA Log form. The cases recorded in former column 7e primarily addressed heat and cold disorders, such as heat stroke and hypothermia; hyperbaric effects, such as caisson disease; and the effects of radiation, including occupational illnesses caused by x-ray exposure, sun exposure and welder's flash. Because space on the form is at a premium, and because column 7e was not used extensively in the past (recorded column 7e cases accounted only for approximately five percent of all occupational illness cases),

OSHA has not continued this column on the new OSHA 300 Log.

...

Column on the Log for Musculoskeletal Disorders
[OSHA has proposed to delay for one year the definition of MSD and the requirement to check the MSD column. However, the same recording criteria applies to musculoskeletal disorders (MSDs) as to all other injuries and illnesses.]

The OSHA 301 Form
Although the final OSHA 300 Log presents information on injuries and illnesses in a condensed format, the final OSHA 301 Incident Record allows space for employers to provide more detailed information about the affected worker, the injury or illness, the workplace factors associated with the accident, and a brief description of how the injury or illness occurred. Many employers use an equivalent workers' compensation form or internal reporting form for the purpose of recording more detailed information on each case, and this practice is allowed under paragraph 1904.29(b)(4) of the final rule.

...

OSHA has also added several items to the OSHA Form 301 that were not on the former OSHA No. 101:
- The date the employee was hired;
- The time the employee began work;
- The time the event occurred;
- Whether the employee was treated at an emergency room; and
- Whether the employee was hospitalized overnight as an in-patient (the form now requires a check box entry rather than the name and address of the hospital).

OSHA concludes that these data fields will provide safety and health professionals and researchers with important information regarding the occurrence of occupational injuries and illnesses. The questions pertaining to what the employee was doing, how the injury or illness occurred, what the injury or illness was, and what object or substance was involved have been reworded somewhat from those contained on the former OSHA No. 101, but do not require employers or employees to provide additional information.

...

The final 301 form contains four questions eliciting case detail information (i.e., what was the employee doing just before the incident occurred?, what happened?, what was the injury or illness?, and what object or substance directly harmed the employee?). The language of these questions on the final 301 form has been modified slightly from that used in the proposed questions to be consistent with the language used on the BLS Survey of Occupational Injuries and Illnesses collection form. The BLS performed extensive testing of the language used in these questions while developing its survey form and has subsequently used these questions to collect data for many years. The BLS has found that the order in which these questions are presented and the wording of the questions on the survey form elicit the most complete answers to the relevant questions. OSHA believes that using the time-tested language and ordering of these four questions will have the same benefits for employers using the OSHA Form 301 as they have had for employers responding to the BLS Annual Survey. Matching the BLS wording and order will also result in benefits for those employers selected to participate in the BLS Annual Survey. To complete the BLS survey forms, employers will only need to copy information from the OSHA Injury and Illness Incident Report to the BLS survey form. This should be easier and less confusing than researching and rewording responses to the questions on two separate forms.

...

Subpart D. Other OSHA injury and illness recordkeeping requirements [p. 6035]

Subpart D of the final rule contains all of the 29 CFR Part 1904 requirements for keeping OSHA injury and illness records that do not actually pertain to entering the injury and illness data on the forms. The nine sections of Subpart D are:

- Section 1904.30, which contains the requirements for dealing with multiple business establishments;
- Section 1904.31, which contains the requirements for determining which employees' occupational injuries and illnesses must be recorded by the employer;
- Section 1904.32, which requires the employer to prepare and post the annual summary;
- Section 1904.33, which requires the employer to retain and update the injury and illness records;
- Section 1904.34, which requires the employer to transfer the records if the business changes owners;
- Section 1904.35, which includes requirements for employee involvement, including employees' rights to access the OSHA injury and illness information;
- Section 1904.36, which prohibits an employer from discriminating against employees for exercising their rights under the Act;
- Section 1904.37, which sets out the state recordkeeping regulations in OSHA approved State-Plan states; and
- Section 1904.38, which explains how an employer may seek a variance from the recordkeeping rule.

Section 1904.30 Multiple Establishments [p. 6035]

Section 1904.30 covers the procedures for recording injuries and illnesses occurring in separate establishments operated by the same business. For many businesses, these provisions are irrelevant because the business has only one establishment. However, many businesses have two or more establishments, and thus need to know how to apply the recordkeeping rule to multiple establishments. In particular, this section applies to businesses where separate work sites create confusion as to where injury and illness records should be kept and when separate records must be kept for separate work locations, or establishments. OSHA recognizes that the recordkeeping system must accommodate operations of this type, and has adopted language in the final rule to provide some flexibility for employers in the construction, transportation, communications, electric and gas utility, and sanitary services industries, as well as other employers with geographically dispersed operations. The final rule provides, in part, that operations are not considered separate establishments unless they continue to be in operation for a year or more. This length-of-site-operation provision increases the chances of discovering patterns of occupational injury and illness, eliminates the burden of creating OSHA 300 Logs for transient work sites, and ensures that useful records are generated for more permanent facilities.

...

The basic requirement of Sec. 1904.30(a) of this final rule states that employers are required to keep separate OSHA 300 Logs for each establishment that is expected to be in business for one year or longer. Paragraph 1904.30(b)(1) states that for short-term establishments, i.e., those that will exist for less than a year, employers are required to keep injury and illness records, but are not required to keep separate OSHA 300 Logs. They may keep one OSHA 300 Log covering all short-term establishments, or may include the short-term establishment records in logs that cover individual company divisions or geographic regions. For example, a construction company with multi-state operations might have separate OSHA 300 Logs for each state to show the injuries and illnesses of its employees engaged in short-term projects, as well as a separate OSHA 300 Log for each construction project expected to last for more than one year. If the same company had only one office location and none of its projects lasted for more than one year, the company would only be required to have one OSHA 300 Log.

Paragraph 1904.30(b)(2) allows the employer to keep records for separate establishments at the business' headquarters or another central location, provided that information can be transmitted from the establishment to headquarters or the central location within 7 days of the occurrence of the injury or illness, and provided that the employer is able to produce and send the OSHA records to each establishment when Sec. 1904.35 or Sec. 1904.40 requires such transmission. The sections of the final rule are consistent with the corresponding provisions of the proposed rule.

Paragraph 1904.30(b)(3) states that each employee must be linked, for recordkeeping purposes, with one of the employer's estab-lishments. Any injuries or illnesses sustained by the employee must be recorded on his or her home establishment's OSHA 300 Log, or on a general OSHA 300 Log for short-term establishments. This provision ensures that all employees are included in a company's records. If the establishment is in an industry classification partially exempted under Sec. 1904.2 of the final rule, records are not required. Under paragraph 1904.30(b)(4), if an employee is injured or made ill while visiting or working at another of the employer's establishments, then the injury or illness must be recorded on the 300 Log of the establishment at which the injury or illness occurred.

...

Recording Injuries and Illnesses Where They Occur

For the vast majority of cases, the place where the injury or illness occurred is the most useful recording location. The events or exposures that caused the case are most likely to be present at that location, so the data are most useful for analysis of that location's records. If the case is recorded at the employee's home base, the injury or illness data have been disconnected from the place where the case occurred, and where analysis of the data may help reveal a workplace hazard. Therefore, OSHA finds that it is most useful to record the injury or illness at the location where the case occurred. Of course, if the injury or illness occurs at another employer's workplace, or while the employee is in transit, the case would be recorded on the OSHA 300 Log of the employee's home establishment.

For cases of illness, two types of cases must be considered. The first is the case of an illness condition caused by an acute, or short term workplace exposure, such as skin rashes, respiratory ailments, and heat disorders. These illnesses generally manifest themselves quickly and can be linked to the workplace where they occur, which is no different than most injury cases. For illnesses that are caused by long-term exposures or which have long latency periods, the illness will most likely be detected during a visit to a physician or other health care professional, and the employee is most likely to report it to his or her supervisor at the home work location.

Recording these injuries and illnesses could potentially present a problem with incidence rate calculations. In many situations, visiting employees are a minority of the workforce, their hours worked are relatively inconsequential, and rates are thus unaffected to any meaningful extent. However, if an employer relies on visiting labor to perform a larger amount of the work, rates could be affected. In these situations, the hours of these personnel should be added to the establishment's hours of work for rate calculation purposes.

Section 1904.31 Covered employees [p. 6037]

Final Rule Requirements and Legal Background Section 1904.31 requires employers to record the injuries and illnesses of all their employees, whether classified as labor, executive, hourly, salaried, part-time, seasonal, or migrant workers. The section also requires the employer to record the injuries and illnesses of employees they supervise on a day-to-day basis, even if these workers are not carried on the employer's payroll. Implementing these requirements requires an understanding of the Act's definitions of "employer" and "employee." The statute defines "employer," in relevant part, to mean "a person engaged in a business affecting interstate commerce who has employees." 29 U.S.C. 652 (5). The term "person" includes "one or more individuals, partnerships, associations, corporations, business trusts, legal representatives, or any organized group of persons." 29 U.S.C. 652 (4). The term "employee" means "an employee of an employer who is employed in a business of his employer which affects interstate commerce." 29 U.S.C. 652(6). Thus, any individual or entity having an employment relationship with even one worker is an employer for purposes of this final rule, and must fulfill the recording requirements for each employee.

The application of the coverage principles in this section presents few issues for employees who are carried on the employer's payroll, because the employment relationship is usually well established in these cases. However, issues sometimes arise when an individual or entity enters into a temporary relationship with a worker. The first question is whether the worker is an employee of the hiring party. If an employment relationship exists, even if

temporary in duration, the employee's injuries and illnesses must be recorded on the OSHA 300 Log and 301 form. The second question, arising in connection with employees provided by a temporary help service or leasing agency, is which employer—the host firm or the temporary help service—is responsible for recordkeeping.

Whether an employment relationship exists under the Act is determined in accordance with established common law principles of agency. At common law, a self-employed "independent contractor" is not an employee; therefore, injuries and illnesses sustained by independent contractors are not recordable under the final Recordkeeping rule. To determine whether a hired party is an employee or an independent contractor under the common law test, the hiring party must consider a number of factors, including the degree of control the hiring party asserts over the manner in which the work is done, and the degree of skill and independent judgment the hired party is expected to apply. Loomis Cabinet Co. v. OSHRC, 20 F.3d 938, 942 (9th Cir. 1994).

Other individuals, besides independent contractors, who are not considered to be employees under the OSH Act are unpaid volunteers, sole proprietors, partners, family members of farm employers, and domestic workers in a residential setting. See 29 CFR Sec. 1975.4(b)(2) and Sec. 1975.6 for a discussion of the latter two categories of workers. As is the case with independent contractors, no employment relationship exists between these individuals and the hiring party, and consequently, no recording obligation arises.

A related coverage question sometimes arises when an employer obtains labor from a temporary help service, employee leasing firm or other personnel supply service. Frequently the temporary workers are on the payroll of the temporary help service or leasing firm, but are under the day-to-day supervision of the host party. In these cases, Section 1904.31 places the recordkeeping obligation upon the host, or utilizing, employer. The final rule's allocation of recordkeeping responsibility to the host employer in these circumstances is consistent with the Act for several reasons.

First, the host employer's exercise of day-to-day supervision of the temporary workers and its control over the work environment demonstrates a high degree of control over the temporary workers consistent with the presence of an employment relationship at common law. See Loomis Cabinet Co., 20 F.3d at 942. Thus, the temporary workers will ordinarily be the employees of the party exercising day-to-day control over them, and the supervising party will be their employer.

Even if daily supervision is not sufficient alone to establish that the host party is the employer of the temporary workers, there are other reasons for the final rule's allocation of recordkeeping responsibility. Under the OSH Act, an employer's duties and responsibilities are not limited only to his own employees. Cf. Universal Constr. Co. v. OSHRC, 182 F.3d 726, 728-731 (10th Cir. 1999). Assuming that the host is an employer under the Act (because it has an employment relationship with someone) it reasonably should record the injuries of all employees, whether or not its own, that it supervises on a daily basis. This follows because the supervising employer is in the best position to obtain the necessary injury and illness information due to its control over the worksite and its familiarity with the work tasks and the work environment.

Section 1904.32 Annual Summary [p. 6042]

At the end of each calendar year, section 1904.32 of the final rule requires each covered employer to review his or her OSHA 300 Log for completeness and accuracy and to prepare an Annual Summary of the OSHA 300 Log using the form OSHA 300-A, Summary of Work-Related Injuries and Illnesses, or an equivalent form. The summary must be certified for accuracy and completeness and be posted in the workplace by February 1 of the year following the year covered by the summary. The summary must remain posted until April 30 of the year in which it was posted. Preparing the Annual Summary requires four steps: reviewing the OSHA 300 Log, computing and entering the summary information on the Form 300-A, certification, and posting. First, the employer must review the Log as extensively as necessary to make sure it is accurate and complete.

Second, the employer must total the columns on the Log; transfer them to the summary form; and enter the calendar year covered, the name of the employer, the name and address of the establishment, the average number of employees on the establishment's payroll for the calendar year, and the total hours worked by the covered employees. If there were no recordable cases at the establishment for the year covered, the summary must nevertheless be completed by entering zeros in the total for each column of the OSHA 300 Log. If a form other than the OSHA 300-A is used, as permitted by paragraph 1904.29(b)(4), the alternate form must contain the same information as the OSHA 300-A form and include identical statements concerning employee access to the Log and Summary and employer penalties for falsifying the document as are found on the OSHA 300-A form.

Third, the employer must certify to the accuracy and completeness of the Log and Summary, using a two-step process. The person or persons who supervise the preparation and maintenance of the Log and Summary (usually the person who keeps the OSHA records) must sign the certification statement on the form, based on their direct knowledge of the data on which it was based. Then, to ensure greater awareness and accountability of the recordkeeping process, a company executive, who may be an owner, a corporate officer, the highest ranking official working at the establishment, or that person's immediate supervisor, must also sign the form to certify to its accuracy and completeness. Certification of the summary attests that the individual making the certification has a reasonable belief, derived from his or her knowledge of the process by which the information in the Log was reported and recorded, that the Log and summary are "true" and "complete."

Fourth, the Summary must be posted no later than February 1 of the year following the year covered in the Summary and remain posted until April 30 of that year in a conspicuous place where notices are customarily posted. The employer must ensure that the Summary is not defaced or altered during the 3 month posting period.

Changes from the former rule. Although the final rule's requirements for preparing the Annual Summary are generally similar to those of the former rule, the final rule incorporates four important changes that OSHA believes will strengthen the recordkeeping process by ensuring greater completeness and accuracy of the Log and Summary, providing employers and employees with better information to understand and evaluate the injury and illness data on the Annual Summary, and facilitating greater employer and employee awareness of the recordkeeping process.

1. **Company Executive Certification of the Annual Summary.** The final rule carries forward the proposed rule's requirement for certification by a higher ranking company official, with minor revision. OSHA concludes that the company executive certification process will ensure greater completeness and accuracy of the Summary by raising accountability for OSHA recordkeeping to a higher managerial level than existed under the former rule. OSHA believes that senior management accountability is essential if the Log and Annual Summary are to be accurate and complete. The integrity of the OSHA recordkeeping system, which is relied on by the BLS for national injury and illness statistics, by OSHA and employers to understand hazards in the workplaces, by employees to assist in the identification and control of the hazards identified, and by safety and health professionals everywhere to analyze trends, identify emerging hazards, and develop solutions, is essential to these objectives. Because OSHA cannot oversee the preparation of the Log and Summary at each establishment and cannot audit more than a small sample of all covered employers' records, this goal is accomplished by requiring employers or company executives to certify the accuracy and completeness of the Log and Summary.

The company executive certification requirement imposes different obligations depending on the structure of the company. If the company is a sole proprietorship or partnership, the certification may be made by the owner. If the company is a corporation, the certification may be made by a corporate officer. For any management structure, the certification may be made by the highest ranking company official working at the establishment covered by the Log (for example, the plant manager or site supervisor), or the latter official's supervisor (for example, a corporate or regional director who works at a different establishment, such as company headquarters).

The company executive certification is intended to ensure that a high ranking company official with responsibility for the recordkeeping activity and the authority to ensure that the recordkeeping function is performed appropriately has examined the records and has a reasonable belief, based on his or her knowledge of that process, that the records are accurate and complete.

The final rule does not specify how employers are to evaluate their recordkeeping systems to ensure their accuracy and completeness or what steps an employer must follow to certify the accuracy and completeness of the Log and Summary with confidence. However, to be able to certify that one has a reasonable belief that the records are complete and accurate would suggest, at a minimum, that the certifier is familiar with OSHA's recordkeeping requirements, and the company's recordkeeping practices and policies, has read the Log and Summary, and has obtained assurance from the staff responsible for maintaining the records (if the certifier does not personally keep the records) that all of OSHA's requirements have been met and all practices and policies followed. In most if not all cases, the certifier will be familiar with the details of some of the injuries and illnesses that have occurred at the establishment and will therefore be able to spot check the OSHA 300 Log to see if those cases have been entered correctly. In many cases, especially in small to medium establishments, the certifier will be aware of all of the injuries and illnesses that have been reported at the establishment and will thus be able to inspect the forms to make sure all of the cases that should have been entered have in fact been recorded.

The certification required by the final rule may be made by signing and dating the certification section of the OSHA 300-A form, which replaces the summary portion of the former OSHA 200 form, or by signing and dating a separate certification statement and appending it to the OSHA Form 300-A. A separate certification statement must contain the identical penalty warnings and employee access information as found on the OSHA Form 300-A. A separate statement may be needed when the certifier works at another location and the certification is mailed or faxed to the location where the Summary is posted.

The certification requirement modifies the certification provision of the former rule (former paragraph 1904.5(c)), which required a certification of the Annual Summary by the employer or an officer or employee who supervised the preparation of the Log and Summary. The former rule required that individual to sign and date the year-end summary on the OSHA Form 200 and to certify that the summary was true and complete. Alternatively, the recordkeeper could, under the former rule, sign a separate certification statement rather than signing the OSHA form.

...

2. **Number of employees and hours worked.** Injury and illness records provide a valuable tool for OSHA, employers, and employees to determine where and why injuries and illnesses occur, and they are crucial in the development of prevention strategies. The final rule requires employers to include in the Annual Summary (the OSHA Form 300-A) the annual average number of employees covered by the Log and the total hours worked by all covered employees.

...

OSHA's view is that the value of the total hours worked and average number of employees information requires its inclusion in the Summary, and the final rule reflects this determination. Having this information will enable employers and employees to calculate injury and illness incidence rates, which are widely regarded as the best statistical measure for the purpose of comparing an establishment's injury and illness

experience with national statistics, the records of other establishment, or trends over several years. Having the data available on the Form 300-A will also make it easier for the employer to respond to government requests for the data, which occurs when the BLS and OSHA collect the data by mail, and when an OSHA or State inspector visits the facility. In particular, it will be easier for the employer to provide the OSHA inspector with the hours worked and employment data for past years.

OSHA does not believe that this requirement creates the time and cost burden some commenters to the record suggested, because the information is readily available in payroll or other records required to be kept for other purposes, such as income tax, unemployment, and workers' compensation insurance records. For the approximately 10% of covered employers who participate in the BLS's Annual Survey of Occupational Injuries and Illnesses, there will be no additional burden because this information must already be provided to the BLS. Moreover, the rule does not require employers to use any particular method of calculating the totals, thus providing employers who do not maintain certain records—for example the total hours worked by salaried employees—or employers without sophisticated computer systems, the flexibility to obtain the information in any reasonable manner that meets the objectives of the rule. Employers who do not have the ability to generate precise numbers can use various estimation methods. For example, employers typically must estimate hours worked for workers who are paid on a commission or salary basis. Additionally, the instructions for the OSHA 300-A Summary form include a worksheet to help the employer calculate the total numbers of hours worked and the average number of employees.

3. **Extended posting period.** The final rule's requirement increasing the summary Form 300-A posting period from one month to three months is intended to raise employee awareness of the recordkeeping process (especially that of new employees hired during the posting period) by providing greater access to the previous year's summary without having to request it from management. The additional two months

of posting will triple the time employees have to observe the data without imposing additional burdens on the employer. The importance of employee awareness of and participation in the recordkeeping process is discussed in the preamble to sections 1904.35 and 1904.36. The requirement to post the Summary on February 1 is unchanged from the posting date required by the former rule.

...

After a review of all the comments received and its own extensive experience with the recordkeeping system and its implementation in a variety of workplaces, OSHA has decided to adopt a 3-month posting period. The additional posting period will provide employees with additional opportunity to review the summary information, raise employee awareness of the records and their right to access them, and generally improve employee participation in the recordkeeping system without creating a "wallpaper" posting of untimely data. In addition, OSHA has concluded that any additional burden on employers will be minimal at best and, in most cases, insignificant. All the final rule requires the employer to do is to leave the posting on the bulletin board instead of removing it at the end of the one-month period. In fact, many employers preferred to leave the posting on the bulletin board for longer than the required one-month period in the past, simply to provide workers with the opportunity to view the Annual Summary and increase their awareness of the recordkeeping system in general and the previous year's injury and illness data in particular. OSHA agrees that the 3-month posting period required by the final rule will have these benefits which, in the Agency's view, greatly outweigh any minimal burden that may be associated with such posting. The final rule thus requires that the Summary be posted from February 1 until April 30, a period of three months; OSHA believes that the 30 days in January will be ample, as it has been in the past, for preparing the current year's Summary preparatory to posting.

4. **Review of the records.** The provisions of the final rule requiring the employer to review the Log entries before totaling them for the Annual Summary are intended as an additional quality control measure that will improve the accuracy of the information in the Annual Summary, which is posted to provide information to employees and is also used as a data source by OSHA and the BLS. Depending on the size of the establishment and the number of injuries and illnesses on the OSHA 300 Log, the employer may wish to cross-check with any other relevant records to make sure that all the recordable injuries and illnesses have been included on the Summary. These records may include workers' compensation injury reports, medical records, company accident reports, and/or time and attendance records.

...

Section 1904.33 Retention and Updating [p. 6048]

Section 1904.33 of the final rule deals with the retention and updating of the OSHA Part 1904 records after they have been created and summarized. The final rule requires the employer to save the OSHA 300 Log, the Annual Summary, and the OSHA 301 Incident Report forms for five years following the end of the calendar year covered by the records. The final rule also requires the employer to update the entries on the OSHA 300 Log to include newly discovered cases and show changes that have occurred to previously recorded cases. The provisions in section 1904.33 state that the employer is not required to update the 300A Annual Summary or the 301 Incident Reports, although the employer is permitted to update these forms if he or she wishes to do so.

As this section makes clear, the final rule requires employers to retain their OSHA 300 and 301 records for five years following the end of the year to which the records apply. Additionally, employers must update their OSHA 300 Logs under two circumstances. First, if the employer discovers a recordable injury or illness that has not previously been recorded, the case must be entered on the forms. Second, if a previously recorded injury or illness turns out, based on later information, not to have been recorded properly, the employer must modify the previous entry. For example, if the description or outcome of a case changes (a case requiring medical treatment becomes worse and the employee must take days off work to recuperate), the employer must remove or line out the original entry and enter the new information. The employer also has a duty to enter the date of an employee's return to work or the date of an injured worker's death on the Form 301; OSHA considers the entering of this information an integral part of the recordkeeping for such cases. The Annual Summary and the Form 301 need not be updated, unless the employer wishes to do so. The requirements in this section 1904.33 do not affect or supersede any longer retention periods specified in other OSHA standards and regulations, e.g., in OSHA health standards such as Cadmium, Benzene, or Lead (29 CFR 1910.1027, 1910.1028, and 1910.1025, respectively).

...

Section 1904.34 Change in Business Ownership [p. 6050]

Section 1904.34 of the final rule addresses the situation that arises when a particular employer ceases operations at an establishment during a calendar year, and the establishment is then operated by a new employer for the remainder of the year. The phrase "change of ownership," for the purposes of this section, is relevant only to the transfer of the responsibility to make and retain OSHA-required injury and illness records. In other words, if one employer, as defined by the OSH Act, transfers ownership of an establishment to a different employer, the new entity becomes responsible for retaining the previous employer's past OSHA-required records and for creating all new records required by this rule.

The final rule requires the previous owner to transfer these records to the new owner, and it limits the recording and recordkeeping responsibilities of the previous employer only to the period of the prior owner. Specifically, section 1904.34 provides that if the business changes ownership, each employer is responsible for recording and reporting work-related injuries and illnesses only for that period of the year during which each employer owned the establishment. The selling employer is required to transfer his or her Part 1904 records to the new owner, and the new owner must save all records of the establishment kept by the prior owner. However, the new owner is not required to update or correct the records of the prior owner, even if new information about old cases becomes available.

...

Sections 1904.35 Employee Involvement, and 1904.36, Prohibition Against Discrimination [p. 6050]

One of the goals of the final rule is to enhance employee involvement in the recordkeeping process. OSHA believes that employee involvement is essential to the success of all aspects of an employer's safety and health program. This is especially true in the area of recordkeeping, because free and frank reporting by employees is the cornerstone of the system. If employees fail to report their injuries and illnesses, the "picture" of the workplace that the employer's OSHA forms 300 and 301 reveal will be inaccurate and misleading. This means, in turn, that employers and employees will not have the information they need to improve safety and health in the workplace. Section 1904.35 of the final rule therefore establishes an affirmative requirement for employers to involve their employees and employee representatives in the recordkeeping process. The employer must inform each employee of how to report an injury or illness, and must provide limited access to the injury and illness records for employees and their representatives. Section 1904.36 of the final rule makes clear that Sec. 11(c) of the Act prohibits employers from discriminating against employees for reporting work-related injuries and illnesses. Section 1904.36 does not create a new obligation on employers. Instead, it clarifies that the OSH Act's anti-discrimination protection applies to employees who seek to participate in the recordkeeping process.

Under the employee involvement provisions of the final rule, employers are required to let employees know how and when to report work-related injuries and illnesses. This means that the employer must establish a procedure for the reporting of work-related injuries and illnesses and train its employees to use that procedure. The rule does not specify how the employer must accomplish these objectives. The size of the workforce, employees' language proficiency and literacy levels, the workplace culture, and other factors will determine what will be effective for any particular workplace.[footnote omitted]

Employee involvement also requires that employees and their representatives have access to the establishment's injury and illness records. Employee involvement is further enhanced by other parts of the final rule, such as the extended posting period provided in section 1904.32 and the access statements on the new 300 and 301 forms.

...

Employee access to OSHA injury and illness records The Part 1904 final rule continues OSHA's long-standing policy of allowing employees and their representatives access to the occupational injury and illness information kept by their employers, with some limitations. However, the final rule includes several changes to improve employees' access to the information, while at the same time implementing several measures to protect the privacy interests of injured and ill employees. Section 1904.35 requires an employer covered by the Part 1904 regulation to provide limited access to the OSHA recordkeeping forms to current and former employees, as well as to two types of employee representatives. The first is a personal representative of an employee or former employee, who is a person that the employee or former employee designates, in writing, as his or her personal representative, or is the legal representative of a deceased or legally incapacitated employee or former employee. The second is an authorized employee representative, which is defined as an authorized collective bargaining agent of one or more employees working at the employer's establishment.

Section 1904.35 accords employees and their representatives three separate access rights. First, it gives any employee, former employee, personal representative, or authorized employee representative the right to a copy of the current OSHA 300 Log, and to any stored OSHA 300 Log(s), for any establishment in which the employee or former employee has worked. The employer must provide one free copy of the OSHA 300 Log(s) by the end of the next business day. The employee, former employee, personal representative or authorized employee representative is not entitled to see, or to obtain a copy of, the confidential list of names and case numbers for privacy cases. Second, any employee, former employee, or personal representative is entitled to one free copy of the OSHA 301 Incident Report describing an injury or illness to that employee by the end of the next business day. Finally, an authorized employee representative is entitled to copies of the right-hand portion of all OSHA 301 forms for the establishment(s) where the agent represents one or more employees under a collective bargaining agreement. The right-hand portion of the 301 form contains the heading "Tell us about the case," and elicits information about how the injury occurred, including the employee's actions just prior to the incident, the materials and tools involved, and how the incident occurred, but does not contain the employee's name. No information other than that on the right-hand portion of the form may be disclosed to an authorized employee representative. The employer must provide the authorized employee representative with one free copy of all the 301 forms for the establishment within 7 calendar days.

Employee privacy is protected in the final rule in paragraphs 1904.29(b)(7) to (10). Paragraph 1904.29(b)(7) requires the employer to enter the words "privacy case" on the OSHA 300 Log, in lieu of the employee's name, for recordable privacy concern cases involving the following types of injuries and illnesses: (i) an injury from a needle or sharp object contaminated by another person's blood or other potentially infectious material; (ii) an injury or illness to an intimate body part or to the reproductive system; (iii) an injury or illness resulting from a sexual assault; (iv) a mental illness; (v) an illness involving HIV, hepatitis, or tuberculosis, or (vi) any other illness, if the employee independently and voluntarily requests that his or her name not be entered on the log. Musculoskeletal disorders (MSDs) are not considered privacy concern cases, and thus employers are required to enter the names of employees experiencing these disorders on the log. The employer must keep a separate, confidential list of the case numbers and employee names for privacy cases. The employer may take additional action in privacy concern cases if warranted. Paragraph 1904.29(b)(9) allows the employer to use discretion in describing the nature of the injury or illness in a privacy concern case, if the employer has a reasonable basis to believe that the injured or ill employee may be identified from the records even though the employee's name has been removed. Only the six types of injuries and illnesses listed in Paragraph 1904.29(b)(7) may be considered privacy concern cases, and thus the additional protection offered by paragraph 1904.29(b)(9) applies only to such cases.

Paragraph 1904.29(b)(10) protects employee privacy if the employer decides voluntarily to disclose the OSHA 300 and 301 forms to persons other than those who have a mandatory right of access under the final rule. The paragraph requires the employer to remove or hide employees' names or other personally identifying information before disclosing the forms to persons other than government representatives, employees, former employees or authorized representatives, as required by paragraphs 1904.40 and 1904.35, except in three cases. The employer may disclose the forms, complete with personally identifying information, (2) only: (i) to an auditor or consultant hired by the employer to evaluate the safety and health program; (ii) to the extent necessary for processing a claim for workers' compensation or other insurance benefits; or (iii) to a public health authority or law enforcement agency for uses and disclosures for which consent, an authorization, or opportunity to agree or object is not required under section 164.512 of the final rule on Standards for Privacy of Individually Identifiable Health Information, 45 CFR 164.512.

Section 1904.37 State Recordkeeping Regulations [p. 6060]

Section 1904.37 addresses the consistency of the recordkeeping and reporting requirements between Federal OSHA and those States where occupational safety and health enforcement is provided by an OSHA-approved State Plan. Currently, in 21 States and 2 territories, the State government has been granted authority to operate a State OSHA Plan covering both the private and public (State and local government) sectors under section 18 of the OSH Act (see the State Plan section of this preamble for a listing of these States). Two additional States currently operate programs limited in scope to State and local government employees only. State Plans, once approved, operate under authority of State law and provide programs of standards, regulations and enforcement which must be "at least as effective" as the Federal program. (State Plans must extend their coverage to State and local government employees, workers not otherwise covered by Federal OSHA regulations.) Section 1904.37 of the final rule describes what State Plan recordkeeping requirements must be identical to the Federal requirements, which State regulations may be different, and provides cross references to the State Plan regulations codified in Section 1902.3(k), 1952.4, and 1956.10(i). The provisions of Subpart A of 29 CFR part 1952 specify the regulatory discretion of the State Plans in general, and section 1952.4 spells out the regulatory discretion of the State Plans specifically for the recordkeeping regulation.

...

Under Section 18 of the OSH Act, a State Plan must require employers in the State to make reports to the Secretary in the same manner and to the same extent as if the Plan were not in effect. Final section 1904.37 makes clear that States with approved State Plans must promulgate new regulations that are substantially identical to the final Federal rule. State Plans must have recording and reporting regulations that impose identical requirements for the recordability of occupational injuries and illnesses and the manner in which they are entered. These requirements must be the same for employers in all the States, whether under Federal or State Plan jurisdiction, and for State and local government employers covered only through State Plans, to ensure that the occupational injury and illness data for the entire nation are uniform and consistent so that statistics that allow comparisons between the States and between employers located in different States are created.

For all of the other requirements of the Part 1904 regulations, the regulations adopted by the State Plans may be more stringent than or supplemental to the Federal regulations, pursuant to paragraph 1952.4(b). This means that the States' recording and reporting regulations could differ in several ways from their Federal Part 1904 counterparts. For example, a State Plan could require employers to keep records for the State, even though those employers are within an industry exempted by the Federal rule. A State Plan could also require employers to keep additional supplementary injury and illness information, require employers to report fatality and multiple hospitalization incidents within a shorter timeframe than Federal OSHA does, require other types of incidents to be reported as they occur, or impose other requirements. While a State Plan must assure that all employee participation and access rights are assured, the State may provide broader access to records by employees and their representatives. However, because of the unique nature of the national recordkeeping program, States must secure Federal OSHA approval for these enhancements.

...

OSHA understands the advantages to multi-State businesses of following identical OSHA rules in both Federal and State Plan jurisdictions, but also recognizes the value of allowing the States to have different rules to meet the needs of each State, as well as the States' right to impose different rules as long as the State rule is at least as effective as the Federal rule. Accordingly, the Part 1904 rules impose identical requirements where they are needed to create consistent injury and illness statistics for the nation and allows the States to impose supplemental or more stringent requirements where doing so will not interfere with the maintenance of comprehensive and uniform national statistics on workplace fatalities, injuries and illnesses.

Section 1904.38 Variances From the Recordkeeping Rule [p. 6061]

Section 1904.38 of the final rule explains the procedures employers must follow in those rare instances where they request that OSHA grant them a variance or exception to the recordkeeping rules in Part 1904.

The rule contains these procedures to allow an employer who wishes to maintain records in a manner that is different from the approach required by the rules in Part 1904 to petition the Assistant Secretary.

Section 1904.8 allows the employer to apply to the Assistant Secretary for OSHA and request a Part 1904 variance if he or she can show that the alternative recordkeeping system: (1) Collects the same information as this Part requires; (2) Meets the purposes of the Act; and (3) Does not interfere with the administration of the Act.

The variance petition must include several items, namely the employer's name and address; a list of the State(s) where the variance would be used; the addresses of the business establishments involved; a description of why the employer is seeking a variance; a description of the different recordkeeping procedures the employer is proposing to use; a description of how the employer's proposed procedures will collect the same information as would be collected by the Part 1904 requirements and achieve the purpose of the Act; and a statement that the employer has informed its employees of the petition by giving them or their authorized representative a copy of the petition and by posting a statement summarizing the petition in the same way notices are posted under paragraph 1903.2(a).

The final rule the describes how the Assistant Secretary will handle the variance petition by taking the following steps:

- The Assistant Secretary will offer employees and their authorized representatives an opportunity to comment on the variance petition. The employees and their authorized representatives will be allowed to submit written data, views, and arguments about the petition.
- The Assistant Secretary may allow the public to comment on the variance petition by publishing the petition in the Federal Register. If the petition is published, the notice will establish a public comment period and may include a schedule for a public meeting on the petition.

- After reviewing the variance petition and any comments from employees and the public, the Assistant Secretary will decide whether or not the proposed recordkeeping procedures will meet the purposes of the Act, will not otherwise interfere with the Act, and will provide the same information as the Part 1904 regulations provide. If the procedures meet these criteria, the Assistant Secretary may grant the variance subject to such conditions as he or she finds appropriate.
- If the Assistant Secretary grants the variance petition, OSHA will publish a notice in the Federal Register to announce the variance. The notice will include the practices the variance allows, any conditions that apply, and the reasons for allowing the variance.

The final rule makes clear that the employer may not use the proposed recordkeeping procedures while the Assistant Secretary is processing the variance petition and must wait until the variance is approved. The rule also provides that, if the Assistant Secretary denies the petition, the employer will receive notice of the denial within a reasonable time and establishes that a variance petition has no effect on the citation and penalty for a citation that has been previously issued by OSHA and that the Assistant Secretary may elect not to review a variance petition if it includes an element which has been cited and the citation is still under review by a court, an Administrative Law Judge (ALJ), or the OSH Review Commission.

The final rule also states that the Assistant Secretary may revoke a variance at a later date if the Assistant Secretary has good cause to do so, and that the procedures for revoking a variance will follow the same process as OSHA uses for reviewing variance petitions. Except in cases of willfulness or where necessary for public safety, the Assistant Secretary will: Notify the employer in writing of the facts or conduct that may warrant revocation of a variance and provide the employer, employees, and authorized employee representatives with an opportunity to participate in the revocation procedures.

...

Like the former variance section of the rule, the final rule does not specifically note that the states operating OSHA-approved state plans are not permitted to grant recordkeeping variances. Paragraph (b) of former section 1952.4, OSHA's rule governing the operation of the State plans, prohibited the states from granting variances, and paragraph (c) of that rule required the State plans to recognize any Federal recordkeeping variances. The same procedures continue to apply to variances under section 1904.37 and section 1952.4 of this final rule. OSHA has not included the provisions from these two sections in the variance sections of this recordkeeping rule, because doing so would be repetitive.

The final rule adds several provisions to those of the former rule. They include (1) the identification of petitioning employers' pending citations in State plan states, (2) the discretion given to OSHA not to consider a petition if a citation on the same subject matter is pending, (3) the clarification that OSHA may provide additional notice via the Federal Register and opportunity for comment, (4) the clarification that variances have only prospective effect, (5) the opportunity of employees and their representatives to participate in revocation procedures, and (6) the voiding of all previous variances and exceptions.

Variance procedures were not discussed in the Recordkeeping Guidelines (Ex. 2), nor have there been any letters of interpretations or OSHRC or court decisions on recordkeeping variances. As noted in the proposal, at 61 FR 4039, only one recordkeeping variance has ever been granted by OSHA. This variance was granted to AT&T and subsequently expanded to its Bell subsidiaries to enable them to centralize records maintenance for workers in the field.

...

Subpart E. Reporting Fatality, Injury and Illness Information to the Government [p. 6062]

Subpart E of this final rule consolidates those sections of the rule that require employers to give recordkeeping information to the government. In the proposed rule, these sections were not grouped together. OSHA believes that grouping these sections into one Subpart improves the overall organization of the rule and will make it easier for employers to find the information when needed. The four sections of this subpart of the final rule are:

(a) Section 1904.39, which requires employers to report fatality and multiple hospitalization incidents to OSHA.

(b) Section 1904.40, which requires an employer to provide his or her occupational illness and injury records to a government inspector during the course of a safety and health inspection.

(c) Section 1904.41, which requires employers to send their occupational illness and injury records to OSHA when the Agency sends a written request asking for specific types of information.

(d) Section 1904.42, which requires employers to send their occupational illness and injury records to the Bureau of Labor Statistics (BLS) when the BLS sends a survey form asking for information from these records.

Each of these sections, and the record evidence pertaining to them, is discussed below.

Section 1904.39 Reporting Fatality or Multiple Hospitalization Incidents to OSHA [p. 6062]

...

Making oral reports of fatalities or multiple hospitalization incidents and the OSHA 800 number.

...

It is essential for OSHA to speak promptly to any employer whose employee(s) have experienced a fatality or multiple hospitalization incident to determine whether the Agency needs to begin an investigation. Therefore, the final rule does not permit employers merely to leave a message on an answering machine, send a fax, or transmit an e-mail message. None of these options allows an Agency representative to interact with the employer to clarify the particulars of the catastrophic incident. Additionally, if the Area Office were closed for the weekend, a holiday, or for some other reason, OSHA might not learn of the incident for several days if electronic or facsimile transmission were permitted. Paragraph 1904.39(b)(1) of the final rule makes this clear.

As noted, OSHA allows the employer to report a fatality or multiple hospitalization incident by speaking to an OSHA representative at the local Area Office either on the phone or in person, or by using the 800 number. This policy gives the employer flexibility to report using whatever mechanism is most convenient. The employer may use whatever method he or she chooses, at any time, as long as he or she is able to speak in person to an OSHA representative or the 800 number operator. Therefore, there is no need to define business hours or otherwise add additional information about when to use the 800 number; it is always an acceptable option for complying with this reporting requirement.

This final rule also includes the 800 number in the text of the regulation. OSHA has decided to include the number in the regulatory text at this time to provide an easy reference for employers. OSHA will also continue to include the 800 number in any interpretive materials, guidelines or outreach materials that it publishes to help employers comply with the reporting requirement.

...

Motor vehicle and public transportation accidents.

...

[OSHA believes] that there is no need for an employer to report a fatality or multiple hospitalization incident when OSHA is clearly not going to make an investigation. When a worker is killed or injured in a motor vehicle accident on a public highway or street, OSHA is only likely to investigate the incident if it occurred in a highway construction zone. Likewise, when a worker is killed or injured in an airplane crash, a train wreck, or a subway accident, OSHA does not investigate, and there is thus no need for the employer to report the incident to OSHA. The text of paragraphs 1904.39(b)(3) and (4) of the final rule clarifies that an employer is not required to report these incidents to OSHA. These incidents are normally investigated by other agencies, including local transit authorities, local or State police, State transportation officials, and the U.S. Department of Transportation.

However, although there is no need to report these incidents to OSHA under the 8-hour reporting requirement, any fatalities and hospitalizations caused by motor vehicle accidents, as well as commercial or public transportation accidents, are recordable if they meet OSHA's recordability criteria. These cases should be captured by the Nation's occupational fatality and injury statistics and be included on the employer's injury and illness forms. The statistics need to be complete, so that OSHA, BLS, and the public can see where and how employees are being made ill, injured and killed. Accordingly, the final rule includes a sentence clarifying that employers are still required to record work-related fatalities and injuries that occur as a result of public transportation accidents and injuries.

Although commenters are correct that OSHA only rarely investigates motor vehicle accidents, the Agency does investigate motor vehicle accidents that occur at street or highway construction sites. Such accidents are of concern to the Agency, and OSHA seeks to learn new ways to prevent these accidents and protect employees who are exposed to them. For example, OSHA is currently participating in a Local Emphasis Program in the State of New Jersey that is designed to protect highway construction workers who are exposed to traffic hazards while performing construction work. Therefore, the final rule provides provisions that require an employer to report a fatality or multiple hospitalization incident that occurs in a construction zone on a public highway or street.

...

Section 1904.40 Providing Records to Government Representatives [p. 6065]

Under the final rule, employers must provide a complete copy of any records required by Part 1904 to an authorized government representative, including the Form 300 (Log), the Form 300A(Summary), the confidential listing of privacy concern cases along with the names of the injured or ill privacy case workers, and the Form 301 (Incident Report), when the representative asks for the records during a workplace safety and health inspection. This requirement is unchanged from the corresponding requirement in OSHA's former recordkeeping rule.

However, the former rule combined the requirements governing both government inspectors' and employers' rights of access to the records into a single section, section 1904.7 "Access to Records." The final rule separates the two. It places the requirements governing access to the records by government inspectors in Subpart E, along with other provisions requiring employers to submit their occupational injury and illness records to the government or to provide government personnel access to them. Provisions for employee access to records are now in section 1904.35, Employee Involvement, in Subpart D of this final rule.

The final regulatory text of paragraph (a) of section 1904.40 requires an employer to provide an authorized government representative with records kept under Part 1904 within four business hours. As stated in paragraph 1904.40(b)(1), the authorized government representatives who have a right to obtain the Part 1904 records are a representative of the Secretary of Labor conducting an inspection or investigation under the Act, a representative of the Secretary of Health and Human Services (including the National Institute for Occupational Safety and Health (NIOSH) conducting an investigation under Section 20(b) of the Act, or a representative of a State agency responsible for administering a State plan approved under section 18 of the Act. The government's right to ask for such records is limited by the jurisdiction of that Agency. For example, a representative of an OSHA approved State plan could only ask for the records when visiting an establishment within that state.

The final rule allows the employer to take into account difficulties that may be encountered if the records are kept at a location in a different time zone from the establishment where the government representative has asked for the records. If the employer maintains the records at a location in a different time zone, OSHA will use the business hours of the establishment at which the records are located when calculating the deadline, as permitted by paragraph 1904.40(b)(2).

...

Government Representatives. Each employer shall provide, upon a request made in person or in writing, copies of the OSHA Forms 300 and 301 or equivalents, and year-end summaries for their own employees, and injury and illness records for "subcontractor employees" as required under this Part to any authorized representative of the Secretary of Labor or Secretary of Health and Human Services or to any authorized representative of a State accorded jurisdiction for occupational safety and health for the purposes of carrying out the Act.

(1) When the request is made in person, the information must be provided in hard copy (paper printout) within 4 hours. If the information is being transmitted to the establishment from some other location, using telefax or other electronic transmission, the employer may provide a copy to the government representative present at the establishment or to the government representative's office.

(2) When the request is made in writing, the information must be provided within 21 days of receipt of the written request, unless the Secretary requests otherwise.

...

Privacy of medical records.

...

This section of the final rule does not give unfettered access to the records by the public, but simply allows a government inspector to use the records during the course of a safety and health inspection. As discussed above in the section covering access to the records for employees, former employees, and employee representatives (Section 1904.35), OSHA does not consider the Forms 300 and 301 to be medical records, for the following reasons. First, they do not have to be completed by a physician or other licensed health care professional. Second, they do not contain the detailed diagnostic and treatment information usually found in medical records. Finally, the injuries and illnesses found in the records are usually widely known among other employees at the workplace where the injured or ill worker works; in fact, these co-workers may even have witnessed the accident that gave rise to the injury or illness.

OSHA does not agree that its inspectors should be required to obtain permission from all injured or ill employees before accessing the full records. Gaining this permission would make it essentially impossible to obtain full access to the records, which is needed to perform a meaningful workplace investigation. For example, an inspector would not be able to obtain the names of employees who were no longer working for the company to perform follow-up interviews about the specifics of their injuries and illnesses. The names of the injured or ill workers are needed to allow the government inspector to interview the injured and ill workers and determine the hazardous circumstances that led to their injury or illness. The government inspector may also need the employee's names to access personnel and medical records if needed (medical records can only be accessed after the inspector obtains a medical access order). Additionally, refusing the inspector access to the names of the injured and ill workers would effectively prohibit any audit of the Part 1904 records by the government, a practice necessary to verify the accuracy of employer recordkeeping in general and to identify problems that employers may be having in keeping records under OSHA's recordkeeping rules. Adopting the inefficient access method suggested by these commenters would also place a substantial administrative burden on the employer, the employees, and the government. Further, since OSHA inspectors do not allow others to see the medical records they have accessed, the privacy of employees is not compromised by CSHO access to the records.

Time for response to requests for records. Paragraphs 1904.40(a) and (b) of the final rule require records to be made available to a government inspector within 4 business hours of an oral request for the records, using the business hours of the establishment at which the records are located.

...

OSHA has concluded that 4 hours is a reasonable and workable length of time for employers to respond to governmental requests for records. The 4-hour time period for providing records from a centralized source strikes a balance between the practical limitations inherent in record maintenance and the government official's need to obtain these records and use the information to conduct a workplace inspection.

...

OSHA believes that it is essential for employers to have systems and procedures that can produce the records within the 4-hour time. However, the Agency realizes that there may be unusual or unique circumstances where the employer cannot comply. For example, if the records are kept by a health care professional and that person is providing emergency care to an injured worker, the employer may need to delay production of the records. In such a situation, the OSHA inspector may allow the employer additional time.

If a government representative requests records of an establishment, but those records are kept at another location, the 4-hour period can be measured in accordance with the normal business hours at the location where the records are being kept.

...

OSHA has designed the final rule to give each employer considerable flexibility in maintaining records. It permits an employer to centralize its records, to use computer and facsimile technologies, and to hire a third party to keep its records. However, an employer who chooses these options must also ensure that they are sufficiently reliable to comply with this rule. In other words, the flexibility provided to employers for recordkeeping must not impede the Agency's ability to obtain and use the records.

Provide copies.

...

OSHA's experience has been that the vast majority of employers willingly provide copies to government representatives during safety and health inspections. Making copies is a routine office function in almost every modern workplace. With the widespread availability of copying technology, most workplaces have copy machines on-site or readily available. The cost of providing copies is minimal, usually less than five cents per copy. In addition, the government representative needs to obtain copes of records promptly, so that he or she can analyze the data and identify workplace hazards. Therefore, in this final rule, OSHA requires the employer to provide copies of the records requested to authorized government representatives.

Section 1904.41 Annual OSHA Injury and Illness Survey of Ten or More Employers [p. 6069]

Section 1904.41 of this final rule replaces section 1904.17, "Annual OSHA Injury and Illness Survey of Ten or More Employers," of the former rule issued on February 11, 1997. The final rule does not change the contents or policies of the corresponding section of the former rule in any way. Instead, the final rule simply rephrases the language of the former rule in the plain language question-and-answer format used in the rest of this rule.

...

Section 1904.42 Requests From the Bureau of Labor Statistics for Data [p. 6069]

...

Section 1904.42 of the final rule derives from the subpart of the former rule titled "Statistical Reporting of Occupational Injuries and Illnesses." The former rule described the Bureau of Labor Statistics annual survey of occupational injuries and illnesses, discussed the duty of employers to answer the survey, and explained the effect of the BLS survey on the States operating their own State plans.

Both OSHA and the BLS collect occupational injury and illness information, each for separate purposes. The BLS collects data from a statistical sample of employers in all industries and across all size classes, using the data to compile the occupational injury and illness statistics for the Nation. The Bureau gives each respondent a pledge of confidentiality (as it does on all BLS surveys), and the establishment-specific injury and illness data are not shared with the public, other government agencies, or OSHA. The BLS's sole purpose is to create statistical data.

OSHA collects data from employers from specific size and industry classes, but collects from each and every employer within those parameters. The establishment-specific data collected by OSHA are used to administer OSHA's various programs and to measure the performance of those programs at individual workplaces.

...

Paragraph 1904.42(a) states the general obligation of employers to report data to the BLS or a BLS designee. Paragraph 1904.42(b)(1) states that some employers will receive a BLS survey form and others will not, and that the employer should not send data unless asked to do so. Paragraph 1904.42(b)(2) directs the employer to follow the instructions on the survey form when completing the information and return it promptly.

Paragraph 1904.42(b)(3) of this final rule notes that the BLS is authorized to collect data from all employers, even those who would otherwise be exempt, under section 1904.1 to section 1904.3, from keeping OSHA injury and illness records. This enables the BLS to produce comprehensive injury and illness statistics for the entire private sector. Paragraph 1904.42(b)(3) combines the requirements of former rule paragraphs 1904.15(b) and 1904.16(b) into this paragraph of the final rule.

In response to the question "Am I required to respond to a BLS survey form if I am normally exempt from keeping OSHA injury and illness records?," the final rule states

"Yes. Even if you are exempt from keeping injury and illness records under Sec. 1904.1 to Sec. 1904.3, the BLS may inform you in writing that it will be collecting injury and illness information from you in the coming year. If you receive such a survey form, you must keep the injury and illness records required by Sec. 1904.4 to Sec. 1904.12 and make survey reports for the year covered by the survey."

Paragraph 1904.42(b)(4) of this final rule replaces section 1904.22 of the former rule. It provides that employers in the State-plan States are also required to fill out and submit survey forms if the BLS requests that they do so. The final rule thus specifies that the BLS has the authority to collect information on occupational fatalities, injuries and illnesses from: (1) employers who are required to keep records at all times; (2) employers who are normally exempt from keeping records; and (3) employers under both Federal and State plan jurisdiction. The information collected in the annual survey enables BLS to generate consistent statistics on occupational death, injury and illness for the entire Nation.

Subpart F. Transition From the Former Rule to the New Rule [p. 6070]

The transition interval from the former rule to the new rule involves several issues, including training and outreach to familiarize employers and employees about the new forms and requirements, and informing employers in newly covered industries that they are now required to keep OSHA Part 1904 records. OSHA intends to make a major outreach effort, including the development of an expert software system, a forms package, and a compliance assistance guide, to assist employers and recordkeepers with the transition to the new rule. An additional transition issue for employers who kept records under the former system and will also keep records under the new system is how to handle the data collected under the former system during the transition year. Subpart F of the final rule addresses some of these transition issues.

Subpart F of the new rule (sections 1904.43 and 1904.44), addresses what employers must do to keep the required OSHA records during the first five years the new system required by this final rule is in effect. This five-year period is called the transition period in this subpart. The majority of the transition requirements apply only to the first year, when the data from the previous year (collected under the former rule) must be summarized and posted during the month of February. For the remainder of the transition period, the employer is simply required to retain the records created under the former rule for five years and provide access to those records for the government, the employer's employees, and employee representatives, as required by the final rule at sections 1904.43 and 44.

...

The transition also raises questions about what should be done in the year 2002 with respect to posting, updating, and retaining the records employers compiled in 2001 and previous years. In the transition from the former rule to the present rule, OSHA intends employers to make a clean break with the former system. The new rule will replace the old rule on the effective date of the new rule, and OSHA will discontinue the use of all previous forms, interpretations and guidance on that date (see, e.g., Exs. 21, 22, 15: 184, 423). Employers will be required to prepare a summary of the OSHA Form 200 for the year 2001 and to certify and post it in the same manner and for the same time (one month) as they have in the past. The following time table shows the sequence of events and postings that will occur:

Date	Activity
2001	Employers keep injury and illness information on the OSHA 200 form
January 1, 2002	Employers begin keeping data on the OSHA 300 form
February 1, 2002	Employers post the 2001 data on the OSHA 200 Form
March 1, 2002	Employers may remove the 2001 posting
February 1, 2003	Employers post the 2002 data on the OSHA 300A form
May 1, 2003	Employers may remove the 2002 posting

The final rule's new requirements for dual certification and a 3-month posting period will not apply to the Year 2000 Log and summary. Employers still must retain the OSHA records from 2001 and previous years for five years from the end of the year to which they refer. The employer must provide copies of the retained records to authorized government representatives, and to his or her employees and employee representatives, as required by the new rule.

However, OSHA will no longer require employers to update the OSHA Log and summary forms for years before the year 2002. The former rule required employers to correct errors to the data on the OSHA 200 Logs during the five-year retention period and to add new information about recorded cases. The former rule also required the employer to adjust the totals on the Logs if changes were made to cases on them (Ex. 2, p. 23). OSHA believes it would be confusing and burdensome for employers to update and adjust previous years' Logs and Summaries under the former system at the same time as they are learning to use the new OSHA occupational injury and illness recordkeeping system.

Subpart G. Definitions [p. 6071]

The Definitions section of the final rule contains definitions for five terms: "the Act," "establishment," "health care professional," "injury and illness," and "you." To reduce the need for readers to move back and forth from the regulatory text to the Definitions section of this preamble, all other definitions used in the final rule are defined in the regulatory text as the term is used. OSHA defines the five terms in this section here because they are used in several places in the regulatory text.

The Act

The Occupational Safety and Health Act of 1970 (the "OSH Act") is defined because the term is used in many places in the regulatory text. The final rule's definition is essentially identical to the definition in the proposal. OSHA received no comments on this definition. The definition of "the Act" follows:

The Act means the Occupational Safety and Health Act of 1970 (84 Stat. 1590 et seq., 29 U.S. 651 et seq.), as amended. The definitions contained in section (3) of the Act and related interpretations shall be applicable to such terms when used in this Part 1904.

Establishment

The final rule defines an establishment as a single physical location where business is conducted or where services or industrial operations are performed. For activities where employees do not work at a single physical location, such as construction; transportation; communications, electric, gas and sanitary services; and similar operations, the establishment is represented by main or branch offices, terminals, stations, etc. that either supervise such activities or are the base from which personnel carry out these activities.

The final rule also addresses whether one business location can include two or more establishments. Normally, one business location has only one establishment. However, under limited conditions, the employer may consider two or more separate businesses that share a single location to be separate establishments for recordkeeping purposes. An employer may divide one location into two or more establishments only when: each of the proposed establishments represents a distinctly separate business; each business is engaged in a different economic activity; no one industry description in the Standard Industrial Classification Manual (1987) applies to the joint activities of the proposed establishments; and separate reports are routinely prepared for each establishment on the number of employees, their wages and salaries, sales or receipts, and other business information. For example, if an employer operates a construction company at the same location as a lumber yard, the employer may consider each business to be a separate establishment.

The final rule also deals with the opposite situation, and explains when an establishment includes more than one physical location. An employer may combine two or more physical locations into a single establishment only when the employer operates the locations as a single business operation under common management; the locations are all located in close proximity to each other; and the employer keeps one set of business records for the locations, such as records on the number of employees, their wages and salaries, sales or receipts, and other kinds of business information. For example, one manufacturing establishment might include the main plant, a warehouse serving the plant a block away, and an administrative services building across the street. The final rule also makes it clear that when an employee telecommutes from home, the employee's home is not a business establishment for recordkeeping purposes, and a separate OSHA 300 Log is not required.

The definition of "establishment" is important in OSHA's recordkeeping system for many reasons. First, the establishment is the basic unit for which records are maintained and summarized. The employer must keep a separate injury and illness Log (the OSHA Form 300), and prepare a single summary (Form 300A), for each establishment. Establishment-specific records are a key component of the recordkeeping system because each separate record represents the injury and illness experience of a given location, and therefore reflects the particular circumstances and hazards that led to the injuries and illnesses at that location. The establishment-specific summary, which totals the establishment's injury and illness experience for the preceding year, is posted for employees at that establishment and may also be collected by the government for statistical or administrative purposes. Second, the definition of establishment is important because injuries and illnesses are presumed to be work-related if they result from events or exposures occurring in the work environment, which includes the employer's establishment. The presumption that injuries and illnesses occurring in the work environment are by definition work-related may be rebutted under certain circumstances, which are listed in the final rule and discussed in the section of this preamble devoted to section 1904.5, Determination of work-relatedness. Third, the establishment is the unit that determines whether the partial exemption from recordkeeping requirements permitted by the final rule for establishments of certain sizes or in certain industry sectors applies (see Subpart B of the final rule). Under the final rule's partial exemption, establishments classified in certain Standard Industrial Classification codes (SIC codes) are not required to keep injury and illness records except when asked by the government to do so. Because a given employer may operate establishments that are classified in different SIC codes, some employers may be required to keep OSHA injury and illness records for some establishments but not for others, e.g. if one or more of the employer's establishments falls under the final rule's partial exemption but others do not.

Fourth, the definition of establishment is used to determine which records an employee, former employee, or authorized employee representative may access. According to the final rule, employees may ask for, and must be given, injury and illness records for the establishment they currently work in, or one they have worked in, during their employment.

...

Subpart G of the final rule defines "establishment" as "a single physical location where business is conducted or where services or industrial operations are performed. For activities such as construction; transportation; communications, electric and gas utility, and sanitary services; and similar operations, the establishment is represented for record-keeping purposes by main or branch offices, terminals, stations, etc. that either supervise such activities or are the base from which personnel carry out these activities." This part of the definition of "establishment" provides flexibility for employers whose employees (such as repairmen, meter readers, and construction superintendents) do not work at the same workplace but instead move between many different workplaces, often in the course of a single day.

How the definition of "establishment" must be used by employers for recordkeeping purposes is set forth in the answers to the questions posed in this paragraph of Subpart G:

(1) Can one business location include two or more establishments?

(2) Can an establishment include more than one physical location?

(3) If an employee telecommutes from home, is his or her home considered a separate establishment?

The employer may consider two or more economic activities at a single location to be separate establishments (and thus keep separate OSHA Form 300s and Form 301s for each activity) only when: (1) Each such economic activity represents a separate business, (2) no one industry description in the Standard Industrial Classification Manual (1987) applies to the activities carried out at the separate locations; and (3) separate reports are routinely prepared on the number of employees, their wages and salaries, sales or receipts, and other business information. This part of the definition of "establishment" allows for separate establishments when an employer uses a common facility to house two or more separate businesses, but does not allow different departments or divisions of a single business to be considered separate establishments. However, even if the establishment meets the three criteria above, the employer may, if it chooses, consider the physical location to be one establishment.

The definition also permits an employer to combine two or more physical locations into a single establishment for recordkeeping purposes (and thus to keep only one Form 300 and Form 301 for all of the locations) only when (1) the locations are all geographically close to each other, (2) the employer operates the locations as a single business operation under common management, and (3) the employer keeps one set of business records for the locations, such as records on the number of employees, their wages and salaries, sales or receipts, and other business information. However, even for locations meeting these three criteria, the employer may, if it chooses, consider the separate physical locations to be separate establishments. This part of the definition allows an employer to consider a single business operation to be a single establishment even when some of his or her business operations are carried out on separate properties, but does not allow for separate businesses to be joined together. For example, an employer operating a manufacturing business would not be allowed to consider a nearby storage facility to be a separate establishment, while an employer who operates two separate retail outlets would be required to consider each to be a separate establishment.

...

Health Care Professional

The final rule defines health care professional (HCP) as "a physician or other state licensed health care professional whose legally permitted scope of practice (i.e. license, registration or certification) allows the professional independently to provide or be delegated the responsibility to provide some or all of the health care services described by this regulation."

...

OSHA recognizes that injured employees may be treated by a broad range of health care practitioners, especially if the establishment is located in a rural area or if the worker is employed by a small company that does not have the means to provide on-site access to an occupational nurse or a physician. Although the rule does not specify what medical specialty or training is necessary to provide care for injured or ill employees, the rule's use of the term health care professional is intended to ensure that those professionals providing treatment and making determinations about the recordability of certain complex cases are operating within the scope of their license, as defined by the appropriate state licensing agency.

Injury or Illness

The final rule's definition of injury or illness is based on the definitions of injury and illness used under the former recordkeeping regulation, except that it combines both definitions into a single term "injury or illness." Under the final rule, an injury or illness is an abnormal condition or disorder. Injuries include cases such as, but not limited to, a cut, fracture, sprain, or amputation. Illnesses include both acute and chronic illnesses, such as, but not limited to, a skin disease, respiratory disorder, or systemic poisoning. The definition also includes a note to inform employers that some

injuries and illnesses are recordable and others are not, and that injuries and illnesses are recordable only if they are new, work-related cases that meet one or more of the final rule's recording criteria.

…

"You"

The last definition in the final rule, of the pronoun "you," has been added because the final rule uses the "you" form of the question-and-answer plain-language format recommended in Federal plain-language guidance. "You," as used in this rule, mean the employer, as that term is defined in the Act. This definition makes it clear that employers are responsible for implementing the requirements of this final rule, as mandated by the Occupational Safety and Health Act of 1970 (29 U.S.C. 651 et seq.)

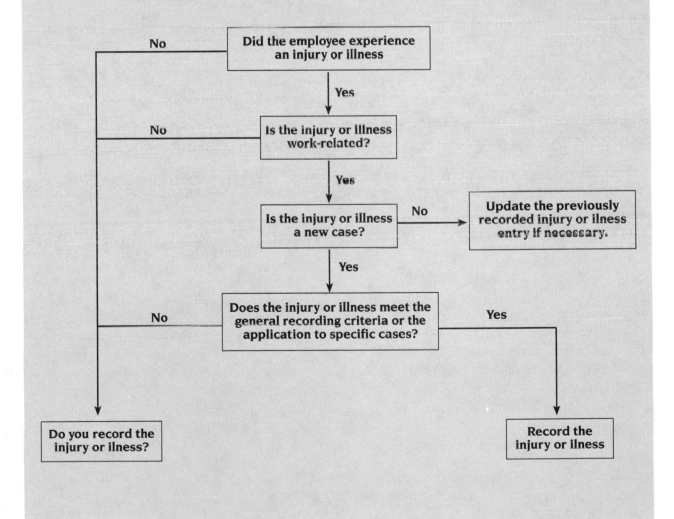

TRAINING

Training that brings about no change is as effective as a parachute that opens on the first bounce.

As an OSHA Outreach trainer you are a key player in helping OSHA's goal to reduce accidents and injuries. Workers do not want to get hurt and employers want to provide a safe workplace. Unfortunately, many safety training sessions are conducted in a manner that leaves the worker with a less-than-enthusiastic regard for safety training sessions. It is necessary to liven up the topic to keep workers' attention. A good training philosophy is to present the material three different times in three different ways so the student is not bored, and yet the material is emphasized in such a way that he or she cannot forget it. A good trainer will establish the climate for training by introducing him or herself to the class as well as any guest speakers. Group discussions and workshops enhance training. A good rule to follow when setting up a class is to stress the key points of the topic.

- **Tell them what you are going to teach them.**
- **Teach them.**
- **Tell them what you have taught them.**

Presenting the material in a lecture is one way of presenting the material. Then have the students refer to written material that you have provided in a handout. Finally, show them a video of the subject as a third method of instruction. This allows different learners to obtain information in different ways and helps to break up the monotony of a class. Use stories, life experiences, statistics, and court decisions to lend credence to the topics.

Good trainers realize that they are working with an adult audience that has needs and expectations. These trainers also realize that they are the key element in the company safety training program. Trainers must be confident of their own skills and technical knowledge to provide benefit to the learners. This confidence enhances the importance of the message.

Children versus Adult Learners

We've learned that children rely on others for information and tend to accept the material presented to them at face value. They are looking for a return on their educational investment some time in the distant future. They know that without a high school education they aren't going to succeed easily, and that an investment in some college, or even getting a college degree, will increase their ability to earn an income in the long run. Still, they have little experience in these matters and usually do not contribute to class discussions. Children generally.

- Rely on others
- Accept the lessons at face value
- Look for long term payback
- Little experience
- Seldom contribute to class

Adult learners, on the other hand, have generally graduated from the school of hard knocks already. They rely on their own experiences, question facts that you present and will challenge what you are presenting. They are very experienced with the topic material and contribute on a regular basis to the class discussions. This sometimes makes it a challenge to keep the class on track and trainers must be ever watchful that they do not "take off on a tangent" discussion.

Adult learners want a quick return on their investment. They are paying for the course and want to be able to use the information today. Adult learners generally:

- Are self reliant
- Question facts
- Are very experienced
- Can contribute significantly to the class
- Expect quick return on their investment

If you attempt to treat adult learners as children, you will lose them. Your class will suffer and your evaluations will reflect that. So remember to treat all learners as adults. Find out what their goals are for the class. A good technique is to introduce yourself and the class topic, then ask the students to stand up, introduce themselves and to mention what they would want to get out of this class. Capture their goals on a sheet of display paper and leave it taped to the wall during the class. This will allow your class to focus on the real world as perceived by the students.

Emphasize how the training can be applied. Talk to the students about how OSHA is enforcing the regulations strictly using recent newspaper articles to illustrate this point. Relate the course topics to the students' experiences and learn from the experiences and opinions of your students. Always encourage discussion.

Treat learners as adults and identify the goals of the learners in the class.

Focus on "real world" situations instead of academic solutions, emphasize how the training can be applied to their day to day jobs and relate the material to their experiences. Encourage discussion within the group and listen to and respect their opinions.

When it comes to the actual learning process, psychologists have found that we learn information through sight, then by hearing, then by smell and finally by touch. By combining these senses in a class setting you can compound the learning process.

Students learn with their senses:

Touch	(1.5%)
Smell	(3.5%)
Hearing	(11%)
Sight	(83%)

Psychologists also conducted tests to find out how different methods of learning affected the ability to remember and recall material later on. While we learn using sight 83% of the time students were found to recall only 10% of what they read. They recall 20% of what they hear and 30% of what they see. Instructors who combine the training techniques have discovered that students recall 50% of what they see and hear. Compare that to 10% of what they read in a safety flyer, or 30% of what they see in the worksite.

If students repeat what they've just heard, they will recall 80% of the information, and if they repeat what they've heard and take action, such as building a scaffold and explaining the procedures as they do it, they recall 90% of the information.

That's why hands on training is so very important in the safety field as the numbers show:

What they read ....(10%)
What they hear ....(20%)
What they see ....(30%)
What they see AND hear ....(50%)
What they SAY..........................(80%)
What they say AND act ....(90%)

Studies reveal that only 30% of the students are actually listening to you. The other 70% are thinking about what they have to do after class is over, wondering how the company is doing without them, or what they should get as a gift for someone important to them. So your class must be vibrant enough to bring them back from their mental vacation to concentrate on the task at hand: learning safety. Remember that only 30% of your students are listening to you at any time during the class. Seventy percent are taking mental vacations, thinking of a past event or planning a future one.

Human beings have a natural potential for learning. Trainers must understand that people are naturally curious, yet they are simultaneously eager and *not* eager to learn. The tendency to learn is more likely to appear when people see relevance to themselves in the learning process.

Significant learning takes place when the subject matter is perceived by students as having usefulness for their own purposes.

Confronting students with practical, social, and ethical problems is effective in promoting learning. Brief, intensive experiences for individuals facing immediate problems are especially effective.

Learning is facilitated when the student participates responsively in the learning process. When students set their own goals, locate and learn to use their resources, and take responsibility for their actions, they tend to learn quickly. Students should be involved in and participate in the class to enhance their educational experience.

Classroom Training in General
Students will not normally pursue the learning objectives on their own and must be prompted to do so. Tests and quizzes can be used as motivators to get students focused on the learning objectives. These evaluations are part of the education itself as students learn what they

need to master and build upon their skill levels "one brick at a time."

Instructors must assign projects and tasks to the students and supervise the work to ensure it is completed. The facilitator must provide guidance to the learners and some form of evaluation.

As a trainer, you are expected to know the subject inside and out, as well as the objective of the training session. Prepare your materials the day before the training session and be prepared to teach an outstanding class. The reason that many instructors carry their own LCD projectors and laptop computers with them is that often different brands are not compatible and simply do not work together. Check out your equipment so that you know how it works. Do a function check of the equipment to ensure your material works with your equipment. Do not wait until the last minute to plan, prepare, and practice.

Check out your facility before the students arrive. Many instructors plan their schedule to arrive at least one hour prior to the students to arrange the classroom. This lets them establish the seating arrangement, find the controls for air conditioning and heating, and electrical plugs for their equipment. Good instructors commit themselves to their class and analyze the audience to best approach them. For example, classes will be different for apprentice construction workers than for construction engineers with vast amounts of experience. Instructors prepare for the different types of audiences and think "sight and sound" as they practice to deliver their presentation in a dynamic, energetic manner. Keep the class lively, since at any one time during the lecture only about 30 percent of the students are listening; the other 70 percent are taking mental naps, planning their next project, or thinking about their vacation!

It is the trainer's responsibility to set the initial mood of the group and establish a climate of learning. Students may be motivated by allowing them to have input into the learning structure. One way of doing this is to have the students introduce themselves at the beginning of a class and identify one particular problem that they seek to have resolved during this class. The trainer can write those concerns on a chalkboard and tailor the session to ensure that those concerns are met. Facilitators can provide a range of resources for the students, including the instructor. Facilitators should keep a close eye on the climate of the class and modify the presentation to maximize class learning.

Confidence comes from being thoroughly prepared. Instructors can expect to be nervous. Some instructors use acting skills and exercises to overcome this natural nervousness. They realize that trainers who *act* enthusiastic will *be* enthusiastic. Keep a positive attitude when you are training and commit yourself to the training session preparation and the class time itself. Speak loudly and clearly. Your clothes say a lot about you, so dress appropriately. Wear comfortable shoes and match your dress to your audience. An executive briefing may require a coat and tie, while the same set of clothes would not be appropriate for forklift operator training.

Understand how long you have to conduct the class and meet that time expectation. Start and finish the class on time. This may require that the class be rehearsed and timed. Understanding the audience is also important. Giving a presentation to new employees is different than giving a presentation to experienced workers or job foremen. Executive briefings and seminars require an entirely different presentation.

What you hear- you forget
What you hear and see- you remember
　Use PowerPoints, videos, flipcharts
What you do- you understand and remember
　Use field trips, demonstrations, hands on activity

There are several ways that training can be presented. Each of these methods has its own advantages and disadvantages. The simplest form of education is the lecture, where the instructor talks to the students about the subject. A foreman getting the workers together and talking to them about how to set up and use a ladder can accomplish ladder safety training.

Using a chalkboard or easel and paper to show the workers the 1:4 pitch, how to tie off the ladder, and the 3-ft. extension can enhance a ladder presentation.

The presentation could be further enhanced by using PowerPoint slides to show photo-graphs of ladders being used correctly and incorrectly. Pictures help to maintain focus on the material. Another teaching aid is a videotape or DVD that brings in sound and action. Other things that can add to the class are personal experiences of the instructor or the students, case studies, and handouts (available from OSHA www.osha.gov) as well as diagrams and sketches. Training is always enhanced when the students receive a handout to refer to after the class. Use a variety of teaching techniques to present your materials to keep the information interesting.

In some cases, students cannot be brought together in one location for the training. In these cases a remote broadcast or tele-conference may be used to provide training over long distances. Some companies use computer-based training via CD-ROM or the Internet. Both of these systems provide sound, action, and student interaction so that the training is effective.

About Your Session
It is all about you! You are the instructor and your personal style is what sets you apart from the thousands of other instructors out there. Learn what your strengths and weaknesses are and work to correct and minimize the weak parts of your style. Use your strong points to your advantage.

If you are getting ready for a class and don't feel nervous, you are unusual. In other words, everyone gets butterflies in their stomach from time to time. It's natural. To counter this feeling, realize that you are the expert in this subject and have a positive attitude. Don't try to be someone else, their tricks and jokes may not work for you.

The best thing to do is to be prepared. Study the slides the night before, go over what you are going to present. Wear the right clothes. If it's a construction class, you don't want to wear a suit and tie, but if you are presenting a class to executives blue jeans and a flannel shirt probably won't fit the occasion.

Be enthusiastic about the subject and don't forget to project your voice to the student sitting in the last row. That way all the students will hear you.

- Expect to be nervous
- Have a positive attitude and be yourself, be flexible, be accessible
- Be prepared and speak loudly to be heard
- Dress appropriately and show enthusiasm

Use a three step procedure for training. Tell the student what you are going to teach them, teach them, and then tell them what you've taught them. More formal institutions have developed a five step method, but the procedure is the same. Review the material you are going to present with the class, giving them the reasons why the topic is important. Give the student an overview of the material that you are going to present. Then present the material in a more detailed manner. Provide some form of activity or exercise to reinforce the learning points you presented and finally, summarize what you've taught them. Use the following five steps to organize your training plan:

- Review
- Overview
- Presentation
- Exercise
- Summary

In this first step of the five step process you should introduce the topic that you are going to present. Demonstrate why such training is important, such as the fact that it saves lives, reduces fines and could keep the employee from losing a finger. Ask students if they have any compliance inspection stories to share with the group. Identify any person or group in the class that has experiences that make the topic a valuable lesson.

- Introduce the topic
- Ask students to share experiences
- Recognize resources within the group

Explain the learning objectives of the module that you are going to present. Tell them that in this class we are going to discuss these five points that are the most popular points that OSHA cites when they walk onto a worksite.

- Discuss the learning objectives
- Establish why this material is important
- Explain the most frequently cited violations

During the presentation of the module, try to make the slides and conversation flow into the next module. Don't load the class up with superfluous information when a few short points are all that they are really going to remember.

It's a good idea to reinforce your lecture with real life stories or newspaper clippings. OSHA publishes FATAL FACTS, which are nice handouts for a class since they detail what happened, what should have happened and why the person died in the accident. You can also hand out and discuss letters of interpretation that are available on the OSHA website at www.osha.gov or in the OSHA CD ROM. Other realistic training aids are statistics or court decisions. When presenting the module, lead into the topic from the overview and explain to the students that you are going to cover the material that they need to know. Provide realistic examples of incidents from a number of sources, including:

- Stories or quotes
- Newspaper clippings
- Fatal Facts from OSHA
- Letters of Interpretation
- Statistics or court decisions

Let the students play with handout materials, tools, mock ups. Involve the students by having them relate their experiences with the topic. Often students will learn more by doing something, so get them involved in committee or team activity, have them build a scaffold or put on safety equipment. Even if it is simply a matter of taking a highlighter and having the students highlight a section in the manual and put a tab on the page, they will remember the session! Always give positive feedback to students. Telling students "Yes, that's right", or "You are on the right track, let's explore this further" is a very strong method of keeping students happy and motivated. Students best remember what they do as opposed to what they observe. Involve the students. Have them:

- Relate personal experiences
- Handle safety equipment
- Demonstrate how to do something
- Highlight and tab the applicable regulations

Take a few minutes at the end of each module to summarize key points for the students.

These key points are often brought up again in a quiz or test, so this is an important time to make sure that all students got the same information out of the last hour. Ask the students if they have any questions pertaining to the subject matter. Finally, use these moments to get the students' minds ready for the next lesson. If you are discussing walking and working surfaces and the next topic is scaffolding, tell the students something like "Now that we know how to work safely on level surfaces, let's take it up a notch. When we get back from break we'll get into working surfaces at a higher elevation as we study scaffolds."

- Stressing key points, summarize the lesson
- Answer any question students may present
- Use this as a transition to the next lesson

It cannot be said often enough: Rehearsal is the key to building an excellent class. Act enthusiastically and your students will become enthusiastic about the class as well. Speak to the student in the last row so that your voice will be heard, and move around in the class so that you are accessible to the students. Make eye contact with each student in the class and hold it for a few seconds when you are teaching. And don't forget to smile.

- Be prepared — rehearse your "show"
- Be positive and show enthusiasm
- Speak loud enough to be heard
- Be flexible and accessible
- Make eye contact

When you are preparing for your class, commit yourself and your time to the class. Analyze the audience and prepare for each day as if it was the only day you had the student under your control. Think of what you can do to improve the sight and sound of your class. If the props you are using are getting old and worn, replace them. Practice moves that you use in the class in front of a mirror to make sure that you have all the moves down. And remember that the class is a presentation. Present it, deliver it to your students as if it were a gift. It is a gift of knowledge, after all.

- Commit yourself to the class
- Analyze the audience
- Prepare
- Think "Sight and Sound"

- Practice and time yourself
- Deliver the class

When you show up at the class, check out the room. You should normally try to check out the classroom the night before the class if it is at a hotel. If it is at a company training center make sure you check in at least an hour or two before the class. That way you can re-arrange any seating or chairs and tables, find out where the electrical outlets are, light controls, etc. Find out where the restrooms and telephones are so that you can remind the class. It's important to establish a refreshment and smoking area as well as finding out where students need to go to be contacted by their company in case of emergencies.

- Table and chair arrangement
- Electrical outlets (you may need an extension cord, power strip)
- Light and heating controls
- Restrooms and telephones
- Refreshment area
- Point of contact for emergencies

Safety training doesn't have to be boring and extremely serious all the time. The students know that the subject is deadly serious, so in the class you can have fun, lighten up the session by telling amusing stories and quotations. Remind students of the gravity of the topic by using recent court decisions and statistics as well as real life experiences.

- Stories
- Quotations
- Court Decisions
- Statistics
- Life Experiences

There are all sorts of training aids that you can use, but remember that they are just that, training aids. The purpose of the class is to get knowledge from the instructor into the mind of the student. If your training aid detracts from the learning process, you have to ask yourself why are you using int. Flip charts and blackboards are easy to use and are just about everywhere. Write large enough so that the student in the back can read the printing without their glasses. Overhead transparencies are nice, easy to create and keep current. You can make overhead transparencies using PowerPoint slides, your computer and a printer. Once the ink is dry, you can place the transparency inside a clear document protector to keep the slide from getting scratched or damaged. Keep the modules in a three ring binder for ease of transportation and filing. Laptop computers and a projector make presentations easy, too. They are state of the art for presenters. Models of industrial plants and equipment can be shown in the class, and the best way to make a point about safety equipment is the safety equipment itself. Hand out eyeglasses, hard hats, gloves and test equipment in the classes so that the students can touch and feel the equipment that they'll be using.

- Flip chart/blackboard
- Overhead transparency
- Slides, movies
- Computer LCD with power point
- Models
- Actual tools and instruments

Whenever there is a change in the flow of education, introduce that change. If you are coming on platform, take a moment to introduce yourself. If you are being followed by another speaker, introduce that speaker, talk about any awards or credentials that you or the next speaker have. If you are going to show a film or video, introduce that as well, saying, "Now we'll take a look at a short film that reinforces the things we've been talking about." Remember how important introductions are and introduce yourself with some background that makes you credible. Always do the same for the guest speaker or the speaker who will follow you. Films and videos should also be introduced so that students can get into the right frame of mind and be more receptive to the video since they know why it is being shown.

Students in groups learn better when there is an informal structure that is relaxed and comfortable. Make sure that discussions within the groups remain fixed on the topic at hand, and make sure that everyone participates in the discussions. It is natural for a leader to emerge in the group, and you may have to rotate among the groups, quietly involving the student who is more shy than the others by asking them what they think about

the task. Make sure that the group members listen to each other to get the most of their collective experiences.

- Atmosphere is informal, comfortable and relaxed
- Center discussions on pertinent issues
- Everyone participates in discussions
- Members of the group listen to each other

The biggest mistake that trainers make is not being prepared. No matter how good you are, how well you know the material, always practice and review your material. Make sure that your equipment is checked and functional before the students arrive. Batteries die and liquids dry up, so check your laser pointers, equipment and markers to make sure that they all work.

Be natural. Don't try to copy someone else if their method is drastically different from yours. Relax, this is your class. Keep control of the class and never, never embarrass a student or belittle them. If the student asks a question and you don't know the answer, it's all right to say that you don't know, but that you'll check and get the answer to the student by the end of the class.

- Don't try to "wing it"
  - Be prepared
  - Check your equipment before class starts
- Don't try to be someone you are not
  - Be yourself, natural
  - Relax
- Don't lose control
- Try not to embarrass students
- Don't be afraid to say that you don't know
- Tell the student you'll get the answer to them.

Don't apologize for your lack of preparedness, the room conditions or the lunch. Don't bring up something that is negative for the students to dwell on. Watch out for those human traits that creep up on us, like rattling your keys in your pocket or jingling change when you walk. Shuffling papers and the repeating phrase "uh", "well" should be trained out of your vocabulary.

- Don't apologize
  - "Your friends don't need it, your enemies won't believe it" Mark Twain

- Distracting mannerisms
  - Rattling keys or change
  - Shuffling papers
  - Verbal annoyances ("uh", "you know")

You may find that you need to be more forceful when leading a group so the students do not get out of control. Or you may find that you need to speak more deliberately, slowly, or loudly. Gestures work for some instructors and are a disaster for others. Stress the point that everyone involved in the session is going to learn from each other, instructor and student alike. Most adult students have experiences to share with the class, so stress the equality of the group as opposed to the superiority of any one person. Focus on solving problems that the group has identified and try to avoid ego trips of individual students...and the instructor.

Involve the students as much as possible using your personal style, attitude, and philosophy. Be open and honest with the students and do not be afraid to display your weaknesses as well as your strengths. This allows the group to open up. When students realize that everyone has foibles and shortcomings, they tend to become more involved. Make eye contact with the students and smile.

Some in the group may initially be a little defensive. They may be a little tense, wondering what they have gotten into and wonder what demands will be made on them. The instructor must allay their fears and lower their tension levels by creating a climate that is open and positive and encourages discussion. Remind the group that their combined experience is far greater than yours and that the instructor is there to serve as a guide to help them use the resources of the group constructively and positively. Mention that quite often they will learn more from one another than they will from the programmed course of instruction.

Handling Problem Situations

When you find a student who talks incessantly, you should realize that they may be eager to demonstrate their skills. On the other hand, some students just like to talk.

Don't embarrass the student or use sarcasm. Slow them down by giving them challenges to solve. Try to involve the group in the handling of the constant talker. When they make a point, steer the attention to the group by asking how the group feels about that point.

- Why
  - May be eager to show off
  - May be well informed and want to show it
  - Some folks are just naturally talkative
- What to do
  - Don't embarrass them or use sarcasm
  - Slow them down with challenging questions
  - Try to let the group handle it -"Hmm, that's interesting, how does the group feel about it?"

Sometimes there are student personalities that mix about the same as oil and water, and this can divide the group into different factions. This occurrence can be the result of different personalities or experiences that the students have. In these cases, emphasize the points that the parties do agree on. Minimize those parts that they don't agree on, and remind the class that it is alright to disagree. Keep the topic and discussion focused on the class objectives, and invite the students to be frank, but note that personalities should be left out of the discussion.

- Why
  - Two or more personalities/experiences
  - Can divide group into factions
- What to do
  - Emphasize points of agreement
  - Minimize disagreements
  - Keep focused on objectives
  - Be frank, ask that personalities be left out

Side conversations can be disconcerting to the instructor, and you won't find out until the end of the class that those conversations were keeping other students from hearing what you had to say. When those conversations take place, and they will, ask the participants if they could leave the class to conclude their discussion without your interrupting them. Ask easy questions, and call on the side conversationalist by name to answer the question. Move towards them when you are making a point and your presence within their personal space is usually enough to disrupt their conversation.

- What
  - May be personal, may be related to the topic, but is usually distracting
- What to do
  - Never embarrass
  - Ask an easy question, call one of them by name
  - Move over towards the group that is talking so that your presence disrupts them

Students who tend to ramble get lost in their own conversation, linking related topics to unrelated topics until you don't know where they are going. They seem to want to talk about everything but the topic you are trying to teach. When they pause to take a breath, thank them for their comments, restate their positive points and move on with your lecture. Smile, and remind them that the class only has one hour to master this particular topic and let him know that you'd love to chat after class or during lunch, but that the class must be focused on the training material at hand.

- What
  - Get lost, use far fetched analogies
  - Talk about everything BUT the topic
- What to do
  - When they pause to breath, thank them for their comments, restate the relevant points and move on
  - Smile, tell them its an interesting point, but mention that we only have one hour to complete this topic
  - Ask them to continue this discussion during lunch or after class

Obstinate people are usually prejudiced and refuse to see your point. Try to use the group and stories to swing the obstinate student around to your way of thinking. Ask the student to keep an open mind, that you see his point, too.

- What
  - Won't budge, Prejudiced, can't see your point
- What to do
  - Use the group to straighten out the student
  - Ask the student to keep an open mind and see this point for the time being

Some students just won't participate. They won't talk. They may be bored, timid, insecure or they may feel superior to you as an expert in this field. You have to find out why they are not speaking and try to arouse their interest by asking them direct questions that they can answer. Try to draw out the person next to the timid person, and then ask the shy student to comment on the response. Make eye contact with them and smile to make them feel comfortable.

- What
  - Bored, indifferent, timid, insecure or feels superior
- What to do
  - Find the motivation for non speaking
  - Arouse interest by asking direct questions
  - Draw out the person next to him, then ask the shy person to comment on the response
  - Smile at them a lot

There are students who really know their field, but they can't convey the meaning with the spoken word. When the student speaks and the words come out wrong, rephrase the words and ask the student if that's their meaning, or if they agree with you. It is important to make them feel a part of the class because they want to contribute. Some of us just don't have a lot of opportunity to speak publicly and get nervous. Tell them to take a deep breath, pause, and then make their point.

- What
  - Cannot put thoughts into words
  - Get the idea, cannot convey it
- What to do
  - Say "Let me repeat that for the class" and restate it more clearly

When a student is heading off on the wrong track, you have to get him back on track. You can say that perhaps you misled the conversation and then restate what you are saying, or use one of the responses below to try to get the person back. One instructor who told a student, "You are absolutely incorrect and this is why..." disoriented the student, who became quiet for the rest of the class, spoke with the other students about how terrible the instructor was, and wrote a scathing letter about the instructor's lack of educational skills to the program director. This situation has to be handled delicately.

- What
  - Student offers a comment that is obviously incorrect
- What to do
  - "I can see how you feel" or "That is one way of looking at it"
  - "Hmm, good point, let's look at it from another direction"

Handling Questions

Skillfully used questions help guide discussions and extract and develop information. Questions invite participation and test the effectiveness of the communication. Questions should motivate student thought and opinion and should be directed to everyone in the group. The purpose of questions is to get the students to participate and think.

There are several types of questions that instructors can ask:

- Open. Allows great freedom, is less threatening, and the student controls the amount of detail in answer.
- Closed. The instructor limits the response length and allows for re-direction of the discussion.
- Direct. Directed at one student.
- Overhead. Covers the class as a whole.
- Return. Redirects the question back to the person who asked it.
- Relay. Takes a question from one student and redirects it at another.

Good questions require the students to think so after you ask a question, allow adequate time for answer formulation and response. Be patient. As a rule of thumb, count to 12 before asking the class another question.

Presenting Material

You have had time to prepare, but most people in the group are hearing the material for the first time. Understanding this new material can be difficult. Presenting it in a way that others understand is even more difficult.

Preparation enables you to organize your thoughts, plan your approach, expand your understanding and develop illustrations, examples, and analogies. Only preparation will give you the

skill and confidence you need to achieve your goals. Rehearsal is difficult, but it is one of the key tools of good preparation. So run through your act before you go on stage. Concentrate on the things you will say and go over it a few times.

Make sure you allow students time to become familiar with a topic before moving on to the next topic. Stress how the concepts can be applied to add value for the students in their own lives. Increase their understanding by relating concepts presented to their own experiences.

Stories hold a group's interest a lot more than explaining something. Everybody loves a story; they are "the propelling power of persuasion". Good stories are: real, vital, timely, specific, and about people. The best stories are drawn from your own experience and tailored to fit the topic.

Construction Training Requirements

The following training requirements have been excerpted from Title 29, Code of Federal Regulations Part 1926. Note that in addition to these requirements, Part 1910, relating to general industry, also contains applicable training standards.

General Safety and Health Provisions—1926.20

(b)(2) Such programs [as may be necessary to comply with this part] shall provide for frequent and regular inspections of the job sites, materials, and equipment to be made by competent persons [capable of identifying existing and predictable hazards in the surroundings or working conditions which are unsanitary, hazardous, or dangerous to employees, and who have authorization to take prompt corrective measures to eliminate them] designated by the employers.

(b)(4) The employer shall permit only those employees qualified [one who, by possession of a recognized degree, certificate, or professional standing, or who by extensive knowledge, training, and experience, has successfully demonstrated his ability to solve or resolve problems relating to the subject matter; the work, or the project] by training or experience to operate equipment and machinery.

Education—1926.21

(a) **General requirements.** The Secretary shall, pursuant to section 107(f) of the Act, establish and supervise programs for the education and training of employers and employees in the recognition, avoidance and prevention of unsafe conditions in employments covered by the act.

(b) **Employer responsibility.** (1) The employer should avail himself of the safety and health training programs the Secretary provides.

(2) The employer shall instruct each employee in the recognition and avoidance of unsafe conditions and the regulations applicable to his work environment to control or eliminate any hazards or other exposure to illness or injury.

(3) Employees required to handle or use poisons, caustics, and other harmful substances shall be instructed regarding their safe handling and use, and be made aware of the potential hazards, personal hygiene, and personal protective measures required.

(4) In job site areas where harmful plants or animals are present, employees who may be exposed shall be instructed regarding the potential hazards and how to avoid injury, and the first-aid procedures to be used in the event of injury.

(5) Employees required to handle or use flammable liquids, gases, or toxic materials shall be instructed in the safe handling and use of these materials and made aware of the specific requirements contained in Subparts D, F, and other applicable subparts of this part.

(6) (i) All employees required to enter into confined or enclosed spaces shall be instructed as to the nature of the hazards involved, the necessary precautions to be taken, and in the use of protective and emergency equipment

required. The employer shall comply with any specific regulations that apply to work in dangerous or potentially dangerous areas.

(ii) For purposes of subdivision (i) of this subparagraph, *confined or enclosed space* means any space having a limited means of egress, which is subject to the accumulation of toxic or flammable contaminants or has an oxygen deficient atmosphere. Confined or enclosed spaces include, but are not limited to, storage tanks, process vessels, bins, boilers, ventilation or exhaust ducts, sewers, underground utility vaults, tunnels, pipelines, and open top spaces more than 4 feet (1.2 meters) in depth such as pits, tubs, vaults, and vessels.

Employee Emergency Action Plans—1926.35

(e) **Training.** (1) Before implementing the emergency action plan, the employer shall designate and train a sufficient number of persons to assist in the safe and orderly emergency evacuation of employees.

(2) The employer shall review the plan with each employee covered by the plan at the following times:

(i) Initially when the plan is developed,

(ii) Whenever the employee's responsibilities or designated actions under the plan change, and

(iii) Whenever the plan is changed.

(3) The employer shall review with each employee upon initial assignment those parts of the plan which the employee must know to protect the employee in the event of an emergency. The written plan shall be kept at the workplace and made available for employee review. For those employers with 10 or fewer employees the plan may be communicated orally to employees and the employer need not maintain a written plan.

Medical Services and First-Aid—1926.50

(c) In the absence of an infirmary, clinic, hospital, or physician, that is reasonably accessible in terms of time and distance to the worksite, which is available for the treatment of injured employees, a person who has a valid certificate in first-aid training from the U.S. Bureau of Mines, the American Red Cross, or equivalent training that can be verified by documentary evidence, shall be available at the worksite to render first aid.

Ionizing Radiation—1926.53

(b) Any activity which involves the use of radioactive materials or X-rays, whether or not under license from the Nuclear Regulatory Commission shall be performed by competent persons specially trained in the proper and safe operation of such equipment. In the case of materials used under Commission license, only persons actually licensed, or competent persons under the direction and supervision of the licensee, shall perform such work.

Nonionizing Radiation—1926.54

(a) Only qualified and trained employees shall be assigned to install, adjust, and operate laser equipment.

(b) Proof of qualification of the laser equipment operator shall be available and in possession of the operator at all times.

Gases, Vapors, Fumes, Dusts, and Mists—1926.55

(b) To achieve compliance with paragraph (a) of this section, administrative or engineering controls must first be implemented whenever feasible. When such controls are not feasible to achieve full compliance, protective equipment or other protective measures shall be used to keep the exposure of employees to air contaminants within the limits prescribed in this section. Any equipment and technical measures used for this purpose must first be approved for each particular use by a competent industrial hygienist or other technically qualified person. Whenever respirators are used, their use shall comply with § 1926.103.

Hazard Communication—1926.59

Note: The requirements applicable to construction work under this section are identical to those set forth at 29 CFR 1910.1200 of this chapter.

Methylenedianiline—1926.60

(3) **Information and training.** (i) The employer shall provide employees with information and training on MDA, in accordance with 29 CFR 1910.1200(h), at the time of initial assignment and at least annually thereafter.

 (ii) In addition to the information required under 29 CFR 1910.1200, the employer shall:

(A) Provide an explanation of the contents of this section, including appendices A and B of this section, and indicate to employees where a copy of the standard is available;

(B) Describe the medical surveillance program required under paragraph (n) of this section, and explain the information contained in appendix C of this section; and

(C) Describe the medical removal provision required under paragraph (n) of this section.

Lead—1926.62

(1) **General.** (i) The employer shall communicate information concerning lead hazards according to the requirements of OSHA's Hazard Communication Standard for the construction industry, 29 CFR 1026.59, including but not limited to the requirements concerning warning signs and labels, material safety data sheets (MSDS), and employee information and training. In addition, employers shall comply with the following requirements:

(ii) For all employees who are subject to exposure to lead at or above the action level on any day or who are subject to exposure to lead compounds which may cause skin or eye irritation (e.g., lead arsenate, lead azide), the employer shall provide a training program in accordance with paragraph (1)(2) of this section and assure employee participation.

(iii) The employer shall provide the training program as initial training prior to the time of job assignment or prior to the start up date for this requirement, whichever comes last.

(iv) The employer shall also provide the training program at least annually for each employee who is subject to lead exposure at or above the action level on any day.

(2) **Training program.** The employer shall assure that each employee is trained in the following:

(i) The content of this standard and its appendices;

(ii) The specific nature of the operations which could result in exposure to lead above the action level;

(iii) The purpose, proper selection, fitting, use, and limitations of respirators;

(iv) The purpose and a description of the medical surveillance program, and the medical removal protection program including information concerning the adverse health effects associated with excessive exposure to lead (with particular attention to the adverse reproductive effects on both males and females and hazards to the fetus and additional precautions for employees who are pregnant);

(v) The engineering controls and work practices associated with the employee's job assignment including training employees to follow relevant good work practices described in Appendix B of this section;

(vi) The contents of any compliance plan in effect;

(vii) Instructions to employees that chelating agents should not routinely be used to remove lead from their bodies and should not be used at all except under the direction of a licensed physician; and

(viii) The employee's right of access to records under 29 CFR 1910.20.

(3) **Access to information and training materials.**

(i) The employer shall make readily available to all affected employees a copy of this standard and its appendices.

(ii) The employer shall provide, upon request, all materials relating to the employee information and training program to affected employees and their designated representatives, and to the Assistant Secretary and the Director.

Process Safety Management of Highly Hazardous Chemicals—1926.64

(g) **Training**—(1) **Initial training.** (i) Each employee presently involved in operating a process, and each employee before being involved in operating a newly assigned process, shall be trained in an overview of the process and in the operating procedures as specified in paragraph (f) of this section. The training shall include emphasis on the specific safety and health hazards, emergency operations including shutdown, and safe work practices applicable to the employee's job tasks.

(ii) In lieu of initial training for those employees already involved in operating a process on May 26, 1992, an employer may certify in writing that the employee has the required knowledge, skills, and abilities to safely carry out the duties and responsibilities as specified in the operating procedures.

(2) **Refresher training.** Refresher training shall be provided at least every three years, and more often if necessary, to each employee involved in operating a process to assure that the employee understands and adheres to the current operating procedures of the process. The employer, in consultation with the employees involved in operating the process, shall determine the appropriate frequency of refresher training.

(3) **Training documentation.** The employer shall ascertain that each employee involved in operating a process has received and understood the training required by this paragraph. The employer shall prepare a record which contains the identity of the employee, the date of training, and the means used to verify that the employee understood the training.

Hazardous Waste Operations and Emergency Response—1926.65

(e) **Training**—(1) **General.** (i) All employees working on site (such as but not limited to equipment operators, general laborers and others) exposed to hazardous substances, health hazards, or safety hazards and their supervisors and management responsible for the site shall receive training meeting the requirements of this paragraph before they are permitted to engage in hazardous waste operations that could expose them to hazardous substances, safety, or health hazards, and they shall receive review training as specified in this paragraph.

(ii) Employees shall not be permitted to participate in or supervise field activities until they have been trained to a level required by their job function and responsibility.

(2) **Elements to be covered.** The training shall thoroughly cover the following:

(i) Names of personnel and alternates responsible for site safety and health;

(ii) Safety, health and other hazards present on the site;

(iii) Use of personal protective equipment;

(iv) Work practices by which the employee can minimize risks from hazards;

(v) Safe use of engineering controls and equipment on the site;

(vi) Medical surveillance requirements, including recognition of symptoms and signs which might indicate overexposure to hazards; and

(vii) The contents of paragraphs (G) through (J) of the site safety and health plan set forth in paragraph (b)(4)(ii) of this section.

(3) **Initial training.** (i) General site workers (such as equipment operators, general laborers and supervisory personnel) engaged in hazardous substance removal or other activities which expose or potentially expose workers to hazardous substances and health hazards shall receive a minimum of 40 hours of instruction off the site, and a minimum of three days actual field experience under the direct supervision of a trained, experienced supervisor.

(ii) Workers on site only occasionally for a specific limited task (such as, but not limited to, ground water monitoring, land surveying, or geo-physical surveying) and who are unlikely to be exposed over permissible exposure limits and published exposure limits shall receive a minimum of 24 hours of instruction off the site, and the minimum of one day actual field experience under the direct supervision of a trained, experienced supervisor.

(iii) Workers regularly on site who work in areas which have been monitored and fully characterized indicating that exposures are under permissible exposure limits and published exposure limits where respirators are not necessary, and the character-

ization indicates that there are no health hazards or the possibility of an emergency developing, shall receive a minimum of 24 hours of instruction off the site and the minimum of one day actual field experience under the direct supervision of a trained, experienced supervisor.

(iv) Workers with 24 hours of training who are covered by paragraphs (e)(3)(ii) and (e)(3)(iii) of this section, and who become general site workers or who are required to wear respirators, shall have the additional 16 hours and two days of training necessary to total the training specified in paragraph (e)(3)(i).

(4) **Management and supervisor training.** On-site management and supervisors directly responsible for, or who supervise employees engaged in, hazardous waste operations shall receive 40 hours initial training, and three days of supervised field experience (the training may be reduced to 24 hours and one day if the only area of their responsibility is employees covered by paragraphs (e)(3)(ii) and (e)(3)(iii)) and at least eight additional hours of specialized training at the time of job assignment on such topics as, but not limited to, the employer's safety and health program and the associated employee training program, personal protective equipment program, spill containment program, and health hazard monitoring procedure and techniques.

(5) **Qualifications for trainers.** Trainers shall be qualified to instruct employees about the subject matter that is being presented in training. Such trainers shall have satisfactorily completed a training program for teaching the subjects they are expected to teach, or they shall have the academic credentials and instructional experience necessary for teaching the subjects. Instructors shall demonstrate competent instructional skills and knowledge of the applicable subject matter.

(6) **Training certification.** Employees and supervisors that have received and successfully completed the training and field experience specified in paragraphs (e)(1) through (e)(4) of this section shall be certified by their instructor or the head instructor and trained supervisor as having suc-

cessfully completed the necessary training. A written certificate shall be given to each person so certified. Any person who has not been so certified or who does not meet the requirements of paragraph (e)(9) of this section shall be prohibited from engaging in hazardous waste operations.

Hearing Protection—1926.101

(b) Ear protective devices inserted in the ear shall be fitted or determined individually by competent persons.

Respiratory Protection—1926.103

Note: The requirements applicable to construction under this section are identical to those set forth 29 CFR 1910.134 of this chapter.

Fire Protection—1926.150

(5) As warranted by the project, the employer shall provide a trained and equipped fire fighting organization (Fire Brigade) to ensure adequate protection to life. ["Fire Brigade" means an organized group of employees that are knowledgeable, trained, and skilled in the safe evacuation of employees during emergency situations and in assisting in fire fighting operations.]

(c)(1)(viii) Portable fire extinguishers shall be inspected periodically and maintained in accordance with Maintenance and Use of Portable Fire Extinguishers, NFPA No. 10A-1970.

The owner or occupant of a property in which fire extinguishers are located has an obligation for the care and use of these extinguishers at all times. By doing so, he is contributing to the protection of life and property. The nameplate(s) and instruction manual should be read and thoroughly understood by all persons who may be expected to use extinguishers.

1120. To discharge this obligation he should give proper attention to the inspection, maintenance, and recharging of this fire protective equipment. He should also train his personnel in the correct use of fire extinguishers on the different types of fires which may occur on his property.

3020. Persons responsible for performing maintenance operations come from three major groups: Trained industrial safety or maintenance personnel; Extinguisher service agencies; Individual owners (e.g., self-employed).

Signaling—1926.201

(a) **Flaggers.** Signaling by flaggers and the use of flaggers, including warning garments worn by flaggers shall conform to Part VI of the Manual on Uniform Traffic Control Devices, (1988 Edition, Revision 3 or the Millennium Edition), which are incorporated by reference in §1926.200(g)(2).

(b) **Crane and hoist signals.** Regulations for crane and hoist signaling will be found in applicable American National Standards Institute standards.

Powder-Operated Hand Tools—1926.302

(e) **Powder-actuated tools.** (1) Only employees who have been trained in the operation of the particular tool in use shall be allowed to operate a powder-actuated tool.

(12) Powder-actuated tools used by employees shall meet all other applicable requirements of American National Standards Institute, A10.3-1970, Safety Requirements for Explosive-Actuated Fastening Tools.

Woodworking Tools—1926.304

(f) **Other requirements.** All woodworking tools and machinery shall meet other applicable requirements of American National Standards Institute, 01.1-1961, Safety Code for Woodworking Machinery

From ANSI Standard 01.1-1961, Selection and Training of Operators:

Before a worker is permitted to operate any woodworking machine, he shall receive instructions in the hazards of the machine and the safe method of its operation. Refer to A9.7 of the Appendix. "A9.7 Selection and Training of Operators. Operation of Machines, Tools, and Equipment. General."

(1) Learn the machine's applications and limitations, as well as the specific potential hazards peculiar to this machine. Follow available operating instructions and safety rules carefully.

(2) Keep working area clean and be sure adequate lighting is available.

(3) Do not wear loose clothing, gloves, bracelets, necklaces, or ornaments. Wear face, eye, ear, respiratory, and body protection devices, as indicated for the operation or environment.

(4) Do not use cutting tools larger or heavier than the machine is designed to accommodate. Never operate a cutting tool at greater speed than recommended.

(5) Keep hands well away from saw blades and other cutting tools. Use a push stock or push block to hold or guide the work when working close to a cutting tool.

(6) Whenever possible, use properly locked clamps, jig, or vise to hold the work.

(7) Combs (feather boards) shall be provided for use when an applicable guard cannot be used.

(8) Never stand directly in line with a horizontally rotating cutting tool. This is particularly true when first starting a new tool, or a new tool is initially installed on the arbor.

(9) Be sure the power is disconnected from the machine before tools are serviced.

(10) Never leave the machine with the power on.

(11) Be positive that hold-downs and anti-kickback devices are positioned properly, and that the workpiece is being fed through the cutting tool in the right direction.

(12) Do not use a dull, gummy, bent, or cracked cutting tool.

(13) Be sure that keys and adjusting wrenches have been removed before turning power on.

(14) Use only accessories designed for the machine.

(15) Adjust the machine for minimum exposure of cutting tool necessary to perform the operation."

Gas Welding and Cutting—1926.350

(d) **Use of fuel gas.** The employer shall thoroughly instruct employees in the safe use of fuel gas as follows:

(1) Before a regulator to a cylinder valve is connected, the valve shall be opened slightly and closed immediately. (This action is generally termed "cracking"" and is intended to clear the valve of dust or dirt that might otherwise enter the regulator.) The person cracking the valve shall stand to one side of the outlet, not in front of it. The valve of a fuel gas cylinder shall not be cracked where the gas would reach welding work, sparks, flame, or other possible sources of ignition.

(2) The cylinder valve shall always be opened slowly to prevent damage to the regulator. For quick closing, valves on fuel gas cylinders shall not be opened more than 1-1/2 turns. When a special wrench is required, it shall be left in position on the stem of the valve while the cylinder is in use so that the fuel gas flow can be shut off quickly in case of an emergency. In the case of manifolded or coupled cylinders, at least one such wrench shall always be available for immediate use. Nothing shall be placed on top of a fuel gas cylinder, when in use, which may damage the safety device or interfere with the quick closing of the valve.

(3) Fuel gas shall not be used from cylinders through torches or other devices which are equipped with shutoff valves without reducing the pressure through a suitable regulator attached to the cylinder valve or manifold.

(4) Before a regulator is removed from a cylinder valve, the cylinder valve shall always be closed and the gas released from the regulator.

(5) If, when the valve on a fuel gas cylinder is opened, there is found to be a leak around the valve stem, the valve shall be closed and the gland nut tightened. If this action does not stop the leak, the use of the cylinder shall be discontinued, and it shall be properly tagged and removed from the work area. In the event that fuel gas should leak from the cylinder valve, rather than from the valve stem, and the gas cannot be shut off, the cylinder shall be properly tagged and removed from the work area. If a regulator attached to a cylinder valve will effectively stop a leak through the valve seat, the cylinder need not be removed from the work area.

(6) If a leak should develop at a fuse plug or other safety device, the cylinder shall be removed from the work area.

(j)(1) **Additional rules.** For additional details not covered in this subpart, applicable technical portions of American National Standards Institute, Z49.1-1967, Safety in Welding and Cutting, shall apply.

From ANSI Standard Z49.1-1967, Fire Watch Duties: "Fire watchers shall be trained in the use of fire extinguishing equipment. They shall be familiar with facilities for sounding an alarm in the event of a fire. They shall watch for fires in all exposed areas, try to extinguish them only when obviously within the capacity of the equipment available, or otherwise sound the alarm. A fire watch shall be maintained for at least a half hour after completion of welding or cutting operations to detect and extinguish possible smoldering fires."

Arc Welding and Cutting—1926.351

(d) **Operating instructions.** Employers shall instruct employees in the safe means of arc welding and cutting as follows:

(1) When electrode holders are to be left unattended, the electrodes shall be removed and the holders shall be so placed or protected that they cannot make electrical contact with employees or conducting objects.

(2) Hot electrode holders shall not be dipped in water; to do so may expose the arc welder or cutter to electric shock.

(3) When the arc welder or cutter has occasion to leave his work or to stop work for any appreciable length of time, or when the arc welding or cutting machine is to be moved, the power supply switch to the equipment shall be opened.

(4) Any faulty or defective equipment shall be reported to the supervisor.

(5) See §1926.406(c) for additional requirements.

Fire Prevention—1926.352

(e) When the welding, cutting, or heating operation is such that normal fire prevention precautions are not sufficient, additional personnel shall be assigned to guard against fire while the actual welding, cutting, or heating operation is being performed, and for a sufficient period of time after completion of the work to ensure that no possibility of fire exists. Such personnel shall be instructed as to the specific anticipated fire hazards and how the firefighting equipment provided is to be used.

Welding, Cutting and Heating in Way of Preservative Coatings—1926.354

(a) Before welding, cutting, or heating is commenced on any surface covered by a preservative coating whose flammability is not known, a test shall be made by a competent person to determine its flammability. Preservative coatings shall be considered to be highly flammable when scrapings burn with extreme rapidity.

Wiring Design and Protection—1926.404

(b)(iii)(B) The employer shall designate one or more competent persons (as defined in §1926.32(f)) to implement the program.

Scaffolding—Training Requirements—1926.454

(a) The employer shall have each employee who performs work while on a scaffold trained by a person qualified in the subject matter to recognize the hazards associated with the type of scaffold being used and to understand the procedures to control or minimize those hazards. The training shall include the following areas, as applicable:

(1) The nature of any electrical hazards, fall hazards and falling object hazards in the work area;

(2) The correct procedures for dealing with electrical hazards and for erecting, maintaining, and disassembling the fall protection systems and falling object protection systems being used;

(3) The proper use of the scaffold and the proper handling of materials on the scaffold;

(4) The maximum intended load and the load-carrying capacities of the scaffolds used; and

(5) Any other pertinent requirements of this subpart.

(b) The employer shall have each employee who is involved in erecting, disassembling, moving, operating, repairing, maintaining, or inspecting a scaffold trained by a competent person to recognize any hazards associated with the work in question. The training shall include the following topics, as applicable:

(1) The nature of scaffold hazards;

(2) The correct procedures for erecting, disassembling, moving, operating, repairing, inspecting, and maintaining the type of scaffold in question;

(3) The design criteria, maximum intended load-carrying capacity and intended use of the scaffold;

(4) Any other pertinent requirements of this subject.

(c) When the employer has reason to believe that an employee lacks the skill or understanding needed for safe work involving the erection use or dismantling of scaffolds, the employer shall retrain each such employee so that the requisite proficiency is regained. Retraining is required in at least the following situations:

(1) Where changes at the worksite present a hazard about which an employee has not been previously trained; or

(2) Where changes in the types of scaffolds, fall protection or other equipment present a hazard about which an employee has not been previously trained; or

(3) Where inadequacies in an affected employee's work involving scaffolds indicate that the employee has not retained the requisite proficiency.

Fall Protection—Training Requirements— 1926.503

(a) **Training Program.** (1) The employer shall provide a training program for each employee who might be exposed to fall hazards. The program shall enable each employee to recognize the hazards of falling and shall train each employee in the procedures to be followed in order to minimize these hazards.

(2) The employer shall assure that each employee has been trained, as necessary, by a competent person qualified in the following areas:

(i) The nature of fall hazards in the work area;

(ii) The correct procedures for erecting, maintaining, disassembling, and inspecting the fall protection systems to be used;

(iii) The use and operation of guardrail systems, personal fall arrest systems, safety net systems, warning line systems, safety monitoring systems, controlled access zones, and other protection to be used;

(iv) The role of each employee in the safety monitoring system when this system is used;

(v) The limitations on the use of mechanical equipment during the performance of roofing work on low-slope roofs;

(vi) The correct procedures for the handling and storage of equipment and materials and the erection of overhead protection; and

(vii) The standards contained in this subpart.

Cranes and Derricks—1926.550

(a) **General requirements.** (1) The employer shall comply with the manufacturer's specifications and limitations applicable to the operation of any and all cranes and derricks. Where manufacturer's specifications are not available, the limitations assigned to the equipment shall be based on the determinations of a qualified engineer competent in this field and such determinations will be appropriately documented and recorded. Attachments used with cranes shall not exceed the capacity, rating, or scope recommended by the manufacturer.

(5) The employer shall designate a competent person who shall inspect all machinery and equipment prior to each use, and during use, to make sure it is in safe operating condition. Any deficiencies shall be repaired, or defective parts replaced, before continued use.

(6) A thorough, annual inspection of the hoisting machinery shall be made by a competent person or by a government or private agency recognized by the U.S. Department of Labor. The employer shall maintain a record of the dates and results of inspections for each hoisting machine and piece of equipment.

(g) **Crane or derrick suspended personnel platforms**—(4) **Personnel platform**—(i) Design criteria. (A) The personnel platform and suspension system shall be designed by a qualified engineer or a qualified person competent in structural design.

(5) **Trial lift, inspection, and proof testing.** (iv) A visual inspection of the crane or derrick, rigging, personnel platform, and the crane or derrick base support or ground shall be conducted by a competent person immediately after the trial lift to determine whether the testing has exposed any defect or produced any adverse effect upon any component or structure.

Material Hoists, Personnel Hoists, and Elevators—1926.552

(a) **General requirements.** (1) The employer shall comply with the manufacturer's specifications and limitations applicable to the operation of all hoists and elevators. Where manufacturer's specifications are not available, the limitations assigned to the equipment shall be based on the determinations of a professional engineer competent in the field.

(c) **Personnel hoists.** (15) Following assembly and erection of hoists, and before being put in service, an inspection and test of all functions and safety devices shall be made under the supervision of a competent person. A similar inspection and test is required following major alterations of an existing installation. All hoists shall be inspected and tested at not more than 3-month intervals. The employer shall prepare a certification record which includes the date the inspection and test of all functions and safety devices was performed; the signature of the person who performed the inspection and test; and a serial number, or other identifier, for the hoist that was inspected and tested. The most recent certification record shall be maintained on file.

(17)(i) Personnel hoists used in bridge tower construction shall be approved by a registered professional engineer and erected under the supervision of a qualified engineer competent in this field.

Material Handling Equipment—1926.602

(c) **Lifting and hauling equipment (other than equipment covered under Subpart N of this part).**

(1)(vi) All industrial trucks in use shall meet the applicable requirements of design, construction, stability, inspection, testing, maintenance, and operation, as defined in American National Standards Institute B56.1-1969, Safety Standards for Powered Industrial Trucks.

From ANSI Standard B56.1-1969: Operator Training: "Only trained and authorized operators shall be permitted to operate a powered industrial truck. Methods shall be devised to train operators in the safe operation of powered industrial trucks. Badges or other visual indication of the operators' authorization should be displayed at all times during the work period."

Site Clearing—1926.604

(a) **General requirements.** (1) Employees engaged in site clearing shall be protected from hazards of irritant and toxic plants and suitably instructed in the first aid treatment available.

Specific Excavation Requirements—1926.651

(c) **Access and egress**—(1) **Structural ramps.** (i) Structural ramps that are used solely by employees as a means of access or egress from excavations shall be designed by a competent person. Structural ramps used for access or egress of equipment shall be designed by a competent person qualified in structural design, and shall be constructed in accordance with the design.

(h) **Protection from hazards associated with water accumulation.**

(2) If water is controlled or prevented from accumulating by the use of water removal equipment, the water removal equipment and operations shall be monitored by a competent person to ensure proper operation.

(3) If excavation work interrupts the natural drainage of surface water (such as streams), diversion ditches, dikes, or other suitable means shall be used to prevent surface water from entering the excavation and to provide adequate drainage of the area adjacent to the excavation. Excavations subject to runoff from heavy rains

will require an inspection by a competent person and compliance with paragraphs (h)(1) and (h)(2) of this section.

1926.651 (i)(1)

(i) **Stability of adjacent structures.**

(2)(iii) A registered professional engineer has approved the determination that the structure is sufficiently removed from the excavation so as to be unaffected by the excavation activity; or

(iv) A registered profession al engineer has approved the determination that such excavation work will not pose a hazard to employees.

1926.651(k)(1) and (2)

(k) **Inspections.** (1) Daily inspections of excavations, the adjacent areas, and protective systems shall be made by a competent person for evidence of a situation that could result in possible cave-ins, indications of failure of protective systems, hazardous atmospheres, or other hazardous conditions. An inspection shall be conducted by the competent person prior to the start of work and as needed throughout the shift. Inspections shall also be made after every rainstorm or other hazard increasing occurrence. These inspections are only required when employee exposure can be reasonably anticipated.

(2) Where the competent person finds evidence of a situation that could result in a possible cave-in, indications of failure of protective systems, hazardous atmospheres, or other hazardous conditions, exposed employees shall be removed from the hazardous area until the necessary precautions have been taken to ensure their safety.

Concrete and Masonry Construction—General Requirements—1926.701

(a) **Construction loads.** No construction loads shall be placed on a concrete structure or portion of a concrete structure unless the employer determines, based on information received from a person who is qualified in structural design, that the structure or portion of the structure is capable of supporting the loads.

Requirements for Cast-in-Place Concrete—1926.703

(b) **Shoring and reshoring.**

(8) Whenever single post shores are used one on top of another (tiered), the employer shall comply with the following specific requirements in addition to the general requirements for formwork:

(i) The design of the shoring shall be prepared by a qualified designer and the erected shoring shall be inspected by an engineer qualified in structural design.

Underground Construction—1926.800

(d) **Safety instruction.** All employees shall be instructed in the recognition and avoidance of hazards associated with underground construction activities including, where appropriate, the following subjects:

(1) Air monitoring;

(2) Ventilation;

(3) Illumination;

(4) Communications;

(5) Flood control;

(6) Mechanical equipment;

(7) Personal protective equipment;

(8) Explosives;

(9) Fire prevention and protection; and

(10) Emergency procedures, including evacuation plans and check-in/check-out systems.

1926.800(g)(2)

(g) **Emergency provisions—(2) Self Rescuers.** The employer shall provide self-rescuers Approved by the National Institute for Occupational Safety and Health under 42 CFR part 84. The respirators must be immediately available to all employees at work stations in underground areas where employees might be trapped by smoke or gas. The selection, issuance, use, and care of respirators must be in accordance with 29 CFR 1926.103.

(g) **Emergency provisions.** (5) Rescue teams.

(iii) Rescue team members shall be qualified in rescue procedures, the use and limitations of breathing apparatus, and the use of firefighting equipment. Qualifications shall be reviewed not less than annually.

(iv) On job sites where flammable or noxious gases are encountered or anticipated in hazardous quantities, rescue team members shall practice donning and using self-contained breathing apparatus monthly.

(v) The employer shall ensure that rescue teams are familiar with conditions at the jobsite.

(j) **Air quality and monitoring—**(1) **General.** Air quality limits and control requirements for construction are found in § 1926.55, except as modified by this section.

(i)(A) The employer shall assign a competent person who shall perform all air monitoring required by this section.

(B) Where this paragraph requires monitoring of airborne contaminants "as often as necessary," the competent person shall make a reasonable determination as to which substances to monitor and how frequently to monitor considering at least the following factors:

(1) Location of jobsite: Proximity to fuel tanks, sewers, gas lines, old landfills, coal deposits, and swamps;

(2) Geology: Geological studies of the jobsite, particularly involving the soil type and its permeability;

(3) History: Presence of air contaminants in nearby jobsites, changes in levels of substances monitored on the prior shift; and

(4) Work practices and jobsite conditions: The use of diesel engines, use of explosives, use of fuel gas, volume and flow of ventilation, visible atmospheric conditions, decompression of the atmosphere, welding, cutting and hot work, and employees' physical reactions to working underground.

(vi) When the competent person determines, on the basis of air monitoring results or other information, that air contaminants may be present in sufficient quantity to be dangerous to life, the employer shall:

(A) Prominently post a notice at all entrances to the underground jobsite to inform all entrants of the hazardous condition; and

(B) Ensure that the necessary precautions are taken.

(o) **Ground support—**(3) **Underground areas** (i)(A) A competent person shall inspect the roof, face, and walls of the work area at the start of each shift and as often as necessary to determine ground stability.

(iv)(B) A competent person shall determine whether rock bolts meet the necessary torque, and shall determine the testing frequency in light of the bolt system, ground conditions and the distance from vibration sources.

1926.800(t)(3)(xix) and (xx)

(t) Hoisting unique to underground construction. (3) Additional requirements for hoists.

(xix) A competent person shall visually check all hoisting machinery, equipment, anchorages, and hoisting rope at the beginning of each shift and during hoist use, as necessary.

(xx) Each safety device shall be checked by a competent person at least weekly during hoist use to ensure suitable operation and safe condition.

Compressed Air—1926.803

(a) **General provisions.** (1) There shall be present, at all times, at least one competent person designated by and representing the employer, who shall be familiar with this subpart in all respects, and responsible for full compliance with these and other applicable subparts.

(2) Every employee shall be instructed in the rules and regulations which concern his safety or the safety of others.

(b) **Medical attendance, examination, and regulations.** (1) There shall be retained one or more licensed physicians familiar with and experienced in the physical requirements and the medical aspects of compressed air work and the treatment of decompression illness. He shall be available at all times while work is in progress in order to provide medical supervision of employees employed in compressed air work. He shall himself be physically qualified and be willing to enter a pressurized environment.

(10) The medical lock shall:

(xii) Be in constant charge of an attendant under the direct control of the retained physician. The attendant shall be trained in the use of the lock and suitably instructed regarding steps to be taken in the treatment of employees exhibiting symptoms compatible with a diagnosis of decompression illness.

(e) **Compression.** (1) Every employee going under air pressure for the first time shall be instructed on how to avoid excessive discomfort.

(f) **Decompression.** (2) In the event it is necessary for an employee to be in compressed air more than once in a 24-hour period, the appointed physician shall be responsible for the establishment of methods and procedures of decompression applicable to repeated exposures.

(3) If decanting is necessary, the appointed physician shall establish procedures before any employee is permitted to be decompressed by decanting methods. The period of time that the employees spend at atmospheric pressure between the decompression following the shift and recompression shall not exceed 5 minutes.

(h) **Compressor plant and air supply.** (1) At all times there shall be a thoroughly experienced, competent, and reliable person on duty at the air control valves as a gauge tender who shall regulate the pressure in the working areas. During tunneling operations, one gauge tender may regulate the pressure in not more than two headings: **Provided**, That the gauge and controls are all in one location. In caisson work, there shall be a gauge tender for each caisson.

Demolition—Preparatory Operations— 1926.850

(a) Prior to permitting employees to start demolition operations, an engineering survey shall be made, by a competent person, of the structure to determine the condition of the framing, floors, and walls, and possibility of unplanned collapse of any portion of the structure. Any adjacent structure where employees may be exposed shall also be similarly checked. The employer shall have in writing evidence that such a survey has been performed.

Chutes—1926.852

(c) A substantial gate shall be installed in each chute at or near the discharge end. A competent employee shall be assigned to control the operation of the gate, and the backing and loading of trucks.

Mechanical Demolition—1926.859

(g) During demolition, continuing inspections by a competent person shall be made as the work progresses to detect hazards resulting from weakened or deteriorated floors, or walls, or loosened material. No employee shall be permitted to work where such hazards exist until they are corrected by shoring, bracing, or other effective means.

Blasting and Use of Explosives—General Provisions—1926.900

(a) The employer shall permit only authorized and qualified persons to handle and use explosives.

(k)(3)(i) The prominent display of adequate signs, warning against the use of mobile radio transmitters, on all roads within 1,000 feet of blasting operations. Whenever adherence to the 1,000-feet distance would create an operational handicap, a competent person shall be consulted to evaluate the particular situation, and alternative provisions may be made which are adequately designed to prevent any premature firing of electric blasting caps. A description of any such alternatives shall be reduced to writing and shall be certified as meeting the purposes of this subdivision by the competent person consulted. The description shall be maintained at the construction site during the duration of the work, and shall be available for inspection by representatives of the Secretary of Labor.

(q)(4) All loading and firing shall be directed and supervised by competent persons thoroughly experienced in this field.

Blaster Qualifications—1926.901

(c) A blaster shall be qualified, by reason of training, knowledge, or experience, in the field of transporting, storing, handling, and use of explosives, and have a working knowledge of State and local laws and regulations which pertain to explosives.

(d) Blasters shall be required to furnish satisfactory evidence of competency in handling explosives and performing in a safe manner the type of blasting that will be required.

(e) The blaster shall be knowledgeable and competent in the use of each type of blasting method used.

Surface Transportation of Explosives— 1926.902

(b) Motor vehicles or conveyances transporting explosives shall only be driven by, and be in the charge of, a licensed driver who is physically fit. He shall be familiar with the local, State, and Federal regulation governing the transportation of explosives.

(i) Each vehicle used for transportation of explosives shall be equipped with a fully charged fire extinguisher, in good condition. An Underwriters Laboratory-approved extinguisher of not less than 10-ABC rating will meet the minimum requirement. The driver shall be trained in the use of the extinguisher on his vehicle.

Firing the Blast—1926.909

(a) A code of blasting signals equivalent to Table U-1, shall be posted on one or more conspicuous places at the operation, and all employees shall be required to familiarize themselves with the code and conform to it. Danger signs shall be placed at suitable locations.

Table U

Warning signal—A 1-minute series of long blasts 5 minutes prior to blast signal.

Blast signal—A series of short blasts 1 minute prior to the shot.

All clear signal—A prolonged blast following the inspection of blast area.

Power Transmission and Distribution— General Requirements—1926.950

(1) When deenergizing lines and equipment operated in excess of 600 volts, and the means

of disconnecting from electric energy is not visibly open or visibly locked out, the provisions of paragraphs (d)(1)(i) through (vii) of this section shall be complied with:

(ii) Notification and assurance from the designated employee [a qualified person delegated to perform specific duties under the conditions existing shall be obtained that asserts that:

(a) All switches and disconnectors through which electric energy may be supplied to the particular section of line or equipment to be worked have been deenergized;

(b) All switches and disconnectors are plainly tagged indicating that men are at work;

(c) And that where design of such switches and disconnectors permits, they have been rendered inoperable.

(vi) When more than one independent crew requires the same line or equipment to be deenergized, a prominent tag for each such independent crew shall be placed on the line or equipment by the designated employee in charge.

(vii) Upon completion of work on deenergized lines or equipment, each designated employee in charge shall determine that all employees in his crew are clear, that protective grounds installed by his crew have been removed, and he shall report to the designated authority that all tags protecting his crew may be removed.

1926.950(d)(2)(ii)

(2) When a crew working on a line or equipment can clearly see that the means of disconnecting from electric energy are visibly open or visibly locked-out, the provisions of paragraph (d)(i), and (ii) of this section shall apply:

(ii) Upon completion of work on deenergized lines or equipment, each designated employee in charge shall determine that all employees in his crew are clear, that protective grounds installed by his crew have been removed, and he shall report to the designated authority that all tags protecting his crew may be removed.

1926.950(e)(1)(i) and (ii) and (2)

(e) **Emergency procedures and first aid.**

(1) The employer shall provide training or require that his employees are knowledgeable and proficient in:

(i) Procedures involving emergency situations, and

(ii) First-aid fundamentals including resuscitation.

(2) In lieu of paragraph (e)(1) of this section the employer may comply with the provisions of §1926.50(c) regarding first-aid requirements.

Overhead Lines—1926.955

(b) **Metal tower construction.**

(3)(i) A designated employee shall be used in directing mobile equipment adjacent to footing excavations.

(8) A designated employee shall be utilized to determine that required clearance is maintained in moving equipment under or near energized lines.

(d) **Stringing adjacent to energized lines.** (1) Prior to stringing parallel to an existing energized transmission line a competent determination shall be made to ascertain whether dangerous induced voltage buildups will occur, particularly during switching and ground fault conditions. When there is a possibility that such dangerous induced voltage may exist the employer shall comply with the provisions of paragraphs (d)(2) through (9) of this section in addition to the provisions of paragraph (c) of this § 1926.955, unless the line is worked as energized.

(e) **Live-line bard-hand work.** (1) Employees shall be instructed and trained in the live-line bare-hand technique and the safety requirements pertinent thereto before being permitted to use the technique on energized circuits.

(4) All work shall be personally supervised by a person trained and qualified to perform live-line, bare-hand work.

Underground Lines—1926.956

(b) **Work in manholes.** (1) While work is being performed in manholes, an employee shall be available in the immediate vicinity to render emergency assistance as may be required. This shall not preclude the employee in the immediate vicinity from occasionally entering a manhole to provide assistance, other than emergency. This requirement does not preclude a qualified employee [a person who by reason of experience or training is familiar with the operation to be performed and the hazards involved], working alone, from entering for brief periods of time, a manhole where energized cables or equipment are in service, for the purpose of inspection, housekeeping, taking readings, or similar work if such work can be performed safely.

Construction in Energized Substations—1926.957

(a) **Work near energized equipment facilities.** (1) When construction work is performed in an energized substation, authorization shall be obtained from the designated, authorized person [a qualified person delegated to perform specific duties under the conditions existing] before work is started.

(d) **Control panels.** (1) Work on or adjacent to energized control panels shall be performed by designated employees.

1926.957(e)(1)

(e) **Mechanized equipment.** (1) Use of vehicles, gin poles, cranes, and other equipment in restricted or hazardous areas shall at all times be controlled by designated employees.

Ladders—1926.1053

(b) **Use.** (15) Ladders shall be inspected by a competent person for visible defects on a periodic basis and after any occurrence that could affect their safe use.

Stairways and Ladders—Training Requirements—1926.1060

The following training provisions clarify the requirements of § 1926.21(b)(2) regarding the hazards addressed in subpart X.

(a) The employer shall provide a training program for each employee using ladders and stairways, as necessary. The program shall enable each employee to recognize hazards related to ladders and stairways, and shall train each employee in the procedures to be followed to minimize these hazards.

(1) The employer shall ensure that each employee has been trained by a competent person in the following areas, as applicable:

   (i) The nature of fall hazards in the work area;

   (ii) The correct procedures for erecting, maintaining, and disassembling the fall protection systems to be used;

   (iii) The proper construction, use, placement, and care in handling of all stairways and ladders;

   (iv) The maximum intended load carrying capacities of ladders used; and

   (v) The standards contained in this subpart.

(b) Retraining shall be provided for each employee as necessary so that the employee maintains the understanding and knowledge acquired through compliance with this section.

Qualifications of Dive Team—1926.1076

Note: The requirements applicable to construction work under this section are identical to those set forth at §1910.410 of this chapter.

§1910.410 Qualifications of dive team.

(a) General.

(1) Each dive team member shall have the experience or training necessary to perform assigned tasks in a safe and healthful manner.

(2) Each dive team member shall have experience or training in the following:

   (i) The use of tools, equipment and systems relevant to assigned tasks;

   (ii) Techniques of the assigned diving mode; and

   (iii) Diving operations and emergency procedures.

(3) All dive team members shall be trained in cardiopulmonary resuscitation and first aid (American Red Cross standard course or equivalent).

(4) Dive team members who are exposed to or control the exposure of others to hyperbaric conditions shall be trained in diving-related physics and physiology.

(b) Assignments.

(1) Each dive team member shall be assigned tasks in accordance with the employee's experience or training, except that limited additional tasks may be assigned to an employee undergoing training provided that these tasks are performed under the direct supervision of an experienced dive team member.

(2) The employer shall not require a dive team member to be exposed to hyperbaric conditions against the employee's will, except when necessary to complete decompression or treatment procedures.

(3) The employer shall not permit a dive team member to dive or be otherwise exposed to hyperbaric conditions for the duration of any temporary physical impairment or condition which is known to the employer and is likely to affect adversely the safety or health of a dive team member.

(c) Designated person-in-charge.

(1) The employer or an employee designated by the employer shall be at the dive location in charge of all aspects of the diving operation affecting the safety and health of dive team members.

(2) The designated person-in-charge shall have experience and training in the conduct of the assigned diving operation.

Asbestos—1926.1101

(k) Communication of hazards.

(9) Employee information and training (i) The employer shall, at no cost, to the employee, institute a training program for all employees who are likely to be exposed in excess of a PEL and for all employees who perform Class I through IV asbestos operations, and shall ensure their participation in the program.

   (ii) Training shall be provided prior to or at the time of initial assignment and at least annually thereafter.

   (iii) Training for Class I operations and for Class II operations that require the use of critical barriers (or equivalent isolation methods) and/or negative pressure enclosures under this section shall be the equivalent in curriculum, training method and length to the EPA Model Accreditation Plan (MAP) asbestos abatement workers training (40 CFR Part 763, subpart E, appendix C).

(iv) Training for other Class II work.

(A) For work with asbestos containing roofing materials, flooring materials, siding materials, ceiling tiles, or transite panels, training shall include at a minimum all the elements included in paragraph (k)(9)(viii) of this section and in addition, the specific work practices and engineering controls set forth in paragraph (g) of this section which specifically relate to that category. Such course shall include "hands-on" training and shall take at least 8 hours.

(B) An employee who works with more than one of the categories of material specified in paragraph (k)(9)(iv)(A) of this section shall receive training in the work practices applicable to each category of material that the employee removes and each removal method that the employee uses.

(C) For Class II operations not involving the categories of material specified in paragraph (k)(9)(iv)(A) of this section, training shall be provided which shall include at a minimum all the elements included in paragraph (k)(9)(viii) of this section and in addition, the specific work practices and engineering controls set forth in paragraph (g) of this section which specifically relate to the category of material being removed, and shall include "hands-on" training in the work practices applicable to each category of material that the employee removes and each removal method that the employee uses.

(v) Training for Class III employees shall be consistent with EPA requirements for training of local education agency maintenance and custodial staff as set forth at 40 CFR 763.92(a)(2). Such a course shall also include "hands-on" training and shall take at least 16 hours. Exception: For Class III operations for which the competent person determines that the EPA curriculum does not adequately cover the training needed to perform that activity, training shall include as a minimum all the elements included in paragraph (k)(9)(viii) of this section and in addition, the specific work practices and engineering controls set forth in paragraph (g) of this section

which specifically relate to that activity, and shall include "hands-on" training in the work practices applicable to each category of material that the employee disturbs.

(vi) Training for employees performing Class IV operations shall be consistent with EPA requirements for training of local education agency maintenance and custodial staff as set forth at 40 CFR 763.92(a)(1). Such a course shall include available information concerning the locations of thermal system insulation and surfacing ACM/PACM, and asbestos-containing flooring material, or flooring material where the absence of asbestos has not yet been certified; and instruction in recognition of damage, deterioration, and delamination of asbestos containing building materials. Such course shall take at least 2 hours.

(vii) Training for employees who are likely to be exposed in excess of the PEL and who are not otherwise required to be trained under paragraph (k)(9)(iii) through (vi) of this section, shall meet the requirements of paragraph (k)(9)(viii) of this section.

(viii) The training program shall be conducted in a manner that the employee is able to understand. In addition to the content required by provisions in paragraphs (k)(9)(iii) through (vi) of this section, the employer shall ensure that each such employee is informed of the following: (A) Methods of recognizing asbestos including the requirement in paragraph (k)(1) of this section to presume that certain building materials contain asbestos;

(B) The health effects associated with asbestos exposure;

(C) The relationship between smoking and asbestos in producing lung cancer.

(D) The nature of operations that could result in exposure to asbestos, the importance of necessary protective controls to minimize exposure including, as applicable, engineering controls, work practices, respirators, housekeeping procedures, hygiene facilities, protective clothing, decontamination procedures, emergency procedures, and waste disposal procedures, and any necessary instruction in the use of these controls and procedures where Class III and IV work will be or is performed, the contents of EPA 20T-2003, 'Managing Asbestos In-Place" July 1990 or its equivalent in content;

(E) The purpose, proper use, fitting instructions, and limitations of respirators as required by 29 CFR 1910.134;

(10) Access to training materials. (i) The employer shall make readily available to affected employees without cost, written materials relating to the employee training program, including a copy of this regulation.

13 Carcinogens—1926.1103

Note: The requirements applicable to construction work under this section are identical to those set forth at §1910.1003 of this chapter.

Vinyl Chloride—1926.1117

Note: The requirements applicable to construction work under this section are identical to those set forth at §1910.1017 of this chapter.

Inorganic Arsenic—1926.1118

Note: The requirements applicable to construction work under this section are identical to those set forth at §1910.1018 of this chapter.

Cadmium—1926.1127

(m) **Communication of cadmium hazards to employees**—(4) Employee information and training. (i) The employer shall institute a training program for all employees who are potentially exposed to cadmium, assure employee participation in the program, and maintain a record of the contents of such a program.

(ii) Training shall be provided prior to or at the time of initial assignment to a job involving potential exposure to cadmium and at least annually thereafter.

(iii) The employer shall make the training program understandable to the employee and shall assure that each employee is informed of the following:

(A) The health hazards associated with cadmium exposure, with special attention to the information incorporated in appendix A to this section;

(B) The quantity, location, manner of use, release, and storage of cadmium in the workplace and the specific nature of operations that could result in exposure to cadmium, especially exposures above the PEL;

(C) The engineering controls and work practices associated with the employee's job assignments;

(D) The measures employees can take to protect themselves from exposure to cadmium, including modification of such habits as smoking and personal hygiene, and specific procedures the employer has implemented to protect employees from exposure to cadmium such as appropriate work practices, emergency procedures, and the provision of personal protective equipment;

(E) The purpose, proper selection, fitting, proper use, and limitations of respirators and protective clothing.

Benzene—1926.1128

Note: The requirements applicable to construction work under this section are identical to those set forth at §1910.1028 of this chapter.

Coke Oven Emissions—1926.1129

Note: The requirements applicable to construction work under this section are identical to those set forth at §1910.1029 of this chapter.

1, 2-dibromo-3-chloro-propane—1926.1144

Note: The requirements applicable to construction work under this section are identical to those set forth at §1910.1044 of this chapter.

Acrylonitrile—1926.1145

Note: The requirements applicable to construction work under this section are identical to those set forth at §1910.1045 of this chapter.

Ethylene Oxide—1926.1147

Note: The requirements applicable to construction work under this section are identical to those set forth at §1910.1047 of this chapter.

Formaldehyde—1926.1148

Note: The requirements applicable to construction work under this section are identical to those set forth at §1910.1048 of this chapter.

Methylene Chloride—1926.1152

Note: The requirements applicable to construction work under this section are identical to those set forth at §1910.1052 of this chapter.

End of Course Quiz

1. What is the most frequently cited OSHA Standard?
   a. Lockout/tagout
   b. Machine guarding
   c. Recordkeeping
   d. Hazardous communication

2. If you feel that a citation that was issued to you was unfair, you have _____ days to contest the charge.
   a. 5
   b. 10
   c. 15
   d 20

3. Even though OSHA has not published an Ergonomics Standard, you can still be cited for an ergonomics problem, such as making workers perform repetitive tasks.
   a. True
   b. False

4. The CD-ROM for OSHA Regulations (available from the Government Printing Office) is updated _____.
   a. Monthly
   b. Quarterly
   c. Annually

5. A Type A fire is one that consists of:
   a. Trash, paper and wood
   b. Oil and tar
   c. Electrical circuits that are still energized
   d. A combination of the above

6. The top four events that kill construction workers are falls from elevations, struck by, struck against, and _____.
   a. Chemical exposure
   b. Electrocution
   c. Collapsing trenches
   d. OSHA inspections

7. Even though the computer system is locked in the job shack at night, MSDSs can be kept on the computer and meet the accessibility requirements when workers who have no computer skills are working at night.
   a. True
   b. False

8. A ground-fault circuit interrupter does not require a grounding wire because it is a type of circuit breaker.
   a. True
   b. False

9. While mopping a spill in the bathroom, Millie the Maid splashes her mop against the GFCI outlet. The electricity flows through the wet mop to Millie's hands until the circuit interrupter breaks the flow of electricity, saving her life. At what level of milliamps should the circuit breaker trip to keep Millie on the pay roll?

  a. 3 milliamps
  b. 5 milliamps
  c. 7 milliamps
  d. 9 milliamps

10. A straight, portable ladder extends to a 20-ft. high roof. To meet OSHA requirements, the worker must ensure the ladder extends 3 ft. past the roof and the base of the ladder is _____ feet from the edge of the building.

  a. 2 ft.
  b. 3 ft.
  c. 5 ft.
  d. 7 ft.

RISK MANAGEMENT

INTRODUCTION:

WHY USE A RISK MANAGEMENT APPROACH

The risk management process and the benefits and opportunities it provides have given companies a way to fix responsibility and accountability at the appropriate level. It requires managers and supervisors to accept responsibility for safety actions in a written form that reinforces their responsibility and liability, resulting in more safe decision making.

Risk Management enhances the workplace environment by eliminating or controlling hazards before they result in losses, whether personnel or materiel, losses that can degrade or halt the operation.

Effective use of Risk Management techniques provides worker, manager and leader with a workplace for which the risks are acceptable, in fact, a safe workplace. The Occupational Health and Safety Act mandates that every workplace be free of recognized hazards. This 'general duty' clause is used when there are no specific standards applicable to a particular hazard.

WHAT IS RISK MANAGEMENT?

Risk Management is a disciplined, organized, and logical decision making process to identify, evaluate and control hazards. With training and practice, personnel will be better able to spot hazards, analyze risk and make risk decisions at the appropriate level of control.

All work and daily routines involve risk. All job tasks and daily living require decisions that include assessing and managing hazards. Each supervisor, along with every individual, is responsible for identifying potential risks and adjusting or compensating appropriately. Decisions must then be made at a level of responsibility that corresponds to the degree of risk and the ability to apply resources, taking into consideration the significance of the task and the timeliness of the required decision. The decision-making techniques apply to all operations.

Risk Management is a process that gives an added edge to those with a long history of meeting "minimum" requirements, or, of meeting standards. It is an opportunity to go beyond the minimum, to reach greater effectiveness in any task or operation. Its prerequisite is a firm foundation in standards. One must understand the standards well enough to know the consequences of compromising them, and therefore how to control the task with a new set of 'standards' that provide risk controls or that the decision authority accepts the risk of loss.

Managers, supervisors and individuals must:

- Take ownership of workplace hazards.
- Not allow uncontrolled hazards.

Risk management is not a radical new way of doing business. Each of us manages risk on a daily basis, while working, driving, shopping, investing, etc. Most decisions are automatic, guided by years of experience coping with the same or similar situations. In a sense, we are all experienced "Risk Managers".

Simply put, Risk Management is an organized framework for decision-making. The aim is to minimize losses, whether associated with money, equipment or personnel safety, while maximizing operation success. It is the rational decision process: Weigh expected costs against expected benefits; if benefits outweigh costs—go for it; otherwise don't. The dilemma most often is how to quantify expected costs and benefits.

WHAT ABOUT COMPLIANCE?

Meeting OSHA standards is required in the workplace. It's important to understand there is no conflict between standards and the application of Risk Management techniques. The OSHA standards provide a foundation for hazard identification and control. Knowledge of OSHA standards provides valuable insight into understanding and implementing safety programs and systems. Application of OSHA standards provides safe workplaces from recognized hazards. However OSHA standards don't cover all hazards. Risk Management provides a process to make the workplace safer by reviewing and prioritizing tasks and operations either not covered, or not covered effectively, by OSHA standards.

HOW DOES IT WORK?

The basic decision making principles are applied before any job, action, or operation is executed. As an operation progresses and evolves, risk management controls are continuously reevaluated. Risk Management requires that owners and CEOs accept the process and take an active part in it. This is done by enforcing its use and establishing the amount of risk that workers can accept. For example, a low risk task, such as setting up a ladder and

changing a light bulb can be approved by the worker doing the task. On the other hand, if the light bulb has electrical wiring that is shorting out and exposing that worker to an electrical shock, and it is in a wet environment, the task may be defined as a high risk task. The CEO may require that all high risk tasks be approved by the plant manager, thereby shifting the authority and acceptance of liability to the plant manager. This is an important concept that eliminates the situation where a plant manager tells a subordinate to engage in a risky task with impunity. Under the Risk Management system, the worker would be required by company policy to inform the supervisor that as performed, this is a highly dangerous risk that cannot be accepted by the worker or the supervisor. It must be sent up the chain of command to someone who can accept the risk and liability. This protects the company, its officers and the workers by forcing a process to be enacted.

Integrate into planning.

- Risks are more easily assessed and managed in the early planning stages.
- The acceptable plans are in proportion to risks and worth the anticipated cost.
- Operation is accomplished without incurring excessive losses in personnel, equipment, time, or position.

Accept no Unnecessary Risk.

- Unnecessary risk has no payback in terms of real benefits or available opportunities.
- RM provides tools to determine which risk or what level of risk is unnecessary. CEOs

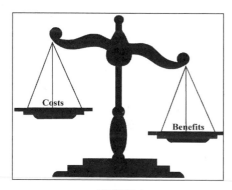

FIGURE 1.
COST AND BENEFIT SCALES

must make this decision to protect their company from lawsuits.

Make Risk Decisions at the Appropriate Level.

- Appropriate level for risk decisions is the one that can allocate the resources to reduce the risk or eliminate the hazard and implement controls.

Accept Risk When Benefits Outweigh the Costs.

- All identified benefits should be compared to all identified costs.
- Figure 1 depicts this principle. Balancing costs and benefits may be a subjective process and open to interpretation.

Ultimately, the balance may have to be determined by the appropriate decision authority.

Integrate RM into Company Doctrine and Planning at all Levels.

Risks are more easily assessed and managed in the planning stages of an operation. Integrating risk management into planning as early as possible provides the decision maker the greatest opportunity to apply RM principles.

Five-Step Risk Management Process. RM is a continuous process designed to detect, assess, and control risk while enhancing performance and maximizing capabilities. Figure 2 depicts the five-step process.

- **Identify Hazards.** A hazard is any real or potential condition that can cause (mission degradation) injury, illness, death to personnel or damage to or loss of equipment or property. Experience, common sense, and specific risk management tools help identify real or potential hazards.
- **Assess the Hazards.** Risk is the probability and severity of loss from exposure to the hazard. Assessment is the application of quantitative or qualitative measures to determine the level of risk associated with a specific hazard. The assessment step in the process defines the probability and severity of a mishap that could result from the hazard and determines the exposure of personnel or assets to that hazard.

- **Develop Control Measures and Make Risk Decision.** Investigate specific strategies and tools that reduce, mitigate, or eliminate the risk. Effective control measures reduce one or more of the three components (probability, severity, or exposure) of risk. Decision makers at the appropriate level choose controls based on the analysis of overall costs and benefits.
- **Implement Controls.** Once control strategies have been selected, an implementation strategy needs to be developed and then applied by management and the work force. Implementation requires commitment of time and resources.
- **Supervise and Evaluate.** Risk management is a process that continues throughout the life cycle of the system, mission, or activity. Once controls are in place, the process must be scrutinized and reevaluated to determine its effectiveness. Mission performance is periodically evaluated to determine the effectiveness of risk control measures.

WHAT IS RISK?

The following chart depicts risk: as risk is evaluated some emerge as clearly unacceptable. The unacceptable risk will either be controlled or the task will not be performed as planned. Some risk is not identified until later in the planning process or in the actual operation phase. That risk is evaluated as it's identified and additional controls either put into place or the risk is accepted or eliminated. Risk perception, risk tolerance, and risk acceptance play major roles in an individual's definition of "risk". Diversity of age, experience, and training are among the filters individuals use to consider risk. Level of experience with the specific mission or task adds another dimension to each individual's concept of "risk".

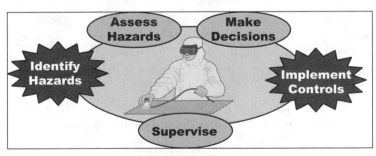

FIGURE 2.
FIVE-STEP PROCESS OF RISK MANAGEMENT

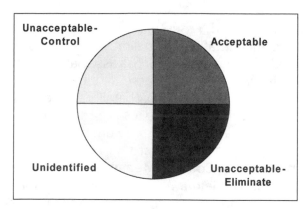

FIGURE 3.
TYPES OF RISK

WHAT ARE THE BENEFITS?

Benefits are not limited to reduced accident rates or decreased injuries, but may be actual increases in efficiency or job effectiveness. Examples of potential benefits include:

- Improved ability to protect the workforce by minimizing accidents—analysis of current processes may reduce risks.
- Enhanced job efficiency—reducing hazards by placing controls may make the task flow decisions are based on a reasoned and repeatable process instead of guess work or intuition.
- Improved confidence in capabilities—adequate risk analysis provides a clear picture of workforce strengths and weaknesses.

WHAT IS UNNECESSARY RISK?

Applying risk management requires a clear understanding of what constitutes "unnecessary risk", when benefits actually outweigh costs, and some guidance as to the appropriate level. Accepting risk is a function of both risk assessment and risk management. Risk acceptance is not as simple a matter as it may first appear. Several points must be kept in mind.

- Some risk is a fundamental reality.
- Risk management is a process of tradeoffs.
- Quantifying risk doesn't ensure safety.

General risk management guidelines are:

- Many activities involving a technical device or complex process entail some risk during their execution.
- Weigh risks and make judgments according to knowledge, experience, and mission requirements.
- Encourage other disciplines to adopt risk management principles. Hazard analysis

and risk assessment do not free us from reliance on good judgment.

- It is more important to establish clear objectives and parameters for risk assessment than to find a "cookbook" approach and procedure.
- There may be no "best solution." There are a variety of directions to go. Each of these directions may produce some degree of risk reduction.
- Point out improvements to established controls rather than to say their approach will not work.
- Complete risk control is not the goal; total risk elimination is seldom achieved in a practical manner.

WHO DOES WHAT?

CEOs/plant managers:

- Set the example
- Establish the acceptable level of risk for subordinates..
- Establish, endorse, and enforce established standards.
- Reinforce personal accountability.
- Accept responsibility for effective management of risk.
- Select from risk reduction options provided by the staff.
- Accept or reject risk based on the benefit to be derived.
- Train and motivate leaders to use risk management.
- Elevate to the appropriate decision maker; based on clearly defined risk levels.

Supervisors:

- Apply the risk management process and direct personnel to use it both on and off duty.
- Consistently apply effective risk management concepts and methods to operations and tasks.
- Elevate risk issues beyond their control or authority to superiors for resolution.

Individuals:

- Understand, accept, and implement risk management processes.
- Maintain a constant awareness of the hazards associated with a task.

- Make supervisors immediately aware of any unrealistic risk reduction measures or high risk procedures.

HOW MUCH IS ENOUGH?

Somewhere between the back of an envelope and a multi-year, multi-million dollar, contractor-engineered PERT chart lies the right amount of risk management for the task or mission at hand. How much is enough? How do you advise the CEO or manager as to the most appropriate level of detail for a particular task or operation? What criteria would you use to make your recommendation?

- We've talked about "effective application of the Risk Management process". It means that "hands on", not just following the "fine print", defines an efficient and effective process when it comes to Risk Management. It's easy to fall into using some format that soon becomes a thoughtless process. That road may be efficient; but it's rarely effective and it's full of potholes. We've talked about Risk Management providing insights into balancing cost and benefit. Some of the costs and benefits are subjective. The question arises "What 'criteria' would you use to advise the CEO on how much Risk Management is enough?" There is no easy answer. We recognize that the cost benefit of effective Risk Management for a major mobilization would likely be greater than for an everyday delivery of goods and services already in the pipeline. "Enough" Risk Management for continued operations is different than "enough" for an office staff with little change in their day to day operations.

Some suggested criteria:

- Is hasty or is deliberate decision making underway?
- Is time available to plan?
- What's the Importance of operation success—100% OK? 75%, 50%? What if it fails completely?
- Is the operation or task a new one or an old familiar one?
- Are personnel involved new to the operation or task? Unit? Experienced/Inexperienced?
- What's been their operation tempo recently?

HOW DO I EVALUATE OUR PROGRAM?

Use structured internal and external assessments. Leaders and managers take advantage of the entrepreneurial genius of the people within the organization to develop better ways of helping people and getting work done. It is a process which encourages ideas and initiatives to float upward. Embedding the risk management process into organizational processes is one way to help achieve better results. The idea behind risk management is to identify strengths and weaknesses in planning and execution with emphasis on hazard control. The value of self-assessments is the awakening of self awareness. With this self awareness, change is more readily accepted.

Risk management integration and self assessment can help change the thinking from "minimal essential" to "maximum possible" philosophies in providing support to workers. Employees are deserving of nothing less than excellence. Authority and responsibility must be pushed down into the organization.

WHERE DOES THE SAFETY PROFESSIONAL FIT IN?

The safety professional is the link between the compliance world and the world of uncontrolled risk. The first step the safety professional makes is to help leaders recognize that risks can be controlled, that accidental losses need not be the cost of doing business. Whether an individual views a task or operation as having group or individual risk plays a major role in whether the individual believes he can take action to reduce the risk. The safety professional can facilitate a change of attitude from the idea that "warehousemen have back injuries", or group risk about which little can be done; to the reality of individual risk, where worksite redesign, individual work-hardening, or use of manual materials handling equipment and eliminate the hazard. Once leaders believe that losses are unnecessary, the next step is that the safety professional can provide the Risk Management process as a deliberative, logical decision making methodology to control the hazards that lead to unnecessary losses. Now, the safety professional must advise leaders on how much Risk Management is appropriate to the task at hand and facilitate the process.

Professional safety personnel provide knowledge of Occupational Health and Safety standards, application of safety practices to recognize, avoid/eliminate hazards, and for hazard control and evaluation techniques that provide the foundation of a safe workplace. Safety professionals are investigators when hazardous conditions turn into accidents or incidents related to inadequately controlled hazards. Safety offices assist in training, program management and coordinating with health and safety related offices; to include preventive medicine, engineers, security and others.

AUDITS. Measurements are necessary to ensure accurate evaluations of how effectively controls eliminated hazards or reduced risks. After action reports, surveys, and in progress reviews provide great starting places for measurements. To be meaningful, measurements must quantitatively or qualitatively identify reductions of risk, improvements in operation success, or enhancement of capabilities. The Risk Management Evaluation Profile (an adaptation of OSHA's Program Evaluation Profile) in appendix B, provides an audit process of a safety program's overall effectiveness. Benefits of conducting an audit include:

- Formally going through the internal audit process with managers and employees,
- Formally reviewing the elements of a safety and health program,
- Getting managers involved in the audit process,
- Making managers, supervisors and employees aware of the scope and complexity of a formal safety and health program, and of their roles and responsibilities in the programs success.

After finishing your audit share the results with managers and legal personnel since the process of doing an audit creates a paper trail of the program's weaknesses. The audit is a formal tool to uncover weak points in the management system that create unsafe work practices and unsafe conditions that can injure workers, diminish their health, interrupt production, or damage products and property.

CONCLUSION. Risk management provides a logical and systematic means of organizing information for rational decision-making, to identify and control risk. Risk management is a process that requires individuals, supervisors and leaders to support and implement the basic principles, along with the discipline to apply them on a continuing basis. Risk management offers individuals and organizations a powerful tool for eliminating accidents and increasing effectiveness. This process has the unique advantage of being accessible to and usable by everyone in every conceivable setting or scenario.

Appendix A: Risk Management Steps

Tools to accomplish the various steps are explained and examples are given in, The Risk Manager's *Hazard Identification Tool Box*.

Step 1. IDENTIFY THE HAZARDS

Hazards lead to risk, so the first step is to identify relevant hazards. Consider all aspects of current and future situations, environment, and known historical problems.

In identifying hazards, experience and training cannot be overemphasized; it is the most effective tool available. Those who have experience must use it, if an organization is to effectively use the RM process. Still, everyone is responsible for, and should be involved in finding potential hazards and informing their supervisor.

Visualization is an effective method to identify hazards. Picture the planned operation, think of what could go wrong—**ask yourself what if**? This can be done by an individual or a group, and can also use quality techniques such as brainstorming, "five whys", mental imaging, affinity diagrams, or cause-effect diagrams. The bottom line is: Honestly assess the planned procedure—**Think of what could go wrong, no matter how unlikely**.

Recognize Hazards: The Activity Hazard Analysis and Job Hazard Analysis (JHA) are both excellent tools to help identify risk as you think through a course of action to be examined. This is accomplished by reviewing current and planned operations describing the task. The supervisor defines what is required to accomplish the tasks and the conditions under which these tasks are to be conducted.

Construct a list or chart depicting the major steps in the job process, normally in time

RESOURCE

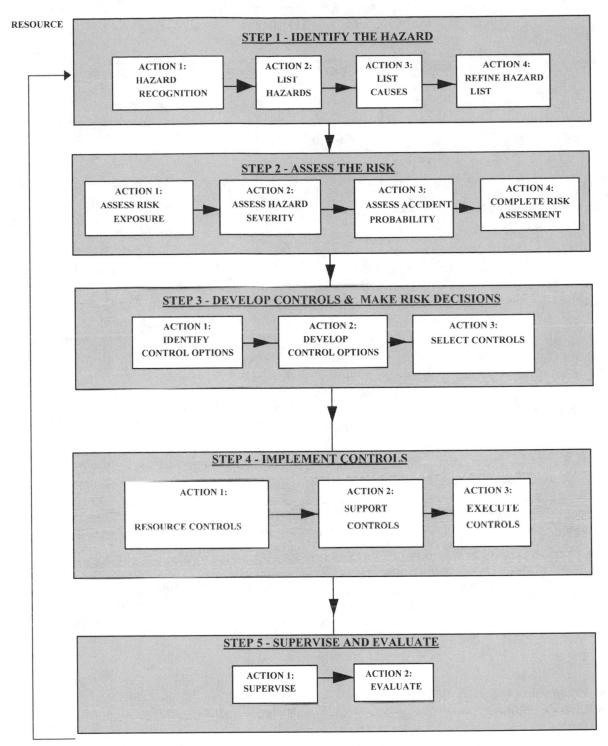

FIGURE 4
RISK MANAGEMENT STEPS

sequence. Break the operation down into 'bite size' chunks.

Some tools that will help perform mission/ task analysis are:

- Activity Hazard Analysis
- Job Hazard Analysis

- Flow Diagram
- Multilinear Event Sequence (MES)
- Sequentially Timed Event Plot (STEP)

List Hazards: Hazards, and factors that could generate hazards, are identified based

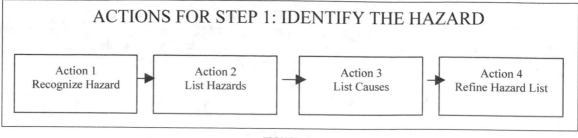

FIGURE 5
STEP 1 ACTIONS

on the deficiency to be corrected and the definition of the task and system requirements. The identification phase produces a listing of hazards or adverse conditions and the accidents which could result. Examples of inherent hazards in any one of the elements include fire, explosion, collision with objects, or electrocution. The analysis must also search for factors that can lead to hazards such as alertness, ambiguity, or escape route. In addition to a hazard list for the elements above, interfaces between or among these elements should be investigated for hazards. An individual required to make critical and delicate adjustment to equipment on a cold, dark night may be at risk to a frost-bite injury, maybe an example of the "interface hazards." Make a list of the hazards associated with each step in the task process. Stay focused on the specific steps in the task being analyzed. Try to limit your list to "big picture" hazards (the final link in the chain of events leading to task degradation, personnel injury, death, or property damage). Hazards should be tracked on paper or in a computer spreadsheet/database system to organize ideas and serve as a record of the analysis for future use. Tools that help list hazards are:

- Preliminary Hazard Analysis.
- Change Analysis.
- Brainstorming.
- "What if" Analysis.

Identify hazards associated with these three categories:
- Task Degradation.
- Personal Injury or Death.
- Property Damage.

List Causes: Make a list of the causes associated with each hazard identified in the hazard list. A hazard may have multiple causes related to man, machine and environments. In each case, try to identify the root cause (the first link in the chain of events leading to mission degradation, personnel injury, death, or property damage). Risk controls can be effectively applied to root causes. Causes should be annotated with the associated hazards in the same paper or computer record mentioned in the previous action. Suggested tools are:
- Change Analysis.
- Brainstorming.
- "What if" Analysis.
- Job Hazard Analysis.

Refine Hazard Lists: If time and resources permit, and additional hazard information is required, use strategic hazard analysis techniques. These are normally used for medium and long term planning, complex tasks, or operations in which the hazards are not well understood. The first step of in-depth analysis should be to examine existing databases or available historical and hazard information regarding the operation. Suggested tools are:
- Database analysis.
- Accident History.
- Cause and effect diagrams.
- Tree Diagrams

The following tools are particularly useful for complex, coordinated operations in which multiple units, participants, and system components and simultaneous events are involved: Complex operations risk management tools are:
- Sequentially timed event plot.
- Multilinear event sequence.
- Interface analysis.
- Failure mode and effect analysis.

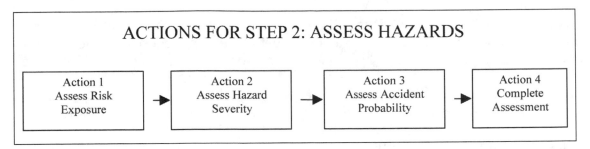

ACTIONS FOR STEP 2: ASSESS HAZARDS

| Action 1 Assess Risk Exposure | Action 2 Assess Hazard Severity | Action 3 Assess Accident Probability | Action 4 Complete Assessment |

FIGURE 6
STEP 2 ACTIONS

There are many additional tools that can help identify hazards. One of the best is through a group process involving representatives directly from the workplace. A simple brainstorming process with a trained facilitator is very productive. The following is a partial list of sources of hazard identification:

- *Accident Reports*: These can come from within the organization, from tenants, within the chain of command, the safety department, etc. Other sources might be medical reports, maintenance records, and fire and police reports.
- *Quality reports*: Quality audits provide important feedback and written documentation on local process management.
- *Accident Databases*: The OSHA 300 and insurance claims are information resources.
- *Surveys*: These can be unit generated. Target an audience and ask some very simple questions related to such topics as: What will your next accident be? Who will have it? What task will cause it? When will it happen? The survey can be a powerful tool because it pinpoints people in the workplace with first hand knowledge of the job. Often, first line supervisors in the same workplace won't have as good an understanding of risk as those who confront it every day.
- *Inspections*: Safety inspections can consist of spot checks, walk-throughs, checklist inspections, site surveys, and mandatory inspections. Use onsite workers to provide input beyond the standard third-party inspection.

Step 2. ASSESS HAZARDS.

For each hazard identified in the previous step:

Assess Hazards. Once hazards are found, the next step is to analyze the associated risk—how likely and how big a loss is possible? **Recognition and assessment is the core of the Risk Management process.** Risk Management process depends on doing good analyses at each step in the process.

Assess Hazard Exposure: Probability is effected by exposure. Repeated exposure to a hazard greatly increases the total likelihood of an accident. This can be expressed in terms of time, proximity, volume, or repetition. Does it happen often, or near personnel or equipment? Does the event happen to a lot of people or equipment? This level can aid in determining the severity or the probability of the event. Additionally, it may serve as a guide for devising control measures to limit exposure. Another important concept is **interaction.** Interaction occurs when two (or more) hazards are present and their total risk is much greater than simply adding their separate risks. It's more like multiplying than adding. Often it is the combination of several factors that make a situation hazardous, rather than any single factor. Experience and clear thinking are the best ways to consistently assess interaction.

Assess Hazard Severity: Determine the severity of the hazard in terms of its potential impact on the people, equipment, or mission. Cause and effect diagrams, scenarios and "What-If" analysis are some of the best tools for assessing the hazard severity. Severity assessment should be based upon the worst possible outcome that can reasonably be expected. Severity categories are defined to provide a qualitative measure of the worst credible accident resulting from personnel error, environmental FIGURE 7conditions; design inadequacies; procedural deficiencies; or system, subsystem, or component failure or malfunction. Using severity categories provide guidance to a wide variety of missions and systems.

Assess Accident Probability: Determine the probability that the hazard will cause an accident or loss of the severity assessed above. Accident probability is proportional to the cumulative probability of the identified causes for the hazard. Probability may be determined through estimates or actual numbers, if they are available. Assigning a quantitative accident probability to a new mission or system may not be possible early in the planning process.

A qualitative accident probability may be derived from research, analysis, and evaluation of historical safety data from similar missions and systems. The typical accident sequence is much more complicated than a single line of erect dominos where tipping the first domino (hazard) triggers a clearly predictable reaction. Supporting rationale for assigning a accident probability should be documented for future reference.

Complete Risk Assessment: Combine severity and probability estimates to form a risk assessment for each hazard. By combining the probability of occurrence with severity, a matrix is created where intersecting rows and columns define a Risk Assessment Index (RAI), table 3-3, AR 385-10. The Risk Assessment Index forms the basis for judging both the acceptability of a risk and the management level at which the decision of acceptance will be made.

The index may also be used to prioritize resources to resolve risks due to hazards or to standardize hazard notification or response actions. Severity, probability, and risk assessment should be recorded to serve as a record of the analysis for future use. Existing databases,

Risk Assessment Index matrix, or a panel of personnel experienced with the mission and hazards can be used to help complete the risk assessment.

The following are some analytical pitfalls that should be avoided in the assessment:

- *Overoptimism*: "It can't happen to us. We're already doing it." This pitfall results from not being totally honest and not looking for root causes of risk.
- *Misrepresentation*: Individual perspectives may distort data.
- *Alarmist*: "The sky's falling" approach, or "worst case" estimates are used.
- *Indiscrimination*: All data is given equal weight.
- *Prejudice*: Subjectivity and/or hidden agendas are used, rather than facts.
- *Inaccuracy*: Bad or misunderstood data nullifies accurate risk assessment.
  - It is difficult to assign a numerical value to human behavior.

SEVERITY	PROBABILITY				
	Frequent	Likely	Occasional	Seldom	Unlikely
Catastrophic	E	E	H	H	M
Critical	E	H	H	M	L
Marginal	H	M	M	L	L
Negligible	M	L	L	L	L

Risk Level: E-Extremely High, H-High, M-Moderate, L-Low

PROBABILITY- The likelihood that an event will occur.
FREQUENT- Occurs often, continuously experienced.
LIKELY - Occurs several times.
OCCASIONAL- Occurs sporadically.
SELDOM- Unlikely, but could occur at some time.
UNLIKELY- Can assume it will not occur.

SEVERITY- The expected consequence of an event in terms of degree of injury, property damage, or other mission-impairing factors.
CATASTROPHIC- Death or permanent total disability, system loss, major property damage, not able to accomplish mission.
CRITICAL - Permanent partial disability, temporary total disability in excess of 3 months, major system damage, significant property damage, significantly degrades mission capability.
MARGINAL- Minor injury, lost workday accident, minor system damage, minor property damage, some degradation of mission capability.
NEGLIGIBLE- First aid or minor medical treatment, minor system impairment, little/no impact on accomplishment of mission.

FIGURE 7

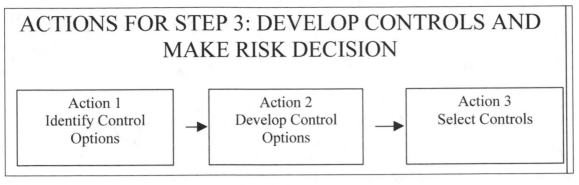

FIGURE 8
STEP 3 ACTIONS

- Numbers may oversimplify real life situations.
- It may be difficult to get enough applicable data, which could force inaccurate estimates.
- Oftentimes simple numbers take the place of reasoned judgment.
- Risk can be unrealistically traded off against benefit by relying solely on numbers.

Step 3. DEVELOP CONTROLS & MAKE RISK DECISIONS.

In this area, one must "develop control measures that eliminate the hazard or reduce its risk. As control measures are developed, risks are re-evaluated until all risks are reduced to a level where benefits outweigh potential cost."

Identify Control Options: The process of developing controls starts by taking the risk levels determined in Step 2, then identifying as many risk control options as possible for all hazards which exceed an acceptable level of risk. Refer to the list of possible causes from Step 1 for control ideas. Brainstorming, mission accident analysis and "What-If" analysis are excellent tools to identify control options. Risk control options include: **avoidance, reduction, spreading** and **transference**.

Avoiding risk altogether requires canceling or delaying the job, mission, or operation, but is an option that is rarely exercised due to mission importance. However, it may be possible to avoid specific risks: like wearing proper personal protective equipment can reduce risks in most job areas.

Risk can be **reduced**. The overall goal of risk management is to plan missions or design systems that do not contain uncontrolled hazards. A proven order of precedence for dealing with hazards and reducing the resulting risks is:

- **Plan or Design for Minimum Risk.** From the first, plan the mission or design the system to eliminate hazards. Without a hazard there is no probability, severity or exposure. If an identified hazard cannot be eliminated, reduce the associated risk to an acceptable level.

- **Incorporate Safety Devices.** If identified hazards cannot be eliminated or their associated risk adequately reduced by modifying the mission or system elements or their inputs, that risk should be reduced to an acceptable level through the use of safety design features or devices. Safety devices usually do not effect probability but reduce severity: an automobile seat belt doesn't prevent a collision but reduces the severity of injuries. Nomex gloves and steel toed boots won't prevent the hazardous event, or even change the probability of one occurring, but they prevent, or decrease the severity of, injury. Physical barriers fall into this category.

- **Provide Warning Devices.** When mission planning, system design, and safety devices cannot effectively eliminate identified hazards or adequately reduce associated risk, devices should be used to detect the condition and warn personnel of the hazard. Warning signals and their application should be designed to minimize the probability of the incorrect personnel reaction to the signals and should be standardized. Flashing red lights or sirens are a common warning device that most people understand.

ACTIONS FOR STEP 4: IMPLEMENT CONTROLS

| Action 1
Identify Control Options | → | Action 2
Develop Control Options |

FIGURE 9
STEP 4. CONTROL ACTION

- **Develop Procedures and Training.** Where it is impractical to eliminate hazards through design selection or adequately reduce the associated risk with safety and warning devices, procedures and training should be used. If the system is well designed and the mission well planned, the only remaining risk reduction strategies may be procedures and training. *Emergency procedure training and disaster preparedness exercises improve human response to hazardous situations.*

Risk is commonly **spread** out by either increasing the exposure distance or by lengthening the time between exposure events. Administratively controlling exposure events, substitution of less hazardous chemicals or re-engineering an operation to reduce exposures to chemicals or toxic agents are examples.

Risk **transference** does not change probability or severity, however, possible losses or costs are shifted to another entity. An example is locating a remote sensing device in a high risk environment instead of risking personnel.

COMMON WAYS TO CONTROL RISK

- Protective equipment, clothing, or safety devices (PPE)
- Highlight hazards for extra care and handling
- Warnings (signs, color coding, audio/visual alarms)
- Repair hazards or build new facilities
- Limit exposure consistent with mission needs
- Train and educate
- Incorporate firm, fail-safe go/no-go criteria
- Select experienced or specialized personnel
- Increase and/or select more highly qualified and experienced supervision

- New policy—formal/informal, written/unwritten
- Develop new procedures

Develop Control Options: Determine the controls for the risk associated with the hazard. A computer spread sheet or data form (Job Hazard Analysis) may be used to list control ideas and indicate control effects. The estimated value(s) for severity and/or probability after implementation of control measures and the change in overall risk assessed from the Risk Assessment Index should be recorded. Scenario building and next accident assessment provide the greatest ability to determine control effects.

Select Controls: For each hazard, select those risk controls that will reduce the risk to an acceptable level.. The decision maker selects the control options after being briefed on all the possible controls. The best controls will be consistent with mission objectives and optimum use of available resources (manpower, material, equipment, money, time. It is not an ad hoc decision, but rather a logical, sequenced part of the risk management process. Decisions are made with awareness of hazards and how important hazard control is to success or failure of the mission (cost versus benefit).

Step 4. IMPLEMENT CONTROLS.

The decision maker must allocate resources to control risk. Control decisions must be made at the appropriate level. The standard for risk management is leadership at the appropriate level of authority making informed decisions control hazards or accept risks.

Safety advisors and consultants do not control the necessary resources to implement the

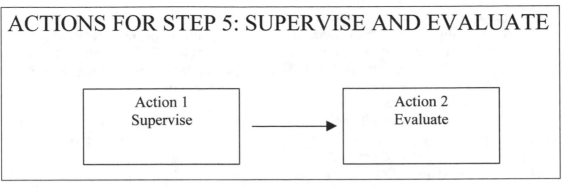

ACTIONS FOR STEP 5: SUPERVISE AND EVALUATE

Action 1 Supervise	→	Action 2 Evaluate

FIGURE 10
STEP 5 ACTIONS

control decisions. Appropriate levels of decisions making reflect the ability of the decision maker to resource the controls.

Resource Controls: For each identified hazard, resource controls that will reduce the risk to an acceptable level. The best controls will be consistent with mission objectives and optimum use of available resources (manpower, material, equipment, money, and time). Record implementation decisions for future reference. Should management determine that the controls require resources beyond their authority, they should elevate the risk decision to higher authority.

Order Controls: To be successful, command must support the control measures put in place. Then, explore appropriate ways to demonstrate command commitment. Provide the personnel and resources necessary to implement the control measures. Design in sustainability from the beginning. Deploy the control measure with a feedback mechanism that provides information on whether the control measure is achieving the intended purpose.

Step 5. SUPERVISE AND EVALUATE.

Supervise: Monitor the operation to ensure:
- The controls are effective and remain in place.
- Changes which require further risk management are identified.
- Action is taken when necessary to correct ineffective risk controls and reinitiate the risk management steps in response to new hazards.

Any time personnel, equipment or operations change or new operations are anticipated in an environment not covered in the initial risk management analysis, the risks and control measures should be reevaluated. The goal of measurement is to answer the question of whether the control measure in fact controlled the associated hazard. The best tool for accomplishing this action of supervision is Change Analysis.

Evaluation: The process review must be systematic. After assets are expended to control risks, then a cost benefit analysis must be accomplished to see if risk and cost are in balance. Any changes in the system (the flow charts from the earlier steps provide convenient benchmarks to compare the present system to the original) are recognized and appropriate risk management controls are applied

To accomplish an effective review:
- Identify whether the actual cost is in line with expectations.
- What effect the control measure has had on mission performance.

Provide operation feedback to ensure that the corrective or preventive action taken was effective and that any new hazards identified during the mission are analyzed and corrective action taken.

Audits: Measurements are necessary to ensure accurate evaluations of how effectively controls eliminated hazards or reduced risks. After action reports, surveys, and in progress reviews provide great starting places for measurements. To be meaningful, measurements must quantitatively or qualitatively identify reductions of risk, improvements in operation success, or enhancement of capabilities. The Risk Management Evaluation Profile (OSHA's PEP) in appendix B, provides an audit process of a programs overall effectiveness.

Benefits of conducting an audit includes:

- Formally going through the internal audit process with managers and employees,
- Formally reviewing the elements of a safety and health program,
- Getting managers involved in the audit process,
- Making managers, supervisors and employees aware of the scope and complexity of a formal safety and health program, and of their roles and responsibilities in the programs success.

After finishing your audit share the results with managers and legal personnel. However the process of doing an audit creates a paper trail of the programs weaknesses. The audit is a formal tool to uncover weak points in the management system that create unsafe work practices and unsafe conditions that can injure workers, diminish their health, interrupt production, or damage products and property.

Conclusion. Risk management provides a logical and systematic means of organizing information for rational decision-making, to identify and control risk. Risk management is a process that requires individuals, supervisors and leaders to support and implement the basic principles, along with the discipline to apply them on a continuing basis. Risk management offers individuals and organizations a powerful tool for eliminating accidents and increasing effectiveness. This process has the unique advantage of being accessible to and usable by everyone in every conceivable setting or scenario.

Appendix B: The Risk Management Evaluation Profile (RMEP)

Subject: The Risk Management Evaluation Profile (RMEP)

A. **Purpose.** To establish policies and procedures for the Risk Management Evaluation Profile (RMEP), the RMEP form, which can be used in assessing safety and health programs in general workplaces.

B. **Scope.** The RMEP is applicable to all company workplaces.

C. **References.**
1. AR 385-10, Army Safety Program.
2. OSHA Instruction CPL 2.103, September 26, 1994, Field Inspection Reference Manual (FIRM).

D. **Action.** CEOs, directors and managers should ensure that the guidelines and procedures set forth here are followed in using the RMEP.

E. **Background.** Assessment of safety and health conditions in the workplace depends on a clear understanding of the programs and management systems that an employer is using for safety and health compliance. The organization places a high priority on safety and health programs and mandates their implementation.

F. **Application.**
1. The RMEP should be completed for a general evaluation of workplace safety and health programs.
   a. The RMEP is an educational document for workers and employers, as well as a source of information for use in the inspection process.
   b. In multi-employer workplaces, a RMEP shall be completed for the safety and health program of the host organization. This RMEP will normally apply to all subordinate organizations, and individual RMEPs need not be completed for them.
   c. The RMEP shall be used in experimental programs that require evaluation of an organizations safety and health program, except where other program evaluation methods/tools are specifically approved.
2. The evaluation of the safety and health program contained in the RMEP shall be shared with the employer and with employee representatives.

G. **Using the RMEP.** The RMEP will be used as a source of safety and health program evaluation for the employer, employees.
1. **Gathering Information for the RMEP** begins during the opening conference

and continues through the inspection process.

a. The evaluator shall explain the purpose of the RMEP and obtain information about the employer's safety and health program in order to make an initial assessment about the program.

b. This initial assessment shall be verified—or modified—based on information obtained in interviews of an appropriately representative number of employees and by observation of actual safety and health conditions during the inspection process.

2. **Recording the Score.** The program elements in the RMEP correspond generally to the major elements of the Guidelines.

a. **Elements.** The **six** elements to be scored in the RMEP are:

  (1) Management.
  (2) Leadership.
  (3) Employee Participation.
  (4) Hazard Identification.
  (5) Hazard Control.
  (6) Training.

b. **Factors.** These elements will also be scored. The score for an element will be determined by the factor scores. The factors are:

  ■ Management
  ■ Leadership.
    − Employee participation.
    − Contractor safety.
    − Survey and hazard identification.
    − Reporting.
    − Investigation of accidents and near-miss incidents
    − Data analysis.
    − Hazard control.
    − Maintenance.
  ■ Medical program.
  ■ Training (as a whole).

c. **Scoring.** The evaluator shall objectively score the organization on each of the individual factors and elements after obtaining the necessary information to do so. These shall be given a score of 1, 2, 3, 4, or 5. If the element or factor does not apply to the worksite being inspected, a notation of **"Not Applicable"** shall be made in the space provided. This shall not affect the score.

(1) The attachment contains the **RMEP Tables**, which provide verbal descriptors of workplace characteristics for each factor for each of the five levels. Evaluators shall refer to these tables as appropriate to ensure that the score they assign to a factor corresponds to the descriptor that best fits the worksite.

(2) Determine scores for each of the six elements as follows:

NOTE: The factors of "Management", "Leadership" and "Employee Participation" are given greater weight because they are considered the foundation of a safety and health program.

  (a) For each of the other elements, **average** the scores for the factors.

  (b) In **averaging** factor scores, round to the nearest whole number (1, 2, 3, 4, or 5). Round up from one-half (.5) or greater; round down from less than one-half (.5).

3. **Program Levels.** The Overall Score on the RMEP constitutes the "level" at which the establishment's safety and health program is scored. **Remember: This level is a relatively informal assessment.** The following chart summarizes the levels:

Score	Level of Safety and Health Program
5	Outstanding program
4	Superior program
3	Basic program
2	Developmental program
1	No program or ineffective program

4. **Specific Scoring Guidance.** The following shall be taken into account in assessing specific factors:

a. **Written Programs.** Employer safety and health programs should be in writing in order to be effectively implemented and communicated.

   (1) Nevertheless, a program's **effectiveness** is more important than whether it is in writing.

      (a) An employer's failure to comply with a paperwork requirement is normally penalized only when there is a serious hazard related to this requirement.

      (b) An employer's failure to comply with a written program requirement is normally not penalized if the employer is actually taking the actions that are the subject of the requirement.

   (2) Thus, evaluators should follow the general principle that "performance counts more than paperwork." In using the RMEP, the evaluator is responsible for evaluating the organizations actual management of safety and health in the workplace, not just the organizations documentation of a safety and health program.

b. **Employee Participation.**

   (1) Employee involvement in an establishment's safety and health program is essential to its effectiveness. Thus, evaluation of safety and health programs must include objective assessment of the ways in which workers' rights and responsibilities are addressed in form and practice.

   (2) Employee involvement should also include participation walk-around inspections, interviews, informal conferences, and formal settlement discussions, as may be appropriate. Many methods of employee involvement may be encountered in individual workplaces.

c. **Comprehensiveness.** The importance of a safety and health program's comprehensiveness is implicitly addressed in Hazard Identification under both hazard identification and Data analysis. An effective safety and health program shall address all known and potential sources of workplace injuries and illnesses, whether or not they are covered by a specific OSHA standard.

d. **Consistency with Violations/Hazards Found.** The RMEP evaluation and the scores assigned to the individual elements and factors should be consistent with the types and numbers of violations or hazards found during the inspection.

5. **Scope of the RMEP Review.** The duration of the RMEP review will vary depending on the circumstances of the workplace and the inspection. In all cases, however, this review shall include:

a. A review of any appropriate employer documentation relating to the safety and health program.

b. A walk-around inspection of pertinent areas of the workplace.

c. Interviews with an appropriate number of employer and employee representatives.

The RMEP Tables

- The text in each block provides a description of the program element or factor that corresponds to the level of program that the employer has implemented in the workplace.
- To avoid duplicative language, each level should be understood as containing all positive factors included in the level below it.

MANAGEMENT, LEADERSHIP and EMPLOYEE PARTICIPATION	
Management	
Visible management provides the motivating force for an effective safety and health program.	
1	Management demonstrates no policy, goals, objectives, or interest in safety and health issues at this worksite.
2	Management sets and communicates safety and health policy and goals, but remains detached from all other safety and health efforts.
3	Management follows all safety and health rules, and gives | visible support to the safety and health efforts of others.
4	Management participates in significant aspects of the site's safety and health program, such as site inspections, incident reviews, and program reviews. Incentive programs that discourage reporting of accidents, symptoms, injuries, or hazards are absent. Other incentive programs may be present.
5	Site safety and health issues are regularly included on agendas of management operations meetings. Management clearly demonstrates—by involvement, support, and example—the primary importance of safety and health for everyone on the worksite. Performance is consistent and sustained or has improved over time.
Notes:	

Employee Participation
Employee participation provides the means through which workers identify hazards, recommend and monitor abatement, and otherwise participate in their own protection.

1	Worker participation in workplace safety and health concerns is not encouraged. Incentive programs are present which have the effect of discouraging reporting of incidents, injuries, potential hazards or symptoms. Employees/employee representatives are not involved in the safety and health program.
2	Workers and their representatives can participate freely in safety and health activities at the worksite without fear of reprisal. Procedures are in place for communication between employer and workers on safety and health matters. Worker rights under the Occupational Safety and Health Act to refuse or stop work that they reasonably believe involves imminent danger are understood by workers and honored by management. Workers are paid while performing safety activities.
3	Workers and their representatives are involved in the safety and health program, involved in inspection of work area, and are permitted to observe monitoring and receive results. Workers' and representatives' right of access to information is understood by workers and recognized by management. A documented procedure is in place for raising complaints of hazards or discrimination and receiving timely employer responses.
4	Workers and their representatives participate in hazard identification analysis, inspections and investigations, and development of control strategies throughout facility, and have necessary training and education to participate in such activities. Workers and their representatives have access to all pertinent health and safety information, including safety reports and audits. Workers are informed of their right to refuse job assignments that pose serious hazards to themselves pending management response.
5	Workers and their representatives participate fully in development of the safety and health program and conduct of training and education. Workers participate in audits, program reviews conducted by management or third parties, and collection of samples for monitoring purposes, and have necessary training and education to participate in such activities. Employer encourages and authorizes employees to stop activities that present potentially serious safety and health hazards.
Notes:

	LEADERSHIP
	Implementation
	Implementation means tools, provided by management, that include: — budget — information — personnel — assigned responsibility — adequate expertise and authority — means to hold responsible persons accountable (line accountability) — program review procedures.
1	Tools to implement a safety and health program are inadequate or missing.
2	Some tools to implement a safety and health program are adequate and effectively used; others are ineffective or inadequate. Management assigns responsibility for implementing a safety and health program to identified person(s). Management's designated representative has authority to direct abatement of hazards that can be corrected without major capital expenditure.
3	Tools to implement a safety and health program are adequate, but are not all effectively used. Safety representative is knowledgeable in hazard recognition and applicable OSHA requirements. Management keeps or has access to applicable OSHA standards at the facility, and seeks appropriate guidance information for interpretation of OSHA standards. Management representative has authority to order/purchase safety and health equipment.
4	All tools to implement a safety and health program are more than adequate and effectively used. Written safety procedures, policies, and interpretations are updated based on reviews of the safety and health program. Safety and health expenditures, including training costs and personnel, are identified in the facility budget. Hazard abatement is an element in management performance evaluation.
5	All tools necessary to implement a good safety and health program are more than adequate and effectively used. Management safety and health representative has expertise appropriate to facility size and process, and has access to professional advice when needed. Safety and health budgets and funding procedures are reviewed periodically for adequacy.
	Notes:

Hazard Identification

Hazard Recognition and Evaluation

Survey and hazard analysis: An effective, proactive safety and health program will seek to identify and evaluate all hazards. In large or complex workplaces, components of such analysis are the **comprehensive survey** and **evaluations of job hazards and changes in conditions**.

1	No system or requirement exists for hazard review of planned/changed/new operations. There is no evidence of a comprehensive survey for safety or health hazards or for routine job hazard analysis.
2	Surveys for violations of standards are conducted by knowledgeable person(s), but only in response to accidents or complaints. The employer has identified principal OSHA standards which apply to the worksite.
3	Process, task, and environmental surveys are conducted by knowledgeable person(s) and updated as needed and as required by applicable standards. Current hazard analyses are written (where appropriate) for all high-hazard jobs and processes; analyses are communicated to and understood by affected employees. Hazard analyses are conducted for jobs/tasks/workstations where injury or illnesses have been recorded.
4	Methodical surveys are conducted periodically and drive appropriate corrective action. Initial surveys are conducted by a qualified professional. Current hazard analyses are documented for all work areas and are communicated and available to all the workforce; knowledgeable persons review all planned/changed/new facilities, processes, materials, or equipment.
5	Regular surveys including documented comprehensive workplace hazard evaluations are conducted by certified safety and health professional or professional engineer, etc. Corrective action is documented and hazard inventories are updated. Hazard analysis is integrated into the design, development, implementation, and changing of all processes and work practices.
Notes:	

WORKPLACE ANALYSIS	
Hazard Assessment	
Inspection: To identify new or previously missed hazards and failures in hazard controls, an effective safety and health program will include regular **site inspections.**	
1	No routine physical inspection of the workplace and equipment is conducted.
2	Supervisors dedicate time to observing work practices and other safety and health conditions in work areas where they have responsibility.
3	Competent personnel conduct inspections with appropriate involvement of employees. Items in need of correction are documented. Inspections include compliance with relevant OSHA standards. Time periods for correction are set.
4	Inspections are conducted by specifically trained employees, and all items are corrected promptly and appropriately. Workplace inspections are planned, with key observations or check points defined and results documented. Persons conducting inspections have specific training in hazard identification applicable to the facility. Corrections are documented through follow-up inspections. Results are available to workers.
5	Inspections are planned and overseen by certified safety or health professionals. Statistically valid random audits of compliance with all elements of the safety and health program are conducted. Observations are analyzed to evaluate progress.
Notes:	

	WORKPLACE ANALYSIS
	Hazard Reporting

A reliable **hazard reporting system** enables employees, without fear of reprisal, to notify management of conditions that appear hazardous and to receive timely and appropriate responses. [Guidelines, (c)(2)(iii)]

1	No formal hazard reporting system exists, or employees are reluctant to report hazards.
2	Employees are instructed to report hazards to management. Supervisors are instructed and are aware of a procedure for evaluating and responding to such reports. Employees use the system with no risk of reprisals.
3	A formal system for hazard reporting exists. Employee reports of hazards are documented, corrective action is scheduled, and records maintained.
4	Employees are periodically instructed in hazard identification and reporting procedures. Management conducts surveys of employee observations of hazards to ensure that the system is working. Results are documented.
5	Management responds to reports of hazards in writing within specified time frames. The workforce readily identifies and self-corrects hazards; they are supported by management when they do so.

Notes:

WORKPLACE ANALYSIS
Accident Investigation

Accident investigation: An effective program will provide for **investigation of accidents and "near miss" incidents**, so that their causes, and the means for their prevention, are identified. [Guidelines, (c)(2)(iv)]

1	No investigation of accidents, injuries, near misses, or other incidents is conducted.
2	Some investigation of incidents takes place, but root cause may not be identified, and correction may be inconsistent. Supervisors prepare injury reports for lost time cases.
3	OSHA-101 is completed for all recordable incidents. Reports are generally prepared with cause identification and corrective measures prescribed.
4	OSHA-recordable incidents are always investigated, and effective prevention is implemented. Reports and recommendations are available to employees. Quality and completeness of investigations are systematically reviewed by trained safety personnel.
5	All loss-producing accidents and "near-misses" are investigated for root causes by teams or individuals that include trained safety personnel and employees.

Notes:

WORKPLACE ANALYSIS	
Data Analysis	
Data analysis: An effective program will **analyze injury and illness records** for indications of sources and locations of hazards, and jobs that experience higher numbers of injuries. By analyzing injury and illness trends over time, patterns with common causes can be identified and prevented.	
1	Little or no analysis of injury/illness records; exposure monitoring) are kept or conducted.
2	Data is collected and analyzed, but not widely used for prevention. Reports are completed for all recordable cases. Exposure records and analyses are organized and are available to safety personnel.
3	Injury/illness logs and exposure records are kept correctly, are audited by facility personnel, and are essentially accurate and complete. Rates are calculated so as to identify high risk areas and jobs. Workers compensation claim records are analyzed and the results used in the program. Significant analytical findings are used for prevention.
4	Employer can identify the frequent and most severe problem areas, the high risk areas and job classifications, and any exposures responsible for OSHA recordable cases. Data are fully analyzed and effectively communicated to employees. Illness/injury data are audited and certified by a responsible person.
5	All levels of management and the workforce are aware of results of data analyses and resulting preventive activity. External audits of accuracy of injury and illness data, including review of all available data sources are conducted. Scientific analysis of health information, including non-occupational data bases is included where appropriate in the program.
Notes:	

	HAZARD CONTROL
	Hazard Control

Hazard Control: Workforce exposure to all current and potential hazards should be prevented or controlled by using **engineering controls** wherever feasible and appropriate, **work practices** and **administrative controls**, and **personal protective equipment** (PPE).

1	Hazard controls are seriously lacking or absent from the facility.
2	Hazard controls are generally in place, but effectiveness and completeness vary. Serious hazards may still exist. Employer has achieved general compliance with applicable OSHA standards regarding hazards with a significant probability of causing serious physical harm. Hazards that have caused past injuries in the facility have been corrected.
3	Appropriate controls (engineering, work practice, and administrative controls, and PPE) are in place for significant hazards. Some serious hazards may exist. Employer is generally in compliance with voluntary standards, industry practices, and manufacturers, and suppliers' safety recommendations. Documented reviews of needs for machine guarding, energy lockout, ergonomics, materials handling, bloodborne pathogens, confined space, hazard communication, and other generally applicable standards have been conducted. The overall program tolerates occasional deviations.
4	Hazard controls are fully in place, and are known and supported by the workforce. Few serious hazards exist. The employer requires strict and complete compliance with all OSHA, consensus, and industry standards and recommendations. All deviations are identified and causes determined.
5	Hazard controls are fully in place and continually improved upon based on workplace experience and general knowledge. Documented reviews of needs are conducted by certified health and safety professionals or professional engineers, etc.

Notes:

HAZARD CONTROL
Maintenance
Maintenance: An effective safety and health program will provide for **facility and equipment maintenanc**e, so that hazardous breakdowns are prevented.

1	No preventive maintenance program is in place; break-down maintenance is the rule.
2	There is a preventive maintenance schedule, but it does not cover everything and may be allowed to slide or performance is not documented. Safety devices on machinery and equipment are generally checked before each production shift.
3	A preventive maintenance schedule is implemented for areas where it is most needed; it is followed under normal circumstances. Manufacturers' and industry recommendations and consensus standards for maintenance frequency are complied with. Breakdown repairs for safety related items are expedited. Safety device checks are documented. Ventilation system function is observed periodically.
4	The employer has effectively implemented a preventive maintenance schedule that applies to all equipment. Facility experience is used to improve safety-related preventative maintenance scheduling.
5	There is a comprehensive safety and preventive maintenance program that maximizes equipment reliability.
Notes:	

HAZARD CONTROL

Medical Program

An effective safety and health program will include a suitable **medical program** where it is appropriate for the size and nature of the workplace and its hazards.

1	Employer is unaware of, or unresponsive to medical needs. Required medical surveillance, monitoring, and reporting are absent or inadequate.
2	Required medical surveillance, monitoring, removal, and reporting responsibilities for applicable standards are assigned and carried out, but results may be incomplete or inadequate.
3	Medical surveillance, removal, monitoring, and reporting comply with applicable standards. Employees report early signs/symptoms of job-related injury or illness and receive appropriate treatment.
4	Health care providers provide follow-up on employee treatment protocols and are involved in hazard identification and control in the workplace. Medical surveillance addresses conditions not covered by specific standards. Employee concerns about medical treatment are documented and responded to.
5	Health care providers are on-site for all production shifts and are involved in hazard identification and training. Health care providers periodically observe the work areas and activities and are fully involved in hazard identification and training.

Notes:

TRAINING

Safety and health training should cover the safety and health responsibilities of all personnel who work at the site or affect its operations. It is most effective when incorporated into other training about performance requirements and job practices. It should include all subjects and areas necessary to address the hazards at the site.

1	Facility depends on experience and peer training to meet needs. Managers/supervisors demonstrate little or no involvement in safety and health training responsibilities.
2	Some orientation training is given to new hires. Some safety training materials (e.g., pamphlets, posters, videotapes) are available or are used periodically at safety meetings, but there is little or no documentation of training or assessment of worker knowledge in this area. Managers generally demonstrate awareness of safety and health responsibilities, but have limited training themselves or involvement in the site's training program.
3	Training includes OSHA rights and access to information. Training required by applicable standards is provided to all site employees. Supervisors and managers attend training in all subjects provided to employees under their direction. Employees can generally demonstrate the skills/knowledge necessary to perform their jobs safely. Records of training are kept and training is evaluated to ensure that it is effective.
4	Knowledgeable persons conduct safety and health training that is scheduled, assessed, and documented, and addresses all necessary technical topics. Employees are trained to recognize hazards, violations of OSHA standards, and facility practices. Employees are trained to report violations to management. All site employees—including supervisors and managers—can generally demonstrate preparedness for participation in the overall safety and health program. There are easily retrievable scheduling and record keeping systems.
5	Knowledgeable persons conduct safety and health training that is scheduled, assessed, and documented. Training covers all necessary topics and situations, and includes all persons working at the site (hourly employees, supervisors, managers, contractors, part-time and temporary employees). Employees participate in creating site-specific training methods and materials. Employees are trained to recognize inadequate responses to reported program violations. Retrievable record keeping system provides for appropriate retraining, makeup training, and modifications to training as the result of evaluations.

Notes:

OSHA Outreach Program

The OSHA Outreach Training Program is a voluntary train-the-trainer program and OSHA's primary way to train workers in the basics of occupational safety and health. Through the program, individuals who complete a one-week OSHA trainer course are authorized to teach 10-hour or 30-hour courses in construction or general industry safety and health standards. Authorized trainers can receive OSHA course completion cards for their students.

The outreach program has grown rapidly in the past 10 years. In 1990 only 12,000 student cards were issued. In 2000, more than 200,000 student cards were distributed and more than 12,600 classes were held—an average of more than 240 classes per week. On any given day, there are approximately 1,500 workers attending OSHA outreach training.

To become an authorized trainer, instructors must complete a required OSHA trainer course. These courses provide an overview of the most hazardous and referenced standards. The courses are one week long and are conducted by the OSHA Training Institute and the OSHA Training Institute Education Centers that are located around the country.

Outreach trainers are authorized to conduct 10- and 30-hour outreach courses and receive OSHA course completion cards to issue to the students.

Becoming an Authorized Trainer

To become an authorized trainer, you must complete a 500-level course and pass a test at the end of the course.

For the construction industry, prospective trainers must take and pass Course 500, Trainer Course in Occupational Safety and Health Standards for the Construction Industry. Prerequisites include five years of construction safety experience and completion of Course 510, Occupational Safety and Health Standards for the Construction Industry, or equivalent construction training.

To train for general industry, prospective trainers must take and pass Course 501, Trainer Course in Occupational Safety and Health Standards for General Industry. When the course has been completed, the trainer will be authorized to train for four years. Before the end of four years, the trainer must take an update course to renew authorization for another four years. There are two update courses available:

Course 502: Update for Construction Industry Outreach Trainers

Course 503: Update for General Industry Outreach Trainers.

Trainers also may retake Course 500 to maintain their trainer status. If the trainer authorization status has expired, taking a 500 course available through the OSHA Training Institute Education Centers for course scheduling information can reinstate it.

Outreach Training Program Guidelines

Designated Training Topics

The 10-hour program is intended to provide a variety of instruction on construction industry safety and health standards to entry-level workers. Of the topics listed below, three hours are mandatory and three hours must be chosen from the options provided. For the remainder of the class, the instructor may teach any other construction standards and policies and/or expand on the required topics.

The required course topics are:

Introduction to OSHA, OSH Act/General Duty Clause 5(a)(1), General Safety and Health Provision, Competent Person, Recordkeeping (29 CFR 1904);

Electrical, Subpart K; and

Fall Protection, Subpart M.

Instructors may choose three topics from the following list:

- Personal Protective and Lifesaving Equipment, Subpart E;
- Materials Handling, Storage, Use, and Disposal, Subpart H;
- Tools, Hand and Power, Subpart I;
- Scaffolds, Subpart L;
- Cranes, Derricks, Hoists, Elevators, and Conveyors, Subpart N;
- Excavations, Subpart P; or
- Stairways and Ladders, Subpart X.

Instructors may then select four more construction-related topics to complete a 10-hour training program.

Topic Length

Training sessions for each course topic should last for at least one hour. In most cases, one hour is the least amount of time necessary to cover a topic adequately. The minimum amount of time spent on any topic is 30 minutes.

Trainers must spend at least 10 or 30 class hours covering course topics. Breaks and lunch periods are not counted as class time.

Conducting a Class over a Period of Time

Trainers may teach classes in segments. Each segment must be at least one hour and the course must be completed within six months.

10 + 20 Hours = 30 Hours

If a student that was trained in the 10-hour training course is interested in taking the 30-hour course, trainers may supplement the training with 20 additional hours and receive a 30-hour card for the trainee. The limitations are that the same trainer must do the training and all the training must take place within six months. Trainees who do this should only receive the 30-hour card.

Guest Trainers

Trainers may have other trainers help conduct classes. An authorized outreach trainer must design and coordinate the course, teach more of the class than anyone else, and attend all sessions to answer questions and ensure the topics are adequately covered and all students are in attendance.

In-Person Training

Outreach training must be delivered in-person, unless the trainer has received an individual exception. Trainers considering using other training methods, such as online, CDROM, and video conferencing, must contact the OSHA Outreach Coordinator. The basic guidelines for video conferencing are that the trainer be able to ensure the full attendance of all trainees, that off-site locations have a training monitor, and that there is a setup to answer trainee questions quickly and effectively.

Class Size

If class size will exceed 50 students, the instructor should contact the OSHA Outreach Coordinator before the class begins to get permission for the class to be considered an outreach training class. Trainers must have a way for students to ask questions apart from the classroom. E-mail is the usual method. It is a good idea to have more than one trainer in large classes and to break the class into work groups whenever possible. Small classes encourage trainee involvement through discussion and group participation and through sharing of knowledge and experiences.

Combined 10-Hour Construction and General Industry Class

A person who is authorized as a trainer in Construction and General Industry may *not* receive 10-hour student cards for both Construction and General Industry when holding a class for less than 20 full hours.

Outreach Training Tips

Worker Emphasis

The outreach classes are designed to be presented to workers; therefore, they must emphasize hazard identification, avoidance, control, and prevention—not OSHA standards. Trainers must tailor their presentations to the needs and understanding of their audience.

Site-Specific Training

The most rewarding classes for students are the ones they can relate to because the trainer uses examples, pictures, and scenarios that come from the students' workplaces.

Homogeneous Class

The ideal class to teach is one in which students have similar needs because they hold comparable positions. Therefore, it is best to conduct separate training for supervisors, managers, and workers. Also, separate workers into like groups (e.g., office personnel, machine operators, and maintenance staff).

Use Objectives

Inform students what is expected of them after receiving training on each topic. Describe the skills and abilities the students should have or exhibit, be specific, and relate the objectives to the students' work if possible.

Presentation Assortment

Students learn in different manners and get tired of one style of training over a lengthy period. Use different trainers, computer presentations, videos, case studies, exercises, and graphics to make the course interesting and enjoyable. By doing this you will be employing the three levels of training techniques:

- Presentation (presenting the material in a variety of ways);
- Discussion (getting the students involved in the learning); and
- Performance (students practice the material they have learned).

Testing

Use quizzes and tests to ensure the students understand key objectives of the training. Students should receive feedback on incorrect answers.

Student Evaluations

Have students evaluate the class. This feedback will help the trainer determine whether the course is accomplishing its goals and provide input that can be used to improve the training.

Monitoring

Staff from the OSHA Office of Training and Education periodically attend outreach training classes to observe training, obtain feedback from the trainer and the students on the training, and to ensure awareness of the outreach guidelines and the materials and assistance that are available to help trainers conduct classes. Through these visits, OSHA aims to help trainers, improve the outreach-training program, ensure consistent program implementation, and assist the trainer in designing the class to meet the needs of the audience.

Advertising

When advertising outreach-training courses, trainers must take the proper care to correctly describe their outreach trainer designation and outreach courses. Trainer authorization is limited to conducting the 10- and 30-hour Construction and/or General Industry outreach training courses.

Outreach advertising restrictions include the following:
- **Certified.** Neither the trainer, the students, nor the curriculum is certified or accredited. The trainer is authorized, the students receive course completion cards, and the OSHA-produced curriculum is approved.
- **OSHA.** Do not make it appear that you are an OSHA employee or that the course is an OSHA course.

- **Course 500.** Do not refer to your outreach course as a 500 course. The 500 course is the train-the-trainer course that is conducted by the OSHA Training Institute or its OSHA Training Institute Education Centers.
- **Department of Labor Logo.** Do not use the logo that you see on outreach cards in your advertising.
- **Train-the-Trainer Course.** Students who complete the 10- or 30-hour training are not entitled to receive cards for students they may train.

If OSHA notifies a trainer that their advertising appears false or misleading and the advertising is not corrected, that trainer will be removed from the program.

Program Administration

Obtaining Student Course Completion Cards

After the class has been conducted, trainers must submit documentation about the course to the OSHA Training Institute to receive OSHA student course completion cards. Prepare a separate packet for each class taught that contains the Outreach Training Program Report, a list of the topics that were taught, and the student roster.

- Submit course documentation within six months of course completion.
- Send one list of legible student names; do not send multiple sign-in sheets.
- You may send more than one class submission in one envelope.
- Do not staple the documentation.

For each outreach class completed, send the following, in this order, to OSHA (**Note:** OSHA may return submittals that are not complete):

- The **OSHA Outreach Training Program Report**, which includes information on the course and the trainer. Make sure to include the most recent trainer date and the address to send the cards. (An excerpt of the format is shown on the following pages.)
- **Instructor's course certificate.** A copy of the instructor's course certificate/trainer card (note the place where the training was taken) if:
  - This is a first outreach training class; or

- The instructor is a trainer with an ID number, who has taken a more recent trainer course than the one shown on the preprinted Outreach Training Program Report.
- **Student names.** The names of students who completed the course. Keep a copy of the students' names and addresses before sending them to OSHA. The trainer will need them to complete and distribute the cards
- **Topic outline.** A topic outline that lists the topics taught and the amount of time spent on each. For 10-hour classes, the trainer may complete the topic outline on the bottom of the OSHA Outreach Training Program Report or send a separate outline. For 30-hour classes, the trainer must send a separate outline.

Mail course documentation to the Education Center that issued the instructor a trainer card. The OSHA Training Institute oversees the program and can be reached at:

Construction (or General Industry)
Outreach Program Coordinator
OSHA Training Institute
2020 S. Arlington Heights Road
Arlington Heights, IL 60005

Student course completion cards are sent to the trainer for completion and distribution.

The trainer completes the card by listing the student's name, the end date of the course, and signing it. If the trainer is unavailable, the trainer's name may be typed in (See Exhibit 25-1.).

Exhibit 25-1. Sample completed student card.

Cards may be laminated. Trainers may use the back of the cards for other identification or training information purposes, but no other alterations are permitted.

The student course completion cards do not expire.

Trainers may provide students with a certificate of training. This may help students have proof they took the training before they receive their pocket student cards. The advertising restrictions also apply to a certificate.

The OSHA Training Institute will send a few extra cards to trainers for each class completed in case of card errors or to enable trainers to replace lost student cards for students trained.

OSHA recommends Outreach Training Program courses as an orientation to occupational safety and health for workers. Participation is voluntary. Workers must receive additional training on specific hazards of their job.

Replacing Lost or Damaged Trainer or Student Cards

Trainer Cards

Contact the organization that issued the card. Inform them what course was taken and when it was taken. After they validate the class was taken and the test was passed, they will issue a replacement card.

Student Cards

Trainers receive a few extra cards when OSHA sends them student cards. Trainers can use these cards to replace student cards, after the proper verification is made. If the trainer does not have an extra card, the trainer or the student may contact OSHA for the replacement, with the following information:

- Student name;
- Trainer name;
- Training date; and
- Type of class (10- or 30-hour, construction or general industry).

OSHA training records are only kept for five years plus the present year. If the training took place prior to this, OSHA will not be able to issue a new card.

OSHA OUTREACH TRAINING PROGRAM REPORT

Construction (or General Industry) Outreach Program Coordinator

Course Conducted (Document each class with a separate Report):

        10-Hour Construction   10-Hour General Industry

        30-Hour Construction   30-Hour General Industry

End Date of Course: _____

Number of Students: _____
(List students' names on back, or on a separate sheet)

Primary Trainer Course Information

ID Number* (see note below):_____

Name:_____

Course (500/501/502/503) Expiration Date:_____
*ID *number* – new trainers do not have one – this only applies to trainers who have received student cards)

Address – cards will be sent here:
(*If you have an ID number and your address is the same, you do not need to complete this*)
❏ **Check if this is a new address**
Name: _____
Company / Dept: _____
Address: _____
City /State /Zip: _____

Phone No: _____   extension:_____   Best time(s) to call:_____

Your documentation must include these items:
- OSHA Outreach Training Program Report
- Student names
- List of course topics and the time spent on each

Do not include these items with your documentation: Student evaluation forms, Student sign-in sheets, Long topic outline, stapled pages

OSHA OUTREACH TRAINING PROGRAM REPORT (continued)
10 Hour Topics (for a 30-hour class, send in a separate topic list)

Construction   General Industry

HOURS*   HOURS*
_____ Required Introduction to OSHA   _____ Required Introduction to OSHA
_____ Required Electrical (K)   _____ Required Walking and Working Surfaces (D)
_____ Required Fall Protection (M)   _____ Required Egress and Fire Prot. (E & L)
_____ Required Electrical (S)

Required - Choose three or more:

_____ Personal Protective and Lifesaving Equipment (E)
_____ Required - Choose three or more
_____ Materials Handling, Storage, Use and Disposal (H)
_____ Flammable and Combustible Liquids (H)
_____ Tools - Hand and Power (1)
_____ Personal Protective Equipment (1)
_____ Scaffolds (L)
_____ Machine Guarding (0)
_____ Cranes, Derricks, Hoists, Elevators, and Conveyors (N)
_____ Hazard Communication (Z)
_____ Excavations (P)
_____ Introduction to Industrial Hygiene/Bloodborne Pathogens (Z)
_____ Stairways and Ladders (X)
_____ Ergonomics
_____ Safety and Health Programs
_____ Electives: Any OSHA Construction standard or policy _____
_____ Electives: Any OSHA General Industry standard or policy_____

Indicate the amount of time spent on each of the topics in the class.

Shortcut Procedures for Outreach Trainers with ID Numbers

OSHA will accept student card requests by e-mail and fax if the trainer has an ID number.

OSHA also will accept a short mail-in format, which lessens the paperwork required. These procedures are only available to trainers with ID numbers. Trainers should carefully read the instructions below before using these procedures.

1. **Who is Eligible? Outreach Trainers with ID Numbers.**
   - ID Numbers are provided to trainers on preprinted Outreach Training Reports that are returned with the student cards.
   - If you've never received student cards from OSHA, you do not have an ID number.
   - ID numbers are not assigned to each person that takes a trainer class (#500 or #502).
   - If you are sending in your first submission, you must use the standard procedure.
   - ID numbers cannot be provided over the phone.

2. **Sending Requests for Student Cards – Procedures (also see the following pages)**
   a. E-mail to the Education Center that issued the instructor card. OTI email addresses are:
      Construction: diane.uramkin@osha.gov
      General Industry: diana.ward@osha.gov
      Subject: 10- or 30-Hour; Construction or General Industry
      Format your e-mail request based on the format that follows these procedures
      Do not send attachments
   b. Fax to the Education Center that issued the instructor card. OTI FAX number is:
      (847) 297-6636
      Send a cover page and indicate the number of pages you are sending
      Subject: 10- or 30-Hour; Construction or General Industry
      Format your fax request based on the format that follows these procedures
   c. Short Mail-in Format

Use in place of preprinted Outreach Training Report. Use the short mail-in format that follows these procedures. Mail to the Education Center that issued the instructor card. OTI address is:

OSHA Training Institute
2020 S. Arlington Heights Road
Arlington Heights, IL 60005

3. **Instructions**
   - Use your ID Number when requesting cards using one of these procedures
   - For each class – send a separate e-mail, fax, or mail-in format
   - Keep a file on each course that includes:
     - Topics taught and time spent on each
     - Student names and addresses – the student's work or home address.
     - A copy of the e-mail or fax you sent to request cards.

4. **Monitoring.** At times, OSHA may ask for a copy of your training topics. They conduct monitoring visits for the OSHA Outreach Training Program and may ask to see documentation of the topics and students taught for each outreach training class conducted.

E-Mail Format ~ Request for Outreach Training Cards ~ For Trainers with ID Numbers

This is a sample of the format you may send to us. You will have to create the format. Send a separate format for each class. Do not send attachments. Your e-mail should look like this:

TO:

SUBJECT: 10-Hour Construction or 30-Hour Construction
               10-Hour General Industry or 30-Hour General Industry

Course End Date: ____/_____/_____

Number of Students_____

ID #:   _____
(IDs are provided on Outreach Training Reports that are sent with student cards to all trainers)

Trainer Name: _____

Trainer Course Data: *If the Trainer or Update Course information shown on your Outreach Training Report is incorrect, please enter the following information:*

Check one, as applicable:
Construction ~ 500 ~ 502   Training Date: _____
General Industry ~ 501 ~ 503   Training Date: _____

Education Center that provided/sponsored the training

Trainer Address: (Only needed if your address has changed)
Street: _____
City: _____   State: _____ ZIP: _____

___(Check) I certify *that the topics taught and the time spent on the topics in this class met the requirements of the OSHA Outreach Training Program.*

Student Names (addresses are not necessary): (list names or attach a separate sheet)

FAX Format Request for Outreach Training, Cards – For Trainers with ID Numbers

Fax:

Course: 10-hour Construction   10-hour General Industry
           30-hour Construction   30-hour General Industry

Course End Date: _____

Number of Students: _____

ID Number: _____
(ID is provided on Outreach Training Report that is sent with student cards to trainer)

Trainer Name: _____

Trainer Course Data: *If the Trainer or Update Course information shown on your Outreach Training Report is incorrect, please enter the following information:*

Check one, as applicable:
Construction ~ 500 ~ 502   Training Date: _____
General Industry ~ 501 ~ 503   Training Date: _____

Education Center that provided/sponsored the training: _____

Trainer Address: (Only needed if your address has changed)
Street: _____
City: _____   State: _____ ZIP: _____

I *certify that the topics taught and the time spent on the topics in this class met the requirements of the OSHA Outreach Training Program*   (sign) _____

Student Names (addresses are not necessary):

1_____   11_____
2_____   12_____
3_____   13_____
4_____   14_____
5_____   15_____
6_____   16_____
7_____   17_____
8_____   18_____
9_____   19_____
10_____   20_____

Continue on another page if more students

Short Mail Format – Request for Outreach Training Cards – For Trainers with ID Numbers

Course: 10-hour Construction   10-hour General Industry
          30-hour Construction   30-hour General Industry

Course End Date: _____

Number of Students: _____

ID Number: _____
(ID is provided on Outreach Training Report sent with student cards to trainer)

Trainer Name: _____

Trainer Course Data: If the Trainer or Update Course information shown on your Outreach Training Report is incorrect, please enter the following information:

Check one, as applicable:
Construction   500 – 502   Training Date: _____
General Industry   501 – 503   Training Date: _____

Education Center that provided/sponsored the training: _____

Trainer Address: (Only needed if your address has changed)
Street: _____   _____
City: _____   State _____ ZIP: _____

I certify that the topics taught and the time spent on the topics in this class met the requirements of the OSHA Outreach Training Program   (Sign)_____

Student Names (addresses are not necessary):

1_____   11_____
2_____   12_____
3_____   13_____
4_____   14_____
5_____   15_____
6_____   16_____
7_____   17_____
8_____   18_____
9_____   19_____
10_____   20_____

Continue on another page if more students

OSHA OUTREACH PROGRAM

Further Information

OSHA Web Sites

To keep up on OSHA and to obtain training materials, there are two main Web sites:

- The OSHA home page at www.osha.gov; and
- The OSHA Outreach Training Program page at www.osha.gov/outreach.
- The OSHA Outreach Training Program site includes the outreach program guidelines, teaching aids, and frequently asked questions. All pertinent program changes however are communicated at OSHA's home page.

Additional information can be found online for:

- OSHA Technical Links atwww.osha-slc.cov/SLTC;
- Multimedia at www.osha-slc.gov/SLTC/multimedia.html;
- OSHA Video Loan Program at www.osha-sle.gov/Publications/video/video.html;
- Training Materials at www.osha-slc.gov/Training/OutReach.html;
- Industry Profiles at www.osha-slc.gov/SLTC/industries.html; and
- OSHA Small Business Page at www.osha-slc.gov/SmallBusiness/index.html.

OSHA Publications

OSHA has many helpful publications, forms, posters, and fact sheets. You can find information on these at www.osha-slc.gov/OshDoc/Additional.html. Single free copies of some of these are available by calling (202) 693-1888, faxing (202) 6932498, or contacting your nearest OSHA Area or Regional Office.

One helpful publication you can order or download is the OS114 Handbook for Small Businesses, OSHA 2209. This handbook assists small business owners in implementing OSHA's recommended safety and health program management guidelines.

U.S. Government Bookstores

These bookstores sell OSHA standards, publications, and subscriptions to the OSHA CD-ROM and Job Safety and Health Quarterly (OSHA's magazine). The bookstores are located throughout the country. The U.S. Government Printing Office (GPO) in Washington, D.C., is the main office. Materials may be ordered by calling (202) 512-1800 or visiting www.osha.gov/oshpubs/gpopubs.html.

National Technical Information Service (NTIS)

NTIS sells some OSHA informational and training, associated materials. NTIS is the federal government's central source for the sale of scientific, technical, engineering, and related business information produced by or for the U.S. government. You can reach them at 1-800-553-6847 or visit their web site at www.ntis.gov/nac/safety.htm.

General Industry Outreach Training Program

If you cannot find the answers for your outreach questions in this guide or at the OSHA Web site, contact:

Mr. Don Guerra
Outreach Program Coordinator
OSHA Office of Training and Education
OSHA Training Institute
2020 S. Arlington Heights Rd.
Arlington Heights, IL 60005
(847) 759-7735
e-mail: outreachgosha.gov

Resource Center

The Resource Center Audiovisual Catalog is distributed in all 501 and 503 classes. The catalog is also available at the Outreach Training Program Web site. To receive an updated catalog or for further information contact:

Ms. Linda Vosburgh
Librarian
OSHA Office of Training and Education
(847) 759-7736
e-mail: linda-vosburgh@osha.gov

Outreach Trainer State Lists

OSHA distributes lists of active trainers (two or more classes conducted within a year), by state, to persons looking for 10- or 30-hour outreach training and also to trainers who need assistance. To obtain a state list contact:

Diana Ward
OSHA Training Institute
2020 S. Arlington Heights Rd.
Arlington Heights, IL 60005
(847) 759-7737
e-mail: diana.ward@osha.gov

Provide:

- The state(s) you are looking for (up to three);
- Whether you want the list(s) for General Industry or Construction; and
- Your fax number or mailing address.

OSHA Support

Outreach trainers can also receive assistance from OSHA Regional and Area Offices. These offices provide publications, answer questions on OSHA standards, and provide other reference services. Contact information for these offices can be found at www.osha-slc.gov/html/RAmap.html

OSHA Training Institute Education Centers

The OSHA Training Institute (OTI) has authorized other educational institutions to conduct selected OSHA training courses. The education centers conduct all outreach courses, including:

- Course 500 Trainer Course in Occupational Safety and Health Standards for the Construction Industry
- Course 501 Trainer Course in Occupational Safety and Health Standards for General Industry
- Course 502 Update for Construction Industry Outreach Trainers
- Course 503 Update for General Industry Outreach Trainers

Region I

Keene State College
OSHA Education Center
175 Ammon Drive
Manchester, NH 03103-3308
Phone: (800) 449-6742
Fax: (603) 358-2569
www.keene.edu/conted/osha.cfm

Region II

Rochester Institute of Technology
31 Lomb Memorial Dr.
Rochester, NY 14623-5603
Phone: (866) 385-7470 x-2919
Fax: (585) 475-6292
www.rit.edu/osha

Atlantic OSHA Training Center
Univ. of Medicine & Dentistry NJ
683 Hoes Lane West
Piscataway, NJ 08854
Phone: (732) 235-9450
Fax: (732) 235-9460
sph.umdnj.edu/ophp

Atlantic OSHA Training Center
University at Buffalo
3435 Main Street Room 134
Buffalo, NY 14214-3000
Phone: (716) 829-2125
Fax: (716) 829-2806
wings.buffalo.edu/trc

Atlantic OSHA Training Center
Universidad Metropolitana
PO Box 21150
San Juan, PR 00928-1150
Phone: (787) 766-1717 x-6553
Fax: (787) 751-5540
www.suagm.edu/umet

Region III

National Labor College
George Meany Campus
10000 New Hampshire Avenue
Silver Spring, MD 20903-1706
Phone: (800) 367-6724
Fax: (301) 431-5411
www.georgemeany.org/html/nrc_for_osha_training.html

Bldg. Const. Trades Dept. AFL-CIO/
Center to Protect Workers' Rights
815 16th St. NW Ste 600
Washington, D.C. 20006-4101
Phone: (202) 756-4636
Fax: (202) 756-4675
www.cpwr.com/nrccoursecat.html

OSHA Outreach Program

West Virginia University
Safety and Health Extension
130 Tower Lane
Morgantown, WV 26506-6615
Phone: (800) 626-4748
Fax: (304) 293-5905
www.wvu.edu/~exten/depts/she/osha.htm

Indiana University of Pennsylvania
1010 Oakland Ave
Indiana, PA 15705-1087
Phone: (724) 357-3019
Fax: (724) 357-3992
www.hhs.iup.edu/sa/oti/index.shtm

Region IV

Eastern Kentucky University
521 Lancaster Ave. Room 202
Richmond, KY 40475-3100
Phone: (888) 401-1956
Fax: (859) 622-6205
www.extendedprograms.eku.edu/osha

Georgia Institute of Technology
151 Sixth Street
Atlanta, GA 30332-0837
Phone: (404) 385-3500
Fax: (404) 894-8275
www.conted.gatech.edu/courses/oti/oti.html

University of South Florida
13201 Bruce B. Downs Blvd.
MDC 56
Tampa, FL 33612-3805
Phone: (866) 697-0975
Fax: (813) 974-9972
www.usfoticenter.org

Region V

Mid-America OSHA Trng. Inst.
Sinclair Community College
444 W. 3rd St.
Dayton, OH 45402-1460
Phone: (937) 512-3242
Fax: (937) 512-2279
midamericaosha.org

Mid-America OSHA Trng. Inst.
Ohio Valley Const. Ed. Foundation
33 Greenwood Lane
Springboro, OH 45066-3034
Phone: (866) 444-4412
Fax: (937) 704-9394
midamericaosha.org

National Safety Education Center
Northern Illinois University
590 Garden Rd. RM 318
DeKalb, IL 60115-2854
Phone: (800) 656-5317
Fax: (815) 753-4203
www.earnyourcard.com

National Safety Education Center
Construction Safety Council
4100 Madison Street
Hillside, IL 60162-1768
Phone: (800) 552-7744
Fax: (708) 544-2371
www.buildsafe.org

National Safety Education Center
National Safety Council
1121 Spring Lake Drive
Itasca, IL 60143-3201
Phone: (800) 621-7615
Fax: (630) 285-1613

Great Lakes Regional
OTI Education Center
UAW Health and Safety Dept.
8000 East Jefferson Ave
Detroit, MI 48214-3963
Phone: (800) 932-8689
Fax: (734) 481-0509
tp://www.uaw.org/hs/02/05/hs01.html

Great Lakes Regional
OTI Education Center
Eastern Michigan University
2000 Huron River Drive, Ste. 101
Ypsilanti, MI 48197-1699
Phone: (800) 932-8689
Fax: (734) 481-0509
www.emich.edu/public/osha

Great Lakes Regional
OTI Education Center
MWC for Occup. Safety & Health
2221 Univ. Ave. SE Ste. 350
Minneapolis, MN 55414-3078
Phone: (800) 493-2060
Fax: (612) 626-4525
www1.umn.edu/mcohs

Great Lakes Regional
OTI Education Center
University of Cincinnati
P.O. Box 670567
Cincinnati, OH 45267-0567
Phone: (800) 207-9399
Fax: (513) 558-1756
www.greatlakesosha.org

Region VI

Southwest Education Center
Texas Engineering Ext. Service
15515 IH-20 at Lumley
Mesquite, TX 75181-3710
Phone: (800) 723-3811
Fax: (972) 222-2978
teexweb.tamu.edu/osha

Region VII

Metropolitan Community Colleges/
Business & Technology College
1775 Universal Avenue
Kansas City, MO 64120-1313
Phone: (800) 841-7158
Fax: (816) 482-5408
kcmetro.edu/btcnew/oshatrain.asp

Midwest OSHA Education Centers
Saint Louis University
3545 Lafayette Ste. 300
St. Louis, MO 63104-8150
Phone: (888) 382-3756
Fax: (314) 977-8150
ceet.slu.edu

Midwest OSHA Education Center
National Safety Council
11620 M Circle
Omaha, NE 68137-2231
Phone: (800) 592-9004
Fax: (402) 896-6331
www.safenebraska.org

Midwest OSHA Education Center
Kirkwood Community College
6301 Kirkwood Blvd. SW
Cedar Rapids, IA 52404-5260
Phone: (800) 464-6874
Fax: (319) 398-1250
www.hmtri.org/moec/moec_index.htm

Region VIII

Rocky Mountain Education Center
Red Rocks Community College
13300 West Sixth Avenue
Lakewood, CO 80228-1255
Phone: (800) 933-8394
Fax: (303) 980-8339
www.rrcc.cccoes.edu/rmec

Mountain West
OSHA Training Center
Consortium of Salt Lake C.C./
University of Utah
75 South 2000 East
Salt Lake City, UT 84112-5120
Phone: (801) 581-4055
Fax: (801) 585-5275
www.rmcoeh.utah.edu/ce/otc.html

Region IX

University of California, San Diego
15373 Innovation Drive, Ste. 105
San Diego, CA 92128-3424
Phone: (800) 358-9206
Fax: (858) 485-7390
osha.ucsd.edu

WESTEC
Westside Energy Services
210 East Center Street
Taft, CA 93268-3605
Phone: (866) 493-7832
Fax: (661) 763-5162
www.westec.org/osha

Region X

University of Washington
4225 Roosevelt Way NE #100
Seattle, WA 98105-6099
Phone: (800) 326-7568
Fax: (206) 685-3872
depts.washington.edu/ehce

OSHA Outreach Training Program Fact Sheet—West Coast

As of October 1, 2003, outreach trainers will send their requests for 10- and 30-hour general industry and construction student cards to the OSHA Training Institute Education Center where they last took their trainer course (500, 501, 502, or 503).

WHEN:

Instructors must send requests to the OSHA Education Center that issued your trainer card (OSHA 500)

Note: Trainers who took their last general industry and construction trainer courses at different Education Centers will have to send their requests to different Education Centers.

WHERE:

Effective October 1, 2003, fax, mail or e-mail requests for student cards to:

Region IX OSHA Training Institute
ATTN: Outreach Training Coordinator
15373 Innovation Drive, Ste 105
San Diego, CA 92128
FAX: 858-485-7390
Online: http://osha.ucsd.edu

Region X OSHA Training Institute
ATTN: Registrar
4225 Roosevelt Way NE #100
Seattle, WA 98105
FAX: 206-685-3872
Online: http://depts.washington.edu/ehce

QUESTIONS:

If you have questions about the outreach training program, including the new administration procedures, contact either of the following staff members.

Region IX ~ UCSD
OSHA Outreach Coordinator
800 358-9206

Region X ~ UW
Lauren Baker, Registrar
Program Support Supervisor
(206) 685-3089

HOW THE PROGRAM ADMINISTRATION WORKS FOR EDUCATION CENTERS:

Education Centers will administer the outreach card requests the same way that the OSHA Training Institute does. Refer to the outreach guidelines for details, the guidelines are also available at *www.osha.gov/fso/ote/training/outreach/training_program.html*.

Requests require the same information: Provide a copy of your trainer certificate if this is your first request. We will review requests for: trainer qualification (valid authorization status), compliance to the guidelines (topics, time, etc.), and completeness of information. Discrepancies will be reviewed with the trainer, and complete, valid requests will be filled within three weeks of receipt.

ACCIDENT INVESTIGATION

Thousands of workplace accidents occur throughout the United States every day. The failure of people, equipment, supplies or surroundings to behave or react as expected cause most accidents. Accident investigations determine how and why these failures occur. By using the information gained through an investigation, a similar or perhaps more disastrous accident may be prevented. Conduct accident investigations with accident prevention in mind. Investigations are *not* to place blame.

An accident is any unplanned event that results in personal injury or property damage. When the personal injury requires little or no treatment, it is minor. If it results in a fatality or in a permanent total, permanent partial or temporary total (lost-time) disability, it is serious. Similarly, property damage may be minor or serious. Investigate all accidents regardless of the extent of injury or damage.

Accidents are part of a broad group of events that adversely affect the completion of a task. These events are incidents. For simplicity, the procedures discussed in later sections refer only to accidents. They are, however, also applicable to incidents.

Accident Prevention

Accidents are usually complex. An accident may have 10 or more events that can be causes. A detailed analysis of an accident will normally reveal three cause levels: basic, indirect and direct. At the lowest level, an accident results only when a person or object receives an amount of energy or hazardous material that cannot be absorbed safely. This energy or hazardous material is the *direct cause* of the accident. The direct cause is usually the result of one or more unsafe acts, unsafe conditions or both. Unsafe acts and conditions are the *indirect causes* or symptoms. In turn, indirect causes are usually traceable to poor management policies and decisions or to personal or environmental factors. These are the *basic causes*.

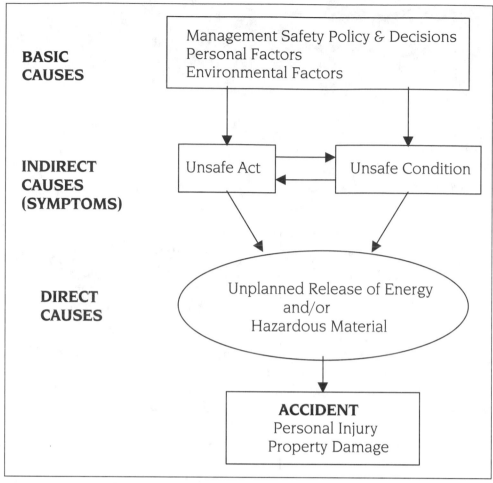

Exhibit 26-1.
A detailed analysis of an accident will normally reveal three cause levels: basic, indirect and direct.

Despite their complexity, most accidents can be prevented by eliminating one or more causes. Accident investigations determine not only what happened, but also how and why. Accident investigators are interested in each event as well as in the sequence of events that led to an accident. The accident type is also important to the investigator. The recurrence of accidents of a particular type or those with common causes shows areas needing special accident-prevention emphasis.

Investigative Procedures

The actual procedures used in a particular investigation depend on the nature and results of the accident. The agency having jurisdiction over the location determines the administrative procedures. In general, responsible officials will appoint an individual to be in charge of the investigation. The investigator uses most of the following steps:

1. Define the scope of the investigation.
2. Select the investigators. Assign specific tasks to each (preferably in writing).
3. Present a preliminary briefing to the investigating team, including:
   a. Description of the accident, with damage estimates.
   b. Normal operating procedures.
   c. Maps (local and general).
   d. Location of the accident site.
   e. List of witnesses.
   f. Events that preceded the accident.
4. Visit the accident site to get updated information.
5. Inspect the accident site:
   a. Secure the area. Do not disturb the scene unless a hazard exists.
   b. Prepare the necessary sketches and photographs. Label each carefully and keep accurate records.
6. Interview each victim and witness. Also interview those who were present before

the accident and those who arrived at the site shortly after the accident. Keep accurate records of each interview. Use a tape recorder if desired and approved.

7. Determine:
   a. What was not normal before the accident.
   b. Where the abnormality occurred.
   c. When it was first noted.
   d. How it occurred.
8. Analyze the data obtained in step 7. Repeat any of the prior steps, if necessary.
9. Determine:
   a. Why the accident occurred.
   b. A likely sequence of events and probable causes (direct, indirect, basic).
   c. Alternative sequences.
10. Check each sequence against the data from step 7.
11. Determine the most likely sequence of events and the most probable causes.
12. Conduct a post-investigation briefing.
13. Prepare a summary report, including the recommended actions to prevent a recurrence. Distribute the report according to applicable instructions.

An investigation is not complete until all data is analyzed and a final report is completed. In practice, the investigative work, data analysis and report preparation often occur simultaneously.

Fact-Finding

The investigator should gather evidence from many sources during an investigation, obtaining information from witnesses and reports as well as by observation. Interview witnesses as soon as possible after an accident. Inspect the accident site before any changes occur. Take photographs and draw sketches of the accident scene. Record all pertinent data on maps. Get copies of all reports. Documents containing normal operating procedures, flow diagrams, maintenance charts, or reports of difficulties or abnormalities are particularly useful. Record pre-accident conditions, the accident sequence, and post-accident conditions. In addition, document the location of victims, witnesses, machinery, energy sources, and hazardous materials. Keep complete and accurate notes in a bound notebook.

In some investigations, a particular physical or chemical law, principle or property may explain a sequence of events. Include laws in the notes taken during the investigation or in the later analysis of data. In addition, gather data during the investigation that may lend itself to analysis by these laws, principles or properties. An appendix in the final report can include an extended discussion.

Interviews

In general, experienced personnel should conduct interviews. If possible, the team assigned to this task should include an individual with a legal background. In conducting interviews, the team should:

1. Appoint a speaker for the group.
2. Get preliminary statements as soon as possible from all witnesses.
3. Locate the position of each witness on a master chart (including the direction of view).
4. Arrange for a convenient time and place to talk to each witness.
5. Explain the purpose of the investigation (accident prevention) and put each witness at ease.
6. Listen. Let each witness speak freely, and be courteous and considerate.
7. Take notes without distracting the witness. Use a tape recorder only with the consent of the witness.
8. Use sketches and diagrams to help the witness.
9. Emphasize areas of direct observation. Label hearsay accordingly.
10. Be sincere and do not argue with the witness.
11. Record the exact words used by the witness to describe each observation. Do not "put words into a witness's mouth."
12. Word each question carefully and be sure the witness understands.
13. Identify the qualifications of each witness (e.g., name, address, occupation, years of experience).
14. Supply each witness with a copy of his or her statements. Have each witness sign his or her statement if possible.

After interviewing all witnesses, the team should analyze each witness statement. They may wish to re-interview one or more witnesses to confirm or clarify key points. While there may be inconsistencies in witnesses' statements, investigators should assemble the available testimony into a logical order. Analyze this information along with data from the accident site.

Not all people react in the same manner to a particular stimulus. For example, a witness within close proximity to the accident may have an entirely different story from one who saw it at a distance. Some witnesses may also change their stories after they have discussed it with others. The reason for the change may be an additional clue.

A witness who has had a traumatic experience may not be able to recall the details of the accident. A witness who has a vested interest in the results of the investigation may offer biased testimony. Finally, eyesight, hearing, reaction time and the general condition of each witness may affect his or her powers of observation. A witness may omit entire sequences because of a failure to observe them or because their importance was not realized.

Problem Solving Techniques

Accidents represent problems that must be solved through investigations. Several formal procedures solve problems of any degree of complexity. This section considers these problem-solving procedures.

The Scientific Method

The scientific method forms the basis of nearly all problem-solving techniques. It is used for conducting research. In its simplest form, it involves the following sequence: making observations, developing hypotheses and testing the hypotheses.

Even a simple research project may involve many observations. A researcher records all observations immediately. A good investigator must do the same thing. Where possible, the observations should involve quantitative measurements. Quantitative data is often important in later development and testing of the hypotheses. Such measurements may require the use of many instruments in the field as well as in the laboratory.

When making observations, the investigator develops one or more hypotheses that explain the observations. The hypothesis may explain only a few of the observations or it may try to explain all of them. At this stage, the hypothesis is merely a preliminary idea. Even if later rejected, the investigator has a goal toward which to proceed.

Test the hypothesis against the original observations. A series of controlled experiments is often useful in performing this evaluation. If the hypothesis explains all of the observations, testing may be a simple process. If not, either make additional observations, change the hypothesis or develop additional hypotheses.

As with scientific research, the most difficult part of any investigation is the formulation of worthwhile hypotheses. Use the following three principles to simplify this step:

- **The principle of agreement.** An investigator uses this principle to find one factor that associates with each observation.
- **The principle of differences.** This principle is based on the idea that variations in observations are due only to differences in one or more factors and no other factors.
- **The principle of concomitant variation.** This principle is the most important because it combines the ideas of both of the preceding principles. In using this principle, the investigator is interested in the factors that are common as well as those that are different in the observations.

In using the scientific method, the investigator must be careful to eliminate personal bias. The investigator must be willing to consider a range of alternatives. Finally, he or she must recognize that accidents often result from the chance occurrence of factors that are too numerous to evaluate fully.

Change Analysis

As its name implies, this technique emphasizes change. To solve a problem, an investigator must look for deviations from the norm. As with the scientific method, change analysis also follows a logical sequence. It is based on the principle of differences described in the discussion of the scientific method. Consider all problems to result from some unanticipated change. Make an analysis of the change to determine its causes. Use the following steps in this method:

- Define the problem (What happened?).
- Establish the norm (What should have happened?).

- Identify, locate and describe the change (What, where, when and to what extent?).
- Specify what was and what was not affected.
- Identify the distinctive features of the change.
- List the possible causes.
- Select the most likely causes.

Sequence Diagrams

Gantt charts are sequence diagrams. Use them for scheduling investigative procedures. They can also aid in the development of the most probable sequence of events that led to the accident. Such a chart is especially useful in depicting events that occurred simultaneously.

Gross Hazard Analysis

Perform a gross hazard analysis (GHA) to get a rough assessment of the risks involved in performing a task. It is "gross" because it requires further study. It is particularly useful in the early stages of an accident investigation in developing hypotheses. A GHA will usually take the form of a logic diagram or table. In either case, it will contain a brief description of the problem or accident and a list of the situations that can lead to the problem. In some cases, analysis goes a step further to determine how the problem could occur. A GHA diagram or table thus shows at a glance the potential causes of an accident. One of the following analysis techniques can then expand upon a GHA.

Job Safety Analysis

Job safety analysis (JSA) is part of many existing accident prevention programs. In general, a JSA breaks a job into basic steps and identifies the hazards associated with each step. The JSA also prescribes controls for each hazard. A JSA is a chart listing these steps, hazards and controls. If available, review the JSA during the investigation. If not available, perform a JSA if one is not available. Perform a JSA as a part of the investigation to determine the events and conditions that led to the accident.

Failure Mode and Effect Analysis

Failure mode and effect analysis (FMEA) determines where failures occurred. Consider all items used in the task involved in the accident (e.g., people, equipment, machine parts, materials). In the usual procedure, FMEA lists each item on a chart. The chart lists the manner or mode in which each item can fail and determines the effects of each failure. Included in the analysis are the effects on other items and on overall task performance. In addition, make evaluations about the risks associated with each failure. That is, project the chance of each failure and the severity of its effects. Determine the most likely failures that led to the accident. Comparing these projected effects and risks with actual accident results does this.

Fault Tree Analysis

Fault tree analysis (FTA) is a logic diagram. It shows all the potential causes of an accident or other undesired event. The undesired event is at the top of the "tree." Reasoning backward from this event, determine the circumstances that can lead to the problem. These circumstances are then broken down into the events that can lead to them and so on. Continue the process until the identification of all events can produce the undesired event. Use a logic tree to describe each of these events and the manner in which they combine. This information determines the most probable sequence of events that led to the accident.

Report of Investigation

As noted earlier, an accident investigation is not complete until a report is prepared and submitted to proper authorities. Special report forms are available in many cases. Other instances may require a more extended report. Such reports are often very elaborate and may include a cover page, title page, abstract, table of contents, commentary or narrative portion, discussion of probable causes and a section on conclusions and recommendations.

The following outline is useful when developing the formal report:

1. Background information
   a. Where and when the accident occurred
   b. Who and what were involved
   c. Operating personnel and other witnesses
2. Account of the accident (What happened?)
   a. Sequence of events
   b. Extent of damage

    c. Accident type

    d. Agency or source (of energy or hazardous material)

3. Discussion (Analysis of the accident—how, why?)

    a. Direct causes (energy sources, hazardous materials)

    b. Indirect causes (unsafe acts, conditions)

    c. Basic causes (management policies, personal or environmental factors)

4. Recommendations (to prevent a recurrence) for immediate and long-range action to remedy

    a. Basic causes

    b. Indirect causes

    c. Direct causes (e.g., reduced quantities, protective equipment, structures)

Summary

A successful accident investigation determines not only what happened, but also finds how and why the accident occurred. Investigations are an effort to prevent a similar or perhaps more disastrous sequence of events.

Accident investigations involve gathering and analyzing facts, and developing hypotheses to explain these facts. Each hypothesis must then be tested against the facts. An investigation is not complete, however, until a final report is written. Responsible officials can then use the resulting information and recommendations to prevent future accidents.

FIELD INSPECTION REFERENCE MANUAL

The following is the official Field Inspection Reference Manual from the Occupational Safety and Health Administration, including change memos. The index has been excluded.

July 13, 1999
MEMORANDUM FOR: REGIONAL ADMINISTRATORS
STATE DESIGNEES

THROUGH: CHARLES N. JEFFRESS
ASSISTANT SECRETARY

FROM: R. DAVIS LAYNE
DEPUTY ASSISTANT SECRETARY

SUBJECT: Child Labor: Probability Assessment and Good
Faith Penalty Adjustment Considerations

This is to advise you of a change to OSHA's probability assessment and "good faith" penalty adjustment considerations for violations involving minor employees which will be effective on the date of this memorandum. This change is being made to provide more effective protection for young workers, who are especially vulnerable to workplace hazards. Young workers in this situation are those employees who are less than 18 years old.

Please make the following pen-and-ink changes at C.2.f.(2)(f) on page IV-10 of the OSHA Field Inspection Reference Manual (FIRM):

C. 2. f. **Probability Assessment...**

  (2)**Violations**. The following circumstances may normally be considered, as appropriate, when violations likely to result in injury or illness are involved.

    (a)Number of workers exposed

    ...

    (f) Other pertinent working conditions

    (f) Youth and inexperience of workers, especially those under 18 years old.

    (g)Other pertinent working conditions.

Please make the following pen-and-ink changes at C.2.i.(5)(b) on page IV-14 of the FIRM:

C. 2. i. (5)(b) *Good Faith.* A penalty reduction of up to 25 percent, based on the CSHO's professional judgment, is permitted in recognition of an employer's "good faith".
<add>
5. Where young workers (i.e., less than 18 years old) are employed, the CSHO's evaluation must consider whether the employer's safety and health program appropriately addresses the particular needs of such workers with regard to the types of work they perform and the hazards to which they are exposed.
<add>

State Plan States. OSHA believes that this policy change is an effective tool for dealing with employers who expose children to safety and health violations. We strongly encourage the States to adopt a similar penalty adjustment policy for violations exposing young workers and to notify their Regional Administrator as to their intent.

If you have any questions, please contact Patrick Kapust or William Smith in the Office of General Industry Compliance Assistance at (202) 693-1850.

June 21, 1996

MEMORANDUM FOR: ALL REGIONAL ADMINISTRATORS

FROM: MICHAEL G. CONNORS
Deputy Assistant Secretary

SUBJECT: FIRM Change: Mandatory Collection of OSHA-200 and Lost Workday Injury and Illness (LWDII) Data During Inspections

This is to advise you that effective July 1, 1996 all OSHA Compliance Safety and Health Officers (CSHOs) shall review the employer's injury and illness records for three prior calendar years, record the information on a copy of the OSHA-200 screen, and enter the employer's data using the IMIS Application on the NCR (micro). This shall be done for all general industry, construction, maritime, and agriculture inspections and investigations.

For construction inspections/investigations, only the OSHA-200 information for the prime/general contractor need be recorded. It will be left to the discretion of the area office or the CSHO as to whether OSHA-200 data should also be recorded for any of the subcontractors.

CSHOs will not need to calculate the LWDII rate since it is automatically calculated when the OSHA-200 data is entered into the micro. If one of the three years is a partial year, so indicate, and the software will calculate accordingly. CSHOs shall, however collect the Number of Employee Hours Worked in each of the reference years, or if the information is not available, the Average Number of Full Time Employees (FTEs).

CSHOs can print blank OSHA-200 screens through any form containing establishment processing (1A, 7, 36, 90, 55). The NCR's Systems Administrator can also print blank 200 forms from selection **N. Blankforms Menu** on the Systems Administration Screen.

Select **Q. UnNumbered 200 & PEP**.

It will be necessary for training to be provided, in each area office, for CSHOs who are not using the CSHO Application, to ensure that they can gather and enter the necessary data for calculation of the LWDII. The PC-CSHO Application on the laptops for the OSHA-200 is not yet available.

This memorandum supersedes any policy or procedure to the contrary that is found in the Field Inspection Reference Manual (FIRM) or what might be found in any memorandum issued before the date of this memorandum. This has been cleared with NCFLL.

If you have any questions, contact Art Buchanan at (202) 219-8041 x114.

March 23, 1995

MEMORANDUM FOR: REGIONAL ADMINISTRATORS

FROM: JAMES W. STANLEY
                       Deputy Assistant Secretary
SUBJECT: FIRM Change: Minimum Serious Willful Penalty

This is to advise you of a change to OSHA's civil willful penalty which will be effective as of the date of this memorandum. The change concerns the proposed minimum serious willful penalties for the smaller employers. The small employers in this situation are those with 50 or fewer employees. In no case will the proposed penalty be less than the statutory minimum, i.e., $5,000 for these employers.

Please make the following pen-and-ink changes at C.2.b.(1) on page IV-8 of the OSHA Field Inspection Reference Manual (FIRM):

C.2.b.(1) Minimum Penalties. The following guidelines apply:

(1) ~~The proposed penalty for any willful violation shall not be less than $5,000 for other than serious and regulatory violations, and shall not be less than $25,000 for serious violations. The $5,000 penalty is a statutory minimum and not subject to administrative discretion.~~

<add>

(1) The proposed penalty for any willful violation shall not be less than $5,000. The $5,000 penalty is a statutory minimum and not subject to administrative discretion. See C.2.m.(1)(a)1, below, for applicability to small employers.

<add>

Please make the following pen-and-ink changes at C.2.m.(1)(a)1, 3, and 4 on page IV-18 of the FIRM:

C.2.m.(1)(a)   Serious Violations. For willful serious violations, a gravity of **high, ~~medium~~,** <add>**moderate**<add>, or **low** shall be assigned based on the GBP of the underlying serious violation, as described at C.2.g.(2).

1   ~~The adjustment factor for size shall be applied at **one half** of the values stated at C.2.c(5)(A) 1, i.e., a reduction of 30 percent (1-25 employees), 20 percent (26-100 employees), 10 percent (101-250 employees), or no reduction (251 or more employees).~~

<add>

1   The adjustment factor for size shall be applied as shown in the following chart:

Employees	Percent Reduction
10 or less	80
11-20	60
21-30	50
31-40	40
41-50	30
51-100	20
101-250	10
251 or more	0

2 The adjustment factor for history shall be applied as described at C.2.i.(5)(c); i.e., a reduction of 10 percent shall be given to employers who have not been cited by OSHA for any serious, willful, or repeated violations in the past 3 years. There shall be no adjustment for good faith.

3 The proposed penalty shall then be determined from the table below:

Penalties to be Proposed			
Total percentage reduction for size and/or history	High Gravity	Moderate Gravity	Low Gravity
0%	$70,000	$55,000	$40,000
10%	$63,000	$49,500	$36,000
20%	$56,000	$44,000	$32,000
30%	$49,000	$38,500	$28,000
40%	$42,000	$33,000	$24,000
50%	$35,000	$27,500	$20,000
60%	$28,000	$22,000	$16,000
70%	$21,000	$16,500	$12,000
80%	$14,000	$11,000	$8,000
90%	$7,000	$5,500	$5,000

Penalties to be proposed					
Total percentage reduction for size and/or history	0%	10%	20%	30%	40%
High Gravity	$70,000	$63,000	$56,000	$49,000	$42,000
Moderate Gravity	$55,000	$49,500	$44,000	$38,500	$33,000
Low Gravity	$40,000	$36,000	$32,000	$28,000	$25,000[1]

[1] See C.2.m.(1)(a)1 below.

4 In no case shall the proposed penalty be less than ~~$25,000~~ <add>$5,000<add>.

State Plan States. Regional Administrators shall ensure that this memorandum is promptly forwarded to each State designee and explain its content as requested. This changes the minimum willful penalty policy which was previously transmitted by memorandum on June 14, 1994 and later incorporated in CPL 2.103, the Field Inspection Reference Manual (FIRM), on September 26, 1994. OSHA believes that this policy change is an effective tool for dealing with significant willful safety and health violations especially as modified in the above table which minimizes penalties for employers with 50 or fewer employees. States are encouraged to adopt this or an equivalent policy. State designees shall advise the Regional Administrator of their intention within 30 days.

States that adopt an identical or alternative policy should submit appropriate plan documentation. States wishing to pilot alternatives may do so and should consider entering into limited Performance Agreements on this issue.

If you have any questions, please contact Helen Rogers or William Smith in the Office of General Industry Compliance Assistance at (202) 219-8031.

OSHA Instruction CPL 2.103
September 26, 1994
Office of General Industry Compliance Assistance

SUBJECT: Field Inspection Reference Manual (FIRM)

A. Purpose. The purpose of this instruction is to transmit the Field Inspection Reference Manual (FIRM). The FIRM was developed by the Field Operations Manual (FOM) Revision Team to provide the field offices a reference document for identifying the responsibilities associated with the majority of their inspection duties.

B. Scope. This instruction applies OSHA-wide.

C. References.

1. OSHA Instruction CPL 2.45B, June 15, 1989, Field Operations Manual (FOM).
2. OSHA Instruction CPL 2.51H, March 22, 1993, Exemptions and limitations under the Current Appropriations Act.
3. OSHA Instruction CPL 2.77, December 30, 1986, Critical Fatality/Catastrophe Investigation.
4. OSHA Instruction CPL 2.80, October 21, 1990, Handling of Cases to be Proposed for Violation-by-Violation Penalties.
5. OSHA Instruction CPL 2.90, June 3, 1991, Guidelines for Administration of Corporate-Wide Settlement Agreements.
6. OSHA Instruction CPL 2.94, July 22, 1991, OSHA Response to Significant Events of Potentially Catastrophic Consequences.
7. OSHA Instruction CPL 2.97, January 26, 1993, Fatality/Catastrophe Reports to the National Office ("Flash Reports").
8. OSHA Instruction CPL 2.98, October 12, 1993, Guidelines for Case File Documentation for Use with Videotapes and Audiotapes.
9. OSHA Instruction CPL 2.102, March 28, 1994, Procedures for Approval of Local Emphasis Programs (LEPs) and Experimental Programs.
10. OSHA Instruction CPL 2-2.20B, April 19, 1993, OSHA Technical Manual.
11. OSHA Instruction CPL 2-2.35A, December 19, 1983, 29 CFR 1910.95(b)(1), Guidelines for Noise Enforcement, Appendix A, Noise Control Guidelines.
12. OSHA Instruction CPL 2-2.54, February 10, 1992, Respiratory Protection Program Manual.
13. OSHA Instruction ADM 1-1.31, September 20, 1993, The IMIS Enforcement Data Processing Manual
14. OSHA Instruction ADM 4.4, August 19, 1991, Administrative Subpoenas. 15. OSHA Instruction ADM 11.3A, July 29, 1991, Revision A to the OSHA Mission and Function Statements.
16. Memorandum dated March 31, 1994, to the Regional Administrators from H. Berrien Zettler, Deputy Director, Directorate of Compliance Programs regarding Policy Regarding Voluntary Rescue Activities.

D. Action. The issuance of the FIRM will require a change to the FOM, but until this change is accomplished, if there are any discrepancies between the FIRM and the FOM, the FIRM prevails. Regional Administrators and Area Directors shall ensure that the policies and procedures established in this instruction are transmitted to all Area and District Offices, and to appropriate staff.

E. Effective Date. September 30, 1994.

F. Federal Agencies. This instruction describes a change that affects Federal agencies. Executive Order 12196, Section 1-201, and 29 CFR 1960.16, maintains that Federal agencies must also follow the enforcement policy and procedures contained in this instruction.

G. Federal Program Change. This instruction describes a Federal program change which affects State programs. Each Regional Administrator shall:

1. Ensure that this change is promptly forwarded to each State designee using a format consistent with the Plan Change Two-way Memorandum in Appendix P, OSHA Instruction STP 2.22A, CH-3. Explain the content of this change to the State designee as requested.

2. Encourage the State designees to review the streamlined procedures contained in the Field Inspection Reference Manual (FIRM) and adopt parallel procedures through a State FIRM or changes to the State Field Operations Manual (FOM).

3. Advise the State designees that specific policy changes have been made in the following areas, through the FIRM, which require a State response:
   a. serious willful penalty increase (previously transmitted by June 14, 1994, memorandum "Revised Penalties and Willful Violations") – FIRM Chapter IV, C.2.m.
   b. good faith credit – FIRM Chapter IV, C.2.i.(5)(b)
   c. definitions concerning complaints – FIRM Chapter I, C.2.
   d. nonformal complaint procedures – FIRM Chapter I, C.7.
   e. voluntary rescue operations – FIRM Chapter II, B.2.e.
   f. imminent danger investigations – FIRM Chapter II, B.3.
   g. unobserved exposure – FIRM Chapter III, C.1.b.(4)
   h. reporting of fatalities/catastrophe (1904.8) – FIRM Chapter II, B.2.a.
   i. reporting time for fatalities (1904.8) – FIRM Chapter IV, C.2.n.(3)(c)
   j. notification of employee representatives of citation issuance – FIRM Chapter IV, B.1.b.
   k. economic feasibility – FIRM Chapter IV, A.6.a.(4)(b) and NOTE
   l. employee involvement in informal conferences/settlements – FIRM Chapter IV, D.1.b.

4. Ensure that the State designees are asked to acknowledge receipt of this Federal program change in writing to the Regional Administrator as soon as possible, but not later than 70 calendar days after the date of issuance (10 days for mailing and 60 days for response). The acknowledgment must include a statement indicating the State's general intention with regard to adopting the FIRM or incorporating the FIRM's procedures into its Field Manual and specific intention in regard to the 12 policy changes specified above.

5. Ensure that State designees submit an appropriate State plan supplement within 6 months and that it is reviewed and processed in accordance with paragraphs I.1.a.(3)(a) and (b), Part I of the State Plan Policies and Procedures Manual (SPM).

6. Review policies, instructions and guidelines issued by the State to determine that this change has been communicated to State compliance personnel.

Joseph A. Dear   Ron Yarman
Assistant Secretary Executive Vice President, NCFLL

DISTRIBUTION: National, Regional, and Area Offices
All Compliance Officers State Designees
NIOSH Regional Program Directors 7(c)(1) Project Managers

OSHA Instruction CPL 2.103
September 26, 1994
Office of General Industry Compliance Assistance

This manual is intended to provide guidance regarding some of the internal operations of the Occupational Safety and Health Administration (OSHA), and is solely for the benefit of the Government. No duties, rights, or benefits, substantive or procedural, are created or implied by this manual. The contents of this manual are not enforceable by any person or entity against the Department of Labor or the United States. Guidelines which reflect current Occupational Safety and Health Review Commission or court precedents do not necessarily indicate acquiescence with those precedents.

TABLE OF CONTENTS
(Page numbers deleted)

Chapter I. Pre-inspection Procedures

Chapter II. Inspections Procedures

A. GENERAL INSPECTION PROCEDURES

1. Inspection Scope
   a. Comprehensive
   b. Partial
2. Conduct of the Inspection
   a. Time of Inspection
   b. Presenting Credentials
   c. Refusal to Permit Inspection
      (1) Refusal of Entry or Inspection
      (2) Employer Interference
      (3) Administrative Subpoena
      (4) Obtaining Compulsive Process
      (5) Compulsory Process
      (6) Action to be Taken Upon Receipt of Compulsory Process
      (7) Federal Marshal Assistance
      (8) Refused Entry or Interference with a Compulsory Process
   d. Forcible Interference with Conduct of Inspection or Other Official Duties
   e. Release for Entry
   f. Bankrupt or Out of Business
   g. Strike or Labor Dispute
   h. Employee Participation
3. Opening Conference
   a. Attendance at Opening Conference
   b. Scope
   c. Forms Completion
   d. Employees of Other Employers
   e. Voluntary Compliance Programs
      (1) Section 7(c)(1) and Contract Consultations
      (2) Voluntary Protection Programs (VPP)
   f. Walkaround Representatives
      (1) Employees Represented by a Certified or Recognized Bargaining Agent
      (2) Safety Committee
      (3) No Certified or Recognized Bargaining Agent
   g. Preemption by Another Agency
   h. Disruptive Conduct
   i. Trade Secrets
   j. Classified Areas
   k. Examination of Record Programs and Posting Requirements
      (1) Records
      (2) Lost Workday Injury (LWDI) Rate
      (3) Posting
4. Walkaround Inspection
   a. Evaluation
   b. Record All Facts Pertinent to an Apparent Violation
   c. Collecting Samples
   d. Taking Photographs and/or Videotapes
   e. Interviews
      (1) Purpose
      (2) Employee Right of Complaint
      (3) Time and Location

Chapter III. Inspection Documentation

Chapter IV. Post-Inspection Procedures

    d. Gravity of Violation
    e. Severity Assessment
    f. Probability Assessment
    g. Gravity-Based Penalty
    h. Gravity Calculations for Combined or Grouped Violations
    i. Penalty Adjustment Factors
    j. Effect on Penalties if Employer Immediately Corrects
    k. Failure to Abate
    l. Repeated Violations
    m.Willful Violations
    n. Violation of 29 CFR Parts 1903 and 1904 Regulatory Requirements
  3. Criminal Penalties

D. POST-CITATION PROCESSES

  1. Informal Conferences
    a. General
    b. Procedures
    c. Participation by OSHA Officials
    d. Conduct of the Informal Conference
    e. Decisions
    f. Failure to Abate
  2. Petitions for Modification of Abatement Date (PMA)
    a. Filing Date
    b. Failure to Meet All Requirements
    c. Delayed Decisions
    d. Area Office Position on the PMA
    e. Employee Objections
  3. Services Available to Employers
  4. Settlement of Cases by Area Directors
    a. General
    b. Pre-Contest Settlement (Informal Settlement Agreement)
    c. Procedures for Preparing an Informal Settlement Agreement
    d. Post-Contest Settlement (Formal Settlement Agreement)
    e. Corporate-Wide Settlement Agreement
  5. Guidance for Determining Final Dates of Settlements and Review Commission Orders

E. REVIEW COMMISSION

  1. Transmittal of Notice of Contest and Other Documents to Review Commission
    a. Notice of Contest
    b. Documents to Executive Secretary
    c. Petitions for Modification of Abatement Dates (PMAs)
  2. Transmittal of File to Regional Solicitor
    a. Notification of the Regional Solicitor
    b. Subpoena
  3. Communications with Commission Employees
  4. Dealings with Parties while Proceedings are Pending Before the Commission

CHAPTER I
PRE-INSPECTION PROCEDURES

A. **General Responsibilities and Administrative Procedures.** The following are brief descriptions of the general responsibilities for positions within OSHA. Reference OSHA Instruction ADM 11.3A for complete information on OSHA mission and function statements. Employees should refer to their position descriptions for individual job responsibilities. This document empowers OSHA personnel to make decisions as situations warrant with the ability to act efficiently to accomplish the mission of OSHA and to enforce the Occupational Safety and Health Act.

1. **Regional Administrator.** It is the duty or mission of the Regional Administrator to manage, execute and evaluate all programs of the Occupational Safety and Health Administration (OSHA) in the region. The Regional Administrator reports to the Assistant Secretary through the career Deputy Assistant Secretary.

2. **Area Director (AD).** It is the duty or mission of the Area Director to accomplish OSHA's programs within the delegated area of responsibility of the Area Office. This includes administrative and technical support of the Compliance Safety and Health Officers (CSHOs) assigned to the Area Office, and the issuing of citations.

3. **Assistant Area Director (AAD).** The Assistant Area Director has first level supervisory responsibility over CSHOs in the discharge of their duties and may also conduct compliance inspections. Assistant Area Directors ensure technical adequacy in applying the policies and procedures in effect in the Agency. The Assistant Area Director shall implement a quality assurance system suitable to the work group, including techniques such as random review of selected files, review based on CSHO recommendation/request, and verbal briefing by CSHOs and/or review of higher profile or non-routine cases.

4. **Compliance Safety and Health Officer.**

   a. **General.** The primary responsibility of the Compliance Safety and Health Officer (CSHO) is to carry out the mandate given to the Secretary of Labor, namely, "to assure so far as possible every working man and woman in the Nation safe and healthful working conditions...." To accomplish this mandate the Occupational Safety and Health Administration employs a wide variety of programs and initiatives, one of which is enforcement of standards through the conduct of effective inspections to determine whether employers are:

      (1) Furnishing places of employment free from recognized hazards that are causing or are likely to cause death or serious physical harm to their employees, and

      (2) Complying with safety and health standards and regulations. Through inspections and other employee/employer contact, the CSHO can help ensure that hazards are identified and abated to protect workers. During these processes, the CSHO must use professional judgment to adequately document hazards in the case file, as required by the policies and procedures in effect in the Agency. The CSHO will be responsible for the technical adequacy of each case file.

   A.4.b. **Subpoena Served on CSHO.** If a CSHO is served with a subpoena, the Area Director shall be informed immediately and shall refer the matter to the Regional Solicitor.

   c. **Testifying in Hearings.** The CSHO is required to testify in hearings on OSHA's behalf. The CSHO shall be mindful of this fact when recording observations during inspections. The case file shall reflect conditions observed in the workplace as accurately as possible. If the CSHO is called upon to testify, the case file will be invaluable as a means for recalling actual conditions.

   d. **Release of Inspection Information.** The information obtained during inspections is confidential, but is to be determined as disclosable or nondisclosable on the basis of criteria established in the Freedom of Information Act, as amended, in 29 CFR Part 70, and in Chapter XIV of OSHA Instruction CPL 2.45B or a superseding directive. Requests for release of inspection information shall be directed to the Area Director.

   e. **Disposition of Inspection Records.** "Inspection Records" are any records made by a CSHO that concern, relate to, or are part of any inspection or that concern, relate to, or are part of the performance of any official duty. Such original material and all copies shall be included in the case file. These records are the property of the United States Government and a part of the case file. Inspection records are not the property of the CSHO and under no circumstances are they to be retained or used for any private purpose. Copies of documents, notes or other recorded information not necessary or pertinent, or not suitable for inclusion in the case file shall, with the concurrence and permission of the Area Director, be destroyed in accordance with an approved record disposition schedule.

5. **General Area Office Responsibilities.** The Area Director shall ensure that the Area Office maintains an outreach program appropriate to local conditions and the needs of the service area. The plan may include utilization of Regional Office Support Services, training and education services, referral services, voluntary compliance programs, abatement assistance, and technical services.

B. **Inspection Scheduling.**

1. **Program Planning.** Effective and efficient use of resources requires careful, flexible planning. In this way, the overall goal of hazard abatement and worker protection is best served.

2. **Inspection/Investigation Types.**

   a. **Unprogrammed.** Inspections scheduled in response to alleged hazardous working conditions that have been identified at a specific worksite are unprogrammed. This type of inspection responds to reports of imminent dangers, fatalities/catastrophes, complaints and referrals. It also includes followup and monitoring inspections scheduled by the Area Office. **NOTE:** This category includes all employers directly affected by the subject of the unprogrammed activity, and is especially applicable on multiemployer worksites.

   b. **Unprogrammed Related.** Inspections of employers at multiemployer worksites whose operations are not directly affected by the subject of the conditions identified in the complaint, accident, or referral are unprogrammed related. An example would be a trenching inspection conducted at the unprogrammed worksite, where the trenching hazard was not identified in the complaint, accident report, or referral.

   c. **Programmed.** Inspections of worksites which have been scheduled based upon objective or neutral selection criteria are programmed. The worksites are selected according to national scheduling plans for safety and for health or special emphasis programs.

d. **Programmed Related.** Inspections of employers at multiemployer worksites whose activities were not included in the programmed assignment, such as a low injury rate employer at a worksite where programmed inspections are being conducted for all high injury rate employers. All high hazard employers at the worksite shall normally be included in the programmed inspections. (See Chapter II, F.2. of OSHA Instruction CPL 2.45B or a superseding directive).

3. **Inspection Priorities.**

a. **Order of Priority.** Generally, priority of accomplishment and assignment of staff resources for inspection categories shall be as follows:

Priority	Category
First	Imminent Danger
Second	Fatality/Catastrophe Investigations
Third	Complaints/Referrals Investigation
Fourth	Programmed Inspections

b. **Efficient Use of Resources.** Based on the nature of the alleged hazard, unprogrammed inspections normally shall be scheduled and conducted prior to programmed inspections. Deviations from this priority list are allowed so long as they are justifiable, lead to efficient use of resources, **and** contribute to the effective protection of workers. An example of such a deviation would be for Area Directors to commit a certain percentage of IH resources to programmed Local Emphasis Program (LEP) inspections.

c. **Followup Inspections.** In cases where followup inspections are necessary, they shall be conducted as promptly as resources permit. Except in unusual circumstances, followup inspections shall take priority over all programmed inspections and any unprogrammed inspections with hazards evaluated as other than serious. Followup inspections should not normally be conducted within the 15 working day contest period unless high gravity serious violations were issued. See Chapter IV at A.4. regarding effect of contest upon abatement period.

4. **Inspection Selection Criteria.**

a. **General Requirements.** OSHA's priority system for conducting inspections is designed to distribute available OSHA resources as effectively as possible to ensure that maximum feasible protection is provided to the working men and women of this country.

(1) **Scheduling.** The Area Director shall ensure that inspections are scheduled within the framework of this chapter, that they are consistent with the objectives of the Agency, and that appropriate documentation of scheduling practices is maintained. (See OSHA Instruction CPL 2.51H, or most current version, for congressional exemptions and limitations on OSHA inspection activity.)

B. 4. a. (2) **Effective Use of Resources.** The Area Director shall ensure that OSHA resources are effectively distributed during inspection activities. If an inspection is of a complex nature, the Area Director may consider utilizing outside OSHA resources (e.g., the Health Response Team) to more effectively employ the Area or District Office resources. The Area Office will retain control of the inspection.

(3) **Effect of Contest.** If an employer scheduled for inspection, either programmed or unprogrammed, has contested a citation and/or a penalty received as a result of a previous inspection and the case is still pending before the Review Commission, the following guidelines apply.

(a) If the employer has contested the penalty only, the inspection shall be scheduled as though there were no contest.

(b) If the employer has contested the citation itself or any items thereon, then programmed and unprogrammed inspections shall be scheduled in accordance with the guidelines in B.3.a. of this chapter. The scope of unprogrammed inspections normally shall be partial. All items under contest shall be excluded from the inspection unless a potential imminent danger is involved.

b. **Employer Contacts.** Contacts for information initiated by employers or their representatives shall not trigger an inspection, nor shall such employer inquiries protect them against regular inspections conducted pursuant to guidelines established by the agency. Further, if an employer or its representative indicates that an imminent danger exists or that a fatality or catastrophe has occurred, the Area Director shall act in accordance with established inspection priority procedures.

C. **Complaints & Other Unprogrammed Inspections.**

1. **General.** This section relates to information received and processed at the area office before an inspection rather than information which is given to the CSHO during an inspection. Complaints will be evaluated according to local Area Office procedures, including using the criteria established in Chapter III, C.2. for classifying the alleged violations as serious or other. When essential information is not provided by the complainant, the complaint is too vague to evaluate, or the Area Office has other specific information that the complaint is not valid, an attempt shall be made to clarify or supplement available information. If a decision is made that the complaint is not valid, a letter will be sent to the complainant advising of the decision and its reasons.

2. **Definitions.**

a. **Complaint (OSHA-7).** Notice of an alleged hazard (over which OSHA has jurisdiction), or a violation of the Act, given by a past or present employee, a representative of employees, a concerned citizen, or an 11(c) officer seeking resolution of a discrimination complaint.

b. **Referral (OSHA-90).** Notice of an alleged hazard or a violation of the Act given by any source not listed under C.2.a., above, including media reports.

c. **Formal Complaint.** A signed complaint alleging an imminent danger or the existence of a violation threatening physical harm, submitted by a current employee, a representative of employees (such as unions, attorneys, elected representatives, and family members), or present employee of another company if that employee is exposed to the hazards of the complained-about workplace. Reference Section 8(f) of the Act and 29 CFR 1903.11.

d. **Nonformal Complaint.** Oral or unsigned complaints, or complaints by former employees or non-employees.

3. **Identity of Complainant.** The identity of the complainant shall be kept confidential unless otherwise requested by the complainant, in accordance with Section 8(f)(1) of the Act. No information shall be given to employers which would allow them to identify the complainant.

4. **Formalizing Oral Complaints.**
   a. If the complainant meets the criteria in C.2.c., above, for filing formal complaints and wishes to formalize an oral complaint, all pertinent information will be entered on an OSHA-7 form, or equivalent, by the complainant or a member of the Area Office staff. A copy of this completed form can be sent to the complainant for signature, or the complainant shall be asked to sign a letter with the particular details of the complaint to the area office.
   b. The complainant shall be informed that, if the signed complaint is not returned within 10 working days, it shall be treated as a nonformal complaint. If the signed complaint arrives after the 10 working days but prior to OSHA's contact with the employer, it will be treated as a formal complaint.
   c. The following are examples of deficiencies which would result in the failure of an apparent formal complaint to meet the requirements of the definition:
      (1) A thorough evaluation of the complaint does not establish reasonable grounds to believe that the alleged violation can be classified as an imminent danger or that the alleged hazard is covered by a standard or, in the case of an alleged serious condition, by the general duty clause (Section 5(a)(1)).
      (2) The complaint concerns a workplace condition which has no direct relationship to safety or health and does not threaten physical harm; e.g., a violation of a regulation or a violation of a standard that is classified as de minimis.
      (3) The complaint alleges a hazard which violates a standard but describes no actual workplace conditions and gives no particulars which would allow a proper evaluation of the hazard. In such a case the Area Director shall make a reasonable attempt to obtain such information.

5. **Imminent Danger Report Received By the Field.** Any allegation of imminent danger received by an OSHA office shall be handled in accordance with the following procedures:
   a. The Area Director shall immediately determine whether there is a reasonable basis for the allegation.
   b. Imminent danger investigations shall be scheduled with the highest priority.
   c. When an immediate inspection cannot be made, the Area Director or CSHO shall contact the employer (and when known, the employee representative) immediately, obtain as many pertinent details as possible concerning the situation and attempt to have any employees affected by imminent danger voluntarily removed. Such notification shall be considered advance notice and shall be handled in accordance with the procedures given in E.3. of this chapter.

6. **Formal Complaints.** All formal complaints meeting the requirements of Section 8(f)(1) of the Act and 29 CFR 1903.11 shall be scheduled for workplace inspections.
   a. **Determination.** Upon determination by the Assistant Area Director that a complaint is formal, an inspection shall be scheduled in accordance with the priorities in C.6.b.
   b. **Priorities for Responding by Inspections to Formal Complaints.** Inspections resulting from formal complaints shall be conducted according to the following priority:
      (1) Formal complaints, other than imminent danger, shall be given a priority based upon the classification and the gravity of the alleged hazards as defined in Chapters III and IV.
      (2) Formal serious complaints shall be investigated on a priority basis within 30 working days and formal other-than-serious complaints within 120 days.
      (3) If resources do not permit investigations within the time frames given in (2), a letter to the complainant shall explain the delay and shall indicate when an investigation may occur. The complainant shall be asked to confirm the continuation of the alleged hazardous conditions.
      (4) If a late complaint inspection is to be conducted, the Area Director may contact the complainant to ensure that the alleged hazards are still existent.

7. **Nonformal Complaints.**
   a. **Serious.** If a decision is made to handle a serious nonformal complaint by letter, a certified letter shall be sent to the employer advising the employer of the complaint items and the need to respond to OSHA within a specified time. When applicable, the employer shall be informed of Section 11(c) requirements, and that the complainant will be kept informed of the complaint progress. Follow-up contact may be by telephone at the option of the Area Office.
   b. **Other-Than-Serious and De Minimis.** Nonformal complaints about other-than-serious hazards or de minimis conditions may be investigated by telephone if they can be satisfactorily resolved in that manner, with follow-up telephone contact to the complainant with the results of the employer's investigation and corrective actions. Corrective action shall be documented in the case file. If, however, the telephone contact is inadequate, a letter will be sent to the employer.
   c. **Letter to Complainant.** Concurrent with the letter to the employer, a letter to the complainant shall be sent containing a copy of the letter to the employer. The complainant will be asked to notify OSHA if no corrective action is taken within the indicated time frame, or if any adverse or discriminatory action or threats are made due to the complainant's safety and health activities. Copies of subsequent correspondence related to the complaint shall be sent to the complainant, if requested.
   d. **Inspection of Nonformal Complaint.**
      (1) Where the employer fails to respond or submits an inadequate response, the employer may be contacted to find out what corrections will be made, or the nonformal complaint will be activated for inspection. If no action has been taken, the nonformal complaint shall normally be activated for inspection.
      (2) Nonformal complaints, when received by the Area Office, may be activated for inspection if the Area Director or representative judges the hazard to be high gravity serious in nature, and the inspection can be performed with efficient use of resources.

8. **Results of Inspection to Complainant.** After an inspection, the complainant shall be sent a letter addressing each complaint item, with reference to the citations and/or with a sufficiently detailed description of the findings and why they did not result in a violation. The complainant shall also be informed of the appeal rights under 29 CFR 1903.12.

9. **Discrimination Complaints.** The complainant shall be advised of the protection against discrimination afforded by Section 11(c) of the Act and shall be informed of the procedure for filing an 11(c) complaint.
   a. Safety and/or health complaints filed by former employees who allege that they were fired for exercising their rights under the Act are nonformal complaints and will not be scheduled for investigation.

(1) Such complaints shall be recorded on an OSHA-7 Form and handled in accordance with the procedures outlined in OSHA Instruction DIS .4B. They shall be transmitted to the appropriate 11(c) personnel for investigation of the alleged 11(c) discrimination complaint.

(2) No letter shall be sent to the employer until after the Regional Supervisory Investigator has reviewed the case and decided that no recommendation for inspection will be submitted to the Area Director.

(3) This screening process by the Regional Supervisory Investigator is not anticipated to take more than 3 work days and usually less. The Area Director can expect to be informed by telephone of the decision within that time frame.

b. In those instances where the Regional Supervisory Investigator determines that the existence or nature of the alleged hazard is likely to be relevant to the resolution of the 11(c) discrimination complaint, the complaint shall be sent back to the Area Director for an OSHA inspection to be handled as a referral.

c. When the decision is that no inspection is necessary, the Area Director shall ensure that the complaint has been recorded on an OSHA-7 Form and proceed to send a letter to the employer in accordance with procedures for responding to nonformal complaints.

d. Any 11(c) complaint alleging an imminent danger shall be handled in accordance with the instructions in C.5.

10. **Referrals.** Referrals shall be handled in a manner similar to that of complaints.

a. **Letters.** Referrals shall normally be handled by letter or telephone. For those referrals handled by letter, complaint letters can be revised to fit the particular circumstances of the referral.

b. **Inspections.** High gravity serious referrals shall normally be handled by inspection. A letter transmitting the results of the investigation shall be sent to any referring agency/department.

11. **Accidents.** Accidents involving significant publicity or any other accident not involving a fatality or a catastrophe, however reported, may be considered as either a complaint or a referral, depending on the source of the report, and shall be handled according to the directions given in Chapter II.

D. Programmed Inspections.

1. Programmed inspections shall be scheduled in accordance with Chapter II, F.2. of OSHA Instruction CPL 2.45B or a superseding directive.

2. Local emphasis programmed inspections shall be conducted in accordance with OSHA Instruction CPL 2.102.

E. Inspection Preparation.

1. **General.** The conduct of effective inspections requires professional judgment in the identification, evaluation and reporting of safety and health conditions and practices. Inspections may vary considerably in scope and detail, depending upon the circumstances in each case.

2. **Planning.** It is most important that the CSHO adequately prepares for an inspection. The CSHO shall also ensure the selection of appropriate inspection materials and equipment, including personal protective equipment, based on anticipated exposures and training received in relation to the uses and limitations of such equipment. Refer to OSHA Instruction CPL 2-2.54 regarding respiratory protection.

a. 29 CFR 1903.7(c) requires that the CSHO comply with all safety and health rules and practices at the establishment and wear or use the safety clothing or protective equipment required by OSHA standards or by the employer for the protection of employees.

b. The CSHO shall not enter any area where special entrance restrictions apply until the required precautions have been taken. It shall be the Assistant Area Director's responsibility to procure whatever materials and equipment are needed for the safe conduct of the inspection.

3. **Advance Notice of Inspections.**

a. **Policy.** Section 17(f) of the Act and 29 CFR 1903.6 contain a general prohibition against the giving of advance notice of inspections, except as authorized by the Secretary or the Secretary's designee.

(1) The Occupational Safety and Health Act regulates many conditions which are subject to speedy alteration and disguise by employers. To forestall such changes in worksite conditions, the Act, in Section 8(a), prohibits unauthorized advance notice.

(2) There may be occasions when advance notice is necessary to conduct an effective investigation. These occasions are narrow exceptions to the statutory prohibition against advance notice.

(3) Advance notice of inspections may be given only with the authorization of the Area Director and only in the following situations:

(a) In cases of apparent imminent danger to enable the employer to correct the danger as quickly as possible;

(b) When the inspection can most effectively be conducted after regular business hours or when special preparations are necessary;

(c) To ensure the presence of employer and employee representatives or other appropriate personnel who are needed to aid in the inspection; and

(d) When the giving of advance notice would enhance the probability of an effective and thorough inspection; e.g., in complex fatality investigations.

(4) Advance notice exists whenever the Area Office sets up a specific date or time with the employer for the CSHO to begin an inspection. Any delays in the conduct of the inspection shall be kept to an absolute minimum. Lengthy or unreasonable delays shall be brought to the attention of the Assistant Area Director. Advance notice generally does not include non-specific indications of potential future inspections.

(5) In unusual circumstances, the Area Director may decide that a delay is necessary. In those cases the employer or the CSHO shall notify affected employee representatives, if any, of the delay and shall keep them informed of the status of the inspection.

b. **Documentation.** The conditions requiring advance notice and the procedures followed shall be documented in the case file.

4. **Pre-Inspection Compulsory Process.** 29 CFR 1903.4 authorizes the agency to seek a warrant in advance of an attempted inspection if circumstances are such that "pre-inspection process (is) desirable or necessary." The Act authorizes the agency to issue administrative subpoenas to obtain relevant information.

a. Although the agency generally does not seek warrants without evidence that the employer is likely to refuse entry, the Area Director may seek compulsory process in advance of an attempt to inspect or investigate whenever circumstances indicate the desirability of such warrants. **NOTE:** Examples of such circumstances would be evidence of denied entry in previous inspections, or awareness that a job will only last a short time or that job processes will be changing rapidly.

b. Administrative subpoenas may also be issued prior to any attempt to contact the employer or other person for evidence related to an OSHA inspection or investigation. (See OSHA Instruction ADM 4.4. and Chapter II, A.2.c.(3).)

5. **Expert Assistance.**

a. The Area Director shall arrange for a specialist and/or specialized training, preferably from within OSHA, to assist in an inspection or investigation when the need for such expertise is identified.

b. OSHA specialists may accompany the CSHO or perform their tasks separately. A CSHO must accompany outside consultants. OSHA specialists and outside consultants shall be briefed on the purpose of the inspection and personal protective equipment to be utilized.

6. **Personal Security Clearance.** Some establishments have areas which contain material or processes which are classified by the U.S. Government in the interest of national security. Whenever an inspection is scheduled for an establishment containing classified areas, the Assistant Area Director shall assign a CSHO who has the appropriate security clearances. The Regional Administrator shall ensure that an adequate number of CSHOs with appropriate security clearances are available within the Region and that the security clearances are current.

7. **Disclosure of Records.** The disclosure of inspection records is governed by the Department's regulations at 29 CFR part 70, implementing the Freedom of Information Act (FOIA).

8. **Classified and Trade Secret Information.** Any classified or trade secret information and/or personal knowledge of such information by OSHA personnel shall be handled in accordance with the regulations of OSHA or of the responsible agency. The collection of such information, and the number of personnel with access to it shall be limited to the minimum necessary for the conduct of compliance activities. The CSHO shall identify classified and trade secret information as such in the case file. Title 18 USC, Section 1905, as referenced by Section 15 of the OSH Act, provides for criminal penalties in the event of improper disclosure.

CHAPTER II
INSPECTION PROCEDURES

A. General Inspection Procedures.

1. **Inspection Scope.** Inspections, either programmed or unprogrammed, fall into one of two categories depending on the scope of the inspection:

a. **Comprehensive.** A substantially complete inspection of the potentially high hazard areas of the establishment. An inspection may be deemed comprehensive even though, as a result of the exercise of professional judgment, not all potentially hazardous conditions, operations and practices within those areas are inspected.

b. **Partial.** An inspection whose focus is limited to certain potentially hazardous areas, operations, conditions or practices at the establishment. A partial inspection may be expanded based on information gathered by the CSHO during the inspection process. Consistent with the provisions of Section 8(f)(2) of the Act, and Area Office priorities, the CSHO shall use professional judgment to determine the necessity for expansion of the inspection scope, based on information gathered during records or program review and walkaround inspection.

2. **Conduct of the Inspection.**

a. **Time of Inspection.** Inspections shall be made during regular working hours of the establishment except when special circumstances indicate otherwise. The Assistant Area Director and CSHO shall confer with regard to entry during other than normal working hours.

b. **Presenting Credentials.**

(1) At the beginning of the inspection the CSHO shall locate the owner representative, operator or agent in charge at the workplace and present credentials. On construction sites this will most often be the representative of the general contractor.

(2) When neither the person in charge nor a management official is present, contact may be made with the employer to request the presence of the owner, operator or management official. The inspection shall not be delayed unreasonably to await the arrival of the employer representative. This delay should normally not exceed one hour. If the person in charge at the workplace cannot be determined, record the extent of the inquiry in the case file and proceed with the physical inspection.

c. **Refusal to Permit Inspection.** Section 8 of the Act "provides that CSHOs may enter without delay and at reasonable times any establishment covered under the Act for the purpose of conducting an inspection". Unless the circumstances constitute a recognized exception to the warrant requirement (i.e., consent, third party consent, plain view, open field, or exigent circumstances) an employer has a right to require that the CSHO seek an inspection warrant prior to entering an establishment and may refuse entry without such a warrant. **NOTE:** On a military base or other Federal Government facility, the following guidelines do not apply. Instead, a representative of the controlling authority shall be informed of the contractor's refusal and asked to take appropriate action to obtain cooperation.

(1) **Refusal of Entry or Inspection.** When the employer refuses to permit entry upon being presented proper credentials or allows entry but then refuses to permit or hinders the inspection in some way, a tactful attempt shall be made to obtain as much information as possible about the establishment. (See A.2.c.(4), below, for the information the CSHO shall attempt to obtain.)

(a) If the employer refuses to allow an inspection of the establishment to proceed, the CSHO shall leave the premises and immediately report the refusal to the Assistant Area Director. The Area Director shall notify the Regional Solicitor.

(b) If the employer raises no objection to inspection of certain portions of the workplace but objects to inspection of other portions, this shall be documented. Normally, the CSHO shall continue the inspection, confining it only to those certain portions to which the employer has raised no objections.

(c) In either case the CSHO shall advise the employer that the refusal will be reported to the Assistant Area Director and that the agency may take further action, which may include obtaining legal process.

(d) On multiemployer worksites, valid consent can be granted by the owner, or another co-occupier of the space, for site entry.

(2) **Employer Interference.** Where entry has been allowed but the employer interferes with or limits any important aspect of the inspection, the CSHO shall determine whether or not to consider this action as a refusal. Examples of interference are refusals to permit the walkaround, the examination of records essential to the inspection, the taking of essential photographs and/or videotapes, the inspection of a particular part of the premises, indispensable employee interviews, or the refusal to allow attachment of sampling devices.

(3) **Administrative Subpoena.** Whenever there is a reasonable need for records, documents, testimony and/or other supporting evidence necessary for completing an inspection scheduled in accordance with any current and approved inspection scheduling system or an investigation of any matter properly falling within the statutory authority of the agency, the Regional Administrator, or authorized Area Director, may issue an administrative subpoena. (See OSHA Instruction ADM 4.4.)

(4) **Obtaining Compulsory Process.** If it is determined, upon refusal of entry or refusal to produce evidence required by subpoena, that a warrant will be sought, the Area Director shall proceed according to guidelines and procedures established in the Region for warrant applications.

(a) With the approval of the Regional Solicitor, the Area Director may initiate the compulsory process.

(b) The warrant sought when employer consent has been withheld shall normally be limited to the specific working conditions or practices forming the basis of the unprogrammed inspection. A broad scope warrant, however, may be sought when the information available indicates conditions which are pervasive in nature or if the establishment is on the current list of targeted establishments.

(c) If the warrant is to be obtained by the Regional Solicitor, the Area Director shall transmit in writing to the Regional Solicitor, within 48 hours after the determination is made that a warrant is necessary, all information necessary to obtain a warrant, as determined through contact with the Solicitor, which may include the following:

1 Area/District Office, telephone number, and name of Assistant Area Director involved.

2 Name of CSHO attempting inspection and inspection number, if assigned. Identify whether inspection to be conducted included safety items, health items or both.

3 Legal name of establishment and address including City, State and County. Include site location if different from mailing address.

4 Estimated number of employees at inspection site.

5 SIC Code and high hazard ranking for that specific industry within the State, as obtained from statistics provided by the National Office.

6 Summary of all facts leading to the refusal of entry or limitation of inspection, including the following:
   a Date and time of entry.
   b Date and time of denial.
   c Stage of denial (entry, opening conference, walkaround, etc.)

7 Narrative of all actions taken by the CSHO leading up to during and after refusal, including the following information.
   a Full name and title of the person to whom CSHO presented credentials.
   b Full name and title of person(s) who refused entry.
   c Reasons stated for the denial by person(s) refusing entry.
   d Response, if any, by CSHO to c, above.
   e Name and address of witnesses to denial of entry.

8 All previous inspection information, including copies of the previous citations.

9 Previous requests for warrants. Attach details, if applicable.

10 As much of the current inspection report as has been completed.

11 If a construction site involving work under contract from any agency of the Federal Government, the name of the agency, the date of the contract, and the type of work involved.

12 Other pertinent information such as description of the workplace; the work process; machinery, tools and materials used; known hazards and injuries associated with the specific manufacturing process or industry.

13 Investigative techniques which will be required during the proposed inspection; e.g., personal sampling, photographs, audio/ videotapes, examination of records, access to medical records, etc.

14 The specific reasons for the selection of this establishment for the inspection including proposed scope of the inspection and rationale:

   a Imminent Danger.
      o Description of alleged imminent danger situation.
      o Date received and source of information.
      o Original allegation and copy of typed report, including basis for reasonable expectation of death or serious physical harm and immediacy of danger.
      o Whether all current imminent danger processing procedures have been strictly followed.

   b Fatality/Catastrophe.
      o The OSHA-36F filled out in as much detail as possible.

   c Complaint or Referral.
      o Original complaint or referral and copy of typed complaint or referral.
      o Reasonable grounds for believing that a violation that threatens physical harm or imminent danger exists, including standards that could be violated if the complaint or referral is true and accurate.
      o Whether all current complaint or referral processing procedures have been strictly followed.
      o Additional information gathered pertaining to complaint or referral evaluation.

d Programmed.
- o Targeted safety—general industry, maritime, construction.
- o Targeted health.
- o Special emphasis program—Special Programs, Local Emphasis Program, Migrant Housing Inspection, etc.

e Followup.
- o Date of initial inspection.
- o Details and reasons followup was to be conducted.
- o Copies of previous citations on the basis of which the followup was initiated.
- o Copies of settlement stipulations and final orders, if appropriate.
- o Previous history of failure to correct, if any.

f Monitoring.
- o Date of original inspection.
- o Details and reasons monitoring inspection was to be conducted.
- o Copies of previous citations and/or settlement agreements on the basis of which the monitoring inspection was initiated.
- o PMA request, if applicable.

(5) **Compulsory Process.** When a court order or warrant is obtained requiring an employer to allow an inspection, the CSHO is authorized to conduct the inspection in accordance with the provisions of the court order or warrant. All questions from the employer concerning reasonableness of any aspect of an inspection conducted pursuant to compulsory process shall be referred to the Area Director.

(6) **Action to be Taken Upon Receipt of Compulsory Process.** The inspection will normally begin within 24 hours of receipt of a warrant or of the date authorized by the warrant for the initiation of the inspection.

(a) The CSHO shall serve a copy of the warrant on the employer and make a separate notation as to the time, place, name and job title of the individual served.

(b) The warrant may have a space for a return of service entry by the CSHO in which the exact dates of the inspection made pursuant to the warrant are to be entered. Upon completion of the inspection, the CSHO will complete the return of service on the original warrant, sign and forward it to the Assistant Area Director for appropriate action.

(c) Even where the walkaround is limited by a warrant or an employer's consent to specific conditions or practices, a subpoena for production of records shall be normally served, if necessary, in accordance with A.2.c.(3), above. The records specified in the subpoena shall include (as appropriate) injury and illness records, exposure records, the written hazards communication program, the written lockout-tagout program, and records relevant to the employer's safety and health management program, such as safety and health manuals or minutes from safety meetings.

(d) The Regional Administrator, or Area Director authorized to do so, may issue, for each inspection, an administrative subpoena which seeks production of the above specified categories of documents. The subpoena may call for immediate production of the records with the exception of the documents relevant to the safety and health management program, for which a period of 5 working days normally shall be allowed.

(e) If circumstances make it appropriate, a second warrant may be sought based on the review of records or on "plain view" observations of other potential violations during a limited scope walkaround.

(7) **Federal Marshal Assistance.** A U.S. Marshal may accompany the CSHO when the compulsory process is presented.

(8) **Refused Entry or Interference with a Compulsory Process.**

(a) When an apparent refusal to permit entry or inspection is encountered upon presenting the warrant, the CSHO shall specifically inquire whether the employer is refusing to comply with the warrant.

(b) If the employer refuses to comply or if consent is not clearly given, the CSHO shall not attempt to conduct the inspection but shall leave the premises and contact the Assistant Area Director concerning further action. The CSHO shall make notations (including all witnesses to the refusal or interference) and fully report all relevant facts. Under these circumstances the Area Director shall contact the Regional Solicitor and they shall jointly decide what further action shall be taken.

d. **Forcible Interference with Conduct of Inspection or Other Official Duties.** Whenever an OSHA official or employee encounters forcible resistance, opposition, interference, etc., or is assaulted or threatened with assault while engaged in the performance of official duties, all investigative activity shall cease.

(1) The Assistant Area Director shall be advised by the most expeditious means.

(2) Upon receiving a report of such forcible interference, the Area Director or designee shall immediately notify the Regional Administrator.

e. **Release for Entry.**

(1) The CSHO shall not sign any form or release or agree to any waiver. This includes any employer forms concerned with trade secret information.

(2) The CSHO may obtain a pass or sign a visitor's register, or any other book or form used by the establishment to control the entry and movement of persons upon its premises. Such signature shall not constitute any form of a release or waiver of prosecution of liability under the Act.

f. **Bankrupt or Out of Business.** If the establishment scheduled for inspection is found to have ceased business and there is no known successor, the CSHO shall report the facts to the Assistant Area Director. If an employer, although adjudicated bankrupt, is continuing to operate on the date of the scheduled inspection, the inspection shall proceed. An employer must comply with the Act until the day the business actually ceases to operate.

g. **Strike or Labor Dispute.** Plants or establishments may be inspected regardless of the existence of labor disputes involving work stoppages, strikes or picketing. If the CSHO identifies an unanticipated labor dispute at a proposed inspection site, the Assistant Area Director shall be consulted before any contact is made.

(1) **Programmed Inspections.** Programmed inspections may be deferred during a strike or labor dispute, either between a recognized union and the employer or between two unions competing for bargaining rights in the establishment.

(2) **Unprogrammed Inspections.** Unprogrammed inspections (complaints, fatalities, etc.) will be performed during strikes or labor disputes. However, the seriousness and reliability of any complaint shall be thoroughly investigated by the supervisor prior to scheduling an inspection to ensure as far as possible that the complaint reflects a good faith belief that a true hazard exists. If there is a picket line at the establishment, the CSHO shall inform the appropriate union official of the reason for the inspection prior to initiating the inspection.

h. **Employee Participation.** The CSHO shall advise the employer that Section 8(e) of the Act and 29 CFR 1903.8 require that an employee representative be given an opportunity to participate in the inspection.

(1) CSHOs shall determine as soon as possible after arrival whether the employees at the worksite to be inspected are represented and, if so, shall ensure that employee representatives are afforded the opportunity to participate in all phases of the workplace inspection.

(2) If an employer resists or interferes with participation by employee representatives in an inspection and this cannot be resolved by the CSHO, the continued resistance shall be construed as a refusal to permit the inspection and the Assistant Area Director shall be contacted in accordance with A.2.c. of this chapter. **NOTE:** For the purpose of this chapter, the term "employee representative" refers to (1) a representative of the certified or recognized bargaining agent, or, if none, (2) an employee member of a safety and health committee who has been chosen by the employees (employee committee members or employees at large) as their OSHA representative, or (3) an individual employee who has been selected as the walkaround representative by the employees of the establishment.

3. **Opening Conference.** The CSHO shall attempt to inform all effected employers of the purpose of the inspection, provide a copy of the complaint if applicable, and shall include employees unless employer objects. The opening conference shall be kept as brief as possible and may be expedited through use of an opening conference handout. Conditions of the worksite shall be noted upon arrival as well as any changes which may occur during the opening conference. **NOTE:** The CSHO shall determine if the employer is covered by any of the exemptions or limitations noted in the current Appropriations Act (see OSHA Instruction CPL 2.51H, or the most current version), or deletions in OSHA Instruction CPL 2.45B Chapter II, F.2.b.(1)(b)**5 b** or superseding directive.

a. **Attendance at Opening Conference.** OSHA encourages employers and employees to meet together in the spirit of open communication. The CSHO shall conduct a joint opening conference with employer and employee representatives unless either party objects. If there is objection to a joint conference, the CSHO shall conduct separate conferences with employer and employee representatives.

b. **Scope.** The CSHO shall outline in general terms the scope of the inspection, including private employee interviews, physical inspection of the workplace and records, possible referrals, discrimination complaints, and the closing conference(s).

c. **Forms Completion.** The CSHO shall obtain available information for the OSHA-1 and other appropriate forms.

d. **Employees of Other Employers.** During the opening conference, the CSHO shall determine whether the employees of any other employers are working at the establishment. If these employers may be affected by the inspection, the scope may be expanded to include others or a referral made at the discretion of the CSHO. At multiemployer sites, copies of complaint(s), if applicable, shall be provided to all employers affected by the alleged hazard(s), and to the general contractor.

e. **Voluntary Compliance Programs.** Employers who participate in selected voluntary compliance programs may be exempted from programmed inspections. The CSHO shall determine whether the employer falls under such an exemption during the opening conference.

(1) **Section 7(c)(1) and Contract Consultations.** In accordance with 29 CFR 1908.7 and Chapter IX of the Consultation Policies and Procedures Manual (CPPM), the CSHO shall ascertain at the opening conference whether an OSHA-funded consultation is in progress or whether the facility is pursuing or has received an inspection exemption through consultation under current procedures.

(a) An on site consultation visit in progress has priority over programmed inspections except as indicated in 29 CFR 1908.7(b) (2)(iv), which allows for critical inspections as determined by the Assistant Secretary.

(b) If a consultation visit is in progress, the inspection may be rescheduled.

(c) If a followup inspection (including monitoring) or an imminent danger, fatality/catastrophe, complaint or referral investigation is to be conducted, the inspection shall not be deferred, but its scope shall be limited to those areas required to complete the purpose of the investigation. The consultant must interrupt the onsite visit until the compliance inspection shall have been completed (Ref. 29 CFR 1908.7).

(2) **Voluntary Protection Programs (VPP).** In the event a CSHO enters a facility that has been approved for participation in a VPP and is currently under an inspection exemption, the approval letter shall be copied and the inspection either be terminated (if it is a programmed inspection) or limited to the specified items in the complaint or referral (if it is unprogrammed).

f. **Walkaround Representatives.** Those representatives designated to accompany the CSHO during the walkaround are considered walkaround representatives, and will generally include employer designated and employee designated representatives. At establishments where more than one employer is present or in situations where groups of employees have different representatives, it is acceptable to have a different employer/employee representative for different phases of the inspection. More than one employer and/or employee representative may accompany the CSHO throughout or during any phase of an inspection if the CSHO determines that such additional representatives will aid, and not interfere with, the inspection (29 CFR 1903.8(a)).

(1) **Employees Represented by a Certified or Recognized Bargaining Agent.** During the opening conference, the highest ranking union official or union employee representative on-site shall designate who will participate in the walkaround. OSHA regulation 29 CFR 1903.8(b) gives the CSHO the authority to resolve all disputes as to who is the representative authorized by the employer and employees. Title 29 CFR 1903.8(c) states that the representative authorized by the employees shall be an employee of the employer. The CSHO can decide to include others.

(2) **Safety Committee.** The employee members of an established plant safety committee or the employees at large may have designated an employee representative for OSHA inspection purposes or agreed to accept as their representative the employee designated by the committee to accompany the CSHO during an OSHA inspection.

(3) **No Certified or Recognized Bargaining Agent.** Where employees are not represented by an authorized representative, where there is no established safety committee, or where employees have not chosen or agreed to an employee representative for OSHA inspection purposes whether or not there is a safety committee, the CSHO shall determine if any other employees would suitably represent the interests of employees on the walkaround. If selection of such an employee is impractical, the CSHO shall consult with a reasonable number of employees during the walkaround.

g. **Preemption by Another Agency.** Section 4(b)(1) of the OSH Act states that the OSH Act does not apply to working conditions over which other Federal agencies exercise statutory responsibility. The determination of preemption by another Federal agency is, in many cases, a highly complex matter. Any such situations shall be brought to the attention of the Area Director as soon as they arise, and dealt with on a case by case basis.

h. **Disruptive Conduct.** The CSHO may deny the right of accompaniment to any person whose conduct interferes with a full and orderly inspection (29 CFR 1903.8(d)). If disruption or interference occurs, the CSHO shall use professional judgment as to whether to suspend the walkaround or take other action. The Assistant Area Director shall be consulted if the walkaround is suspended. The employee representative shall be advised that during the inspection matters unrelated to the inspection shall not be discussed with employees.

i. **Trade Secrets.** The CSHO shall ascertain from the employer if the employee representative is authorized to enter any trade secret area(s). If not, the CSHO shall consult with a reasonable number of employees who work in the area (29 CFR 1903.9(d)).

j. **Classified Areas.** In areas containing information classified by an agency of the U.S. Government in the interest of national security, only persons authorized to have access to such information may accompany a CSHO (29 CFR 1903.8(d)).

k. **Examination of Record Programs and Posting Requirements.**

(1) **Records.** As appropriate, the CSHO shall review the injury and illness records to the extent necessary to determine compliance and identify trends. Other OSHA programs and records will be reviewed at the CSHO's professional discretion as necessary.

(2) **Lost Workday Injury (LWDI) Rate.** The LWDI may in the CSHO's discretion be used in determining trends in injuries and illnesses. The LWDI rate is calculated according to the following formula:

It the number of employees hours worked is available from the employer, use:

$$\text{LWDI Rate} = \frac{\# \text{ LWDI's} \times 200,000}{\# \text{ employee hours worked}}$$

Where:
- LWDI's = sum of LWDI's in the reference years.
- employee hours worked = sum of employee hours in the reference years.
- 200,000 = base for 100 full-time workers, working 40 hours per week, 50 weeks per year.

EXAMPLE: An establishment scheduled for inspection in October 1993 employed an average of 54 workers in 1992, 50 workers in 1991, and 50 workers in 1990. Therefore, injury and employment data for the two preceding calendar years will be used.

- LWDI's in 1991 = 5
- LWDI's in 1992 = 3
- Employee hours worked in 1991 = 100,000
- Employee hours worked in 1992 = 108,000

$$\text{LWDI Rate} = \frac{(5+3) \times 200,000}{100,000 + 108,000}$$

$$= \frac{1,600,000}{208,000}$$

$$= 7.69 \text{ (rounded to 7.7)}$$

(3) **Posting.** The CSHO shall determine if posting requirements are met in accordance with 29 CFR Parts 1903 and 1904.

4. **Walkaround Inspection.** The main purpose of the walkaround inspection is to identify potential safety and/or health hazards in the workplace. The CSHO shall conduct the inspection in such a manner as to eliminate unnecessary personal exposure to hazards and to minimize unavoidable personal exposure to the extent possible.

a. **Evaluation.** The employer's safety and health program shall be evaluated to determine the employer's good faith. See Chapter IV, C.2.i.(5)(b).

b. **Record All Facts Pertinent to an Apparent Violation.** Apparent violations shall be brought to the attention of employer and employee representatives at the time they are documented. CSHOs shall record at a minimum the identity of the exposed employee, the hazard to which the employee was exposed, the employee's proximity to the hazard, the employer's knowledge of the condition, and the manner in which important measures were obtained.

NOTE: If employee exposure (either to safety or health hazards) is not observed, the CSHO shall document facts on which the determination is made that an employee has been or could be exposed.

c. **Collecting Samples.**

(1) The CSHO shall determine as soon as possible after the start of the inspection whether sampling, such as but not limited to air sampling and surface sampling, is required by utilizing the information collected during the walkaround and from the pre-inspection review.

(2) If either the employer or the employee representative requests sampling results, summaries of the results shall be provided to the requesting representative as soon as practicable.

(3) The CSHO may reference the sampling strategy located in OSHA Instruction CPL 2-2.20B for additional information on sampling techniques.

d. **Taking Photographs and/or Videotapes.** Photographs and/or videotapes shall be taken whenever the CSHO judges there is a need. Photographs that support violations shall be properly labeled, and may be attached to the appropriate OSHA-1B. The CSHO shall ensure that any photographs relating to confidential or trade secret information are identified as such. All film and photographs shall be retained in the case file. Videotapes shall be properly labeled and stored. Refer to OSHA Instruction CPL 2.98 for further information on videotaping.

e. **Interviews.** A free and open exchange of information between the CSHO and employees is essential to an effective inspection. Interviews provide an opportunity for employees or other individuals to point out hazardous conditions and, in general, to provide assistance as to what violations of the Act may exist and what abatement action should be taken. Employee interviews are also an effective means to determine if advance notice of inspection, when given under the guidelines in Chapter I, E.3., has adversely affected the inspection conditions.

(1) **Purpose.** Section 8(a)(2) of the Act authorizes the CSHO to question any employee privately during regular working hours in the course of an OSHA inspection. The purpose of such interviews is to obtain whatever information the CSHO deems necessary or useful in carrying out the inspection effectively. Such interviews shall be kept as brief as possible. Individual interviews are authorized even when there is an employee representative present.

(2) **Employee Right of Complaint.** The CSHO may consult with any employee who desires to discuss a possible violation. Upon receipt of such information, the CSHO shall investigate the alleged hazard, where possible, and record the findings. If a written complaint is received, the written response procedures in Chapter I shall be followed.

(3) **Time and Location.** Interviews shall be conducted in a reasonable manner and normally will be conducted during the walkaround; however, they may be conducted at any time during an inspection. If necessary, interviews may be conducted at locations other than the workplace.

(4) **Privacy.** Employers shall be informed that the interview is to be in private. Whenever an employee expresses a preference that an employee representative be present for the interview, the CSHO shall make a reasonable effort to honor that request. Any employer objection to private interviews with employees may be construed as a refusal of entry and handled in accordance with the procedures in A.2.c. of this chapter.

(5) **Interview Statements.** Interview statements of employees or other individuals shall be obtained whenever the CSHO determines that such statements would be useful in documenting adequately an apparent violation.

(a) Interviews shall normally be reduced to writing, and the individual shall be encouraged to sign and date the statement. The CSHO shall assure the individual that the statement will be held confidential to the extent allowed by law, but they may be used in court/hearings. See OSHA Instruction CPL 2.98 for guidance on videotaping.

(b) Interview statements shall normally be written in the first person and in the language of the individual.

1 Any changes or corrections shall be initialed by the individual; otherwise, the statement shall not be changed, added to or altered in any way.

2 The statements shall end with wording such as: "I have read the above, and it is true to the best of my knowledge." The statement shall also include the following: "I request that my statement be held confidential to the extent allowed by law." The individual, however, may waive confidentiality. The individual shall sign and date the statement and the CSHO shall then sign it as a witness.

3 If the individual refuses to sign the statement, the CSHO shall note such refusal on the statement. The statement shall, nevertheless, be read to the individual and an attempt made to obtain agreement. A note that this was done shall be entered into the case file.

(c) A transcription of a recorded statement shall be made if necessary.

f. **Employer Abatement Assistance.**

(1) **Policy.** CSHOs shall offer appropriate abatement assistance during the walkaround as to how workplace hazards might be eliminated. The information shall provide guidance to the employer in developing acceptable abatement methods or in seeking appropriate professional assistance. CSHO's shall not imply OSHA endorsement of any product through use of specific product names when recommending abatement measures. The issuance of citations shall not be delayed.

(2) **Disclaimers.** The employer shall be informed that:

(a) The employer is not limited to the abatement methods suggested by OSHA;

(b) The methods explained are general and may not be effective in all cases; and

(c) The employer is responsible for selecting and carrying out an effective abatement method.

g. **Special Circumstances.**

(1) **Trade Secrets.** Trade secrets are matters that are not of public or general knowledge. A trade secret is any confidential formula, pattern, process, equipment, list, blueprint, device or compilation of information used in the employer's business which gives an advantage over competitors who do not know or use it.

(a) **Policy.** It is essential to the effective enforcement of the Act that the CSHO and all OSHA personnel preserve the confidentiality of all information and investigations which might reveal a trade secret.

(b) **Restrictions and Controls.** When the employer identifies an operation or condition as a trade secret, it shall be treated as such. Information obtained in such areas, including all negatives, photographs, videotapes, and OSHA documentation forms, shall be labeled:
"ADMINISTRATIVELY CONTROLLED INFORMATION"
"RESTRICTED TRADE INFORMATION"

1 Under Section 15 of the Act, all information reported to or obtained by a CSHO in connection with any inspection or other activity which contains or which might reveal a trade secret shall be kept confidential. Such information shall not be disclosed except to other OSHA officials concerned with the enforcement of the Act or, when relevant, in any proceeding under the Act.

2 Title 18 of the United States Code, Section 1905, provides criminal penalties for Federal employees who disclose such information. These penalties include fines of up to $1,000 or imprisonment of up to one year, or both, and removal from office or employment.

3 Trade secret materials shall not be labeled as "Top Secret," "Secret," or "Confidential," nor shall these security classification designations be used in conjunction with other words unless the trade secrets are also classified by an agency of the U.S. Government in the interest of national security.

(c) **Photographs and Videotapes.** If the employer objects to the taking of photographs and/or videotapes because trade secrets would or may be disclosed, the CSHO should advise the employer of the protection against such disclosure afforded by Section 15 of the Act and 29 CFR 1903.9. If the employer still objects, the CSHO shall contact the Assistant Area Director.

(2) **Violations of Other Laws.** If a CSHO observes apparent violations of laws enforced by other government agencies, such cases shall be referred to the appropriate agency. Referrals shall be made using appropriate Regional procedures (see A.3.g. of this chapter).

5. **Closing Conference.**

a. At the conclusion of an inspection, the CSHO shall conduct a closing conference with the employer and the employee representatives, jointly or separately, as circumstances dictate. The closing conference may be conducted on site or by telephone as deemed appropriate by the CSHO.

NOTE: When conducting separate closing conferences for employers and labor representatives (where the employer has declined to have a joint closing conference with employee representatives), the CSHO shall normally hold the conference with employee representatives first, unless the employee representative requests otherwise. This procedure will ensure that worker input, if any, is received—and that any needed changes are made—before employers are informed of violations and proposed citations.

b. The CSHO shall describe the apparent violations found during the inspection and other pertinent issues as deemed necessary by the CSHO. Both the employer and the employee representatives shall be advised of their rights to participate in any subsequent conferences, meetings or discussions, and their context rights. Any unusual circumstances noted during the closing conference shall be documented in the case file.

(1) Since the CSHO may not have all pertinent information at the time of the first closing conference, a second closing conference may be held by telephone or in person to inform the employer and the employee representatives whether the establishment is in compliance.

(2) The CSHO shall advise the employee representatives that:

(a) Under 29 CFR 2200.20 of the Occupational Safety and Health Review Commission regulations, if the employer contests, the employees have a right to elect "party status" before the Review Commission.

(b) They must be notified by the employer if a notice of contest or a petition for modification of abatement date is filed.

(c) They have Section 11(c) rights.

(d) They have a right to contest the abatement date. Such contest must be in writing and must be filed within 15 working days after receipt of the citation.

B. Special Inspection Procedures.

1. **Followup and Monitoring Inspections.**

a. **Inspection Procedures.** The primary purpose of a followup inspection is to determine if the previously cited violations have been corrected. Monitoring inspections are conducted to ensure that hazards are being corrected and employees are being protected, whenever a long period of time is needed for an establishment to come into compliance, or to verify compliance with the terms of granted variances. Issuance of willful, repeated and high gravity serious violations, failure to abate notifications, and/or citations related to imminent danger situations are examples of prime candidates for followup or monitoring inspections. Followup or monitoring inspections would not normally be conducted when evidence of abatement is provided by the employer or employee representatives. Normally, there shall be no additional inspection activity unless, in the judgment of the CSHO, there have been significant changes in the workplace which warrant further inspection activity.

b. **Failure to Abate.**

(1) A failure to abate exists when the employer has not corrected a violation for which a citation has been issued and abatement date has passed or which is covered under a settlement agreement, or has not complied with interim measures involved in a long-term abatement within the time given.

(2) If the cited items have not been abated, a Notice of Failure to Abate Alleged Violation shall normally be issued. If a subsequent inspection indicates the condition has still not been abated, the Regional Solicitor shall be consulted for further guidance.

NOTE: If the employer has exhibited good faith, a late PMA may be considered in accordance with Chapter IV, D.2 where there are extenuating circumstances.

(3) If it is determined that the originally cited violation was abated but then recurred, a citation for repeated violation may be appropriate.

c. **Reports.**

(1) A copy of the previous OSHA-1B, OSHA-1BIH, or citation can be used, and "corrected" written on it, with a brief explanation of the correction if deemed necessary by the CSHO, for those items found to be abated. This information may alternately be included in the narrative or in video/audio documentation.

(2) In the event that any item has not been abated, complete documentation shall be included on an OSHA-1B.

d. **Followup Files.** The followup inspection reports shall be included with the original (parent) case file.

2. **Fatality/Catastrophe Investigations.** For guidance on conducting fatality and catastrophe inspections, refer to OSHA Instruction CPL 2.77 and CPL 2.94.

a. **Definitions.** The following definitions apply for purposes of this section:

(1) **Fatality.** An employee death resulting from a work-related incident or exposure; in general, from an accident or illness caused by or related to a workplace hazard.

(2) **Catastrophe.** The hospitalization of three or more employees resulting from a work-related incident; in general, from an accident or illness caused by a workplace hazard.

(3) **Hospitalization.** To be admitted as an **inpatient** to a hospital or equivalent medical facility for examination or treatment.

(4) **Reporting.** Area Directors shall report all job-related fatalities and catastrophes which may result in high media attention or have national implications and that appear to be within OSHA's jurisdiction as soon as they become aware of them to the Regional Administrator. See CPL 2.97.

b. **Selection of CSHO.** A CSHO, preferably with expertise in the particular industry or operation involved in the accident or illness, shall be selected by the Area Director and sent to the establishment as soon as possible. If a potential criminal violation appears possible during the inspection, staff who have received criminal investigation training at the Federal Law Enforcement Training Center shall be assigned, if available.

c. **Families of Victims.**

   (1) Family members of employees involved in fatal occupational accidents or illnesses shall be contacted at an early point in the investigation, given an opportunity to discuss the circumstances of the accident or illness, and provided timely and accurate information at all stages of the investigations as directed in (2), below.

   (2) All of the following require special tact and good judgment on the part of the CSHO. In some situations, these procedures should not be followed to the letter; e.g., in some small businesses, the employer, owner, or supervisor may be a relative of the victim. In such circumstances, such steps as issuance of the form letter may not be appropriate without some editing.

      (a) As soon as practicable after initiating the investigation, the CSHO shall attempt to compile a list of all of the accident victims and their current addresses, along with the names of individual(s) listed in the employer's records as next-of-kin (family member(s)) or person(s) to contact in the event of an emergency.

      (b) The standard information letter should be sent to the family member(s) or the person(s) listed as the emergency contact person(s) indicated on the victims' employment records within 5 working days of the time their identities have been established.

      (c) The compliance officer, when taking a statement from families of victims, shall explain that the interview will be kept confidential to the extent allowed by law and that the interview will be handled following the same procedures as employee interviews. The greatest sensitivity and professionalism is required for such an interview. The information received must be carefully evaluated and corroborated during the investigation.

      (d) Followup contact shall be maintained with a key family member or other contact person, when requested, so that the survivors can be kept up-to-date on the status of the investigation. The victim's family members shall be provided a copy of all citations issued as a result of the accident investigation within 5 working days of issuance.

d. **Criminal.** Section 17(e) of the Act provides criminal penalties for an employer who is convicted of having willfully violated an OSHA standard, rule or order when that violation caused the death of an employee. In an investigation of this type, therefore, the nature of the evidence available is of paramount importance. There shall be early and close liaison between the OSHA investigator, the Area Director, the Regional Administrator and the Regional Solicitor In developing any finding which might involve a violation of Section 17(e) of the Act. An OSHA investigator with criminal investigation training shall be assigned at an early stage to assist in developing the case.

e. **Rescue Operations.** OSHA has no authority to direct rescue operations—this is the responsibility of the employer and/or of local political subdivisions or State agencies. OSHA does have the authority to monitor and inspect the working conditions of covered employees engaged in rescue operations to make certain that all necessary procedures are being taken to protect the lives of the rescuers. See also memorandum on Policy Regarding Voluntary Rescue Activities, dated March 31, 1994, to the Regional Administrators from H. Berrien Zettler, Deputy Director, Directorate of Compliance Programs

f. **Public Information Policy.** The OSHA public information policy regarding response to fatalities and catastrophes is to explain Federal presence to the news media. It is not to provide a continuing flow of facts nor to issue periodic updates on the progress of the investigation. The Area Director or his/her designee shall normally handle responses to media inquiries.

3. **Imminent Danger Investigations.**

   a. **Definition.** Section 13(a) of the Act defines imminent danger as "...any conditions or practices in any place of employment which are such that a danger exists which could reasonably be expected to cause death or serious physical harm immediately or before the imminence of such danger can be eliminated through the enforcement procedures otherwise provided by this Act."

   b. **Requirements.** The following conditions must be met before a hazard becomes an imminent danger:

      (1) It must be reasonably likely that a serious accident will occur immediately (see B.3.c.(2)(b), below) **or**, if not immediately, then before abatement would otherwise be required (see B.3.c.2.(c), below). If an employer contests a citation, abatement will not be required until there is a final order of the Review Commission affirming the citation.

      (2) The harm threatened must be death or serious physical harm. For a health hazard, exposure to the toxic substance or other health hazard must cause harm to such a degree as to shorten life or cause substantial reduction in physical or mental efficiency even though the resulting harm may not manifest itself immediately.

   c. **Inspection.**

      (1) **Scope.** CSHO may consider expanding the scope of inspection based on the information available during the inspection process.

      (2) **Elimination of the Imminent Danger.** As soon as reasonably practicable after it is concluded that conditions or practices exist which constitute an imminent danger, the employer shall be so advised and requested to notify its employees of the danger and remove them from exposure to the imminent danger. The employer should be encouraged to do whatever is possible to eliminate the danger promptly on a voluntary basis.

         (a) **Voluntary Elimination of the Imminent Danger.** The employer may voluntarily and permanently eliminate the imminent danger as soon as it is pointed out. In such cases, no imminent danger proceeding need be instituted; and, no Notice of Alleged Imminent Danger completed. An appropriate citation and notification of penalty shall be issued.

         (b) **Action Where the Danger is Immediate and Voluntary Elimination Is Not Accomplished.** If the employer either cannot or does not voluntarily eliminate the hazard or remove employees from the exposure and the danger is immediate, the following procedures shall be observed:

            1 The CSHO shall post the OSHA-8 and call the Area Director, who will decide whether to contact the Regional Solicitor to obtain a Temporary Restraining Order (TRO). The Regional Administrator shall be notified of the TRO proceedings.

NOTE: The CSHO has no authority to order the closing of the operation or to direct employees to leave the area of the imminent danger or the workplace.

    2 The CSHO shall notify employees and employee representatives of the posting of the OSHA-8 and shall advise them of their Section 11(c) rights.

    3 The employer shall be advised that Section 13 of the Act gives United States District Courts jurisdiction to restrain any condition or practice which is an imminent danger to employees.

    4 The Area Director and the Regional Solicitor shall assess the situation and make arrangements for the expedited initiation of court action, if warranted, or instruct the CSHO to remove the OSHA-8.

    5 The CSHO's first priority in scheduling activities is to prepare for litigation related to TRO's in imminent danger matters.

(c) **Action Where the Danger is that the Harm will Occur Before Abatement is Required.** If the danger is that the harm will occur before abatement is required, i.e. before a final order of the Commission can be obtained in a contested case, the CSHO shall contact the Area Director and Regional Solicitor.

    1 In many cases, the CSHO or the AD may not decide there is such an imminent danger at the time of the physical inspection of the plant. Further evaluation of the file or additional evidence may warrant consultation with the Regional Solicitor.

    2 In appropriate cases, the imminent danger notice may be posted at the time citations are delivered or even after the notice of contest is filed.

4. **Construction Inspections.**

    a. **Standards Applicability.** The standards published as 29 CFR Part 1926 have been adopted as occupational safety and health standards under Section 6(a) of the Act and 29 CFR 1910.12. They shall apply to every employment and place of employment of every employee engaged in construction work, including non-contract construction work.

    b. **Definition.** The term "construction work" means work for construction, alteration, and/or repair, including painting and decorating. These terms are discussed in 29 CFR 1926.13. If any question arises as to whether an activity is deemed to be construction for purposes of the Act, the Director of Compliance Programs shall be consulted.

    c. **Employer Worksite.**

        (1) **General.** Inspections of employers in the construction industry are not easily separable into distinct worksites. The worksite is generally the site where the construction is being performed (e.g., the building site, the dam site). Where the construction site extends over a large geographical area (e.g., road building), the entire job will be considered a single worksite. In cases when such large geographical areas overlap between Area Offices, generally only operations of the employer within the jurisdiction of any Area Office will be considered as the worksite of the employer.

        (2) **Beyond Single Area Office.** When a construction worksite extends beyond a single Area Office and the CSHO believes that the inspection should be extended, the affected Area Directors shall consult with each other and take appropriate action.

    d. **Entry of the Workplace.**

        (1) **Other Agency.** The CSHO shall ascertain whether there is a representative of a Federal contracting agency at the worksite. If so, the CSHO shall contact the representative, advise him/her of the inspection and request that he/she attend the opening conference. (For Federal Agencies, see Chapter XIII and following Appendix A, of OSHA Instruction CPL 2.45B or a superseding directive).

        (2) **Complaints.** If the inspection is being conducted as a result of a complaint, a copy of the complaint is to be furnished to the general contractor and any affected sub-contractors.

    e. **Closing Conference.** Upon completion of the inspection, the CSHO shall confer with the general contractors and all appropriate subcontractors or their representatives, together or separately, and advise each one of all the apparent violations disclosed by the inspection to which each one's employees were exposed, or violations which the employer created or controlled. Employee representatives participating in the inspection shall also be afforded the right to participate in the closing conference(s).

5. **Federal Agency Inspections.** Policies and procedures for Federal agencies are to be the same as those followed in the private sector, except as specified in Chapter XIII, and the following Appendix A, of OSHA Instruction CPL 2.45B or a superseding directive.

CHAPTER III
INSPECTION DOCUMENTATION

A. Four Stage Case File Documentation.

  1. **General.**

    a. **Guidelines.** These guidelines are developed to assist the CSHO in determining the minimum level of written documentation appropriate for each of four case file stages. **All necessary information relative to violations shall be obtained during the inspection, using any means deemed appropriate by the CSHO (i.e., notes, audio/videotapes, photographs, and employer records).**

    b. **Solicitor Coordination.** Consultation in accordance with regional procedures, including Solicitor procedures, shall be considered when the inspection or investigation could involve important, novel or complex litigation or when consultation is necessary in the CSHO or Area Director's professional judgment. If consultation is deemed necessary, such consultation shall be conducted at the earliest stage possible of the investigation.

  2. **Case File Stages.** The following paragraphs indicate what documentation is required for each of the four case file stages. **NOTE:** The difference between Stage III and Stage IV is one of format and organization only. A Stage III case file is not understood as involving a lesser degree of documentation.

    a. **Stage I.**

No on-site inspection conducted —

      o OSHA-1 or equivalent, and brief statement expanding upon the reason for not conducting the inspection.

      o If refusal of entry, information necessary to secure a warrant (see Chapter II, A.2.c.).

      o Complainant/referral response, if complaint/referral inspection.

b. **Stage II.**

In-compliance inspection —-

- o OSHA-1 or equivalent.
- o OSHA-1A or pertinent information (see B.1. of this chapter).
- o Records obtained during the inspection, based on the CSHO's professional judgment as to what should be obtained.

    NOTE: The CSHO need not document that a condition was in compliance beyond a general statement that no conditions were observed in violation of any standard.

- o Complainant/referral response, if complaint/referral inspection.

c. **Stage III.**

Inspection conducted, citations to be issued —-

- o SHA-1 or equivalent.
- o OSHA-1A or equivalent (see B.1. of this chapter).
- o Records obtained during the inspection which, based on the CSHO's professional judgment, are necessary to support the violations.
- o OSHA-1B forms or the equivalent with the following included: Inspection # Instances on page (a,b,/) Type of violation (S,W,R,O,FTA) Citation number and item number Number exposed REC Abatement Period SAVE, AVD, and/or standard reference Photo/video location Severity Rating (H,M,L) and brief justification Probability Rating (G,L) and brief justification GBP and multiplier if applicable % reduction (adjustment) Proposed penalty

    NOTE: Information in relation to exposed employees shall be documented on the OSHA-1B, or referenced on the OSHA-1B as to the specific location of this information.

- o Complainant/referral response, if complaint/referral inspection.

d. **Stage IV.**

Citations are contested —-

- o CSHO's will determine after consultation with the Solicitor if the documentation obtained during the inspection needs to be transferred to a different format or location within the file (e.g., transfer of video/audio information to a written format). The information will then be transferred to the appropriate areas as needed. Items which may be considered include transfer of exposed employee information, instance description, employer knowledge, employer's affirmative defenses, employer/ employee comments, and other employer information to the OSHA-1B or equivalent.

B. Specific Forms.

1. Narrative, Form OSHA-1A.

a. **General.** The OSHA-1A Form, or its equivalent, shall be used to record information relative to the following, at a minimum:

   ITEM: Establishment Name.

   ITEM: Inspection Number.

   ITEM: Additional Citation Mailing Addresses.

   ITEM: Names and Addresses of all Organized Employee Groups.

   ITEM: Names, Addresses, and Phone Numbers of Authorized Representatives of Employees.

   ITEM: Employer Representatives Contacted and extent of their participation in the inspection.

   ITEM: Comment on S&H program to the extent necessary, based on CSHO's professional judgment, including penalty reduction justifications for good faith.

   ITEM: Document whether closing conference was held, describe any unusual circumstances

   ITEM: Additional Comments (CSHO's shall use their professional judgment to determine if any additional information shall be added to the case file.)

b. **Specific.** The following information may be located on the OSHA-1A Form or referenced on the OSHA-1A as to the specific location of this information:

   ITEM: Names, Addresses, and Phone Numbers of Other Persons Contacted.

   ITEM: Accompanied By.

2. **Photo Mounting Worksheet, Form OSHA-89.** This worksheet may be utilized by the CSHO, if mounting is necessary. Other methods of mounting the photograph may be used, such as attaching it to the OSHA-1B. The photograph shall be annotated "trade secret," if applicable.

3. **Inspection Case File Activity Diary Insert.** The Inspection Case File Activity Diary is designed to provide a ready record and summary of all actions relating to a case. The diary sheet will be used to document important events related to the case, especially those not found elsewhere in the case file.

C. Violations.

1. Basis of Violations.

a. **Standards and Regulations.** Section 5(a)(2) of the Occupational Safety and Health Act states that each employer has a responsibility to comply with the occupational safety and health standards promulgated under the Act. The specific standards and regulations are found in Title 29 Code of Federal Regulations (CFR) 1900 series. Subparts A and B of 29 CFR 1910 specifically establish the source of all the standards which are the basis of violations.

   NOTE: The most specific subdivision of the standard shall be used for citing violations.

   (1) **Definition and Application of Universal Standards (Horizontal) and Specific Industry Standards (Vertical).** Specific Industry standards are those standards which apply to a particular industry or to particular operations, practices, conditions, processes, means, methods, equipment or installations. Universal standards are those standards which apply when a condition is not covered by a specific industry standard. Within both universal and specific industry standards there are general standards and specific standards.

   (a) When a hazard in a particular industry is covered by both a specific industry (e.g., 29 CFR Part 1915) standard and a universal (e.g., 29 CFR Part 1910) standard, the specific industry standard shall take precedence. **This is true even if the universal standard is more stringent.**

(b) When determining whether a universal or a specific industry standard is applicable to a work situation, the CSHO shall focus attention on the activity in which the employer is engaged at the establishment being inspected rather than the nature of the employer's general business.

(2) **Variances.** The employer's requirement to comply with a standard may be modified through granting of a variance, as outlined in Section 6 of the Act.

    (a) An employer will not be subject to citation if the observed condition is in compliance with either the variance or the standard.

    (b) In the event that the employer is not in compliance with the requirements of the variance, a violation of the standard shall be cited with a reference in the citation to the variance provision that has not been met.

b. **Employee Exposure.**

(1) **Definition of Employee.** Whether or not exposed persons are employees of an employer depends on several factors, the most important of which is who controls the manner in which the employees perform their assigned work. The question of who pays these employees may not be the determining factor. Determining the employer of an exposed person may be a very complex question, in which case the Area Director may seek the advice of the Regional Solicitor.

(2) **Proximity to the Hazard.** The proximity of the workers to the point of danger of the operation shall be documented.

(3) **Observed Exposure.** Employee exposure is established if the CSHO witnesses, observes, or monitors exposure of an employee to the hazardous or suspected hazardous condition during work or work-related activities. Where a standard requires engineering or administrative controls (including work practice controls), employee exposure shall be cited regardless of the use of personal protective equipment.

(4) **Unobserved Exposure.** Where employee exposure is not observed, witnessed, or monitored by the CSHO, employee exposure is established if it is determined through witness statements or other evidence that exposure to a hazardous condition has occurred, continues to occur, or could recur.

    (a) In fatality/catastrophe (or other "accident") investigations, employee exposure is established if the CSHO determines, through written statements or other evidence, that exposure to a hazardous condition occurred at the time of the accident.

    (b) In other circumstances, based on the CSHO's professional judgment and determination, exposure to hazardous conditions has occurred in the past, and such exposure may serve as the basis for a violation when employee exposure has occurred in the previous six months.

(5) **Potential Exposure.** A citation may be issued when the possibility exists that an employee could be exposed to a hazardous condition because of work patterns, past circumstances, or anticipated work requirements, and it is reasonably predictable that employee exposure could occur, such as:

    (a) The hazardous condition is an integral part of an employer's recurring operations, but the employer has not established a policy or program to ensure that exposure to the hazardous condition will not recur; or

    (b) The employer has not taken steps to prevent access to unsafe machinery or equipment which employees may have reason to use.

2. **Types of Violations.**

a. **Other-Than-Serious Violations.** This type of violation shall be cited in situations where the most serious injury or illness that would be likely to result from a hazardous condition cannot reasonably be predicted to cause death or serious physical harm to exposed employees but does have a direct and immediate relationship to their safety and health.

b. **Serious Violations.**

(1) Section 17(k) of the Act provides ". . . a serious violation shall be deemed to exist in a place of employment if there is a substantial probability that death or serious physical harm could result from a condition which exists, or from one or more practices, means, methods, operations, or processes which have been adopted or are in use, in such place of employment unless the employer did not, and could not with the exercise of reasonable diligence, know of the presence of the violation."

(2) The CSHO shall consider four elements to determine if a violation is serious.

    (a) **Step 1.** The **types of accident** or health hazard exposure which the violated standard or the general duty clause is designed to prevent.

    (b) **Step 2.** The most serious **injury or illness** which could reasonably be expected to result from the type of accident or health hazard exposure identified in Step 1.

    (c) **Step 3.** Whether the results of the injury or illness identified in Step 2 could **include death or serious physical harm.** Serious physical harm is defined as:

        1 Impairment of the body in which part of the body is made **functionally useless** or is **substantially reduced in efficiency** on or off the job. Such impairment may be permanent or temporary, chronic or acute. Injuries involving such impairment would usually require treatment by a medical doctor.

        2 Illnesses that could shorten life or significantly reduce physical or mental efficiency by inhibiting the normal function of a part of the body.

    (d) **Step 4.** Whether the **employer knew,** or with the exercise of reasonable diligence, could have known of the presence of the hazardous condition.

        1 In this regard, the supervisor represents the employer and a supervisor's knowledge of the hazardous condition amounts to employer knowledge.

        2 In cases where the employer may contend that the supervisor's own conduct constitutes an isolated event of employee misconduct, the CSHO shall attempt to determine the extent to which the supervisor was trained and supervised so as to prevent such conduct, and how the employer enforces the rule.

        3 If, after reasonable attempts to do so, it cannot be determined that the employer has actual knowledge of the hazardous condition, the knowledge requirement is met if the CSHO is satisfied that the employer could have known through the exercise of reasonable diligence. As a general rule, if the CSHO was able to discover a hazardous condition, and the condition was not transitory in nature, it can be presumed that the employer could have discovered the same condition through the exercise of reasonable diligence.

c. **Violations of the General Duty Clause.** Section 5(a)(1) of the Act requires that "Each employer shall furnish to each of his (sic) employees employment and a place of employment which are free from recognized hazards that are causing or are likely to cause death or serious physical harm to his (sic) employees." The general duty provisions shall be used only where there is no standard that applies to the particular hazard involved, as outlined in 29 CFR _1910.5(f).

(1) **Evaluation of Potential Section 5(a)(1) Situations.** In general, Review Commission and court precedent has established that the following elements are necessary to prove a violation of the general duty clause:

(a) The employer failed to keep the workplace free of a hazard to which employees of that employer were exposed;

(b) The hazard was recognized;

(c) The hazard was causing or was likely to cause death or serious physical harm; and

(d) There was a feasible and useful method to correct the hazard.

(2) **Discussion of Section 5(a)(1) Elements.** The above four elements of a Section 5(a)(1) violation are discussed in greater detail as follows:

(a) **A Hazard to Which Employees Were Exposed.** A general duty citation must involve both a serious hazard and exposure of employees.

1 **Hazard.** A hazard is a danger which threatens physical harm to employees.

a **Not the Lack of a Particular Abatement Method.** In the past some Section 5(a)(1) citations have incorrectly alleged that the violation is the failure to implement certain precautions, corrective measures or other abatement steps rather than the failure to prevent or remove the particular hazard. It must be emphasized that Section 5(a)(1) does not mandate a particular abatement measure but only requires an employer to render the workplace free of certain hazards by any feasible and effective means which the employer wishes to utilize.

EXAMPLE: In a hazardous situation involving high pressure gas where the employer has failed to train employees properly, has not installed the proper high pressure equipment, and has improperly installed the equipment that is in place, there are three abatement measures which the employer failed to take; there is only one hazard (that is, exposure to the hazard of explosion due to the presence of high pressure gas) and hence only one general duty clause citation.

b **The Hazard Is Not a Particular Accident.** The occurrence of an accident does not necessarily mean that the employer has violated Section 5(a)(1) although the accident may be evidence of a hazard. In some cases a Section 5(a)(1) violation may be unrelated to the accident. Although accident facts may be relevant and shall be gathered, the citation shall address the hazard in the workplace, not the particular facts of the accident.

EXAMPLE: A fire occurred in a workplace where flammable materials were present. No employee was injured by the fire itself but an employee, disregarding the clear instructions of his/her supervisor to use an available exit, jumped out of a window and broke a leg. The danger of fire due to the presence of flammable materials may be a recognized hazard causing or likely to cause death or serious physical harm, but the action of the employee may be an instance of unpreventable employee misconduct. The citation should deal with the fire hazard, not with the accident involving the employee who broke his/her leg.

c **The Hazard Must Be Reasonably Foreseeable.** The hazard for which a citation is issued must be reasonably foreseeable.

i. All the factors which could cause a hazard need not be present in the same place at the same time in order to prove foreseeability of the hazard; e.g., an explosion need not be imminent.

EXAMPLE: If combustible gas and oxygen are present in sufficient quantities in a confined area to cause an explosion if ignited but no ignition source is present or could be present, no Section 5(a)(1) violation would exist. If an ignition source is available at the workplace and the employer has not taken sufficient safety precautions to preclude its use in the confined area, then a foreseeable hazard may exist.

ii. It is necessary to establish the reasonable foreseeability of the general workplace hazard, rather than the particular hazard which led to the accident.

EXAMPLE: A titanium dust fire may have spread from one room to another only because an open can of gasoline was in the second room. An employee who usually worked in both rooms was burned in the second room from the gasoline. The presence of gasoline in the second room may be a rare occurrence. It is not necessary to prove that a fire in both rooms was reasonably foreseeable. It is necessary only to prove that the fire hazard, in this case due to the presence of titanium dust, was reasonably foreseeable.

2 **The Hazard Must Affect the Cited Employer's Employees.** The employees exposed to the Section 5(a)(1) hazard must be the employees of the cited employer.

(b) **The Hazard Must be Recognized.** Recognition of a hazard can be established on the basis of industry recognition, employer recognition, or "common-sense" recognition. The use of common-sense as the basis for establishing recognition shall be limited to special circumstances. Recognition of the hazard must be supported by satisfactory evidence and adequate documentation in the file as follows:

1 **Industry Recognition.** A hazard is recognized if the employer's industry recognizes it. Recognition by an industry other than the industry to which the employer belongs is generally insufficient to prove this element of a Section 5(a)(1) violation. Although evidence of recognition by the employer's specific branch within an industry is preferred, evidence that the employer's industry recognizes the hazard may be sufficient.

a In cases where State and local government agencies not falling under the preemption provisions of Section 4(b)(1) have codes or regulations covering hazards not addressed by OSHA standards, the Area Director shall determine whether the hazard is to be cited under Section 5(a)(1) or referred to the appropriate local agency for enforcement.

    b Regulations of other Federal agencies or of State atomic energy agencies generally shall not be used. They raise substantial difficulties under Section 4(b)(1) of the Act, which provides that OSHA is preempted when such an agency has statutory authority to deal with the working condition in question.

  2 **Employer Recognition.** A recognized hazard can be established by evidence of actual employer knowledge. Evidence of such recognition may consist of written or oral statements made by the employer or other management or supervisory personnel during or before the OSHA inspection, or instances where employees have clearly called the hazard to the employer's attention.

  3 **Common-Sense Recognition.** If industry or employer recognition of the hazard cannot be established in accordance with (a) and (b), recognition can still be established if it is concluded that any reasonable person would have recognized the hazard. This theory of recognition shall be used only in flagrant cases.

(c) **The Hazard Was Causing or Was likely to Cause Death or Serious Physical Harm.** This element of Section 5(a)(1) violation is identical to the elements of a serious violation, see C.2.b. of this chapter.

(d) **The Hazard Can Be Corrected by a Feasible and Useful Method.**

  1 To establish a Section 5(a)(1) violation the agency must identify a method which is feasible, available and likely to correct the hazard. The information shall indicate that the recognized hazard, rather than a particular accident, is preventable.

  2 If the proposed abatement method would eliminate or significantly reduce the hazard beyond whatever measures the employer may be taking, a Section 5(a)(1) citation may be issued. A citation shall not be issued merely because the agency knows of an abatement method different from that of the employer, if the agency's method would not reduce the hazard significantly more than the employer's method. It must also be noted that in some cases only a series of abatement methods will alleviate a hazard. In such a case all the abatement methods shall be mentioned.

(3) **Limitations on Use of the General Duty Clause.** Section 5(a)(1) is to be used only within the guidelines given in C.2.c. of this chapter.

(a) Section 5(a)(1) may be cited in the alternative when a standard is also cited to cover a situation where there is doubt as to whether the standard applies to the hazard.

(b) Section 5(a)(1) violations shall not be grouped together, but may be grouped with a related violation of a specific standard.

(c) Section 5(a)(1) shall not normally be used to impose a stricter requirement than that required by the standard. For example, if the standard provides for a permissible exposure limit (PEL) of 5 ppm, even if data establishes that a 3 ppm level is a recognized hazard, Section 5(a)(1) shall not be cited to require that the 3 ppm level be achieved unless the limits are based on different health effects. If the standard has only a time-weighted average permissible exposure level and the hazard involves exposure above a recognized ceiling level, the Area Director shall consult with the Regional Solicitor.

    NOTE: An exception to this rule may apply if it can be documented that "an employer knows a particular safety or health standard is inadequate to protect his workers against the specific hazard it is intended to address." **International Union, U.A.W. v. General Dynamics Land Systems Div.,** 815 F.2d 1570 (D.C. Cir. 1987). Such cases shall be subject to pre-citation review.

(d) Section 5(a)(1) shall normally not be used to require an abatement method not set forth in a specific standard. If a toxic substance standard covers engineering control requirements but not requirements for medical surveillance, Section 5(a)(1) shall not be cited to require medical surveillance.

(e) Section 5(a)(1) shall not be used to enforce "should" standards.

(f) Section 5(a)(1) shall not normally be used to cover categories of hazards exempted by a standard. If, however, the exemption is in place because the drafters of the standard (or source document) declined to deal with the exempt category for reasons other than the lack of a hazard, the general duty clause may be cited if all the necessary elements for such a citation are present.

(4) **Pre-Citation Review.** Section 5(a)(1) citations shall undergo a pre-citation review following established area office procedures when required by the Area Director or Assistant Area Director.

    NOTE: If a standard does not apply and all criteria for issuing a Section 5(a)(1) citation are not met, but it is determined that the hazard warrants some type of notification, a letter shall be sent to the employer and the employee representative describing the hazard and suggesting corrective action.

d. **Willful Violations.** The following definitions and procedures apply whenever the CSHO suspects that a willful violation may exist:

(1) A willful violation exists under the Act where the evidence shows either an intentional violation of the Act or plain indifference to its requirements.

(a) The employer committed an intentional and knowing violation if:

  1 An employer representative was aware of the requirements of the Act, or the existence of an applicable standard or regulation, and was also aware of a condition or practice in violation of those requirements, and did not abate the hazard.

  2 An employer representative was not aware of the requirements of the Act or standards, but was aware of a comparable legal requirement (e.g., state or local law) and was also aware of a condition or practice in violation of that requirement, and did not abate the hazard.

(b) The employer committed a violation with plain indifference to the law where:

  1 Higher management officials were aware of an OSHA requirement applicable to the company's business but made little or no effort to communicate the requirement to lower level supervisors and employees.

  2 Company officials were aware of a continuing compliance problem but made little or no effort to avoid violations.

    EXAMPLE: Repeated issuance of citations addressing the same or similar conditions.

  3 An employer representative was not aware of any legal requirement, but was aware that a condition or practice was hazardous to the safety or health of employees and made little or no effort to determine the extent

of the problem or to take the corrective action. Knowledge of a hazard may be gained from such means as insurance company reports, safety committee or other internal reports, the occurrence of illnesses or injuries, media coverage, or, in some cases, complaints of employees or their representatives.

4   Finally, in particularly flagrant situations, willfulness can be found despite lack of knowledge of either a legal requirement or the existence of a hazard if the circumstances show that the employer would have placed no importance on such knowledge even if he or she had possessed it, or had no concern for the health or safety of employees.

(2) It is not necessary that the violation be committed with a bad purpose or an evil intent to be deemed "willful." It is sufficient that the violation was deliberate, voluntary or intentional as distinguished from inadvertent, accidental or ordinarily negligent.

(3) The CSHO shall carefully develop and record, during the inspection, all evidence available that indicates employer awareness of and the disregard for statutory obligations or of the hazardous conditions. Willfulness could exist if an employer is advised by employees or employee representatives of an alleged hazardous condition and the employer makes no reasonable effort to verify and correct the condition. Additional factors which can influence a decision as to whether violations are willful include:

(a) The nature of the employer's business and the knowledge regarding safety and health matters which could reasonably be expected in the industry.

(b) The precautions taken by the employer to limit the hazardous conditions.

(c) The employer's awareness of the Act and of the responsibility to provide safe and healthful working conditions.

(d) Whether similar violations and/or hazardous conditions have been brought to the attention of the employer.

(e) Whether the nature and extent of the violations disclose a **purposeful disregard** of the employer's responsibility under the Act.

(4) If the Area Office cannot determine whether to issue a citation as a willful or a repeat violation due to the raising of difficult issues of law and policy which will require the evaluation of complex factual situations, the Area Director shall normally consult with the Regional Solicitor.

e. **Criminal/Willful Violations.** Section 17(e) of the Act provides that: "Any employer who willfully violates any standard, rule or order promulgated pursuant to Section 6 of this Act, or of any regulations prescribed pursuant to this Act, and that violation caused death to any employee, shall, upon conviction, be punished by a fine of not more than $10,000 or by imprisonment for not more than six months, or by both; except that if the conviction is for a violation committed after a first conviction of such person, punishment shall be a fine of not more than $20,000 or by imprisonment for not more than one year, or by both."

(1) The Area Director, in coordination with the Regional Solicitor, shall carefully evaluate all willful cases involving worker deaths to determine whether they may involve criminal violations of Section 17(e) of the Act. Because the nature of the evidence available is of paramount importance in an investigation of this type, there shall be early and close liaison between the OSHA investigator, the Area Director, the Regional Administrator, and the Regional Solicitor in developing any finding which might involve a violation of Section 17(e) of the Act.

(2) The following criteria shall be considered in investigating possible criminal/willful violations:

(a) In order to establish a criminal/willful violation OSHA must prove that:

1   The employer violated an OSHA standard. A criminal/willful violation cannot be based on violation of Section 5(a)(1)

2   The violation was willful in nature.

3   The violation of the standard caused the death of an employee. In order to prove that the violation of the standard caused the death of an employee, there must be evidence in the file which clearly demonstrates that the violation of the standard was the cause of or a contributing factor to an employee's death.

(b) Although it is generally not necessary to issue "Miranda" warnings to an employer when a criminal/willful investigation is in progress, the Area Director shall seek the advice of the Regional Solicitor on this question.

(c) Following the investigation, if the Area Director decides to recommend criminal prosecution, a memorandum containing that recommendation shall be forwarded promptly to the Regional Administrator. It shall include an evaluation of the possible criminal charges, taking into consideration the greater burden of proof which requires that the Government's case be proven beyond a reasonable doubt. In addition, if the correction of the hazardous condition appears to be an issue, this shall be noted in the transmittal memorandum because in most cases the prosecution of a criminal/willful case delays the affirmance of the civil citation and its correction requirements.

(d) The Area Director shall normally issue a civil citation in accordance with current procedures even if the citation involves allegations under consideration for criminal prosecution. The Regional Administrator shall be notified of such cases, and they shall be forwarded to the Regional Solicitor as soon as practicable for possible referral to the U.S. Department of Justice.

(3) When a willful violation is related to a fatality, the Area Director shall ensure the case file contains succinct documentation regarding the decision **not** to make a criminal referral. The documentation should indicate which elements of a criminal violation make the case unsuitable for criminal referral.

f. **Repeated Violations.** An employer may be cited for a repeated violation if that employer has been cited previously for a **substantially similar condition** and the citation has become a final order.

(1) **Identical Standard.** Generally, similar conditions can be demonstrated by showing that in both situations the identical standard was violated.

EXCEPTION: Previously a citation was issued for a violation of 29 CFR 1910.132(a) for not requiring the use of safety-toe footwear for employees. A recent inspection of the same establishment revealed a violation of 29 CFR 1910.132(a) for not requiring the use of head protection (hard hats). Although the same standard was involved, the hazardous conditions found were not substantially similar and therefore a repeated violation would not be appropriate.

(2) **Different Standards.** In some circumstances, similar conditions can be demonstrated when different standards are violated. Although there may be different standards involved, the hazardous conditions found could be substantially similar and therefore a repeated violation would be appropriate.

(3) **Time limitations.** Although there are no statutory limitations upon the length of time that a citation may serve as a basis for a repeated violation, the following policy shall be used in order to ensure uniformity.

  (a) A citation will be issued as a repeated violation if:

    1 The citation is issued within 3 years of the final order of the previous citation, or,

    2 The citation is issued within 3 years of the final abatement date of that citation, whichever is later.

  (b) When a violation is found during an inspection, and a repeated citation has been issued for a substantially similar condition which meets the above time limitations, the violation may be classified as a second instance repeated violation with a corresponding increase in penalty (see Chapter IV, C.2.l.).

  (c) For any further repetition, the Area Director shall be consulted for guidance.

(4) **Obtaining Inspection History.** For purposes of determining whether a violation is repeated, the following criteria shall apply:

  (a) **High Gravity Serious Violations.** When high gravity serious violations are to be cited, the Area Director shall obtain a history of citations previously issued to this employer at all of its identified establishments, nationwide, (Federal enforcement only) within the same two-digit SIC code. If these violations have been previously cited within the time limitations described in C.2.f.(3), above, and have become a final order of the Review Commission, a repeated citation may be issued. Under special circumstances, the Area Director, in consultation with the Regional Solicitor, may also issue citations for repeated violations without regard for the SIC code.

  (b) **Violations of Lesser Gravity.** When violations of lesser gravity than high gravity serious are to be cited, Agency policy is to encourage the Area Director to obtain a national inspection history whenever the circumstances of the current inspection will result in a large number of serious, repeat, or willful citations. This is particularly so if the employer is known to have establishments nationwide and if significant citations have been issued against the employer in other areas, or at other mobile worksites.

  (c) **Geographical limitations.** Where a national inspection history has **not** been obtained, the following criteria regarding geographical limitations shall apply:

    1 **Multifacility Employer.** A multifacility employer shall be cited for a repeated violation if the violation recurred at any worksite within the same OSHA Area Office jurisdiction.

    EXAMPLE: Where the construction site extends over a large area and/or the scope of the job is unclear (such as road building), that portion of the workplace specified in the employer's contract which falls within the Area Office jurisdiction is the establishment. If an employer has several worksites within the same Area Office jurisdiction, a citation of a violation at Site A will serve as the basis for a repeated citation in Area B.

    2 **Longshoring Establishment.** A longshoring establishment will encompass all longshoring activities of a single stevedore within any single port area. Longshoring employers are subject to repeated violation citations based on prior violations occurring anywhere. Other maritime employers covered by OSHA standards (e.g., shipbuilding, ship repairing) are multifacility employers as defined in **a.**, above.

(5) **Repeated vs. Willful.** Repeated violations differ from willful violations in that they may result from an inadvertent, accidental or ordinarily negligent act. Where a repeated violation may also meet the criteria for willful but not clearly so, a citation for a repeated violation shall normally be issued.

(6) **Repeated vs. Failure to Abate.** A failure to abate situation exists when an item of equipment or condition previously cited has never been brought into compliance and is noted at a later inspection. If, however, the violation was not continuous (i.e., if it had been corrected and then reoccurred), the subsequent occurrence is a repeated violation.

(7) Alleged Violation Description (AVD). If a repeated citation is issued, the CSHO must ensure that the cited employer is fully informed of the previous violations serving as a basis for the repeated citation, by notation in the AVD portion of the citation, using the following or similar language:

THE (COMPANY NAME) WAS PREVIOUSLY CITED FOR A VIOLATION OF THIS OCCUPATIONAL SAFETY AND HEALTH STANDARD OR ITS EQUIVALENT STANDARD (NAME PREVIOUSLY CITED STANDARD) WHICH WAS CONTAINED IN OSHA INSPECTION NUMBER_____, CITATION NUMBER_____, ITEM NUMBER_____, ISSUED ON (DATE), WITH RESPECT TO A WORKPLACE LOCATED AT _____.

g. **De Minimis Violations.** De Minimis violations are violations of standards which have no direct or immediate relationship to safety or health and shall not be included in citations. An OSHA-1B/1BIH is no longer required to be completed for De Minimis violations. The employer should be verbally notified of the violation and the CSHO should note it in the inspection case file. The criteria for finding a de minimis violation are as follows:

(1) An employer complies with the clear intent of the standard but deviates from its particular requirements in a manner that has no direct or immediate relationship to employee safety or health. These deviations may involve distance specifications, construction material requirements, use of incorrect color, minor variations from recordkeeping, testing, or inspection regulations, or the like.

EXAMPLE #1: 29 CFR 1910.27(b)(1)(ii) allows 12 inches (30 centimeters) as the maximum distance between ladder rungs. Where the rungs are 13 inches (33 centimeters) apart, the condition is de minimis.

EXAMPLE #2: 29 CFR 1910.28(a)(3) requires guarding on all open sides of scaffolds. Where employees are tied off with safety belts in lieu of guarding, often the intent of the standard will be met, and the absence of guarding may be de minimis.

EXAMPLE #3: 29 CFR 1910.217(e)(1)(ii) requires that mechanical power presses be inspected and tested at least weekly. If the machinery is seldom used, inspection and testing prior to each use is adequate to meet the intent of the standard.

(2) An employer complies with a proposed standard or amendment or a consensus standard rather than with the standard in effect at the time of the inspection and the employer's action clearly provides equal or greater employee protection or the employer complies with a written interpretation issued by the OSHA Regional or National Office.

(3) An employer's workplace is at the "state of the art" which is technically beyond the requirements of the applicable standard and provides equivalent or more effective employee safety or health protection.

3. **Health Standard Violations.**

   a. **Citation of Ventilation Standards.** In cases where a citation of a ventilation standard may be appropriate, consideration shall be given to standards intended to control exposure to recognized hazardous levels of air contaminants, to prevent fire or explosions, or to regulate operations which may involve confined space or specific hazardous conditions. In applying these standards, the following guidelines shall be observed:

     (1) **Health-Related Ventilation Standards.** An employer is considered in compliance with a health-related airflow ventilation standard when the employee exposure does not exceed appropriate airborne contaminant standards; e.g., the PELs prescribed in 29 CFR 1910.1000.

       (a) Where an over-exposure to an airborne contaminant is detected, the appropriate air contaminant engineering control requirement shall be cited; e.g., 29 CFR 1910.1000(e). In no case shall citations of this standard be issued for the purpose of requiring specific volumes of air to ventilate such exposures.

       (b) Other requirements contained in health-related ventilation standards shall be evaluated without regard to the concentration of airborne contaminants. Where a specific standard has been violated **and** an actual or potential hazard has been documented, a citation shall be issued.

     (2) **Fire. and Explosion-Related Ventilation Standards.** Although they are not technically health violations, the following guidelines shall be observed when citing fire. and explosion-related ventilation standards:

       (a) **Adequate Ventilation.** In the application of fire. and explosion. related ventilation standards, OSHA considers that an operation has **adequate** ventilation when both of the following criteria are met:

        1 The requirement of the specific standard has been met.

        2 The concentration of flammable vapors is 25 percent or less of the lower explosive limit (LEL).

        EXCEPTION: Certain standards specify violations when 10 percent of the LEL is exceeded. These standards are found in maritime and construction exposures.

       (b) **Citation Policy.** If 25 percent (10 percent when specified for maritime or construction operations) of the LEL has been exceeded and:

        1 The standard requirements have not been met, the standard violation normally shall be cited as serious.

        2 There is no applicable specific ventilation standard, Section 5(a)(1) of the Act shall be cited in accordance with the guidelines given in C.2.c. of this chapter.

   b. **Violations of the Noise Standard.** Current enforcement policy regarding 29 CFR 1910.95(b)(1) allows employers to rely on personal protective equipment and a hearing conservation program rather than engineering and/or administrative controls when hearing protectors will effectively attenuate the noise to which the employee is exposed to acceptable levels as specified in Tables G-16 or G-16a of the standard.

     (1) Citations for violations of 29 CFR 1910.95(b)(1) shall be issued when engineering and/or administrative controls are feasible, both technically and economically; and

       (a) Employee exposure levels are so high that hearing protectors alone may not reliably reduce noise levels received by the employee's ear to the levels specified in Tables G-16 or G-16a of the standard. Given the present state of the art, hearing protectors which offer the greatest attenuation may not reliably be used when employee exposure levels border on 100 dBA (See OSHA Instruction CPL 2-2.35A, Appendix.); or

       (b) The costs of engineering and/or administrative controls are less than the cost of an effective hearing conservation program

     (2) A control is not reasonably necessary when an employer has an ongoing hearing conservation program and the results of audiometric testing indicate that existing controls and hearing protectors are adequately protecting employees. (In making this decision such factors as the exposure levels in question, the number of employees tested, and the duration of the testing program shall be taken into consideration.)

     (3) When employee noise exposures are less than 100 dBA but the employer does not have an ongoing hearing conservation program or the results of audiometric testing indicate that the employer's existing program is not working, the CSHO shall consider whether:

       (a) Reliance on an effective hearing conservation program would be less costly than engineering and/or administrative controls.

       (b) An effective hearing conservation program can be established or improvements can be made in an existing hearing conservation program which could bring the employer into compliance with Tables G-16 or G-16a.

       (c) Engineering and/or administrative controls are both technically and economically feasible.

     (4) If noise levels received by the employee's ear can be reduced to the levels specified in Tables G-16 or G-16a by means of hearing protectors and an effective hearing conservation program, citations under the hearing conservation shall normally be issued rather than citations requiring engineering controls. If improvements in the hearing conservation program cannot be made or, if made, cannot be expected to reduce exposure sufficiently and feasible controls exist, a citation under 1910.95(b)(1) shall normally be issued.

     (5) When hearing protection is required but not used and employee exposure exceeds the limits of Table G-16, 29 CFR 1910.95(i)(2)(i) shall be cited and classified as serious (see (8), below) whether or not the employer has instituted a hearing conservation program. 29 CFR 1910.95(a) shall no longer be cited except in the case of the oil and gas drilling industry.

     NOTE: Citations of 29 CFR 1910.95(i)(2)(ii)(b) shall also be classified as serious.

     (6) If an employer has instituted a hearing conservation program and a violation of the hearing conservation amendment (other than 1910.95 (i)(2)(i) or (i)(2)(ii)(b)) is found, a citation shall be issued if employee noise exposures equal or exceed an 8-hour time-weighted average of 85 dB.

     (7) If the employer has not instituted a hearing conservation program and employee noise exposures equal or exceed an 8-hour time-weighted average of 85 dB, a citation for 1910.95(c) only shall be issued.

     (8) Violations of 1910.95(i)(2)(i) from the hearing conservation amendment may be grouped with violations of 29 CFR 1910.95(b)(1) and classified as serious when an employee is exposed to noise levels above the limits of Table G-16 and:

(a) Hearing protection is not utilized or is not adequate to prevent overexposure to an employee; or

(b) There is evidence of hearing loss which could reasonably be considered:

1 To be work-related, and

2 To have been preventable, at least to some degree, if the employer had been in compliance with the cited provisions.

(9) When an employee is overexposed but effective hearing protection is being provided and used, an effective hearing conservation program has been implemented and no feasible engineering or administrative controls exist, a citation shall not be issued.

c. **Violations of the Respirator Standard.** When considering a citation for respirator violations, the following guidelines shall be observed:

(1) **In Situations Where Overexposure Does Not Occur.** Where an overexposure has not been established:

(a) But an improper type of respirator is being used (e.g., a dust respirator being used to reduce exposure to organic vapors), a citation under 29 CFR 1910.134(b)(2) shall be issued, provided the CSHO documents that an overexposure is possible.

(b) And one or more of the other requirements of 29 CFR 1910.134 is not being met; e.g., an unapproved respirator is being used to reduce exposure to toxic dusts, generally a de minimis violation shall be recorded in accordance with OSHA procedures. (Note that this policy does **not** include emergency use respirators.) The CSHO shall advise the employer of the elements of a good respirator program as required under 29 CFR 1910.134.

(c) In **exceptional** circumstances a citation may be warranted if an adverse health condition due to the respirator itself could be supported and documented. Examples may include a dirty respirator that is causing dermatitis, a worker's health being jeopardized by wearing a respirator due to an inadequately evaluated medical condition or a significant ingestion hazard created by an improperly cleaned respirator.

(2) **In Situations Where Overexposure Does Occur.** In cases where an overexposure to an air contaminant has been established, the following principles apply to citations of 1910.134:

(a) 29 CFR 1910.134(a)(2) is the general section requiring employers to provide respirators "... when such equipment is necessary to protect the health of the employee" and requiring the establishment and maintenance of a respiratory protection program which meets the requirements outlined in 29 CFR 1910.134(b). Thus, if no respiratory program at all has been established, 1910.134(a)(2) alone shall be cited; if a program has been established and some, but not all, of the requirements under 1910.134(b) are being met, the specific standards under 1910.134(b) that are applicable shall be cited.

(b) An acceptable respiratory protection program includes all of the elements of 29 CFR 1910.134; however, the standard is structured such that essentially the same requirement is often specified in more than one section. In these cases, the section which most adequately describes the violation shall be cited.

d. **Additive and Synergistic Effects.**

(1) Substances which have a known additive effect and, therefore, result in a greater probability/severity of risk when found in combination shall be evaluated using the formula found in 29 CFR _ 1910.1000(d)(2). The use of this formula requires that the exposures have an additive effect on the same body organ or system.

(2) If the CSHO suspects that synergistic effects are possible, it shall be brought to the attention of the supervisor, who shall refer the question to the Regional Administrator. If it is decided that there is a synergistic effect of the substances found together, the violations shall be grouped, when appropriate, for purposes of increasing the violation classification severity and/or the penalty.

e. **Absorption and Ingestion Hazards.** The following guidelines apply when citing absorption and ingestion violations. Such citations do **not** depend on measurements of airborne concentrations, but shall normally be supported by wipe sampling.

(1) Citations under 29 CFR 1910.132, 1910.141 and/or Section 5(a)(1) may be issued when there is reasonable probability that employees will be exposed to these hazards.

(2) Where, for any substance, a serious hazard is determined to exist due to the potential of ingestion or absorption of the substance for reasons other than the consumption of contaminated food or drink (e.g., smoking materials contaminated with the toxic substance), a serious citation shall be considered under Section 5(a)(1) of the Act.

f. **Biological Monitoring.** If the employer has been conducting biological monitoring, the CSHO shall evaluate the results of such testing. The results may assist in determining whether a significant quantity of the toxic material is being ingested or absorbed through the skin.

4. Writing Citations.

a. **General.** Section 9 of the Act controls the writing of citations.

(1) **Section 9(a).** "... the Secretary or his authorized representative ... shall with reasonable promptness issue a citation to the employer." To facilitate the prompt issuance of citations, the Area Director may issue citations which are unrelated to health inspection air sampling, prior to receipt of sampling results.

(2) **Section 9(c).** "No citation may be issued ... after the expiration of six months following the occurrence of any violation." Accordingly, a citation shall not be issued where any violation alleged therein last occurred 6 months or more prior to the date on which the citation is actually signed and dated. Where the actions or omissions of the employer concealed the existence of the violation, the time limitation is suspended until such time that OSHA learns or could have learned of the violation. The Regional Solicitor shall be consulted in such cases.

b. **Alternative Standards.**

(1) In rare cases, the same factual situation may present a possible violation of more than one standard. For example, the facts which support a violation of 29 CFR 1910.28(a)(1) may also support a violation of 1910.132(a) if no scaffolding is provided when it should be and the use of safety belts is not required by the employer.

(2) Where it appears that more than one standard is applicable to a given factual situation and that compliance with any of the applicable standards would effectively eliminate the hazard, it is permissible to cite alternative standards using the words "in the alternative." A reference in the citation to each of the standards involved shall be accompanied by a separate Alleged Violation Description (AVD) which clearly alleges all of the necessary elements of a violation of that standard. Only one penalty shall be proposed for the violative condition.

5. **Combining and Grouping of Violations.**

a. **Combining.** Violations of a single standard having the same classification found during the inspection of an establishment or worksite generally shall be combined into one alleged citation item. Different options of the same standard shall normally also be combined. Each instance of the violation shall be separately set out within that item of the citation. Other-than-serious violations of a standard may be combined with serious violations of the same standard when appropriate.

   NOTE: Except for standards which deal with multiple hazards (e.g., Tables Z-1, Z-2 and Z-3 cited under 29 CFR 1910.1000 (a), (b), or (c)), the same standard may not be cited more than once on a single citation. The same standard may be cited on different citations on the same inspection, however.

b. **Grouping.** When a source of a **hazard** is identified which involves interrelated violations of different standards, the violations may be grouped into a single item. The following situations normally call for grouping violations:

   (1) **Grouping Related Violations.** When the CSHO believes that violations classified either as serious or as other-than-serious are so closely related as to constitute a single hazardous condition.

   (2) **Grouping Other-Than-Serious Violations Where Grouping Results in a Serious Violation.** When two or more individual violations are found which, if considered individually represent other-than-serious violations, but if grouped create a substantial probability of death or serious physical harm.

   (3) **Where Grouping Results in Higher Gravity Other-Than-Serious Violation.** Where the CSHO finds during the course of the inspection that a number of other-than-serious violations are present in the same piece of equipment which, considered in relation to each other affect the overall gravity of possible injury resulting from an accident involving the combined violations.

   (4) **Violations of Posting and Recordkeeping Requirements.** Violations of the posting and recordkeeping requirements which involve the same document; e.g., OSHA-200 Form was not posted or maintained. (See Chapter IV, C.2.n. for penalty amounts.)

   (5) **Penalties for Grouped Violations.** If penalties are to be proposed for grouped violations, the penalty shall be written across from the first violation item appearing on the OSHA-2.

c. **When Not to Group.** Times when grouping is normally inappropriate.

   (1) **Multiple Inspections.** Violations discovered in multiple inspections of a single establishment or worksite may not be grouped. An inspection in the same establishment or at the same worksite shall be considered a single inspection even if it continues for a period of more than one day or is discontinued with the intention of resuming it after a short period of time if only one OSHA-1 is completed.

   (2) **Separate Establishments of the Same Employer.** Where inspections are conducted, either at the same time or different times, at two establishments of the same employer and instances of the same violation are discovered during each inspection, the employer shall be issued separate citations for each establishment. The violations shall not be grouped.

   (3) **General Duty Clause Violations.** Because Section 5(a)(1) of the Act is cited so as to cover all aspects of a serious hazard for which no standard exists, **no** grouping of separate Section 5(a)(1) violations is permitted. This provision, however, does not prohibit grouping a Section 5(a)(1) violation with a related violation of a specific standard.

   (4) **Egregious Violations.** Violations which are proposed as violation-by-violation citations shall **not** normally be combined or grouped. (See OSHA Instruction CPL 2.80.)

6. This paragraph has been replaced by a revised multi-employer policy contained in OSHA Instruction CPL 2-0.124. ~~Multiemployer Worksites. On multiemployer worksites, both construction and non-construction, citations normally shall be issued to employers whose employees are exposed to hazards (the exposing employer).~~

   a. ~~Additionally, the following employers normally shall be cited, whether or not their own employees are exposed, but see C.2.c.(2)(a)2 of this chapter for Section 5(a)(1) violation guidance:~~

      (1) ~~The employer who actually creates the hazard (the creating employer);~~

      (2) ~~The employer who is responsible, by contract or through actual practice, for safety and health conditions on the worksite; i.e., the employer who has the authority for ensuring that the hazardous condition is corrected (the controlling employer);~~

      (3) ~~The employer who has the responsibility for actually correcting the hazard (the correcting employer).~~

   b. ~~Prior to issuing citations to an exposing employer, it must first be determined whether the available facts indicate that employer has a legitimate defense to the citation, as set forth below:~~

      (1) ~~The employer did not create the hazard;~~

      (2) ~~The employer did not have the responsibility or the authority to have the hazard corrected;~~

      (3) ~~The employer did not have the ability to correct or remove the hazard;~~

      (4) ~~The employer can demonstrate that the creating, the controlling and/or the correcting employers, as appropriate, have been specifically notified of the hazards to which his/her employees are exposed;~~

      (5) ~~The employer has instructed his/her employees to recognize the hazard and, where necessary, informed them how to avoid the dangers associated with it.~~

         (a) ~~Where feasible, an exposing employer must have taken appropriate alternative means of protecting employees from the hazard.~~

         (b) ~~When extreme circumstances justify it, the exposing employer shall have removed his/her employees from the job to avoid citation.~~

   c. ~~If an exposing employer meets all these defenses, that employer shall not be cited. If all employers on a worksite with employees exposed to a hazard meet these conditions, then the citation shall be issued only to the employers who are responsible for creating the hazard and/or who are in the best position to correct the hazard or to ensure its correction. In such circumstances the controlling employer and/or the hazard-creating employer shall be cited even though no employees of those employers are exposed to the violative condition. Penalties for such citations shall be appropriately calculated, using the exposed employees of all employers as the number of employees for probability assessment.~~

7. **Employer/Employee Responsibilities.**

    a. Section 5(b) of the Act states: "Each employee shall comply with occupational safety and health standards and all rules, regulations, and orders issued pursuant to the Act which are applicable to his own actions and conduct." The Act does not provide for the issuance of citations or the proposal of penalties against employees. Employers are responsible for employee compliance with the standards.

    b. In cases where the CSHO determines that employees are systematically refusing to comply with a standard applicable to their own actions and conduct, the matter shall be referred to the Area Director who shall consult with the Regional Administrator.

    c. Under no circumstances is the CSHO to become involved in an **onsite** dispute involving labor-management issues or interpretation of collective-bargaining agreements. The CSHO is expected to obtain enough information to understand whether the employer is using all appropriate authority to ensure compliance with the Act. Concerted refusals to comply will not bar the issuance of an appropriate citation where the employer has failed to exercise full authority to the maximum extent reasonable, including discipline and discharge.

8. **Affirmative Defenses.**

    a. **Definition.** An affirmative defense is any matter which, if established by the employer, will excuse the employer from a violation which has otherwise been proved by the CSHO.

    b. **Burden of Proof.** Although affirmative defenses must be proved by the employer at the time of the hearing, OSHA must be prepared to respond whenever the employer is likely to raise or actually does raise an argument supporting such a defense. The CSHO, therefore, shall keep in mind the potential affirmative defenses that the employer may make and attempt to gather contrary evidence when a statement made during the inspection fairly raises a defense. The CSHO should bring the documentation of the hazards and facts related to possible affirmative defenses to the attention of the Assistant Area Director. Where it appears that each and every element of an affirmative defense is present, the Area Director may decide that a citation is not warranted.

    c. **Explanations.** The following are explanations of the more common affirmative defenses with which the CSHO shall become familiar. There are other affirmative defenses besides these, but they are less frequently raised or are such that the facts which can be gathered during the inspection are minimal.

        (1) **Unpreventable Employee Misconduct or "Isolated Event".** The violative condition was:

            (a) Unknown to the employer; and

            (b) In violation of an adequate work rule which was effectively communicated and uniformly enforced.

                EXAMPLE: An unguarded table saw is observed. The saw, however, has a guard which is reattached while the CSHO watches. Facts which the CSHO shall document may include: Who removed the guard and why? Did the employer know that the guard had been removed? How long or how often had the saw been used without guards? Did the employer have a work rule that the saw guards not be removed? How was the work rule communicated? Was the work rule enforced?

        (2) **Impossibility.** Compliance with the requirements of a standard is:

            (a) Functionally impossible or would prevent performances of required work; and

            (b) There are no alternative means of employee protection.

                EXAMPLE: During the course of the inspection an unguarded table saw is observed. The employer states that the nature of its work makes a guard unworkable. Facts which the CSHO shall document may include: Would a guard make performance of the work impossible or merely more difficult? Could a guard be used part of the time? Has the employer attempted to use guards? Has the employer considered alternative means or methods of avoiding or reducing the hazard?

        (3) **Greater Hazard.** Compliance with a standard would result in greater hazards to employees than noncompliance and:

            (a) There are no alternative means of employee protection; and

            (b) An application of a variance would be inappropriate.

                EXAMPLE: The employer indicates that a saw guard had been removed because it caused particles to be thrown into the operator's face. Facts which the CSHO shall consider may include: Was the guard used properly? Would a different type of guard eliminate the problem? How often was the operator struck by particles and what kind of injuries resulted? Would safety glasses, a face mask, or a transparent shelf attached to the saw prevent injury? Was operator technique at fault and did the employer attempt to correct it? Was a variance sought?

        (4) **Multiemployer Worksites.** Refer to C.6. of this chapter.

CHAPTER IV
POST-INSPECTION PROCEDURES

A. Abatement.

1. **Period.** The abatement period shall be the shortest interval within which the employer can **reasonably** be expected to correct the violation. An abatement date shall be set forth in the citation as a specific date, not a number of days. When the abatement period is very short (i.e., 5 working days or less) and it is uncertain when the employer will receive the citation, the abatement date shall be set so as to allow for a mail delay and the agreed-upon abatement time. When abatement has been witnessed by the CSHO during the inspection, the abatement period shall be "Corrected During Inspection" on the citation.

2. **Reasonable Abatement Date.** The establishment of the shortest practicable abatement date requires the exercise of professional judgment on the part of the CSHO.

        NOTE: Abatement periods exceeding 30 calendar days should not normally be necessary, particularly for safety violations. Situations may arise, however, especially for health violations, where extensive structural changes are necessary or where new equipment or parts cannot be delivered within 30 calendar days. When an initial abatement date is granted that is in excess of 30 calendar days, the reason, if not self-evident, shall be documented in the case file.

3. Verification of Abatement. The Area Director is responsible for determining if abatement has been accomplished. When abatement is not accomplished during the inspection or the employer does not notify the Area Director by letter of the abatement, verification shall be determined by telephone and documented in the case file.

NOTE: If the employer's abatement letter indicates that a condition has not been abated, but the date has passed, the Area Director shall contact the employer for an explanation. The Area Director shall explain Petition for Modification of Abatement (PMA) procedures to the employer, if applicable.

4. **Effect of Contest Upon Abatement Period.** In situations where an employer contests either (1) the period set for abatement or (2) the citation itself, the abatement period generally shall be considered not to have begun until there has been an affirmation of the citation and abatement period. In accordance with the Act, the abatement period begins when a final order of the Review Commission is issued, and this abatement period is not tolled while an appeal to the court is ongoing unless the employer has been granted a stay. In situations where there is an employee contest of the abatement date, the abatement requirements of the citation remain unchanged.

   a. Where an employer has contested only the proposed penalty, the abatement period continues to run unaffected by the contest.

   b. Where the employer does not contest, he must abide by the date set forth in the citation even if such date is within the 15-working-day notice of contest period. Therefore, when the abatement period designated in the citation is 15 working days or less and a notice of contest has not been filed, a followup inspection of the worksite may be conducted for purposes of determining whether abatement has been achieved within the time period set forth in the citation. A failure to abate notice may be issued on the basis of the CSHO's findings.

   c. Where the employer has filed a notice of contest to the initial citation within the contest period, the abatement period does not begin to run until the entry of a final Review Commission order. Under these circumstances, any followup inspection within the contest period shall be discontinued and a failure to abate notice shall not be issued.

   NOTE: There is one exception to the above rule. If an early abatement date has been designated in the initial citation and it is the opinion of the CSHO and/or the Area Director that a situation classified as imminent danger is presented by the cited condition, appropriate imminent danger proceedings may be initiated notwithstanding the filing of a notice of contest by the employer.

   d. If an employer contests an abatement date in good faith, a Failure to Abate Notice shall not be issued for the item contested until a final order affirming a date is entered, the new abatement period, if any, has been completed, and the employer has still failed to abate.

5. **Long-Term Abatement Date for Implementation of Feasible Engineering Controls.** Long-term abatement is abatement which will be completed more than one year from the citation issuance date. In situations where it is difficult to set a specific abatement date when the citation is originally issued; e.g., because of extensive redesign requirements consequent upon the employer's decision to implement feasible engineering controls and uncertainty as to when the job can be finished, the CSHO shall discuss the problem with the employer at the closing conference and, in appropriate cases, shall encourage the employer to seek an informal conference with the Area Director.

   a. **Final Abatement Date.** The CSHO and the Assistant Area Director shall make their best judgment as to a reasonable abatement date. A specific date for final abatement shall, in all cases, be included in the citation. The employer shall not be permitted to propose an abatement plan setting its own abatement dates. If necessary, an appropriate petition may be submitted later by the employer to the Area Director to modify the abatement date. (See D.2. of this chapter for PMA's.)

   b. **Employer Abatement Plan.** The employer is required to submit an abatement plan outlining the anticipated long-term abatement procedures.

   NOTE: A statement agreeing to provide the affected Area Offices with written periodic progress reports shall be part of the long-term abatement plan.

6. **Feasible Administrative, Work Practice and Engineering Controls.** Where applicable, the CSHO shall discuss control methodology with the employer during the closing conference.

   a. Definitions.

   (1) **Engineering Controls.** Engineering controls consist of substitution, isolation, ventilation and equipment modification.

   (2) **Administrative Controls.** Any procedure which significantly limits daily exposure by control or manipulation of the work schedule or manner in which work is performed is considered a means of administrative control. The use of personal protective equipment is not considered a means of administrative control.

   (3) **Work Practice Controls.** Work practice controls are a type of administrative controls by which the employer modifies the manner in which the employee performs assigned work. Such modification may result in a reduction of exposure through such methods as changing work habits, improving sanitation and hygiene practices, or making other changes in the way the employee performs the job.

   (4) **Feasibility.** Abatement measures required to correct a citation item are feasible when they can be accomplished by the employer. The CSHO, following current directions and guidelines, shall inform the employer, where appropriate, that a determination will be made as to whether engineering or administrative controls are feasible.

   (a) **Technical Feasibility.** Technical feasibility is the existence of technical know-how as to materials and methods available or adaptable to specific circumstances which can be applied to cited violations with a reasonable possibility that employee exposure to occupational hazards will be reduced.

   (b) **Economic Feasibility.** Economic feasibility means that the employer is financially able to undertake the measures necessary to abate the citations received.

   NOTE: If an employer's level of compliance lags significantly behind that of its industry, allegations of economic infeasibility will not be accepted.

   b. **Responsibilities.**

   (1) The CSHO shall document the underlying facts which give rise to an employer's claim of infeasibility.

   (a) When economic infeasibility is claimed the CSHO shall inform the employer that, although the cost of corrective measures to be taken will generally not be considered as a factor in the issuance of a citation, it may be considered during an informal conference or during settlement negotiations.

   (b) Serious issues of feasibility should be referred to the Area Director for determination.

   (2) The Area Director is responsible for making determinations that engineering or administrative controls are or are not feasible.

c. **Reducing Employee Exposure.** Whenever feasible engineering, administrative or work practice controls can be instituted even though they are not sufficient to eliminate the hazard (or to reduce exposure to or below the permissible exposure limit (PEL)). Nonetheless, they are required in conjunction with personal protective equipment to reduce exposure to the lowest practical level.

B. Citations.

1. **Issuing Citations.**

   a. **Sending Citations to the Employer.** Citations shall be sent by certified mail; hand delivery of citations to the employer or an appropriate agent of the employer may be substituted for certified mailing if it is believed that this method would be more effective. A signed receipt shall be obtained whenever possible; otherwise the circumstances of delivery shall be documented in the file.

   b. **Sending Citations to the Employee.** Citations shall be mailed to employee representatives no later than one day after the citation is sent to the employer. Citations shall also be mailed to any employee upon request.

   c. **Followup Inspections.** If a followup inspection reveals a failure to abate, the time specified for abatement has passed, and no notice of contest has been filed, a Notification of Failure to Abate Alleged Violation (OSHA-2B) may be issued immediately without regard to the contest period of the initial citation.

2. **Amending or Withdrawing Citation and Notification of Penalty in Part or In Its Entirety.**

   a. **Citation Revision Justified.** Amendments to or withdrawal of a citation shall be made when information is presented to the Area Director which indicates a need for such revision under certain conditions which may include:

      (1) Administrative or technical error.
         (a) Citation of an incorrect standard.
         (b) Incorrect or incomplete description of the alleged violation.
      (2) Additional facts establish a valid affirmative defense.
      (3) Additional facts establish that there was no employee exposure to the hazard.
      (4) Additional facts establish a need for modification of the correction date, or the penalty, or reclassification of citation items.

   b. **Citation Revision Not Justified.** Amendments to or withdrawal of a citation shall not be made by the Area Director under certain conditions which include:

      (1) Valid notice of contest received.
      (2) The 15 working days for filing a notice of contest has expired and the citation has become a final order.
      (3) Employee representatives have not been given the opportunity to present their views unless the revision involves only an administrative or technical error.
      (4) Editorial and/or stylistic modifications.

   c. **Procedures for Amending or Withdrawing Citations.** The following procedures are to be followed in amending or withdrawing citations. The instructions contained in this section, with appropriate modification, are also applicable to the amendment of the Notification of Failure to Abate Alleged Violation, OSHA-2B Form:

      (1) Withdrawal of or modifications to the citation and notification of penalty, shall normally be accomplished by means of an informal settlement agreement (ISA). (See D.4.b. of this chapter for further information in ISA's).
      (2) Changes initiated by the Area Director without an informal conference are exceptions. In such cases the procedures given below shall be followed:
         (a) If proposed amendments to citation items change the classification of the items; e.g., serious to other-than-serious, the original citation items shall be withdrawn and new, appropriate citation items issued.
         (b) The amended Citation and Notification of Penalty Form (OSHA-2) shall clearly indicate that:
            1 The employer is obligated under the Act to post the amendment to the citation along with the original citation until the amended violation has been corrected or for 3 working days, whichever is longer;
            2 The period of contest of the amended portions of the OSHA-2 will begin from the day following the date of receipt of the amended Citation and Notification of Penalty; and
            3 The contest period is not extended as to the unamended portions of the original citation.
         (c) A copy of the original citation shall be attached to the amended Citation and Notification of Penalty Form when the amended form is forwarded to the employer.
         (d) When circumstances warrant it, a citation may be withdrawn in its entirety by the Area Director. Justifying documentation shall be placed in the case file. If a citation is to be withdrawn, the following procedures apply:
            1 A letter withdrawing the Citation and Notification of Penalty shall be sent to the employer. The letter shall refer to the original citation and penalty, state that they are withdrawn and direct that the letter be posted by the employer for 3 working days in those locations where the original citation was posted.
            2 When applicable to the specific situation (e.g., an employee representative participated in the walkaround inspection, the inspection was in response to a complaint signed by an employee or an employee representative, or the withdrawal resulted from an informal conference or settlement agreement in which an employee representative exercised the right to participate), a copy of the letter shall also be sent to the employee or the employee representative as appropriate.

C. Penalties.

1. **General Policy.** The penalty structure provided under Section 17 of the Act is designed primarily to provide an incentive toward correcting violations voluntarily, not only to the offending employer but, more especially, to other employers who may be guilty of the same infractions of the standards or regulations.

   a. While penalties are not designed primarily as punishment for violations, the Congress has made clear its intent that penalty amounts should be sufficient to serve as an effective deterrent to violations.

   b. Large proposed penalties, therefore, serve the public purpose intended under the Act; and criteria guiding approval of such penalties by the Assistant Secretary are based on meeting this public purpose. (See OSHA Instruction CPL 2.80.)

   c. The penalty structure outlined in this section is designed as a general guideline. The Area Director may deviate from this guideline if warranted, to achieve the appropriate deterrent effect.

2. **Civil Penalties.**

   a. **Statutory Authority.** Section 17 provides the Secretary with the statutory authority to propose civil penalties for violations of the Act.

     (1) Section 17(b) of the Act provides that any employer who has received a citation for an alleged violation of the Act which is determined to be of a serious nature shall be assessed a civil penalty of up to $7,000 for each violation. (See OSHA Instruction CPL 2.51H, or the most current version, for congressional exemptions and limitations placed on penalties by the Appropriations Act.)

     (2) Section 17(c) provides that, when the violation is specifically determined not to be of a serious nature, a proposed civil penalty of up to $7,000 may be assessed for each violation.

     (3) Section 17(i) provides that, when a violation of a posting requirement is cited, a civil penalty of up to $7,000 shall be assessed.

   b. **Minimum Penalties. The following guidelines apply:**

     (1) The proposed penalty for any willful violation shall not be less than $5,000. The $5,000 penalty is a statutory minimum and not subject to administrative discretion. See C.2.m.(1)(a)1, below, for applicability to small employers.

     (2) When the adjusted proposed penalty for an other-than-serious violation (citation item) would amount to less than $100, no penalty shall be proposed for that violation.

     (3) When, however, there is a citation item for a posting violation, this minimum penalty amount does not apply with respect to that item since penalties for such items are mandatory under the Act.

     (4) When the adjusted proposed penalty for a serious violation (citation item) would amount to less than $100, a $100 penalty shall be proposed for that violation.

   c. **Penalty Factors.** Section 17(j) of the Act provides that penalties shall be assessed on the basis of four factors:

     (1) The gravity of the violation,

     (2) The size of the business,

     (3) The good faith of the employer, and

     (4) The employer's history of previous violations.

   d. **Gravity of Violation.** The gravity of the violation is the primary consideration in determining penalty amounts. It shall be the basis for calculating the basic penalty for both serious and other violations. To determine the gravity of a violation the following two assessments shall be made:

   (1) The severity of the injury or illness which could result from the alleged violation.

   (2) The probability that an injury or illness could occur as a result of the alleged violation.

   e. **Severity Assessment.** The classification of the alleged violations as serious or other-than-serious, in accordance with the instructions in Chapter III, C.2., is based on the severity of the injury or illness that could result from the violation. This classification constitutes the first step in determining the gravity of the violation. A severity assessment shall be assigned to a hazard to be cited according to the most serious injury or illness which could reasonably be expected to result from an employee's exposure as follows:

     (1) **High Severity:** Death from injury or illness; injuries involving permanent disability; or chronic, irreversible illnesses.

     (2) **Medium Severity:** Injuries or temporary, reversible illnesses resulting in hospitalization or a variable but limited period of disability.

     (3) **Low Severity:** Injuries or temporary, reversible illnesses not resulting in hospitalization and requiring only minor supportive treatment.

     (4) **Minimal Severity:** Other-than-serious violations. Although such violations reflect conditions which have a direct and immediate relationship to the safety and health of employees, the injury or illness most likely to result would probably not cause death or serious physical harm.

   f. **Probability Assessment.** The probability that an injury or illness will result from a hazard has no role in determining the classification of a violation but does affect the amount of the penalty to be proposed.

     (1) **Categorization.** Probability shall be categorized either as greater or as lesser probability.

       (a) Greater probability results when the likelihood that an injury or illness will occur is judged to be relatively high.

       (b) Lesser probability results when the likelihood that an injury or illness will occur is judged to be relatively low.

     (2) **Violations.** The following circumstances may normally be considered, as appropriate, when violations likely to result in injury or illness are involved:

       (a) Number of workers exposed.

       (b) Frequency of exposure or duration of employee overexposure to contaminants.

       (c) Employee proximity to the hazardous conditions.

       (d) Use of appropriate personal protective equipment (PPE).

       (e) Medical surveillance program.

       (f) Youth and inexperience of workers, especially those under 18 years old.

       (g) Other pertinent working conditions.

     (3) **Final Probability Assessment.** All of the factors outlined above shall be considered together in arriving at a final probability assessment. When strict adherence to the probability assessment procedures would result in an unreasonably high or low gravity, the probability may be adjusted as appropriate based on professional judgment. Such decisions shall be adequately documented in the case file.

   g. **Gravity-Based Penalty.** The gravity-based penalty (GBP) is an unadjusted penalty and is calculated in accordance with the following procedures:

     (1) The GBP for each violation shall be determined based on an appropriate and balanced professional judgment combining the severity assessment and the final probability assessment.

     (2) For serious violations, the GBP shall be assigned on the basis of the following scale:

Severity	Probability	GBP	Gravity
High	Greater	$5,000	high ($5,000+)
Medium	Greater	$3,500	——
LowGreater		$2,500	|— moderate
High	Lesser	$2,500	|
Medium	Lesser	$2,000	——
LowLesser		$1,500	low

NOTE: The gravity of a violation is defined by the GBP.
- o A high gravity violation is one with a GBP of $5,000 or greater.
- o A moderate gravity violation is one with GBP of $2,000 to $3,500.
- o A low gravity violation is one with a GBP of $1,500.

(3) The highest gravity classification (high severity and greater probability) shall normally be reserved for the most serious violative conditions, such as those situations involving danger of death or extremely serious injury or illness. If the Area Director determines that it is appropriate to achieve the necessary deterrent effect, a GBP of $7,000 may be proposed. The reasons for this determination shall be documented in the case file.

(4) For other-than-serious safety and health violations, there is no severity assessment.

(5) The Area Director may authorize a penalty between $l,000 and $7,000 for an other-than-serious violation when it is determined to be appropriate to achieve the necessary deterrent effect. The reasons for such a determination shall be documented in the case file.

Probability	GBP
Greater	$1,000 – $7,000
Lesser	$0

(6) A GBP may be assigned in some cases without using the severity and the probability assessment procedures outlined in this section when these procedures cannot appropriately be used.

(7) The Penalty Table (Table IV-1) may be used for determining appropriate adjusted penalties for serious and other-than-serious violations.

h. **Gravity Calculations for Combined or Grouped Violations.** Combined or grouped violations will normally be considered as one violation and shall be assessed one GBP. The following procedures apply to the calculation of penalties for combined and grouped violations:

(1) The severity and the probability assessments for combined violations shall be based on the instance with the highest gravity. It is not necessary to complete the penalty calculations for each instance or subitem of a combined or grouped violation if it is clear which instance will have the highest gravity.

(2) For grouped violations, the following special guidelines shall be adhered to:

(a) **Severity Assessment.** There are two considerations to be kept in mind in calculating the severity of grouped violations:

1   The severity assigned to the grouped violation shall be no less than the severity of the most serious reasonably predictable injury or illness that could result from the violation of any single item.

2   If a more serious injury or illness is reasonably predictable from the grouped items than from any single violation item, the more serious injury or illness shall serve as the basis for the calculation of the severity factor of the grouped violation.

(b) **Probability Assessment.** There are two considerations to be kept in mind in calculating the probability of grouped violations:

1   The probability assigned to the grouped violation shall be no less than the probability of the item which is most likely to result in an injury or illness.

2   If the overall probability of injury or illness is greater with the grouped violation than with any single violation item, the greater probability of injury or illness shall serve as the basis for the calculation of the probability assessment of the grouped violation.

(3) In egregious cases an additional factor of up to the number of violation instances may be applied. Such cases shall be handled in accordance with OSHA Instruction CPL 2.80. Penalties calculated with this additional factor shall not be proposed without the concurrence of the Assistant Secretary. (See also C.2.k.(2)(c)4 of this chapter.)

i. **Penalty Adjustment Factors.** The GBP may be reduced by as much as 95 per cent depending upon the employer's "good faith," "size of business," and "history of previous violations." Up to 60-percent reduction is permitted for size; up to 25-percent reduction for good faith, and 10-percent for history.

(1) Since these adjustment factors are based on the general character of a business and its safety and health performance, the factors generally shall be calculated only once for each employer. After the classification and probability ratings have been determined for each violation, the adjustment factors shall be applied subject to the limitations indicated in the following paragraphs.

(2) Penalties assessed for violations that are classified as high severity and greater probability shall be adjusted only for size and history.

(3) Penalties assessed for violations that are classified as repeated shall be adjusted only for size.

(4) Penalties assessed for regulatory violations, which are classified as willful, shall be adjusted for size. Penalties assessed for serious violations, which are classified as willful, shall be adjusted for size and history.
NOTE: If one violation is classified as willful, no reduction for good faith can be applied to any of the violations found during the same inspection. The employer cannot be willfully in violation of the Act and at the same time, be acting in good faith.

(5) The rate of penalty reduction for size of business, employer's good faith and employer's history of previous violations shall be calculated on the basis of the criteria described in the following paragraphs:

(a) **Size.** A maximum penalty reduction of 60 percent is permitted for small businesses. "Size of business" shall be measured on the basis of the maximum number of employees of an employer at all workplaces at any one time during the previous 12 months.

   1   The rates of reduction to be applied are as follows:

Employees	Percent reduction
1–25	60
26–100	40
101–250	20
251 or more	None

   2   When a small business (1–25 employees) has one or more serious violations of high gravity or a number of serious violations of moderate gravity, indicating a lack of concern for employee safety and health, the CSHO may recommend that only a partial reduction in penalty shall be permitted for size of business.

(b) **Good Faith.** A penalty reduction of up to 25 percent, based on the CSHO's professional judgment, is permitted in recognition of an employer's "good faith".

   1   The 25% credit for "good faith" normally requires a written safety and health program. In exceptional cases, the compliance officer may recommend the full 25% for a smaller employer (1–25 employees) who has implemented an efficient safety and health program, but has not reduced it to writing.

      a   Provides for appropriate management commitment and employee involvement; worksite analysis for the purpose of hazard identification; hazard prevention and control measures; and safety and health training.

         NOTE: One example of a framework for such a program is given in OSHA's voluntary "Safety and Health Program Management Guidelines" (Federal Register, Vol. 54, No. 16, January 26, 1989, pp. 3904-3916, or later revisions as published).

      b   Has deficiencies that are only incidental.

   2   A reduction of 15 percent shall normally be given if the employer has a documentable and effective safety and health program, but with more than only incidental deficiencies.

   3   No reduction shall be given to an employer who has no safety and health program or where a willful violation is found.

   4   Only these percentages (15% or 25%) may be used to reduce penalties due to the employer's good faith. No intermediate percentages shall be used.

   5   Where young workers (i.e., less than 18 years old) are employed, the CSHO's evaluation must consider whether the employer's safety and health program appropriately addresses the particular needs of such workers with regard to the types of work they perform and the hazards to which they are exposed.

(c) **History.** A reduction of 10 percent shall be given to employers who have not been cited by OSHA for any serious, willful, or repeated violations in the past three years.

(d) **Total.** The total reduction will normally be the sum of the reductions for each adjustment factors.

j. **Effect on Penalties If Employer Immediately Corrects or Initiates Corrective Action.** Appropriate penalties will be proposed with respect to an alleged violation even though, after being informed of such alleged violation by the CSHO, the employer immediately corrects or initiates steps to correct the hazard.

k. **Failure to Abate.** A Notification of Failure to Abate an Alleged Violation (OSHA-2B) shall be issued in cases where violations have not been corrected as required.

  (1) **Failure to Abate.** Failure to abate penalties shall be applied when an employer has not corrected a previously cited violation which had become a final order of the Commission. Citation items become final order of the Review Commission when the abatement date for that item passes, if the employer has not filed a notice of contest prior to that abatement date. See D.5. of this chapter for guidance on determining final dates of settlements and Review Commission orders.

  (2) **Calculation of Additional Penalties.** A GBP or unabated violations is to be calculated for failure to abate a serious or other-than-serious violation on the basis of the facts noted upon reinspection. This recalculated GBP, however, shall not be less than that proposed for the item when originally cited, except as provided in C.2.k.(4), below.

    (a) In those instances where no penalty was initially proposed, an appropriate penalty shall be determined after consulting with the Assistant Area Director. In no case shall the unadjusted penalty be less than $1,000 per day.

    (b) Only the adjustment factor for size—based upon the circumstances noted during the reinspection—shall then be applied to arrive at the daily proposed penalty.

    (c) The daily proposed penalty shall be multiplied by the number of calendar days that the violation has continued unabated, except as provided below:

      1   The number of days unabated shall be counted from the day following the abatement date specified in the citation or the final order. It will include all calendar days between that date and the date of reinspection, excluding the date of reinspection.

      2   Normally the maximum total proposed penalty for failure to abate a particular violation shall not exceed 30 times the amount of the daily proposed penalty.

      3   At the discretion of the Area Director, a lesser penalty may be proposed with the reasons for doing so (e.g., achievement of an appropriate deterrent effect) documented in the case file.

      4   If a penalty in excess of the normal maximum amount of 30 times the amount of the daily proposed penalty is deemed appropriate by the Area Director, the case shall be treated under the violation-by-violation (egregious) penalty procedures established in OSHA Instruction CPL 2.80.

  (3) Partial Abatement.

    (a) When the citation has been partially abated, the Area Director may authorize a reduction of 25 percent to 75 percent to the amount of the proposed penalty calculated as outlined in C.2.k.(2), above.

    (b) When a violation consists of a number of instances and the followup inspection reveals that only some instances of the violation have been corrected, the additional daily proposed penalty shall take into consideration the extent that the violation has been abated.

EXAMPLE: Where 3 out of 5 instances have been corrected, the daily proposed penalty (calculated as outlined in C.2.k.(2), above, without regard to any partial abatement) may be reduced by 60 per cent.

(4) **Good Faith Effort to Abate.** When the CSHO believes, and so documents in the case file, that the employer has made a good faith effort to correct the violation and had good reason to believe that it was fully abated, the Area Director may reduce or eliminate the daily proposed penalty that would otherwise be justified.

l. **Repeated Violations.** Section 17(a) of the Act provides that an employer who repeatedly violates the Act may be assessed a civil penalty of not more than $70,000 for each violation.

  (1) **Gravity-Based Penalty Factors.** Each violation shall be classified as serious or other-than-serious. A GBP shall then be calculated for repeated violations based on facts noted during the current inspection. Only the adjustment factor for size, appropriate to the facts at the time of the reinspection, shall be applied.

  (2) **Penalty Increase Factors.** The amount of the increased penalty to be assessed for a repeated violation shall be determined by the size of the employer.

    (a) **Smaller Employers.** For employers with 250 or fewer employees, the GBP shall be doubled for the first repeated violation and quintupled if the violation has been cited twice before. If the Area Director determines that it is appropriate to achieve the necessary deterrent effect, the GBP may be multiplied by 10.

    (b) **Larger Employers.** For employers with more than 250 employees, the GBP shall be multiplied by 5 for the first repeated violation and multiplied by 10 for the second repeated violation.

  (3) **Other-Than-Serious, No Initial Penalty.** For a repeated other-than-serious violation that otherwise would have no initial penalty, a GBP penalty of $200 shall be assessed for the first repeated violation, $500 if the violation has been cited twice before, and $1,000 for a third repetition.

    NOTE: This penalty will not have the penalty increase factors applied as discussed under C.2.l.(2).

  (4) **Regulatory Violations.** For repeated instances of regulatory violations, the initial penalty shall be doubled for the first repeated violation and quintupled if the violation has been cited twice before. If the Area Director determines that it is appropriate to achieve the necessary deterrent effect, the initial penalty may be multiplied by 10.

    NOTE: See Chapter III, C.2.f., for additional guidance on citing repeated violations.

m. **Willful Violations.** Section 17(a) of the Act provides that an employer who willfully violates the Act may be assessed a civil penalty of not more than $70,000 but not less than $5,000 for each violation.

  (1) **Gravity-Based Penalty Factors.** Each willful violation shall be classified as serious or other-than-serious.

    (a) Serious Violations. For willful serious violations, a gravity of high, medium moderate, or low shall be assigned based on the GBP of the underlying serious violation, as described at C.2.g.(2).

     1 The adjustment factor for size shall be applied as shown in the following chart:

Employees	Percent Reduction
10 or less	80
11–20	60
21–30	50
31–40	40
41–50	30
51–100	20
101–250	10
251 or more	0

     2 The adjustment factor for history shall be applied as described at C.2.i.(5)(c); i.e., a reduction of 10 percent shall be given to employers who have not been cited by OSHA for any serious, willful, or repeated violations in the past 3 years. There shall be no adjustment for good faith.

     3 The proposed penalty shall then be determined from the table below:

Penalties to be proposed

Total percentage reduction for size and/or history	0%	10%	20%	30%	40%	50%	60%	70%	80%	90%
High Gravity	$70,000	$63,000	$56,000	$49,000	$42,000	$35,000	$28,000	$21,000	$14,000	$7,000
Moderate Gravity	$55,000	$49,000	$44,000	$38,000	$33,000	$27,500	$22,000	$16,500	$11,000	$5,500
Low Gravity	$40,000	$36,000	$32,000	$28,000	$24,000	$20,000	$16,000	$12,000	$8,000	$5,000

     4 In no case shall the proposed penalty be less than $25,000 $5,000.

    (b) **Other-Than-Serious Violations.** For willful other-than-serious violations, the minimum willful penalty of $5,000 shall be assessed.

  (2) **Regulatory Violations.** In the case of regulatory violations (see C.2.n., below) that are determined to be willful, the unadjusted initial penalty shall be multiplied by 10. In no event shall the penalty, after adjustment for size, be less than $5,000.

n. **Violation of 29 CFR Parts 1903 and 1904 Regulatory Requirements.** Except as provided in the Appropriations Act, Section 17 of the Act provides that an employer who violates any of the posting requirements shall be assessed a civil penalty of up to $7,000 for each violation and may be assessed a like penalty for recordkeeping violations.

  (1) **General Application.** Unadjusted penalties for regulatory violations, including posting requirements, shall have

the adjustment factors for size and history applied (excluding willful violations, see C.2.m.(2), above).

(2) **Posting Requirements.** Penalties for violation of posting requirements shall be proposed as follows:

    (a) **OSHA Notice (Poster).** If the employer has not displayed (posted) the notice furnished by the Occupational Safety and Health Administration as prescribed in 29 CFR 1903.2 (a), an other-than-serious citation shall normally be issued. The unadjusted penalty for this alleged violation shall be $1,000 provided that the employer has received a copy of the poster or had knowledge of the requirement.

    (b) **Annual Summary.** If an employer fails to post the summary portion of the OSHA-200 Form during the month of February as required by 29 CFR 1904.5(d)(1), and/or fails to complete the summary prior to February 1, as required by 29 CFR 1904.5(b), even if there have been no injuries, an other-than-serious citation shall be issued. The unadjusted penalty for this violation shall be $1,000.

    (c) **Citation.** If an employer received a citation that has not been posted as prescribed in 29 CFR 1903.16, an other-than-serious citation shall normally be issued. The unadjusted penalty shall be $3,000.

(3) **Reporting and Recordkeeping Requirements.** Section 17(c) of the Act provides that violations of the recordkeeping and reporting requirements may be assessed civil penalties of up to $7,000 for each violation.

    (a) **OSHA-200 Form.** If the employer does not maintain the Log and Summary of Occupational Injuries and Illnesses, OSHA-200 Form, as prescribed in 29 CFR Part 1904, an other-than-serious citation shall be issued. There shall be an unadjusted penalty of $1,000 for each year the form was not maintained, for each of the preceding 3 years.

        1   When no recordable injuries or illnesses have occurred at a workplace during the current calendar year, the OSHA 200 need not be completed until the end of the calendar year for certification of the summary.

        2   An OSHA-200 with significant deficiencies shall be considered as not maintained.

    (b) **OSHA-101 Forms.** If the employer does not maintain the Supplementary Record, OSHA 101 Form (or equivalent), as prescribed in 29 CFR Part 1904, an other-than-serious citation shall be issued. There shall be an unadjusted penalty of $1000 for each OSHA-101 Form not maintained.

        1   A penalty of $1000 for each OSHA-101 Form not maintained at all up to a maximum of $7000.

        2   A penalty of $1,000 for each OSHA-101 Form inaccurately maintained up to a maximum of $3000.

        3   Minor inaccuracies shall be cited, but with no penalties.

        4   If large numbers of violations or other circumstances indicate that the violations are willful, then other penalties including, violation-by-violation, may be applied.

    (c) **Reporting.** Employers are required to report either orally or in writing to the nearest Area Office within 8 hours, any occurrence of an employment accident which is fatal to one or more employees or which results in the hospitalization of three or more employees.

        1   An other-than-serious citation shall be issued for failure to report such an occurrence. The unadjusted penalty shall be $5,000.

        2   If the Area Director determines that it is appropriate to achieve the necessary deterrent effect, an unadjusted penalty of $7,000 may be assessed.

        3   If the Area Director becomes aware of an incident required to be reported under 29 CFR 1904.8 through some means other than an employer report, prior to the elapse of the 8-hour reporting period and an inspection of the incident is made, a citable violation for failure to report does not exist.

(4) **Grouping.** Violations of the posting and recordkeeping requirements which involve the same document (e.g., summary portion of the OSHA-200 Form was neither posted nor maintained) shall be grouped as an other-than-serious violation for penalty purposes. The unadjusted penalty for the grouped violations would then take on the highest dollar value of the individual items, which will normally be $1,000.

(5) **Access to Records.**

    (a) **29 CFR Part 1904.** If the employer fails upon request to provide records required in 1904.2 for inspection and copying by any employee, former employee, or authorized representative of employees, a citation for violation of 29 CFR 1904.7(b)(1) shall normally be issued. The unadjusted penalty shall be $1,000 for each form not made available.

        1   Thus, if the OSHA-200 for the 3 preceding years is not made available, the unadjusted penalty would be $3,000.

        2   If the employer is to be cited for failure to maintain these records, no citation of 1904.7 shall be issued.

    (b) **29 CFR 1910.20.** If the employer is cited for failing to provide records as required under 29 CFR 1910.20 for inspection and copying by any employee, former employee, or authorized representative of employees, an unadjusted penalty of $1,000 shall be proposed for each record; i.e., either medical record or exposure record, on an individual employee basis. A maximum $7,000 may be assessed for such violations. This policy does not preclude the use of violation-by-violation penalties where appropriate. (See OSHA Instruction CPL 2.80.)

        EXAMPLE: If all the necessary evidence is established where an authorized employee representative requested exposure and medical records for 3 employees and the request was denied by the employer, a citation would be issued for 6 instances of violation of 29 CFR 1910.20, with an unadjusted penalty of $6,000.

(6) **Notification Requirements.** When an employer has received advance notice of an inspection and fails to notify the authorized employee representative as required by 29 CFR 1903.6, an other-than-serious citation shall be issued. The violation shall have an unadjusted penalty of $2,000.

TABLE IV-1
PENALTY TABLE

Percent Reduction				PENALTY (in dollars)				
0	1,000	1,500	2,000	2,500	3,000	3,500	5,000	7,000
10	900	1,350	1,800	2,250	2,700	3,150	4,500	6,300
15	850	1,275	1,700	2,125	2,550	2,975	4,250*	5,950
20	800	1,200	1,600	2,000	2,400	2,800	4,000	5,600
25	750	1,125	1,500	1,875	2,250	2,625	3,750*	5,250*
30	700	1,050	1,400	1,750	2,100	2,450	3,500	4,900
35	650	975	1,300	1,625	1,950	2,275	3,250*	4,550*
40	600	900	1,200	1,500	1,800	2,100	3,000	4,200
45	550	825	1,100	1,375	1,650	1,925	2,750*	3,850*
50	500	750	1,000	1,250	1,500	1,750	2,500	3,500
55	450	675	900	1,125	1,350	1,575	2,250*	3,150*
60	400	600	800	1,000	1,200	1,400	2,000	2,800
65	350	525	700	875	1,050	1,225	1,750*	2,450*
70	300	450	600	750	900	1,050	1,500	2,100
75	250	375	500	625	750	875	1,250*	1,750*
85	150	225	300	375	450	525	750*	1,050*
95	100**	100**	100	125	150	175	250*	350*

* Starred figures represent penalty amounts that would not normally be proposed for high gravity serious violations because no adjustment for good faith is made in such cases. They may occasionally be applicable for other-than-serious violations where the Area Director has determined a high unadjusted penalty amount to be warranted.

** Administratively, OSHA will not issue a penalty less than $100 for a serious violation.

3. Criminal Penalties.
   a. The Act and the U.S. Code provide for criminal penalties in the following cases:
      (1) Willful violation of an OSHA standard, rule, or order causing the death of an employee (Section 17(e)).
      (2) Giving unauthorized advance notice. (Section 17(f).)
      (3) Giving false information. (Section 17(g).)
      (4) Killing, assaulting or hampering the work of a CSHO. (Section 17(h)(2).)
   b. Criminal penalties are imposed by the courts after trials and not by the Occupational Safety and Health Administration or the Occupational Safety and Health Review Commission.

D. Post-Citation Processes.
1. Informal Conferences.
   a. **General.** Pursuant to 29 CFR 1903.19, the employer, any affected employee or the employee representative may request an informal conference. When an informal conference is conducted, it shall be conducted within the 15 working day contest period. If the employer's intent to contest is not clear, the Area Director shall contact the employer for clarification.
   b. **Procedures.** Whenever an informal conference is requested by the employer, an affected employee or the employee representative, both parties shall be afforded the opportunity to participate fully. If either party chooses not to participate in the informal conference, a reasonable attempt shall be made to contact that party to solicit their input prior to signing an informal settlement agreement if the adjustments involves more than the penalty. If the requesting party objects to the attendance of the other party, separate informal conferences may be held. During the conduct of a joint informal conference, separate or private discussions shall be permitted if either party so requests. Informal conferences may be held by any means practical.
      (1) The employer shall be requested to complete and post the form found at the end of the informal conference letter until after the informal conference has been held.
      (2) Documentation of the Area Director's actions notifying the parties of the informal conference shall be placed in the case file.
   c. **Participation by OSHA Officials.** The inspecting CSHOs and their Assistant Area Directors shall be notified of an upcoming informal conference and, if practicable, given the opportunity to participate in the informal conference (unless, in the case of the CSHO, the Area Director anticipates that only a penalty adjustment will result).
      (1) At the discretion of the Area Director, one or more additional OSHA employees (in addition to the Area Director) may be present at the informal conference. In cases in which proposed penalties total $100,000 or more, a second OSHA staff member shall attend the informal conference.
      (2) The Area Director shall ensure that notes are made indicating the basis for any decisions taken at or as a result of the informal conference. It is appropriate to tape record the informal conference and to use the tape recording in lieu of written notes.
   d. **Conduct of the Informal Conference.** The Area Director shall conduct the informal conference in accordance with the following guidelines:
      (1) **Opening Remarks.** The opening remarks shall include discussions of the following:
         (a) Purpose of the informal conference.
         (b) Rights of participants.
         (c) Contest rights and time restraints.
         (d) limitations, if any.
         (e) Settlements of cases.
         (f) Other relevant information.
         (g) If the Area Director states any views on the legal merits of the employer's contentions, it should be made clear that those views are personal opinions only.

(2) **Closing.** At the conclusion of the discussion the main issues and potential courses of action shall be summarized. A copy of the summary, together with any other relevant notes or tapes of the discussion made by the Area Director, shall be placed in the case file.

  e. **Decisions.** At the end of the informal conference, the Area Director shall make a decision as to what action is appropriate in the light of facts brought up during the conference.

    (1) Changes to citations, penalties or abatement dates normally shall be made by means of an informal settlement agreement in accordance with current OSHA procedures; the reasons for such changes shall be documented in the case file. For more detail on settlement agreements, see D.4.b., below.

    (2) Employers shall be informed that they are required by 29 CFR 1903.19 to post copies of all amendments to the citation resulting from informal conferences. Employee representatives must also be provided with copies of such documents. This regulation covers amended citations, citation withdrawals and settlement agreements.

  f. **Failure to Abate.** If the informal conference involves an alleged failure to abate, the Area Director shall set a new abatement date in the informal settlement agreement, documenting for the case file the time that has passed since the original citation, the steps that the employer has taken to inform the exposed employees of their risk and to protect them from the hazard, and the measures that will have to be taken to correct the condition.

2. **Petitions for Modification of Abatement Date (PMA).** Title 29 CFR 1903.14a governs the disposition of PMAs. If the employer requests additional abatement time after the 15-working-day contest period has passed, the following procedures for PMAs are to be observed:

  a. **Filing Date.** A PMA must be filed in writing with the Area Director who issued the citation no later than the close of the next working day following the date on which abatement was originally required.

    (1) If a PMA is submitted orally, the employer shall be informed that OSHA cannot accept an oral PMA and that a written petition must be mailed by the end of the next working day after the abatement date. If there is not sufficient time to file a written petition, the employer shall be informed of the requirements below for late filing of the petition.

    (2) A late petition may be accepted only if accompanied by the employer's statement of exceptional circumstances explaining the delay.

  b. **Failure to Meet All Requirements.** If the employer's letter does not meet all the requirements of 1903.14a(b)(1)-(5), the employer shall be contacted within 10 working days and notified of the missing elements. A reasonable amount of time for the employer to respond shall be specified during this contact with the employer.

    (1) If no response is received or if the information returned is still insufficient, a second attempt (by telephone or in writing) shall be made. The employer shall be informed of the consequences of a failure to respond adequately; namely, that the PMA will not be granted and the employer may, consequently, be found in failure to abate.

    (2) If the employer responds satisfactorily by telephone and the Area Director determines that the requirements for a PMA have been met, appropriate documentation shall be placed in the case file.

  c. **Delayed Decisions.** Although OSHA policy is to handle PMAs as expeditiously as possible, there are cases where the Area Director's decision on the PMA is delayed because of deficiencies in the PMA itself, a decision to conduct a monitoring inspection and/or the need for Regional Office or National Office involvement. Requests for additional time (e.g., 45 days) for the Area Director to formulate a position shall be sent to the Review Commission through the Regional Solicitor. A letter conveying this request shall be sent at the same time to the employer and the employee representatives.

  d. **Area Office Position on the PMA.** After 15 working days following the PMA posting, the Area Director shall determine the Area Office position, agreeing with or objecting to the request. This shall be done within 10 working days following the 15 working days (if additional time has not been requested from the Review Commission; in the absence of a timely objection, the PMA is automatically granted even if not explicitly approved). The following action shall be taken:

    (1) If the PMA requests an abatement date which is two years or less from the issuance date of the citation, the Area Director has the authority to approve or object to the petition.

    (2) Any PMA requesting an abatement date which is more than two years from the issuance date of the citation requires the approval of the Regional Administrator as well as the Area Director.

    (3) If the PMA is approved, the Area Director shall notify the employer and the employee representatives by letter.

    (4) If supporting evidence justifies it (e.g., employer has taken no meaningful abatement action at all or has otherwise exhibited bad faith), the Area Director or the Regional Administrator, as appropriate and after consultation with the Regional Solicitor, shall object to the PMA. In such a case, all relevant documentation shall be sent to the Review Commission in accordance with 29 CFR 1903.14a(d). Both the employer and the employee representatives shall be notified of this action by letter, with return receipt requested.

      (a) The letters of notification of the objection shall be mailed on the same date that the agency objection to the PMA is sent to the Review Commission.

      (b) When appropriate, after consultation with the Regional Solicitor, a failure to abate notification may be issued in conjunction with the objection to the PMA.

  e. **Employee Objections.** Affected employees or their representatives may file an objection in writing to an employer's PMA with the Area Director within 10 working days of the date of posting of the PMA by the employer or its service upon an authorized employee representative.

    (1) Failure to file such a written objection with the 10-working-day period constitutes a waiver of any further right to object to the PMA.

    (2) If an employee or an employee representative objects to the extension of the abatement date, all relevant documentation shall be sent to the Review Commission.

      (a) Confirmation of this action shall be mailed (return receipt requested) to the objecting party as soon as it is accomplished.

      (b) Notification of the employee objection shall be mailed (return receipt requested) to the employer on the same day that the case file is forwarded to the Commission.

3. Services Available to Employers. Employers requesting abatement assistance shall be informed that OSHA is willing to work with them even after citations have been issued.

4. Settlement of Cases By Area Directors.

a. **General. Area** Directors are granted settlement authority, using the following policy guidelines to negotiate settlement agreements.

(1) Except for egregious cases, or cases which affect other jurisdictions, Area Directors are authorized to enter into Informal Settlement Agreements with an employer before the employer files a written notice of contest. **NOTE:** After the employer has filed a written notice of contest, the Area Director may proceed toward a Formal Settlement Agreement with the concurrence of the Regional Solicitor in cases where a settlement appears probable without the need for active participation by an attorney.

(2) Area Directors are authorized to change abatement dates, to reclassify violations (e.g., willful to serious, serious to other-than-serious), and to modify or withdraw a penalty, a citation or a citation item if the employer presents evidence during the informal conference which convinces the Area Director that the changes are justified.

(a) If an employer, having been cited as willfully or repeatedly violating the Act, decides to correct all violations, but wishes to purge himself or herself of the adverse public perception attached to a willful or repeated violation classification and is willing to pay all or almost all of the penalty and is willing to make significant additional concessions, then a Section 17 designation may be applicable. Decisions to make a Section 17 designation shall be based on whether the employer is willing to make significant concessions. **NOTE:** Significant concessions may include the company entering into a corporate-wide settlement agreement subject to OSHA Instruction CPL 2.90, providing employee training of a specified type and frequency, hiring a qualified safety and health consultant and implementing the recommendations, effecting a comprehensive safety and health program, reporting new construction jobs or other worksites to OSHA, or waiving warrants for specified inspections/periods.

(b) A Section 17 designation also may be considered if the employer has advanced substantial reasons why the original classification is questionable but is willing to pay the penalty as proposed. **NOTE:** Where the original classification clearly was excessive, Section 17 is not appropriate. Instead, the citation shall be amended to the appropriate classification.

(3) The Area Director has authority to actively negotiate the amount of penalty reduction, depending on the circumstances of the case and what improvements in employee safety and health can be obtained in return.

(4) Employers shall be informed that they are required by 29 CFR 1903.19 to post copies of all amendments or changes resulting from informal conferences. Employee representatives must also be provided with copies of such documents. This regulation covers amended citations, citation withdrawals and settlement agreements.

b. **Pre-Contest Settlement (Informal Settlement Agreement).** Pre-contest settlements generally will occur during, or immediately following, the informal conference and prior to the completion of the 15 working day contest period.

(1) If a settlement is reached during the informal conference, an Informal Settlement Agreement shall be prepared and the employer representative shall be invited to sign it. The Informal Settlement Agreement shall be effective upon signature by both the Area Director and the employer representative so long as the contest period has not expired. Both shall date the document as of the day of actual signature.

(a) If the employer representative requests more time to consider the agreement and if there is sufficient time remaining of the 15-working-day period, the Area Director shall sign and date the agreement and provide the signed original for the employer to study while considering whether to sign it. A letter explaining the conditions under which the agreement will become effective shall be given (or mailed by certified mail, return receipt requested) to the employer and a record kept in the case file.

(b) The Area Director shall sign and date the agreement and provide the original (in person, or by certified mail, return receipt requested) to the employer if any other circumstances warrant such action; the agreement may also be sent to the employer for signature, and returned to the Area Director, via facsimile if circumstances warrant.

1 If the signed agreement is provided to the employer, a copy shall be kept in the case file and the employer informed in writing that no changes are to be made to the original by the employer without explicit prior authorization for such changes from the Area Director.

2 In every case the Area Director shall give formal notice in writing to the employer that the citation will become final and unreviewable at the end of the contest period unless the employer either signs the agreement or files a written notice of contest.

3 If the employer representative wishes to make any changes to the text of the agreement, the Area Director must agree to and authorize the proposed changes prior to the expiration of the contest period.

a If the changes proposed by the employer are acceptable to the Area Director, they shall be authorized and the exact language to be written into the agreement shall be worked out mutually. The employer shall be instructed to incorporate the agreed-upon language into the agreement, sign it and return it to the Area Office as soon as practicable by telefacsimile, if possible.

b Annotations incorporating the exact language of any changes authorized by the Area Director shall be made to the retained copy of the agreement, and a dated record of the authorization shall be signed by the Area Director and placed in the case file.

4 Upon receipt of the Informal Settlement Agreement signed by the employer, the Area Director shall ensure that any modified text of the agreement is in accordance with the notations made in the case file.

a If so, the citation record shall be updated in IMIS in accordance with current procedures.

b If not, and if the variations substantially change the terms of the agreement, the agreement signed by the employer shall be considered as a notice of intent to contest and handled accordingly. The employer shall be so informed as soon as possible.

5 A reasonable time shall be allowed for return of the agreement from the employer.

a After that time, if the agreement has still not been received, the Area Director shall presume that the employer is not going to sign the agreement; and the citation shall be treated as a final order until such time as the agreement is received, properly signed prior to the expiration of the contest period.

        b   The employer shall be required to certify that the informal settlement agreement was signed prior to the expiration of the contest period.

     (2) If the Area Director's settlement efforts are unsuccessful and the employer contests the citation, the Area Director shall state the terms of the final settlement offer in the case file.

  c. **Procedures for Preparing the Informal Settlement Agreement.** The Informal Settlement Agreement shall be prepared and processed in accordance with current OSHA policies and practices. For guidance for determining final dates of settlements and Review Commission orders see D.5., below.

  d. **Post-Contest Settlement (Formal Settlement Agreement).** Post-contest settlements will generally occur before the complaint is filed with the Review Commission.

     (1) Following the filing of a notice of contest, the Area Director shall, unless other procedures have been agreed upon, notify the Regional Solicitor when it appears that negotiations with the employer may produce a settlement. This shall normally be done at the time when the notice of contest transmittal memorandum is sent to the Regional Solicitor.

     (2) If a settlement is later requested by the employer with the Area Director, the Area Director shall communicate the terms of the settlement to the Regional Solicitor who will then draft the settlement agreement.

  e. **Corporate-Wide Settlement Agreements.** Corporate-wide Settlement Agreements (CSAs) may be entered into under special circumstances to obtain formal recognition by the employer of cited hazards and formal acceptance of the obligation to seek out and abate those hazards throughout all workplaces under its control. Guidelines, policies and procedures for entering into CSA negotiations are found in OSHA Instruction CPL 2.90.

5. Guidance for Determining Final Dates of Settlements and Review Commission Orders.

  a. **Citation/Notice of Penalty Not Contested.** The Citation/Notice of Penalty and abatement date becomes a final order of the Commission on the date the 15-working-day contest period expires.

  b. **Citation/Notice of Penalty Resolved by Informal Settlement Agreement (ISA).** The ISA becomes final, with penalties due and payable, 15 working days after the date of the last signature.

    NOTE: A later due date for payment of penalties may be set by the terms of the ISA.

    NOTE: The Review Commission does NOT review the ISA.

  c. **Citation/Notice of Penalty Resolved by Formal Settlement Agreement (FSA).** The Citation/Notice of Penalty becomes final 30 days after docketing of the Administrative Law Judge's (ALJ's) Order "approving" the parties' stipulation and settlement agreement, assuming there is no direction for review. The Commission's Notice of Docketing specifies the date upon which the decision becomes a final order. If the FSA is "approved" by a Commission's Order, it will become final after 60 days.

    NOTE: A later due date for payment of penalties may be set by the terms of the FSA.

    NOTE: Settlement is permitted and encouraged by the Commission at any stage of the proceedings. (See 29 CFR 2200.100(a).)

  d. Citation/Notice of Penalty Resolved by an ALJ Decision. The ALJ decision/report becomes a final order of the Commission 30 days after docketing unless the Commission directs a review of the case. The Commission's Notice of Docketing specifies the date upon which the decision becomes a final order.

  e. ALJ Decision is Reviewed by Commission. According to Section 11 of the OSH Act, the Commission decision becomes final 60 days after the Notice of Commission Decision if no appeal has been filed with the U.S. Court of Appeals. The Notice of Commission Decision specifies the date the Commission decision is issued.

  f. Commission Decision Reviewed by the U.S. Court of Appeals. The U.S. Court of Appeals' decision becomes final 90 days after the entry of the judgment, if no appeal has been filed with the U.S. Supreme Court.

E. Review Commission.

1 Transmittal of Notice of Contest and Other Documents to Commission.

  a. Notice of Contest. In accordance with the Occupational Safety and Health Review Commission (OSHRC) revised Rules of Procedure (51 F.R. 32020, No. 173, September 8, 1986), the original notice of contest, together with copies of all relevant documents (all contested Citations and Notifications of Penalty and Notifications of Failure to Abate Alleged Violation, and proposed additional penalty) shall be transmitted by the Area Director to the OSHRC post-marked prior to the expiration of 15 working days after receipt of the notice of contest (29 CFR 2200.33). The Regional Solicitor shall be consulted in questionable cases.

     (1) The envelope that contained the notice of contest shall be retained in the case file with the postmark intact.

     (2) Where the Area Director is certain that the notice of contest was not mailed; i.e., postmarked, within the 15-working-day period allowed for contest, the notice of contest shall be returned to the employer who shall be advised of the statutory time limitation. The employer shall be informed that OSHRC has no jurisdiction to hear the case because the notice of contest was not filed within the 15 working days allowed and, therefore, that the notice of contest will not be forwarded to the OSHRC. A copy of all untimely notices of contest shall be retained in the case file.

     (3) If the notice of contest is submitted to the Area Director after the 15-working-day period, but the notice contests only the reasonableness of the abatement period, it shall be treated as a Petition for Modification of Abatement and handled in accordance with the instructions in D.2. of this chapter.

     (4) If written communication is received from an employer containing objection, criticism or other adverse comment as to a citation or proposed penalty, which does not clearly appear to be a notice of contest, the Area Director shall contact the employer as soon as possible to clarify the intent of the communication. Such clarification must be obtained within 15 working days after receipt of the communication so that if, in fact, it is a notice of contest, the file may be forwarded to the Review Commission within the allowed time. The Area Director shall make a memorandum for the case file regarding the substance of this communication.

     (5) If the Area Director determines that the employer intends the document to be a notice of contest, it shall be transmitted to the OSHRC in accordance with E.1.a., above. If the employer did not intend the document to be a notice of contest, it shall be retained in the case file with the memorandum of the contact with the employer. If no contact can be made with the employer, communications of the kind referred to in E.1.a.(4), above, shall be timely transmitted to the OSHRC.

(6) If the Area Director's contact with the employer reveals a desire for an informal conference, the employer shall be informed that an informal conference does not stay the running of the 15-working-day period for contest.

b. **Documents to Executive Secretary.** The following documents are to be transmitted within the 15-working day time limit to the Executive Secretary, Occupational Safety and Health Review Commission, 1825 K Street, N.W., Washington, D.C. 20006:

NOTE: In order to give the Regional Solicitor the maximum amount of time to prepare the information needed in filing a complaint with the Review Commission, the notice of contest and other documents shall not be forwarded to the Review Commission until the final day of the 15-working-day period.

(1) **All Notices of Contest.** The originals are to be transmitted to the Commission and a copy of each retained in the case file.

(2) **All Contested Citations and Notices of Proposed Penalty or Notice of Failure to Abate Issued in the Case.** The signed copy of each of these documents shall be taken from the case file and sent to the Commission after a copy of each is made and placed in the case file.

(3) **Certification Form.** The certification form shall be used for all contested cases and a copy retained in the case file. It is essential that the original of the certification form, properly executed, be transmitted to the Commission.

(a) When listing the Region number in the heading of the form, do not use Roman numerals. Use 1, 2, 3, 4, 5, 6, 7, 8, 9, or 10. Insert "C" in the CSHO Job Title block if a safety CSHO or "I," if a health CSHO.

(b) Item 3 on the certification form shall be filled in by inserting only the word "employer" or "employee" in the space provided. This holds true even when the notice of contest is filed by an attorney for the party contesting the action. An item "4" shall be added where other documents, such as additional notices of contest, are sent to the Commission.

(c) Use a date stamp with the correct date for each item in the document list under the column headed "Date".

(d) Be sure to have the name and address of the Regional Solicitor or attorney who will handle the case inserted in the box containing the printed words "FOR THE SECRETARY OF LABOR." The Commission notifies this person of the hearing date and other official actions on the case. If this box is not filled in by the Area Director, delay in receipt of such notifications by the appropriate Regional Solicitor or attorney could result.

(4) **Documents Sent to OSHRC.** In most cases, the envelope sent to the OSHRC Executive Secretary will contain only four documents—the certification form, the employer's letter contesting OSHA's action, and a copy of the Citation and Notification of Penalty Form (OSHA-2) or of the Notice of Failure to Abate Form (OSHA-2B).

c. **Petitions for Modification of Abatement Dates (PMAs).**

(1) In accordance with the OSHRC Rules of Procedure the Secretary or duly authorized agent shall have the authority to approve petitions for modification of abatement filed pursuant to 29 CFR 2200.37(b) and (c).

(2) The purpose of this transfer of responsibility is to facilitate the handling and to expedite the processing of PMAs to which neither the Secretary nor any other affected party objects. The Area Director who issued the citation is the authorized agent of the Secretary and shall receive, process, approve, disapprove or otherwise administer the petitions in accordance with 29 CFR 2200.37 and 2200.38, 29 CFR 1903.14a, and D.2. of this chapter. In general, the Area Director shall:

(a) Ensure that the formal requirements of 2200.37(b) and (c) and 1903.14a are met.

(b) Approve or disapprove uncontested PMA's within 15 working days from the date the petition was posted where all affected employees could have notice of the petition.

(c) Forward to the Review Commission within 10 working days after the 15-working-day approval period all petitions objected to by the Area Director or affected employees.

(d) File a response setting forth the reasons for opposing granting of the PMA within 10 working days after receipt of the docketing by the Commission.

2. **Transmittal of File to Regional Solicitor.**

a. **Notification of the Regional Solicitor.** Under the Commission's Rules of Procedure the Secretary of Labor is required to file a complaint with the Commission within 20 calendar days after the Secretary's receipt of a notice of contest.

b. **Subpoena.** The Commission's rules provide that any person served with a subpoena, whether merely to testify in any Commission hearing or to produce records and testify in such hearing, shall, within 5 days after the serving of the subpoena, move to revoke the subpoena if the person does not intend to comply with the subpoena. These time limitations must be complied with, and expeditious handling of any subpoena served on OSHA employees is necessary. In addition, OSHA personnel may be subpoenaed to participate in nonthird-party OSHA actions. In both types of cases, the Solicitor will move to revoke the subpoena on OSHA personnel. Therefore, when any such subpoena is served on OSHA personnel, the Regional Solicitor shall immediately be notified by telephone.

3. **Communications with Commission Employees.** There shall be no ex parte communication, with respect to the merits of any case not concluded, between the Commission, including any member, officer, employee, or agent of the Commission who is employed in the decisional process, and any of the parties or interveners. Thus, CSHOs, Area Directors, Regional Administrators, or other field personnel shall refrain from any direct or indirect communication relevant to the merits of the case with Administrative Law Judges or any members or employees of the Commission. All inquiries and communications shall be handled through the Regional Solicitor.

4. **Dealings With Parties While Proceedings Are Pending Before the Commission.**

a. **Clearance with Regional Solicitor.** After the notice of contest is filed and the case is within the jurisdiction of the Commission, there shall be no investigations of or conferences with the employer without clearance from the appropriate Regional Solicitor. Such requests shall be referred promptly to the Regional Solicitor for a determination of the advisability, scope and timing of any investigation, and the advisability of participation in any conference. To the maximum extent possible, there shall be consultation with the Solicitor on questions of this nature so as to insure no procedural or legal improprieties.

b. Inquiries. Once a notice of contest has been filed, all inquiries relating to the general subject matter of the Citation and Notification of Penalty raised by any of the parties of the proceedings, including the employer and affected employees or authorized employee representative, shall be referred promptly to the Regional Solicitor. Similarly, all other inquiries, such as from prospective witnesses, insurance carriers, other Government agencies, attorneys, etc., shall be referred to the Regional Solicitor.

Notes

CHAPTER

28

ADDITIONAL SOURCES OF HELP

OSHA standards, interpretations, directives, interactive expert compliance assistance, and additional information are on the Internet at **www.osha.gov** and **www.osha-slc.gov.**

A variety of OSHA materials, including standards, interpretations and directives can be purchased on CD-ROM from the Government Printing Office. Ordering information is available from OSHA Publications at (202) 219-4667. Order publications directly from the Government Printing Office by contacting:

Superintendent of Documents
U.S. Government Printing Office (GPO)
732 N Capitol St, NW
Washington, DC 20401
1-888-293-6498; (202) 512-1530

Safety and Health Organizations and Agencies

The following is a list of organizations and government agencies that are involved in safety and health. Brief descriptions of their responsibilities are included.

American Association of Occupational Health Nurses
2920 Brandywine Rd, #100
Atlanta, GA 30341
(770) 455-7757
www.aaohn.org

Works to ensure occupational health nurses are the authority on health, safety, productivity and disability management for employees. Provides education and guidance for nurses and advocates new legislation, regulations, and public policy whose end goal is to provide healthy and safe workplaces.

American College of Occupational & Environmental Medicine
55 W Seegers Rd
Arlington Heights, IL 60005
(847) 228-6850
www.acoem.org

Promotes the health of workers through preventive medicine, clinical care, research, and education. Holds conferences and seminars and offers publications to healthcare professionals that are knowledgeable and capable of treating job-related diseases, recognizing and resolving workplace hazards, instituting rehabilitation methods, and providing well-managed care.

American Conference of Governmental Industrial Hygienists (ACGIH)
Kemper Woods Center
1330 Kemper Meadow Dr
Cincinnati, OH 45240
(513) 742-2020
www.acgih.org

Professional society of persons employed by official governmental units responsible for full-time programs of industrial hygiene. Devoted to the development of administrative and technical aspects of worker health protection.

American Industrial Hygiene Association (AIHA)
2700 Prosperity Ave, Ste 250
Fairfax, VA 22031
(703) 849-8888
www.aiha.org

Professional society of industrial hygienists. Promotes the study and control of environmental factors affecting the health and well being of industrial workers.

American National Standards Institute (ANSI)
11 W 42nd St
New York, NY 10038
(212) 354-3300
www.ansi.org

Serves as clearinghouse for nationally coordinated voluntary safety, engineering and industrial standards.

American Society for Heating, Refrigeration and Air Conditioning Engineers (ASHRAE)
1791 Tullie Circle, NE
Atlanta, GA 30329
1-800-527-4723; (404) 636-8400
www.ashrae.org

Provides technical and educational information, standards, and guidelines to members.

American Society of Safety Engineers (ASSE)
1800 E Oakton St
Des Plaines, IL 60018
(847) 699-2929
www.asse.org

Professional society of safety engineers, safety directors and others concerned with accident prevention and safety programs.

American Welding Society (AWS)
550 NW LeJeune Rd
Miami, FL 33126
1-800-443-9353
www.asw.org

Professional engineering society in the field of welding. Sponsors seminars and conferences on welding.

ASME International (formerly the American Society of Mechanical Engineers)
Three Park Ave
New York, NY 10016-5990
1-800-843-2763
www.asme.org

Conducts research; develops boiler, pressure vessel and power test codes. Sponsors American National Standards Institute in developing safety codes and standards for equipment.

ASTM International (formerly the American Society for Testing and Materials)
100 Bar Harbor Dr
PO Box C700
West Conshohocken, PA 19428-2959
(610) 832-9585
www.astm.org

Establishes voluntary consensus standards for materials, products, systems and services.

Bureau of Labor Statistics (BLS)
Postal Square Bldg
2 Massachusetts Ave, NE
Washington, DC 20212-0006
(202) 691-5200
www.bls.gov

Compiles and publishes statistics on occupational injuries and illnesses.

Centers for Disease Control and Prevention (CDC)
1600 Clifton Rd
Atlanta, GA 30333
(404) 639-3311
www.cdc.gov

Surveys national disease trends and epidemics and environmental health problems. Promotes national health education program. Administers block grants to states for preventive medicine and health services programs.

CHEMTREC (Chemical Transportation Emergency Center)
1300 Wilson Blvd
Arlington, VA 22209
1-800-262-8200; (703) 741-5523
www.chemtrec.org

Provides information and assistance for emergency incidents involving chemicals and hazardous materials via its 24-hour emergency call center MSDS document storage and retrieval system, which contains more than 2.8 million MSDSs.

Compressed Gas Association (CGA)
4221 Walney Rd, 5th Flr
Chantilly, VA 20151-2923
(703) 788-2700
www.cganet.com

Submits recommendations to appropriate government agencies to improve safety standards and methods of handling, transporting and storing gases. Acts as advisor to regulatory authorities and other agencies concerned with safe handling of compressed gases.

Consumer Product Safety Commission
4330 East-West Hwy
Bethesda, MD
1-800-638-2772
www.cpsc.gov

Protects the public from unreasonable risks of serious injury or death from more than 15,000 types of consumer products, including power tools. Provides industry guidance via recall programs, handbooks on regulated products and recalls, regulatory summaries in plain language, and conference proceedings.

Environmental Protection Agency (EPA)
Ariel Ros Bldg
1200 Pennsylvania Ave, NW
Washington, DC 20460
(202) 272-0167
www.epa.gov

Administers federal environmental policies, research and regulations. Provides information on many environmental subjects.

U.S. Government Printing Office (GPO)
732 N Capitol St, NW
Washington, DC 20401
1-888-293-6498; (202) 512-1530
www.gpoaccess.gov

Prints, distributes, and sells selected publications of the U.S. Congress, government agencies, and executive departments.

Institute of Makers of Explosives
1120 19th St, NW, Ste 310
Washington, DC 20036-3605
(202) 429-9280
www.ime.org

Promotes the safety and security of employees, users, the public, and the environment in all aspects of the manufacture and use of explosive materials in industrial blasting and other essential operations.

582

International Agency for Research on Cancer (IARC)
c/o World Health Organization
Publications Center USA
525 23rd St, NW
Washington, DC 20037
(202) 974-3000
www.iarc.fr

Coordinates and conducts research on the causes of human cancer, the mechanisms of carcinogenesis, and to develop scientific strategies for cancer control. The agency is involved in epidemiological and laboratory research and disseminates scientific information through publications, meetings, courses, and fellowships.

International Association of Drilling Contractors
15810 Park 10 Place, #242
Houston, TX 77084-5134
(281) 578-7171
www.iadc.org

Fosters education and communications within the upstream petroleum industry through conferences, training seminars and a comprehensive network of technical publications, it

Mine Safety and Health Administration (MSHA)
1100 Wilson Blvd, 21st Flr
Arlington, VA 22209-3939
(202) 693-9400
www.msha.gov

Administers and enforces the health and safety provisions of the Federal Mine Safety and Health Act of 1977. Has a training facility in Beckley, West Virginia. (Mine Health and Safety Academy, PO Box 1166, Beckley, WV 25801)

National Audiovisual Center (NAC)
National Technical Information Service
5285 Port Royal Rd
Springfield, VA 22161
(703) 605-6000
www.ntis.gov

Serves as the central source for all federally produced audiovisual materials and makes them available to the public through information and distribution services.

National Fire Protection Association (NFPA)
1 Batterymarch
Park Quincy, MA 02169-7471
1-800-344-3555; (617) 770-3000
www.nfpa.org

Develops, publishes and disseminates standards, prepared by approximately 175 technical committees, intended to minimize the possibility and effects of fire and explosion.

National Institute for Occupational Safety and Health (NIOSH)
U.S. Department of Health and Human Services
Education and Information Division
4676 Columbia Pkwy
Cincinnati, OH 45226
1-800-356-4674; (513) 533-8302
www.cdc.gov/niosh

NIOSH Publications
(513) 533-8287

NIOSH Technical Assistance
1-800-35-NIOSH

Part of the Centers for Disease Control and Prevention. Supports and conducts research on occupational safety and health issues. Provides technical assistance and training. Develops recommendations for OSHA. Operates an occupational safety and health informational bibliographic database.

National Institute of Standards and Technology (NIST)
100 Bureau Dr
Stop 3460
Gaithersburg, MD 20899-3460
(301) 975-6478
www.nist.gov

Formerly the National Bureau of Standards, NIST develops engineering measurements, data and test methods. Produces the technical base for proposed engineering standards and code changes. Generates new engineering practices. Aids international competitiveness of small- and medium-sized companies and consortia through technology development and transfer programs.

National Institutes of Health (NIH)
9000 Rockville Pike
Bethesda, MD 20892
(301) 496-4000
www.nih.gov

Supports and conducts biomedical research into the causes and prevention of diseases and furnishes information to health professionals and the public.

National Safety Council (NSC)
1121 Spring Lake Dr
Itasca, IL 60143-3201
(630) 285-1121
www.nsc.org

A voluntary, non-governmental organization that promotes accident reduction by providing a forum for the exchange of safety and health ideas, techniques, experiences and accident prevention methods.

National Technical Information Service (NTIS)
5285 Port Royal Rd
Springfield, VA 22161
(703) 605-6000
www.ntis.gov

Distribution center that sells to the public government-funded research and development reports and other technical analyses prepared by federal agencies, their contractors, or grantees. Offers microfiche and computerized bibliography search services.

National Toxicology Program
PO Box 12233
111 Alexander Dr
Research Triangle Park, NC 27709
(919) 541-3991
ntp-server.niehs.nih.gov

An interagency program whose mission is to evaluate agents of public health concern by developing and applying tools of modern toxicology and molecular biology.

Occupational Safety and Health Administration (OSHA)
200 Constitution Ave, NW
Washington, DC 20210
1-800-321-6742
www.osha.gov

Sets policy, develops programs and implements the Occupational Safety and Health Act of 1970.

Occupational Safety and Health Review Commission (OSHRC)
1120 20th St, NW
Washington, DC 20036
(202) 606-5398
www.oshrc.gov

Independent executive agency that adjudicates disputes between private employers and OSHA arising from citations of occupational safety and health standards

We're Into Safety
1015 S 233rd Pl
Des Moines, WA 98198-7442
206-824-4189
www.wisafety.com

Provides a variety of training aids and services, including free, downloadable materials.

World Health Organization
525 23rd St, NW
Washington, DC 20037
(202) 974-3000
www.who.ch

The United Nations' specialized agency for health. Its objective is "the attainment by all peoples of the highest possible level of health." Offers a variety of information and publications.

World Safety Organization
106 W Young Ave, Ste G
PO Box 518
Warrensburg, MO 64093
(606) 747-3132
www.worldsafety.org

Coordinates functions, activities, operations and related works with other international bodies and organizations to promote safety and accident prevention.

ANSWERS TO TEST AND QUIZZES

Answers to Construction Pre-Test

1. The controlling employer can be cited whether or not his or her own employees are exposed to a hazard.
   a. True
   b. False

2. What is a key element of a comprehensive safety and health program?
   a. Identification and control of hazards
   b. Tool box meetings
   c. Exchange of Hazard Communication Programs
   d. OSHA Poster on site
   e. None of the above

3. On a multi-employer worksite, penalties for employers with no exposed employees will be calculated using the exposed employees of all employers as the number of employees for probability assessment.
   a. True
   b. False

4. The four hazards which are relevant to a focused inspection include: falls, electrocutions, struck-by and caught in between.
   a. True
   b. False

5. Employers are required to have a program in which frequent and regular safety and health inspections are made by a competent person.
   a. True
   b. False

6. Employers are not responsible for instructing each employee in the recognition and avoidance of unsafe conditions, but he/she does have to instruct them on the regulations that are applicable to their own work environment.
   a. True
   b. False

7. Each employee who is constructing a leading edge 5 feet or more above lower levels shall be protected from falling by the use of guardrail systems, safety net systems or personal fall arrest systems.
   a. True
   b. False

8. On residential construction, when the employer can demonstrate that it is infeasible or creates a greater hazard to use the conventional fall protections including: guard rails, safety nets, and personal fall arrest systems, the employer shall develop and implement a:

a. System of interventions designed to protect employees at the moment they appear to be falling.

b. Fall protection plan that meets the requirements of paragraph K. of 1926.502

c. Blue prints, detailing scaffold availability throughout each construction phase.

d. None of the above

9. **A stairway or ladder shall be provided at all personnel points of access where there is a break in elevation of 12 inches or more and no ramp, runway, sloped embankment or personnel hoist is provided.**

a. True

b. False

10. **Fixed ladders shall be provided with cages, wells, ladder safety devices or self-retracting lifelines where the length of climb is less than 24 feet, but the top of the ladder is at a distance greater than 24 feet above lower levels.**

a. True

b. False

11. **No scaffold shall be erected, moved, dismantled, or altered except under the supervision of competent persons.**

a. True

b. False

12. **When freestanding mobile scaffold towers are used, the height shall not exceed ____ times the minimum base dimension.**

a. Five times

b. Six times

c. Eight times

d. Four times

13. **In steel erection operations, when bolts or drift pins are being knocked out, means shall be provided to keep them from falling.**

a. True

b. False

14. **In steel erection operations, when rivet heads are knocked off or backed out, means shall be provided to keep them from_____.**

a. Bouncing

b. Falling

c. Curling

d. Sticking

e. None of the above

15. **The employer shall be responsible for the development of a fire protection program to e followed throughout all phases of the construction and demolition work, and he shall provide for the firefighting equipment as specified in this subpart. As fire hazards occur, there shall be no delay in providing the necessary equipment.**

a. True

b. False

16. **Not more than _____ gallons of flammable or _____ gallons of combustible liquids shall be store in any one storage cabinet. Not more than three such cabinets may be located in a single storage area. Quantities in excess of this shall be stored in an inside storage room.**

a. 50 & 100

b. 40 and 150

c. 60 and 120

d. none of the above

17. **Portable heaters, including salamanders, shall be equipped with an approved automatic device to shut off the flow of gas to the main burner and pilot, if used, in the event of flame failure. Such heaters, having inputs above 50,000 B.T.U. per hour shall be equipped with either a pilot, which must be lighted and proved before the burner can be turned on, or an electrical ignition system.**

a. True

b. False

18. **All construction equipment cab glass shall be ____ glass, or equivalent, that introduces no visible distortion affect-**

ing the safe operation of any machine covered by this subpart.

a. Clear
b. Stained
c. Safety
d. Rust resistant
e. None of the above

19. **Employers can use any motor vehicle equipment having an obstructed view to the rear whether or not it is equipped with a reverse signal alarm that is audible above the surrounding noise level.**

a. True
b. False

20. **No grounded conductor shall be attached to any terminal or lead so as to reverse designated polarity.**

a. True
b. False

21. **A written description of the employers assured equipment grounding conductor program, including the specific procedures adopted by the employer, shall be available at the _____ for inspection and copying by the Assistant Secretary and any affected employee.**

a. Home office
b. Employees house
c. Job site
d. General Contractors headquarters
e. None of the above

22. **Condition of tools. All hand and power tools and similar equipment, whether** furnished by the employer or the employee, shall be maintained in a safe condition.

a. True
b. False

23. **All hand-held powered platen sanders, grinders with wheels 2-inch diameter or less, routers, planers, laminate trimmers, nibblers, shears, scroll saws and jigsaws with blade shanks one-fourth of an inch or less may be equipped with only a positive _____ control.**

a. Toggle switch
b. Trigger finger
c. Quick release
d. On/Off
e. All of the above

24. **"Limited access zone" means an area alongside a masonry wall that is under construction, which is clearly demarcated to limit access by employees.**

a. True
b. False

25. **No construction loads shall be placed on a concrete structure or portion of a concrete structure unless the employer determines, based on information received from a person who is competent in structural design, that the structure or portion of the structure is capable of supporting the loads.**

a. True
b. False

Answers to Introduction to OSHA Quiz

1. **OSHA was formed in 1970 in order to:**
   a. Provide income to the Federal Government
   b. Establish and enforce occupational health and safety rules and to preserve human resources.
   c. Establish an Agency that would work with the EPA to enforce pollution.
   d. Provide for worker safety by reducing the need for unions.

2. **On a construction site, the OSHA inspector conducting a FOCUS inspection will look mainly at hazards caused by Falls, Struck by, Struck against and :**
   a. Drowning
   b. Chemical Exposure
   c. Electrical Exposure
   d. Safety Program Violations

3. **On a large construction site the general contractor and subcontractors can be viewed as one organization under the multi-employer rule. OSHA may NOT issue citations to companies that:**
   a. Created the hazard
   b. Controlled the hazard
   c. Are responsible for correcting the hazard
   d Observe the hazard indirectly

4. **The General Duty Clause states that each employer shall furnish to each employee a place of employment which:**
   a. is free from recognized hazards
   b. comply with OSHA regulations
   c. recognize organized bargaining units
   d. provide minimum safety and health provisions

5. **States that develop their own safety and health rules must ensure that those rules are:**
   a. Identical to the Federal rules
   b. providing safety to workers that equal or exceed federal standards
   c. in the best interest of the state
   d. available to all workers in the state

6. **OSHA has the authority to conduct inspections. Employers may:**
   a. Require the inspector to wait until the safety director arrives
   b. Reschedule the inspection for a more appropriate time
   c. Be informed of the name of the employee who filed an anonymous complaint
   d. Request a search warrant

Answers to Hazard Communication Quiz

1. **The Hazard Communication Act is also known as the:**
   a. Chemical Identification Act of 1984
   b. MSDS Law
   c. Chemical Protective Act
   d. Right to Know Law

2. **PEL Stands for:**
   a. Permissible Exposure Level
   b. Priority Evacuation Ladder
   c. Permissive Exposure Limit
   d. Post-mortem Exposure Level

3. The Hazcom standard requires that construction firms have a site specific program that must be in writing, at the location that:
   a. Lists chemicals on site and how they are labeled
   b. Lists chemicals on site and what they look like
   c. List chemicals on site and where they are stored
   d. List chemicals on site and how to safely dispose of them

4. **Material Safety Data Sheets must be:**
   a. Available to the supervisor on shift
   b. Stored in a central location at the company headquarters
   c. Available to all workers
   d. Available to workers who are exposed to the chemical

5. **Two common types of labels are the HMIS label and the:**
   a. NFPA label
   b. ANSI label
   c. CGA label
   d. PEL label

6. **Regarding chemicals, workers must be trained to:**
   a. Identify the chemical they are using
   b. Protect themselves from the chemical they are using
   c. Know what chemicals they are occupationally exposed to
   d. All of the above

Answers to Personal Protective Equipment Quiz

1. **On a construction site, who is responsible to ensure that workers have the PPE?**
   a. The employee
   b. The labor service company
   c. The employer
   d. OSHA

2. **For head protection, workers should wear a hard hat that complies with:**
   a. ANSI Standard Z64
   b. ANSI Standard Z89
   c. NFPA 101
   d. NFPA 93

3. **Safety shoes must meet the requirements of:**
   a. LeHigh Safety Shoe specification
   b. ANSI Standard Z89
   c. ANSI Standard Z41.1
   d. ANSI Standard Z87.1

4. **Eye protection must have the name of the manufacturer and the ANSI Standard stamped on them. In order to be effective, they must:**
   a. Have side shields
   b. Be tinted to preclude sun glare
   c. Not disturb other types of PPE such as hard hats or respirators
   d. Be provided by the employee

5. **When working over water if there is a danger of falling in, workers must:**
   a. Be provided with a US Coast Guard approved life jacket
   b. Have a certified swimmer available to fish them out
   c. Be trained in basic life saving techniques
   d. Understand the danger of hyphothermia

6. **Hard hats must be worn:**
   a. With the bill facing front at all times
   b. Over the top of any other type of hat, such as baseball caps
   c. At all times
   d. When there is a danger of objects striking the head

Answers to Permit Required Confined Space Entry Quiz - Answers

1. **By definition, a confined space must be:**
   a. Large enough to enter, have restricted entry and be dangerous
   b. Large enough to enter, be dangerous, have a confined space sign posted
   c. Large enough to enter, restricted access, not be designed for continuous occupancy.
   d. Large enough to enter, be posted as a restricted area

2. **The construction standard requires that workers entering a confined space:**
   a. Know about the hazards they will encounter
   b. Be instructed on the hazards, what precautions must be taken and how to use PPE and emergency equipment.
   c. Wear a self contained breathing apparatus
   d. Be trained in permit required entry rescue techniques.

3. **Examples of construction related confined spaces are:**
   a. A tool shop, an enclosed trailer and a sewage tank.
   b. A manhole, a building foundation, and the job shack.
   c. A manhole, a condenser pit or an underground vault.
   d. A classroom with no windows, a tool shop and a job shack.

4. **Under the 1910 permit required entry rules, entry into a permit required confined space requires:**
   a. An authorized entrant, an attendant, a supervisor of the operation.
   b. An authorized entrant, a certified engineer, a supervisor of the operation.

c. An authorized entrant, an attendant, a stand-by rescue team

d. An authorized entrant, a supervisor, a stand-by rescue team

5. **The ANSI standard for entry into permit required confined spaces is:**
   a. ANSI Z87.1
   b. ANSI Z41
   c. ANSI Z 117.1
   d. ANSI Z93.3

6. **OSHA will enforce the rules for entry into permit required confined spaces for construction workers using:**
   a. General Duty Clause and ANSI Z 117.1
   b. 29CFR 1910.146
   c. 29CFR 1910.147
   d. There are no rules for construction workers entering permit required confined spaces

---

Answers to Electrical Quiz

1. **Workers exposed to electrical shock on construction sites must be protected by:**
   a. Ground fault circuit interrupter or an assured grounding program
   b. Grounding of all electrical systems
   c. Low voltage tools
   d. Ohms Law

2. **A ground fault circuit interrupter is designed to trip at about:**
   a. 10 milli-amps
   b. 20 milli-amps
   c. 3 milli-amps
   d. 5 milli-amps

3. **Electrical conductors and equipment used in construction must be:**
   a. Approved for the type of use they will be used for.
   b. Registered with the General Contractor
   c. Protected by a GFCI.
   d. Labeled with the name of the owner of the conductor or equipment

4. **Using an assured protection program all equipment must be tested by a competent person:**
   a. Before first use, after repairs, after suspected damage, at least every 90 days
   b. Before first use, and every 90 days
   c. Annually
   d. As determined by the competent person

5. **The assured grounding program requires that the following tests be performed on all cord sets and receptacles that are not a permanent part of the building:**
   a. Continuity and proper insulation
   b. Continuity, correct attachment of the cap or plug
   c. Continuity and correct type of wiring for the use anticipated
   d. Continuity and use of GFCI

6. **Assured grounding tests shall be:**
   a. Conducted daily
   b. Recorded
   c. Performed by a licensed electrician
   d. Performed by an authorized individual

Answers to Stairs and Ladders Quiz

1. **A stairway or ladder must be provided at all points of access where there is a break in elevation of:**
   a. 12 inches
   b. 19 inches
   c. 24 inches
   d. 36 inches

2. **Ladders must extend beyond the working surface by:**
   a. 1 foot
   b. 2 feet
   c. 3 feet
   d. 4 feet

3. **Ladders must be secured from movement and self supporting ladders must:**

a. Have a ¼ ratio: for every four feet up, the base must come out 1 foot.

b. Be held by a competent person

c. Be made of fiberglass

d. Have a 1/3 ration: for every three feet up, the base must come out 1 foot

4. Workers must be trained by a competent person on how to use ladders and stairways. This training must include:

a. Nature of hazards of falls, correct procedures for using the equipment, maximum load.

b. Nature of hazards of falls, the requirements of the OSHA regulation

c. The ANSI standard that governs ladder use.

d. A written test that may be inspected by OSHA

5. Ladders that have structural defects such as missing rungs or steps:

a. May be used if they cannot be immediately repaired.

b. Must be removed to the job trailer.

c. Must be immediately marked defective or tagged with a "do not use" sign

d. Must be repaired immediately

6. Around electrical lines:

a. Ladders may not be made of metal.

b. Ladders must remain over 30 feet from powerlines.

c. Ladders must be protected with a coating of varnish

d. Ladders may come into contact with the insulation on the powerlines.

Answers to Fall Protection Quiz

1. A general rule for all construction activities is that workers must be protected from falls at:

a. 4 feet

b. 6 feet

c. 10 feet

d. 20 feet

2. A personal fall arrest system consists of:

a. Anchor point, fall arrest harness, shock absorbing lanyard

b. Anchor point, locking snap hooks, shock absorbing lanyard

c. Anchor point, fall arrest harness, locking snap hooks

d. Anchor point, locking snap hooks, guardrail.

3. A body belt may be used for fall protection

a. True

b. False

4. Guardrails consist of:

a. Top rail, intermediate posts, toeboard

b. Top rail, intermediate posts, fiber webbing

c. Top rail, intermediate posts, midrail

d. Top rail, fiber webbing, toeboard

5. A safety net that is placed 7 feet below the working deck must exend:

a. 8 feet horizontally

b. 10 feet horizontally

c. 13 feet horizontally

d. 15 feet horizontally

6. A positioning device such as a body belt or harness may allow free fall of:

a. 1 foot

b. 2 feet

c. 6 feet

d. 10 feet

Answers to Scaffolding Quiz

1. **During assembly or disassembly of a scaffold what fall protection standard applies?**
   a. Scaffold section rules
   b. Fall protection rules
   c. Stairways and ladder rules
   d. General Duty Clause

2. **Assembly or disassembly of a scaffold must be supervised by:**
   a. A qualified supervisor
   b. An authorized supervisor
   c. A competent supervisor
   d. A professionally licensed Engineer

3. **When the scaffold is correctly built and used, fall protection is provided by:**
   a. Training of the users on the scaffold.
   b. Personal Fall Arrest Systems on the users
   c. The competent person conducting periodic worksite inspections
   d. The guardrail and midrail system of the scaffold

4. **Mobile Scaffolds may be moved while occupied when:**
   a. The competent person says it is ok to do so.
   b. All abutting ends of the scaffold are tied with #200 wire
   c. Flooring planks are secured
   d. Never

5. **Planking on scaffolds must be of scaffold grade lumber and:**
   a. Complete with no openings over six inches
   b. Complete with no openings at all
   c. Should provide a safe working platform as determined by the competent person
   d. Should be secured to the scaffold at all times with #200 wire

6. **The base of scaffolds should rest on:**
   a. The steel leg of the scaffold placed on a cement block
   b. The steel leg of the scaffold placed on the 4 inch metal base
   c. The steel leg of the scaffold placed on the 4 inch metal base which rests on a mudsill.
   d. A sound and secure surface, such as dry soil.

Answers to Fire Protection Quiz

1. **For every 3,000 square feet of a building there must be:**
   a. A fire extinguisher with a rating of at least 2A
   b. A Type C fire extinguisher
   c. A Type B fire extinguisher
   d. A garden hose

2. **Flammable and combustible liquids must be stored in a storage cabinet:**
   a. If the amount is over 15 gallons
   b. If the amount is over 25 gallons
   c. If the amount is over 35 gallons
   d. If the flash point is below 65 degrees

3. **When pouring 10 gallons of gasoline from one tank to another the area must be separated by:**
   a. 25 feet from other operations
   b. A construction with a one hour fire rating
   c. Both of the above
   d. Either of the above
   e. None of the above

4. **On a multiple story building, fire extinguishers must be located:**
   a. At the base of the stairway
   b. On each floor
   c. Within 200 feet of flammable gas
   d. Based on the operation taking place

5. **Temporary heating devices such as torpedo heaters must:**
   a. Have sufficient fresh air supply and be used according to manufacturers directions.
   b. Be set on solid wood flooring
   c. Be directly plumbed to the gas source

d. Be located at least 25 feet from coverings such as canvas or tarps.

6. Which statement is not correct?

a. Fire extinguishers must be within 100 feet of the workers

b. Fire extinguishers must be on vehicles that transport flammables

c. Fire extinguishers must be within 100 feet of open storage yards

d. Fire extinguishers must be within 100 feet of a service/fuel area

---

Answers to Trenching and Excavation Quiz

1. **Regarding trenching and excavations-what are the requirements to be considered a "competent person"?**
   Be able to recognize and predict hazards. Have the authority to correct those hazards.

2. **Prior to beginning a dig at a construction site, who should be called and why?**
   Underground utility companies to locate wires, pipes and cables.

3. **While digging a trench, how close to the edge of the trench may materials be placed?**
   No closer than two feet

4. **Workers in a trench must be protected by an adequate protective system whenever a trench is more than _____ feet.**
   Five feet

5. **Workers in a trench must have a ladder, stairway or ramp with how many feet of them?**
   25 feet

6. **A shield system for a trench box must be built to manufacturers specifications or be designed by _____.**
   Licensed Professional Engineer (LPE)

7. **The trench has been dug in soil classified as Class C soil. The competent person decides to slope the trench. What is the angle of the slope?**
   1 ½ to 1

8. **How often must the competent person inspect the trench?**
   Daily and whenever conditions change that may affect the stability of the trench

9. **A walkway is built over a trench that is ten feet deep. What must the walkway have?**
   Guardrails that meet OSHA specifications

10. **Class B soil is being dug, but there is water seeping freely from the bottom of the excavation. What must the competent person do?**
    Reclassify the soil to a lower classification (class C) and remove the water from the trench.

Answers to End of Course Quiz

1. What is the most frequently cited OSHA Standard?
   a. Lockout/tagout
   b. Machine guarding
   c. Recordkeeping
   d. Hazardous communication

2. If you feel that a citation that was issued to you was unfair, you have _____ days to contest the charge.
   a. 5
   b. 10
   c. 15
   d 20

3. Even though OSHA has not published an Ergonomics Standard, you can still be cited for an ergonomics problem, such as making workers perform repetitive tasks.
   a. True
   b. False

4. The CD-ROM for OSHA Regulations (available from the Government Printing Office) is updated _____.
   a. Monthly
   b. Quarterly
   c. Annually

5. A Type A fire is one that consists of:
   a. Trash, paper and wood
   b. Oil and tar
   c. Electrical circuits that are still energized
   d. A combination of the above

6. The top four events that kill construction workers are falls from elevations, struck by, struck against, and _____.
   a. Chemical exposure
   b. Electrocution
   c. Collapsing trenches
   d. OSHA inspections

7. Even though the computer system is locked in the job shack at night, MSDSs can be kept on the computer and meet the accessibility requirements when workers who have no computer skills are working at night.
   a. True
   b. False

8. A ground-fault circuit interrupter does not require a grounding wire because it is a type of circuit breaker.
   a. True
   b. False

9. While mopping a spill in the bathroom, Millie the Maid splashes her mop against the GFCI outlet. The electricity flows through the wet mop to Millie's hands until the circuit interrupter breaks the flow of electricity, saving her life. At what level of milliamps should the circuit breaker trip to keep Millie on the pay roll?
   a. 3 milliamps
   b. 5 milliamps
   c. 7 milliamps
   d. 9 milliamps

10. A straight, portable ladder extends to a 20-ft. high roof. To meet OSHA requirements, the worker must ensure the ladder extends 3 ft. past the roof and the base of the ladder is _____ feet from the edge of the building.
   a. 2 ft.
   b. 3 ft.
   c. 5 ft.
   d. 7 ft.

GLOSSARY

Acid. Any chemical with a low pH that in a water solution can burn the skin or eyes. Acids turn litmus paper red and have pH values of 0 to 6.

Action level. Term used by OSHA and NIOSH to express the level of toxicant that requires medical surveillance, usually one half of the PEL.

Activated charcoal. Charcoal is an amorphous form of carbon formed by burning wood, nutshells, animal bones, and other carbonaceous materials. Heating it with steam to 800°C to 900°C activates charcoal. During this treatment, a porous, submicroscopic internal structure is formed which gives it an extensive internal surface area. Activated charcoal is commonly used as a gas or vapor adsorbent in air-purifying respirators and as a solid sorbent in air sampling.

Acute effect. Adverse effect on a human or animal that has severe symptoms developing rapidly and coming quickly to a crisis. Also see Chronic effect.

Adsorption. The condensation of gases, liquids, or dissolved substances on the surfaces of solids.

Air. The mixture of gases that surround the earth; its major components are as follows: 78.08 percent nitrogen, 20.95 percent oxygen, 0.03 percent carbon dioxide, and 0.93 percent argon. Water vapor (humidity) varies.

Airline respirator. A respirator that is connected to a compressed breathing air source by a hose of small inside diameter. The air is delivered continuously or intermittently in a sufficient volume to meet the wearer's breathing requirements.

Air-purifying respirator. A respirator that uses chemicals to remove specific gases and vapors from the air or that uses a mechanical filter to remove particulate matter. An air-purifying respirator must only be used when there is sufficient oxygen to sustain life and the air contaminant level is below the concentration limits of the device.

Alkali. Any chemical with a high pH that in a water solution is irritating or caustic to the skin. Strong alkalis in solution are corrosive to the skin and mucous membranes. Alkalis turn litmus paper blue and have pH values from 8 to 14. Example: sodium hydroxide, also known as caustic soda or lye. See also Base.

Allergy. An abnormal response of a hypersensitive person to chemical and physical stimuli. Allergic manifestations of major importance occur in about 10 percent of the population.

Anchorage (point). A secure point of attachment for lifelines, lanyards or deceleration devices.

American Conference of Governmental Industrial Hygienists (ACGIH). A professional organization that develops and publishes recommended occupational exposure limits for hundreds of chemical substances and physical agents.

American Table of Distances (Quantity Distance Tables). American Table of Distances for Storage of Explosives as reviewed and approved by the Makers of Explosives IME, June 1964.

American National Standards Institute (ANSI). A voluntary membership organization that develops consensus standards nationally for a variety of devices and procedures.

Approved. Equipment that has been listed or approved by a nationally recognized testing laboratory, such as Factory Mutual Engineering Corp. or Underwriters' Laboratories, Inc., or federal agencies, such as the Bureau of Mines or U.S. Coast Guard.

Approved storage facility. A facility for the storage of explosive materials conforming to the requirements of OSHA and covered by a license or permit issued under authority of the Bureau of Alcohol, Tobacco and Firearms.

Asphyxiant. A vapor or gas that can cause unconsciousness or death by suffocation (lack of oxygen). Asphyxiation is one of the principal potential hazards of working in confined spaces.

Atmosphere-supplying respirator. A respirator that provides breathing air from a source independent of the surrounding atmosphere. There are two types: airline and self-contained breathing apparatus.

Atmospheric pressure. The pressure exerted in all directions by the atmosphere. At sea level, mean atmospheric pressure is 29.92 inches Hg, 14.7 psi, or 407 inches Hg.

Authorized person. A person who is authorized by the employer to perform a task.

Base. A compound that reacts with an acid to form a salt. See also Alkali.

Bearer. A horizontal member of a scaffold that may be supported by ledgers and upon which the platform rests.

Benign. Not malignant. A benign tumor is one that does not metastasize or invade tissue. Benign tumors may still be lethal, due to pressure on vital organs.

Blast area. The area in which explosives loading and blasting operations are being conducted.

Blaster. The person or persons authorized to use explosives for blasting purposes and meeting the qualifications outlined in the OSHA regulations.

Blasting agent. Any material or mixture consisting of a fuel and oxidizer used for blasting, but is not classified as an explosive in which none of the ingredients is classified as an explosive provided the product cannot be detonated with a No. 8 test blasting cap when confined. A common blasting agent is a mixture of ammonium nitrate and carbonaceous combustibles, such as fuel oil or coal. This agent may be procured, premixed and packaged from explosives companies or mixed in the field

Blasting cap. A metallic tube closed at one end, containing a charge of one or more detonating compounds and designed for and capable of detonation from the sparks or flame from a safety fuse inserted and crimped into the open end.

Blocking hole. The breaking of boulders by firing a charge of explosives that has been loaded into a drill hole.

Boatswains chair. A seat supported by slings attached to a suspended rope, designed to accommodate one worker in a sitting position

Body belt. A strap with means both for securing it about the waist and for attaching it to a lanyard, lifeline or deceleration device. Only to be used for positioning purposes. Not an acceptable method of fall protection.

Body harness. Straps that may be secured about the person in a manner that distributes the fall-arrest forces over at least the thighs, pelvis, waist, chest and shoulders, with a means for attaching the harness to other components of a personal fall arrest system.

Biohazard. A combination of the words biological hazard. Organisms or products of organisms that present a risk to humans.

Brace. A tie that holds one scaffold member in a fixed position with respect to another member.

Bricklayers square scaffold. A scaffold composed of framed wood squares that support a platform, limited to light and medium duty.

Carpenters bracket scaffold. A scaffold consisting of wood or metal brackets supporting a platform.

Boiling point. The temperature at which the vapor pressure of a liquid equals atmospheric pressure.

Carbon monoxide. A colorless, odorless toxic gas produced by any process that involves the incomplete combustion of carbon-containing substances. It is emitted through the exhaust of gasoline-powered vehicles.

Carcinogen. A substance or agent capable of causing or producing cancer in mammals, including humans. A chemical is considered to be a carcinogen if:

- It has been evaluated by the International Agency for Research on Cancer and found to be a carcinogen or potential carcinogen;
- It is listed as a carcinogen or potential carcinogen in the Annual Report on Carcinogens published by the National Toxicology Program; or
- It is regulated by OSHA as a carcinogen.

Chemical Abstracts Service (CAS). An organization within the American Chemical Society that abstracts and indexes chemical literature from all over the world. "CAS Numbers" are used to identify specific chemicals or mixtures.

Ceiling limit (C). An airborne concentration of a toxic substance in the work environment that should never be exceeded.

Chemical cartridge respirator. A respirator that uses various chemical substances to rid inhaled air of certain gases and vapors. This type of respirator is effective for concentrations no more than 10 times the TLV of the contaminant if the contaminant has warning properties (odor or irritation below the TLV).

Chemical Transportation Emergency Center (CHEMTREC). Public service of the Chemical Manufacturers Association that provides immediate advice for those at the scene of hazardous materials emergencies. There is a 24-hour toll-free telephone number (1-800-424-9300) to provide assistance during chemical transportation emergencies.

Chronic effect. an adverse effect on a human or animal body, with symptoms that develop over a long period of time or recur frequently. See also Acute.

Cleat. A ladder crosspiece of rectangular cross section placed on edge upon which a person may step while ascending or descending a ladder.

Closed container. A container so sealed by means of a lid or other device that neither liquid nor vapor will escape from it at ordinary temperatures.

Combustible liquid. Any liquid having a flash point at or greater than 100°F and below 200°F.

Combustion. Any chemical process that involves oxidation sufficient to produce light or heat.

Competent person. A person who is qualified and authorized to perform the task. A competent person must have the ability to identify hazardous conditions and must have the authority to take action to maintain a safe workplace.

Concentration. The amount of a given substance in a stated unit of measure. Common methods of stating concentration are percent by weight, by volume, weight per unit volume and normality.

Connector. A device that is used to couple, or connect, parts of a personal fall arrest system or positioning device system.

Confined space. An area that has adequate size and configuration for employee entry, has limited means of access or egress, and is not designed for continuous employee occupancy.

Construction work. Work that consists of construction, alteration, and/or repair, including painting and decorating.

Controlled access zone. A work area clearly marked and designated in which certain types of work (e.g., overhand bricklaying) may take place without the use of conventional fall protection systems, such as guardrails, personal arrest systems or safety nets.

Conveyance. Any unit for transporting explosives or blasting agents. Includes, but not limited to, trucks, trailers, rail cars, barges and vessels.

Corrosive. A substance that causes visible destruction or permanent changes in human skin tissue at the site of contact.

Coupler. A device for locking together the component parts of a tubular metal scaffold. The material used for the couplers shall be of a structural type, such as drop forged steel, malleable iron, or structural grade aluminum.

Crawling board. A plank with cleats spaced and secured at equal intervals, for use by a worker on roofs. Not designed to carry any material. Also known as Chicken ladder.

Cutaneous. Pertaining to or affecting the skin.

De minimis violations. Violations of standards that have no direct or immediate relationship to safety or health. Whenever de minimis conditions are found during an inspection, they are documented in the same way as any other violation, but are not included on the citation.

Deceleration device. Any mechanism, such as rope, grab, rip stitch lanyard, specially woven lanyard, tearing or deforming lanyards, or automatic self-retracting lifelines/lanyards, that serves to dissipate a substantial amount of energy during a fall arrest or otherwise limits the energy imposed on an employee during fall arrest.

Deceleration distance. The additional vertical distance a falling person travels, excluding lifeline elongation and free-fall distance, before stopping. It is at this point that a deceleration device begins to operate.

Degrees Celsius (Centigrade). The temperature on a scale in which the freezing point of water is 0°C and the boiling point is 100°C. To convert to Degrees Fahrenheit, use the following formula: $F = (C \times 1.8) + 32$.

Degrees Fahrenheit. The temperature on a scale in which the boiling point of water is 212°F and the freezing point is 32°F. To convert to Degrees Celsius, use the following formula: $C = 5/9(F - 32)$

Density. The mass per unit volume of a substance. For example, lead is much denser than aluminum.

Dermatitis. Inflammation of the skin from any cause.

Dermatosis. A broader term than dermatitis; it includes any cutaneous abnormality thus encompassing follicullitis, pigmentary changes, and nodules and tumors.

Detonating cord. A flexible cord containing a center core of high explosives that when detonated will have sufficient strength to detonate other cap-sensitive explosives with which it is in contact.

Detonator. Blasting caps, electric blasting caps, delay electric blasting gaps and nonelectric delay blasting caps.

Dose-response relationship. Correlation between the amount of exposure to an agent or toxic chemical and the resulting effect on the body.

Double-cleat ladder. A ladder with a center rail to allow simultaneous two-way traffic for workers ascending or descending.

Double pole scaffold. A scaffold supported from the base by a double row of uprights, independent of support from the walls and constructed of uprights, ledgers, horizontal platform bearers and diagonal bracing. Also known as Independent pole scaffold.

Dusts. Solid particles generated by handling, crushing, grinding, rapid impact, detonation, and decrepitation of organic or inorganic materials, such as rock, ore, metal, coal, wood and grain. Dusts do not tend to flocculate, except under electrostatic forces. They do not diffuse in air but settle under the influence of gravity.

Dyspnea. Shortness of breath, difficult or labored breathing.

Electric blasting cap. A blasting cap designed for and capable of detonation by means of an electric current.

Electric blasting circuitry. Circuitry comprising electric blasting caps and several wires, including bus, connecting, leading and permanent blasting:

Bus wire. An expendable wire, used in parallel or series, in parallel circuits, to which the leg wires of electric blasting caps are connected.

Connecting wire. An insulated expendable wire used between electric blasting caps and the leading wires or between the bus wire and the leading wires.

Leading wire. An insulated wire used between the electric power source and the electric blasting cap circuit.

Permanent blasting wire. A permanently mounted insulated wire used between the electric power source and the electric blasting cap circuit.

Electric delay blasting caps. Caps designed to detonate at a predetermined period of time after energy is applied to the ignition system.

Evaporation. The process by which a liquid is changed into the vapor state.

Evaporation rate. The ratio of the time required to evaporate a measured volume of a liquid to the time required to evaporate the same volume of a reference liquid (e.g., butyl acetate, ethyl ether) under ideal test conditions. The higher the ratio, the slower the evaporation rate. The evaporation rate can be useful in evaluating the health and fire hazards of a material.

Explosives. Any chemical compound, mixture or device whose primary or common purpose is to function by explosion; that is, with substantially instantaneous release of gas and heat, unless such compound, mixture or device is specifically classified otherwise by the U.S. Department of Transportation. All material that is classified as an Class A, B or C explosive by the U.S. Department of Transportation.

Class A. Poses a detonating hazard, such as dynamite, nitroglycerin, picric acid, fulminate of mercury, black powder, blasting caps or detonating primers.

Class B. Poses a flammable hazard, such as propellant explosives, including some smokeless propellants.

Class C. Includes certain types of manufactured articles that contain Class A or B explosives, or both, as components, but in restricted quantities.

Failure. Load refusal or breakage. Also describes a separation of ladder components.

Failure to abate prior violation. A type of OSHA violation where an employer is cited for failing to fix a previously cited hazard. This violation may bring a civil penalty of up to $7,000 for each day the violation continues beyond the prescribed abatement date.

Federal Register. A publication of U.S. government documents officially promulgated under the law, whose validity depends upon such publication. It is published on each day following a government working day. It is, in effect, the daily supplement to the Code of Federal Regulations.

Fire brigade. An organized group of employees that is knowledgeable, trained and skilled in the safe evacuation of employees during emergency situations and in assisting in firefighting operations.

Fire point. The lowest temperature at which a material can evolve vapors fast enough to support continuous combustion.

Fire resistance. So resistant to fire that for a specified time and under conditions of a standard heat intensity, it will not fail structurally and will not permit the side away from the fire to become hotter than a specified temperature. Determined by NFPA 251-1969.

First aid. Emergency measures to be taken before regular medical help can be obtained when a person is suffering from overexposure to a hazardous material.

Fixed ladder. A ladder that cannot be readily moved or carried because it is an integral part of a building or structure.

Flammable limits. Flammables have a minimum concentration below which propagation of flame does not occur on contact with a source of ignition. This is known as the lower flammable explosive limit (LEL). There is also a maximum concentration of vapor or gas in air above which propagation of flame does not occur. This is known as the upper flammable explosive limit (UEL). These units are expressed in percent of gas or vapor in air by volume.

Flammable. Capable of being easily ignited, burning intensely, or having a rapid rate of flame spread.

Flammable liquid. Any liquid having a flash point of less than 100°F, except any mixture having components with flashpoints of 100°F or higher, the total of which make up 99 percent or more of the total volume of the mixture.

Flammable range. The difference between the lower and upper flammable limits, expressed in terms of percentage of vapor or gas in air by volume. Also known as Explosive range.

Flash point. The minimum temperature at which a liquid gives off vapor within a test vessel in sufficient concentration to form an ignitable mixture with air near the surface of the liquid. Two tests are used: open cup and closed cup.

Float or ship scaffold. A scaffold hung from overhead supports by means of ropes and consisting of a substantial platform having diagonal bracing underneath, resting upon and securely fastened to two parallel plank bearers at right angles to the span.

Fume. Airborne particulate formed by the evaporation of solid materials (e.g. metal fume emitted during welding). Usually less than one micron in diameter.

Fuse lighters. Special devices for the purpose of igniting safety fuses.

Gage pressure. Pressure measured with respect to atmospheric pressure.

Gas. A state of matter in which the material has very low density and viscosity, can greatly expand and contract in response to changes in temperature and pressure, easily diffuses into other gases, readily and uniformly distributes itself throughout any container. A gas can be changed to the liquid or solid state only by the combined effect of increased pressure and decreased temperature. Examples include sulfur dioxide, ozone, and carbon monoxide.

Gram (g). A metric unit of weight (1 oz = 28.4 g).

Guardrail. A rail secured to uprights and erected along the exposed sides and ends of platforms.

Guardrail system. A barrier erected to prevent employees from falling to lower levels.

Handrail. A rail used to provide employees with a handhold for support.

Heavy duty scaffold. A scaffold designed and constructed to carry a working load not to exceed 75 pounds per square foot.

High efficiency particulate air (HEPA) filter. A disposable, extended medium, dry type filter with a particle removal efficiency of no less than 99.97 percent for 0.3pm particles.

Horse scaffold. A scaffold for light or medium duty, composed of horses supporting a work platform.

Hole. A void or gap measuring 2 inches or more in the least dimension in a floor, roof or other walking/working surface.

Immediately dangerous to life and health (IDLH). An atmospheric concentration of any toxic, corrosive or asphyxiant substance that poses an immediate threat to life or would cause irreversible or delayed adverse health effects or would interfere with an individual's ability to escape from a dangerous atmosphere.

Ignition source. Anything that provides heat, sparks or flame sufficient to cause combustion/explosion.

Ignition temperature. The minimum temperature to initiate or cause self-sustained combustion in the absence of any source of ignition.

Impervious. A material that does not allow another substance to pass through or penetrate it. Frequently used to describe gloves.

Inches of mercury column. A unit used in measuring pressures. One inch of mercury column equals a pressure of 1.66 kPa (0.491 psi).

Inches of water column. A unit used in measuring pressures. One inch of water column equals a pressure of 0.25 kPa (0.036 psi).

Incompatible materials. Materials that could cause dangerous reactions when they come into direct contact with one another.

Ingestion. Taking in by the mouth.

Inhalation. Breathing of a substance in the form of a gas, vapor, fume, mist, or dust.

Insoluble. Incapable of being dissolved in a liquid.

Interior hung scaffold. A scaffold suspended from the ceiling or roof structure.

Irritant. A chemical that is not corrosive, but causes a reversible inflammatory effect on living tissue by chemical action at the site of contact.

Job-made ladder. A ladder that is fabricated by employees, typically at the construction site. A ladder that is not commercially manufactured.

Ladder jack scaffold. A light-duty scaffold supported by brackets attached to ladders.

Lanyard. A flexible line of rope, wire rope or strap that generally has a connector at each end for connecting the body belt or body harness to a deceleration device, lifeline or anchorage.

Latent period. The time that elapses between exposure and the first manifestation of damage.

Lethal concentration (LC). The concentration level that will kill 50 percent of the test animals within a specified time.

Lethal dose (LD). The dose required to produce the death in 50 percent of the exposed species within a specified time.

Ledgers (Stringers). A horizontal member that extends from post to post and supports the putlogs or bearers forming a tie between the posts.

Light-duty scaffold. A scaffold designed and constructed to carry a working load not to exceed 25 pounds per square foot.

Liter (L). A measure of capacity (1 qt = 0.9 L).

Load refusal. The point where the structural members lose their ability to carry the load. Lower explosive limit (LEL). The lower limit of flammability of a gas or vapor at ordinary ambient temperatures expressed in percent of the gas or vapor in air by volume. This limit is assumed constant for temperatures up to 120°C (250°F). Above this, it should be decreased by a factor of 0.7 because explosability increases with higher temperatures.

Leading edge. The edge of a floor, roof or formwork for a floor or other walking/working surface (e.g., the deck) that changes location as additional floor, roof, decking or formwork sections are placed, formed or constructed.

Lifeline. A component consisting of a flexible line for connection to an anchorage point at one end to hang vertically (vertical lifeline) or for connection to anchorages at both ends to stretch horizontally (horizontal lifeline) and that serves as a means for connecting other components of a personal fall arrest system to the anchorage.

Liquid petroleum gases (LPG or LP Gas). Any material that is composed predominantly of any of the following hydrocarbons, or mixtures of them: propane, propylene, butane and butylenes.

Low slope roof. A roof having a slope less than or equal to 4 in 12 (vertical to horizontal)

Magazine. Any building or structure, other than an explosives manufacturing building, used for the storage of explosives.

Malignant. As applied to a tumor. Cancerous and capable of undergoing metastasis or invasion of surrounding tissue.

Manually propelled mobile scaffold. A portable rolling scaffold supported by casters.

Mason's adjustable multiple point suspension scaffold. A scaffold having a continuous platform supported by bearers suspended by wire rope from overhead supports, so arranged and operated as to permit the raising or lowering of the platform to desired working positions.

Maximum rated load. The total of all loads, including the working load, the weight of the scaffold and such other loads as may be reasonably anticipated.

Medium-duty scaffold. A scaffold designed and constructed to carry a working load not to exceed 50 pounds per square foot.

Midrail. A rail approximately midway between the guardrail and platform, secured to the uprights erected along the exposed sides and ends of platforms.

Misfire. An explosive charge that failed to detonate.

Metastasis. Transfer of the causal agent (cell or microorganism) of a disease from a primary focus to a distant one through the blood or lymphatic vessels. Also, spread of malignancy from site of primary cancer to secondary site(s).

Meter. A metric unit of length, equal to about 39 inches.

Micron micrometer. A unit of length equal to one millionth of a meter, approximately 1/25 of an inch.

Milligram (mg). A unit of weight in the metric system (1,000 mg = 1 g).

Milligrams per cubic meter (mg/m). Unit used to measure air concentrations of dusts, gases, mists, and fumes.

Milliliter (mL). A metric unit used to measure volume (1 mL = 1 cu cm).

Millimeter of mercury (mmHg). The unit of pressure equal to the pressure exerted by a column of liquid mercury 1 mm high at a standard temperature.

Mists. Suspended liquid droplets generated by condensation from the gaseous to the liquid state or by breaking up a liquid into a dispersed state, such as by splashing, foaming, or atomizing. Mist is formed when a finely divided liquid is suspended in air.

Mucous membranes. Lining of the hollow organs of the body, notably the nose, mouth, stomach, intestines, bronchial tubes, and urinary tract.

Mud capping. The blasting of boulders by placing a quantity of explosives against a rock, boulder or other object without confining the explosives in a drill hole. Also known as Bulldozing, Adobe blasting and Dobying.

Needle beam scaffold. A light-duty scaffold consisting of needle beams supporting a platform.

National Fire Protection Association (NFPA). A voluntary member-ship organization whose aim is to promote and improve fire protection and prevention. The NFPA publishes 16 volumes of codes known as the National Fire Codes.

National Institute for Occupational Safety and Health (NIOSH). A federal agency that conducts research on health and safety concerns, tests and certifies respirators, and trains occupational health and safety professionals.

Nonelectric delay blasting cap. A blasting cap with an integral delay element in conjunction with and capable of being detonated by a detonation impulse or signal from a miniaturized detonating cord.

National Toxicology Program (NTP). The NTP publishes an annual report on carcinogens.

Nuisance dust. Dust with little adverse effect on the lungs that does not produce significant organic disease or toxic effect when exposures are kept under reasonable control.

Opening. A gap or void 30 inches or more high and 18 inches or more wide in a wall or partition through which employees can fall to a lower level.

Other than serious violation. A violation that has a dire relationship to job safety and health, but probably would not cause death or serious physical harm. A proposed penalty of up to $7,000 for each violation is discretionary.

Outrigger scaffold. A scaffold supported by outriggers or thrust outs projecting beyond the wall or face of the building or structure, the inboard ends of which are secured inside of such building or structure.

Oxidizer. A substance that gives up oxygen readily. The presence of an oxidizer increases the fire hazard.

Oxygen deficiency. The concentration of oxygen by volume below which atmosphere-supplying respiratory protection must be provided. It exists in atmospheres where the percentage of oxygen by volume is less than 19.5 percent oxygen.

Oxygen-enriched atmosphere. An atmosphere containing more than 23.5 percent oxygen by volume.

Particulate matter. A suspension of fine solid or liquid particles in air, such as dust, fog, fume, smoke or sprays. Particulate matter suspended in air is commonly known as an aerosol.

Parts per million (ppm). Parts per million parts of air by volume of vapor or gas or other contaminant. Used to measure air concentrations of vapors and gases.

Permissible exposure limit (PEL). An exposure limit that is published and enforced by OSHA as a legal standard.

Permit-required confined space. A confined space that presents or has the potential for hazards related to atmospheric conditions (e.g., toxic, flammable, asphyxiating), engulfment, configuration or any other recognized serious hazard.

Personal protective equipment (PPE). Devices worn by the worker to protect against hazards in the environment. Examples include respirators, gloves and hearing protectors.

Personal fall arrest system. A system including, but not limited to, an anchorage point, connectors, and a body belt or body harness used to arrest an employee in a fall from a working level.

pH. Means used to express the degree of acidity or alkalinity of a solution with neutrality indicated as seven.

Point of access. All areas used by employees for work-related passage from one area or level to another.

Portable ladder. A ladder that can be readily moved or carried.

Positioning device system. A body belt or body harness system rigged to allow an employee to be supported on an elevated vertical surface such as a wall and work with both hands free while leaning backwards

Polymerization. A chemical reaction in which two or more small molecules (monomers) combine to form larger molecules (polymers) that contain repeating structural units of the original molecules. A hazardous polymerization is the above reaction with an uncontrolled release of energy.

Portable tank. A closed container having a liquid capacity of more than 60 US gallons and not intended for fixed installation.

Pounds per square inch (psi) For MSDS purposes, this is the pressure a material exerts on the walls of a confining vessel or enclosure. For technical accuracy, pressure must be expressed as pounds per square inch gauge (psig) or pounds per square inch absolute (psia); that is, gauge pressure plus sea level atmospheric pressure or psig plus approximately 14.7 pounds per square inch.

Primary blasting. The blasting operation by which the original rock formation is dislodged from its natural location.

Primer. A cartridge or container of explosives into which a detonator or detonating cord is inserted or attached.

Putlog. A scaffold member upon which the platform rests.

Qualified person. A person who has the knowledge to perform that task through education, schooling, training or experience.

Reactivity (chemical). A substance's susceptibility to undergo a chemical reaction or change that may result in dangerous side effects, such as an explosion, burns, and corrosive or toxic emission.

Respirable size particulates. Particulates in the size range that permit them to penetrate deep into the lungs upon inhalation.

Respirator (approved). A device that has met the requirements of 30 CFR Part 11 and is designed to protect the wearer from inhalation of harmful atmospheres and has been approved by the National Institute for Occupational Safety and Health and the Mine Safety and Health Administration.

Respiratory system. Consists of (in descending order) the nose, mouth, nasal passages, nasal pharynx, pharynx, larynx, trachea, bronchi, bronchioles, air sacs (alveoli) of the lungs and the muscles of respiration

Repeated violation. A violation of any standard, regulation, rule, or order where, upon reinspection, a substantially similar violation is found. A fine of up to $70,000 can be brought for each such violation. To be the basis of a repeated citation, the original citation must be final; a citation under contest may not serve as the basis for a subsequent repeated citation.

Riser height. The vertical distance from the top of a tread or platform/landing to the top of the next higher tread or platform/landing.

Rope grab. A deceleration device that travels on a lifeline and automatically engages the lifeline and lock to arrest a fall.

Roofing or bearer bracket. A bracket used in slope roof construction, having provisions for fastening to the roof or supported by ropes fastened over the ridge and secured to some suitable object.

Route of entry. The path by which chemicals can enter the body. There are three main routes of entry: inhalation, ingestion and skin absorption.

Runner. The lengthwise horizontal bracing or bearing members, or both.

Safety can. An approved closed container, of not more than five gallon capacity, having a flash-arresting screen, spring-closing lid and spout cover. It is so designed that it will safely relieve internal pressure when subjected to fire exposure

Safety fuse. A flexible cord containing an internal burning medium by which fire is conveyed at a continuous and uniform rate for the purpose of firing blasting caps.

Safety-monitoring system. A safety system in which a competent person is responsible for recognizing and warning employees of fall hazards.

Scaffold. Any temporary elevated platform and its supporting structure used for supporting workers, materials, or both

SCBA. Self-contained breathing apparatus.

Secondary blasting. The reduction of oversize material by the use of explosives to the dimension required for handling, including mud capping and block holing.

Self retracting lifeline/lanyard. A deceleration device containing a drum-wound line that can be slowly extracted from, or retracted onto, the drum under minimal tension during normal employee movement and, after onset of a fall, will automatically lock the drum and arrest the fall.

Semi-conductive hose. A hose with an electrical resistance high enough to limit flow of stray electric currents to safe levels, yet not so high as to prevent drainage of static electric charges to ground. Hose of not more than 2 megohms resistance over its entire length and of not less than 5,000 ohms per foot meets the requirement.

Sensitizer. A substance that on first exposure causes little or no reaction but that on repeated exposure may cause a marked response not necessarily limited to the contact site. Skin sensitization is the most common form of sensitization in the industrial setting.

Serious violation. A violation where there is substantial probability that death or serious physical harm could result and that the employer knew, or should have known, of the hazard. A mandatory penalty of up to $7,000 for each violation is proposed. A penalty for a serious violation may be adjusted downward, based on the employer's good faith, history of previous violations, the gravity of the alleged violation and size of business.

Short-term exposure limit (STEL). Maximum concentration to which workers can be exposed for a short period of time (15 minutes) for only four times throughout the day with at least one hour between exposures. An ACGIH-recommended exposure limit.

Side-step fixed ladder. A ladder that requires a person to get off at the top to step to the side of the ladder side rails to reach the landing.

Single-cleat ladder. A ladder consisting of a pair of side rails connected together by cleats, rungs or steps.

Single-point adjustable suspension scaffold. A manually or power-operated unit designed for light-duty use, supported by a single wire rope from an overhead support so arranged and operated as to permit the raising or lowering of the platform to desired working positions.

Single pole scaffold. Platforms resting on putlogs or cross beams, the outside ends of which are supported on ledgers secured to a single row of posts or uprights, and the inner ends of which are supported on or in a wall.

"Skin." A notation (sometimes used with PEL or TLV exposure data) that indicates that the stated substance may be absorbed by the skin, mucous membranes, and eyes—either airborne or by direct contact—and that this additional exposure must be considered part of the total exposure to avoid exceeding the PEL or TLV for that substance.

Snaphook. A connector consisting of a hook-shaped member with a normally closed keeper, or similar arrangement, that may be opened to permit the hook to receive an object, but when released, automatically closes to retain the object.

Solubility in water. A term expressing the percentage of a material (by weight) that will dissolve in water at ambient temperature. Solubility information can be useful in determining spill cleanup methods and re-extinguishing agents and methods for a material.

Solvent. A substance, usually a liquid, in which other substances are dissolved. The most common solvent is water.

Sorbent. 1. A material that removes toxic gases and vapors from air inhaled through a canister or cartridge. 2. Material used to collect gases and vapors during air sampling.

Specific gravity. The ratio of the mass of a unit volume of a substance to the mass of the same volume of a standard substance at a standard temperature. Water at 4°C (39.2°F) is the standard usually referred to for liquids; for gases, dry air (at the same temperature and pressure as the gas) is often taken as the standard substance. See also Density.

Springing. The creation of a pocket in the bottom of a drill hole by the use of a moderate quantity of explosives so that larger quantities of explosives may be inserted therein.

Stability. An expression of the ability of a material to remain unchanged. For HBDS purposes, a material is stable if it remains in the same form under expected and reasonable conditions of storage or use. Conditions that may cause instability (i.e., dangerous change) are stated. Examples are temperatures above 150°F, shock from dropping.

Stair rail system. A vertical barrier erected along the unprotected sides and edges of a stairway to prevent employees from falling to lower levels.

Stemming. A suitable inert incombustible material or device used to confine or separate explosives in a drill hole or to cover explosives in mud capping.

Steep roof. A roof having a slope greater than 4 in 12 (vertical to horizontal)

Stone setters adjustable multiple-point suspension scaffold. A swinging type scaffold having a platform supported by hangers suspended at four points so as to permit the raising or lowering of the platform to the desired working position by the use of hoisting machines.

Synergistic. Cooperative action of substances whose total effect is greater than the sum of their separate effects.

Systemic. Spread throughout the body, affecting all body systems and organs. Not localized in one spot or area.

Temporary service stairway. A stairway where permanent treads or landings are to be filled in at a later date.

Threshold. The lowest dose or exposure to a chemical at which a specific effect is observed.

Threshold limit value (TLV). A time-weighted average concentration under which most people can work consistently for eight hours a day, day after day, with no harmful effects. A table of these values and accompanying precautions is published annually by the ACGIH.

Through fixed ladder. A fixed ladder that requires a person getting off at the top to step between the side rails of the ladder to reach the landing.

Time weighted average concentration (TWA) Refers to concentrations of airborne toxic materials that have been weighted for certain time duration, usually eight hours.

Toeboard. A low protective barrier that prevents material and equipment from falling to lower levels and protects personnel from falling.

Toxicity. A relative property of a chemical agent. Refers to a harmful effect on some biologic mechanism and the conditions under which this effect occurs.

Tread depth. The horizontal distance from front to back of a tread, excluding nosing, if any.

Tube and coupler scaffold. An assembly consisting of tubing that serves as posts, bearers, braces, ties, and runners; a base supporting the posts; and special couplers that serve to connect the uprights and join the various members.

Tubular welded frame scaffold. A sectional panel or frame metal scaffold substantially built or prefabricated; a welded section that consists of posts and horizontal bearers with intermediate members.

Two-point suspension scaffold. A scaffold, the platform of which is supported by hangers (stirrups) at two points, suspended from overhead supports so as to permit the raising or lowering of the platform to the desired working position by tackle or hoisting machines. Also known as a Swinging scaffold.

Unprotected sides and edges. Any side or edge (except at entrances to points of access) of a walking/working surface (e.g., floor, roof, ramp or runway) where there is no wall or guardrail system at least 39 inches high.

Upper explosive limit (UEL). The highest concentration (expressed in percent vapor or gas in the air by volume) of a substance that will burn or explode when an ignition source is present.

Vapor pressure. Pressure (measured in pounds per square inch absolute (psia)) exerted by a vapor. If a vapor is kept in confinement over its liquid so that the vapor can accumulate above the liquid (the temperature being held constant), the vapor pressure approaches a fixed limit called the maximum (or saturated) vapor pressure, dependent only on the temperature and the liquid.

Vapors. The gaseous form of substances that are normally in the solid or liquid state (at room temperature and pressure). The vapor can be changed back to the solid or liquid state either by increasing the pressure or decreasing the temperature alone. Vapors also diffuse. Evaporation is the process by which a liquid is changed into the vapor state and mixed with the surrounding air. Solvents with low boiling points will volatilize readily. Examples include benzene, methyl alcohol, mercury and toluene.

Viscosity. The property of a fluid that resists internal flow by releasing counteracting forces.

Volatility. The tendency or ability of a liquid to vaporize. Such liquids as alcohol and gasoline, because of their tendency to evaporate rapidly, are called volatile liquids.

Walking/working surface. Any horizontal or vertical surface on which an employee walks or works, or is permitted to walk or work. This includes, but is not limited to, floors, roofs, ramps, bridges, runways, formwork and concrete reinforcing steel. It does not include ladders, vehicles or trailers on which employees must be located to perform their assigned duties.

Warning line system. A barrier erected on a roof to warn employees that they are approaching an unprotected roof side or edge and designates an area in which roofing work may take place without the use of guardrail, body belt or safety net systems to protect employees in the area.

Water column. A unit used in measuring pressure. See also Inches of water column.

Water gels. A variety of materials used for blasting. They contain substantial proportions of water and high proportions of ammonium nitrate (some of which also are in the water solution). Two broad classes of water gels are (1) Those that are sensitized by a material classed as an explosive, such as TNT or smokeless powder, and (2) those that contain no ingredient classified as an explosive; these are sensitized with metals such as aluminum or with other fuels. Water gels may be premixed at an explosives plant or mixed at the site immediately before delivery into the bore hole. Also known as Slurry explosives.

Willful violation. A violation that the employer knowingly commits or commits with plain indifference to the law. The employer either knows that what it is doing constitutes a violation or is aware that a hazardous condition existed and made no reasonable effort to eliminate it.

Window jack scaffold. A scaffold, the platform of which is supported by a bracket or jack that projects through a window opening.

Working load. Load imposed by workers, materials and equipment on a scaffold.